Second Edition

Business Information Management

Improving Performance Using Information Systems

Dave Chaffey

Gareth White

**Financial Times
Prentice Hall
is an imprint of**

Harlow, England • London • New York • Boston • San Francisco • Toronto
Sydney • Tokyo • Singapore • Hong Kong • Seoul • Taipei • New Delhi
Cape Town • Madrid • Mexico City • Amsterdam • Munich • Paris • Milan

Pearson Education Limited
Edinburgh Gate
Harlow
Essex CM20 2JE
England

and Associated Companies throughout the world

Visit us on the World Wide Web at:
www.pearsoned.co.uk

First published 2005
Second edition published 2011

ISBN: 978-0-273-71179-7

British Library Cataloguing-in-Publication Data
A catalogue record for this book is available from the British Library

Library of Congress Cataloging-in-Publication Data
Chaffey, Dave, 1963-
  Business information management : improving performance using information
systems / Dave Chaffey, Gareth White. -- 2nd ed.
       p. cm.
  Includes index.
  ISBN 978-0-273-71179-7 (pbk.)
 1. Management information systems. 2. Information resources management.
3. Business--Communication systems--Management. 4. Information
technology--Management. I. White, Gareth. II. Title.
  HD30.213.C43 2011
  658.4'038011--dc22
                                                    2010039883

10 9 8 7 6 5 4 3 2 1
14 13 12 11 10

Typeset in 9/12pt Stone Serif by 30

Printed and bound by Rotolito Lombarda, Italy

PEARSON Copyright © 1995 - 2011 Pearson Education. All rights reserved.
Legal Notice | Privacy Policy | Permissions

Dr Dave Chaffey is CEO and co-founder of Smart Insights (www.smartinsights.com), a digital marketing portal and consultancy who provide advice and software to help businesses succeed online.

He has consulted for companies of a range of sizes from larger organizations like 3M, Arco, BP, HSBC, Intel, Mercedes-Benz UK to smaller organizations like Euroffice, Hornbill and i-to-i.

Dave's passion is empowering businesses to improve their online performance through getting the most value from their business information, especially web analytics and market insight.

He is proud to have been recognized by the Department of Trade and Industry as one of the leading individuals who have provided input and influence on the development and growth of E-commerce and the Internet in the UK over the last 10 years. Dave has also been recognized by the Chartered Institute of Marketing as one of 50 marketing 'gurus' worldwide who have shaped the future of Marketing.

Between 1995 and 2001 he was Senior Lecturer in the Business School at the University of Derby where his research specialism was 'Approaches to measuring and improving e-marketing performance'. He developed the MSc in Electronic Commerce and also taught on the MBA and MA Marketing Management Programmes. He continues to lecture in e-business and e-marketing in business schools at UK universities including Birmingham, Cranfield, Leeds and Warwick.

Between 1988 and 1995 Dave worked in industry as a business analyst/project manager developing IT marketing solutions for companies such as Ford Europe, WH Smith and the Halifax. He was on the senior management team of an engineering software vendor for five years.

Dave is author of five other best-selling business books including *Internet Marketing: Strategy, Implementation and Practice*, *E-business and E-commerce Management*, *eMarketing eXcellence* (with PR Smith) and *Total E-mail Marketing*. He is also author of the E-consultancy best practice guides to Search Engine Optimisation, Paid Search Marketing, Web site design and Managing Digital Channels.

Gareth RT White, MSc, PGCert(TLHE), MCMI, FHEA, has worked in automotive, Formula 1 and nuclear electronics sectors in Engineering, Senior Management and Consultative capacities. He is Senior Lecturer in Operations and Information Systems Management at Bristol Business School, University of the West of England, teaching under-graduate modules in information systems management, operations management and a variety of postgraduate courses, as well as supervising undergraduate and post-graduate research.

Gareth undertakes training and consultancy with businesses operating on the South West supervising several Knowledge Transfer Partnership projects and is currently reading for a PhD in the areas of knowledge acquisition. He also participates in AimHigher and Outreach programmes that unite universities with local schools and colleges and encourage young people to consider the benefits and opportunities of higher education.

Brief contents

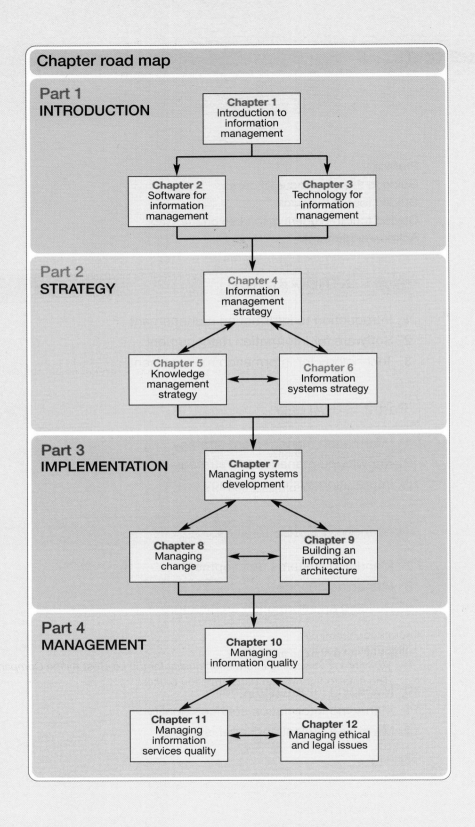

Chapter road map

Part 1
INTRODUCTION

Chapter 1
Introduction to information management

Chapter 2
Software for information management

Chapter 3
Technology for information management

Part 2
STRATEGY

Chapter 4
Information management strategy

Chapter 5
Knowledge management strategy

Chapter 6
Information systems strategy

Part 3
IMPLEMENTATION

Chapter 7
Managing systems development

Chapter 8
Managing change

Chapter 9
Building an information architecture

Part 4
MANAGEMENT

Chapter 10
Managing information quality

Chapter 11
Managing information services quality

Chapter 12
Managing ethical and legal issues

Detailed contents

Part 1 INTRODUCTION

Chapter 1
Introduction to information management   2

Chapter 3
Technology for information management 92

Part 2 STRATEGY

Chapter 6
Information systems strategy   259

Part 3 IMPLEMENTATION

Chapter 7
Managing systems development   316

Chapter 8
Managing change

Part 4 MANAGEMENT

Chapter 10
Managing information quality   474

Chapter 12
Managing ethical and legal issues

Supporting resources

Visit **www.pearsoned.co.uk/chaffey** to find valuable online resources:

Companion Website for students
- Learning outcomes for each chapter
- Multiple-choice questions for each chapter with instant feedback
- Annotated weblinks to relevant, specific Internet resources to facilitate in-depth independent research
- Searchable online glossary

For instructors
- PowerPoint slides that can be downloaded and used for presentations
- Complete instructors' manual
- Testbank of additional multiple-choice questions, that can help assessment

Also: The Companion Website provides the following features:
- Search tool to help locate specific items of content
- E-mail results and profile tools to send results of quizzes to instructors
- Online help and support to assist with website usage and trouble-shooting

For more information please contact your local Pearson Education sales representative or visit **www.pearsoned.co.uk/chaffey**

Why business information management?

The volume of information that organizations need to manage continues to increase relentlessly. Today this includes both internal information about managing processes within an organization and increasingly, external information that customers, partners and other stakeholders may discuss through social networks or their systems.

As information volumes increase, so do the challenges of managing the information and trying to find value in it. Some of the challenges of managing such huge volumes of information, increasing at this rate are:

- *Relevancy* – How do we find information relevant to our decisions?
- *Accessibility* – How do organizations make relevant information available to employees and partners through computer applications, web and e-mail? How is the knowledge used to apply information captured and shared between employees?
- *Legality* – How do organizations ensure they are using customer, employee and market information in accordance with legal and ethical standards?
- *Security* – How do we protect this information from accidental or deliberate threats?
- *Value* – How can this information help organizations reach their business objectives?

Traditionally, the study of information systems has often had a strong focus on managing *technology* – the hardware and software components and different applications of information systems. This is evident in the many textbooks available on business information systems and the technology orientation of their content. This focus was in response to a need to educate students in technology concepts since business and management students typically had limited direct experience of using information systems. But today, primary school children are introduced to using Office and Internet applications from the age of five. By the time they reach further and higher education, they will be well versed in hardware and software concepts and applications through instruction and use at school, home and work. What they are less likely to be prepared for is the challenges of managing information in organizations. Similarly, many postgraduate students who are studying will have experience of the problems of information and knowledge management and will want to know how organizations can cope with the challenges of information and knowledge management. The purpose of *Business Information Management*, second edition is to raise awareness of these challenges and opportunities and to discuss solutions which involve proactive management of information as a corporate resource.

From a descriptive approach to a problem-based learning approach

Traditionally, introductory information systems texts have used a largely descriptive approach. Typical questions answered in many previous texts include: What is hardware? What is software? What types of information systems are there? Where can they be applied in organizations? What are the types of local area network or database systems? What are the merits of sequential file access, token ring networks, hierarchical databases or chip designs, etc.

Yet most business and management students will never be involved with the implementation of such technologies. What all will be involved with is managing information to improve their personal performance and the performance of the work area they are responsible for. This will involve assessing the quality of information available and working with colleagues to develop processes and introduce applications to make better use of this information.

This book does not focus solely on the hardware and software technology for managing information technology – the 'T' in 'IT', instead the emphasis is on the 'I' in 'IT'. It acknowledges the major problems with implementing information systems which deliver value to the business. It explores the reasons for these problems and management solutions to reduce these problems.

So the approach taken in *Business Information Management*, is to place the emphasis on managing information by replacing questions such as those above with management questions more relevant to managers in the modern organization such as:

- How can we assess and improve information quality?
- How should we help employees manage information overload?
- How much should we decide where to invest in information systems (IS)?
- How do we select the best hardware, software, applications?
- How should we protect organizational information and protect customer privacy?
- How can organizational knowledge be managed?
- How should we manage the organizational change involved with introducing information systems?

Such key management questions are outlined at the start of each chapter and are used to help structure the chapters.

An organization stakeholder orientation

The information and knowledge management challenges mentioned above are faced by a range of employees who will view the challenge from a different perspective. *Business Information Management* uses a stakeholder-based approach considering key issues faced by different types of staff in an organization. The different information management issues and their coverage in the text are shown in Table 1. Note that each stakeholder also faces all the concerns of those at the level above – for example every type of manager is also an end-user.

Table 1 Key issues in business information management and their influence on stakeholders with a business

Information management issue or problem	Relevant concept and coverage in BIM
End users (internal, customers and partners)	
Availability of good quality information	Information quality, C1, 4, 10
Availability of the right tools and service levels	Service quality, C2, 11
Managing own or a team's data/time	Project management, C7 Information architecture, C9
Searching for information online	Search engine skills, C1

Department or process managers	
Selecting applications	Applications portfolio. C2, 6
Selecting providers	Procuring applications, C2, 3, 6, 11
Integrating with other functions	IS/IM/KM Strategy, C4, 5, 6
Senior manager or CEO perspective	
Contribution to business, Delivering value from IT – achieving competitive advantage, aligning with business strategy, cost control	IS Strategy, C1, 4 Investment appraisal, C4
Managing and improving organizational performance	Corporate performance management, C1, 4
Legal – are we compliant with data protection and employee monitoring law – am I personally culpable?	Legal and ethical considerations, C12
Maximizing staff productivity (people resource management) – minimizing unproductive use of technology, e.g. e-mail and web usage, SPAM, viruses, configuring systems and fixing problems	IS Governance, C6, 11
Capturing, storing and disseminating knowledge held by employees	Knowledge Management Strategy, C5
Project failure rates and managing change – failure rates of business transformation initiatives including IS components	Managing systems development, C7 Risk management, C7
Resourcing and structuring information management, knowledge management and IS	IM, KM, IS Strategy, C4, 5, 6
IT manager or CIO perspective	
Delivering quality information	Information quality, C1, 4, 10
Delivering quality services	Services quality, C11 Information architecture, C9
Protecting information	Information security, C4, 9, 11
Balancing resources	Outsourcing, C10
Managing introduction of new applications	Managing systems development, C7
Implementing e-business	E-business, C2, 4, 10
Managing cost of technology	Total cost of ownership, C10 Utility computing, C3

Key: CEO = chief executive officer, CIO = chief information officer.

Who is this book for?

The book is for students and managers who need to understand the concepts and best practice for effective business information management. The book has been designed to support students on a range of study programmes including:

● *Postgraduates students on MBA, Certificate in Management, Diploma in Management Studies or specialist masters degrees* which involve modules on information management or IS strategy or electives in knowledge management.

- *Students on specialist undergraduate and postgraduate courses in Information Management and Information and Library Management.*
- *Undergraduates taking general business or management courses* such as Business Administration and Business Studies or specialised business courses such as Accounting, Marketing, Tourism and Human Resources Management. These programmes often include modules such as information management, IT or IS for Business for which this book is designed.
- *Undergraduates on specialist computer science courses* in Business Information Systems or Business Information Technology which involve the study of business applications of information technology and the management of the development of IS.
- *Students at college aiming for vocational qualifications* such as the HNC/HND in Business Management or Computer Studies.

Practising managers in all types of organizations including business-to-business, business-to-consumer and not-for-profit organizations will also find the strategic approaches and practical guidance on information and knowledge management valuable:

- *Senior managers* looking to improve the contribution of information systems to organizational performance.
- *Departmental managers* planning how information management solutions can support the work processes in their departments.
- *Information managers, Chief Information Officers and IT managers* responsible for implementing information management and knowledge management programmes within their organization.

How does the book support lecturers teaching these courses?

The book is intended to bring the subject of information management to life through illustrating the major information management issues facing modern managers. Research and case studies on topical practical issues such as coping with information overload, SPAM and viruses are allied to strategic initiatives such as developing strategies for information systems, information management and knowledge management.

The student learning features detailed in the next section will support lecturers through providing lecture and seminar material such as activities, case studies and assessments which can be integrated into a range of different programmes. These features have been selected to be relevant to UK and European students following business programmes.

How this book differs from information systems texts

The content and pedagogy of this book have been created to enable it to be used on both information management and information systems modules. Many of the chapter topics can be used to support individual lectures or a series of lectures on either type of module, for example: Applications (Chapter 2), Technology (Chapter 3), Information Systems Strategy (Chapter 6), Managing Systems Development (Chapter 7) and Legal and ethical issues (Chapter 12). However, there are significant differences in *Business Information Management*:

1 Emphasis on managing information and knowledge as strategic issues. Separate chapters on Information Management Strategy (Chapters 4 and 10) and Knowledge Management Strategy (Chapter 5).
2 Technology described on a 'need to know' basis. i.e. what managers of IS need to know to select the appropriate hardware or software and what users of systems need to know to work with them.

3 Less detailed coverage of traditional systems analysis and design techniques for bespoke systems. Many systems are now standard packages hosted inside or outside an organization and managing projects to reduce risks in implementing these types of system is the emphasis (Chapter 7).

4 Recognises major problems of delivering value from IS and implementing IS rather than concentrating on the benefits of applications. The reasons for these problems and possible solutions to them are explored.

5 A problem-based learning approach is used to help students understand the issues and question the solutions. Detailed activities and questions for debate are integrated into the chapters and can be used as pre-reading or activities during lectures or tutorials.

Student learning features

The book has been designed to assist you to rapidly learn and apply the concepts of business information management through the inclusion of many standard features. In each chapter you will find these features:

At the start of each chapter:

- *Learning outcomes*: a list describing what readers can learn through reading the chapter and outcomes completing the activities.
- *Management issues*: a summary of main issues or decisions faced by managers related to the Chapter topic area.
- *Chapter at a glance*: a list of main topics and case studies.
- *Links to other chapters*: a summary of related topics in other chapters.
- *Introductions*: succinct summaries of the relevance of the topic to students and practitioners together with content and structure.

In each chapter:

- *Activities*: A number of short activities in the main text that develop concepts and understanding often by relating to student experience or through reference to websites.
- *Case studies*: real-world examples of issues facing companies that implement e-business. Questions at the end of the case study highlight the main learning points from each case study.
- *Mini case studies*: Shorter examples illustrating concepts described in the main text.
- *Running case study* based on 'The Lo-cost Airline Company' – a low-cost airline company which can be easily related to, to illustrate concepts.
- *Research Insights*: Further details on behaviour through research conducted by academics, analysts or sponsored by vendors.
- *Debates*: Suggestions for discussion of significant issues for managers involved with the transformation required for e-business.
- *Definitions*: when significant terms are first introduced, the main text contains succinct definitions in the margin for easy reference.

At the end of each chapter:

- *Chapter summaries*: intended as revision aids and to summarize the main learning points from the chapter.
- *Self-assessment questions* and *Essay and discussion questions*.
- *Weblinks*: Web addresses are given for further information, particularly those to update information.

The running case study

To provide context and to help explain the concepts and theories introduced in *Business Information Management*, one company is used throughout this book, both in the text and activities. This is the '*Lo-cost Airline company*'. Many of the business information management issues highlighted are most likely to occur in earlier high growth phases of companies from medium-sized to large organizations which accentuate the challenges of business information management.

This is a fictitious regional airline, which would have an operation covering an area such as Europe, the Americas, Australasia or part of Asia. It is around 10 years old and employs thousands of staff. The core product is flights booked by both individuals and businesses. Additional revenue is also derived from a car rental business and package holidays.

Products are sold directly by phone or booked online using the Internet ticketing service. Over 90 per cent of tickets are sold online with 40 per cent of customer service contacts serviced by the website which has local language versions for each of the major markets it operates in.

This is a fiercely competitive market with several other prominent low-cost carriers and traditional airlines competing in each market. All competitors have e-commerce sites offering online booking and customer service.

The Lo-cost Airline Company is a fictitious low-cost airline used for the activities throughout this book. Similar companies that can be referred to gain an idea of the company and its markets are: easyJet (**www.easyjet.com**), Ryanair (**www.ryanair.com**), South Western Airlines (**www.southwestern.com**) and Virgin Blue in Australia (**www.virginblue.com**).

What's new in this second edition

In addition to refreshing and expanding the many smaller case studies, research notes and references to contemporary literature, this edition sees the inclusion of many new areas of discussion and several new case studies.

Topical subjects include environmental issues and 'green IT' (chapter 4); business process management and business process reengineering (chapter 1); the benefits offered by cloud computing (chapter 3); research into the relative benefits and drawbacks of RFID versus barcode technologies (chapter 3); the use of QR codes to link the tangible and virtual worlds (chapter 3); the increasing hazards presented by computer viruses (chapter 11); and concerns over the ethical use and retention of private and personal information (chapter 12).

The World Wide Web continues to impact on the way we do business and the ways that we interact with family and friends. The amount of data that is stored 'somewhere out there' is truly phenomenal yet only a small fraction of this is readily searchable. In chapter 1 we examine the scale of this 'hidden web' and also highlight the importance of safely securing personal data, drawing specific reference to the measures taken by the authors during the creation of this text (p24).

Open-source software is highlighted in chapter 2 as becoming increasingly attractive to modern business, offering high levels of functionality and affordability. We also include a case study that discusses the software and technology that are employed by the Royal Navy to manage and order spares (p57).

Building upon the importance of taking care of data, in chapter 3 we look at how arrays of disks may be used as backup devices and include a case study that outlines the use of RAID in a veterinarian practice (p119). The subject of assistive technologies that enable people with physical or visual impairments to use computing devices is also introduced.

The globalization of commerce has significant implications for organizations that span many cultures, time zones, languages and legislative requirements. The development of supportive information and knowledge strategies is therefore becoming of even greater importance in order to gain and maintain a competitive advantage. The traditional dilemma of centralization versus decentralization is now significantly more complex and in chapter 6 we discuss how information systems can be seen to comprise many levels of architectural asymmetry.

Despite much academic and practitioner attention over several decades, the task of developing new and improved information systems remains problematic. Chapter 7 presents examples of some of the biggest information system disasters of all time, expands upon the many approaches towards systems development, and provides a case study that portrays the problems encountered in a Police Force communications and control room (p345).

The quality of data that is stored directly relates to the quality of decisions that can be made from analysing that data. Consequently, data quality is a feature to be proactively managed and is covered in chapters 10 and 11. We provide a case study that explores the importance of capturing high quality data in the operating theatres of an NHS hospital, and highlights the problems that are caused when data is improperly defined (p499). A further case study that outlines a recent assessment of online customer service is also included (p531).

Dave Chaffey and Gareth White
Autumn 2010

Guide to the main focus of cases

Case	Description	Ch. 1 Introduction	Ch. 2 Software	Ch. 3 Technologies	Ch. 4 IM strategy	Ch. 5 KM strategy	Ch. 6 IS strategy	Ch. 7 Systems development	Ch. 8 Managing change	Ch. 9 Information architecture	Ch. 10 Information quality	Ch. 11 Services quality	Ch. 12 Ethical and legal issues
1.1 Avoiding disasters	Considers the measures taken to protect the data used in the production of this text	●			●					●			
1.2 Has IT failed to deliver?	Explores problems in achieving value from IT investments	●					●	●				●	
2.1 Spares ordering in the Navy	Reviews the way that maintenance records and spares and managed in the Navy		●									●	
2.2 Utility computing	Discusses the advantages and disadvantages of web services		●				●					●	
2.3 Open-source software	Asks whether open-source is a realistic choice for large corporations and gives example deployments		●				●	●				●	
3.1 SANs	Looks at the relevance of storage area networks to information management			●								●	
3.2 Veterinary clinic	Depicts the information requirements of a small veterinarian clinic			●	●								
3.3 easyJet	Reviews how adoption of technology standards at easyJet has supported their internet sales service			●								●	
4.1 Ten commandments	These are guidelines from practitioners advising on improving information management				●						●		
4.2 GlaxoSmithKline	The approach to creation of an information management group at this company from an information management perspective				●						●		
4.3 GlaxoSmithKline	Considers the same company, but from the technologist's perspective				●							●	
5.1 Social networks, banking example	An example from the banking sector on applying social network analysis					●							
5.2 Department of Trade and Industry	An overview of how the DTI has developed a KM strategy					●					●		
6.1 Renault	Illustrates the challenges involved with managing 1400 applications in a large company					●	●				●		
6.2 Tesco	Discusses the technology adoption strategy followed by Tesco			●			●						

Case	Description	Ch. 1 Introduction	Ch. 2 Software	Ch. 3 Technologies	Ch. 4 IM strategy	Ch. 5 KM strategy	Ch. 6 IS strategy	Ch. 7 Systems development	Ch. 8 Managing change	Ch. 9 Information architecture	Ch. 10 Information quality	Ch. 11 Services quality	Ch. 12 Ethical and legal issues
7.1 Reading Council	Reviews issues with the introduction of PRINCE2 project management methodology							●					
7.2 Police force	Reviews the problems faced by the users of a critical information system		●	●				●	●				
8.1 Business process management	Gives a modern perspective on approaches to improve business processes using information systems. It summarizes the tools, benefits and some of the problems associated with business process management	●							●				
8.2 Data analysis	Outlines some analytical techniques used for decision making								●		●		
8.3 Business intelligence software	Examines the relevance of this software through reference to different organizations	●	●						●				
9.1 Database administrators	Looks at the role of these staff in information management									●			
9.2 Sainsbury's	Illustrates the approach used to classify intranet information sources		●						●	●			
10.1 NHS	Discusses the information system used within an operating theatre and the importance of clearly defining data types								●		●	●	
10.2 Chartered surveyors (SME)	Illustrates the process of creating and information policy for a small organization		●					●			●		
11.1 Transversal	Outlines the results of a study of the problems with online services				●	●						●	
11.2 To scrap or not to scrap?	Explores the arguments for and against extending the lifetime of PC hardware		●				●						●
12.1 Monitoring employee use	Summarizes the extent of non-work-related computer activities in the workplace and explores approaches to limit them					●				●			●
12.2 Plagiarism	Reviews controls on plagiarism in an academic setting												●

Key: ● = Main reference ● = Case supports learning in this chapter

Guided tour of the book

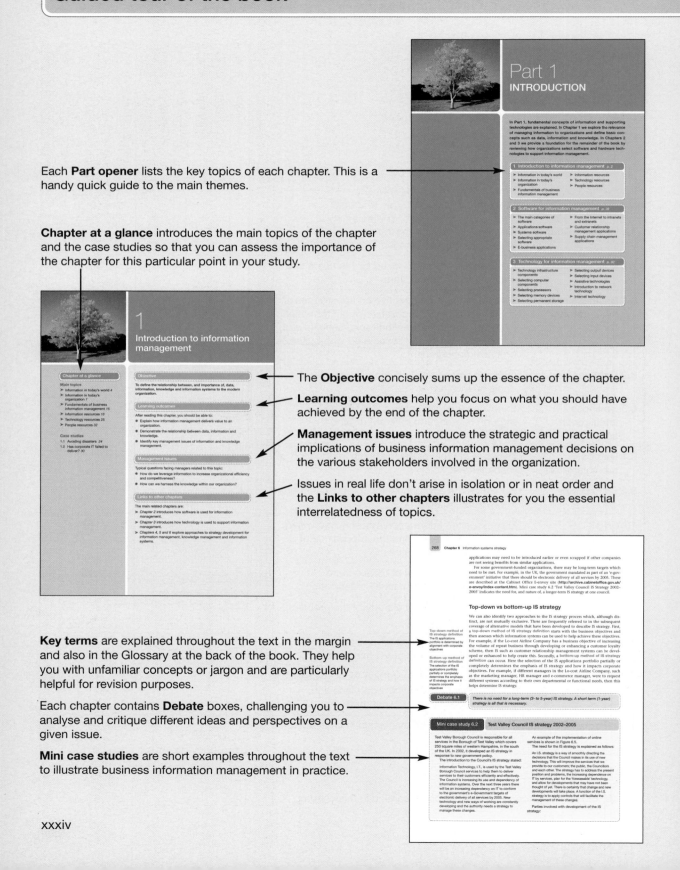

Each **Part opener** lists the key topics of each chapter. This is a handy quick guide to the main themes.

Chapter at a glance introduces the main topics of the chapter and the case studies so that you can assess the importance of the chapter for this particular point in your study.

The **Objective** concisely sums up the essence of the chapter.

Learning outcomes help you focus on what you should have achieved by the end of the chapter.

Management issues introduce the strategic and practical implications of business information management decisions on the various stakeholders involved in the organization.

Issues in real life don't arise in isolation or in neat order and the **Links to other chapters** illustrates for you the essential interrelatedness of topics.

Key terms are explained throughout the text in the margin and also in the Glossary at the back of the book. They help you with unfamiliar concepts or jargon and are particularly helpful for revision purposes.

Each chapter contains **Debate** boxes, challenging you to analyse and critique different ideas and perspectives on a given issue.

Mini case studies are short examples throughout the text to illustrate business information management in practice.

The **Activities**, many of which are web-based, reinforce your
learning with problems and practical applications.

Figures and **tables** illustrate key points, concepts and
processes visually to reinforce your learning. This text also
includes colour screenshots to illustrate case studies and
make for a more stimulating read.

The **Research insight** boxes highlight innovative studies
from both industry and academia. They provide you with an
advantage in more advanced study by offering insights into
ground-breaking research.

Up-to-date **Case studies**, many taken from the *Financial Times*
newspaper, consolidate your learning of the major themes by
encouraging you to apply what you have learnt to real-life
business information management scenarios.

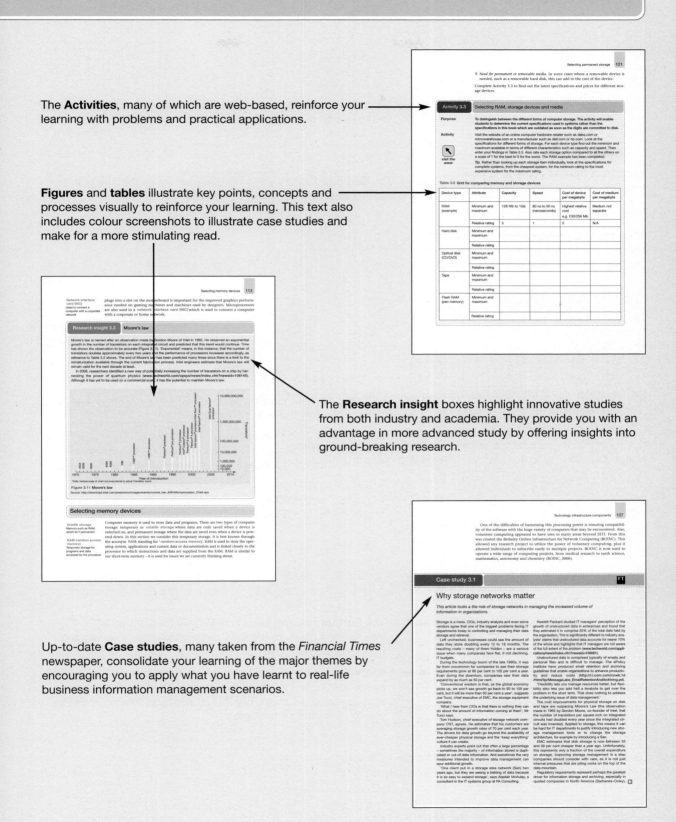

Guided tour *continued*

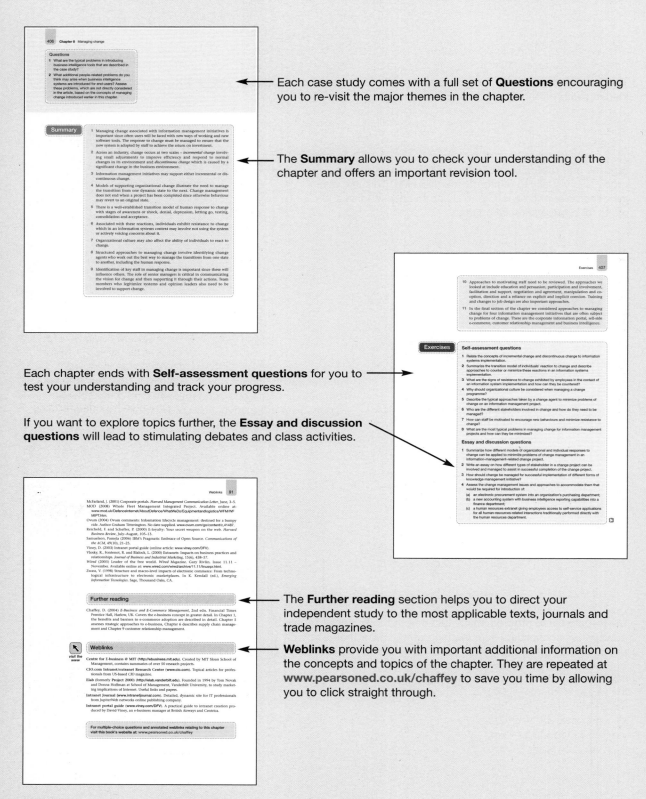

Each case study comes with a full set of **Questions** encouraging you to re-visit the major themes in the chapter.

The **Summary** allows you to check your understanding of the chapter and offers an important revision tool.

Each chapter ends with **Self-assessment questions** for you to test your understanding and track your progress.

If you want to explore topics further, the **Essay and discussion questions** will lead to stimulating debates and class activities.

The **Further reading** section helps you to direct your independent study to the most applicable texts, journals and trade magazines.

Weblinks provide you with important additional information on the concepts and topics of the chapter. They are repeated at **www.pearsoned.co.uk/chaffey** to save you time by allowing you to click straight through.

Guided tour to the student resources on the Web

Business Information Management, 2nd edition, is supported by a fully interactive Companion Website, available at **www.pearsoned.co.uk/chaffey**, that contains a wealth of additional learning material.

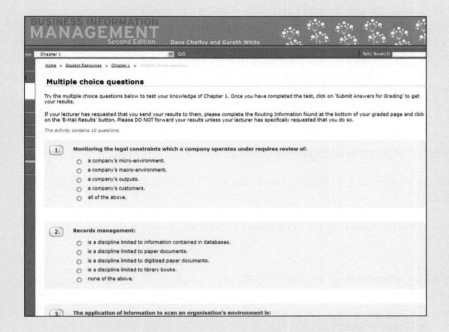

Extensive **Multiple-choice questions**, all with helpful feedback on incorrect answers, help develop your subject knowledge and improve your understanding.

Interactive **Flashcards**, with the key term on one side and the definition on the other, aid your revision by testing your understanding of core terms and concepts.

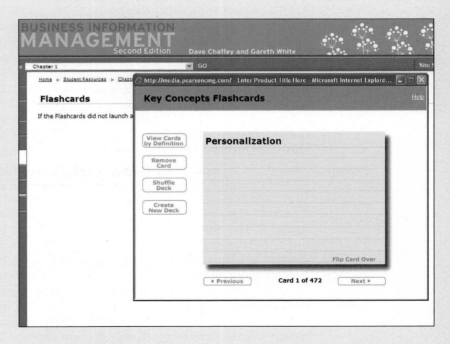

Acknowledgements

Author's acknowledgements

The detailed comments and insights from the panel of reviewers are always appreciated and help shape the book, so first, I'd like to thank the reviewers for their input.

Next, I'd like to thank my co-author for this edition, Gareth White, who has put a tremendous amount of effort into updating this edition.

Finally, at Pearson Education, I would like to thank our editor, Philippa Fiszzon, for her efforts in ensuring the quality of the book and Gabrielle James for her help in commissioning the research and design for the book.

Publisher's acknowledgements

The publishers would like to thank Fiona Shearer for her extremely helpful and valued input.

We are grateful to the following for permission to reproduce copyright material:

Figures

Figure 1.1 from Global Best Practice guidelines, www.globalbestpractices.com/ Bestpractices, PricewaterhouseCoopers, (2002); Figure 1.3 from *Mastering Information Management*, Financial Times Prentice Hall (Marchand, D., Davenport, T. and Dickson, T. (eds) 2000) pp.295-300; Figure 1.4 from Business in the Information Age:The International Benchmarking Study 2003. A report prepared for the UK Department of Trade and Industry by Booz, Allen and Hamilton, www.ukonlinefor-business.gov.uk/benchmarking2003, Crown Copyright material is reproduced with permission under the terms of the Click-Use Licence; Figure 1.7 from www.flightmapping.com/Europe/flights-map.swf, flightmapping.com; Figure 1.9 from Searchenginewatch, http://searchenginewatch.com/reports; Figure 1.10 from Autonomy Corporation plc; Figures 2.4, 2.13, 2.16, 2.17, 3.22, 3.23, 3.24, 3.25, 6.12, 7.9 from *E-Business and E-Commerce Management*, 2nd ed., Financial Times Prentice Hall (Chaffey, D. 2004); Figure 2.9 from http://www.netmarketshare.com/os-market-share.aspx?qprid=11&qptimeframe=M&qpsp=112&qpnp=25; Figures 2.11, 7.4, 7.5, 7.6, 9.4, 9.24, 9.25 from Microsoft Corporation , Microsoft product (box or screen) shot(s) reprinted with permission from Microsoft Corporation; Figure 2.12 from University of Aberdeen website, http://www.abdn.ac.uk/helpdesk/self-service; Figure 2.15 from The British Council, http://www.educationuk.org/UK/Careers-in-different-fields, © The British Council; Figure 2.18 from Edinburgh Napier University, http://staff.napier.ac.uk; Figure 2.19 from UCAS, www.ucas.ac.uk; Figure 2.20 from UK Freedom of Information Blog (http://foia.blogspot.com/) established by Steve Wood and now produced by the Campaign for Freedom of Information (http://www.cfoi.org.uk); Figure 3.5 from Rune's PC Museum, Photo: Rune Tapper, pc-museum.com; Figure 3.6 from Hewlett-Packard Company Inc, Palo Alto, CA, www.hp.com; Figure 3.12 from Kingston Technology Company, Fountain Valley, California, http://www.kingston.com/ press/primages/contents.asp; Figure 3.16 from Kingston Technology Company, Fountain

Valley, California, http://www.kingston.com/ press/primag/contents.asp; Figure 3.19 from Dell, Inc., Round Rock, Texas (www.dell.com); Figure 3.20 from Xerox Corporation (www.xerox.xom); Figure 3.27 from http://text.it/mediacentre/sms_figures.cfm, Source: Mobile Data Association; Figure 4.2 from *Global Data Management survey*, PricewaterhouseCoopers (2001); Figure 4.3 from *The PricewaterhouseCoopers Global Information Security survey 2010. Research report, published September 2010.* PricewaterhouseCoopers (2010); Figure 5.5 from Snowden, D. (2003) Complex Knowledge. Gurteen Knowledge Conference, London, June, www.gurteen.com; Figure 5.6 from *The Knowledge Creating Company: How Japanese Companies Create the Dynamics of Innovation*, Oxford University Press, New York (Nonaka, I. and Takeuchi, H. 1995), By permission of Oxford University Press, Inc.; Figure 5.7 from *Competitive Knowledge Management*, Palgrave (Bahra, N. 2001), Reproduced with permission of Palgrave Macmillan; Figure 5.15 from *Developing a knowledge strategy. In C. Choo and N. Bontis (eds) The Strategic Management of Intellectual Capital and Organizational Knowledge*, Oxford University Press (Zak, M 2002), By permission of Oxford University Press, Inc.; Figure 5.19 from *Integrated IT systems to capitalise on market knowledge .In G. Krogh, I. Nonaka and T. Nishiguchi (eds) Knowledge Creation: A Source of Value*, Palgrave (Nonaka, I, Reinmoeller, P. and Senoo, D. 2000), Reproduced with permission of Palgrave Macmillan; Figure 5.20 from TFPL (2003) Knowledge and Information Management Competency Dictionary www.tfpl.com/resources/competencydictionary.cfm; Figure 6.1 from COBIT 4.1, www.isaca.org/cobit, © 1996-2007 ITGI. All rights reserved. Used by permission.; Figure 6.4 from www.nhsia.nhs.gov.uk, Crown Copyright material is reproduced with permission under the terms of the Click-Use Licence; Figure 6.7 from *Business and E-Commerce Management*, Financial Times Prentice Hall (Chaffey, D. 2002); Figure 6.8 from Information systems management and strategy formulation: the stages of growth model revisited, *Journal of Information Systems*, 1 (2), 89-114 (Galliers, R. and Sutherland, A. 1991), © American Accounting Association; Figure 6.9 from Information systems management strategy formulation: the stages of growth model revisited, *Journal of Information Systems*, 1 (2) (Galliers, R. and Sutherland, A. 1991), © American Accounting Association; Figure 6.11 from www.archive.org; Figure 6.14 from Ofcom (2010) The Communications Market 2010. Research report published at: http://stakeholders.ofcom.org.uk/market-data-research/market-data/communications-market-reports/; Figure 6.16 from *ProSight Portfolio Management;* Figure 6.17 from *Strategic Planning for Information Systems*, 3rd ed., Wiley (Ward, J. and Peppard, J. 2002); Figure 7.1 from Standish Group (2010); Figure 7.14 from UK Office of Government Commerce 'Why projects fail guide', www.ogc.gov.uk/sdtoolkit/reference/ogc_library/bpbriefings/it projects.pdf, Crown Copyright material is reproduced with permission under the terms of the Click-Use Licence; Figure 8.1 from *Discontinuous Change*, Jossey-Bass, San Francisco (Nadler et al 1995), Reproduced with permission of John Wiley & Sons, Inc.; Figure 8.5 from DTI (2002), Crown Copyright material is reproduced with permission under the terms of the Click-Use Licence; Figure 8.7 from Siebel (2002); Figure 8.8 from *Business Information Systems: Technology, Development and Management*, 2nd ed., Financial Times Prentice Hall (Bocij, P., Chaffey, D., Greasley, A. and Hickie, S. 2003); Figure 9.23 from BSI, BS 7799-2:2002, Figure 1, Permission to reproduce extracts from BS 7799-2:2002 is granted by the British Standards Institution (BSI). No other use of this material is permitted. British Standards can be obtained in PDF or hard copy formats from the BSI online shop: http://shop.bsigroup.com or by contacting BSI Customer Servcies for hard copies only: Tel: +44 (0)20 8996 9001, Email: cservices@bsigroup.com; Figure 9.26 from http://www.cabinetoffice.gov.uk/govtalk/schemasstandards/e-gif/datastandars.aspx, Crown Copyright material is reproduced with permission under the terms of the Click-Use Licence; Figure 9.33 from *Information Architecture for the World Wide Web*, 2nd ed., O'Reilly (Rosenfeld, L. and Morville, P. 2002), All rights reserved. Used with permission from O'Reilly Media Inc.;

Figures 9.34 from www.hm-treasury.gov.uk, Crown Copyright material is reproduced with permission under the terms of the Click-Use Licence; Figures 9.35 from www.hm-treasury.gov.uk, Crown Copyright material is reproduced with permission under the terms of the Click-Use Licence; Figures 9.37 from http://www.audit-commission.gov.uk, Crown Copyright material is reproduced with permission under the terms of the Click-Use Licence; Figures 9.38 from http://www.audit-commission.gov.uk, Crown Copyright material is reproduced with permission under the terms of the Click-Use Licence; Figure 9.41 from (HMSO), Crown Copyright material is reproduced with permission under the terms of the Click-Use Licence; Figures 9.42 from *HMSO*, Crown Copyright material is reproduced with permission under the terms of the Click-Use Licence; Figures 9.43 from *HMSO*, Crown Copyright material is reproduced with permission under the terms of the Click-Use Licence; Figures 9.45, 9.46 from www.guardian.co.uk, Copyright Guardian News & Media Ltd 2004; Figure 9.47 from www.guardian.co.uk; www.feeddemon.com, Copyright Guardian News & Media Ltd 2004; Figure 10.9 from www.factiva.com; Figure 10.11 from *Practical Information Policies*, 2nd ed., Gower Publishing (Orna, E. 1999); Figure 11.2 from A conceptual model of service quality and its implications for future research, *Journal of Marketing*, 49, Fall:48 (Parasuraman, A., Zeithaml, V. and Berry, L. 1985), Reprinted with permission from the Journal of Marketing, published by the American Marketing Association, Parasuraman, A., Zeithaml, V. and Berry, L. 1985; Reprinted with permission from the Journal of Marketing, published by the American Marketing Association, ; Figure 11.4 from DTI (2004), Crown Copyright material is reproduced with permission under the terms of the Click-Use Licence; Figure 11.5 from University of Berkeley, http://www.caida.org/publications/papers/2003/sapphire/sapphire.html, Copyright 2003 The Regents of the University of California. All Rights Reserved.; Figures 11.10, 11.11 from Toolbox.com (2003); Figure 12.6 from *Seventh Annual BSA/IDC Global Software Piracy Study*, Business Software Alliance (2010).

Tables

Table 1.2 from Lyman, P. and Varian, H. (2003) How Much Information? - Online research summary, http://www.ischool.berkeley.edu/research/projects; Table 2.1 from Gartner, 2010; Table 3.1 from *Closing the Cognitive Gaps: how people process information in Marchand, T., Davenport and Dickson, T. (eds) Mastering Information Management*, Financial Times Prentice Hall (Wei Choo, C. 2000); Table 3.4 from Lyman, P. and Varian, H (2003) How much information? – online research summary., http://www2.sims.berkeley.edu/research/projects/how-much-info-2003/; Table 3.7 from Information taken from DCMI Recommendation http://dublincore.org/documents/2008/01/14/dces/, Copyright © 2008 Dublin Core Metadata Initiative. All Rights Reserved. http://www.dublincore.org/about/copyright/; Table 6.2 from *An organizational approach to IS strategy-making. In M.Earl (ed.) Information Management: The Organizational Dimension*, Oxford University Press (Earl, M. 1996) p.142, By permission of Oxford University Press; Table 8.5 from Business in the Information Age - International Benchmarking Study, 2001. UK Department of Trade and Industry, www.ukonlinefor-business.gov.uk/benchmarking2002, Crown Copyright material is reproduced with permission under the terms of the Click-Use Licence; Table 9.3 from *Modern Systems Analysis and Design*, 3rd ed., Prentice Hall (Hoffer, J., George, J. and Valacich, J. 2002), Hoffer, Jeffrey A; George, Joey; Valacich, Joseph, Modern Systems Analysis and Design, 3rd Edition, © 2002. Reprinted by permission of Pearson Education, Inc., Upper Saddle River, NJ; Table 10.3 from *Practical Information Policies*, 2nd ed., Gower Publishing (Orna, E. 1999); Table 12.1 from Seventh Annual BSA/IDC Global Software Piracy Study, Business Software Alliance, 2010.

Text

Case Study 2.1 from http://www.mod.uk/DefenceInternet/AboutDefence/WhatWeDo/ScienceandTechnology/CBML http://www.mod.uk/DefenceInternet/AboutDefence/WhatWeDo/ InformationManagement/ICAD/, Crown Copyright material is reproduced with permission under the terms of the Click-Use Licence; Case Study 2.2 from The Myth About IT as a Utility, *Educause Review*, July/August 2007 (Hawkins, B. and Oblinger, D.), © Brian Hawkins and Diana Oblinger; Case Study 12.2 from Philip Delves Broughton, MBA students swap integrity for plagiarism, *FT.com*, 19/05/2008 (Philip Delves Broughton); Research Insight 5.1 from *California Management Review*, Vol.40, No.3 (Fahey and Prusak 1998), Copyright 1988, by The Regents of the University of California. Reprinted from the California Management Review, Vol 40, No.3. By permission of The Regents.; Case Study 5.2 from Department of Trade and Industry Strategy web pages, www.dti.gov.uk/ ckmu/unit.html, Crown Copyright material is reproduced with permission under the terms of the Click-Use Licence; Case Study 7.1 from www.ogc.gov.uk/prince/downloads/templatercase.htm, Crown Copyright material is reproduced with permission under the terms of the Click-Use Licence; Case Study 8.2 from Fair Isaac Corporation, whitepaper, A Discussion of Data Analysis, April 2006, © FICO; Case Study 9.1 from *Choosing a Remote DBA instead of a full-time consultant* (Michael J Corey, Ntirety 2007); Research Insight 10.2 from www.jiscinfonet.ac.uk/Resources/external-resources/glamorgan-is-case-study/view, JISC; Mini Case Study 10.3 from David Stephens, Business Intelligence Solutions.

The Financial Times

Quote on page 29 from Buried Treasure, *The Financial Times*, 10/12/2003 (Simon London), Buried Treasure, Financial Times, 10/12/2003 (Simon London). The Financial Times Ltd. (FT); Case Study 1.2 from Richard Waters, 'Corporate computing tries to find a new path' (4 June, 2003), www.FT.com; Mini Case Study 2.2 adapted from Munich makes the move, *FT.com*, 15/10/2003 (Stephen Pritchard), and Putting Linux on desktops, FT.Com, 07/11/2007 (Sam Hiser); Case Study 2.3 from Twin forces stir desktop debate, *FT.com*, 15/10/2003 (Nuala Moran); Mini Case Study 2.7 from Iceland gets wise before the event, *Ft.com*, 01/10/2003 (Penelope Ody); Case Study 3.1 from Drowning in a deluge of data, *FT.com*, 12/11/2003 (Stephen Pritchard); Case Study 4.3 from Corporate profile: GlaxoSmithKline, Feather in cap for Sherwood leader, *FT.com*, 16/10/2002 (Michael Dempsey); Article on pages 296-7 from Inside Track article: An optimist's vision of tomorrow's technology: Interview George Colony, Forrester Research, *Financial Times* (Fiona Harvey, 2002); Case Study 6.1 from Bringing business technology out into the open – Jean-Pierre Corniou of Renault, *FT.com*, 16/09/2003 (Fiona Harvey); Mini Case Study 6.4 from Bringing the rigour of financial investing to IT, *FT.com*, 01/10/2003 (Geoffrey Nairn); Case Study 8.1 from Smoothing the workflow, *FT.com*, 15/05/2003 (Douglas Hayward); Case Study 8.3 from Fighting the flood of data, *FT.com*, 07/05/2003 (Stephen Pritchard); Case Study 11.2 from Working life gets longer for corporate PCs, *FT.com*, 07/05/2003 (Scott Morrison), and Spending rebound set to spur IT revival, FT.com, 14/01/2010 (Chris Nuttall); Case Study 12.1 from Prevention better than litigation? Monitoring of employee computer use, *Financial Times*, 02/10/2002 (Mark Vernon).

Photographs

Corbis: Alfredo Dagli Orti, The Art Archive, page 147; **Digital Vision**: page 47; **Pioneer Electronics**: page 120.

Part 1
INTRODUCTION

In Part 1, fundamental concepts of information and supporting technologies are explained. In Chapter 1 we explore the relevance of managing information to organizations and define basic concepts such as data, information and knowledge. In Chapters 2 and 3 we provide a foundation for the remainder of the book by reviewing how organizations select software and hardware technologies to support information management.

1

Introduction to information management

Objective

To define the relationship between, and importance of, data, information, knowledge and information systems to the modern organization.

Learning outcomes

After reading this chapter, you should be able to:

● Explain how information management delivers value to an organization.
● Demonstrate the relationship between data, information and knowledge.
● Identify key management issues of information and knowledge management.

Management issues

Typical questions facing managers related to this topic:

● How do we leverage information to increase organizational efficiency and competitiveness?
● How can we harness the knowledge within our organization?

Links to other chapters

The main related chapters are:

➤ *Chapter 2* introduces how software is used for information management.
➤ *Chapter 3* introduces how technology is used to support information management.
➤ *Chapters 4, 5 and 6* explore approaches to strategy development for information management, knowledge management and information systems.

Introduction

Information. Technology. Both resources are increasingly important as organizations seek to improve their performance. Information and technology resources coupled with human resources help deliver value to organizations in many different ways. Applying information and technology offers new ways to do business, increases the efficiency of business processes, reduces costs, and provides the performance measures used to control improvement.

What is the relative importance of these resources to organizations? When we talk about management of information technology, with the two words coupled together, it seems that often the emphasis is firmly placed on the technology. But, as Professor Thomas Davenport has noted, the managerial emphasis should be placed more on approaches to managing information rather than technology – the stress is on the 'I' rather than the 'T' in 'IT' (Davenport, 2000). Similarly, Peter Drucker stressed the importance of information to organizational competitiveness in 1993 when he wrote:

> The industries that have moved into the center of the economy in the last forty years, have as their business, the production and distribution of knowledge and information rather than the production and distribution of things.

Ultimately, value is delivered not through technology, but through applying information; by improved flows of information which require less resources; by better-quality information and knowledge sharing which improves decision making. In the same way that energy, water and nutrients are transported between different parts of a tree in order for it to survive, information needs to be transmitted efficiently through an organization for it to thrive.

For an organization to gain value from information raises many management issues which are not limited to technology. In *Business Information Management*, we will explore the key issues facing managers in all types of organizations as they try to harness their information resources. In each part of the book a major theme in managing business information will be investigated:

In Part 1, *Introduction*, the key management question is:

> *How do we select the appropriate hardware and software technologies and standards for information management?*

In Part 2, *Strategy*, the key management question is:

> *How we do create strategies to resource and control information flows and usage within the organization for effective delivery of value?*

In Part 3, *Implementation*, the key management question is:

> *How do we manage the projects and the impact of change on staff within our organization associated with the introduction of new ways of using information and new technologies?*

In Part 4, *Management*, the key management question is:

> *How do we use technology and people resources to continually improve the quality of information and information services within an organization while meeting legal and ethical requirements?*

In Chapter 1, we will discuss some of the fundamental principles involved with managing information as a resource. We start by looking at the importance of information in today's world and also at some of the common issues that businesses face in managing the information resource. We will then look at basic concepts and definitions needed to underpin the study of information, such as the distinction between data, information and knowledge; the role of technology and information systems; and different approaches to using information as a resource.

We also show how effective information management requires careful control of three types of resource:

- *information resources* such as data, information and knowledge;
- *technology resources* such as the hardware and software that forms information and communications technology and information systems;
- *people resources* such as the different types of employee and manager within a company and also third parties such as suppliers and customers who also determine information quality.

Information in today's world

The significance of information in the modern world can be gauged from three terms that have been coined to highlight the importance of information in the modern world: the information society, the information economy and the information age.

The information society

Information society
A society with widespread access to and transfer of digital information within business and the community

The importance of information in the world today has led to social commentators and governments referring to an **information society**. Martin (1995) says of information:

> Without an uninterrupted flow for this vital resource, society as we know it would quickly run into difficulties, with business and industry, education, leisure, travel and communications, national and international affairs all vulnerable to disruption. In more advanced societies, this vulnerability is heightened by an increasing dependence on the enabling powers of information and communications technologies.

This quotation stresses the importance of information and our dependence on it as a resource within organizations and society at large. Given the importance of information to society, governments launch initiatives and pass laws to ensure that businesses use information competitively, that their citizens' personal information is protected and that relevant information is accessible to all in society. For example, the European Community Information Society initiative **(http://ec.europa.eu/information_society/eeurope/i2010/index_en.htm)** was launched in 1998 with the aims of increasing public awareness of the impact of the information society and stimulating people's motivation and ability to participate (reducing social exclusion), increasing socio-economic benefits and enhancing the role of Europe in influencing the global information society. The European Community initiative describes the growth of the information society as follows:

> The last few years have witnessed a transformation in the industrial landscape of the developed world. Telecommunications liberalisation, the explosive growth of the Internet and a growing tide of mergers between computer, media and telecommunications companies all point to one thing – the birth of the information society.

The information society was defined by the UK INSINC Working Party on Social Inclusion in the Information Society in 1997 as:

> A society characterised by a high level of information intensity in the everyday life of most citizens, in most organisations and workplaces; by the use of common or compatible technology for a wide range of personal, social, educational and business activities; and by the ability to transmit and receive digital data rapidly between places irrespective of distance.

In Chapter 12 we review the ethical issues raised by the information society and the organizational implications of government attempts to manage the 'information society' through legal and investment initiatives.

The information economy

Information economy
An economy that is highly dependent upon the collection, storage and exchange of information

The concept of the information economy also recognizes the importance of information in the modern world, but this time with an emphasis on the impact on the economy. An information economy suggests an economy that is highly dependent upon the collection, storage and exchange of information. The dependence on information is suggested by the data in Table 1.1 and also the proportion of GDP spent on information management hardware and software, which averages 5 per cent in many countries. Additionally, many business services now deal exclusively with managing and adding value to data and by selling information derived from the data. Examples include:

- *Financial Times* (business news and information at **www.ft.com**)
- Factiva (detailed information about business performance at **www.factiva.com**)
- Experian (information about customers such as credit ratings and profiling for targeted marketing communications from **www.experian.com**)
- Questia (online subscription-based access is provided to published books and articles for students at **www.questia.com**)
- ScienceDirect.com (online journal access for science and business researchers at **www.sciencedirect.com**).

Evans and Wurster of Harvard Business School have argued in their paper 'Strategies and the new economics of information' that there are three characteristics of information in any market that will determine its importance (Evans and Wurster, 1997). These are:

1 *Reach.* The number or rather proportion of people in a market who are exchanging information.

2 *Richness.* This is defined by the information itself. It is constrained by *bandwidth* (the volume of information that can be transmitted using a communications link in a given time), hence as high-speed broadband access to the Internet increases, increasingly rich information can be delivered to customers. *Richness* is also determined by the degree to which information can be customized. For example, an e-mail received by a customer offering discounts on a product is more likely to be acted on if the product is tailored to its recipient. Interactivity is also important to richness. A dialogue is a more effective way of exchanging information. So for a customer to solve a query about their account it will often be more efficient to speak to them by phone rather than sending an e-mail since the phone is a more interactive medium.

3 *Affiliation.* This refers to links with partners. In an online context, an organization that has the most links to other organizations will be able to gain a larger reach and influence.

In markets such as air travel, where ticket sales have been transformed by the Internet, understanding how to improve reach, richness and affiliation is crucial. This is not only because a large proportion of people buy their flights online, but because they also research their route and carrier online.

The information age

The increasing importance of information through time both to society and economies has been used to suggest that we are now in the 'information age'. When did the information age begin? Decide for yourself from Table 1.1. The 'information age' takes over from the 'industrial age' which in turn follows the 'agricultural age'. In the agricultural age, the key resources were the land and the people who worked on it and defended it. When products were first produced, it was usually one person who produced the whole product. In the industrial age, mass-production of products became commonplace, with different people working on different aspects of the product, supported by machinery. Capital became a key strategic resource in addition to people. In the information age, information and knowledge are critical to organizational success and information becomes a key strategic resource also. Information is used to understand the needs of markets, support the development of products, and govern and control the direction of businesses. Furthermore, in the information age, individuals and organizations pay for pure information services, ranging from online newspaper subscriptions to analysts' reports and alerts about particular industries to marketing databases to promote products to potential customers.

Table 1.1 Possible starting points for the information age

Time	Event
40,000 BC	Clay tablets from ancient Mesopotamia, where Iraq now stands, have a precursor of cuneiform writing
1300 BC	Basic Chinese characters, such as that for the horse, first formed in bone
387 BC	Plato founded his academy devoted to research in philosophy and the sciences on land which had belonged to Academos
1455	The printing of the Bible with movable type by Gutenberg in Germany
1564	Graphite is discovered
1651	John Dury first describes the role of information manager (actually a librarian at the University of Oxford, usually referred to as the first modern library)
1860	First commercial typewriters use the QWERTY keyboard
1876	Alexander Graham Bell introduced the first telephone to an audience at the Centennial Exposition in Philadelphia
1901	Marconi sends a radio signal of the Morse code letter 's' across the Atlantic from Cornwall, England, to St John's, Newfoundland
1937	Atanasoff–Berry Computer (ABC), the world's first electronic digital computer built by John Vincent Atanasoff and Clifford Berry at Iowa State University
1947	First commercial computer – ENIAC (Electronic Numerical Integrator and Computer). It weighed thirty tons and used 18,000 vacuum tubes
1953	IBM produced the first computer system that was widely adopted by organizations
1969	First node on the US ARPANET, forerunner of the Internet
1971	A computer engineer named Ray Tomlinson sent the first e-mail message. He can't remember the message, but he does remember choosing the @ symbol!
1991	First website (**http://info.cern.ch**) published by Tim Berners-Lee

A light-hearted guide to changes in our society is available online at **www.out-a-time.com** or **www.futurefeedforward.com/timeline.php** which highlights some of the technological developments in the information age and places them in the context of earlier and later ages through to 2072!

Information in today's organization

The greatest contribution that information makes to organizations is as a resource to improve the performance of organizations and the individuals that work within them. Organizational performance can be improved by utilizing information resources to help deliver better-quality products or services more profitably. Individual performance can be improved by providing employees with more relevant, timely information to support their decisions.

The importance of information to organizational performance has been recognized by the IT Governance Institute, which has developed with its member organizations COBIT, a framework intended to assist organizations in managing their information resources. COBIT stands for Control Objectives for Information and related Technology. It was first released by the Information Systems Audit and Control Foundation (ISACF) in 1996. It is not a methodology or a standard, but a practical tool drawn from other standards and methodologies. It focuses on delivering quality information and distinguishes between 'information and related information technology (IT)'. COBIT is used by organizations in Europe, Asia and the Americas. In COBIT 4.1 (COBIT, 2008), the reasons for the importance of managing information are stated as follows:

> Increasingly, top management is realising the significant impact that information can have on the success of the enterprise. Management expects heightened understanding of the way IT is operated and the likelihood of its being leveraged successfully for competitive advantage. In particular, top management needs to know if information is being managed by the enterprise so that it is:
>
> - Likely to achieve its objectives
> - Resilient enough to learn and adap
> - Judiciously managing the risks it faces
> - Appropriately recognising opportunities and acting upon them

We consider in more detail in Chapter 6 how the COBIT framework can be used to manage and control information technology and refer extensively to it in the following chapters. We will now look at how information can be used to support organizational improvement through support of business process and as a means of value creation. But, first, we highlight one of the main challenges of information management today – information overload.

Information overload

Information overload
The capacity of individuals and systems within an organization to derive value from information is exceeded by the volume and complexity of information

The flow of information within and between organizations and their stakeholders increases relentlessly. The amount of corporate data is doubling roughly every 6 months. A SNIA (2003) survey showed that in many European companies, data storage requirements more than doubled in the previous 12 months. Research insight 1.1 'How much information?' further highlights the scale of the problem. Within organizations, information overload, or if you prefer, 'drowning in data,' is a common complaint of employees as they see the potential value of information, yet are frustrated in their ability to derive benefit from it owing to its volume and complexity. A

Research insight 1.1	How much information?

An indication of the mind-boggling magnitude of information overload is provided by the estimates of Lyman and Varian (2003), researchers at the School of Information Management and Systems, University of California, Berkeley.

They calculated that in 2002, the world's total yearly creation of print, film, optical and magnetic content would require 5 exabytes of storage (Table 1.2). An exabyte is 1,000,000,000,000,000,000 bytes or 10^{18} bytes, where a byte is equivalent to one character. Assuming that the world's population is 6.3 billion, annually 800 megabytes of recorded information are produced for each man, woman and child on Earth. In a more understandable context it would take about 30 feet of books to store the equivalent information for each person on paper. The annual rate of increase is estimated at 30 per cent across all media.

The World Wide Web is one area where it is easy to see the rate at which data is duplicated and stored. Social networking sites such as Facebook and MySpace, for example, allow people to upload photographs and videos to their personal spaces which take up room on servers. Also, the more people that join the site, the more personal data has to be stored, including usernames, passwords, e-mail addresses and preferences. Membership of social networking sites is expected to continue to grow until 2012 (PublicTechnology, 2008), yet even after this peak is reached the members will undoubtedly continue to add materials.

Even though much of the data that is stored around the web can be seen via a browser, still more exists 'behind the scenes' in what is known as the 'deep Web'. It has been estimated that this hidden web contains 500 times more data than the visible web, being in the region of 7,500 terabytes (Bin, Patel, Zhen and Chen-Chuan Chang, 2007).

Table 1.2 shows the importance of magnetic media in information storage. Ninety-two per cent of new information is stored on magnetic media, primarily computer hard disks (see Chapter 3).

Table 1.2 Worldwide production of original information, if stored digitally, in terabytes circa 2002

Storage medium	2002 Terabytes, upper estimate	2002 Terabytes, lower estimate	1999–2000, upper estimate	1999–2000, lower estimate	% change, upper estimate
Paper	1,634	327	1,200	240	36%
Film	420,254	74,202	431,690	58,209	–3%
Magnetic	4,999,230	3,416,230	2,779,760	2,073,760	80%
Optical	103	51	81	29	28%
TOTAL	5,421,221	3,490,810	3,212,731	2,132,238	69%

Source: Lyman and Varian (2003)

Upper estimates assume information is digitally scanned, lower estimates assume digital content has been compressed. A terabyte is approximately one trillion bytes, 1,024 gigabytes.

The researchers provide these estimates of information flows across different media:

- *Telephone calls worldwide* – on both landlines and mobile phones – contained 17.3 exabytes of new information if stored in digital form; this represents 98 per cent of the total of all information transmitted in electronic information flows, most of it person-to-person.
- *Most radio and TV broadcast* content is not new information. About 70 million hours (3500 terabytes) of the 320 million hours of radio broadcasting are original programming. TV worldwide produces about 31 million hours of original programming (70,000 terabytes) out of 123 million total hours of broadcasting.
- *The World Wide Web* contains about 170 terabytes of information on its surface; in volume this is seventeen times the size of the Library of Congress print collections.
- Instant messaging generates five billion messages a day (750 GB), or 274 terabytes a year.
- *E-mail* generates about 400,000 terabytes of new information each year worldwide.
- *Person-to-person (P2P)* file exchange on the Internet is growing rapidly. Seven per cent of users provide files for sharing, while 93 per cent of P2P users only download files. The largest files exchanged are video files larger than 100 MB, but the most frequently exchanged files contain music (MP3 files).

For a description of the different storage capacities, see Chapter 3 or search at **www.whatis.com.**

Source: Based on Lyman and Varian (2003)

simple example of this problem is e-mail. A survey in 2002 showed that the average UK office worker spends nearly an hour of the average seven-and-a-half hour day working through their e-mails (BBC, 2002). Time spent by employees searching for information is a further and perhaps more serious problem. It is estimated that US companies spend $107 billion a year paying their employees to search for external information (Outsell, 2001). Researchers interviewed over 6000 **knowledge workers** in large organizations with revenue of more than $10 million, ranging from senior managers to more junior staff. They found that knowledge workers spend around four hours per week looking for and gathering external information and a further four hours reviewing and applying information. An average salary of $30 per hour or $240 per week was used to estimate the total of $107 billion.

In spite of information overload, information is still a vital asset of every organization. To exploit this asset effectively, organizations have to counter information overload by improving information quality. Managing information quality will ensure that information is fit for purpose, that it is *relevant* to the needs of employees, customers and suppliers. Practical, technology-enabled techniques are available to improve information quality, such as:

- *Aggregating* – the 'big picture' is presented by summing up individual data items.
- *Summarizing* – an abstract of a technical report is one form of summarizing.
- *Filtering* – less relevant information can be removed, for example only news items that contain the company's name or competitors' names are sent through to managers.
- *Alerting* – messages are displayed on-screen or sent via e-mail to alert managers to a newsworthy piece of information.

Later in this chapter we will introduce the concept of information quality and in Chapter 10 we will look at management approaches to improve information quality.

Using information to support processes

Knowledge workers
A term referring to employees who spend a large part of their time searching, analysing and disseminating information within an organization

Business processes
The activities undertaken by organizations to develop and deliver products or services to stakeholders

Information is vital to all organizations since all **business processes** that make up an organization's operations and management make extensive use of information. Organizational performance is improved by reviewing how well processes work and making adjustments to make them operate more efficiently and effectively (see Chapter 10). Davenport and Short (1990) defined a process as

> a set of logically related tasks performed to achieve a defined business outcome.

Typical business processes involve activities to deliver a service to an internal or external customer and are illustrated in Figure 1.1.

There are many different types of information that support these processes. The Hawley Committee (1995), which was created to help organizations make better use of their information assets, identifies these information groupings:

- Market and customer information
- Product information
- Specialist knowledge
- Business process information
- Management information and plans
- Human resource information
- Supplier information
- Accountable information.

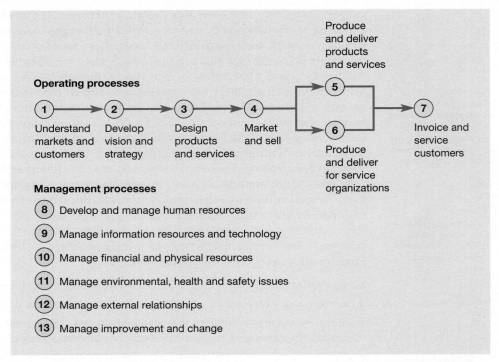

Figure 1.1 Generic organizational operating processes and management processes
Source: PricewaterhouseCoopers, 2002

From these information groups it is evident that information enables organizations to:

1 *Sense* what is happening in the external environment and respond accordingly through their strategy and tactics. For example, they can monitor competitor activity such as the introduction of new products or the winning of new contracts.

2 *Research* demand for new products – customers in different markets can be surveyed for their needs for products.

3 *Monitor and control* operating processes for efficiency and improve them to save time or money.

4 *Exchange information* with partners such as suppliers as part of their operational processes.

5 *Communicate* messages about brands and products internally and externally.

We can see why Evans and Wurster (1997) wrote: '*every business is an information business … information is the glue that holds together the structure of all businesses*'. But information is more than a glue; we will see that information management can help deliver strategic advantage to organizations through better sensing of the business environment, offering distinctive services and driving down costs. Evans and Wurster (1997) give the examples of three companies that they feel compete as much on the basis of the way they use information as through their physical products. They cite American Airlines using its control of its SABRE reservations system to achieve higher seat capacity utilization on its flights, Wal-Mart's use of electronic data interchange to increase efficiency in its supply chain, and Nike's detailed knowledge of its customer segments to produce specific products.

To illustrate the different concepts of business information management in this text, we will use a common running example – the *Lo-cost Airline Company*, which was introduced in the Preface. Consider how this fictitious company would use information to support the processes shown in Figure 1.1. For example, the process 'understand customers and markets' requires information collected inside the company about individual customers, such as where they live, the routes they fly and how much they spend with the airline. This information also needs to be aggregated (summed) so that we know the total size of a market such as the business flights market or flights originating in one country. Such internal information which helps managers review and improve the performance of an organization is known as '**business intelligence**'. The process for improving both the quality of the information and the performance of the oganization is '**business performance management**'. External information is also needed to support processes. For the process 'Develop vision and strategy' it is necessary to monitor trends such as the total number of flights, market share and competitor activity, which together are known as '**market intelligence**'. The use of information and software to support business performance management is explored further in Chapters 8 and 10.

Business intelligence
Internal information about the performance of an organization reviewed at either a detailed or summary level

Business performance management
A process for improving the performance of organizations based on performance metrics

Market intelligence
External information about a specific market which is used to understand a company's competitive position

Using information to create value

We have seen that business information management is vital to supporting the operation of organizational processes and improving organizational performance and how organizations need to counter information overload. But, perhaps the most critical reason for the study and practice of business information management is its strategic importance to organizations. The information management capabilities of organizations impact their position in the markets in which they operate. As an example of how one company has taken information to the heart of its strategy read Mini case study 1.1 'Capital One creates value through information'.

Mini case study 1.1 | **Capital One creates value through information** **FT**

Capital One was established in 1995. It offers credit cards, savings, loans and insurance products in the UK, Canada and the US. It is a financially successful company achieving high returns of 20 per cent earnings per share growth and 20 per cent return on equity growth. It had been profitable in every quarter of the first ten years of its existence, only suffering losses during the global financial meltdown in 2008.

The organisation is quick to point out that its success, due in no small part to customer loyalty, is generated through more than just advertising:

> ...our brand is not defined by our television commercials. It is defined by the quality of our products and our customer experience. At Capital One, our brand is premised on empowering our customers with informed choice, great value, and excellent service. We are building on our heritage of bringing our customers great value without the hassle by investing in our customer experience to drive ongoing customer loyalty. We also are investing in world-class customer infrastructure, such as an integrated view of customer relationships and enhanced online servicing capabilities. These investments will enable us to provide all of our national

Figure 1.2 Capital One website
Source: www.capitalone.com

and local customers with better products at lower cost. We have a franchise of over 50 million customer accounts and 36 million unique customers. We interact with our customers around 300 million times a year, not counting the billion times they use our cards. I am grateful for our customers' loyalty, and our job is to sustain and build on it to make Capital One the best choice for all their banking needs. (CapitalOne, 2007)

Capital One uses what it calls an 'Information-Based Strategy' (IBS), which brings marketing, credit, risk, operations and IT together to enable flexible decision making. It describes IBS as 'a rigorously scientific test-and-learn methodology that has enabled us to excel at product innovation, marketing and risk management – the essentials of success in consumer financial services'. For customers it is able to offer financial solutions that are tailored to individual customers' needs. It does this through mass-customization: offering different rates and fees structures to different customers depending on their risk status.

Information technology also plays an important part in capturing new custom at Capital One:

'We are making it easier than ever to become a customer of our bank. In 2007, we introduced SmartSwitch®, which enables our customers to reliably and easily move their entire banking relationship from another bank to Capital One, including the seamless transfer of electronic bill pay information.' (CapitalOne, 2007)

The scale of use of information is indicated by different operations in the business. In corresponding with customers, *The Banker* reported that Capital One sends out one billion items of mail per year and handles 90 million inbound calls, 300 million outbound calls, 230 million Internet impressions and 40 million transactions per day. Together with its subsidiaries, the company had 50 million worldwide customers and $147 billion in managed loans as of September 2010.

The IBS is managed by the Chief Information Officer, Gregor Bailar. He is in charge of operations related to computer systems, analysis of customer data, data protection, setting data standards, business continuity and information security.

According to *The Banker*, Gregor says:

CIOs today need to be technology alchemists. They need to be strong in professional technical methodologies so that their conversation is a disciplined one but, at the same time, they need to understand the business, be it banking, credit cards or loans.

Their job is not to know the future of technology, nor the latest and greatest of delivery networks, but to be focused on balancing the set of business needs, and choosing or creating the best possible solutions that can be provided from a technical perspective.

On the one hand, the CIO has to be an advocate for the business into the technology world, and on the other hand, the voice of technology in the best respect of how it can respond to the business. This is a relatively new role and the challenge is to interpret and prioritise correctly the business's needs and make the technology systems really responsive.

The CIO is expected to be involved not only in strategy development, but also in business and product innovation. Now, more than ever, CIOs are being held accountable for driving the business value, not just for keeping the lights blinking on the computers.

Source: Based on company annual reports and an article in *The Banker* (2003)

The strategic importance of business information management in an organization can be assessed using Figure 1.3. This analytic tool devised by Professor Don Marchand shows different ways in which information can create value for organizations. The main methods are:

1 *Add value.* Value is added through providing better-quality products and services to an organization's customers. Information can be used to better understand customer characteristics and needs and their level of satisfaction with services. Information is also used to sense and respond to markets. Information about trends in demands, competitor products and activities must be monitored so that organizations can develop strategies to compete in the marketplace. The Lo-cost Airline Company will use databases to store personal characteristics of customers and details of which routes customers have flown. Analysis of these databases using the approach of data mining described in Chapter 8 can then be used to understand customer preferences and market products that better meet their needs.

2 *Reduce costs.* Cost reduction through information is achieved through making the business processes shown in Figure 1.1 more efficient. Efficiency is achieved through using information to create, market and deliver services using fewer resources than previously. Technology is applied to reduce paperwork, reduce the human resources needed to operate the processes through automation and improve internal and external communications. The Lo-cost Airline Company has used Internet technology so that customers serve themselves when they book tickets or make enquiries online – the concept of 'web self-service' described in Chapter 2.

3 *Manage risks*. Risk management is a well-established use of information within organizations. Marchand (2000) notes how risk management within organizations has created different functions and professions such as finance, accounting, auditing and corporate performance management (Chapter 9). For example, the Lo-cost Airline Company will produce management information on the ticket sales and costs of operating the different routes which will be used by managers to assess whether their strategies are effective and revise them accordingly.

4 *Create new reality*. Marchand uses the expression 'create new reality' to refer to how information and new technologies can be used to innovate, to create new ways in which products or services can be developed. The Lo-cost Airline Company can also use online services to introduce new products more cost-effectively, such as a holiday booking service, a car rental service or web-based services to compare the price of flights from different suppliers – all also potential value-adding activities.

All organizations use a combination of these four approaches to using information. Traditionally, organizations have mainly used information to reduce costs and manage risk (company A in Figure 1.3). Risk management is essential to the operation of businesses. The availability of information technology has eased these activities. IT has also given new opportunities to create value (company B). Company C has a balanced approach to using information to create business value. However, depending on an organization's characteristics such as its size and its markets, it may not be appropriate for all companies to achieve the position occupied by company C. Instead, Figure 1.3 can be used to assess opportunities for improved use of information.

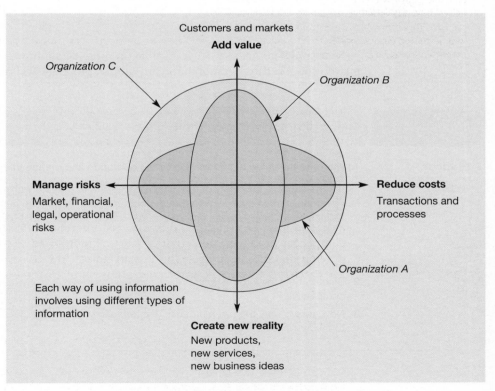

Figure 1.3 An evaluation tool relating information to business value

An organization's use of information on each axis can be assessed from 1 (low use of information) to 10 (high use of information)

Source: Marchand (2000)

Figure 1.4 gives insight into how business perceives the benefits of information technology. It can be seen that cost reduction is the main driver, with enhanced communication to customers, staff and suppliers also well represented. However, using the technology to gain competitive advantage is not frequently cited.

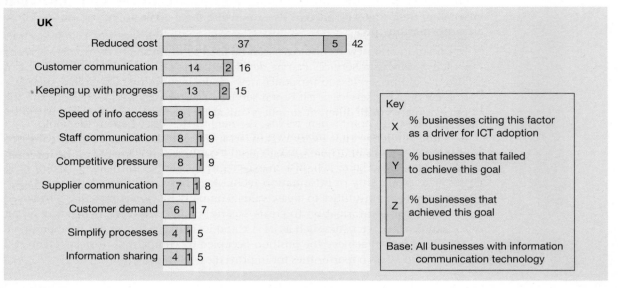

Figure 1.4 Reasons cited by businesses for adoption of information technology
Source: DTI www.ukonlineforbusiness.gov.uk/benchmarking2003

Now complete Activity 1.1 to explore, in more detail, how different types of information support the operation of organizational processes and create value.

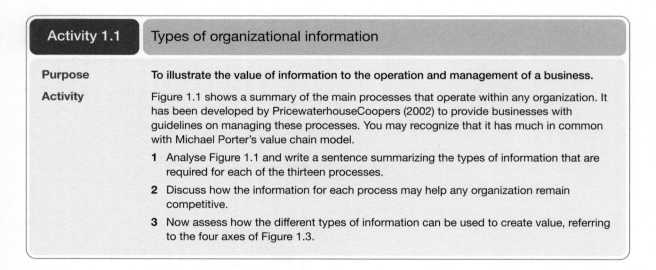

Activity 1.1	Types of organizational information
Purpose	To illustrate the value of information to the operation and management of a business.
Activity	Figure 1.1 shows a summary of the main processes that operate within any organization. It has been developed by PricewaterhouseCoopers (2002) to provide businesses with guidelines on managing these processes. You may recognize that it has much in common with Michael Porter's value chain model.

1 Analyse Figure 1.1 and write a sentence summarizing the types of information that are required for each of the thirteen processes.

2 Discuss how the information for each process may help any organization remain competitive.

3 Now assess how the different types of information can be used to create value, referring to the four axes of Figure 1.3.

Fundamentals of business information management

We have seen that managing information has become a significant challenge for organizations. In this section we introduce key concepts that are used as a basis for studying and improving information management. Effective BIM is dependent on effective management of different types of resources within an organization. These are information, people and technology. The elements of these three types of resources which we introduce in this chapter are summarized in Figure 1.5. These are portrayed as a three-legged stool, since if there are failures in the management of any one of the three of these resources, then BIM will be ineffectual. In the following sections we start by defining business information management and then explore the three different resource types and introduce some of the main issues with managing these resources and point where we discuss them further elsewhere in the book.

A major challenge that every organization faces today is to develop coherent strategies that enable effective management of the different elements of the information–people–technology resource shown in Figure 1.5. In Part 2 of *Business Information Management* we consider how the development of information management (Chapter 4), knowledge management (Chapter 5) and information systems strategies (Chapter 6) can help harness these resources together to deliver value and support organizational processes.

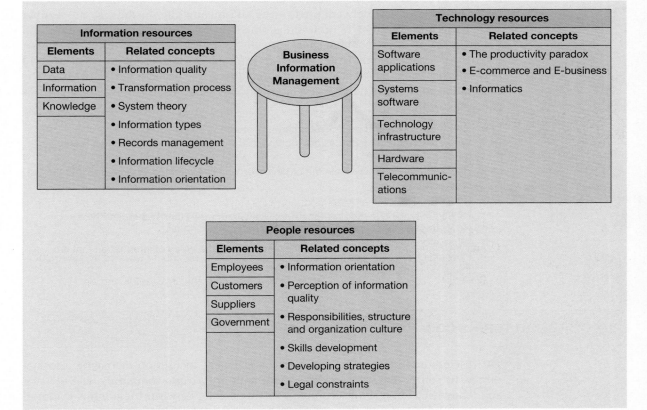

Figure 1.5 The three strands of business information management (information, people and technology resources)

What is business information management?

'Information management' and 'business information management' are increasingly used to refer to courses and business school departments that deliver education for current and future managers. At the same time, in organizations, roles such as chief information officers (CIOs), chief knowledge officers (CKOs) and business information managers are increasing, as Carr (2003) has noted. The use of such terms is useful to suggest the need for a focus on the study and practice of managing information as a strategic resource within organizations. We define business information management (BIM) as:

> *The process of managing information as a strategic resource for improving organizational performance. This process involves developing strategies and introducing systems and controls to improve information quality to deliver value.*

This definition emphasizes the need to treat information as a valuable resource which has an important role to play in delivering value to all types of organizations. It also suggests the need for specific responsibilities, strategies and tools to be created to manage the resource and improve its quality (see later in the chapter and Chapter 10 for discussion of information quality). Note that technology has less emphasis than in terms such as 'information technology' and 'information systems'. Technology is simply used as a tool to implement systems and controls which help deliver information-based value to the business.

However, the degree of adoption of this emphasis on business information management varies in different countries. In the US, one of the leading trade publications for professionals is *CIO (chief information officer)* (**www.cio.com**) reflecting this emphasis. We will see in Chapters 4 and 6 that the role of CIO is commonplace in the US, but it has been less widely adopted in the UK. Meanwhile, in the UK, the leading trade publications read by IT professionals are *Computing* (**www.computing.co.uk**) and *Computer Weekly* (**www.computerweekly.co.uk**), reflecting a more technical emphasis.

The key organizational issues related to information management, which we will cover in this book, have been usefully summarized by Elizabeth Orna (1999), of the Association for Information Management who says that information management is concerned with:

- How information is acquired, recorded and stored
- Where information resources are located in the organization and who has responsibility for them
- How information flows within the organization and between the organization and the outside world
- How the organization uses it
- How people who handle it apply their skills and co-operate with one another
- How information technology supports the users of information
- What information costs and the value it contributes
- How effectively all these information-related activities contribute towards achievement of the organization's objectives.

Business information management
The process of managing information as a strategic resource for improving organizational performance. This process involves developing strategies and introducing systems and controls to improve information quality to deliver value

Information resources

The discipline of business information management focuses on managing information as a resource. But what exactly is information? (We also commonly refer to 'data' and 'knowledge' in a similar context.) Distinguishing between these terms is important for understanding the nature of business information management and to enable information to be managed effectively.

How do the concepts of data, information and knowledge interrelate? Let's take the example of ticket sales for the Lo-cost Airline Company (see Figure 1.6). Here **data** are recorded each time a customer buys a ticket as part of the sales process. The data will be automatically recorded in a digital form as customers or call-centre operators enter the flight booking via a web page. Since an airline will sell millions of tickets each year, in its raw form, these data have little value to managers in the airline. The sheer volume of data means they cannot be used to assess how well the processes are operating. The data need to be transformed into **information** using an **information system** for them to be used for decision making by managers.

English (1999) defines the relationship between data and information as follows:

Information is data in context. Information is usable data. Information is the meaning of data, so facts become understandable.

With this information at hand managers can use the information to ask different questions about the processes, for example:

- What is the split of revenue between sales to business and individual customers? (Operating process 1 – understand markets and customers.)
- What proportion of seats do we sell on each route? (Operating process 4 – market and sell.)
- What is the profitability of each route? (Operating process 5 – produce and deliver products and services.)

It is apparent that to answer these questions, information systems are needed to deliver relevant, timely information which is at the right level of detail to answer each question. The information from millions of ticket sales will be aggregated or summarized to produce totals and averages across the entire year for different routes. Ticket sales will also need to be compared to competitors who use these routes. Visualization using different forms such as charts and maps such as Figure 1.7 is essential to simplify the volume of data. Note that the FlightMapping service (**www.flightmapping.com**) is an example of an online intermediary website with a revenue model based on advertising and commission on referrals which has been created to meet online searchers' need to reduce their information overload. Of course a manual or paper-based information system would be incapable of delivering these information needs, so **information and communication technology (ICT or IT)** is vital to modern business information management. This ICT includes software applications to capture and give access to information, computer hardware to run these applications and networks to facilitate transfer of information within the organization and beyond. In Chapter 2, we describe the different types of software or programs used to support business information management in more detail and in Chapter 3 we look at the hardware and communications technology.

While information from the information system will enable managers to answer the type of questions given above about processes, this, in turn, is of little value to the business if no action is taken. Managers need to apply their skills and experience to use the information to take decisions about how to change the way they use their resources to improve process performance. This application of judgement to take the best action is **knowledge**. For example, managers at the Lo-cost Airline Company will use their knowledge to act on information about unprofitable routes to attempt to improve their profitability. The concept of knowledge is less straightforward than those of data and information and it is explored further in Chapter 5.

English (1999) builds on his definition of information to define knowledge as follows:

Knowledge is not just information known, it is information in context. Knowledge means understanding the significance of the information. Knowledge is the value added to information by people who have the experience and acumen to understand its real potential. Knowledge has value only to the extent that people are empowered to act based on that knowledge. In other words, knowledge has value only when acted on.

Data
Discrete, objective facts about events. Data are transformed into information by adding value through context, categorization, calculations, corrections and condensation

Information
Organized data, meaningful and contextually relevant. Used for decision making

Information system
A computerized or manual system to capture data and transform them into information and/or knowledge

Information and communication technology (ICT or IT)
The software applications, computer hardware and networks used to create information systems

Knowledge
The combination of data and information to which is added expert opinion, skills and experience to result in a valuable asset which can be used to make decisions

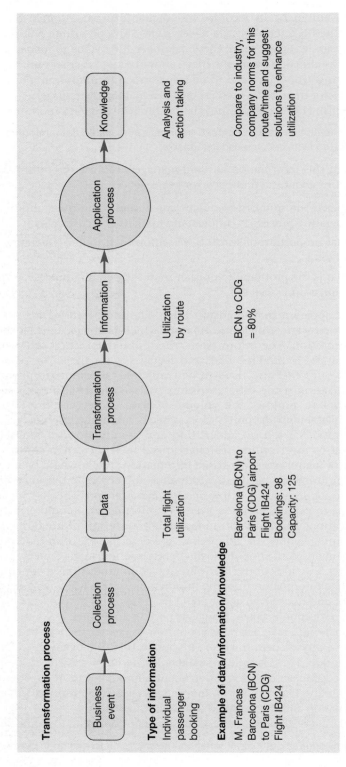

Figure 1.6 The data to information to knowledge transformation process

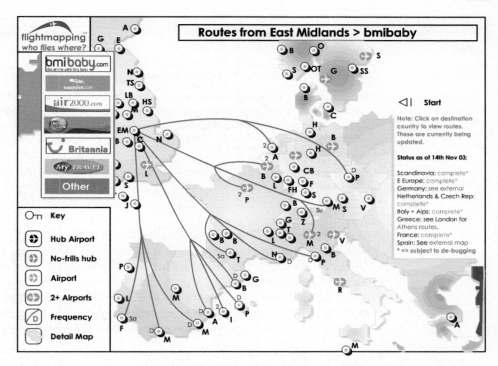

Figure 1.7 Summary information view of European flights from Birmingham International Airport

Source: www.flightmapping.com/Europe/flights-map.swf

The transformation process from data to information to knowledge is explored in a little more detail later in the chapter and in Chapter 5.

Information quality

The effectiveness of business information management within an organization is essentially determined by the quality of information. For information to be effective in supporting organizational processes, its quality, or 'fitness for purpose' is critical. In the context of information quality, 'fitness for purpose', means how well it supports the tasks performed by individuals and the decisions they take. If information quality is poor then tasks will be performed inefficiently, erroneous decisions will be made, or, perhaps worse, information will not be trusted and no decisions will be made.

Think about what characteristics make superior quality information. Activity 1.2 reviews the qualities of information for a manager within an airline who needs to review the effectiveness of their marketing campaigns. It can be seen that the most important attribute of information to managers is *relevance* – the information must support them in their decision making. *Accuracy* is another prerequisite – accuracy must be sufficient to base a decision on it. If the same information is duplicated in different parts of the organization then there will often be a problem with accuracy if the different information repositories are not replicated to be consistent. Activity 1.2 also shows the importance of *timeliness* – delays between the collection of data and their processing should be minimized. The final aspect of information quality is the *form* in which it is presented – some information is more easily visualized in a table, while other information is more easily presented in graph or map form.

Improving the quality of the information attributes described in this section has been a major driver for investment in information systems. For example, the enterprise

<table>
<tr><td>

Activity 1.2

</td><td>

Assessing information quality for the Lo-cost Airline Company

</td></tr>
<tr><td>

Purpose

Activity

</td><td>

To illustrate the meaning of information quality through considering an example.

You are a newly appointed marketing manager within the Lo-cost Airline Company. You want to assess the quality of information on the performance of your marketing campaigns such as advertising a particular route or low-price deal. How would you assess the quality of information available to your team to help them improve the effectiveness and efficiency of their campaigns?

Tip Look at the detailed coverage of information quality in Chapter 10 when completing this activity.

</td></tr>
</table>

Information audit
An approach to reviewing and improving information usage – information quality within an organization

Information policy
A formal declaration of how information management will be managed and information quality will be improved within an organization

Business data
Detailed objective facts about events or items related to business processes and the external environment

Business event
A financial or non-financial transaction within or between organizations that happens at a point in time

Business information
Data that have been transformed into a meaningful, organized form relevant to those who require it to manage business processes

resource planning systems described in Chapter 2 have been introduced in many organizations to increase information accuracy by reducing duplication, increasing timeliness and providing real-time information and drill-down facilities to different parts of the organization.

Managing information quality is a vital part of business information management. In Chapters 4 and 10 we look in more detail at how organizations conduct an **information audit** and create an **information policy** to help improve the quality of information.

The data-to-information transformation process

Information systems take inputs (**business data**) and transform them into outputs (**business information**). Data are typically detailed facts about business events related to business processes or facts about the external environment. A **business event** may include financial transactions such as sales or billing, but also other interactions such as a customer service e-mail enquiry or complaint. For a sales process for an airline, data include sales details such as ticket number and method of payment, customer details such as contact details or product characteristics such as the route flown. Such data items will exist for every sale made, so data often consist of a stream of transactions which for an airline will amount to millions of transactions a year.

Information exists or is held in many media, such as on a piece of paper, in a phone conversation, inside a computer, on a computer screen and in our memories. Some is transient, some permanent. Business information management is essentially about capturing the value in this information. Capturing involves making the most valuable information available to the right people at the right time to support their decisions. Without the best-possible-quality information poor decisions will be made which may result in poor organizational performance, loss of jobs, or even loss of life.

Orna (1996) summarizes the intangible but vital nature of information as follows:

● It must be transformed by human cognition to be of value – information has no inherent value in itself.

● Where inflows of information to maintain knowledge or support appropriate action are blocked, disaster can follow, either immediately (as in an airline flight) or a more gradual decrease in organizational competence.

● Where information is hoarded for the exclusive use of a limited number of people, it does not fulfil its potential value.

● Information is a diffuse resource that enters into all activities of businesses and forms a component of all its products and services.

Information is used to help manage the organizational processes shown in Figure 1.1. For example, consider Operating Process 1 'Understand markets and customers' for an airline. One function of this process is to monitor the environment of the company to assess its implications for the airline's strategy. Environment monitoring requires managers to be supplied with information including competitor activity such as their current routes and fares, the levels of customer demand for different routes and legal constraints in different countries. Detailed information could be distributed, showing, for example, every route for every competitor with number of flights and capacity utilization (number of seats sold). However, the tens of thousands of items would be overwhelming. Instead what is required is summary information such as total number of routes flown by competitors, their average capacity and changes compared to a previous period. This is valuable business information that can be rapidly reviewed by managers as required.

Within an organization, information transformation follows these stages:

1 Capture or input of data.
2 Routeing of data to location for processing.
3 Processing of data to produce information.
4 Distribution of information to its users.
5 Analysis and interpretation of information by users coupled with their knowledge (skills and previous experience) to take actions which give results.

These stages are summarized in Figure 1.6 on page 18.

Activities involved in processing information can be summarized by using the 4 Cs of:

- *Context* – displaying a data item relative to other data items, such as in a time series or trend graph. Sorting data alphabetically or numerically is another example of contextualization.
- *Calculation* – producing derived metrics such as calculating a percentage capacity utilization.
- *Classification or categorization* – grouping information into different categories, for example all flights into a particular country.
- *Condensation* – aggregating or totalling information is always important in presenting business event data as summary information, for example, total sales on a route. Filtering is also used to summarize information, for example 'show me all flights that were delayed by at least two hours'.

Information types and sources

Earlier in the chapter, we introduced different groupings of business information such as customer information, market information and accountable information which are used to support different business processes. These sources of information may be internal or external.

For each one of these information types, different forms of information are available, as is shown with examples in Figure 1.8. Forms of information include:

- *structured* information – presented in reports, tables and graphs;
- *unstructured* information – delivered verbally or on an ad-hoc basis;
- *formal* information – part of established reporting and communication;
- *informal* information – ad-hoc communication such as conversations or e-mail.

Business information management seeks to harness all of these types of information to improve business performance.

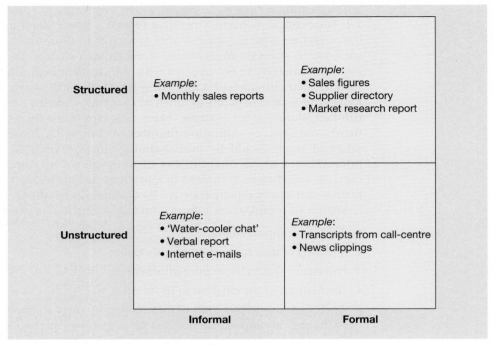

Figure 1.8 Different forms of information

All of the forms of information in Figure 1.8 are available from both internal and external sources and these often need to be managed separately.

Online information sources

One of the factors contributing towards the information overload referred to at the start of the chapter is the rapid increase in growth of online sources of information of the **Internet** and **World Wide Web**. E-mail alerts and e-newsletters have become an important method of updating us about new information as it becomes available on the web. These online information sources may be external or internal.

The public information on company and organizational websites which are accessed by search engines is the best-known online information source. The largest **search engines** now index over 3 billion website pages and are increasing in size rapidly as shown by Figure 1.9. If every one of these pages was printed and stacked, it would form a paper tower 130 miles high. Even the name of search engine Google originates from big numbers – Google is named after the mathematical term 'googol', which refers to the number 1 followed by one hundred zeros.

The most popular search engine services provided by Google, MSN and Yahoo! are used intensively. In 2008, comScore estimated that 235 million searches were performed every day.

A further issue is the time potentially wasted by staff seeking information about their own personal interests. Similarly, staff may use e-mail to communicate with friends and family during work time. The extent of this problem was highlighted in 2003 when the managing director of UK company Phones 4 U banned all use of e-mail by customer-facing staff. Managing staff access to such information resources is discussed further in Chapter 11.

One approach to managing research information is to use software to automatically categorize information and alert users to relevant information. One company

Internet
A global network of computers across the globe. It consists of the infrastructure of network servers and communication links between them that are used to hold and transport information between the client computers such as PCs and the web servers storing the information

World Wide Web (WWW)
A technique for publishing information on the Internet. The web is accessed through web browsers which display web pages of embedded graphics and HTML- or XML-encoded text

Search engines
Automated tools known as 'spiders' or 'robots' index registered sites. Users use a search engine by typing a key phrase and are presented with a list of pages from the index ranked by relevance to the key phrase

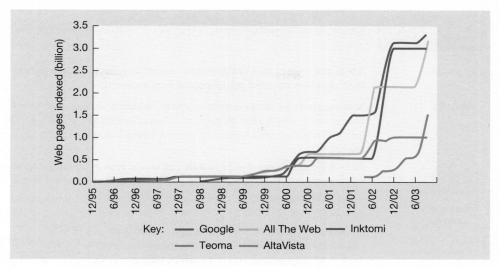

Figure 1.9 Trends in number of web pages indexed by major search engines
Source: Searchenginewatch: http://searchenginewatch.com/reports

providing this solution is UK-based Autonomy. Their Portal-In-A-Box™ product (Figure 1.10) alerts users to relevant information from the internal and external environment through automatic analysis of information based on its content and then matches it to users' previous information preferences.

How good are your information-searching skills? Activity 1.3 gives some detailed guidance on using search engines such as Google to find information more rapidly.

The information accessed in search engines does not include the **invisible web** which is made up of web pages not accessible to search engines since they are

Invisible web
Web pages not accessible by search engines since they are dynamically generated from specialized searchable databases or deliberately or accidentally excluded

Figure 1.10 Autonomy Portal-In-A-Box™
Source: Autonomy Corporation plc

Activity 1.3	Smarter searching using Google

Purpose	Assesses level of skill in information searching using Google through an example and then provides detailed guidelines on improvement.
Activity	You are a researcher for a travel company which is researching markets in Eastern Europe with a view to expanding its presence there. Specifically, you want to assess demand for forms of business and holiday travel in different European countries, and how it will vary in the future.
visit the www	Write a Google query (the keywords you would type into Google) to find a report with this information in it. Use Google Advanced search syntax (different characters) where relevant.
	If you have not used specialized Google syntax such as quotes around a phrase: 'site', 'filetype', '+' or '−', it will be possible to improve your searching, to 'search smarter'.
	To 'search smarter' visit the companion website for this book at **www.booksites.net/chaffey** and download the 'Smarter Searching Guide'. After reading the section on formulating searches rewrite your earlier query to improve your performance.

Intranet
A private network within a single organization using Internet standards to enable employees to share information using e-mail and web publishing

Extranet
Formed by extending selected intranet services beyond an organization to its customers, suppliers and collaborators

dynamically generated from specialized searchable databases or deliberately or accidentally excluded. This is an important source of business information, as is indicated by the Invisible Web directory (**www.invisible-web.net**) which catalogues some of these databases.

As well as external online information sources there are internal online information sources such as company intranets which are used to publish information for employees and extranets which are used to publish information for partners. These also provide a repository for relevant information found by knowledge workers from external sources. In each case access is restricted through a secure network and log-in using passwords. In Chapter 2 we will look in detail at how these tools can be used for information sharing.

Case study 1.1

Avoiding disasters

Before the authors started to write this edition of the textbook the issue of data security and back-up was identified as being of great importance. The text comprises many tens of thousands of words and hundreds of diagrams and charts which would be very difficult and time-consuming to replace should they become lost or damaged.

Subsequently a simple strategy was developed to ensure the safety of the book transcript:

- The files containing the existing text were stored by the publisher and would be protected by their existing system's back-up and retrieval protocols.
- A copy of the files would be held by the authors, Dave and Gareth, which they would modify to become the new edition.
- Gareth would back up his modified text files on the server of the university where he worked and would

therefore be protected by their existing system's back-up and retrieval protocols.
- Dave would back up his modified text files using IBM's Tivoli software (**http://www-306.ibm.com/software/tivoli/products/continuous-data-protection/**) and network-attached storage (NAS) devices.
- Both Gareth and Dave also stored back-ups online at **www.ibackup.com**, online using GMail (**www.viksoe.dk/code/gmail.htm**) and on a variety of other portable storage media including CD-ROM and USB memory sticks.

By utilising the existing back-up and retrieval systems of the publisher and the university it was not necessary for the authors to invest in extra hardware and software to ensure the safety of the book text. Furthermore, the publisher and university use data protection and back-up systems that are far more sophisticated (and expensive!)

than the authors could possibly afford themselves. It is not even necessary to understand 'how' any of these systems work in order to take advantage of the security that they may provide. Adopting this simple strategy gave the paradoxical benefits of being very low cost yet still offering very high security.

Such a 'disaster prevention' strategy is often seen as being unproductive, wasteful and expensive. The time, effort and cost of developing these plans do not contribute to the profitability or effective operation of an organization and are frequently overlooked. However, it is not until disaster strikes that the benefit of having a recovery plan becomes apparent.

It was shortly after adding the 'Simple models of strategic analysis' section to Chapter 6 that the hard disk in Gareth's personal computer failed. Despite being relatively new (less than two years old) and being regularly defragmented and analysed for defects, the disk failed without warning and all data, including the file containing the recent modifications to Chapter 6, were lost.

It took three days to purchase a replacement hard disk and reinstall the operating system and applications. Incidentally, the replacement disk cost half as much as the original failed disk but had twice the capacity and indicates the speed at which computer technology advances and costs decrease!

Once the hardware and software were installed it took a mere moment to download from the university server the 'master' copy of Chapter 6 which had been saved with the additional section 'Simple models of strategic analysis' intact.

During the rewriting of this edition of the textbook Dave's server was brought offline by a fire at the company which physically houses the equipment (TheRegister, 2008). Fortunately there was no permanent damage to the servers or networking equipment but many customers were affected when their websites and services were not functional for several days and were further inconvenienced when subsequent repair work to the building had to be undertaken.

There is a lesson to be learned from this tale, which applies to students as much as to large organizations, and that is to **be prepared!**

UK government statistics indicate that 46 per cent of Internet users rarely or never make back-ups of files (**www.statistics.gov.uk/pdfdir/inta0807.pdf**). Every year we are approached by students who have lost the files containing their assignments, or whose laptops which contained all of their revision notes for the entire year have been stolen. There is little that can be done after the event, but by planning ahead such disasters can be reduced to mere inconveniences. Assignments, lecture slides, notes and presentations can be protected from loss and damage quite inexpensively:

- Antivirus software that will protect your computer and files from viruses and other forms of electronic sabotage is available free of charge. See AVG Antivirus (**http://free.avg.com/**), for example.
- Files can and should be backed up to CD ROM frequently. They may also be copied to USB sticks and drives.
- E-mailing a file as an attachment to yourself can be a simple way of retaining a copy which will then be protected by the back-up and retrieval systems of your Internet and e-mail service provider.
- Similarly, e-mail providers such as Hotmail and GMail provide free storage space where copies of important files may be kept.
- Google offer a free document-sharing service called Google Docs that can be used to store vital information. It is also a useful way for students to work together on team projects.

Technology resources

Information technology
The information and communications technologies used to capture, process, store and transport information in digital form

The technology resources used for business information management are more commonly referred to as information technology (IT). 'IT' refers to the hardware, software and telecommunications networks used to manage information. In the European Union and UK government initiatives IT is often now referred to as 'ICT' or 'Information and communications technology' to stress the importance of networks and the Internet. In this book we use the more succinct and widely adopted acronym 'IT'.

Selecting the appropriate technology is undeniably important to the implementation of the strategies needed to manage the information required to support different organizational processes. In this book, in Chapter 2 we consider software and applications resources as introduced below and in Chapter 3 infrastructure resources.

Software resources

Applications software
A computer program that delivers services to support business processes and their managers

Systems software
Software used to deliver basic computing services for applications software

Software resources include applications software and systems software. Applications software is the different types of business software applications used to deliver business information management facilities to the stakeholders. Examples include Enterprise Resource Planning systems, e-business applications and office applications. Systems software manages the computer resources such as the memory and processor and other hardware and is used to support the applications software. The role of systems software can be best understood by considering what happens as a user works with an application. Take the example of a spreadsheet application. As the user works with this, they use hardware such as the keyboard to enter numbers and formulas and the mouse to select menu options such as saving a file. As they use the mouse and keyboard, it is Microsoft Windows, the systems software, that interprets the movements of the mouse and keyboard from signals sent by the hardware.

Key management issues with different types of software are discussed in Chapter 2. These issues are the concern of the IS manager or CIO, but also closely involve departmental managers or process owners who may need to select specialist applications for their business area. The management issues with applications software include:

- Do we select best-of-breed applications or enterprise-wide systems? (Chapter 2)
- How do we select the most appropriate portfolio of applications? (Chapter 6)
- How do we manage projects to implement new applications? (Chapters 7, 8 and 9)

Technology infrastructure resources

Technology infrastructure resources
The hardware and communications networks used to store, process and transmit the software and information in an organization

Hardware
Physical devices used for information processing and storage

Communications networks
Communications media and communications processors used for transfer of data between systems

Total cost of ownership (TCO)
TCO includes purchase and maintenance price for a technology resource such as a PC

Information systems
The means by which organizations and people, using information technologies, gather, process, store, use and disseminate information

The technology infrastructure resources are the hardware and communications networks used to store, process and transmit the software and information in an organization.

Key management issues with technology infrastructure resources are discussed in Chapter 3. They are mainly the concern of the IS manager or CIO. They include:

- How do we select the most appropriate technology for the organization? (Chapter 3)
- How do we assess when we should upgrade our technology? (Chapter 3)
- Which technology standards should we adopt? (Chapter 3)
- How do we reduce the total cost of ownership (TCO)? (Chapter 11)
- How do we ensure a good quality of service? (Chapter 11).

Information systems

Business information management also involves the management of information systems within an organization.

The UK Academy for Information Systems (**www.ukais.org**) defines information systems as follows:

> Information systems are the means by which organizations and people, using information technologies, gather, process, store, use and disseminate information.

So information systems use information technology as a tool to manage information. Of course, information systems do not have to use technology. There are still occasions where transactions are recorded and processed on paper – this is a manual information system. There is a close relationship between strategies to manage information systems and strategies to manage information and knowledge. These are discussed separately in Chapters 4 to 6, where we shall see that placing the correct emphasis on each of these has proved problematic and is one of the reasons for the disillusionment in corporate IT referred to in Case study 1.2.

E-business and e-commerce

E-business and e-commerce are very new concepts relative to IS and IT. Yet, these concepts have had a significant impact on business practice since the term 'e-business' first came to prominence when IBM launched a campaign built around the term in October 1997. E-business and e-commerce are often used interchangeably and have to some extent replaced the use of terms such as IT and IS, so it is useful to distinguish between them here.

Electronic commerce (e-commerce)
All financial and informational electronically mediated exchanges between an organization and its external stakeholders

Electronic commerce (e-commerce) is often thought to refer simply to buying and selling using the Internet; people immediately think of consumer retail purchases from companies such as Amazon. However, e-commerce includes both financial and informational electronically mediated transactions between an organization and any third party it deals with (Chaffey, 2004). By this definition, non-financial transactions such as customer support enquiries about products and orders are also considered to be part of e-commerce. For the Lo-cost Airline Company, e-commerce activities would include customers checking for flight times and availability, online ordering, enquiries about tickets and baggage, and also the company buying online services. Different applications of electronic commerce are explored in more detail in Chapter 2.

How then does e-business relate to e-commerce? Let's start from the definition by IBM (**www.ibm.com/e-business**), which was one of the first suppliers to coin the term:

> **e-business (e' biz' nis)**: The process of using Web technology to help businesses streamline processes, improve productivity and increase efficiencies. Enables companies to easily communicate with partners, vendors and customers, connect back-end data systems and transact commerce in a secure manner.

E-business
All digital information exchanges supporting business processes that are mediated through Internet technology including transactions within and between organizations

It can be seen that e-business has a broader meaning. It includes e-commerce transactions, but also the use of Internet technology and e-mail to support internal processes. Within the Lo-cost Airline Company e-business activities would include those described above for e-commerce, but would also include use of intranets for scheduling internal resources for flights and extranet links for procuring resources from suppliers. Since Internet technology is increasingly used for all types of application, there is a large and increasing overlap between e-business and information systems.

In this book, the specific management challenges of e-business and e-commerce will not be explored directly, rather the concepts are reviewed throughout the book from an organizational perspective. For specific guidance on development and implementation of e-business and e-commerce strategies, refer to the coverage in Chaffey (2004). Different types of e-business applications are next covered at the end of Chapter 2.

Informatics

Organizational informatics
The study of the development and use of information and information technology within an organization with a focus on the effects on the organization's human resources

In many European countries the term 'informatics' is used to describe the study of how information and information technologies can be used together to support organizations. For example, in France, '*informatique*' is used, while in Germany and the Netherlands it is '*informatik*'. '**Organizational informatics**' is used to distinguish it from informatics in other disciplines such as healthcare or medical informatics. Kling (1993) was one of the first to adopt the term. He describes organizational informatics as follows:

Organizational Informatics denotes a field which studies the development and use of computerized information systems and communication systems in organizations. It includes studies of their conception, design, effective implementation within organizations, maintenance, use, organizational value, conditions that foster risks of failures, and their effects for people and an organization's clients.

This is a useful definition since it highlights the organizational context of information management. But it is apparent that this definition could equally be applied to information management or 'information systems'. Aside from specialist areas such as medical informatics, information management and 'knowledge management' are the terms that are the lingua franca of business professionals in most countries, and it is these terms that are used throughout this book.

Does IT matter?

As the amount of money spent by organizations on information technology has increased, there has been a great deal of argument about the value delivered by this IT. Despite the large-scale investments in IT within organizations, it is still not clear the extent to which investment in information systems benefits organizations.

In 1987, the MIT professor and Nobel economist Robert Solow (We'd better watch out, *New York Times*, 12 July) made the remark:

We see the computer age everywhere except in the productivity statistics.

IT productivity paradox
Research results indicating a poor correlation between organizational investment in information technology and organizational performance measured by return on equity

This expressed in words what many in business and economists had suspected – the feeling that although there was a lot of expenditure on IT, there was relatively little to show for it. Subsequent studies in the late 1980s and 1990s summarized by Brynjolfsson (1993) and Strassman (1997) did indeed suggest that, across companies, there is little or no correlation between a company's investment in information technology and its business performance measured in terms of profitability or shareholder value. This concept is known as the **IT productivity paradox**. Strassman's early work, looking at the paradox at the firm level, was based on a study of 468 major North American and European firms which showed a random relationship between IS spending per employee and return on equity. More recently, Brynjolfsson and Hitt (1998) and studies summarized in the *Financial Times* (2003) suggested that the productivity paradox is no longer valid.

Today, most authors, such as Brynjolfsson and Hitt (1998) and Mcafee and Brynjolfsson (2008), refute the productivity paradox and conclude that it results from mismeasurement, the lag occurring between initial investment and payback and the mismanagement of information systems projects. Mcafee and Brynjolfsson (2008) suggest that to use digital technology to support competition the mantra should be:

'Deploy, innovate, and propagate': First, deploy a consistent technology platform. Then separate yourself from the pack by coming up with better ways of working. Finally, use the platform to propagate these business innovations widely and reliably. In this regard, deploying IT serves two distinct roles – as a catalyst for innovative ideas and as an engine for delivering them.

More recent detailed studies such as that by Sircar et al. (2000) confirm the findings of Brynjolfsson and Hitt (1998). They state that 'Both IT and corporate investments have a strong positive relationship with sales, assets, and equity, but not with net income. Spending on IS staff and staff training is positively correlated with firm performance, even more so than computer capital'. In conclusion they note 'The value of IS staff and staff training was also quite apparent and exceeded that of computer capital. This confirms the positions of several authors, that the effective use of IT is far more important than merely spending on IT'.

These findings highlight the importance of considering the information, people and technology resources together both when studying information management and information systems and when developing strategies to manage the information, people and technogies within an organization. It also suggests that IT contributes to productivity gains only when combined with investments in process redesign, organizational change management and innovation.

Despite this research, in an article that challenged many assumptions about IT spending, Carr (2003) suggested that information technology had become commoditized to such an extent that it no longer delivers a competitive advantage. Carr says:

> What makes a resource truly strategic – what gives it the capacity to be the basis for a sustained competitive advantage is not ubiquity, but scarcity. You only gain an edge over rivals by having something that they can't have or can't do. By now the core functions of IT – data storage, data processing and data transport have become available and affordable to all … They are becoming costs of doing business that must be paid by all but provide distinction to none.

While many would agree that the technology such as PCs, servers and communications technologies have become commoditized, it is arguable whether technology cannot provide distinction. Carr's argument is not necessarily in conflict with the work on the productivity paradox mentioned above since although IT investments may help in increasing productivity, this does not necessarily yield a competitive advantage if all competitors are active in making similar IT investments. As the *Financial Times* (2003) puts it:

> Productivity gains that are easily replicated across an industry usually end up in the hands of customers. Only when gains remain unique to a company do managers get a say in how to distribute the spoils – between customers (in the form of lower prices or higher quality), shareholders (higher profits) and workers (increased pay).

Buried Treasure, *The Financial Times*, 10/12/2003 (Simon London)

The difference between total investment in new information management practices (e.g. business process redesign, external consultants, training and managerial time) and IT (cost of software and new computers) shows that applying technology is only a relatively small part in achieving returns – developing the right approaches to process innovation, business models and change management is more important, and arguably more difficult and less easy to replicate. Some leading companies have managed to align investment in IT with their business strategies to achieve these unique gains. For example, Wal-Mart Stores, Dell, Intel and easyJet have combined extensive use of technology with strategic innovation. Dell has used a range of IT-enabled techniques, discussed further in Chapter 2, such as online ordering, the Dell Premier extranet for large purchasers, vendor-managed inventory, adaptive supply chains and build-to-order to gain competitive advantage.

To explore the issue of how technology delivers value to organizations, refer to Case study 1.2.

Debate 1.1

Information Technologies are costs of doing business that must be paid by all, but provide distinction to none. (Carr, 2003)

Has corporate IT failed to deliver?

This article highlights some of the disappointments with the implementation of corporate IT. The reasons for these disappointments are explored. As you read through the article, evaluate whether you think reasons given are accurate.

In the use of technology to transform business, something has gone badly wrong.

Computers and the internet were meant to put business on a new footing. Newly available information would make everything smarter, from corporate supply chains to the strategic decisions of senior executives. Entire new business models would be made possible: any company that failed to adapt risked extinction.

It has not worked out quite as planned. Despite all it has promised – and in some cases delivered – the explosion of information technology has failed to live up to the hype. Corporate information systems have become complex, ungainly and difficult to manage.

Somewhere in the 1990s, amid the flowering of high-tech innovation, something seems to have gone awry.

'It's almost as though the technology took over', says Irving Wladawsky-Berger, general manager of International Business Machines' latest corporate computing initiative, known as e-business on demand.

The backlash has been powerful. Instead of being an area that corporate executives looked at to give them a competitive advantage, IT has gone back to what it was before the 1990s boom in wishful thinking: a management headache.

Big IT projects are complex and difficult to make work, with a frighteningly high failure rate. Corporate spending on IT has again become an expense to be reined in, not indulged. And the maturing of the wave of technology that arrived with the internet has left companies asking what they got for their money.

The latest symptom of this malaise has been a questioning of the strategic significance of technology to business. What real competitive advantage can be gained from technology, runs this argument, if it is equally available to your competitors? Like electricity and the telephone, it may be a necessity; but also like them, it may have little impact on a company's real competitive position. 'IT doesn't matter', claimed a provocative article in the *Harvard Business Review*. It remains to be seen for example whether emergent communication technologies such as Voice-over-Internet-Protocol (VOIP) – **www.voip.org.uk/** – and Flexible Mobile Convergence (FMC) will really add flexibility to organisations or simply generate complexity and confusion (Mazoudier, 2008).

Faced with this scepticism, the technology industry is preparing for its next big push. The real transformation of business still lies ahead, according to this view. It will happen when corporate IT systems operate flawlessly and work together seamlessly: lost luggage for example is estimated to have cost the airlines $3.8 billion in 2007 alone (Murray, 2008). And while the technology itself may not confer an instant competitive advantage, its effective application is vital to business success.

But can technology companies overcome the shortcomings of the past to fulfil this promise? And how will corporate buyers of IT, still dealing with the after-effects of their last wave of spending, react to the claims?

First, consider the sources of the problem.

Perhaps the biggest was the arrival of a new computing architecture that liberated users from the tyranny of the mainframe, but exposed a failure in technology management.

This client–server architecture brought new control to the individual user in the shape of a desktop PC. It also handed power to IT managers, making it easier to develop department-level applications to run the processes that seemed vital in the new internet era. But in the process, the larger corporate picture was lost.

'It was good at the departmental level but it didn't do much for the enterprise', says Mr Wladawsky-Berger at IBM. Liberated from the data centre, IT managers 'wrote code that was fine if it lived alone', says Bob Napier, chief technology officer at Hewlett-Packard (HP). The trouble was, it did not live alone but had to fit into a complex system. 'For some reason, when the internet came along we forgot all the pain of the past' when adapting to earlier generations of computer architecture, acknowledges Mr Napier. 'We discovered we'd left all the management tools behind us.'

A second source of the problem has been the incompleteness of the technology. While individual applications have proliferated, the tools needed to knit them together have been lacking. 'The components are advancing very rapidly, but critical elements are not there', says Mr Wladawsky-Berger. 'That's a major gap.'

The third reason for technology's disappointment has been a failure to align it with business management. Technology companies tend to blame customers for failing to understand how deeply new IT systems impact their business processes, while the users blame the technology for being too rigid.

'Most people point at the technology as the thing that's slow to change, but usually it's the business process architecture', says Ann Livermore, head of HP's services division. Business Process Management (BPM) is appearing as a favoured approach to managing complex corporate information streams (Cane, 2008). The benefits though of adding a further level of virtual control over an existing system may be challenged by those proponents of alternative approaches such as Business Process Reengineering (BPR) who would seek to eliminate and streamline those existing processes first – see Chapter 8 for a discussion of BPM and BPR.

These forces have combined to create the many headaches that companies have when trying to make modern IT systems live up to their promise.

One symptom has been the high failure rate of IT projects. 'Too many projects are taken on without the basic project management being put in place', says Mr Napier at HP. 'The number of projects that fail is scary.'

Another symptom is the low utilisation of corporate IT assets. During the boom, many companies added servers and storage every time they introduced a new department-level IT application. 'Servers were growing like bacteria', says Mr Napier. As a result, considerably less than half of this IT capacity is actually used.

Still another symptom is the high cost of maintaining corporate information systems. 'The proportion of the IT budget involved in just keeping the lights on and the business running is far too high', says Amnon Landan, chairman and chief executive of Mercury Interactive, a software company whose products measure the performance of IT applications. More than half the money big companies spend on IT is used to employ an army of technicians.

What is the answer to this crisis in corporate computing?

The IT industry's prescription rests on a number of promises. They are aimed at taking the hard work out of building and managing IT systems, freeing companies to concentrate on using the technology to its potential. 'We want to make the technology much more transparent', says Mr Wladawsky-Berger. Though simple in theory, it is likely to take years to achieve.

The main features of the promised new generation of corporate IT systems are:

Integration. The need to knit together the disparate applications is the most pressing issue facing chief information officers.

Much rests on the development of industry-wide technical standards that allow different IT systems to inter-operate. In the past, tech companies have focused much of their effort on developing and maintaining their own proprietary technologies – a strategy that was seen as essential to maintaining high profit margins. Most now claim to see the world differently.

'This is a very different industry', says Mr Wladawsky-Berger. 'Until the internet took over, vendors, including IBM, thought about control points and outmoded ideas like that. Now it's clear that this technology is more valuable when all this stuff works together.'

For buyers, the emergence of standards is having another desirable effect. 'What most companies want to do is reduce their dependence on any one supplier', says Gary Reiner, chief information officer at General Electric. 'That's why everyone is moving to open standards so aggressively.'

Automation. The key to keeping down the soaring headcount in corporate IT departments revolves around creating technology that can maintain itself. 'We need to make everything as automated as possible', says Mr Wladawsky-Berger. 'If not, the costs will go up and up. Let users say what they want, and let the technology figure it out.'

Virtualisation. By using the internet to link corporate IT assets together, it may be possible to tap unused computing or storage resources more efficiently. Turning all these assets into one giant 'virtual' machine holds out the promise of sharing work out where it can be handled most effectively. The grid computing architecture that is making its way out of academia into the corporate world is at the heart of this effort.

Utility computing. Once IT systems have been better integrated and virtualised, it will become easier, in theory, for companies to tap into specialist utility companies to supply some or all their computing needs. Then companies will be able to decide whether they want to stay in the business of building and maintaining technology or whether this is best left to outside suppliers. Although much has been done to develop informatic services over the last few years there is still no unanimous view that utility computing is the logical step for all organisations. But companies that work towards a web-centric future are predicted to be those that are most likely to survive into the long-term (McCormack, 2008).

All of these efforts are geared towards one end: to make IT serve an enterprise's interests better. 'It's almost back to the future', says Mr Wladawsky-Berger. 'That's how IT got into business in the first place.'

Most big buyers of information technology will be hoping that this time around, the promises do not prove to be as hollow.

Source: Based on Richard Waters, Corporate computing tries to find a new path, FT.com, 4 June 2003

Questions

1 What are the problems in deploying IT in corporate environments that are referred to in the article?

2 What is suggested are the main causes for these problems? How do the descriptions of failures with IT relate to technology, people and information resources used to support business information management summarized in Figure 1.5?

People resources

The people or human resources involved in business information management include internal staff and staff at other organizations such as customers, suppliers, distributors, government organizations and the media. Throughout this book we explore the issues involved with managing business information through considering the concerns of the different stakeholders within and beyond the organization. We ask what issues need to be managed to enable different types of stakeholder to use information effectively. In many businesses a high proportion of staff are **knowledge workers** who are actively involved in creating, using and distributing information and applying knowledge for decision making. Considering roles of staff in departments such as finance, human resources management, operations and marketing shows that most staff in these functions would be knowledge workers.

Knowledge worker
An employee who spends a significant amount of their time in creating, using and distributing information and applying knowledge for decision making

Particular emphasis is placed on managing human resources in Chapter 7 Managing systems development, Chapter 8 Managing change, Chapter 10 Managing information quality, Chapter 11 Managing information services quality and Chapter 12 Managing ethical and legal issues.

In Chapters 4, 5 and 6 we consider how people resources should be structured and which responsibilities should be defined as part of information, knowledge and information systems strategies.

The issues for the different stakeholders, from the end-user to different types of managerial user, are summarized below and in Table 1 in the Preface. It can be seen that each stakeholder also faces all the concerns of those at the level above – for example, every type of manager is also an end-user.

Internal end-user concerns include:

- *Data quality* – is it relevant, timely, accurate and easy to understand? (Chapter 10)
- *Service quality* – are the systems available when required at the speed required? (Chapter 11)
- *Developing IT skills* – do I have the best skills to use information and technology? (Chapter 4)
- *Applications* – do I have the right tools to do the job? (Chapters 2, 3, 6 and 9)

Departmental manager or process owner issues include:

- *Selecting providers* – which internal and external suppliers of information management services do I select? (Chapters 2, 3 and 11)
- *Applications selection* – are the right applications available to support the performance of the area I am responsible for? (Chapters 2 and 6)
- *Integrating with other functions* – how can I share information with other departments and shared processes? (Chapters 2 and 10)
- *Knowledge management* – how can the knowledge of my staff be shared and enhanced? (Chapter 5)

Chief executive officer (CEO) perspective includes:

- *Contribution of IS to business* in terms of value-adding and cost control (Chapter 4)
- *Strategic impact of IS* – how can improved information management yield competitive advantage? (Chapter 4)
- *Legal implications of information management* – what are the legal risks? What are senior managers liable for in law? (Chapter 12)

IS manager or CIO perspective includes:

- *IS strategy* – how can IS expenditure support corporate strategy? (Chapter 4)
- *Managing change and minimizing risk* as new applications are introduced (Chapter 7)
- *Resourcing* – which technologies should be outsourced and which should be kept in-house? (Chapters 7 and 10)
- *Security* – are information services secure? (Chapter 11)

Customer or partner perspective:

- *Supply* of quality information from organization
- *Security* of own information
- *Integration of systems* for transfer of information
- *Support* through enquiries made of partner organization.

Information orientation

Information orientation
A concept or metric used to assess how effectively people use information and IT to improve business performance

This book is centred on the concept of business information management to emphasize the strategic importance of managing information to organizations and the need for a stronger **information orientation (IO)** within organizations. 'Information orientation' is a phrase coined by Marchand et al. (2002). It is introduced at this point, since the information orientation concept stresses the importance of managing the way people manage and use information. The concept is explored in more detail in Chapter 4 as part of information management strategy. These authors stress these key characteristics of IO:

1 'IO incorporates a people-centric view of information use [as opposed to a technological orientation].
2 IO is causally linked to business performance [hence our selection of 'improving (organizational) performance' as the subtitle of this text]
3 IO is an organization-wide issue, not limited to the IT department or other information management support functions.
4 IO applies universally across international borders. There are no significant differences between the senior manager responses in North America and Europe.
5 IO can be used as a key performance indicator over time to assess the effectiveness of management actions to improve information behaviours and values, information management practice and IT practices.'

Summary

1 Information is now important to the state of every society and economy since it influences the relative prosperity and quality of living in each country.

2 Information is vital to organizations since it can deliver value, reduce costs and reduce risks.

3 Information supports business performance management where organizational processes are evaluated in order to increase their efficiency.

4 The problem of information overload, where information creation increases in organizations, needs to be carefully managed. Approaches must be found to deliver relevant, high-quality information to staff.

5 Business information management is defined as 'The process of managing information as a strategic resource for improving organizational performance. This process involves developing strategies and introducing systems and controls to improve information quality to deliver value.'

6 Business information is created as part of a transformation process where data are processed to give insights to managers who apply it using their knowledge to support their decisions.

7 Management of information quality is needed to improve the relevance, timeliness and form dimensions of information.

8 Systems theory can be used to model organizations and the use of resources within them. The main elements of a system are input, processing, output, feedback and control.

9 Business information management is supported through a range of resources including:

- information resources such as data, information and knowledge;
- people resources used to manage and use the information;
- technology resources such as the hardware and communications infrastructure and the applications resources for delivering information to users.

Exercises

Self-assessment questions

1 Distinguish between data, information and knowledge. Why is this distinction significant for managers involved in business information management?

2 Explain how information can be used for corporate performance management.

3 Draw a diagram summarizing how an organization processes information.

4 Which different types of information are used in an organization?

5 What are the characteristics of e-business and e-commerce? Which information types are involved in e-business and e-commerce management?

6 Distinguish between information management and knowledge management.

7 Describe the four stages of the business decision-making process and explain how information systems can support this process.

8 Summarize the arguments for the existence of the IT productivity paradox.

Essay and discussion questions

1 Assess the strategic importance of information management to an organization with reference to an organization you are familiar with.

2 Discuss the assertion by Carr that 'They [information systems] are becoming costs of doing business that must be paid by all but provide distinction to none'. Does this imply that investment in information systems should be minimized?

3 You are the managing director of a small manufacturing business with 25 staff. You have recognized the need to adopt a more structured approach to information management within your business. You want to educate staff about the importance of information quality. Develop a policy to improve information quality. You should explain the characteristics of information quality and suggest measures that can be taken at organizational and individual levels to improve information quality.

4 Assess the strengths and weaknesses of the four different schools of management practice and thinking for information management described by Marchand et al. (2002). What approaches can be used to reconcile the disparate principles of the schools?

5 Assess the significance of information management to corporate performance management.

6 Assess the relationship between e-business and information management strategic initiatives in organizations.

References

The Banker (2003) Why does the CIO have so many hats? *The Banker*. Published on 2 December www.thebanker.com/news/fullstory.php/aid/921/WhyrdoesrtherCIOr haversormanyrhatsr.html?PHPSESSID=6127f5720bc3f4cb3bd386bf1f31087a.

BBC (2002) Parenting suffers in e-mail overload, *BBC News* (http://news.bbc.co.uk/1/low/sci/tech/1998334.stm).

Bin, H., Patel, M., Zhen, Z. and Chen-Chuan Chang, K. (2007) Accessing the Deep Web. *Communications of the ACM*, 50(5), 95–101.

Brynjolfsson, E. (1993) The productivity paradox of information technology. *Communications of the ACM*, 36(12), 67–77.

Brynjolfsson, E. and Hitt, L. (1998) Beyond the productivity paradox. *Communications of the ACM*, 41(8), 49–55.

Cane, A. (2008) Process management: Making complex business simpler. FT.com. Available online at: www.ft.com/cms/s/0/b0ec54c4-1fc3-11dd-9216-000077b07658,dwp_uuid=19513b02-2298-11dd-93a9-000077b07658.html.

CapitalOne (2007) Annual Report. Available online at: http://library.corporate-ir.net/library/70/706/70667/items/283356/2007AnnualRpt.pdf.

Carr, N. (2003) IT doesn't matter. *Harvard Business Review*, May, 5–12.

Chaffey, D. (2004) *E-Business and E-Commerce Management*, 2nd edn. Financial Times Prentice Hall, Harlow.

COBIT (2008) Executive Summary & Framework of COBIT. Available online at: www.isaca.org.

Davenport, T. (2000) Putting the I into IT. In D. Marchand, T. Davenport and T. Dickson (eds), *Mastering Information Management*. Financial Times Prentice-Hall, Harlow, pp. 5–9.

Davenport, T. and Short, J. (1990) The new industrial engineering: Information technology and business process redesign. *Sloan Management Review*, 31(4) (Summer), 11–27.

Drucker, P. (1993) *Post Capitalist Society*. Harper Business, New York.

DTI (2003) Business in the Information Age: The International Benchmarking Study 2003. A report prepared for the UK Department of Trade and Industry by Booz, Allen and Hamilton. www.ukonlinefor business.gov.uk/benchmarking2003.

English, L. (1999) *Improving Data Warehouse and Business Information Quality. Methods for Reducing Costs and Increasing Profits*. Wiley, New York.

Evans, P. and Wurster, T. (1997) Strategy and the new economics of information. *Harvard Business Review*, September–October, 70–82.

Financial Times (2003) Buried treasure, Simon, London, 10 December.

Hawley, R. (1995) Information as an asset: The board agenda/The Hawley Committee; a consultative document for chairmen, chief executives and boards of directors developed on behalf of the KPMG IMPACT Programme by a committee under the chairmanship of Dr Robert Hawley, chief executive of Nuclear Electric plc. London: KPMG, 1995. [1]: A consultative report. – 30pp.; 30cm. [2]: Checklist and explanatory notes. – 16pp.; 23cm.

Kling, R. (1993) Organizational analysis in computer science. *The Information Society*, 9(2) (Mar–Jun), 71–87. Available online at: www.ics.uci.edu/~kling/ orginf.html.

Lyman, P. and Varian, H. (2003) How much information? – Online research summary. Available online at: www.sims.berkeley.edu/research/projects/.

Marchand, D. (2000) Hard IM choices for senior managers. In D. Marchand, T. Davenport and T. Dickson (eds), *Mastering Information Management*. Financial Times Prentice Hall, Harlow, pp. 295–300.

Marchand, D., Davenport, T. and Dickson, T. (eds) (2000) *Mastering Information Management*. Financial Times Prentice Hall, Harlow.

Marchand, D., Kettinger, W. and Rollins, J. (2002) *Information Orientation: The Link to Business Performance*. Oxford University Press, Oxford. Explains the information orientation and information lifecycle concepts in more detail.

Martin, W. (1995) *The Global Information Society*. Aslib/Gower, Aldershot.

Mazoudier, F. (2008) Going all-mobile – the real meaning of FMC. FT.com. Available online at: www.ft.com/cms/s/0/52d699f0-3c54-11dd-b958-0000779fd2ac,dwp_uuid=8941d764-3ba2-11dd-9cb2-0000779fd2ac.html.

Mcafee, A. and Brynjolfsson, E. (2008) Investing in the IT that makes a competitive difference. *Harvard Business Review*, 7/8, 98–107.

McCormack, A. (2008) Boardroom debate: Following the herd can lead you astray. FT.com. Available online at: http://www.ft.com/cms/s/0/446e0290-3c54-11dd-b958-0000779fd2ac, dwp_uuid=8941d764-3ba2-11dd-9cb2-0000779fd2ac.html.

Murray, S. (2008) Irport technology: Tags that keep bags on track. FT.com. Available online at: www.ft.com/cms/s/0/46c38934-3c54-11dd-b958-0000779fd2ac,dwp_uuid=8941d764-3ba2-11dd-9cb2-0000779fd2ac.html.

Orna, E. (1996) Valuing information: Problems and opportunities. In D. Best (ed.) *The Fourth Resources: Information and its Management*. Gower, Basingstoke.

Orna, E. (1999) *Practical Information Policies*, 2nd edn. Gower, Basingstoke.

Outsell (2001) Super Information about Information Managers. Report on study conducted by Outsell Inc. for Factiva, Dialog and KPMG.

PricewaterhouseCoopers (2002) PricewaterhouseCoopers Global Best Practice Guidelines. Available online at: www.globalbestpractices.com/Bestpractices.

PublicTechnology (2008) Explosive growth of social networking to level out in 5 years time, says research. Available online at: www.publictechnology.net/modules.php?op=modload&name=News&file=article&sid=12195.

Sircar, S., Turnbow, J. and Bordoloi, B. (2000) A framework for assessing the relationship between information technology investments and firm performance. *Journal of Management Information Systems*, Spring, 16(4), 69–98.

SNIA (2003) Storage requirements doubled in 2002. Press Release – Storage Networking Industry Association Europe 4/22/03. Available online at: www.snia. org/news/pressrreleases/2003/2003r04r22rSNIAE.pdf.

Strassman, P. (1997) *The Squandered Computer*. Information Economics Press, New Canaan, CT.

The Register (2008) Fire at The Planet takes down thousands of websites. Available online at: www.theregister.co.uk/2008/06/01/the_planet_houston_data_center_fire/.

Further reading

English, L. (1999) *Improving Data Warehouse and Business Information Quality. Methods for Reducing Costs and Increasing Profits*. Wiley, New York. A book for information professionals with clear descriptions of differences between data, information and knowledge and approaches to improving their quality.

Marchand, D,. Davenport, T. and Dickson, T. (eds) (2000) *Mastering Information Management*. Financial Times Prentice Hall, Harlow. A compilation of short articles by specialist information management academics and practitioners.

*visit the
www*

Weblinks

ASLIB (**www.aslib.co.uk**) A membership organization promoting best practice in Information Management. Site includes Glossary and Internet resources.

First Monday journal (**www.firstmonday.org**) Freely accessible peer-reviewed articles on the Internet focusing on information management.

Information Orientation (**www.enterpriseiq.com**) More recent papers on this concept from Don Marchand and William Kettinger.

Information Research – an International Journal (**http://informationr.net**) An online journal compiled by staff at the Department of Information Studies, University of Sheffield.

Performance Measurement Association (**www.performanceportal.org**) An association for academics and practitioners interested in the field of Performance Measurement and Management hosted by Cranfield School of Management Centre for Business Performance, UK. Links and free newsletter with in-depth articles.

UK Academy of Information Systems (**www.ukais.org**) An organization created by UK academics to foster the discipline of IS. Includes a free newsletter and links to online IS journals and other resources.

Trade magazines

IT focus

Chief Information Office (**www.cio.com**). US monthly with full access to content online in 20 different 'research centres'.

Computer Weekly (**www.computerweekly.com**) UK weekly for IT managers. Full access to content online.

Computing (**www.computing.com**). UK weekly for IT managers. Full access to content online.

Information management focus

Information World Review – VNU Publishing (**www.iwr.co.uk**) European weekly. No archive at this site, but can be searched from **Computing**.

Intranet Strategist – Ark Group (**www.intranetstrategist.com**) European monthly paid subscription magazine with some limited free content including access to archive.

JISC InfoNet (**www.jiscinfonet.ac.uk**) Funded by the Joint Information Systems Committee, this portal gives resources and case studies and best practice in information management at further and higher education institutions. Further information on records management is available at: **www.jiscinfonet.ac.uk/ InfoKits/records-management**.

Knowledge Management – Ark Group (**www.kmmagazine.com**) European monthly.

Managing Information (**www.managinginformation.com**) ASLIB also publishes the subscription magazine *Managing Information* which has partial content and a newsletter online.

For multiple-choice questions and annotated weblinks relating to this chapter visit this book's website at: **www.pearsoned.co.uk/chaffey**

2

Software for information management

Objective

To define how the different forms of software contribute to an organization and review issues in software selection.

Learning outcomes

After reading this chapter, you will be able to:

● Understand how different types of software support business information management.

● Distinguish between the concepts of e-business and e-commerce.

● Assess how information management applications can support information flows within and between organizations.

Management issues

Typical questions facing managers related to this topic:

● How do we select the appropriate portfolio of information management applications?

● Should we make, buy or rent software?

● Should we adopt open-source software?

Links to other chapters

The main related chapters are:

➤ *Chapter 3* on technologies for information management, describes the hardware components that interact with software and Internet standards.

➤ *Chapter 6* on IS strategy, provides more detail on selection of the applications portfolio.

Introduction

Information system
The combination of hardware and software technology used by an individual to perform tasks including information management

Software
The instructions or programs used to control a computer system through interaction with hardware

Software or web services
Information management facilities are accessed from an external provider – the software is not installed within the company

Hardware
The physical components of a computer system such as its input devices, processor, memory, storage and output devices

When an end-user in an organization uses and manages information using an **information system**, they use two main types of information technology – software and hardware. In the next two chapters we will examine the management issues involved in the selection of software and then of hardware. In this chapter, we start by looking at **software**. 'Software' refers to the instructions or programs used to control a computer system. We start with software since software is arguably the most significant purchase in terms of the experience to the user of the application and the value it delivers to the business. In recent years, the nature of software has changed dramatically. Traditionally software has been purchased as a package such as Microsoft Windows or Office or specialist applications such as an accounting package and then installed on computers within an organization. Alternatively, organizations have created software specific to their needs, which again is installed within the organization. The Internet and the World Wide Web have enabled a new approach of renting **software or web services** where the software is installed and managed outside the organization and typically the information is also managed externally. This concept is part of the move to e-business introduced in Chapter 1, and in the current chapter we will explore the implications of these new approaches for deploying and managing software.

As we saw in Chapter 1 in the discussion on 'Does IT matter?', **hardware** has become commoditized to a great extent. This means that the type of end-user computer or hardware vendor selected will make a relatively small difference to the process of information management since, for a given price, the hardware and resulting performance of systems is similar. It is the selection of the software applications and the approaches to information management that are most important to return on investment in information systems. For this reason we start by considering software and applications for information management in this chapter and then move on to look at the underlying hardware technologies in the following chapter.

The sale of software, hardware, telecommunications equipment and related services is a major industry, accounting for expenditure of over $2 trillion per year (Table 2.1). So it is no surprise that there are many commentators and suppliers who have a vested interest in increasing expenditure on IT. The decline in IT spend at the start of the millennium had a major impact in many economies. As a consequence, potential purchasers of information and communications technology are bombarded by many vendors with marketing messages to upgrade to the latest, greatest technology. It follows that a major issue for many organizations is deciding when to invest in new software and hardware and how to select the most cost-effective solution. The process and criteria for selecting the most appropriate software and hardware are the underlying theme of this chapter and the next.

There are tens of thousands of different types of business software available for an organization to select, ranging from widely used software such as Microsoft Windows or an accounting package that is applicable to all organizations, to more specialist software needed in particular industries such as construction or manufacturing. In this chapter we start by identifying the main categories of software that are needed by every organization, large and small. We then look at the choices for obtaining software for an organization, such as making, buying or renting. The activities in this chapter look at the different options for selection of software for the large organization and a small start-up or high-growth organization.

E-business
All electronically mediated information exchanges, both within an organization and with external stakeholders supporting the range of business processes

In the remainder of the chapter we look at the options for selecting software for different parts of an organization. This includes software both for managing information flows to support internal processes and for managing flows of information through electronic links with customers, suppliers and other third parties. Since late 1997, the management of internal and external information flows using the Internet, the World Wide Web and e-mail has been widely referred to as '**e-business**'. In the last part of this

Table 2.1 IT spending by industry vertical market, worldwide (millions of US dollars)

Industry	Total IT spending 2010	Total IT spending 2009	2009–2010 growth (%)
Banking and securities	390,488	379,855	2.8
Communications media and services	392,506	378,750	3.6
Education	64,148	62,607	2.5
Healthcare	88,996	86,215	3.2
Insurance	159,926	156,573	2.1
Local and regional government	179,664	176,747	1.7
Manufacturing and natural resources	426,085	415,480	2.6
National and international government	244,410	235,086	4.0
Retail	146,239	142,420	2.7
Transportation	105,703	103,689	1.9
Utilities	125,583	119,927	4.7
Wholesale trade	83,315	81,196	2.6
Total	**2,407,063**	**2,338,544**	**2.9**

Source: Gartner Inc. (August 2010)

chapter we look at how different types of e-business applications can be deployed in different parts of the organization to support different business processes. The increased connections within and between organizations enabled by this digital technology are alluded to through the spider's web image of the chapter opener.

The main categories of software

Applications software
Software programs used by business users to support their work

Applications portfolio
The mix of software applications used in an organization or department

E-business applications
Information management applications supporting business processes which are enabled through Internet technology

Systems software
Controls the resources of the computer system as it performs tasks for the end-user through acting as a 'bridge' between the hardware and applications software

Software can be divided into two broad types as shown in Figure 2.1. In this chapter, the focus is on **applications software**. Applications software is used by members of an organization to support the different tasks they need to perform. For example, if you write an assignment or report using a word processor, you are using applications software. If you are working in a finance department or human resource (HR) management department and use specialist finance or HR software to help you do your work, then this is also applications software. One of the key roles of those responsible for managing information within a department, or the organization as a whole, is to decide on the best mix of applications, known as the '**applications portfolio**', to support the business. Investing in the most suitable applications portfolio is a major challenge of developing an information systems strategy. In Chapter 6 we look at a case study where we see the extent of this problem – a large organization such as car manufacturer Renault has over 1,400 applications in their portfolio! When an organization embraces e-business this is closely related to selecting the appropriate Internet-based applications to deploy. For example, Renault uses online customer relationship management and supply chain management systems to improve its organizational performance. We will look at specific **e-business applications** in the final section of this chapter.

The other main type of software is **systems software**. Systems software manages the computer resources such as the memory and processor and other hardware

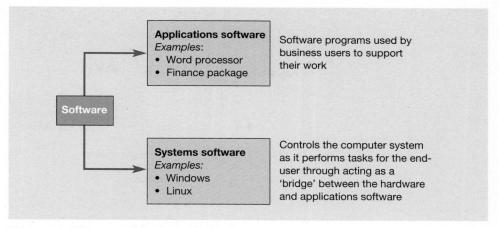

Figure 2.1 Different categories of software

described in Chapter 3. Systems software works in conjunction with the applications software and the hardware to provide a service to the end-user. Microsoft Windows, Apple Computer System 10 and Linux are examples of an important category of systems software – **operating systems software**.

Operating systems software
Software that interacts with the hardware and applications software of a computer system to control its operation

The role of systems software can be best understood by considering what happens as a user works with an application. Take the example of a word processor. As the user works with their applications software, they use hardware such as the keyboard to enter words and the mouse to select menu options such as saving a file. As they use the mouse and keyboard, it is Microsoft Windows, the systems software, that interprets the movements of the mouse and keyboard from signals sent by the hardware. The systems software translates the movements of the mouse by the user and instructs the screen display to update, showing the new position of the cursor. Microsoft Windows also interprets a left mouse click and if a menu option such as File Save is detected it will inform the application that this action has been performed. The application, in turn, sends to the operating system instructions such as saving a file or displaying a character typed. The operating system converts these instructions into specific changes required by the hardware such as saving a file or updating the screen.

This relationship between systems software, applications software and hardware is illustrated by Figure 2.2. In this chapter the majority of the coverage is on applications software since this has the greatest impact on delivering value to the business through applications to support business processes and information management. After the section on applications software, there is a brief review of the different types of systems software.

Applications software

Different forms of applications software are used to support end-users in their information management tasks, whether they be general tasks such as writing a memo using a word-processing application or specific tasks such as analysing the number of company debtors using an accounting system. In this section we review the typical applications which compose the applications portfolio of an organization. Applications software is commonly categorized as shown in Figure 2.3. We start with the applications that are used across an organization, then look at specialist applications and, finally, at personal and group applications.

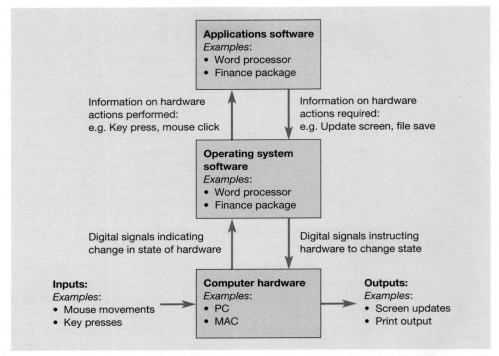

Figure 2.2 The relationship between applications software and systems software

Categorizing applications by level of decision making

The Anthony model
A simple framework for categorizing applications according to their support for planning and control at the strategic, tactical or operational level

Information management applications are also commonly categorized by their role in supporting organizational planning and control. The 1965 'Anthony model' identifies three levels of management decision making that occur in an organization when supporting planning and control (Anthony, 1965). The three levels, which are summarized in Figure 2.4, are:

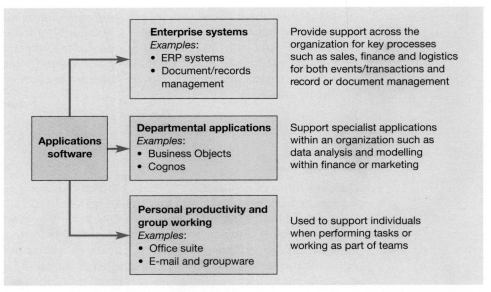

Figure 2.3 Main categories of applications software according to organizational scope

- *Strategic applications*. Support decisions taken by senior managers to direct the future of an organization. Long-term perspective, typically greater than six months. For the Lo-cost Airline Company a strategic decision is which geographical markets to serve. Information is needed on sales to existing customers, but also market research indicating potential sales levels and market characteristics in new markets. Traditionally such strategic applications have been referred to as 'executive information systems', but the term is less widely used now since senior managers often access information available through a 'corporate information portal or intranet dashboard', as described later in this chapter.

- *Tactical applications*. Support decisions taken by less senior departmental managers which control planning to achieve strategic objectives. Medium-term perspective, typically one month to twelve months. In the Lo-cost Airline Company, tactical applications will be used by marketing managers to plan and monitor the success of their marketing campaigns to stimulate ticket sales in different geographical markets or on different routes. The business intelligence systems described in Chapter 10 are typical for this.

- *Operational applications*. Support decisions taken on a day-to-day basis by all types of employees during the operation of the business. Short-term perspective, typically to resolve an immediate issue. An operational marketing application in the Lo-cost Airline Company will be used to send out and monitor the response from marketing campaigns delivered by mail or e-mail. There will be many other operational applications for scheduling how resources such as flight crew and refreshments are deployed to the different routes.

From an information management perspective, the majority of organizational data are captured at the operational level and then made available as information at all levels. As we saw in Chapter 1, data about ticket sales on an individual flight for the Lo-cost Airline Company captured at an operational level will be aggregated with data from all flights to take decisions at tactical and strategic levels about the promotion of routes and their competitiveness. However, data are captured at other levels also as managers create spreadsheets or share knowledge through committing their opinions to a company network.

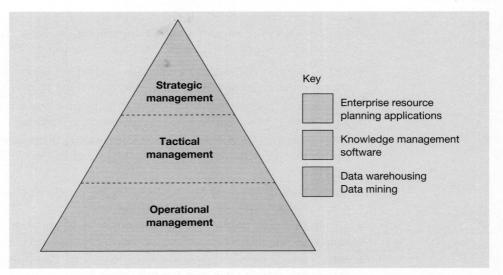

Figure 2.4 Different forms of applications used to support management decision making within an organization

Source: Chaffey (2004)

Although the decisions taken in business have remained similar over the past 40 years, the applications used to support decision making have changed dramatically. An individual application does not often now fit neatly into one of the three levels in Figure 2.4. Figure 2.4 shows that the enterprise resource planning systems, described in the next section, support decision making at all levels, although the main focus is on the operational and tactical levels. Effectively an ERP system supports information flows between the operational, tactical and strategic levels. Different modules or business views supplied by such applications may focus on different levels of decision making. Similarly applications which support knowledge management (Chapter 5) and data mining (Chapter 8) will often support all levels of decision making.

Enterprise applications

In a large organization, arguably the most important type of software is the **enterprise application**. Enterprise applications are used to support business processes such as marketing, sales, logistics and manufacture. A common goal for enterprise applications is to integrate information across these different processes to increase process efficiency, so reducing costs and time-to-market and increasing product quality for manufacturing organizations. Process efficiency is achieved through better management of the information flows between different areas of the organization. For the Lo-cost Airline Company, the ticketing or flight booking system is an example of an enterprise application. This will integrate and share data with other enterprise applications such as finance systems, marketing systems and operational systems for managing the resources involved with flights.

The suppliers of systems such as SAP, Baan, Peoplesoft and Oracle often describe their software as '**enterprise resource planning (ERP) software**'. ERP systems typically provide a single solution from a single supplier, but different modules can be purchased from different vendors. When the concept of ERP systems was introduced in the late 1980s and early 1990s, only medium and large companies could afford the software and the consultants to implement ERP, which will often cost millions of pounds. But, today, smaller companies can implement ERP through lower-cost solutions, often based on integrated accounting packages.

Note that ERP solutions are now often referred to as 'e-business applications' or 'supply chain management solutions', as we will see in later sections in this chapter. Figure 2.5 shows the range of business applications available through a system such as SAP. Modules are available for each of these applications:

- *CRM – customer relationship management* – managing personal details of customers, their product order history and how they have responded to marketing campaigns.
- *SCM – supply chain management* – managing the processes for obtaining raw materials or services from suppliers and the distribution of products.
- *SRM – supplier relationship management* – managing the financial and business relationships with different suppliers – large companies will have thousands of suppliers.
- *PLM – product lifecycle management* – managing the development and production of a new product from conception to manufacture.
- *Financials* – used by the finance department to manage all the financial transactions associated with managing the relationships listed above.
- *HRM – human resource management* – managing the recruitment, development and reward of staff within an organization.

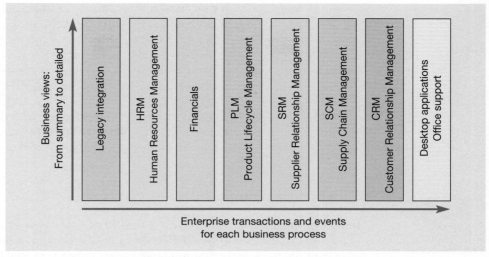

Figure 2.5 Business applications delivered by an enterprise resource planning (ERP) system
Source: SAP

As well as these modules, the ERP system must integrate with existing systems, often known as **legacy systems** and also desktop or office applications. Figure 2.5 also shows how ERP systems give different **business views** of information – from summary reporting views of events for senior managers to more detailed views for different operational staff. For example, a manager of an international company operating in EMEA (Europe, Middle East and Africa) might only want to review sales levels at a country level, while more junior staff would look at sales levels in more detail.

Figure 2.6 suggests the importance of ERP applications to modern organizations. It shows the growth of the German-based company SAP which in 2002 had over 18,000 customers and nearly 30,000 employees worldwide. And SAP is only one of many ERP suppliers. Other ERP vendors include Baan, Oracle, Peoplesoft (mainly dealing with large organizations) and Sage, Microsoft Great Plains and Systems Union (focusing on small to medium companies).

An important goal of ERP systems is to allow integrated access to information across an organization. Traditionally, the different applications shown in Figure 2.5 and their associated databases were separate. These are commonly referred to as 'information silos'– an apt analogy since it is impossible to transfer grain between different silos (Figure 2.7). One of the worst problems this created was in customer service; if a customer enquired about the status of an order, a single employee might not be able to immediately answer the customer's question since the information would be accessed through different applications available in different departments.

Think of an order for office furniture for a new building placed by a business with a furniture manufacturer. Information about this customer order could be contained in the manufacturer's customer database (personal details), order database (product and date ordered), financials database (whether a purchase order had been received from the customer), manufacturing database (whether a bespoke product had been produced) and distribution database (whether the product had been dispatched). ERP systems are designed to avoid this type of problem and instead provide a **single view of the customer** where all customer details can be readily accessed.

Many information management problems are also created through data silos. Information sharing between departments will be poor, thus the potential value of data may not be exploited. For example, the marketing department may know the

Legacy systems
Existing systems with which new systems must be integrated

Business views
Different reports available from a system, from summary to detailed level, to support different types of manager and decision

Information silos
Information is stored in separate databases which are not linked

Single view of the customer
All information related to a customer can be readily accessed using an integrated system

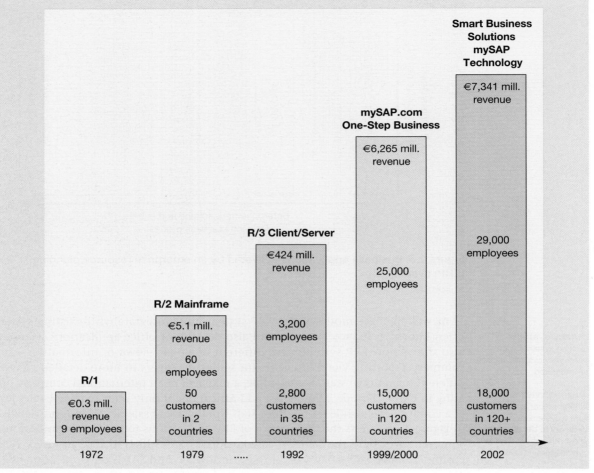

Figure 2.6 The development of the SAP ERP system
Source: SAP

number of customers it has, but it cannot assess their value since information on their purchases is stored in a separate silo. Information quality also tends to be poor since data can be duplicated in different silos and may be up to date in one silo, but out of date in another.

Traditionally, enterprise applications were limited to inside an organization – they were intra-organizational. Today, they are often inter-organizational. That is, there are also electronic links outside an organization to partners such as suppliers or customers which effectively use the same enterprise application and data source. For example, supermarket Tesco uses enterprise applications to enable it to meet fluctuations in consumer demand by rapidly notifying its suppliers of changes in stock inventory that are required. These suppliers can then promptly provide products which meet fluctuations in customer demand. Another example is shown in the Mini case study 2.1 'Enterprise applications improve information access at Minolta Europe', which illustrates the types of benefits and the areas of the business that are affected by this type of software.

Figure 2.7 Grain silos – a great analogy for the problems of separate applications and databases
Source: Digital Vision.

Mini case study 2.1 | **Enterprise applications improve information access at Minolta Europe**

Camera manufacturer Minolta Europe moved to using enterprise applications software SAP R/3 as part of a plan to move to a common global IT infrastructure. The main aim of introducing the new environment was to enable divisions around the world to share data more readily. Query processing times would also be reduced from several minutes to less than a second. Three centralized server hubs in Japan, Germany and the US would provide business applications to more than 60 sites around the world.

The new system would support global sales, finance, procurement and customer service. It did not purchase HR, but this is another option of the SAP system.

The benefits of adopting enterprise applications and consolidating the number of servers are indicated by Holger Mailand, Team Manager, System Planning & Support, Information System Division, Minolta Europe Gmbh. He said:

We found this to be an attractive option because it dramatically cut down the chaos and costs of managing and operating multiple platforms and systems. For a global company to be successful, the sales and communication channels must be open – so that information can be accessed on demand.

Source: Antony Adshead, Technology: servers, *Computer Weekly*, 29 April 2003, online at **www.computerweekly.co.uk**.

Document and records management systems

Electronic document management systems (EDMS)
Used to create, distribute and maintain organizational documentation

Electronic document management systems (EDMS) are used to provide an organization with all the procedures, guidelines, product information and standards necessary for it to operate. EDMS are used to create, distribute and maintain this type of documentation in a controlled way. They are an example of a workflow management system. Now that such information is often stored on the web, software known as 'content management systems' tends to be more widely used and this is described in the section on intranets later in this chapter. Specialist EDMS suppliers such as Documentum (**www.documentum.com**) now provide tools enabling both physical documents such as product brochures and catalogues and their online equivalents to be produced.

The technology used to publish web content for staff, partners and customers is important if the power of the Internet is to be fully utilized by a company. This may not be evident when a simple site is produced which may simply require an HTML editor or Microsoft Frontpage. It becomes more significant when a company wants to make its product catalogue available for queries or to take orders online. As these facilities are added the website changes from an isolated system to one that must be integrated with other technologies such as the customer database, stock control and sales order processing systems. A further technology issue to be addressed is to provide an infrastructure which allows the content developers throughout the company to update copy from their own desktop computer. For example, companies that have standardized on Lotus Notes can use this so that individual content developers can readily contribute their copy and the process of checking can be part-automated using workflow facilities to send messages to reviewers who can then authorize or reject the content. Such authoring and workflow tools, known as **content management systems (CMSs)**, are becoming increasingly popular. Imagine the situation at the BBC which needs to publish hundreds of online news items a day. It would not be practical for each reporter to send it to someone to publish online. Instead, every journalist has access to a CMS which is used to forward items for review, amendment and publishing. Further need for CMS has been accelerated by the ramifications of the Enron financial misreporting case which resulted in the failure of the company and trial of senior executives from 2002 onwards. In the US, the Sarbanes–Oxley regulations and in Europe, the Basel II regulations require capabilities to address the lifecycle of financial reporting, from the initial audit working papers through to the final approval and submittal to the SEC (the Securities and Exchange Commission, a US governmental agency established in 1934 to oversee the trading of all issues of securities by companies offering securities to the public). CMS providers such as Hummingbird (**www.hummingbird.com**) provide services for this purpose. Such systems are also known as 'electronic records management systems'.

In 2003, as is commonly the case with technology solutions, a new category of software came to the forefront, with different vendors offering **information lifecycle management (ILM)** solutions. Graham Titterington, Senior Analyst with Ovum (Ovum, 2004) describes ILM as follows:

> This relatively new discipline recognises that the properties of data change over time – sometimes automatically with time, and sometimes in response to events, such as the appearance of a new version of the data. ILM uses an automated workflow for storing, moving, copying and deleting data. The problem is that to be generally useful, ILM needs to understand something about the data, beyond looking at the routine file attributes.

ILM is closely related to existing solutions such as EDMS and CMS for records management, but it unites the software applications for managing documents and records with the storage hardware solutions. This approach can help improve document availability in large organizations and optimize storage as well as automating the need to manage the creation, modification and deletion of documents as part of their lifecycle. Ovum (2004) explain the reasons for the emergence of ILM solutions as follows:

> Management of information requires competence in both the content management and storage areas. Content management brings an understanding of what the data means and of its business significance. Storage provides the means of delivering the overall information system, and elaborate storage technology is required for satisfying scalability and geographic distribution requirements.

Content management system (CMS)
A software tool for creating, editing and updating documents accessed by intranet, extranet, or Internet

Information lifecycle management (ILM)
Workflow systems to control the creation, storage, modification and deletion of documents

This is why some storage vendors are turning to content management vendors for support, through acquisition, partnership or by working with other product teams in the same vendor. Content management systems can generate and associate metadata with data to assist in its management.

Departmental applications

Departmental applications
Specialist software used to support workers in one area of the business which is not closely integrated with other areas of the business

Specialist applications typically used within a department to meet its specific needs are known as 'departmental applications'. Specialist applications may also be used within a specific vertical market such as the chemical industry or the media. Unlike enterprise applications, it is less important that these departmental applications or their data are accessed by other parts of the business. However, it may be useful to send reports or information from these applications to other departments for review.

Examples of specialist departmental applications include:

- Computer-aided design (CAD) software for producing product or architectural plans
- Computer-aided engineering (CAE)
- Computer-aided manufacturing (CAM)
- Financial modelling software for assessing company growth
- Analysis software to assess the performance of marketing campaigns
- Software for keeping an inventory or audit of IT equipment within a company.

Personal productivity or office software

Office software
Basic document management applications including word-processor, spreadsheet, database, presentation-package and e-mail software

Personal productivity software
Software application to support staff in administrative tasks

Web browsers
Browsers such as Microsoft Internet Explorer provide an easy method of accessing and viewing information stored as web documents on different web servers

Applications software with a more limited scope is used by the individual or to collaborate with co-workers. The best known example of this software is 'office software' such as Microsoft Office. For many years this software has dominated the office market, but as Case study 2.2 and the Mini case study 2.2 'Munich makes the move to Linux' presented later in the chapter show, open- source software such as Star Office (**www.sun.com/software/star/staroffice**), Open Office (**www.openoffice.org**) and KOffice (**www.koffice.org**) is starting to challenge this position. 'Office software' is sometimes referred to as 'personal productivity software', but increasingly documents produced by word processors and spreadsheets will be shared with colleagues during development.

Web browsers are another form of personal application, although they are not usually supplied as part of an office package. They are used to access a static informational website, but many applications are now accessed via a web browser such as Microsoft Internet Explorer, Mozilla Firefox or Opera. The Internet standards on which web browsers access and serve information are described in Chapter 3. Traditionally, ERP systems would have required installation of a special program on every PC. Today, ERP systems can be accessed via web browsers using systems such as MySAP. This is part of the move to e-business described later in this chapter.

Groupware

Groupware
Software supporting group working and collaboration by employees

Groupware is software for team working. Groupware aids communication in a company and helps staff work together on joint tasks. It also equips them with the information needed to complete their work and can help decision making. Groupware has grown to cover a vast range of potential applications. This growth has occurred with the availability of lower-cost networks such as intranets within and between businesses providing the infrastructure for improved communication.

Groupware assists teams of people to work together because it provides key group functions; the 'three Cs' of communication, collaboration and coordination:

● Communication is the core groupware feature which allows information to be shared or sent to others using electronic mail. Groupware for conferencing is sometimes known as 'computer-mediated communication (CMC)' software.

● Collaboration is the act of joint cooperation in solving a business problem, or undertaking a task. Groupware may reduce some of the problems of traditional meetings, such as finding a place and a time to meet, a lack of available information or even dominance by one forceful individual in a meeting. Groupware improves the efficiency of decision making and its effectiveness by encouraging contributions from all group members.

● Coordination is the act of making sure that a team is working effectively and meeting its goals. This includes distributing tasks to team members, reviewing their performance or perhaps steering an electronic meeting.

When a company provides groupware for staff, it is useful to consider the options for sharing information in terms of time and place. These are shown in Table 2.2. To understand these terms, consider the options for using groupware to support student learning by completing Activity 2.1.

Table 2.2 Different uses of collaborative systems classified in time and space

	Synchronous	Asynchronous
Same location	*Same time, same place* Example: meeting support software	*Different time, same place* Example: workflow systems
Different location	*Same time, different place* Example: video-conferencing	*Different time, different place* Example: e-mail and discussion groups

Activity 2.1	Options for using groupware to support student learning

Purpose	To understand the concepts of 'synchronous' and 'asynchronous' and the effect of different locations for using groupware.
Activity	Your university is planning to introduce Internet-based groupware to support e-learning.

1 Place each of these options for groupware in the appropriate category in Table 2.2:
   (a) Online discussion group or forum available through a website
   (b) E-mail-based discussion list
   (c) Real-time chat using a technique such as Instant Messenger, Yahoo! Messenger or ICQ.

2 Assess the strengths and weaknesses of the different techniques.

3 What management measures would help in the adoption of the different alternatives?

The main classes of groupware applications or functions are shown in Table 2.3. Of these applications, there are two that are particularly important for information management in many businesses. These are electronic document management systems and workflow systems. The management of e-mail also presents a challenge to the modern organization, as we will explore in Chapter 11.

Table 2.3 The main applications of groupware

Groupware applications	Application
1 E-mail and messaging	E-mail, electronic forms processing
2 Document management and information sharing	Supports creation and review of documents Improved information dissemination
3 Collaborative authoring	Team development of documents
4 Conferencing	Text conferencing, video-conferencing, whiteboarding
5 Time management	Calendar and group scheduling
6 Groupware management and decision support	Remote and distributed access facilities including replication and access control
7 Ad-hoc workflow	Loosely couple collaboration
8 Structured workflow	Structured management of tasks

Workflow management applications
Applications to manage the flow of information required when several stages and/or different resources are used to process this information

Case management
An approach to managing all the tasks involved with a process concerning an individual customer such as a job or credit applicant or an insurance claimant

Workflow management applications are important in supporting the flow of information in business processes, particularly those involved with **case management**. As an example, imagine a clerk at an insurance company investigating a claim on a car insurance policy. The clerk will have to follow a series of steps over days or weeks in deciding whether to settle the claim. Over this period they will be dealing with many other similar claims and the documentation associated with them. For the Lo-cost Airline Company workflow systems might be used for responding to customer complaints or for managing the refreshments and cleaning of an aircraft between flights.

A workflow system will assist by providing a checklist of tasks to be conducted each day and information on the customer and other insurers. The system will permit collaboration by enabling other clerks to share the same case if necessary or provide a manager doing the final authorization with the information they need to sanction the claim. The workflow system will also provide an overview of the status of the process such as how many claims are completed each day, how long they take on average and what are the bottlenecks. This management information can then be used to improve the process further.

When you applied to the institution where you are studying, your application is likely to have been processed through a workflow or case management system. This would remind the administrator to ask you for certain information such as previous qualifications and to remind you of events such as open days.

Database systems

Database system
Software for management of structured data

Middleware
Software used to facilitate communications between business applications, including data transfer and control

Most applications that manage the input, storage, retrieval and reporting of structured information use a **database system**. Many of the types of applications software we have already mentioned use a database for data maintenance – for example, enterprise resource planning software, groupware, workflow software, human resources management applications, finance systems. Database deployment in a large organization using databases such as Oracle, Microsoft SQL Server or Sybase could be considered to be systems software, with applications accessing the data stored within the database. **Middleware** communications software is used to mediate between the database and different client applications. For example, in a large organization, applications software will be used to enter sales orders data about new customers and their orders in a database. There are also some specialist database systems such as Lotus Notes and Microsoft Exchange Server which have been developed for storage of less structured information such as documents. Personal databases such as Microsoft

Access can be considered to be applications software. A common organizational information management problem is that data may be stored in separate databases, which results in poor data quality. We will look at technical approaches to managing databases in Chapter 9 on information architectures.

Systems software

Systems software manages the computer resources such as the memory and processor and other hardware described at the start of the next chapter. There are several different types of systems software, summarized in Figure 2.8, which we will briefly describe in this section. The coverage is not in depth since the majority of managers will not be involved in selecting systems software. Systems software such as Microsoft Windows or UNIX will usually be an established part of the software infrastructure in most organizations. The main management concerns with operating systems are their reliability and performance and how effectively the operating system can support business applications software and integration of data with other partners in the supply chain. A further issue, discussed in the next section, is whether cost savings are possible through migrating to an open-source solution such as the Linux operating system.

Operating systems software

The best-known operating systems software is Microsoft Windows which is used on personal computers. In large organizations, which use powerful computers that may support thousands of users, other forms of operating system are used. For example, IBM offers operating systems known as 'VM' and 'UNIX' on the mainframes and workstation computers referred to at the start of the next chapter. The functions of operating systems are similar, regardless of their manufacturer. The open-source solution Linux runs on a range of platforms, from desktop PCs to UNIX servers.

Google provides us with a good indication of the global usage of different operating systems, at least for those individuals and companies with Internet access! Figure 2.9 shows that many users of Microsoft operating systems do not immediately upgrade to

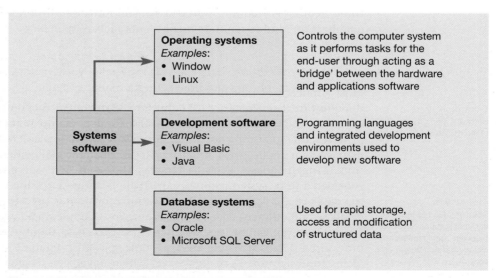

Figure 2.8 Different categories of systems software

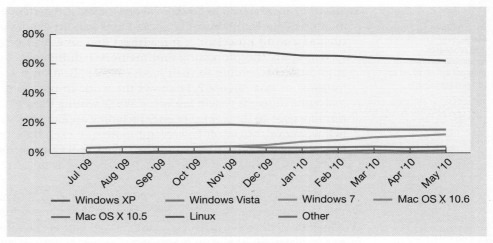

Figure 2.9 Popularity of common operating systems
Sources: www.netmarketshare.com

the latest version. Vista, for instance, did not encourage people to migrate from XP. However, the release of Windows 7 has been met much more favourably and both XP and Vista are seeing a considerable drop in usage. Microsoft Windows is clearly dominant, with other systems including the Macintosh and Linux small by comparison.

The functions of operating systems software include:

Graphical user interface
A visual method to enable the user to control the computer using mouse and keyboard

1 *Managing the user interface.* Modern operating systems use a **graphical user interface** (GUI, pronounce 'gooey') to interact with end-users. Standard features of the Windows GUI include screen windows, menus and the Start task bar. The Windows operating system has evolved through different releases, as shown in Figure 2.10. Windows first became widely used commercially with Windows 3.1 around 1990. It was based on a previous operating system known as 'DOS (Disk Operating System)', used by early PCs; this system had a text-based user interface which used what is known as a 'command line interpreter (CLI)' for users to give instructions such as starting a program. Some mainframes and mini-computers (see Chapter 3) still use such a user interface – you will see this in some retailers where shop assistants enter product codes into a text-based interface. But, for Windows users, it seems peculiar today that to start a word processor required 'winword' to be typed at the CLI. The two columns show a personal or home edition of Windows on the left and a version designed for large organizations – formerly known as 'Windows NT' for 'New Technology' and now known as the 'professional edition'. There are also specialist versions for using on personal digital assistants, phones and home entertainment systems.

2 *Managing data transfer with hardware.* As explained in the previous section, the operating system manages data transfer events from the mouse and keyboard. It also controls saving data to storage devices such as a CD or hard disk.

3 *Managing the file system.* As you will know from using computers, files such as your documents are stored in folders or directories. The operating system enables folders to be created, modified and deleted. For the files, within each folder, the operating system enables each file to be protected (set to read-only) and permissions can be set so that only certain categories of user can access them. For example, only someone working in finance might be able to access data processed by an accounting system.

Access control system
Restricts use of files and resources through a log-in and password system and corresponding permissions for files

4 *Managing access to systems resources.* Related to the permissions mentioned above, the operating system restricts access to certain files or applications. To enable this restricted access users have to log on using an **access control system.**

Multi-tasking
Management of memory and processor requirements enabling different applications to run simultaneously

5 *Managing system resources for different applications.* Modern operating systems enable **multi-tasking**; in other words, several applications can be run at the same time, such as a word processor, a spreadsheet and an e-mail program. The operating system splits the processing and memory requirements between the different applications according to their load. Each application is known technically as a 'process' or task. Figure 2.11 shows the work an operating system has to do in managing different system resources. While writing these words, my computer was running over 40 different processes including applications such as Microsoft Word (winword.exe), Microsoft PowerPoint (powerpnt.exe), the Outlook e-mail and contact manager (outlook.exe) and the Opera web browser (opera.exe). As well as

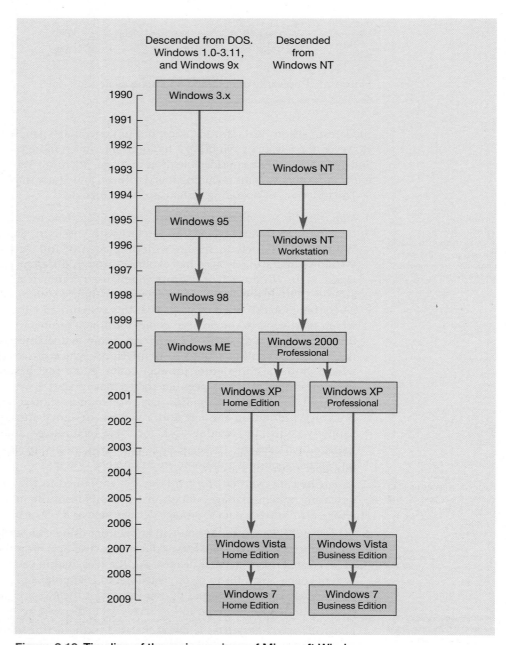

Figure 2.10 Timeline of the main versions of Microsoft Windows

Source: www.microsoft.com/windows/WinHistoryProGraphic.mspx

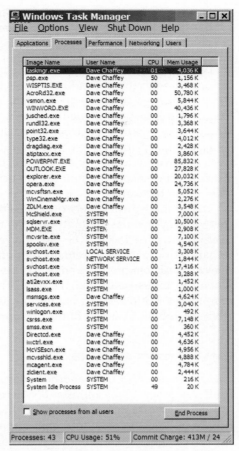

Figure 2.11 Task Manager view of processes in Windows XP

Source: Reprinted by permission of Microsoft Corporation

these applications there are many system processes such as rundll32.exe which are needed to support the applications plus additional software such as anti-virus software (mc*.exe). The implications of selecting different amounts of memory on system performance are discussed in Chapter 3.

6 *Providing utilities for systems management.* An operating system is not a single program, rather there is a main program for the tasks mentioned above which is loaded on start-up. However, there are many other utilities which are used when required. For example, a disk defragmenter is used periodically to improve the performance of the disk access.

Network software

Network operating system (NOS)
Systems software used to control the access to, and flow of, information on a network

Network software or the **network operating system (NOS)** is another type of systems software used to manage the links between a computer and other computers. The NOS has these main functions:

1 *Managing shared hardware resources.* Examples include **file servers, back-up devices** and printers. Servers and networking are described in more detail in the next chapter.

File server
A computer system used to share files from different PCs

2 *Managing shared data resources.* Access to files on the servers is controlled through the NOS.

Back-up devices
Storage using optical media such as a CD-ROM or magnetic tape used to keep a copy of documents

3 *Managing communications between different systems*. The NOS enables data to be transferred between different machines.

4 *Managing access control*. Managing access to different resources as described above.

Directory services
Provided as part of the NOS and used to manage objects associated with the network such as user accounts and servers

Directory services are provided as part of the NOS and are used to manage objects associated with the network. They use a hierarchical organization similar to that for the folders on a single computer that provides a single point of access for management of user accounts, clients, servers, printers and applications. Microsoft Active Directory and Novell Directory are examples of such directories. They interface with directory standards such as X.500 and LDAP (lightweight directory access protocol) which provide a hierarchy of: country, organization, organizational unit and person. Such systems enable communication between members of an organization, wherever they are in the world.

Traditionally, in PC networks, a NOS was installed separately, but, increasingly, networking facilities are built into the operating system. In the early 1990s, Novell Netware was used as a NOS, but, increasingly, Microsoft Windows is used. In large organizations, Novell remain popular. For example, the Novell eDirectory (**www.novell.com/products/edirectory**) is used by BASF, which mainly operates in the chemical industry, to manage network access or directory services to its 103,000 employees worldwide. In mainframe and mini-computer systems, the networking software is built in as part of the operating system.

Development software

Development software is another category of systems software used by programmers to develop new applications and systems software. New software is developed using different **programming languages** which use defined phrases or syntax to instruct the operating system and/or application to perform particular operations. An example of a simple programming language is Visual Basic. In Visual Basic, to open a box alerting the user that a postcode field has not been completed on a data form, the relevant program code is:

Programming languages
Program code used to help develop new systems

MsgBox('Please enter your postcode')

High-level languages
Relatively simple programming languages

Low-level languages
Relatively complex programming languages which interact more directly with the hardware

Programming languages vary in their ease of learning and use. Simple languages such as Visual Basic are known as **high-level languages**. They may still be powerful. One of the challenges for information systems managers is controlling usage of high-level languages by end-users. This is explored further in the section on end-user computing in Chapter 11. Lower-level languages include C#, Java, C++ and Assembler. Assembler is considered to be truly a **low-level language** since it is used to interact directly with hardware such as in programming a set-top box. Low-level languages are used by specialist programmers or systems developers and are beyond the scope of this book. 'High' and 'low' level are relative and not definitive terms – some would consider Java to be a high-level language.

Integrated development environment (IDE)
Tools used to create new software using programming languages and databases

Applications programming interfaces (API)
A standard method of exchanging data and instructions between different pieces of development software

Today, development software is not simply a programming language edited in a text editor. Rather, a suite of tools is used to help design, test and revise the software created by the developer. These tools are usually integrated as an **integrated development environment (IDE)**. The IDE will allow the user to access libraries of previously written functions and data access interfaces which enable them to access different types of database. One of the key features of modern development is to enable interoperability between different systems. To help achieve this, standard interfaces known as an '**applications programming interfaces (APIs)**' are developed to enable integration of different software modules.

Development software is also used to tailor existing software. For example, users of Microsoft Office commonly use specific applications built in Visual Basic.

Case study 2.1

Spares ordering systems in the Navy

The Ministry of Defence (MoD) continuously upgrades and improves its operational systems. It is highly complex, employing around 200,000 personnel, holding over 365,000 hectares of land and using many thousands of vehicles, aircraft and ships, which cost in excess of £34 billion per annum to operate (DASA, 2008). The MOD often work in partnership with other organizations as part of their ongoing improvement programmes, for example collaborating with LogicaCMG to implement JAMES, a software system that manages its many vehicle assets (Logica, 2008; MOD, 2008).

One of the major challenges for this type and size of organization is the acquisition and control of spare parts and the scheduling of equipment maintenance.

Maintenance can be undertaken in three ways:

1 As a repair activity to equipment that has already failed.
2 As a preventive activity whereby equipment is maintained and serviced at regular intervals.
3 As a predictive activity whereby equipment is maintained based upon the time it has been in service and the conditions in which it has been operating. Such an approach is often termed Reliability Centred Maintenance.

Global maintenance information system

Reliability Centred Maintenance (RCM) is orchestrated through the Unit Maintenance Management System (UMMS). UMMS is the information system that tracks the location of equipment, its current state of repair, the date on which the next maintenance activity is expected to be undertaken and the parts and materials that are required to perform that maintenance.

The interval at which maintenance is scheduled to be undertaken on each part is determined in conjunction with the manufacturers and may include anything from simple work such as changing the oil in an engine, to checking the main bearings or even replacing the entire engine after a predetermined number of hours operating at maximum speed.

A ship may be at sea for many weeks or even months, during which time almost all of the equipment is being operated continuously. This high rate of usage means that many of the ship's systems are in need of continuous maintenance while at sea and extensive maintenance when the ship returns to port. A catalogue of spare parts and materials will be produced for each of them, along with a prediction of the time taken to effect the repair and the amount of labour and other tools and equipment that will be needed. A maintenance programme will be drawn up so that work can begin as soon as the ship has docked, thus enabling minimum periods of time where the ship is not active.

Occasionally items of equipment will be damaged or will fail unexpectedly while the ship is at sea. Usually the failed part can be repaired or replaced by the ship's engineers without returning to port: many of the larger warships hold complete diesel engines as spares and regularly practise swapping them without stopping the ship's normal operation.

When a spare part from the ship's inventory is used, a signal will be sent via UMMS to order a replacement. The replacement part will usually be added to the ship stores when it returns to port; however, critical components and systems may be despatched immediately and transported to where the ship is currently located.

UMMS feeds into the central information system at Abbey Wood in Bristol which coordinates the manufacture and delivery of the spare parts and materials required for all maintenance activities that are scheduled to take place when the ship next arrives in port. Many of these parts are held in stores, others need to be manufactured by private companies. The accurate scheduling of these parts is of paramount importance. Without the correct parts and materials the scheduled maintenance cannot take place, and without the correct maintenance the ship cannot return to service.

Ship maintenance information system

While the ship is at sea, all of the items of equipment that are predicted to require maintaining will be identified by UMMS and a list of daily, weekly and monthly tasks to be performed will be generated. These tasks, which can be anything from major engine maintenance to toilet cleaning, are allocated to the relevant sections and maintenance personnel to be carried out.

The maintenance personnel log in to the UMMS to check which tasks have been completed and which still need to be done. UMMS also provides Job Information Cards that provide detailed instructions on how to carry out each particular task. It also records who has performed the maintenance and at what time it was started and completed.

A 'watchkeeping' system is also controlled by UMMS. At regular intervals maintenance personnel patrol the ship, check equipment oil levels and air pressures and enter the readings into a hand-held Personal Data Assistant (PDA). The PDA uploads the readings to UMMS which checks them against the equipment specifications. UMMS may then issue an equipment warning or a maintenance request to rectify a fault, such as topping up oil levels.

Maintenance information system feedback

UMMS tracks every scheduled and unscheduled maintenance activity that takes place on board every vessel along with the readings of the 'watchkeeping'. This enables engineers at Abbey Wood to check that all maintenance activities have been undertaken and that all sectors of the ship are operating within specification.

UMMS also enables details of unexpected faults and failures to be communicated across the fleet. The solution to problems can be distributed so that the fault or failure does not occur on other ships that are in active service and this helps to maintain a high level of operational effectiveness. Furthermore, details of equipment failure can be circulated to the manufacturers so that parts can be redesigned or modified before the next return to port whereupon permanent fixes can be effected.

Questions

1 How can a ship send a request for spare parts without revealing its position?

2 To what extent is the success of UMMS dependent upon the range of spares suppliers and manufacturers throughout the supply chain using an electronic information system?

3 If the central information system at Abbey Wood failed, how could the provision of spares still be managed?

4 Discuss how the Navy's strategic, tactical and operational plans are fulfilled by information systems.

Selecting appropriate software

Selecting the most suitable software for an organization is an involved process. For all organizations, regardless of size, software is a significant investment. If inappropriate software is selected then there will be a poor **return on investment (ROI)**. The return on investment is determined by the value of the benefits achieved through the software in comparison to the costs of purchasing and maintaining the software.

Return on investment (ROI)
A measure of the benefits delivered by the software in comparison to the costs incurred in its purchase and maintenance

The software selection process

Selecting the best type of software requires a methodical approach since the software selected will affect its operational efficiency and effectiveness. A typical approach for an important piece of software is:

1 *Identify criteria and functionality for new system.* The important criteria listed in the next section will be identified.

2 *Take the make-rent-or-buy decision.* For most specialist application software there is a choice of creating the software from scratch, renting it online or purchasing it from a packaged software vendor.

3 *Identify possible suppliers.* A 'longlist' of perhaps five to ten suppliers that can meet the requirements listed below will be drawn up by searching on the web or from articles and ads in relevant magazines.

4 *Produce a shortlist of preferred suppliers.* A shortlist will be produced by using a checklist to select the best suppliers from those that meet the most requirements.

5 *Select supplier from shortlist.* There are a number of methods for finally selecting the supplier, and these depend on the cost and importance of the final system. For software for home use it may be sufficient to see which provides the required features or to check comments on a product review website. It may also be possible to download a trial version of the software. For larger purchases the vendors will be invited to present their software in a 'beauty parade'. Benchmarking may be conducted to see how well the software performs in practice.

It is often tempting for individuals and businesses to upgrade to the latest version of a piece of software. Microsoft frequently releases new editions of its Windows operating system and Office suites. Historically, businesses have been slow to adopt new operating systems but Vista appears to have changed that trend when just one year after its release 48 per cent of organizations reported that they were testing it (Business Centre, 2008). Over half of those engaged in testing expected to make the transition over the next year. Security improvements, performance and productivity improvements along with enhanced networking capabilities were cited as the main reasons for making the change.

In the following sections we look at the first two issues – criteria used for selecting applications and the make, rent or buy decision. We also consider the number of vendors – for enterprise applications, several vendors or a single vendor may be preferred.

Criteria for selecting software

When selecting packaged software which is installed within an organization or hosted on an external server, there are many factors to consider – whether it is software that is made, bought or rented as described in the next section. The main criteria which are used to compare software from different vendors are:

1 *Functionality*. The features of the application. Describes how well the application meets the business need.
2 *Ease of use*. Every system takes some time to learn, but system use should be intuitive to minimize the time needed to learn how to use it. A well-constructed piece of software will make it fast to conduct common tasks.
3 *Performance*. The speed of the application to perform different functions. This is measured by how long the user has to wait for individual functions to be completed, such as data retrieval, calculation and screen display. It will depend on the power of the computer, but can vary significantly between applications.
4 *Scalability*. Scalability is related to performance: it describes how well a system can adapt to higher workloads which arise as a company grows. For example, an ERP system will require more customer details, suppliers and products to be held on it as the company grows. The workload will also be higher as the number of internal and external users of the system increases.
5 *Compatibility or interoperability*. This term refers to how easy it is to integrate the application with other applications. For example, does it have import and export facilities, does it support transfer of data using XML?
6 *Extensibility*. Related to scalability and interoperability, this describes how easy it is to add new functions or features to a package by adding new modules from the original vendor or other vendors.
7 *Stability or reliability*. All applications have errors or bugs and applications vary in the number of times they fail, depending on how well they have been tested since they were first introduced.
8 *Security*. Capabilities for restricting access to applications should be assessed. This is particularly important for hosted solutions.
9 *Support*. Levels of support and the cost of support from the software vendor will vary. There is a risk that small companies may cease trading and the product may no longer be supported.

Now complete Activity 2.2 which explores how the criteria for selecting software vary for different types of software from a small-business perspective. This shows how the criteria listed above will differ for different types of software (and by implication, different types of business).

<table>
<tr><td>Activity 2.2</td><td>Selecting applications software for a small business</td></tr>
</table>

Purpose

To aid understanding of the different factors to assess when selecting applications software and the relative importance of them.

Activity

A start-up business which manufactures furniture requires several different types of software. Each group should select one type of software and discuss the importance of the nine criteria for selecting software described above. A ranked list of the criteria in order of importance should be produced. These can be put on a whiteboard, with one type of software in each column to assess the commonality in requirements.

Software types:

1 Operating system.
2 Office package.
3 Accounting package.
4 Customer relationship management application.
5 Supply chain management application.
6 Employee package.

The make, buy or rent decision

When an organization identifies the need for a new information management application, it has a range of options for obtaining the system. One of the first decisions is whether to make, buy or rent. Traditionally, when a new application was required, it was a choice between developing a new application from scratch using programming ('make') or obtaining an existing packaged solution from a software vendor ('buy'). Even if a packaged solution is selected, some tailoring is often needed. In each case, the system was usually hosted inside the organization on its own computers. Today, there is a third choice where the software is rented and the application and its data are located on servers belonging to the software company. Let's now review these options in a little more detail.

Bespoke development
Information system developed specifically for the purpose

Packaged implementation
Standard software is installed with limited configuration required

Hosted solution
Standard software that is managed externally on the supplier's server

Applications service provider (ASP)
A software supplier that offers hosted solutions to a range of customers

Software or web services
Information management facilities are accessed from an external provider – the software is not installed within the company

1 *Bespoke*. With a **bespoke development**, a completely new, unique application is developed from scratch through programming of a solution. This is the costliest approach to obtaining applications since a team of technical staff is required to design, build and test the application. However, it has the benefit that the application can be created to deliver exactly the correct features the business requires.

2 *Off-the-shelf or packaged*. In a **packaged implementation**, a standard existing system is purchased from a software vendor and installed on computers located within an organization. Alternatively, free or low-cost open-source software as referred to earlier in the chapter may be used. An office application or a simple accounting package is an example of an off-the-shelf packaged implementation. This is a much cheaper approach to obtaining applications since the cost of development is effectively shared with other purchasers. The system is also less likely to contain errors since different users will find errors which must be fixed and a rigorous testing programme is needed to avoid these types of problem. The disadvantage of this approach is that it will not precisely fit an organization's information management needs. Instead it will be produced for the typical organization.

3 *Hosted solution (packaged)*. With a **hosted solution**, a standard system is used, but it is not managed within the company; instead there is a third-party **applications service provider (ASP)** or **web services** approach. Web services are a significant trend in applications procurement since although the advantages and disadvantages of this approach are similar to those of a packaged solution, there are

additional benefits. Cost is the main additional benefit, since installation and upgrades are managed completely by the software provider – so fewer internal IT staff are required. More frequent upgrades also become possible. Furthermore, it is relatively easy to 'try before you buy' – different providers of web services can be tried remotely, usually using example data sets. You may also see the term '**application hosting provider (AHP)**'. This is a managed service that is subtly different from an ASP in that individual application(s) and related data specific to an organization are hosted. In the ASP approach an application or service is made available that is shared by many organizations.

A related concept is **utility computing**. Utility computing involves treating all aspects of IT as a commodity service like water, gas or electricity where payment is according to usage. This includes not only software which may be used on a pay-per-use basis, but also using hardware. Read Case study 2.2 to explore further the benefits and disadvantages of this approach. We return to the concept of utility computing for hardware in Chapter 3. Yet another term used to describe this concept is '**on-demand computing**'. This term, which was coined by IBM, has a broader meaning since IBM refer to it as an extension of the e-business concept. Complete Activity 2.3 to understand the importance of this concept.

4 *Tailored development*. In a **tailored development**, an off-the-shelf system or hosted solution is tailored according to an organization's needs. This form of project is often based on integrating components from one or several vendors. Although the terms are similar, this differs from a bespoke system in that a bespoke system is entirely new, whereas a tailored development is based on an existing packaged solution.

Application hosting provider (AHP)
Service for hosting an organization's application separately

Utility computing
IT resources and in particular software and hardware are utilized on a pay-per-use basis

On-demand computing
This term was coined by IBM

Tailored development
The standard solution requires major configuration or integration of different modules

Activity 2.3	On-demand computing

Purpose	**To understand the significance of the on-demand concept.**
Activity *visit the www*	Visit the IBM microsite which is used to promote the on-demand concept (**www.ibm.com/ondemand, now provided by Oracle**). Summarize the meaning and benefits of on-demand computing according to IBM, explaining how it differs from previous concepts such as e-business.

IBM has co-developed with Siebel Systems CRM On Demand (**www.crmondemand.com**), a hosted system launched in 2003. This competes with Salesforce.com, a company founded in 1999 by former Oracle executive Marc Benioff, which in 2003 boasted 100,000 users across 8,000 companies. In 2010 this has risen to an estimated 4.6 million 'live' users. This number of users indicates the potential of ASP/hosted/utility/on-demand computing.

The implications of choosing standard or packaged software are more far-reaching than they first appear, since selection of standard software for operational purposes often implies that a company must adapt its practices and processes to match the software. With increasing amounts of tailoring it becomes possible to tailor the software to match the processes.

The options for different parties to build applications as part of a systems development project are summarized in Table 2.4 and described in more detail in Chapter 7.

Table 2.4 A summary of the different methods of obtaining applications software

Software acquisition method	Advantages	Disadvantages
Bespoke	• Fits company needs well	• Costly and time-consuming to develop and upgrade • More errors
Packaged	• Relatively inexpensive • Relatively error-free	• Will not meet organization's needs exactly
Hosted	• Can pay for on a pay-per-use model • Relatively rapid to set up • Majority of maintenance costs borne by supplier	• Longer-term costs may be higher • Dependent on supplier for data security and upgrades
Tailored	• Combines the benefits of the bespoke and packaged solutions • Can use modules from different suppliers	• Inflexibility of packaged solutions may make it difficult to tailor software

Best-of-breed or single-vendor?

Best-of-breed
Software is not purchased from a single vendor, but from multiple vendors which are considered to be the best for specialist applications

For large-scale software deployments such as ERP, CRM and SCM a decision also has to be taken about the number of vendors. The choice is essentially whether to use a single software vendor as supplier, or to go for a 'best-of-breed' approach of using multiple packages which are best within their specific application. Read the Research insight 2.1 'Single-vendor or best-of-breed?' to study the arguments for and against.

Research insight 2.1   **Single-vendor or best-of-breed?**

AMR Research (2003) summarized the results of research amongst European retailers on their preferences for a single-vendor or best-of-breed approach. Here are some of the advantages of each, reported by this analyst's report.
   Advantages of single-vendor ERP:

● Integrated and consistent processes throughout the value chain
● Many of the processes are the culmination of industry best-practice
● Consistent data-model for the entire enterprise
● Easier estimation of overall project cost through primary relationship.

Best-of-breed provides:

● Selection of functionally richest system for each business area
● Resilience against single-vendor failure or demise
● Greater flexibility in terms of substitution of individual elements
● Faster response from vendor to adaptation needs
● More specialized vendors.

   Speaking on behalf of the ERP approach was manufacturer and retailer Coca-Cola HBC, the Greek bottling company that holds the franchise of the brand in 26 countries. It made a strategic decision to implement SAP, and anyone in the organization wanting to procure any other functionality through other software had to prove why it could not use SAP.

Speaking for best-of-breed was the IT strategy director for the UK's largest food retailer, Tesco. Tesco uses a range of packaged solutions too. Tesco stated that its route was not taken through any desire to steer away from one end-to-end system. Quite the contrary – Tesco would have selected an ERP suite vendor if one had delivered at least 80 per cent of the functionality needed. It didn't find such a vendor; for example, it believed that SAP would not have satisfied its point-of-sale (POS) requirements. This view was not shared by French retailer Casino and US retailer Wal-Mart which believes that it achieves competitive advantage by developing applications ahead of the packaged vendors. However, Switzerland's second largest retailer, Coop, disagrees with the best-of-breed approach. It selected SAP based on an Oracle database.

Case study 2.2

IT as a utility

Information technology is just a utility – like water or electricity. We'd all like that statement to be true. When we want to connect to the Internet, we want it to be there – instantly. And most of the time, it is. For the most common applications – e-mail or Web browsing – the Internet can be turned on or off. We can get e-mail on our computers. We can get e-mail on our mobile phones. We can get e-mail from kiosks in airports. We can use the campus e-mail system or gmail. But thinking about IT as a utility is misleading. Thirty years ago, e-mail was an exotic application available only to scientists with access to ARPANET. IT has come a long way since then – just like utilities.

On the main street of any small town in the 1950s were a drugstore, a Western Auto store, a grocery, a bakery, a clothes store, a bar, a movie theater, a bank, a dimestore, and a couple of gas stations. What many have forgotten is that there was also an electrical store that sold coffee pots, electric frying pans, toasters, and the like. In the early part of the twentieth century, many local power companies had their own standards for voltage and amperage, and appliances were made to those standards. Not even the plugs and the wall outlets were standardized (many older homes still have these outlets, long since painted over). Rural electrification led to common standards, which allowed for the commoditization of appliances.

For decades, electricity has remained the same. Standards are in place. There is a single service provider. The evolution is in the appliances that use the electricity, not in the electricity itself. In some ways, IT is going through a similar evolution. In the 1980s and early 1990s, technologists were sorting out networking standards and protocols. Only when those differences were resolved did the commoditization of networking become possible.

But the commonality between electricity and IT may end there. What operating system do you use? Are you a Mac user, or do you prefer a PC? Do you have a BlackBerry server to support e-mail on your handheld, or is your mobile device based on Windows or Palm software? You can exchange e-mail, but you can't interchange the devices. If a campus records lectures as podcasts for students, someone made a choice about whether the podcast would be distributed over iTunes U or on the campus Web site, whether it would be saved as an MP4 or an MP3, whether it would be released as audio alone or enhanced with video. Just because something is podcast doesn't mean that it will work on any device. If it doesn't work everywhere, is it a utility?

Assuming that IT is limited to commodity services is incorrect. Beyond the everyday tools are IT applications that are critical to discovery and learning: 3-D graphics, visualization, grid computing, high-throughput computing, large distributed databases, and so on. Even the network – the component most like a utility – is constantly evolving. The third generation of fiber optics carries 10 trillion bits per second on one strand of fiber. Predictions are that by 2013, a supercomputer will be built that exceeds the computation capacity of the human brain. Maybe IT isn't quite like a utility.

Much of IT involves people, not just 'plugging in' a technology. For the faculty member who is exploring how to make his or her class more interactive or the student who needs help using Excel, the personal touch is critical. Disaster recovery is at least as much about staying in touch with students and faculty as it is about making backups. Even 'technical' issues such as identity management, authorization, and security aren't just about IT alone; they concern people, risk, and judgment. None of these issues have yet been simplified to commodity status.

In thinking about IT as a utility, the CIO and other members of the executive team should ask themselves the following strategic questions:

Do we make the assumption that all IT is the same? IT encompasses a range of activities, some routine and others experimental and highly individualized. Although network access, e-mail services, and Web sites may come to mind first, IT also includes advanced decision-making ▶

tools, simulations, high-performance computing, worldwide databases such as for the human genome, and assistive devices. Many IT applications have stabilized, but others are just emerging. Does the institution inadvertently make the assumption that IT changes are in the past?

What systems and applications are commoditized? Some campus applications, such as e-mail, are as readily available from external providers as from internal ones. Other applications may be critical to campus operations without being tied to the core mission. Payroll and administrative systems are certainly critical to the institution but may have routine, stable requirements that make them candidates for outsourcing. Is there an advantage to moving responsibility for selected applications to another provider? Will doing so free up valuable time for the IT organization to provide services of greater value? If there is no competitive advantage to keeping an application in-house, what is the process for identifying another provider?

Is there a regular, systematic process for reviewing which applications are mission-critical, unique, or commoditized and then determining the implications for how these services are delivered? Since IT is ubiquitous, colleges and universities are so often caught in the tyranny of the urgent – applying a patch or upgrading a service – that they fail to examine what they are doing. A periodic 'audit' of services – of who provides them and even whether they are still necessary – is advisable.

How much of IT is about the technology, and how much is about people and the work IT enables? Although IT is a technology, its value is in the service it provides to people, whether through automation, speed, insight, or convenience. Simply applying IT to a problem or process will not necessarily yield benefits: people are a critical part of the equation. How much of those human interactions could be treated as a commodity? How much should?

What opportunities do we miss if we think of IT only as a utility? Higher education cannot afford to assume that IT is a constant or a commodity. If IT were constant, Web 2.0 would not have emerged from the search-and-retrieve Web of a few years ago. We would have missed Flickr, *Wikipedia*, blogs, YouTube, and Facebook. If IT were just a commodity, cyberinfrastructure would not be emerging from the Internet. We would have missed 3-D rendering, virtual reality, and access to worldwide databases and powerful research communities. IT does not stand still.

Most of the time, IT is a utility – ubiquitous and taken for granted. But it is also a rapidly evolving, mission-critical resource. Few institutions can risk underestimating the power of IT to catalyze change and create competitive advantage.

Source: Brian L Hawkins and Diana G Oblinger,The Myth About IT as a Utility, *Educause Review*, July/August 2007

Questions

1 What are the benefits of 'utility computing' suggested by the article?

2 What impact will this have on the way that businesses use IT?

3 Evaluate the facilitators and barriers to the adoption of utility computing.

Open-source software

Open source software
Software for which the underlying program code is freely available

A significant software selection issue for managers in many organizations is the **open-source software** option. Open-source software can be either systems software or applications software. We introduce the concept at this point since the increasingly popular operating system Linux is open-source software.

The 'source' in 'open source' refers to the program code or instructions on which software is based. This is freely available for inspection, unlike proprietary code which is compiled into an executable form which runs on a computer. Once the source is freely available, the software effectively becomes free to users since anyone can install it, compile it and then use it.

The Open Source organization (**www.opensource.org**) explain the benefits of open source software as follows:

> The basic idea behind open source is very simple: When programmers can read, redistribute, and modify the source code for a piece of software, the software evolves. People improve it, people adapt it, people fix bugs. And this can happen at a speed that, if one is used to the slow pace of conventional software development, seems astonishing.

> We in the open source community have learned that this rapid evolutionary process produces better software than the traditional closed model, in which only a very few programmers can see the source and everybody else must blindly use an opaque block of bits.

Linux
An open-source operating system initially developed by Linus Torvalds

Linux open-source systems software has been enthusiastically adopted, both by end-users and by established hardware vendors such as IBM and HP which supply it as an option with their computers. IBM was once a staunch defender of intellectual property rights for software yet now they spend around $100 million per year toward development of Linux and similar open-source systems (Samuelson, 2006).

One of the fêted adopters is Sterling Ball, chief executive of Californian guitar and guitar string manufacturer Ernie Ball, who preached to 2,000 people at the 2003 Linux World Expo. He says that since the changeover productivity has improved. 'We don't have crashes and don't have viruses' and it is also cheaper: he believes he may save $80,000 to $100,000 a year. Two years previously, the company was fined $90,000 when, after an unannounced raid by armed US Marshals instigated by the Business Software Alliance, formed to protect companies' investments in software, it was found to have eight unlicensed copies of Microsoft Office. The company paid the fine, but Ball was so furious that he decided to purge his company of all Microsoft products. It chose open-source software for almost everything; in particular, Linux, the operating system, and OpenOffice, the open-source productivity suite owned by Sun Microsystems that forms the basis of the StarOffice suite. The Mini case study 2.2 'Munich makes the move to Linux' gives an example of where a larger organization switched to open-source.

Mini case study 2.2   Munich makes the move to Linux

Munich City Council has over 14,000 computers and 16,000 staff. In 2001 the council decided to investigate software alternatives to Windows NT, and by 2004 they had decided to implement Linux, as well as an open-source office suite. The new software was rolled out during 2008. The project is one of the largest ever moves from Windows to Linux.

The migration involved 170 business applications and 300 software products. It was self-managed, but Unilog, IBM and Novell assisted with the conceptualisation in 2003.

Munich's decision to move to open-source was taken at the highest political level; according to a statement issued by the council, reasons included greater vendor independence, and a desire to promote greater competition in the software market.

This, the council believed, would lead to cost savings in the long run.

But a more pressing concern, according to Peter Hofmann, Linux project manager in Munich City Council's IT department, was that Microsoft had ended support and production of Windows NT, the council's existing desktop operating system.

'The problem isn't that we don't have a helpline from Microsoft, but that hardware and software vendors no longer support NT. We can't buy NT on new PCs. We change our PCs every five years and the situation is becoming more severe with time,' he said in 2003.

Newer technologies, such as wireless networking and especially USB support, for printers, were also causing problems, said Mr Hofmann. Moving to Microsoft's Windows XP operating system and Office XP would have solved the problem. That was what Microsoft was lobbying for – including chief executive Steve Ballmer, who visited Munich.

However, with 14,000 computers and more than 16,000 staff, this would have been both complex and expensive. As a result, Munich decided to commission an independent survey from Unilog, the German IT consultants.

Unilog looked at three options: moving to XP and Office XP; moving to XP but with an open-source office suite, and moving to an open-source operating system and office suite.

The consultants also examined two intermediate, 'migration' platforms, using either emulation software or terminal server software and the Linux operating system to extend the life of existing Windows applications.

Analysis by Unilog suggested that moving to XP and Office XP would be the cheapest option for Munich in the short term, at a cost of around €34m.

Moving to Linux and an open-source office environment would be a little more, at around €36m, including Linux, an open-source office suite and Windows emulation.

However, Munich council believed that the short-term costs would be outweighed by the potential for greater flexibility and cost savings in the longer term.

By 2007, costs were estimated at €35m, or about €2,500 per desktop. The council acknowledged that training costs would be higher with Linux, but not dramatically higher than a move to XP – and a large part of the budget was earmarked for training.

Much of the final cost, according to the council's IT department, would depend on how quickly Munich Council's departments could make the switch.

'We want whole organisational units to make the switch to Linux, not one PC in 10 from a group of co-workers', he says. 'That would be impossible to administer.'

Source: Adapted from Munich makes the move, by Stephen Pritchard, FT.com, 15 October 2003, and Putting Linux on Desktops, by Sam Hiser, FT.com, 7 November 2007.

Debate 2.1

Since Linux software is free to install, it is a straightforward decision for all organizations to adopt it.

The Mini case study 2.2 'Munich makes the move to Linux' gives a European example of a large Linux implementation, and a further case study is given in the later section on office software. The advantages and disadvantages of open-source software and possible counter-arguments are given in Table 2.5. The development of Linux is a fascinating story and a counterpoint to Bill Gates's rise to power through Microsoft. Linux was initially developed by Linus Torvalds. As *Wired* (2003) explains:

> At 21, wearing a ratty robe in a darkened room in his mother's Helsinki apartment, Torvalds wrote the kernel of an operating system that can now be found inside a boggling array of machines and devices. He posted it on the Internet and invited other programmers to improve it. Since then, tens of thousands of them have, making Linux perhaps the single largest collaborative project in the planet's history.

This highlights a key feature of many open-source projects – they are collaborative developments between software writers. A worldwide workforce of enthusiasts effectively divide the work between them. It seems extraordinary, given the problems of systems development described in Chapter 7, that this approach can deliver software that is stable enough to be used by commercial organizations, but the examples show that it does. Table 2.5 summarizes some of the main advantages and disadvantages of open-source software. To gain an appreciation of the issues faced by a technical manager pondering the open-source dilemma, complete Activity 2.4.

Table 2.5 Three advantages and three disadvantages of open-source software

Advantages of open-source software	Counter-argument
1 Effectively free to purchase	Cost of migration from existing systems may be high and will include costs of disruption and staff training
2 Lower cost of maintenance since upgrades are free	There is not a specific counter-argument for this, but see the disadvantages below
3 Increased flexibility	Organizations with the resources can tailor the code. Frequent patches occur through collaborative development

Disadvantages of open-source software	Counter-argument
1 Has less functionality than commercial software	Simplicity leads to ease of use and fewer errors. Many functions are not used by the majority of users
2 More likely to contain bugs compared to commercial software since it is not tested commercially	Evidence does not seem to suggest this is the case. The modular design needed by collaborative development enables problems to be isolated and resolved
3 Poor quality of support	Organizations with the resources can fix problems themselves since they have access to the code. Companies such as IBM, SuSe and RedHat do offer support for Linux for a fee
4 May infringe software patents	

Activity 2.4	Selecting open-source software

Purpose

The decision on adopting open-source software is a common one facing technical managers developing their technology infrastructure strategy.

Questions

1 For the different alternatives facing a technical manager below, assess:
   (a) Which is most popular (use research figures through performing a Google search referring to the different technologies; for example, a search phrase you might use is: web server software market share 2010)
   (b) The benefits and disadvantages of the Microsoft solution against the alternatives.

2 Make recommendations, with justifications, of which you would choose for a small, medium or large organizations:
   (a) Operating system: Microsoft Windows Vista/Windows 7 v. Linux (open-source) for server and desktop clients
   (b) Browser: Internet Explorer browser or rivals such as Mozilla Firefox or Opera (www.opera.com).
   (c) Programming language for dynamic e-commerce applications: Microsoft ASP.Net as against independent languages/solutions such as PHP/MySQL and Perl.
   (d) Web server for hosting websites: Microsoft Internet Information Server (IIS) against open-source Apache.

visit the www

Case study 2.3		FT

Is open-source software a realistic choice?

This case reviews the advantages and disadvantages of open-source software for both office applications software and operating systems.

With a 95 per cent share of the desktop software market, Microsoft seemed unassailable, but an alternative has emerged in the shape of desktop applications based on the Linux open source operating system.

Two forces are coming together: while the leading Linux desktop applications – StarOffice from Sun Microsystems and the free software OpenOffice – are maturing, a growing band of disgruntled customers have become offended by Microsoft's stranglehold on the desktop software environment, for reasons of cost, security, or simply because they want a choice. Within the first week of OpenOffice being made available, the open source alternative to Microsoft Office, over 3 million copies were downloaded (www.techworld.com/applications/news/index.cfm?newsid=106163).

As a result momentum is building, particularly in the public sector, where there have been declarations by national and local governments in favour of open-source software and Linux. In October 2003 the UK government said it would carry out trials of open-source systems in nine government departments.

While most attention is focused currently on Linux at the server level, a key breakthrough came in early 2003 when the City of Munich announced it was moving 14,000 desktop PCs from Microsoft's Windows operating system to Linux.

The city implemented OpenOffice/StarOffice applications supplied by Nuremberg-based SuSE Linux. 'In the past 18 months there have been significant improvements in the quality and presentation of Linux software,' says David Burger, vice-president of enterprise solutions at SuSE.

'Things like fonts and graphical user interfaces were not historically important because Linux was not looking to compete with Microsoft per se . . . in the last six months there has been work to license fonts, understand what users want, and make it easier to use.'

In September 2003 Sun launched its bid for the desktop software market with Java Desktop System, an integrated package (known as Project Mad Hatter pre-launch) incorporating a new release of StarOffice, along with the Linux user interface Gnome, the Mozilla browser, Ximian Evolution e-mail, and messaging and calendaring tools.

The company promised simplified licensing, savings of 80 per cent over Microsoft Windows running Office XP, greater security, and the ability to interoperate with Microsoft Windows for sharing printers, files and documents.

So is Linux desktop software a realistic alternative for corporate users? Peter Houppermans, senior consultant at PA Consulting Group, says: 'There is a difference between ranting about Microsoft and actually making the change. But I think [Linux-based software] is just as good a choice as any if it fits in your environment.' This is a critical point: although Sun and the other vendors claim their products have the same look and feel, they are not claiming the same overall functionality as Microsoft Office.

'In the typical corporate setting [Staroffice or OpenOffice] would be fine for 70–80 per cent of users – but every company is going to have those users who are more sophisticated,' says Tim Jennings of the consultants Butler Group. Sun says Java Desktop and Microsoft Office can coexist, but this would leave users supporting two operating systems.

Mark Burgbacher, chief technology officer at Computer Sciences' global consulting group, says: 'I don't see any momentum with Linux on the desktop at present. We have certain clients who want to have a choice at the desktop, but the move to Linux is focused more on the application server space.'

This suggests that Microsoft may eventually face most competition not from packaged software vendors, but from centrally managed server- or portal-based applications. While enterprise software vendors previously ceded the desktop territory to Microsoft, advances in portal technology, web services and the development of remotely managed utility-style services are blurring the frontier between desktop and enterprise, and will provide further scope to move applications off the desktop.

Gartner, the IT market analysts, threw cold water on the idea that migrating from Windows on the desktop to Linux on the desktop would reduce costs in a report published in September 2003. David Smith, vice-president, pointed out that while companies may have found it straightforward to implement Linux at the server level, the desktop environment is different.

'Knowledge workers use PCs to run diverse combinations of applications. For those users, migration costs will be very high because all Windows applications must be replaced or rewritten', he says.

One of the central claims made for the superiority of Linux over Windows is that it is inherently more secure. Although not stating that it is immune completely to viruses and worms, Mr Burger at SuSE says: 'There are hundreds and thousands of people [in the open-source community] who will rally to deal with attacks.'

But the psychology of virus writing implies that the more Linux desktops there are, the more attractive a target it becomes. As Mr Jennings points out, 'If 90 per cent of the world's desktops are Microsoft, Microsoft will suffer 90 per cent of the world's viruses.'

Sun readily acknowledges that Java Desktop cannot do everything that Microsoft Office can. So it is targeting customers such as call centres, smaller companies, regional government and education, arguing there is no point in such users paying for the full functionality of Microsoft Office.

Sun had ambitions to take 20 per cent of the total market for desktop software worldwide in the two years after 2003.

But Mr Jennings questions whether Sun is committed enough. 'If Sun is really going to make a go of it it needs to put all its muscle behind it. The company is making noises at the moment but I think it will get distracted.'

Linux has had some high profile wins and defections, but as yet Microsoft is not undermined. However, these straws in the wind could be the start of something. After all, Linux on the server was not a big deal a few years ago.

In 2008, open source vendors are still not a dominant force in the marketplace (**www.techworld.com/opsys/ news/index.cfm?newsid=106027**). However, some people predict that the economic downturn will have a positive effect on open source providers (**www.techworld. com/opsys/news/index.cfm?newsid=105911**) but a large-scale migration from Microsoft to Linux would require significant effort and is more than just a case of purchasing and installing a new operating system (http://blogs.zdnet.com/perlow/?p=9300&tag=nl.e539).

What the experts say

Mark Burgbacher: chief technology officer, CSC Global Consulting Group
The simpler licensing regime promised by Sun is attention getting and will force people to look at the alternatives to Microsoft on the desktop. I believe the push is coming more from the thin client, with the software on the server, rather than Linux software on the desktop, because of the manageability. But you need a large return on investment case to make an operating system swap, and in the office there is not a compelling argument to do that at present.

Peter Houppermans: PA Consulting Group
Linux has come from nowhere to something quite usable. Its richness has driven it in the server market, and is now driving it to the desktop. The user interface has improved but as yet is not as polished as Microsoft Office. It needs someone to put money behind it, and conduct usability studies and so forth. As to whether it is suitable for any particular company, the issue now is less to do with the content or because it doesn't look the same, but what the existing IT infrastructure looks like.

Tim Jennings: Butler Group
Sun Microsystems has been trying to make a breakthrough to the desktop on and off for over three years. Java Desktop is not new in terms of functionality; what is new is the marketing push. Functionality-wise it is catching up with Microsoft Office, but I still feel it is not equivalent. It is okay for typing a letter, but comes unstuck in power uses. If you are just typing a letter it is not much different, but if you are putting a PowerPoint presentation together you will end up tearing your hair out.

David Burger: vice-president of enterprise solutions, SuSE Linux

Without any sensationalism there is no doubt there are alternatives to Microsoft on the desktop. There is heavyweight support for Linux at the server level, including IBM, HP and Oracle, which are all pushing Linux as a legitimate, cost efficient alternative. But the greatest push is coming from users who are offended by changes to Microsoft licensing policies. As Linux has become more accepted and deployed on servers, they want it on the desktop.

Source: Nuala Moran, Twin forces stir desktop debate, FT.com, 15 October 2003

Question

Assess the advantages and disadvantages of switching to open-source office software in a large organization, based on this article, Table 2.5, Research insight 2.2 and discussion with fellow students and your lecturer.

E-business applications

E-business and e-commerce are now widely recognized concepts which determine the types of software applications and information management approaches used by organizations. Occurrences on web pages indexed by Google of the keywords 'e-business' and 'e-commerce' weigh in at 5.3 million and 6 million respectively. This is smaller than 'information technology' and 'information systems', but larger than 'knowledge management' and 'information management', indicating the prevalence of these 'e-concepts'. But what exactly do 'e-business' and 'e-commerce' mean? Is there a difference in meaning of these terms, and how do they relate to established concepts such as information technology and information systems?

We will start by considering electronic commerce and then contrast this with electronic business. In this section, we will take the example of university and college information systems to explore the meaning of e-business concepts. This is intended to be applied by students to a range of organizations such as local government or service businesses rather than the more commonly quoted examples of online retailers such as Amazon.

Electronic commerce (e-commerce)
All financial and informational electronically mediated exchanges between an organization and its external stakeholders

Electronic commerce (e-commerce) is often thought simply to refer to buying and selling using the Internet; people immediately think of consumer retail purchases, using credit cards, from online bookstores, or perhaps home shopping or home banking. However, e-commerce involves much more than electronically mediated *financial* transactions between organizations and customers. Most commentators now consider e-commerce to refer to *both financial and informational* electronically mediated transactions between an organization and any third party it deals with (Chaffey, 2004). In a university context, an online application form for a course is an example of this form of e-commerce transaction – this is typically an information rather than financial exchange. According to this definition, non-financial transactions such as marketing to customers using e-mail and web-initiated customer enquiries and support known as '**web self-service**' are also considered to be part of e-commerce. A web self-service application for a university is illustrated in Figure 2.12. The importance of web self-service in reducing costs is suggested in the Research insight 2.2 'Online transaction costs'. Note that background on the technology standards used to support e-commerce, such as the World Wide Web, web browsers and web servers, is given in Chapter 3.

Web self-service
Customer service enquiries are performed using a website without direct or indirect contact between customer and employee

Research insight 2.2	Online transaction costs

A widely quoted piece of research which highlighted the benefits of e-commerce was produced by analysts Booz Allen Hamilton. They showed that there were significant differences in the cost of processing an inbound enquiry dependent on the channel used:

- Branch banking $1.08
- Phone banking 54¢
- ATM banking 27¢
- PC dial-up banking 28¢
- Internet banking 13¢

Of course, technology is required to support all of these types of interaction, but Internet banking is the lowest-cost transaction since it has the lowest need for physical infrastructure and human resources to support the transaction.

Linux is reputed to offer lower Total Cost of Ownership than a similar Microsoft system and has been used in the financial sector to improve transaction processing throughout and thereby lower the cost of each transaction (**http://news.zdnet.co.uk/software/0.1000000121,39217118,00htm**).

Source: Booz Allen Hamilton: Booz Allen Hamilton (BAH) at www.bah.com/press/jbankstudy.html (6 July 1999), and BAH, cited by www.arraydev.com/commerce/jibc/9811–14.htm (6 July 1999)

Figure 2.12 Web self-service application at a university

Source: University of Aberdeen website

Kalakota and Whinston (1997) refer to a range of different perspectives for e-commerce:

1 *a communications perspective* – the delivery of information, products/services or payment by electronic means;

2 *a business process perspective* – the application of technology towards the automation of business transactions and workflows;

3 *a service perspective* – enabling cost cutting at the same time as increasing the speed and quality of service delivery;

4 *an online perspective* – the buying and selling of products and information online.

Zwass (1998) uses a broad definition of e-commerce, noting the significance of information transfer. He refers to it as:

> the sharing of business information, maintaining business relationships, and conducting business transactions by means of telecommunications networks.

The UK government also uses a broad definition:

> E-commerce is the exchange of information across electronic networks, at any stage in the supply chain, whether within an organisation, between businesses, between businesses and consumers, or between the public and private sector, whether paid or unpaid.
>
> (Cabinet Office, 1999)

All these definitions imply that electronic commerce is not solely restricted to the actual buying and selling of products, but also applies to pre-sale and post-sales activities across the supply chain.

When evaluating the opportunities for e-commerce within an organization, it is useful to identify the role of buy-side and sell-side e-commerce transactions as depicted in Figure 2.13. 'Sell-side e-commerce' refers to transactions involved with selling products to an organization's customers. This is often referred to as **Internet marketing** or **e-marketing**. In a university recruitment context, sell-side e-commerce includes both the **inbound e-marketing activities** referred to above, such as web self-service and online applications, and outbound e-marketing activities. '**Outbound e-marketing activities**'

Sell-side e-commerce
E-commerce transactions between a supplier organization and its customers, possibly through intermediaries

Internet marketing or e-marketing
The application of the Internet and e-mail to support all forms of marketing exchanges with customers and other stakeholders

Inbound e-marketing activities
The Internet is used to support enquiries to an organization referred by offline communications such as advertising or online communications such as search engines, online adverts or e-mail enquiries

Outbound e-marketing activities
The Internet is used to proactively communicate with customers and potential customers using e-mail campaigns and e-newsletters

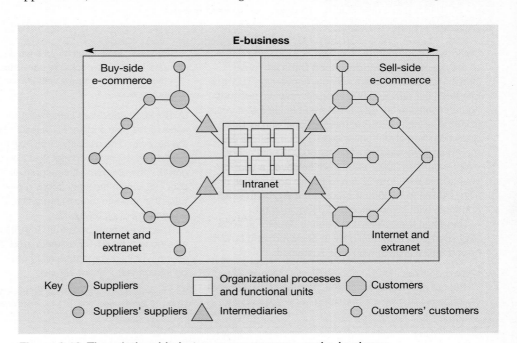

Figure 2.13 The relationship between e-commerce and e-business
Source: Chaffey (2004)

Buy-side e-commerce
E-commerce transactions
between a purchasing
organization and its
suppliers, possibly through
intermediaries

Business-to-consumer (B2C)
Commercial transactions
are between an organization
and consumers

Business-to-business (B2B)
Commercial transactions
are between an organization
and other organizations

E-business
All digital information
exchanges supporting
business processes that
are mediated through
Internet technology
including transactions
within and between
organizations

involve using e-mail to communicate, such as reminding prospective students to visit a university on an open day or sending out an e-newsletter. 'Buy-side e-commerce' refers to business-to-business transactions to procure resources needed by an organization from its suppliers. This is typically the responsibility of those in the operational and procurement functions of an organization. If a university is building a new library or learning centre, the university and its suppliers may use the Internet to procure facilities such as furniture and computers.

It is commonplace to identify both buy-side and sell-side e-commerce transactions in terms of whether an organization is transacting with consumers (business-to-consumer (B2C)) or other businesses (business-to-business (B2B)).

To conclude this section, read Mini case study 2.3 'Dabs.com profit from e-business' to see how small and medium businesses, which operate in the right market and have the right vision and the right execution, have used the Internet to transform their business.

E-business defined

Given that Figure 2.13 depicts different types of e-commerce, where does e-business fit? Let us start from the definition by IBM (www.ibm.com/e-business), which was one of the first suppliers to coin the term in the mid-1990s:

e-business (e' biz' nis): The transformation of key business processes through the use of Internet technologies.

Referring back to Figure 2.13, the key business processes referred to in the IBM definition are the organizational processes or units in the centre of the figure. They include research and development, marketing, manufacturing and inbound and outbound logistics. In a university, organizational processes include managing student applications, development and delivery of courses, research projects and other administration functions such as managing employees.

Mini case study 2.3 — Dabs.com profit from e-business

David Atherton, founder and former managing director of the online company, described Dabs as 'a real British dot-com, bricks-to-clients conversion success. Our first year saw £40,000 in profit; now we see that figure in sales every day. It's incredible.' In just 4 years from the launch of its first transactional site in 1999, dabs.com had about one million unique visitors each month and was adding a further 30,000 new users every month. In 2003, dabs.com achieved a year-on-year profits rise from £2.5m to £5.1m and a sales rise from £150m to £200m. It predicted the growth would continue, with sales reaching £350m in 2005.

Jonathan Wall, Dabs's marketing director in 2003, explained how the initial growth occurred, and how he hoped future growth would be sustained:

We dominate the PC hobbyist/IT professional sector, but our business must evolve. We want to cast our net further so that we are appealing to people who are interested in technology as a whole. New customers need a new approach. We have built a new environment and a new website for this target audience.

In mid-2003 dabs.com launched a site to help it achieve sales to the new audience. Research helped to develop the new site. The usability of the existing website was tested and the new concept was also shown to a focus group. After analysing the responses Dabs created a pilot site, which the same focus group then approved. In total, the new site took 10 months to develop and was an investment of £750,000.

The investment bore fruit. In April 2006, dabs.com was bought by BT for an estimated £3 million. It is now a wholly owned subsidiary of BT and continues to be a successful online retailer.

Source: Adapted from David Neal, E-Shops adds to attractions, *IT Week*, 12 September 2003, p. 24, www.itweek.co.uk

Although support for these internal processes can be referred to as 'e-commerce', more typically, 'e-business' is used to refer to these. So there are two main interpretations of the relationship between e-business and e-commerce:

1 E-commerce is equivalent to e-business.

2 E-commerce is a subset of e-business.

The second interpretation is the more widely held view and the one adopted in this book, since e-business is typically considered to be broader. 'E-business' refers to all internal and external information exchanges involved with organizational processes which are facilitated by Internet technologies. 'E-commerce' is limited to those transactions between an organization and third parties. For the Lo-cost Airline Company, the main focus of e-commerce will be sell-side e-commerce involving online ticket sales and online customer enquiries. It may also include buy-side e-commerce of the different inputs it needs to run the business, such as purchase of office equipment or in-flight items. E-business includes these e-commerce activities, but also includes using the Internet to support information flows inside the company as part of the process of scheduling and resourcing flights.

However, what is important within any given organization is that managers involved in exploring the opportunities for e-commerce or e-business are agreed on the scope of what they are trying to achieve!

Some argue that 'e-business' is just a new label for business information systems that is used to encourage the adoption of technology by businesses. They point to long-standing electronic transfer of information between businesses using electronic data interchange (EDI), which is described in Chapter 3. However, this does not challenge the scale of change, described by some as a 'paradigm shift'. EDI was expensive and was only used by larger businesses. Internet technologies have enabled many small and medium businesses to sell internationally. The Internet is now used by billions of consumers worldwide and this has had a major impact on how products are purchased. Figure 2.14 shows how widely used the Internet is for selection and purchase of

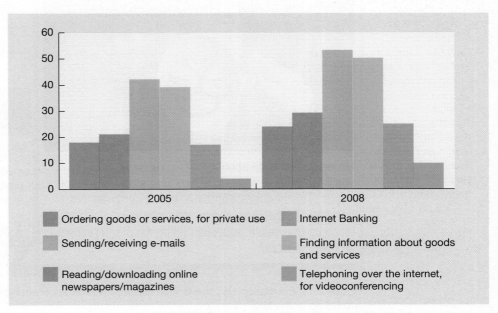

Figure 2.14 Percentage of individuals doing specific online activities in the previous 3 months, EU27

Source: http://ec.europa.eu/information society/eeurope/i2010/docs/annual report/2009/digital competitiveness/pdf from http://ec.europa.eu/information society/eeurope/i2010/key documents/indexen.htm

different products. It can be seen that products vary in how often they are purchased online. Standard products that do not need examination in a shop, such as books, music, electrical goods, holidays and flights, are the most popular purchases. Early in the evolution of e-commerce, only low-ticket-price purchases such as books and music were made, but today more expensive products such as holidays and electrical goods are commonly purchased online.

E-business has also caused major changes in the dynamic of the business market-place, making it easier for businesses to bypass intermediaries and for new electronic intermediaries to be created. Sites such as Kelkoo (**www.kelkoo.com**) make it easy to compare prices of suppliers.

'E-business is often also used to refer to the electronic linkages that become possi-ble with stakeholders. A good example of this for universities is provided by Figure 2.15, which shows how the British Council uses the Internet to promote UK further and higher education. It does this through a partnership with Hotcourses (**www.hot-courses.com**) which has created a searchable database of around 70,000 different courses in the UK. Similar sites exist in local languages for countries such as China, Thailand and India. This service was simply not practical before the advent of the

Figure 2.15 Education UK, the British Council website promoting further and higher education in the UK

Source: The British Council (www.educationuk.org)

Internet. It is apparent that with such services attracting hundreds of thousands of prospective students, it becomes important that universities update the information that describes their courses.

E-business benefits and management issues

The benefits to business of adopting e-business are a mix of cost reduction achieved through lower costs of information transfer and processing and the potential for increased revenue arising from increased reach to a larger audience. The Internet also offers opportunities for building relationships with existing customers through providing online services and e-mail communications. The benefits of e-business are summarized in Table 2.6 and described in more detail in Chaffey (2004).

There are many management issues involved with the adoption of e-business, but perhaps the most significant are involved with managing the organizational transformation needed to support e-business. Chaffey (2004) explains how new organizational structures, new responsibilities, new applications and new marketing and supply chain management tactics may be needed. The Internet can also be used to impact business strategy through offering opportunities for developing online products or exploiting new markets. Chaffey (2004) describes the need for organizations to perform demand analysis to assess the relevance of e-commerce transactions and services for their customers and suppliers and other partners. This will govern the extent of transformation required. According to the level of demand and the types of products sold, different degrees of transformation will be needed in the adoption of e-business. For an airline, the impact of the Internet is significant since many consumers are willing to purchase digital tickets online. For a consumer brand such as for a cereal producer or a perfume manufacturer where the product is purchased through a retailer, the impact is lower. In this case the adoption of buy-side e-commerce for procurement of raw material from suppliers may be more significant. Sell-side e-commerce will centre on using the Internet to link with distributors and retailers to manage the delivery of products to the point of sale. For distributors and intermediaries, a key influence of the Internet is its

Table 2.6 Tangible and intangible benefits from e-commerce and e-business

Tangible benefits	Intangible benefits

• Increased sales from new sales leads, giving rise to increased revenue from:
  – new customers, new markets
  – existing customers (repeat-selling)
  – existing customers (cross-selling)
• Marketing cost reductions from:
  – reduced time in customer service
  – online sales
  – reduced printing and distribution
  – costs of marketing communications
• Supply-chain cost reductions from:
  – reduced levels of inventory
  – increased competition from suppliers
  – shorter cycle time in ordering
• Administrative cost reductions from more efficient routine business processes such as recruitment, invoice payment and holiday authorization
	• Corporate image communication
	• Enhancing brand
	• More rapid, more responsive marketing communications, including PR
	• Faster product development lifecycle enabling faster response to market needs
	• Improved customer service
	• Learning for the future
	• Meeting customer expectations to have a website
	• Identifying new partners, supporting existing partners better
	• Better management of marketing information and customer information
	• Feedback from customers on products

impact on channel structures. It is important that these marketplace phenomena should be assessed and then evaluated as part of strategy:

- *Disintermediation* – the removal of intermediaries such as distributors or brokers that formerly linked a company to its customers, as indicated by the change in Figure 2.16 (a) to (b). An airline selling direct to customers rather than through a travel agent is an example of this.

- *Reintermediation* – the creation of new intermediaries between customers and suppliers providing services such as supplier search and product evaluation, indicated by Figure 2.16 (c). easyJet created a price comparison site easyValue (**www.easyvalue.com**) to compare flights and other products. Kelkoo (**www.kelkoo.co.uk**) is another well-known example.

- *Countermediation* – the creation of a new intermediary by an established company. Here an existing player or players form a new intermediary to compete against other intermediaries. In the European air-travel market, countermediary Opodo (**www.opodo.com**) was formed by airlines Aer Lingus, Air France, Alitalia, Austrian Airlines, British Airways, Finnair, Iberia, KLM, Lufthansa and Amadeus to counter the advances of online specialists such as Lastminute.com (**www.lastminute.com**) and Expedia (**www.expedia.co.uk**).

The strategic response to e-business has been managed by the CIO or information systems manager in many organizations; alternatively, a separate e-business responsibility or department may be created in larger organizations. In Chapter 4 we highlight the impingement of e-business strategy on information systems strategy. In Chapter 8 we examine how adoption of e-commerce services by customers can be encouraged.

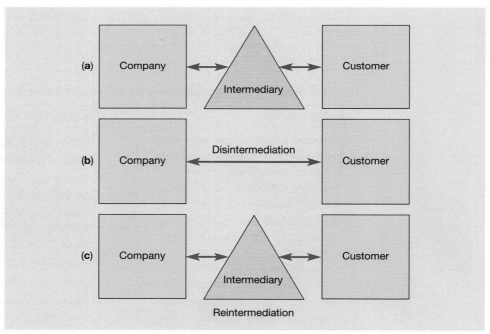

Figure 2.16 **From original marketplace structure (a) to disintermediation (b) and reintermediation (c)**
Source: Chaffey (2004)

From the Internet to intranets and extranets

Intranet
A network within a single company which enables access to company information using the familiar tools of the Internet such as web browsers. Only staff within the company can access the intranet, which will be password-protected

Extranet
Formed by extending the intranet beyond a company to customers, suppliers, collaborators or even competitors. This is again password-protected to prevent access by all Internet users

'Intranet' and 'extranet' are two terms that arose in the 1990s to describe applications of Internet technologies that do not only involve communicating with customers, but rather involve company staff (intranet) and third parties such as suppliers and distributors (extranet). They are both used to deliver e-business applications. They use the same technologies as the public Internet – data transfer over the Internet network and the access of information through web browsers and e-mail. However, the scope of information access is different. While everyone connected to the Internet can access a company Internet website, only those who have been given authorization via a username and password can access an intranet or extranet. This relationship between the Internet, intranets and extranets is indicated by Figure 2.17. It can be seen that an intranet is effectively a private-company Internet with access available to staff only. An extranet permits access to trusted third parties, and the Internet provides global access.

Intranet applications

Intranets are widely used for supporting employee access to organization information. For example, the Lo-cost Airline Company intranet would include:

● phone directories;
● staff newsletters;
● company procedures or quality manuals.

Such static information published on an intranet is accessed using a web browser and simply involves following hyperlinks to web pages in a web browser.

More sophisticated systems such as the ERP applications referred to earlier in the chapter, which are used to access sales or inventory data, for example, are now accessed via a web browser and these are also intranet applications. Human resources applications such as booking holidays or training courses are now also managed through such

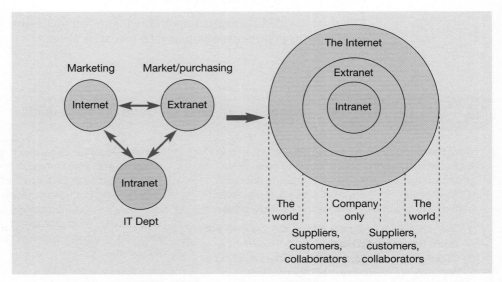

Figure 2.17 The relationship between access to intranets, extranets and the Internet
Source: Chaffey (2004)

intranet applications. In the future, the distinction between information and applications will eventually disappear: users will think only in terms of different pages which contain different types of information to support them in their work!

Mini case study 2.4 is an example of an intranet which features both simple information access and access to more complex applications.

Corporate information portal
Organizational information resources are made accessible via an intranet which gives access to documents and applications

Web-based access to company information and applications is sometimes referred to as a 'corporate information portal', 'portal' meaning a gateway to information. The corporate portal provides structured access to information stored in HTML documents, as shown in Figure 2.18. Documents held on file servers in other standard formats such as those for spreadsheets, word processors and Adobe Acrobat may also be available. A corporate or enterprise portal will also consolidate many existing separate intranets into a single access point. The facility to search through information will also be available. In many large organizations, the corporate information portal is not necessarily delivered through the web browser, but through widely used document management databases such as Lotus Notes, Vignette or Documentum. McFarland (2001) makes a distinction between the corporate information portal and the intranet. She sees the portal as more sophisticated since it will include dynamic content, personalized for the individual employee (like MyYahoo!) and provide access to a range of company applications. Honeywell's Enterprise Information portal includes more than 50 human resources micro-applications to assist employees with managing healthcare benefits, life insurance, sick leave, performance reviews and training (e-learning).

Total cost of ownership (TCO)
The sum of all cost elements of managing information systems for end-users, including purchase, support and maintenance

When web browsers provide an access platform for business applications which were traditionally accessed using separate software programs, this can help reduce the total cost of ownership (TCO) of delivering and managing information systems. Applications delivered through a web-based intranet or extranet can be cheaper to maintain since no installation is required on the end-user's PC, upgrades are easier and there are fewer problems with users reconfiguring software on their PC. See Chapter 10 for more detail on TCO.

Different intranets may be created for different audiences in different departments or different organizational processes. In a university, different intranet content will be available for staff and students, as is shown in Figure 2.18.

Intranet benefits and management issues

In a survey of 275 managers responsible for an intranet featured in *CIO* (2002), the main benefits of intranets mentioned by managers were:

Mini case study 2.4   A modern intranet for Ceva Santé Animale

Ceva Santé Animale is a French SME and one of the largest animal health products and veterinary pharmaceuticals organizations. Its intranet, dubbed 'Ceva en réseau' (or Networked Ceva), has access to both simple information and more complex applications:

1 The company's internal directory, the Ceva Phone Book, first to be put online.
2 Communications department section containing a photo library, corporate graphics guidelines, company standards.

3 Human Resources department section gives access to documents needed for employee management such as internal rules, collective bargaining and working duration agreements.
4 Each business unit has activity reports for each business unit, project progress reports, market and competition surveys and applications for that line of business.

Source: Adapted from IBM (2003)

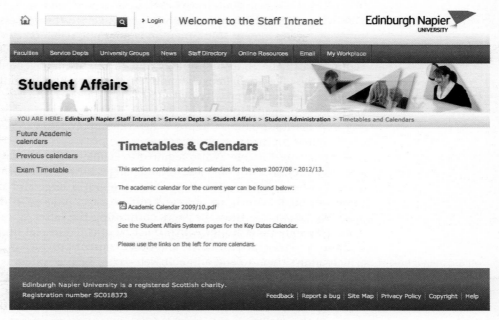

Figure 2.18 Example content from a university intranet
Source: Edinburgh Napier University

1 Improved information sharing (customer service), 97 per cent
2 Enhanced communications and information sharing (communications), 95 per cent
3 Increased consistency of information (customer service), 94 per cent
4 Increased accuracy of information (customer service), 93 per cent
5 Reduced or eliminated processing, 93 per cent
6 Easier organizational publishing, 92 per cent.

It is apparent that benefits focus on information delivery, suggesting that management of information quality is a key to successful use of intranets. Notice that cost saving is not referred to directly in the list of benefits. Direct cost reduction can be achieved through reduced cost of printing and indirectly though reduced staff time needed to access information. However, intranets represent a substantial investment, so careful consideration of the return on investment is required. David Viney, who has managed implementation of intranets at PricewaterhouseCoopers, British Airways and Centrica PLC, estimates that for a large implementation of more than 10,000 staff, the cost could average £250 per user or seat (Viney, 2003). He suggests that this cost breaks down into four categories, software (content management systems), hardware (servers to store content and applications), integration of information sources and applications and process change (staff costs and opportunity costs associated within implementation). He also suggests that if the portal project involves integration with ERP systems, this could add £150 per seat.

The management challenges of implementing and maintaining an intranet are similar to those of an extranet. In the next section, we examine five key management issues of extranets. Each of these issues also applies to intranets.

One of the key attributes needed for a successful intranet is information quality – achieving dynamic, up to date content is a key to the success of public websites, intranets and extranets. If information is not up to date, its relevance falls and repeat visits and use of these online resources will fall also. To achieve up-to-date content requires both the right technology and the right management of staff resources. Perhaps the biggest challenge is motivating staff to update content, since this often won't be viewed as a priority by them. This issue is explored in Chapter 8, from the perspective of managing change, and in Chapter 10, from the perspective of managing information quality. Chapter 9 describes approaches to designing information architectures for intranets and extranets.

A suitable technology is also required to enable staff to manage their own content. For large sites, it is not practical for all changes to web content to be sent through to a webmaster to update the pages. Think about a large site such as the BBC site (**www.bbc.co.uk**) which has around 4 million pages indexed in Google (the search '+a site:www.bbc.co.uk' finds all pages containing the letter 'a' on this site). Many of these pages are news stories which must be updated in real time. The only practical method is to provide journalists and other content providers with access to a system which allows them to add and edit web pages. Such a system is known as a **content management system (CMS)**. As explained earlier in the chapter, a CMS is a means of managing the updating and publication of information on any website, whether intranet, extranet or Internet. Review of content to check it for quality is often necessary and this facility is also provided by content management systems. After a draft document is published a reference to the document will be forwarded to reviewers via e-mail and they will then review it and it will be authorized for publication.

Content management system (CMS)
Software used to manage creation, editing and review of web-based content

Extranet applications

Although an extranet may sound complex, from a user point of view it is straightforward. If you have bought a book or CD online and have been issued with a username and password to access your account, then you have used an extranet. This is a consumer extranet. Extranets are also used to provide online services which are restricted to business customers. If you visit the Ifazone (**www.ifazone.com**) extranet of financial services company Standard Life, which is designed for the independent financial advisers who sell its products, you will see that the website only has three initial options – log-in, register and demonstrations. The Ifazone extranet is vital to Standard Life since 90 per cent of business is now introduced through this source. This usage of the term 'extranet', referring to electronic business-to-business communications, is most typical (see, for example, Vlosky et al., 2000). Hannon (1998) concurs, and also notes the relationship of extranets with intranets; he describes an extranet as

> any network connected to another network for the purpose of sharing information and data. An extranet is created when two businesses connect their respective intranets for business communication and transactions.

For example, Dell provides Premier Dell.com (formerly Premier Pages) for its business customers. This is how Dell describes the service to customers:

> Premier Dell.com is your customized procurement portal. A powerful tool created for you to more efficiently manage all phases of computer ownership: purchasing, asset management and product support.
>
>   Beyond mere customer service or e-commerce, Premier Dell.com empowers organizations to take control. Your organization's Premier Dell.com procurement portal may include a customized online computer store, purchasing and asset management reports and tools, system specific technical information, links to useful information throughout Dell's extensive website and more. All the information you need to do business with Dell, in one place, available to you 24 hours a day, 7 days a week. 'Easy as Dell'.

(Source: http://premier.dell.com/premier/demo)

When a university uploads details of new courses to the Hotcourses system shown in Figure 2.15, or electronically receives details of applications through a central application and clearing system such as UCAS (**www.ucas.ac.uk**), this is an example of an extranet application. Figure 2.19 shows the main e-business services offered by UCAS. These are *search*, *apply* and *track*. Of these, *search* is a public Internet service for which the applicant does not need to log-in, but *applying* and *tracking* are extranet services requiring log-in by the applicant to access their personal details.

Extranets are also used to share information between an organization and other partners such as suppliers and distributors (see Mini case study 2.5 about Herman Miller).

Figure 2.19 UCAS (Universities and Colleges Admission services)
Source: UCAS (www.ucas.ac.uk)

The office furniture maker Herman Miller (**www.hermanmiller.com**) was a relatively early adopter of Internet technology, but unlike many companies it did not embark first on an intranet. Instead, it decided it was more important to communicate more effectively with suppliers. It created its first extranet in 1998, but in 2000 produced MySign or the Supplier Information Global Network. This portal enabled Herman Miller workers and suppliers to access the finance and manufacturing systems maintained in the company's Baan ERP system. Users of the portal can also view demand schedules, supplier performance metrics and pricing lists. E-commerce manager Mike Brunsting explained the company's aims as 'we were exposing financial information from our business system to those key financial people at the supplier'.

By 2003 around 150 suppliers, representing 90 per cent of Herman Miller's procurement spend, were conducting transactions on the portal. Most used the Web page to access demand requirements, to confirm deliveries, and to verify payments.

Source: CFO Europe (2003)

Extranet benefits and management issues

Vlosky et al. (2000) refer to these business benefits of an extranet:

1 *Information sharing in secure environment*. Information needed to support business through a range of business partners can be shared using an extranet. Vlosky et al. (2000) give the example of advertising agency Saatchi using an extranet to allow their advertisers to access draft advertising material during a project. Information for suppliers is often shared by providing a log-in to a database which shows demand for products.

2 *Cost reduction*. Operating processes can be made more efficient through an extranet. The example given by these authors is Merisel, a $3.5 billion computer hardware reseller, reducing its order processing costs by 70 per cent. Such cost reductions are achieved by reducing the number of people involved in placing orders and the need to rekey information from paper documents.

3 *Order processing and distribution*. The authors refer to an 'electronic integration effect'. For example, an extranet can connect a retailer's point-of-sale terminals to a supplier's delivery system, ensuring prompt replenishment of goods sold. This potentially means fewer lost sales because of out-of-stock items, and a lower inventory holding.

4 *Customer service*. Improving levels of service is one of the main benefits of the Premier Dell.com extranet described above, although it also has the other benefits listed above. Distributors or agents of companies can also find information such as customized pricing or advertising materials. For example, 3M provides open web access to individual customers to find information about its office products such as Post-it notes and transparent films (**www.3m.com/uk/office**), but it also offers an extranet for distributors such as Spicers (**www.spicers.net**) and Euroffice (**www.euroffice.co.uk**).

Many of the management issues involved with managing extranets are similar to those for intranets. These are five key questions that need to be asked when reviewing an existing extranet or creating a new extranet:

1 *Are the levels of usage sufficient?* Extranets require a substantial investment, but as with a public-facing website, efforts need to be made to encourage usage since we are asking the users of the service to change their behaviour. It is in the organization's interest to encourage usage, to achieve a return on their investment and achieve the cost savings and efficiencies intended. Take the example of the Standard Life Ifazone referred to above. Many financial advisers may be comfortable with their existing way of selling products using the phone and post. Education will be needed to explain the benefits of the extranet and incentives such as increased commission may also be used.

2 *Is it effective and efficient?* Controls must be put in place to assess how well it is working and improve its performance. Return on investment should be assessed. For example, visitor levels can be measured for different types of audience and the level of usage for accessing different types of information can be assessed. The direct and indirect cost savings achieved through each extranet transaction can be calculated to help assess effectiveness. For example, 3M, manufacturer of many products including office products such as Post-it notes, has an extranet to connect to the office supply retailers (see **www.3m.com/uk/easy**). Retailers download the latest price lists and promotional information such as product pictures. Each digital download represents a significant saving in comparison to shipping physical items to the retailer.

3 *Who has ownership of the extranet?* Functions with an interest in an extranet include IT (technical infrastructure), Finance (setting payments and exchanging purchase

orders and invoices), Marketing (providing marketing materials and sales data to distributors or providing services to customers) and Operations Management (exchanging information about inventory). Clearly the needs of these different parties must be resolved and management controls established.

4 *What are the levels of service quality*? Since an extranet will become a vital part of an organization's operating process, a problem with the speed or availability of the extranet could cause loss of a lot of money; it is arguably more important than the public-facing Internet site.

5 *Is the quality of the information adequate*? The most important attributes of information quality is that it be up to date and accurate. Vlosky et al. (2000) point out the importance of liability if information is inaccurate or the extranet crashes.

Web logs

Blog
An online, publicly accessible, diary or news source prepared by an individual or a group of people

Web logs or '**blogs**' give an easy method of publishing web pages, particularly those with news or events listings. They are essentially online diaries and often have links to related sites. There are many free services which enable anyone to keep their diary online (for example, **www.blogger.com** which was purchased by Google in 2003). An example of a useful blog which can keep marketing professionals up to date about Internet marketing developments is **www.marketingwonk.com** which is based on MovableType (**www.movabletype.com**) software to host it. Steve Wood produced a blog focusing on developments in the Freedom of Information Act – this is shown in Figure 2.20. It is apparent that such blogs could be used for knowledge management with access via a corporate portal. For example, a member of staff could produce a blog to link to news stories about their market, such as market analysts' reports and stories about competitor activity. However, such use of blogs has not been widespread, with many companies preferring to source external services such as Factiva (**www.factiva.com**) for such competitive intelligence (see Chapter 5 for further discussion). Such services deliver such information by e-mail and through a corporate portal.

Figure 2.20 An example of a web log for business people and researchers
Source: UK Freedom of Information Blog (http://foia.blogspot.com)

Really Simple Syndication (RSS) is an extension of blogging where blog, news or any type of content is received by specialist reader software as described in Chapter 9. It offers a method of receiving news that uses a different broadcast method from e-mail, so is not subject to the same conflicts with spam or spam filters (Chapter 12).

Customer relationship management applications

Customer relationship management (CRM)
An approach to building and sustaining long-term business with customers

'**Customer relationship management (CRM)**' describes both a type of application and a business concept that is vital to all businesses. The business concept is based on the belief that building long-term relationships with customers is essential for any sustainable business. Since acquiring new customers through marketing is expensive, companies will achieve greater profitability if they can retain customers through time and sell additional products to them. This concept is clearest for companies that sell service contracts such as mobile phone or utilities companies. The longer a new customer continues to use their services, the more profitable this will be for the business. This is particularly marked online. Research by Reicheld and Schefter (2000) into profitability of online retailers showed that by retaining just 5 per cent more customers, online companies can boost their profits by 25 to 95 per cent.

The implementation of CRM is frequently broken down into four areas, which also correspond to the goals of CRM. These elements of CRM are summarized in Table 2.7. It is apparent that CRM applications are focused on the processes and activities involved in marketing a service to customers. The concept of CRM can be best under-

Table 2.7 A summary of the elements of customer relationship management

Customer acquisition
Techniques used to gain new customers

Customer retention
Techniques to maintain relationships with existing customers

Customer extension
Techniques to encourage customers to increase their involvement with an organization

Customer selection
Picking the ideal customers for acquisition, retention and extension

Element of CRM	Description	Information-based marketing techniques
Customer acquisition	Forming relationships to gain new customers	Tailored marketing communications such as direct mail, e-mail and visits by sales representatives are used to explain the features and benefits of services
Customer retention	Keeping existing customers buying existing products (repeat purchases)	Personalized communications are used to keep the customer informed about the products offered
Customer extension	Part of customer retention that is specifically focused on selling additional similar products (cross-selling) or widening the range of products used to more expensive products (up-selling)	Personalized communications are used to encourage repeat cross-selling and up-selling
Customer selection	Marketing communications for acquisition, retention and extension are targeted to customers likely to give the best response	Database analysis and modelling are used to identify groups of customers, such as those that will be most responsive

stood by imagining a customer lifecycle or their long-term relationship with the customer. Take an online grocery retailer such as Tesco.com. At the customer acquisition stage, it will send direct mail and e-mail to targeted customers such as young professionals that it thinks are likely to buy its products. These communications will be achieved through renting lists from data providers such as Claritas (**www.claritas.com**) and Experian (**www.experian.com**) and they will explain the benefits of using the service, perhaps with an offer such as €5 off the first online shop. After the first purchase, customer retention techniques will be used to encourage repeat purchases. E-mail newsletters and direct mails will be sent out to customers to remind them of the service and give benefits for repeat purchases. With customer extension, Tesco.com will try to persuade customers to purchase more expensive products (up-sell) or different products such as finance or electrical goods (cross-sell). **Personalization** technologies are used to encourage new purchase behaviour – if you regularly buy bottles of wine, an offer to buy a crate of wine from Tesco's online store may be delivered by e-mail.

A CRM system supports the following marketing applications:

1 *Sales force automation (SFA)*. Sales representatives are supported in their account management through tools to arrange and record customer visits.

2 *Customer service management*. Representatives in contact centres respond to customer requests for information by using an intranet to access databases containing information on the customer, products and previous queries.

3 *Managing the sales process*. This can be achieved through e-commerce sites, or in a B2B context by supporting sales representatives by recording the sales process (SFA).

4 *Campaign management*. Managing ad, direct mail, e-mail and other campaigns.

5 *Analysis*. Through technologies such as data warehouses and approaches such as data mining, customers' characteristics, their purchase behaviour and campaigns can be analysed in order to optimize the marketing mix. **Data warehousing** and **data mining** are defined by the Data Warehousing Institute (**www.dw-institute.com**) as:

> Extracting data from legacy systems and other resources; cleaning, scrubbing and preparing data for decision support; maintaining data in appropriate data stores; accessing and analysing data using a variety of end-user tools and mining data for significant relationships. The primary purpose of these efforts is to provide easy access to specially prepared data that can be used with decision support applications such as management report, queries, decision support systems, executive information systems and datamining.

The management issues involved with the implementation of data warehousing are discussed in Chapter 8 under the heading of 'Business intelligence'.

The success of CRM implementations is dependent on the quality of customer data. There are three main types of customer data held as tables in customer databases for CRM:

1 *Personal and profile data*. These include contact details and characteristics for profiling customers such as age, sex, socio-economic group (B2C) and business size, industry sector and individual's role in the buying decision (B2B).

2 *Transaction data*. A record of each purchase transaction, including specific product purchased, quantities, category, location, date and time and channel where purchased.

3 *Communications data*. A record of which customers have been targeted by campaigns, and their response to them (outbound communications). Also includes a record of inbound enquiries and sales representative visits and reports (B2B).

The implementation of CRM systems is often associated with problems owing to the change they introduce on staff and their way of working. In Chapter 8 we look at approaches to managing this change.

Personalization
Relevant products and messages are offered to users of the Internet via websites or e-mails dependent upon their profiles and behaviour

Data warehousing
Data related to customer characteristics and transactions are stored separately from the operational systems to enable analysis and targeting of future communications

Data mining
A technique used to identify patterns within data that may prove valuable in understanding customer behaviour or enable targeting

It is in the interests of organizations to use these data sensitively so that customers are not annoyed by unsolicited communications, and there are also legal constraints which are described in Chapter 12. We will see that using data sensitively is known as 'permission-based marketing' and communications should be anticipated, relevant and personal. As with all information management applications, there are issues involved in demonstrating the return on investment. Mini case study 2.6 'Standard Life Bank justify new data warehouse' describes how a case for investment can be built up, and summarizes the benefits of a data warehouse.

Mini case study 2.6	Standard Life Bank justifies new data warehouse

Mick James, customer data analysis manager at Standard Life, faced a common dilemma. He wanted to introduce a common data warehouse which could be used to better understand customer needs and target them in marketing communications. This would involve pooling of 5.5 million active customer names across the firm's life assurance, health care and savings business into a group-wide data warehouse dubbed 'Marketing the customer view'. Potential benefits were large; a trial involving merging two databases and offering bank products to insurance customers generated £250 million in bank deposits in a single campaign. However, to justify the expenditure to the board was not going to be straightforward. Talking about general benefits such as increasing cross-sell and up-sell (marketing other products to existing customers) would not be sufficient.

James decided to focus on the tangible benefits, and to estimate a monetary value for each benefit. The benefits and savings were as follows:

1 £250,000 incremental revenue through increasing sales to existing customers.

2 £300,000 savings through reduced costs of supplementing internal databases with lists of customers from external brokers.

3 £155,000 through improved data quality and reduced data cleaning costs – data cleaning such as de-duplication for customers' records was previously outsourced.

4 £30,000 through reduced customer complaints about unwanted or misdirected direct marketing.

There were also intangible benefits, but these were not the main part of the argument. These included:

- Improved customer targeting in direct mail campaigns delivering higher response rates leading to …
  - Lower product acquisition costs
  - Better understanding of customer needs leading to better product and pricing decisions
  - Faster speed-to-market for new products.

Source: Presentation to The Customer Relationship Management conference, 7 to 9 October 2003, Olympia, London: Developing an effective business case and calculating ROI on your CRM investment. Mick James, Marketing Manager, The Standard Life Assurance Company

---

Supply chain management applications

Supply chain management
The coordination of all supply activities of an organization from its suppliers and partners to its customers

Value chain
A model for analysis of how supply chain activities can add value to products and services delivered to the customer

Value network
The links between an organization and its strategic and non-strategic partners that form its external value chain

Supply chain management (SCM) is the coordination of all supply activities of an organization from its suppliers and delivery of products to its customers. Information technology has a great impact on SCM since it enables information about demand and supply for products to be more easily exchanged. In this final section of the chapter we consider some of the benefits of using the Internet for supply chain management.

The 'value chain' is a related concept that describes the different value-adding activities that connect a company's supply side with its demand side. We can identify an *internal* value chain within the boundaries of an organization and an *external* value chain where these activities are performed by partners. Note that in the era of e-business a company will manage many interrelated value chains which are sometimes referred to as a 'value network'. Different models of the value chain are explored in Chapter 6 on information systems strategy.

Information systems, and in particular electronic communications, can be used to impact supply chain management in a number of ways. Chaffey (2004) identifies the following benefits:

1 *Increased efficiency of individual processes.* Here the cycle time to complete a process and the resources needed to execute it are reduced. For example, if online ordering or e-procurement is adopted this will result in a shorter cycle time and cost per order will be reduced. Chaffey (2004) refers to the example of Cambridge Consultants which has over 4000 suppliers. Previously the procurement process involved between eight and ten people and cost the company anywhere from £60 to £120 per order, depending on the complexity of the order. The main cost is in requisitioning, when engineers and consultants spend their revenue-producing time in identifying their needs and raising paperwork. Using a combination of purchasing cards and e-procurement using electronic forms and e-mail-based authorization for purchases from strategic supplier RS Components (**www.rswww.com**) has meant that average order costs have been reduced to £10.

   Benefit: reduced cycle time and cost per order.

2 *Reduced complexity of the supply chain.* This is the process of disintermediation described above. A company may be able to order directly from suppliers rather than through distributors, and its own customers may also be able to order directly through the online environment.

   Benefit: reduced cost of channel distribution and sale.

3 *Improved data integration between elements of the supply chain.* A company can share information with its suppliers on the demand for its products to optimize the supply process.

   Inventory management can be improved through sharing data on demand for products within retailers. Inventory management is crucial to both manufacturers and retailers. If there are too many items on the shelves in a warehouse then space and so money is wasted in holding them. For the retailer, out-of-stock shelves means irritated customers and lost revenues. The *Financial Times* (2003) quoted Walter Hitziger, a member of Baumax's executive board, who summarized the benefits to Austrian DIY chain Baumax, which has 120 stores in central and eastern Europe and uses demand optimization applications to improve performance:

   > We have been able to reduce stock-outs by up to 25 per cent, with an inventory reduction of 11 per cent. With up to £250m in stock at any time that is a very major saving.

   An increasingly common approach to reducing out-of-stock items is known as '**vendor-managed inventory (VMI)**'. This relies on shared information systems or extranets which enable the supplier to monitor the levels of demand for its products at a retailer and supply according to the level of demand. Mini case study 2.7 'Iceland brings its suppliers in from the cold' describes this approach and its benefits.

   Benefit: reduced cost of paper processing and lower inventory holdings.

Vendor-managed inventory (VMI)
Suppliers monitor information about the level of demand for products by their customers through shared systems and provide goods to match this demand

4 *Reduced cost through outsourcing.* The company can outsource or use virtual integration to transfer assets and costs such as inventory holding costs to third-party companies. Technology is also an enabler in forming value networks, and in making it faster to change suppliers on the basis of cost and quality.

   Benefits: lower costs through price competition and reduced spend on manufacturing capacity and holding capacity. Better service quality through contractual arrangements.

5 *Innovation.* It may be possible to offer new products or new ways of ordering and servicing products to customers. For example, a chemical company could use e-commerce to enable its customers to specify the mixture of chemical compounds and additives used to formulate their plastics and refer to a history of previous formulations.

   Benefit: better customer responsiveness.

An alternative perspective is to look at the benefits that technology can deliver to customers at the end of the supply chain. These could include:

- increased convenience through 24 hours a day, 7 days a week, 365 days a year ordering;
- increased choice of supplier, leading to lower costs;
- faster lead times and lower costs through reduced inventory holding;
- the facility to tailor products more readily;
- increased information about products and transactions such as technical data sheets and order histories.

Technology is also applied internally to manage resources in the production process. This type of application includes MRP or materials requirements planning, computer-aided design (CAD), computer-aided manufacture (CAM), computer-integrated manufacture (CIM) and flexible manufacturing systems (FMS). Such applications have existed since long before the e-business concept developed. Many such applications have been upgraded so that information can be shared across an intranet, but the core basis of the application remains the same.

Mini case study 2.7   Iceland brings its suppliers in from the cold

Retailers have been sharing sales information with their suppliers for years but, as Ian Kielty, supply chain director at Iceland, points out, 'only after the event, so they couldn't actually do very much with what we gave them'.

Telling suppliers a week after the promotion finished that it had led to stock-outs or left stores with an over-abundance of unwanted merchandise was not particularly helpful for either trading partner. 'We knew there were benefits in collaborating more closely but they had to be mutual', he says.

Iceland, the UK supermarket chain, part of the Big Food Group, has used store and warehousing applications from JDA Software for some time so an obvious solution was to extend these systems to suppliers to give them direct insights into store activity in a simple, seamless approach.

Iceland put significant effort into developing suitable security systems to ensure that its trading partners only saw information relevant to them and – unusually – undertook training its suppliers directly.

'We needed to teach them how to interpret and act on store level information', says Mr Kielty, 'so that they could really start to use the sort of information we had available.' In effect Iceland had to teach its suppliers to think like retailers, capable of identifying the slight changes in customer buying patterns that could signal new trends and developing demands.

Work on security and training began in August 2002, starting with own-label suppliers, and in June [2003] Iceland began signing up additional suppliers to the scheme in earnest. As well as own-label businesses such as Deans Foods and Rye Valley, the company now has branded businesses including Nestlé, Sun Valley and United Biscuits tapping into store-level data. All these suppliers have also paid for the relevant JDA software needed while Iceland's investment has been largely confined to training and support.

'Our planners and buyers start by agreeing supply parameters and setting targets and key performance indicators', says Mr Kielty. 'The supplier can then access our forecasts and monitor sales proactively while the planners monitor the agreed KPIs [key performance indicators].'

The system enables a supplier of frozen pizza, for example, to tap into specific store-level data each morning to check on the performance of its products the previous day. 'They act just like our own planners to adjust forecasts up or down depending on performance', he says.

If business is better than expected, the supplier creates an order for additional stocks, without needing to check with Iceland's buying department – staying, of course, within the previously agreed parameters.

As well as matching stockholdings more closely to demand and reducing stock-outs, there have been real benefits for suppliers, too. 'They are achieving better vehicle utilisation', says Jon Grey, Iceland's group logistics director, 'as they can see how orders are developing and can switch consignments around to fill trucks and match demand more closely. Instead of just responding to our orders they can now see when to respond, which is helping us move to more just-in-time replenishment models.'

Source: Penelope Ody, Iceland gets wise before the event, FT.com, 1 October 2003

Summary

1 Software enables a user to interact with a computer system to complete their work and manage information. There are two major categories of software: systems software and applications software.

2 Systems software such as the Microsoft Windows operating system or Linux manages the resources of the computer system such as its input and output devices, memory and processor, which are described in Chapter 3.

3 Applications software enables users to perform different tasks. Applications can be defined according to their scope – enterprise resource planning applications support users performing tasks across the organization, specialist departmental software may be used in some departments while office software is used to create different forms of document.

4 There are a range of choices when selecting software, including packaged, off-the-shelf versions which may be freely available as open source. Hosted solutions used on a pay-per-use basis are also available. In some cases, organizations may decide to build their own bespoke applications or combine applications from different vendors.

5 E-business is a concept describing how applications can be delivered to stakeholders inside and outside the organization.

6 E-commerce applications are part of e-business and can be divided into buy-side applications such as e-procurement and sell-side applications such as online retail which may be with business organizations (B2B) or consumers (B2C).

7 Information provided via Internet technology can be limited to different audiences. Intranets restrict access to employees only and extranets to partners such as suppliers and distributors.

8 Two key applications of e-business are customer relationship management which is used to support the marketing of products and services and supply chain management which is used to support the sourcing of materials and distribution of goods.

Exercises

Self-assessment questions

1 Distinguish between applications software and systems software.

2 Describe the main functions of operating systems software.

3 Summarize the advantages and disadvantages of open-source software.

4 Describe the different options for obtaining software.

5 How would an organization select software from a particular vendor?

6 Define e-business and e-commerce. What are the main types of applications for e-business services?

7 Explain the concept of customer relationship management and how it can be used to improve organizational performance.

8 Explain the concept of supply chain management and how it can be used to improve organizational performance.

Essay and discussion questions

1　You are an IT analyst. Write a report for business managers, explaining and making recommendations on the suitability of the on-demand approach for buying business organizations.

2　Assess the advantages and disadvantages of the best-of-breed and single supplier options for enterprise resource planning systems.

3　'Open-source office applications such as Star Office and Open Office are not likely to be widely adopted.' Assess the future drivers and barriers to adoption and suggest to what degree the situation will have changed within the next five years.

4　You are introducing a structured approach to selecting software applications at an SME. Which controls would you implement to ensure that the most appropriate software was selected?

5　What management controls are necessary for the implementation of intranets to be successful?

6　As the chairman of a committee tasked with selecting a CRM application, you have to produce a cost–benefit report for a new CRM application. Write a report detailing the benefits for an organization of your choice.

References

AMR Research (2003) European retailers divided over ERP versus best of breed. AMR Research Alert by Nigel Montgomery, 22 April. Available online from *Computer Weekly* (www.computerweekly.com/Article123442.htm).

Anthony, R. (1965) *Planning and Control: A Framework for Analysis*. Harvard University Press, Cambridge, MA.

Business Centre (2008) Business Users Get into the Vista Adoption Curve. 15 January. Available online from PCWorld at: www.pcworld.com/businesscenter/article/141396/business_users_get_into_the_vista_adoption_curve.html.

Cabinet Office (1999) E-commerce@itsbest.uk. A Performance and Innovation Unit report, September. www.pm.gov.uk/output/page3698.asp.

CFO Europe (2003) Portals: Behind the green door. Article, accessed online, December. www.cfoeurope.com/displaystory.cfm/1742005/lrprint.

Chaffey, D. (2004) *E-Business and E-commerce Management*, 2nd edn. Financial Times Prentice Hall, Harlow.

CIO (2002) Measuring the ROIs of intranets – mission possible? Toby Ward. October. Available online at: www.cio.com/research/intranet/studyr2002.html.

DASA (2008) Defence Analytical Services and Advice. Available online at: www.dasa.mod.uk/applications/newWeb/www/index.php.

Financial Times (2003) Baumax sets a demanding challenge. Penelope Ody. 1 October.

Gartner (2002) Press release: Gartner Dataquest says Worldwide IT spending is on pace to increase 3 percent in 2002. September. www.gartner.com/5rabout/pressr releases/2002r10/pr20021007b.jsp.

Hannon, N. (1998) *The Business of the Internet*. Course Technology, New York.

IBM (2003) A clean bill of health for Ceva Santé Animale's portal with IBM WebSphere Portal Express. Case study on IBM website. www-3.ibm.com/software/success/cssdb.nsf/CS/AGON-5TEC5H?OpenDocument&Site=igsww.

Kalakota, R. and Whinston, A. (1997) *Electronic Commerce. A Manager's Guide*. Addison-Wesley, Reading, MA.

Logica (2008) LogicaCMG delivers hosting and helpdesk for Ministry of Defence asset Management Programme, JAMES. Available online at: www.logica.co.uk/ logicacmg+delivers+hosting+and+helpdesk+for+ministry+of+defence+asset+management+programme,+james/400002932.

McFarland, J. (2001) Corporate portals. *Harvard Management Communication Letter*, June, 3–5.

MOD (2008) Whole Fleet Management Integrated Project. Available online at: www.mod.uk/DefenceInternet/AboutDefence/WhatWeDo/Equipmentandlogistics/WFM/WF MIPT.htm.

Ovum (2004) Ovum comments: Information lifecycle management: destined for a bumpy ride. Author Graham Titterington. No date supplied. www.ovum.com/go/content/c,41487.

Reicheld, F. and Schefter, P. (2000) E-loyalty: Your secret weapon on the web. *Harvard Business Review*, July–August, 105–13.

Samuelson, Pamela (2006) IBM's Pragmatic Embrace of Open Source. *Communications of the ACM*, 49(10), 21–25.

Viney, D. (2003) Intranet portal guide (online article: www.viney.com/DFV).

Vlosky, R., Fontenot, R. and Blalock, L. (2000) Extranets: Impacts on business practices and relationships. *Journal of Business and Industrial Marketing*, 15(6), 438–57.

Wired (2003) Leader of the free world. *Wired Magazine*. Gary Rivlin. Issue 11.11 – November. Available online at: www.wired.com/wired/archive/11.11/linusrpr.html.

Zwass, V. (1998) Structure and macro-level impacts of electronic commerce: From technological infrastructure to electronic marketplaces. In K. Kendall (ed.), *Emerging Information Tecnologies*. Sage, Thousand Oaks, CA.

Further reading

Chaffey, D. (2004) *E-Business and E-Commerce Management*, 2nd edn. Financial Times Prentice Hall, Harlow, UK. Covers the e-business concept in greater detail. In Chapter 1, the benefits and barriers to e-commerce adoption are described in detail. Chapter 5 assesses strategic approaches to e-business, Chapter 6 describes supply chain management and Chapter 9 customer relationship management.

visit the www

Weblinks

Centre for E-business @ MIT (http://ebusiness.mit.edu). Created by MIT Sloan School of Management, contains summaries of over 50 research projects.

CIO.com Intranet/extranet Research Center (www.cio.com). Topical articles for professionals from US-based *CIO* magazine.

Elab (formerly Project 2000) (http://elab.vanderbilt.edu). Founded in 1994 by Tom Novak and Donna Hoffman at School of Management, Vanderbilt University, to study marketing implications of Internet. Useful links and papers.

Intranet Journal (www.intranetjournal.com). Detailed, dynamic site for IT professionals from JupiterWeb networks online publishing company.

Intranet portal guide (www.viney.com/DFV). A practical guide to intranet creation produced by David Viney, an e-business manager at British Airways and Centrica.

For multiple-choice questions and annotated weblinks relating to this chapter visit this book's website at: www.pearsoned.co.uk/chaffey

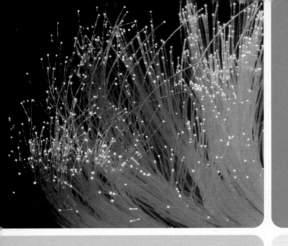

3

Technology for information management

Objective

To understand the purpose and the criteria for selecting different types of hardware and technology standards that are used for business information management.

Learning outcomes

After reading this chapter, you will be able to:

● Explain the relationship between software, hardware and communications components of information systems.
● Evaluate the suitability of different technology components for information management.

Management issues

Typical questions facing managers related to this topic:

● How do we select the appropriate technology for our organization?
● What are the meaning and relevance of different technology standards associated with the Internet?

Links to other chapters

The main related chapters are:

➤ *Chapter 2* introduces software components.
➤ *Chapter 9* on information architecture describe the concept of enterprise architecture and approaches to design of infrastructure.

Introduction

Technology infrastructure
The architecture of hardware, software, content and data used to deliver information services to employees, customers and partners

Hardware
Physical devices or components used for information processing and storage which form computer systems

Creating an effective **technology infrastructure** is vital to all companies. The infrastructure directly affects the quality of service experienced by internal and external users of the systems in terms of speed and responsiveness to their requests for information. The technology infrastructure refers to the combination of **hardware** such as computer systems within the organization, the network used to link this hardware and the software applications used to deliver services to workers within an organization and also to its partners and customers. In the previous chapter we reviewed the selection of the software components of information systems; in this chapter we turn our attention to the hardware and network components.

Understanding the jargon or techno-babble involved in the selection of information and communications technology is a major challenge for non-IT-literate office staff and business managers. Research Insight 3.1 'From techno-speak to common speak' shows the extent of this challenge. In this chapter we will explore the meaning of the most relevant jargon related to information and communications technology. But, only knowing the meaning of technical jargon is not sufficient if a manager is involved in the selection of technology. To choose appropriate technology it is necessary to know the relationship between the different technology and what distinguishes different solutions.

This chapter will review issues involved in selecting the technology infrastructure for information management on a 'need to know' basis. That is, what managers need to know if they are involved in selecting hardware and technology standards. There are four different aspects of technology infrastructure we will review in this chapter:

1 *Organizational technology infrastructure.* We start by looking at the different technology components needed in an organization and how they are arranged – their architecture. This includes the different types of computer systems used in an organization and how they are arranged.

2 *Computer system components.* We then move to a smaller scale when we assess the best specification for individual components which make up a computer such as a PC.

3 *Networking and telecommunications links.* Different forms of computer network for connecting computers within and beyond an organization. Networks are reviewed briefly since non-specialist managers are not involved in selecting networking facilities. The opening image for this chapter shows a type of fibre-optic connection which has been important in increasing the speed of transmission of data.

4 *Inter-organizational technology infrastructure.* Since Internet-based technologies are now the main method of electronic communications between organizations, in

Research insight 3.1   From techno-speak to common speak

In 2003, IT recruitment consultant Computer People conducted a survey into the extent of the problem of IT jargon. A thousand office workers across various industries were surveyed to examine perceptions of IT personnel and to explore how communication between IT professionals and their non-IT colleagues could be improved.

Over two-thirds (67 per cent) of office workers said they felt 'bewildered' and 'inadequate' due to not understanding IT professionals' 'tech jargon'. Over half (56 per cent) of those surveyed said that IT professionals 'speak another language', with two-fifths (40 per cent) saying that they feel IT staff are unaware of the confusion that tech jargon causes.

Source: Computer People: **www.computerpeople.com**

this section we consider how the Internet is used for information transfer. This section covers different technology standards for information transfer and publication on the Internet.

Systems theory

Systems theory
A model of the interdependence between different elements or resources in organizations and the natural world

The data-to-information transformation process is just one example of how systems theory can help us understand and improve business information management and information systems. Systems theory is a powerful concept that can be applied to many business and physical processes to better understand how they work.

The Austrian Ludwig von Bertalanffy was the main instigator of systems theory, developing the idea for organisms in the 1930s, then applying it to thermodynamics in the 1940s, before developing general systems theory in the 1950s. The essence of systems theory is indicated by these quotations from his book, *General Systems Theory* (1976):

> It is necessary to study not only parts and processes in isolation, but also to solve the decisive problems found in organization and order unifying them, resulting from dynamic interaction of parts, and making the behavior of the parts different when studied in isolation or within the whole.

> The whole is more than the sum of its parts is simply that constitutive characteristics are not explainable from the characteristics of the isolated parts.

System
A collection of interrelated components that work together towards a collective goal

The quotations show that in understanding processes it is important to consider the overall performance of the system, not only its constituent parts.

What, then, does this mean in an organizational context? For an organization, the system is made up of all the processes within the organization that work towards achieving its goal. The organizational system interacts with its environment, both responding to it and influencing it. The organizational system makes use of inputs such as finance, raw materials and human resources and will produce outputs such as products and services. The system uses a transformation process to change these inputs to outputs. Take the example of a tree – this receives solar energy, water, carbon dioxide (CO_2) and nutrients as inputs from its environment. It transforms these as it grows and photosynthesizes to produce outputs such as oxygen (O_2) and the leaves that fall from the tree and so leave the system.

Environment
The external influence on a system with which it interacts

Inputs
The physical and virtual resources that feed into a system

Outputs
The physical and virtual products that are created by a system

For an organization to be successful in meeting its objectives, two further elements to the system are required. First, feedback is required on the performance of the system and, second, control needs to be exerted based on this feedback. In an organization, feedback and control are achieved through the corporate performance management systems referred to earlier in the chapter. Feedback is achieved through reviewing metrics such as performance drivers and key performance indicators to assess whether targets have been achieved. Control then occurs as managers apply their knowledge to this information and make corrections to the process by changing the inputs or the way the resources are managed.

Transformation process
The mechanism by which inputs are transformed into outputs

Feedback
Output that is used to evaluate the performance of a system

The relationship between the different elements of the organizational system such as the inputs, outputs, transformation process, feedback and control systems is shown in Figure 3.1. All systems have these basic elements and there is a similar relationship between them.

Figure 3.2 shows the details of the organizational environment with which the organizational systems integrate. It is useful to distinguish between two different aspects of the organizational environment.

Control
Changes to a system through modification of system inputs or resources

Micro-environment
Specific forces on an organization generated by its stakeholders

The micro-environment is the immediate marketplace of an organization. This is shaped by the needs of customers and how services are provided to them through competitors and intermediaries and via suppliers.

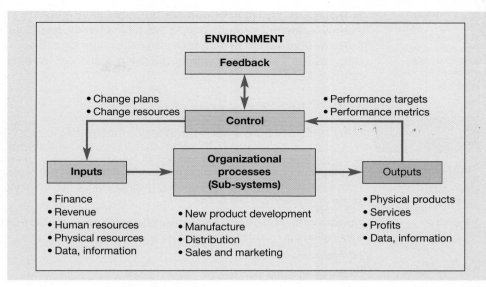

Figure 3.1 The organizational system

The **macro-environment** influences are broader, provided by local and international economic conditions, government initiatives and legislation together with whatever business practices are acceptable to society (ethics). Innovations in technology are part of the macro-environment also. These factors impact equally on all stakeholders within an organization's micro-environment.

These environmental influences on any organization change rapidly, so it is important that the current environment be monitored and future environment trends be anticipated. Organizations that do not monitor these environmental factors and or those that do not respond to them adequately will fail to remain competitive

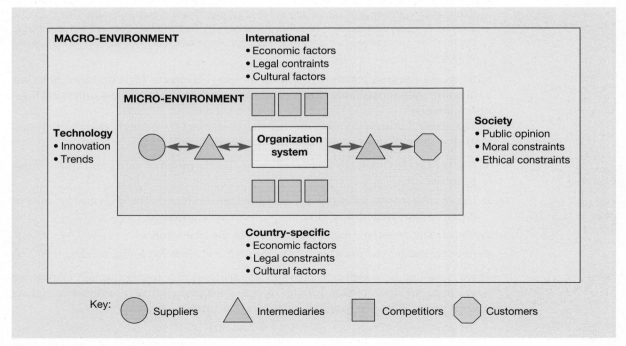

Figure 3.2 The organizational environment

Environmental scanning or sensing
The process of continuously monitoring the environment and events and responding accordingly

and may fail. The process of monitoring the environment is referred to as **environmental scanning or sensing**. As we have already seen in this chapter, effective business information management is vital to achieving this. To understand how business information management can help assist environment sensing, complete Activity 3.1.

Activity 3.1	Why are environmental influences important?

Purpose	To emphasize the role of business information management in organizational scanning from a range of perspectives, including the importance of monitoring and acting on a range of environment influences.
Activity	For each of the roles, (a), (b) and (c), consider which types of macro and micro-environment information it is important to monitor (refer to Figure 3.2). (a) Marketing manager (b) Purchasing manager (c) Information systems manager

Decision-making theory

We have said that information is vital to supporting decisions, but how exactly does this process occur? This is the realm of decision-making theory and should underpin approaches to information management. Managers make many decisions each day and we all do as we go through the day. The process is not mechanical – it involves both logic and intuition to make the best decision, as French mathematician Henri Poincaré noted in 1906:

> But of all these paths, which will lead us most promptly to the goal? Who will tell us which to choose? We need a faculty which will help us perceive the goal from afar. This faculty is intuition ... Logic and intuition both have a necessary part to play. Both are indispensable. Logic alone can convey certainty: it is the instrument of proof. Intuition is the instrument of invention.

More recent research has shown that we all use elements of logic and intuition, but with some individuals favouring a systematic, logical approach and others an intuitive approach.

The classic business decision-making theory defined by Herbert Simon (1955) suggests that there are four main stages in decision making:

1 *Intelligence*. At this stage awareness occurs that a problem exists and that it must be solved.

2 *Design*. Alternative solutions are identified and reviewed. The risks and benefits of different approaches to solving the problem are considered.

3 *Choice*. The decision is made by selection of the best solution.

4 *Implementation*. The decision is implemented and reviewed for its success.

There is overlap between each stage and the manager may iterate through all of these stages until the best decision is made. A less structured approach to decision making is suggested by Research insight 3.2 'How people process information'.

Research insight 3.2   How people process information

The structured approach to decision making presented above may misrepresent the actual process of information seeking and information processing to support decision making. Chun Wei Choo, a specialist in scanning an organization's external environment for information, suggests that the affective (emotional) response may be important too. He notes that often we consider information as a static resource residing in documents, but that an alternative perspective is that it is not an object, but an outcome of people constructing meaning out of messages and cues (Wei Choo, 2000). He says that:

> individuals actively create the meaning of information through their thoughts, actions and feelings

Wei Choo divides information seeking for decision making related to environment scanning into three stages:

1 information needs – the focus of information required, i.e. the type of information;
2 information seeking – the preference for different sources and approaches used to find information;
3 information use – how the information is applied.

In the context of information needs he suggests that determination of information needs of an individual should not simply ask 'What do you want to know?', but also 'Why do you need to know it?', 'What does your problem look like?', 'What do you know already?', 'What do you anticipate finding?' and 'How does this help you?'.

Wei Choo's work builds on previous models of our personality. For example, the well-known Myers–Briggs personality matrix can be applied to identify these traits in information seeking:

1 *Introversion v. extroversion*: Introverts draw mental energy from within whereas extroverts draw energy from others. The implication is that introverts are more likely to consult online information sources to build knowledge rather than colleagues or friends.
2 *Sensing v. intuiting*: Sensing types rely on information received through the five senses whereas intuiting types rely on patterns and hunches.
3 *Thinking v. feeling*: Thinking types use information to make logical decisions based on objective criteria. Feeling types depend on personal values to decide.
4 *Judging v. perceiving*: Judging types rapidly take a decision based on the available information, but feeling types take decisions more slowly and gather more information.

Wei Choo has applied these concepts of information seeking in the context of the World Wide Web. He has identified four modes of scanning to which we can all relate, which are summarized in Table 3.1.

In undirected viewing there is no specific informational need in mind and the purpose is to scan broadly; large amounts of information are scanned; large chunks are quickly dropped as in 'surfing the web'. In conditioned viewing, information seeking is directed to known sources which are also browsed. In informal search, there is an active approach to look for information to deepen knowledge and understanding of a specific issue. This could involve searching using a search engine such as Google. Finally, in formal search, a structured approach to obtain specific information about a particular issue occurs. This is a structured approach according to some pre-established procedure or methodology. This approach could use Google or a more specialist search tool and is only likely to be undertaken by those with formal training in information retrieval.

Chun Wei Choo has also applied the model of information need, seeking and use to organization-level information seeking. In Wei Choo (2001) he shows how organizations differ in how actively they pursue analysis of the external environment and application of the information.

Table 3.1 Modes of scanning when searching on the World Wide Web

Scanning modes	Information need	Information seeking	Information use
Undirected viewing	General areas of interest; specific need to be revealed	**'Sweeping'** Scan broadly a diversity of sources, taking advantage of what's easily accessible	**'Browsing'** Serendipitous discovery
Conditioned viewing	Able to recognize topics of interest	**'Discriminating'** Browse in pre-selected sources on pre-specified topics of interest	**'Learning'** Increase knowledge about topics of interest
Informal search	Able to formulate simple queries	**'Satisfying'** Search is focused on area or topic, but a good-enough search is satisfactory	**'Selecting'** Increase knowledge on area within narrow boundaries
Formal search	Able to specify targets in detail	**'Optimizing'** Systematic gathering of information about an entity, following some method or procedure	**'Retrieving'** Formal use of information for decision and policy making

Source: Wei Choo et al. (2000)

Technology infrastructure components

Infrastructure also includes the architecture of the networks, hardware and software. Additionally, infrastructure can be considered to include the data and documents accessed through e-business applications. A key decision with managing this infrastructure is which elements are located within the company and which are managed externally as third-party-managed applications, data servers and networks.

Figure 3.3 is a model showing one view of how the different components of technology architecture relate to each other. They can be conceived of as different layers with defined interfaces between each layer. The different layers can best be understood in relation to a typical task performed by a user of an information system. For example, an employee who needs to book a holiday will access a specific human resources application that has been created to enable the holiday to be booked (Level I in Figure 3.3). This application will enable a holiday request to be entered and will forward the application to their manager and human resources department for approval. To access the application, the employee will use a web browser such as Microsoft Internet Explorer using an operating system such as Microsoft Windows or Mac OS X (Level II in Figure 3.3). This systems software will then request transfer of the information about the holiday request across a network or transport layer (Level III in Figure 3.3). The information will be stored in computer memory (RAM) or in long-term magnetic storage on a web server (Level IV in Figure 3.3). The information itself which makes up the web pages or content viewed by the employee and the data about their holiday request is shown as a separate layer (Level V in Figure 3.3), although it could be argued that this is the first or second level in the architecture.

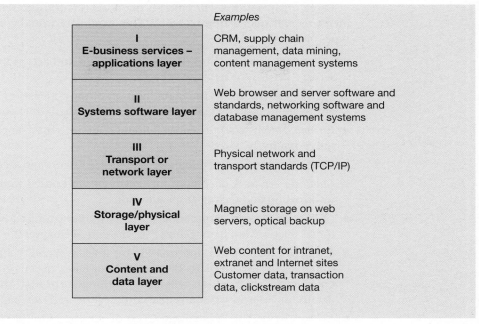

Examples

I **E-business services –** **applications layer**	CRM, supply chain management, data mining, content management systems
II **Systems software layer**	Web browser and server software and standards, networking software and database management systems
III **Transport or** **network layer**	Physical network and transport standards (TCP/IP)
IV **Storage/physical** **layer**	Magnetic storage on web servers, optical backup
V **Content and** **data layer**	Web content for intranet, extranet and Internet sites Customer data, transaction data, clickstream data

Figure 3.3 A five-layer model of technology infrastructure
Source: Adapted from Chaffey (2004)

The relative positions of the five layers of infrastructure are open to different interpretations. Kampas (2000) describes a five-level model where the infrastructure layers are in a different formation:

1 *Storage/physical.* Memory and disk hardware components (equivalent to Level IV in Figure 3.3).

2 *Processing.* Computation and logic provided by the processor (processing occurs at Levels I and II in Figure 3.3).

3 *Infrastructure.* This refers to the human and external interfaces and also the network, referred to as 'extrastructure' by Kampas. (This is Level III in Figure 3.3, although the human or external interfaces are not shown there.)

4 *Application/content.* This is the data processed by the application into information. (This is Levels I and V in Figure 3.3.)

5 *Intelligence.* Additional computer-based logic that transforms information to knowledge. (This is also part of the application layer, I in Figure 3.3.)

The client/server model

Client/server model
A system architecture in which end-user machines such as PCs known as 'clients' run applications while accessing data and possibly software programs from a server

Client
An end-user computer

Server
A computer that provides services such as storage or application to other client computers

Middleware
Software used to facilitate communications between business applications including data transfer and control

At a physical level of different types of computer system, the technology infrastructure shown in Figure 3.3 is usually implemented using a **client/server** arrangement. This arrangement is composed of user machines known as '**clients**', which access data or applications across a network located on a **server**. The server is typically a more powerful machine providing resources to several clients to which it is connected by a network. The client/server arrangement is typically used in larger organizations to produce a distributed computing architecture which we will contrast with other types of architecture shortly. A distributed architecture involves multiple servers accessed by clients. To enable communications between the server software and different client applications, so-called **middleware** is used.

Large organizations will contain many servers for different purposes. An e-commerce retailer such as the Lo-cost Airline Company would contain all these different types of server:

- *Web server.* Manages http requests from client and acts as a passive broker to other servers. Returns or serves web pages.

- *Merchant server.* This is the main location of the application logic and integrates the entire application by making requests to the other server components.

- *Personalization server.* Provides tailored content – may be part of commerce server functionality.

- *Payment commerce server.* Manages payment systems and secure transactions.

- *Catalogue server.* A document management server used to display detailed product information and technical specifications.

- *CRM server.* Stores information on all customer contacts. For more details on customer relationship management see the end of Chapter 2.

- *ERP server.* Required for information on stock availability and pricing from the customer. Will also need to be accessed for sales order processing and histories. Logistics for distribution will also be arranged through the ERP server. For more details on enterprise resource planning see the start of Chapter 2.

- *Network server.* Used to manage access of employees to the company network.

To manage the load on each server, more than one physical machine may be used for each server. For very large loads such as on websites like Google these are called 'server farms' and comprise hundreds of servers.

A key decision when designing the technology infrastructure for the business is how different functions are partitioned between the client and the server. This is not simply a technical exercise since it can significantly affect the combination of service level and cost for the information system. In the design of the architecture, it needs to be agreed how the following functions should be divided between the client and the server.

Cookies
Small files stored on the client used to identify it to the server

- *Data storage.* This should be predominantly on the server. In Internet-based systems, client storage is ideally limited to cookies for identification of users and session tracking. Cookie identifiers for each system user are then related to the data for the user which is stored on a database server. The legal implications of cookie use are described in Chapter 12. The reality is that many users will store data locally on the hard disk of their computer rather than on the storage provided on the server. This is a management problem since local versions of files may contain information that is not synchronized with data elsewhere in the organization; it cannot be readily shared with others in the organization and will not be archived or backed up regularly like the data on servers. Policies are needed to minimize storage of data on their desktop PCs which should be backed up and could be shared with others in the organization. The hard disk also adds to the cost of the machine, so some companies install PCs with no or limited local storage.

- *Query processing.* Database queries are performed on server machines in the modern architecture, although some validation can be performed on the client.

- *Display.* The display of graphics and text is mainly performed on the client machine.

- *Application logic.* Traditionally, in early PC applications, this was a client function, but with the move to hosted or on-demand computing described in Chapter 2, it is now more common for the application logic processing to be performed on the server.

In fact, the client/server model does not, strictly speaking, refer to the physical machines, rather the client and server are different types of software, where the client requests information and the server delivers the relevant information. Sometimes the client and server software will reside on the same machine. Consider a database such as Oracle: in the personal version of Oracle, perhaps run on an employee's laptop, the separate client and server programs run on the same physical machine. Modern client/server architecture in large businesses commonly uses a **three-tier client/server** model where the client is mainly used for display, with application logic and the business rules partitioned on one server, which is the second tier, and the database server is the third tier (Figure 3.4). Often, the application server and database server will be separate physical computers as shown in the figure, but they could be on the same server. Because most of the processing is executed on the servers rather than the client, this architecture is sometimes referred to as a '**thin client**', because the size of the executable program used on the client is smaller. The application server provider (ASP) approach described in Chapter 2 is typically based upon the three-tier model.

Types of client computer

Client computers are available based on several different technologies. The two most widely used client computers in use are the personal computer (PC) and the Apple computer. Less widely used are specialist client machines known as 'workstations' such as those used by engineers and designers which are produced by companies such as Sun Microsystems and Silicon Graphics. In large organizations, there are simple, low-cost **terminals** which may use a text-based interface link to larger servers. All of these technologies share the same types of components for input, output, processing and storage, as described in the next section.

Three-tier client/server
The first tier is the client that handles display, the second is application logic and business rules, the third tier is database storage

Thin client
An end-user access device (terminal) where computing requirements such as processing and storage (and so cost) are minimized

Terminal
A simple computer typically consisting of display, keyboard and mouse. The number of processors and amount of memory are minimized to reduce cost

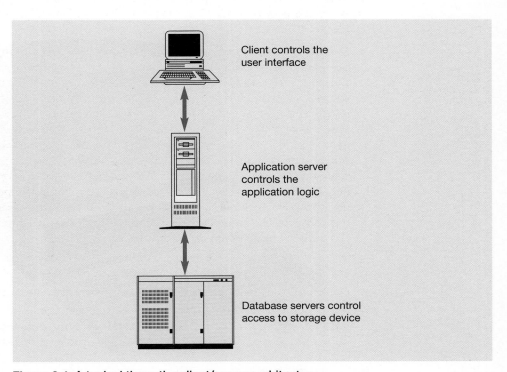

Figure 3.4 A typical three-tier client/server architecture

Personal computer (PC)
The most widely used client machine, originally developed by IBM and now produced by many manufacturers

The **personal computer (PC)** was originally developed in the 1980s by IBM and is still sometimes referred to as 'IBM-compatible'. Figure 3.5 shows the first computer which heralded the arrival of desktop clients in many organizations. The IBM PC followed on from other desktop PCs which can be viewed at **www.pc-history.org**. One of the earliest of these was the MITS Altair 8800 in 1975.

Client PCs are now available in many forms:

System unit
The main body of the PC which is used to house processor and storage

- *Desktop.* The most common arrangement similar to that shown in Figure 3.5. The main body of the computer, known as the '**system unit**', may also be positioned vertically in a tower or mini-tower configuration.

- *Portable or laptop.* Since 1990 it has been practical to carry portable PCs. These are more expensive than the desktop varieties because they need to be engineered differently to achieve compactness. Different sizes of portable have different descriptions according to their size, for example 'notebook' or 'sub-notebook'.

Personal digital assistants (PDAs)
Handheld computers used for managing an individual's tasks

- *Handheld.* Engineering has advanced such that it is now possible to house PC functionality in a device that fits into the palm of the hand. Such PCs are also referred to as '**personal digital assistants (PDAs)**'. Just as with their desktop relations, many PDAs now use a version of the Windows operating system as shown in Figure 3.6. This provides access to limited-functionality versions of office, messaging and diary applications. Such functionality is now also available in some mobile phones – an example of **device convergence**. Ultimately every PDA will have access to office applications, company ERP data, the Internet, digital camera, radio, music players and, of course, a phone.

Device convergence
The functionality of different digital devices is united into a single device

Total cost of ownership (TCO)
The lifetime cost of purchasing, maintaining and supporting any technology component

- *Windows terminal or network computer.* These PCs are designed to minimize cost. They have the minimum processor and memory since they run applications on the client. They are designed to reduce the **total cost of ownership (TCO)** through lower initial purchase price and lower support costs since applications and operating system are not stored locally, but on the server. We return to the role of total cost of ownership in managing information services in Chapter 10.

Figure 3.5 The first personal computer
Source: Rune's PC Museum (http://pc-museum.com/rcm-001.jpg) curator@pc-museum.com

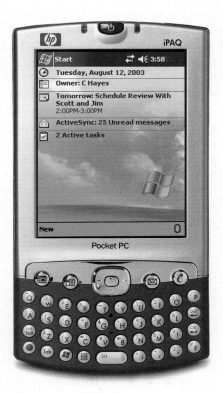

Figure 3.6 A personal digital assistant – the iPaq Pocket PC

Source: Hewlett-Packard Company, Inc., Palo Alto CA (www.hp.com)

Types of server computer

Mainframe
Powerful computers used for large-scale data processing

Mini-computer
A general term, often referred to as 'midrange', typically for computers larger than micro-computers and PCs, but smaller than mainframes

Micro-computer
Typically used to refer to a PC or similar-sized client workstation

Server computers tend to be larger than desktop clients since the system unit has to contain large-capacity storage devices. The earliest servers were large computers that often filled an entire room and were known as '**mainframes**'. Through time, as technology has advanced, these have decreased in size to smaller mainframes, **mini-computers** and now **micro-computers**. The servers used in small organizations are effectively indistinguishable from tower-system PCs and use similar components. In larger organizations, more powerful servers are available from vendors such as IBM, Hewlett-Packard and Sun Microsystems.

Innovation in servers continues, with efforts to improve performance and reduce the total cost of ownership. Current approaches include:

- *Blade servers*. Compact 'high-density' servers comprising microprocessors and memory on a single circuit board. Developed to be low-cost servers which can easily be added to as capacity requirement changes. Each blade often has a particular function such as web serving, file sharing or streaming content. Blade servers have smaller power consumption and space requirements than traditional servers. One product supports 280 blades in a single clustered unit.

- *Clustering*. Servers are connected to increase stability and performance. If one server fails, another will take over; if there is a high load then this will be shared between servers. Google is reputed to have over one million servers. It can readily deal with failure of individual servers. This capacity provides the fast response needed for the over a billion searches performed on a single day, and initiatives such as Google e-mail, known as 'Gmail'.

- *Storage area network (SAN)*. Server clustering is used to connect and manage networked storage devices. This helps ensure that all data are backed up and if new storage capacity is needed, it can be added without disruption of service. Central management of storage replaces an ad-hoc approach to managing storage and back-up on servers throughout the organization. Read Case study 3.1 to understand the importance of storage networks.

- *Grid computing*. The need for powerful servers is reduced by this approach which shares the power of client machines to solve computational problems – the clients are effectively joined to become a powerful server. The best-known application of grid computing is SETI (Search for Extraterrestrial Intelligence, see also 'Voluntary computing' below). The Large Hadron Collider, which smashes protons together to investigate how the universe began, also uses grid computing to harness the processing power necessary to analyse the enormous amounts of data that will be generated. The equivalent of 20 million CDs of data per year will be captured (BBC, 2003b) and processed by around 80,000 computers (Telegraph, 2008).

- *Mainframes*. Mainframes are still widely used in large organizations. While perceived by many as lumbering dinosaurs, in fact they can deliver a better cost/performance ratio than PCs in a large organization. Reference to this site for IS professionals working with mainframes such as the IBM/390 shows how widely used these services are – http://search390.techtarget.com. Mainframes also support innovation – in New Zealand, the TSB Bank has moved to the open-source Linux operating system on its mainframes, as have BP and Banca Commerziale Italiana in Europe.

- *Mini-computers*. Likewise, mini-computers such as the IBM AS/400 are still widely used for the cost/performance and stability they bring to businesses. IBM has renamed the system eServer iSeries/400 and claims that modern information management applications such as data warehousing, groupware and e-commerce services are common applications in medium-to-large organizations.

The concept of utility computing, introduced in Chapter 2, can be applied to hardware resources such as servers. As Case study 3.1 (p.107) on storage area networks shows, it has now become relatively easy to add new server storage and processing capacity. For an example of how this concept has been applied by server vendor Sun Microsystems, see http://www.sun.com/service/utility.

Computing architectures

Centralized computing
A single mainframe or mini-computer performs processing and provides storage for many users

Personal computing
Individual PCs are used for performing users' tasks and storing data

Distributed computing
Clients are networked with multiple servers. The organization's data are physically located on different servers

The different clients and servers introduced in the previous sections can be combined into different architectures. These alternatives and their benefits and disadvantages are summarized in Figure 3.7. The alternatives from (a) to (e) represent a general evolution in architectures over the few decades since the mainframe was introduced.

In (a) centralized computing, a single mainframe or mini-computer performs processing and provides storage for many users. This proved cost-effective and relative easy to administer compared with some of the other alternatives. In (b), personal computing, individual PCs are used for performing user tasks and storing data. This introduced users to multi-tasking (running several applications at the same time), but gave problems of data management and support. In (c), distributed computing, clients are networked with multiple servers. The organization's data are physically located on different servers and may also be stored on the hard disks of clients. This is the classic client/server architecture in medium to large organizations. It gave great flexibility in delivering different applications to different departments, but created problems of information sharing and a high total cost of ownership – an issue which is discussed further in Chapter 11. In (d), network computing, a return to the approach of centralized computing occurred. But, this time, the clients tended to be more sophisticated than the text terminals used previously. They supported multi-tasking through a graphical user interface and tended to have more local memory and processor power on the client. Finally, in (e), the availability of networked PCs gave the opportunity for **peer-to-peer computing** (P2P), where each computer can be used in either a client or a server capacity. This can be used for file transfer, as is the case with networks such as Napster, Grokster or Kazaa where music or video files can be transferred (the transfer is mediated through a server). Alternatively, P2P networking can be used to share information within an office or home. In (f), **cloud computing**, the information system is not physically located in the organization nor is it managed by them. The hardware and software required are effectively leased or rented from one or more providers that exist somewhere 'out there' on the web. Responsibility for maintenance and upgrade of resources rests with the provider, leaving the organization to focus on its core activities and business purpose. While this reduces the complexity of system ownership, it also means that the organization loses a degree of control of it's underlying business information systems. Furthermore, an organization that operates in the UK may have its data stored in any country around the world, or even multiple countries. This raises issues of data security whereby the national laws governing the storage of data may be different for the country where it is stored – a situation highlighted by the Canadian government, which forbids public sector data from being stored on US-based hosting services (BBC, 2008).

Cloud computing is gaining support as a new model for informatic architecture in business though no common approaches have yet been described or have emerged. A broad range of definitions has been compiled (Infoworld, 2008) from a range of industry organizations:

- Software As A Service
- Utility Computing
- Web services in the cloud
- Platform As A Service
- Managed Service Providers
- Service Commerce Platforms
- Internet Integration.

Voluntary computing

Within the academic and research community there is a form of computing architecture which is gaining popularity. Sometimes termed 'volunteer computing', it is an approach that uses the redundant processing power of individuals' computers to solve scientific problems. With the costs of hiring powerful supercomputers beyond the budget of most research teams, volunteer computing invites members of the public to subscribe to a research project and uses the time that their computer lies idle to perform the calculations. Although a supercomputer is vastly more powerful than any personal computer, the sheer number of parallel computations that can be achieved by volunteer computing provides comparable overall processing capability.

It began in 1999 with the launch of SETI@Home (**http://setiathome.berkeley.edu/index.php**) which searched for signs of life within the data received from the radio telescope at Arecibo. Once installed, the SETI project would run as a screensaver, downloading packets of data and uploading them again once analysed. The project has grown rapidly and now comprises over 5 million registered users running 320,000 active computers (SETI, 2008) generating 100 terabytes of analysed data every year.

Peer-to-peer computing
Each computer is used in either a client or a server capacity

Cloud computing
Computing resources and technologies reside off-site under no direct control.

Computing approach	Explanation of typical approach	Avantages	Disadvantages
(a) Centralized computing 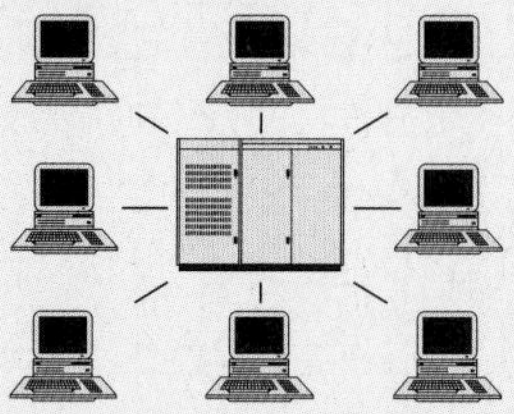	A single mainframe or mini-computer performs processing and provides storage for many users.	Cost-effective since clients have low cost and maintenance of clients is reduced.	Totally reliant on central computer, causing problems when it fails or is overloaded. Graphical applications can be limited. Limited flexibility for users. Usually single application running.
(b) Personal computing 	Individual PCs are used for performing users' tasks and storing data. They may be networked to some extent.	Flexibility for users to install applications necessary and configure system as they wish. Not dependent on reliability or performance of network or central computer. Multiple applications possible.	Information management problems since data cannot be readily shared or backed up. Time wasted in configuration and support. High cost of hardware.
(c) Distributed computing 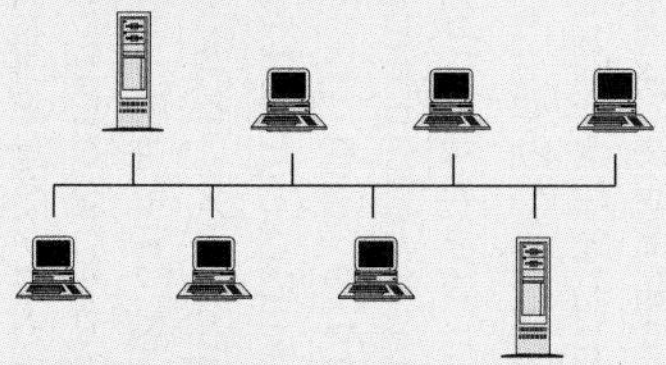	Clients are networked with multiple servers. The organization's data are physically located on different servers.	Less reliant on single central computer. Opportunities to share data greater than personal computing model.	Complex to manage hardware, software and data which are located across different servers and clients. Security may be a problem.
(d) Network computing 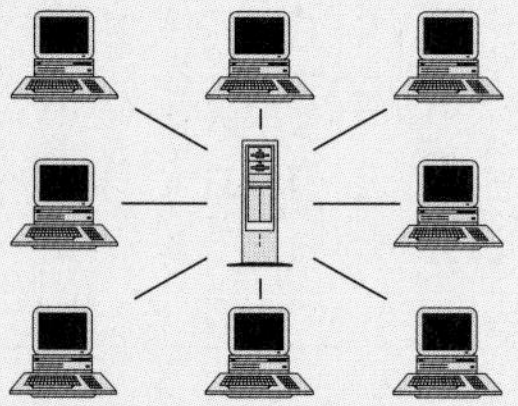	A similar approach to centralized computing, but typically uses more powerful client PCs for data processing and multiple servers. Supports multi-tasking.	Cost-effective since clients are relatively low-cost and maintenance costs of clients are reduced.	Dependent on central server(s) Limited processing on the end-users' clients.
(e) Peer-to-peer computing 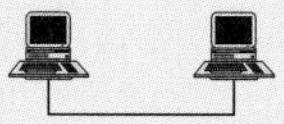	Each computer is used in a client or a server capacity.	Storage and processing power can be divided between computers.	Typically only suitable for smaller networks. Security limitations.

Figure 3.7 Five alternative computing architectures

One of the difficulties of harnessing this processing power is ensuring compatibility of the software with the huge variety of computers that may be encountered. Also, volunteer computing appeared to have uses in many areas beyond SETI. From this was created the Berkeley Online Infrastructure for Network Computing (BOINC). This allowed any research project to utilize the power of voluntary computing, plus it allowed individuals to subscribe easily to multiple projects. BOINC is now used to operate a wide range of computing projects, from medical research to earth science, mathematics, astronomy and chemistry (BOINC, 2008).

Case study 3.1

FT

Why storage networks matter

This article looks a the role of storage networks in managing the increased volume of information in organizations.

Storage is a mess. CIOs, industry analysts and even some vendors agree that one of the biggest problems facing IT departments today is controlling and managing their data storage and retrieval.

Left unchecked, businesses could see the amount of data they store doubling every 12 to 18 months. The resulting costs – many of them hidden – are a serious issue when many companies face flat, if not declining, IT budgets.

During the technology boom of the late 1990s, it was far from uncommon for companies to see their storage requirements grow at 90 per cent to 100 per cent a year. Even during the downturn, companies saw their data expand by as much as 50 per cent.

'Conventional wisdom is that, as the global economy picks up, we won't see growth go back to 90 to 100 per cent, but it will be more than 50 per cent a year', suggests Joe Tucci, chief executive of EMC, the storage equipment company.

'What I hear from CIOs is that there is nothing they can do about the amount of information coming at them', Mr Tucci says.

Tom Hudson, chief executive of storage network company CNT, agrees. He estimates that his customers are averaging storage growth rates of 70 per cent each year. The drivers for data growth go beyond the availability of ever-cheaper physical storage and the 'keep everything' culture it can create.

Industry experts point out that often a large percentage – sometimes the majority – of information stored is duplicated or out-of-date information. And sometimes the very measures intended to improve data management can spur additional growth.

'One client put in a storage area network (San) two years ago, but they are seeing a trebling of data because it is so easy to expand storage', says Alastair McAulay, a consultant in the IT systems group at PA Consulting.

Hewlett Packard studied IT managers' perception of the growth of unstructured data in enterprises and found that they estimated it to comprise 25% of the total data held by the organisation. This is significantly different to industry analysts' claims that unstructured data accounts for nearer 70% of the whole and highlights that IT managers are not aware of the full extent of the problem (**www.techworld.com/applications/news/index.cfm?newsid=106661**).

Unstructured data is comprised typically of emails and personal files and is difficult to manage. The ePolicy Institute have produced email retention and archiving guidelines that enable organisations to enhance productivity and reduce costs (**http://i.i.com.com/cnwk.1d /html/itp/MessageLabs_EmailRetentionAndArchiving.pd**).

'Flexibility lets you manage resources better, but flexibility also lets you add half a terabyte to get over the problem in the short term. That does nothing to address the underlying issue of data management.'

The cost improvements for physical storage on disk and tape are outpacing Moore's Law (the observation made in 1965 by Gordon Moore, co-founder of Intel, that the number of transistors per square inch on integrated circuits had doubled every year since the integrated circuit was invented). Applied to storage, this means it can be hard for IT departments to justify introducing new storage management tools or to change the storage architecture, for example by introducing a San.

EMC estimates that disk storage is now between 35 and 38 per cent cheaper than a year ago. Unfortunately, this represents only a fraction of the overall expenditure on storage. Improving storage management is a step companies should consider with care, as it is not just internal pressures that are piling rocks on the top of the data mountain.

Regulatory requirements represent perhaps the greatest driver for information storage and archiving, especially in quoted companies in North America (Sarbanes–Oxley), financial sector companies in Europe (Basel 2) and in the healthcare sector in the US (HIPAA). Data protection and financial compliance rules, combined with decisions in the courts, mean that many finance directors, compliance officers and security managers are erring on the side of keeping rather than discarding data.

'Compliance and regulatory issues are making the data issue worse', suggests Charles Stevens, vice-president of Microsoft's enterprise storage division. 'You cannot destroy or erase data, and then there is all the information that is moving off paper.'

Regulators want to know that this information is not only being kept, but that it is readily accessible.

Authorities may not be willing to wait days while a company retrieves tapes from its vaults, and then finds the relevant e-mail or document. This is prompting businesses to keep more information, and for much longer, on disk-based storage systems.

Estimates across the IT industry vary, but the more pessimistic suggest that hardware might represent as little as one sixth of the total cost of storing data.

The remainder is human and IT management costs. All too often these costs are not taken into account when departments or users make requests for more storage.

The tools and technologies for improving storage and data management have improved considerably over the last two to three years, with higher performance and greater interoperability between vendors' products.

On the hardware side, the continuing development of storage area networks means that this technology is no longer the preserve of the large business or the centralised data centre.

However, it is vital that a holistic approach is adopted in order to evaluate system design and reliability and thereby reduce the overall Total Cost of Ownership (www.equal-logic.com/uploadedFiles/Resources/Technical_Bulletins / CB108_Reliability_2005_0217.pdf).

A simple San 'kit' can today cost as little as $35,000, and the price differential between direct attached storage and networked storage, at least at the mid to high end, is eroding rapidly.

'I don't think we are anywhere near reaching the floor [in pricing] for San technology', says Tom Clark, marketing director at McData and the author of several books on storage networking. 'Sans have many rich capabilities, and there is a lot of technology that is pushing the price point lower.'

Greg Reyes, chief executive of Brocade, a storage networking hardware company, agrees. '[In] mid-2004 customers will be able to purchase an entry-level San without paying a premium to direct attached storage.'

Among the technologies driving prices down is iSCSI, as a lower cost alternative to fibre-channel Sans, and Serial ATA drives, which allow for cheaper storage arrays.

These hardware trends are contributing, too, to the growth in near-line storage and tape replacement systems, with the benefit of much faster access times than conventional tape.

Vendors such as Quantum, which specialise in back-up systems, report a significant shift towards disk. Employing software techniques such as storage virtualisation means that businesses should no longer be constrained by the location or type of their storage.

'Virtualisation turns storage into a software-managed resource', says John Parkinson, chief technologist for the North America region at Cap Gemini Ernst & Young. 'You will be able to swap media in and out, as long as it is recognised by the software layer.'

Sans, for their part, allow companies to centralise many of the tasks associated with managing data, from provisioning and allocating storage to applications to taking back-ups.

This allows IT managers to deploy a consistent, and often more powerful, set of software-based management tools, and techniques such as information lifecycle management (ILM).

Doing so, however, can create a quite different set of problems, as businesses have to decide on the data they want to keep and, increasingly, justify its cost. 'Getting to grips with that can mean tripping over corporate policies', cautions Bob Zimmerman, a vice-president at Forrester Research. 'The legal department may be saying that you cannot throw that away; it is a management cost that is coming from outside the business.'

But at least CIOs now have the tools to start bringing those costs under control.

Further growth of outsourced data storage and management providers may lessen the burden on organizational Sans (www.jisc.ac.uk/media/documents/ techwatch/tsw_03-07.pdf) but it is not expected to replace them (www.techworld.com.opsys/news/index. cfm?newsid=106091, www.techworld.com/storage/ news/index.cfm?newsid=106386).

What the experts say

John Parkinson, chief technologist, North America, Cap Gemini Ernst & Young
'As a rule of thumb direct attached storage is only 40 per cent utilised. Network attached storage is usually 80 per cent utilised, but badly allocated. Managed network storage is 90 per cent utilised and well allocated. That is data that is . . . accessed frequently and stored in the most appropriate way. Storage management leaves all the data in the right place.'

Bob Zimmerman, analyst, Forrester Research
'The issue is that almost no-one purges [deletes or archives unused] data. Especially in the US there are regulations and rules mandating archiving and long-term maintenance of data. And it is getting worse. The more people try to do secondary and tertiary analysis of their data, the more likely they are to extract what they want. There can be tens of copies of data around the enterprise.'

Greg Reyes, chief executive, Brocade

'For the most part, the storage area network is now mainstream. Whether you want to implement utility computing, or share storage resources more effectively, or have a platform for data management, it is well understood that it requires a San. The market is still massively under penetrated, but people are being more strategic about their investments.'

Tom Hudson, chief executive, CNT

'Software tools can add a whole level of improvements to utilisation, but take longer to implement. You need rules for managing recovery, and for how many generations of data you will back up. You have to address data corruption, but do you use local or remote mirroring? All these things are in the software, but today too much data is treated homogeneously.'

Source: Stephen Pritchard, Drowning in a deluge of data, FT.com, 12 November 2003

Questions

1 What are the reasons for, and the benefits of, implementing a storage area network?
2 What are the management issues involved with storage area networks once they have been implemented?

Selecting computer components

Although it could be argued that the insides of computers are of little relevance to managers, many managers will be involved in selecting hardware such as PCs whether it is for their company, a workgroup or at home. Likewise, students often have to decide which is the best kit to equip themselves with for their studies or advise their family and friends.

We find that the best way to remember all the different parts of a PC is to think about their appearance. To help in this, the main components of a PC system, which we will review in this section, are shown in visual form in Figure 3.8.

To help selection of the most appropriate computer for the application to match the budget it is useful to know in outline the purpose of each component. But a detailed knowledge of how it works is not required. What is most important is knowing how to select the type of component that represents the best price–performance combination within a budget. This will inform the approach we use in this section, which has been written as succinctly as is possible to adequately explain the factors affecting selection of each component. For each of the different types of hardware component, we will briefly explain its purpose and then examine the different options and how to select the most appropriate. We will examine the different components in an approximate order of the difference they make to the system. Selecting the appropriate components is difficult since the hardware requirements of computer systems are constantly increasing as new functionality is built into operating systems and applications software.

Selecting processors

Processor
The computer component that controls the operation of the computer through processing instructions and issuing signals to control other parts of the system

The **processor** of a computer is so called because it processes instructions supplied by the program code within the operating system and applications software. An analogy with the human brain is often made since it controls the other computer components in a similar way to how the brain controls the other parts of the body. Another analogy is with the driver of a car who responds to various inputs to control the vehicle. While both analogies are apt, neither the brain nor the human controlling a vehicle is really analogous to the processor working together with systems and applications software.

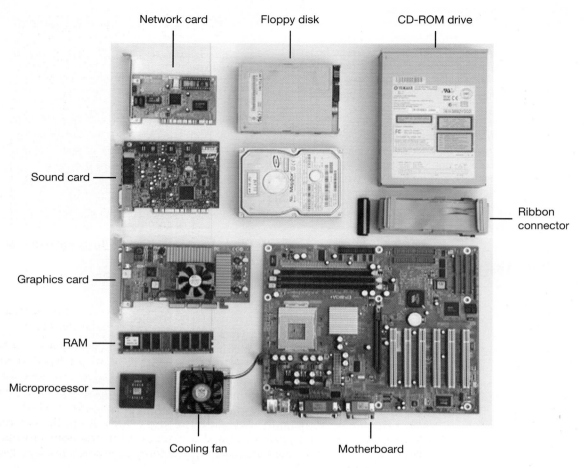

Network card   Floppy disk   CD-ROM drive

Sound card

Ribbon
connector

Graphics card

RAM

Microprocessor

Cooling fan   Motherboard

Figure 3.8 The main components of a PC

Source: Tomshardware (www.tomshardware.com)

**Central processing
unit (CPU)**
The traditional terminology
for the processor

Microprocessor
A modern small-scale
processor

Control unit
Part of the processor that
fetches instructions from
memory and then decodes
them to produce signals
which control other parts
of the computer

**Arithmetic and logic
unit (ALU)**
Part of the processor that
executes operations or
performs calculations

Cache
A temporary storage area
used by the processor

In early computers the processor was formally kown as the **central processing unit
(CPU)** today, in PCs and other small computers it is more commonly referred to as a
'**microprocessor**', see Figure 3.9. It is also sometimes called a 'chip', which is short
for 'silicon chip', since the circuitry is etched on silicon. 'Chips' are also used to refer
to computer memory, which is described in the next section.

A microprocessor consists of several components. The **control unit** fetches instructions from memory and then decodes them to produce signals which control other
parts of the computer. The **arithmetic and logic unit (ALU)** performs operations or calculations – such as addition, subtraction and multiplication of integers. It also has its
own temporary storage area used when it performs calculations – this is known as
the '**cache**'.

Factors in microprocessor selection

There are four main questions to ask when selecting a processor for a PC.

1 *Manufacturer*. Processors are produced with different architectures from different
   manufacturers. Today the two main PC processor manufacturers are Intel and
   Advanced Micro Devices (AMD). The processors from each vendor have the same
   functionality, so effectively we are paying for differences in brand name and the
   speed of the processor. In general, computers built with AMD processors have better

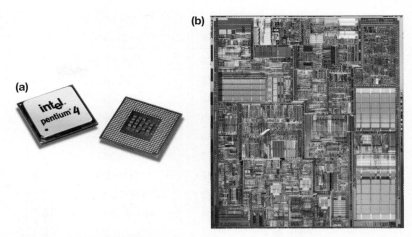

Figure 3.9 Intel Pentium microprocessor: (a) microprocessor, (b) microprocessor circuitry

Source: Intel Corporation (www.intel.com/pressroom/archive/photos/p4rphotos.htm)

price for performance since the AMD brand is less well known. Other manufacturers such as Hitachi and Motorola make processors for other types of computer.

2 *Processor architecture.* Each processor manufacturer is continually striving to improve the performance of their chips. Different designs are produced to improve performance. Table 3.2 shows how microprocessors have advanced since the 8080 processor, the forerunner of the 8088 processor used in the first PC. Each processor has a different design or architecture and more **transistors** are packed in; these have a smaller width of connectors measured in microns. It can be seen that the performance of the processor, measured in millions of instructions processed per second (MIPS), has increased dramatically according to Moore's law (see Research insight 3.3 on Moore's law).

3 *Clock speed.* The **clock speed** gives an indication of how fast a chip can process instructions. It can be seen from Table 3.2 that as the clock speed, measured in hertz or cycles per second increases, so does the performance measured in millions of instructions per second (MIPS). Each of the different chip architectures shown in Table 3.2 will be sold in versions at different clock speeds. So a Pentium 4 is available in different clock speeds such as 2 GHz, 3 GHz and 4 GHz, with each increase in clock speed increasing the performance and cost of the chip.

4 *System bus, chipset and motherboard.* The microprocessor is only one part of a wider range of chips known as a '**chipset**' which is located on the **motherboard** – a large piece of circuitboard inside the computer. Intel has many different chipset and motherboard combinations (see **www.intel.com/products/chipsets/index.htm**). For example, a motherboard supporting an 800 MHz **system bus** has the option for a purchaser to select from different Intel chipsets such as 875P, 865PE, 865G. The chipset is usually only advertised in the small print, but it does affect the performance of the computer. Sound, video and wireless networking are commonly built into the chipset.

Different processor architectures and chipsets may be developed for computers with different purposes – so a server or workstation may use a Xeon processor and in 2003 Intel introduced Centrino which was a combination of Pentium M processor and a specialist chipset and motherboard to enable wireless computing.

Multiple processors are commonly used in modern mini-computers and mainframes. The Unisys ClearPath Libra mainframe server can support up to 32 processors from Intel or other manufacturers each delivering around 1,900 MIPS.

Transistors
Switches or amplifiers used in a circuit

Clock speed
An indication of how fast instructions are processed by the processor, measured as 'cycles per second'

Chipset
A grouping of chips integrated together to perform a particular function such as sounds or video

Motherboard
Circuitboard on which is located processor, chipsets, memory and other components

System bus
Used for transferring data between the components on the motherboard

Table 3.2 History of development of Intel microprocessors for the PC

Name	Date	Transistors	Microns	Clock speed	MIPS
8080	1974	6,000	6	2 MHz	0.64
8088	1979	29,000	3	5 MHz	0.33
80286	1982	134,000	1.5	6 MHz	1
80386	1985	275,000	1.5	16 MHz	5
80486	1989	1,200,000	1	25 MHz	20
Pentium	1993	3,100,000	0.8	60 MHz	100
Pentium II	1997	7,500,000	0.35	233 MHz	300
Pentium III	1999	9,500,000	0.25	450 MHz	510
Pentium 4	2000	42,000,000	0.18	1.5 GHz	1,700
Pentium 4 'Prescott'	2004	125,000,000	0.09	3.6 GHz	7,000

Source: The Intel Microprocessor Quick Guide http://computer.howstuffworks.com/microprocessor1.htm

Graphics and audio microprocessors

Graphics card
A separate card for improved graphics performance, sometimes known as the 'video adapter'

Sound card
A separate card used for audio reproduction

The graphic microprocessor on a system can also affect performance. Microprocessors for managing audio are also required. Traditionally, PCs have required separate **graphics cards** (video adapters) and **sound cards** for this purpose. Graphics cards are mainly supplied by independent manufacturers such as ATI and Radeon, with sound cards such as the 'Sound Blaster' supplied by companies such as Creative. Graphics cards also have their own memory for graphics purposes. An example is shown in Figure 3.10. The monitor is plugged into the connector on the back of the system. Today, cards such as Intel Extreme Graphics and Sound can be built into the chipset, so reducing the cost of the system. However, selecting a separate graphics card that

Figure 3.10 ATI Radeon 9800 graphics card with 128 MB RAM

Source: ATI Technologies, Inc., Ontario, Canada (www.ati.com)

Network interface card (NIC)
Used to connect a computer with a corporate network

plugs into a slot on the motherboard is important for the improved graphics performance needed on gaming machines and machines used by designers. Microprocessors are also used in a **network interface card (NIC)** which is used to connect a computer with a corporate or home network.

Research insight 3.3 | **Moore's law**

Moore's law is named after an observation made by Gordon Moore of Intel in 1965. He observed an exponential growth in the number of transistors on each integrated circuit and predicted that this trend would continue. Time has shown the observation to be accurate (Figure 3.11). 'Exponential' means, in this instance, that the number of transistors doubles approximately every two years and the performance of processors increases accordingly, as reference to Table 3.2 shows. The end of Moore's law has been predicted many times since there is a limit to the miniaturization available through the current fabrication process. Intel engineers estimate that Moore's law will remain valid for the next decade at least.

In 2008, researchers identified a new way of potentially increasing the number of transistors on a chip by harnessing the power of quantum physics (**www.techworld.com/opsys/news/index.cfm?newsid=106145**). Although it has yet to be used on a commercial scale, it has the potential to maintain Moore's law.

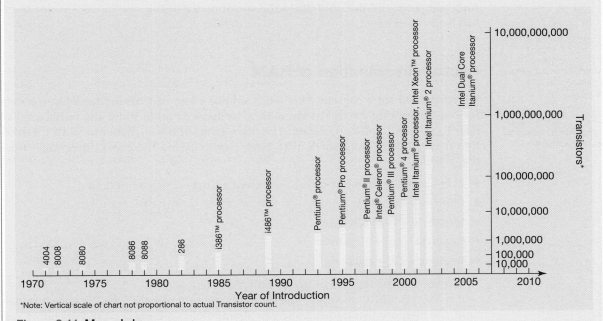

*Note: Vertical scale of chart not proportional to actual Transistor count.

Figure 3.11 Moore's law

Source: http://download.intel.com/pressroom/images/events/moores_law_40th/Microprocessor_Chart.eps

---

Selecting memory devices

Volatile storage
Memory such as RAM which isn't permanent

RAM (random access memory)
Temporary storage for programs and data accessed by the processor

Computer memory is used to store data and programs. There are two types of computer storage: temporary or **volatile storage** where data are only saved when a device is switched on, and permanent storage where the data are saved even when a device is powered down. In this section we consider this temporary storage. It is best known through the acronym **RAM**, standing for '**random-access memory**'. RAM is used to store the operating system, applications and current data or documentation and is linked closely to the processor to which instructions and data are supplied from the RAM. RAM is similar to our short-term memory – it is used for issues we are currently thinking about.

Figure 3.12 RAM (random access memory)

Source: Kingston Technology Company, Fountain Valley, California (www.kingston.com/press/primages/contents.asp)

Physically, RAM is a form of microchip which is typically supplied with several chips making up one memory module as shown in Figure 3.12.

As well as the RAM each computer also contains **read-only memory or ROM**. This is permanent storage used to store the BIOS, which is activated when a computer is first switched on before the operating system is loaded from the hard disk or other permanent media. When you switch a PC on, the first text screen will always refer to the BIOS (binary input and output system) loading. The BIOS is effectively constant, but it can be upgraded if required. This form of ROM is a standard component on each computer and does not affect the performance of the system, so it is not specified for PC purchase.

Read-only memory or ROM
Permanent memory used to store the BIOS

Factors in selection of RAM

Selecting RAM for a computer system is simply a case of selecting the right capacity for our computing needs. To know this, we have to understand the terms used to refer to different volumes of data. The main terms you will encounter with information management, from smallest to largest, with each a thousand times larger than the previous, are:

● Byte – made up of 8 bits used to represent a single character or digit
● Kilobyte – 1024 bytes
● Megabyte – 1024 kilobytes
● Gigabyte – 1024 megabytes
● Terabyte – 1024 gigabytes

To test your understanding of these terms, complete Activity 3.2.

It is always difficult to specify the optimum amount of RAM for a PC since, through time, the memory requirements increase dramatically as more powerful operating systems and applications are used. Additionally, it is dependent on the needs of the user. Each new application that is used will take up additional memory and certain specialist applications tend to take up a lot more memory. For example, the needs of an administrator who is simply running a word processor and an e-mail package will be much lower than those of an architect who is similarly running a word processor and e-mail package, but also a spreadsheet, a graphics package and a computer-aided design package. It is important that sufficient memory be specified for a system since it is possible to exceed the memory capacity. When this happens, operating systems such as Windows will be forced to use 'virtual memory' instead of RAM to keep the system running. The virtual memory uses the permanent storage of the hard disk. Since it is a lot slower to read and write to the hard disk, the performance of the system becomes slow regardless of the power of the processor installed. Figure 3.13 shows how this can happen. As a consequence of the degradation in performance caused by limited amounts of RAM, business or home users should always buy as much RAM as possible and prioritize spending on RAM rather than on processors.

Virtual memory
Memory that is allocated from the hard disk to supplement RAM

Activity 3.2	Understanding storage capacity

Purpose   To engage with the different terms used to represent data volumes or storage capacities.

Activity   Complete Table 3.3, filling in the gaps shown by the question marks with these values:

- Label for volume (size): byte, terabyte, kilobyte, megabyte
- Numeric amount: 1,000,000, 1,000, 1,000,000,000,000, 1

The table has been completed for gigabyte.

Table 3.3 Data volume grid

Label for volume (size)	?	Gigabyte	?	?	?
Numeric amount (bytes)	?	1,000,000,000	?	?	?
Example data amount	A database for a large company	A database for a small company	A high-resolution photo	A low-resolution photo	A character
Example storage amount	1 ?b capacity server	120 ?b hard disk	512?b memory	Old style 720 ?b hard disk mobile phone	100 ?b to store numbers in

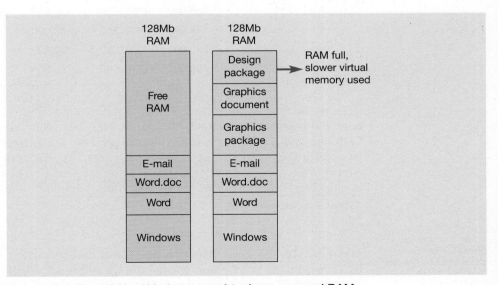

Figure 3.13 The relationship between virtual memory and RAM

For example, when one of the authors bought a PC in 2003, he purchased a relatively large amount of RAM (for the time) of 1 gigabyte, but did not buy the latest, fastest processor.

Note that although storage capacity is the overriding factor in selecting RAM for a personal computer, RAM does differ in speed, rated in nanoseconds access time. The differences are of marginal importance to system performance in comparison with other system components such as processor and hard disk speed and capacity.

Modern mainframes may contain massive amounts of RAM. For example, the Unisys ClearPath Libra 185 offers up to 64 gigabytes whereas most desktop PCs contain less than 1 gigabyte.

Selecting permanent storage

Non-volatile storage
Storage is permanent

Storage device
The unit used for reading and writing data from and to the storage media

Storage media
The form of material used for storing information

Permanent storage is used to store the operating system, applications and data. Unlike RAM, the storage is persistent or non-volatile storage – the data are retained after the hardware is 'powered down'. Some say that permanent storage is equivalent to our long-term memory. But the human analogy breaks down since these memories are not retained when we are 'powered down'!

There are a wide variety of permanent storage devices and these can be classified according to the type of storage media and the form of the storage device. The main media types for permanent storage are magnetic, optical, tape and solid-state. The media may be readily removable from the computer or be a fixed part of the system. The importance of the different forms of storage media is suggested by Table 3.4.

Table 3.4 Worldwide production of magnetic original content, if stored digitally using standard compression methods, in terabytes c. 2002

Storage medium	Type of content	Terabytes/yr Upper estimate	Terabytes/yr Lower estimate	2002 report Upper estimate	2002 report Lower estimate	% change Upper estimates
Magnetic	Videotape	1,340,000	1,340,000	1,420,000	1,420,000	–6
	Audiotape	128,800	128,800	182,000	182,000	–30
	Digital tape	250,000	250,000	250,000	250,000	0
	MiniDV	1,265,000	1,265,000	N/A	N/A	N/A
	Floppy disk	80	80	70	70	14
	Zip	350	350	1,690	1,690	–79
	Audio MD	17,000	17,000	N/A	N/A	N/A
	Flash	12,000	12,000	N/A	N/A	N/A
	Hard disk	1,986,000	403,000	926,000	220,000	114
	TOTAL	**4,999,230**	**3,416,230**	**2,779,760**	**2,073,760**	**80**

Source: Lyman and Varian (2003)

Magnetic storage
Storage on iron ferrite-based disks such as the hard disk

Hard disks
The most common form of permanent storage on computer systems

Magnetic storage stores data in a number of devices such as hard disks. The hard disk is used in all PCs for non-volatile storage and is not usually removable. The hard disk consists of several magnetic platters which rotate at speeds as high as 7,200 revolutions per minute. An arm writes and reads data to and from different tracks (Figure 3.14). Some hard disks are now built to be removable so that they can be kept secure or for transfer of data.

Figure 3.14 Hard disk drive
Source: Seagate Technology LLC (www.seagate.com/newsinfo/newsroom/photo/D2h3.html)

RAID systems

A further complication for many types of magnetic storage, especially in large organizations and for users of large amounts of data, is selecting the type of data protection that will be used. Where large amounts of data are stored and where complex applications are used it is common to find information systems that employ multiple hard disks: it is even becoming common for home computer users to use two or more hard disks to have the capacity to store large numbers of photographs or videos.

One method of protecting the data on these disks is to employ a Redundant Array of Inexpensive Disks (also known as a Redundant Array of Independent Disks and originally described by Patterson, Gibson and Katz, 1988). This is a way of distributing the data across many disks and, by using a number of complex techniques, is able to protect the data from loss, damage or corruption.

RAID is a collective term for a number of techniques of data protection, individually termed RAID0, RAID1...RAID5... etc., each of which is increasingly sophisticated and has specific applications.

RAID0 is most simple and effectively offers no useful data protection.

In a two-disk system (an array of two disks), data are written to both disks (called striping). If one disk fails, due to mechanical failure or other damage, then data on the other disk will still be intact. If the hard disks were being used to store holiday photos, however, it is likely that every single photo will be written, in part, to both disks. In the event of failure of either disk it would therefore not be possible to view any complete photograph.

RAID1 uses data mirroring whereby all data are written first to one disk, then copied to a second disk. In this case, if the hard disks were being used to store holiday photographs and one of the disks failed then the remaining disk would still hold a complete mirror-image of the files containing the photographs. None of the data would have been lost. The failed disk could be replaced and the data could again be mirrored onto it.

The disadvantage of using RAID1 is that you require double the amount of storage space in order to keep the same amount of data.

Mean time before failure or mean time between failures (MTBF)

It is possible to calculate when a disk in an array can be expected to fail. Most equipment manufacturers state their equipment MTBF in the technical specifications. In the 1990s hard disk MTBFs were around 100,000 hours, in 2000 they typically exceeded 1,000,000 hours operation (Hitachi, 2008).

The formula for calculating the time before a simple system fails is:

$$\text{MTBFsystem} = \frac{\text{MTBFcomponent}}{\text{Number of components}}$$

Note, calculating the MTBF of complex systems where different components are used is significantly more complex.

A two-disk array comprising identical hard disks with MTBF = 500,000 hours and 160 Gb storage capacity can be expected to fail at around:

$$\text{MTBFsystem} = \frac{500,000}{2}$$

$$\text{MTBFsystem} = 250,000 \text{ hours}$$

Storing very large amounts of data, for example for video editing, may require many disks in an array. It may seem as though more disks in an array equals greater security, as long as anything better than RAID0 is being used! However, the reverse is true.

Using the same disks in the example above, the MTBF for a four-disk system is:

$$\text{MTBFsystem} = \frac{500,000}{4}$$

$$\text{MTBFsystem} = 125,000 \text{ hours}$$

We can summarize our findings as:

- RAID technologies offer ways to protect stored data.
- RAID0 is the simplest but offers no data recovery and has little use. A RAID0 system can use all the available hard disk space for data storage.
- RAID1 offers useful data recovery but requires half the available storage space to achieve it.
- The more disks that are used in an array, the more quickly it can be expected to fail but less data will be at risk.

Optical storage
Storage using optical media such as CD and DVD that are accessed using a laser

CD or DVD burners
Recording through optical storage devices

Optical storage provides higher-capacity storage than magnetic media, but the access speeds are lower. Optical media are removable since they are used for data back-up and, of course, recording music and film. Optical storage principally uses CD and DVD media. The most expensive optical storage devices can write as well as read these media. These are often referred to as **CD or DVD burners** since the saved data

Case study 3.2

Summerhill Veterinary Surgery

This surgery is located near the centre of a medium-sized city in the UK and deals mainly with small animals such as dogs, cats and other household pets. There are over 2000 animals registered with the surgery, each of which is identified by the following information:

- Animal's name
- Type of animal
- Breed (if applicable)
- Sex
- Owner's first name
- Owner's last name
- Owner's address
- Owner's home telephone number
- Owner's mobile telephone number

In addition, a history of the animal's ailments and treatments is recorded, including any vaccinations and electronic identification tags, along with laboratory test results, measurements of the animal's weight, height, age and any special notes that the vet wishes to record. Occasionally a photograph of the animal is retained.

The surgery employs 5 vets and 10 veterinary nurses, plus 4 administrative staff, and is open 7 days a week. At night and during bank holidays a minimum number of staff operates the surgery.

It comprises a Reception, 3 treatment rooms, 1 operating theatre, 1 pharmacy and a hospital where animals stay to recover after surgery or are treated over long periods of time.

The surgery has several computers and a central server linked across a LAN:

- Reception – 2 PCs
- Treatment Rooms – 1 PC in each
- Pharmacy – 1 PC
- Hospital – 1 PC

The central server is located in a separate room and operates RAID0.

Every night the Head Vet performs a back-up of the data contained on the RAID onto magnetic tape. This tape is duplicated, one copy remaining at the surgery while the other is stored offsite in a fireproof safe.

Questions

1 What would be the best way for Summerhill to collect and retain all the important data about the animals that they treat and their owners?

2 How effective is the RAID0 server setup and their method of backing up important data?

---

are effectively burnt onto the media through the laser. The different types of devices and media may support:

- *Read-only* – traditional CDs and DVDs used for music and film.
- *Recordable* (denoted by CDR and DVDR) – the media can be written to, but once they reach their capacity space cannot be cleared by deleting existing files.
- *Rewritable* (denoted by CDRW and DVDRW) – the media can be written to repeatedly (Figure 3.15).

Tape storage
Magnetic tape used for data storage

Tape storage uses a magnetic tape medium. Its use is declining for personal computers since optical media are faster to read and write. However, digital tape is still used for back-up of servers because of its higher capacity.

Solid-state memory devices confusingly use a non-volatile form of RAM, known as 'flash RAM'. **Flash RAM** is so called since the memory blocks are arranged so that a block of memory is erased instantaneously. Flash memory has become increasingly used in recent years with pen drives or memory keys/USB sticks such as that shown in Figure 3.16, popular with students and business people since they can store from 16 Mb to over 256 Mb of presentations or references. These are the modern version of the floppy drive, but can contain over ten times the data. They are plugged to the USB (universal serial bus) port of a computer.

Flash RAM
Non-volatile storage

Figure 3.15 Optical drive – a DVD rewriter

Source: Pioneer North America, Inc., Long Beach, California (www.pioneerelectronics.com/pna/product/detail/ 0,,2076r17573091r23143977, 00.html). Image courtesy of Pioneer Europe NV, Components Division

Figure 3.16 USB stick

Source: Kingston Technology Company, Fountain Valley, California (www.kingston.com/press/primages/contents.asp)

Factors in selection of storage devices and media

When selecting storage devices the factors that need to be considered are:

1 *Capacity of device or medium.* This is measured in unit of bytes as for RAM, such as megabytes, gigabytes or terabytes. For example, a hard disk may range from 120 gigabytes to higher capacities. A floppy disk is a mere 1.44 Mb. The standard capacity for a CD is 640 Mb and for a DVD is 4.7 Gb.

2 *Speed of reading and writing media.* All permanent storage devices are slower than RAM and speeds decrease from magnetic disk media, through optical media to tape media.

3 *Cost of device.* The most expensive devices are those with the best combination of price, capacity and performance. RAM is more expensive than all permanent media. Rewritable optical drives tend to be more expensive than magnetic disk media.

4 *Cost of removable media.* This is a relatively low cost compared to the cost of the device.

5 *Need for permanent or removable media.* In some cases where a removable device is needed, such as a removable hard disk, this can add to the cost of the device.

Complete Activity 3.3 to find out the latest specifications and prices for different storage devices.

Activity 3.3	Selecting RAM, storage devices and media

Purpose To distinguish between the different forms of computer storage. The activity will enable students to determine the current specifications used in systems rather than the specifications in this book which are outdated as soon as the digits are committed to disk.

Activity Visit the website of an online computer hardware retailer such as dabs.com or microwarehouse.com or a manufacturer such as dell.com or hp.com. Look at the specifications for different forms of storage. For each device type find out the minimum and maximum available in terms of different characteristics such as capacity and speed. Then enter your findings in Table 3.5. Also rate each storage option compared to all the others on a scale of 1 for the best to 5 for the worst. The RAM example has been completed.

visit the www

Tip Rather than looking up each storage item individually, look at the specifications for complete systems, from the cheapest system, for the minimum rating to the most expensive system for the maximum rating.

Table 3.5 Grid for comparing memory and storage devices

Device type	Attribute	Capacity	Speed	Cost of device per megabyte	Cost of medium per megabyte
RAM (example)	Minimum and maximum	128 Mb to 1Gb	80 ns to 50 ns (nanoseconds)	Highest relative cost e.g. £30/256 Mb	Medium not separate
	Relative rating	5	1	5	N/A
Hard disk	Minimum and maximum				
	Relative rating				
Optical disk (CD/DVD)	Minimum and maximum				
	Relative rating				
Tape	Minimum and maximum				
	Relative rating				
Flash RAM (pen memory)	Minimum and maximum				
	Relative rating				

Selecting output devices

Output devices
Used for viewing outputs
from a system

Hard copy
Printed output from a
system, distinct from 'soft'
or electronic copy

There are two main output devices for a computer system which are used to interact
with applications and data. The first is the monitor or display which is, of course,
used for interacting with the system, the second is the printer which is used for keeping hard copy.

Monitors

There are two main types of monitor. The first is the traditional cathode-ray tube
(CRT) variety which works on a similar basis to the TV set (Figure 3.17). These are
bulky and consume a large amount of power. The second is the flat-screen, LCD or
plasma display; these are more compact and use less power, but are more expensive.
They can form multi-panels for specialist applications such as for traders at a stock
exchange (Figure 3.18).

Figure 3.17 A CRT monitor from ViewSonic®
Source: ViewSonic Corporation, Walnut, California (www.viewsonic.com)

Figure 3.18 A flat-screen monitor
Source: ViewSonic Corporation, Walnut, California (www.viewsonic.com)

Printers

There are also two main types of printer commonly in use by business. These are the inkjet and the laser printer. The inkjet printer (Figure 3.19) prints using a print-head containing many small nozzles that squirt droplets of ink onto paper. The laser printer (Figure 3.20) prints using charged sections of a rotating drum which picks up dry toner powder and then deposits it on the paper to form an image. Very high print capacities are needed for printers in large organizations. Multi-function printers of either variety also enable copying, scanning or faxing.

Factors in selecting displays or monitors

The type of monitor and the size, resolution and number of colours supported by a monitor are the main factors to be considered. As the quality of image gets higher, so does the price. Sizes vary from 10 inches to over 21 inches for monitors, with much

Figure 3.19 Multi-function inkjet printer
Source: Dell, Inc., Round Rock, Texas (www.dell.com)

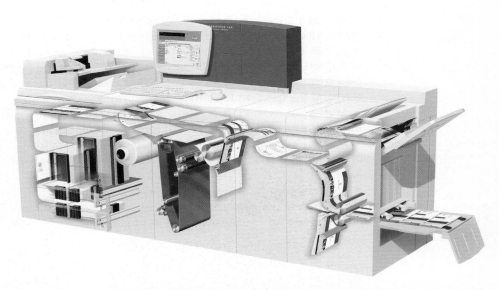

Figure 3.20 Xerox Docutech laser printer with a capacity of 500,000 sheets per month
Source: Xerox Corporation (www.xerox.com)

smaller monitors used in PDAs and mobile phones. Flat-screen monitors over 21 inches can cost over €1000 but small CRT monitors may be less than €100. The size refers to the length of the diagonal. The **resolution** affects the clarity or sharpness of the image. It is dependent on the number of dots or **pixels** that can be displayed on the screen. A maximum is imposed by the monitor, but it is also dependent on the graphics card. The most commonly used screen resolutions can be detected for site visitors by website monitoring software. Data from Onestat (**www.onestat.com**) showed that in 2002, the proportions of different resolutions were:

1024 × 768	46.1%
800 × 600	34.3%
1280 × 1024	13.1%
1152 × 864	3.9%
640 × 480	1.1%
1600 × 1200	1%
1152 × 870	0.2%

This shows that the 640 × 480 pixel resolution used in the early PCs is very rare and it is not necessary for websites to support this. They need to be readily viewable at 1024 × 768 and 800 × 600 resolutions which account for around three-quarters of monitors. A related measure that affects clarity is the **dot pitch**, which is an indication of the physical size of each pixel. For most monitors this is around 0.28 mm. Since it is similar on most monitors, this figure is not used to differentiate between monitors by most purchasers.

The number of colours supported by monitors and graphics cards is now standardized such that they can display 'true colour' – that is, the colour is described by a 24-bit value allowing for 16,777,216 colours. Most graphics cards now support 32-bit colour. In web browsers 256 standard colours are used in the colour palette, so web designers must allow for this.

Factors in selecting printers

The factors involved in the decision to purchase printers are similar to those for monitors. The factors include the type of printer together with its paper size, resolution, number of colours supported and price. An additional factor is the speed of printing.

Whether a laser printer or inkjet printer is purchased is usually dependent on the price. Inkjet printers are less costly, particularly where colour printing is required, and may cost less than €100. However, laser printers are superior in terms of print quality and speed. Over the years the two varieties have become closer together in terms of performance for price, with relatively low-cost colour laser printers becoming available, and the speed and quality of inkjet printers improving.

Most printers support printing in A4 dimensions (210 × 297 mm) and standard-thickness paper and card, but larger formats such as A3 and A2 are available.

Resolution for printers is measured in **dots per inch (dpi)**. A minimum acceptable in modern printers is 600 dpi while 1200 dpi is a higher resolution now available in most models.

Speed of printing is measured in **pages per minute (ppm)**. Laser printers tend to be faster than inkjet printers. Some workgroup models achieve 50 ppm while inkjet printer speeds are usually measured in single figures.

Resolution
An indication of the clarity of screen image

Pixel
A dot on a screen, short for 'picture element'

Dot pitch
The absolute size of a dot on screen in millimetres

Dots per inch (dpi)
A measure of printer resolution

Pages per minute (ppm)
A measure of printer speed

Selecting input devices

There are again two main input devices for the personal computer: the mouse and keyboard. These do not affect the performance of the system overall, but they are important considerations for the health of users. **Repetitive strain injury (RSI)** is a common complaint of computer users. Ergonomic keyboards and mice can reduce the risk of this happening. Laws have been introduced in some countries to encourage employers to audit the use of computers to ensure that the health of staff is not at risk. The company may then have to provide wrist rests or screen glare reducers for staff.

For organizational information systems, other important input devices are the scanner and the barcode reader. Optical scanners are used to scan in documents when they arrive in the post. They are important in case management systems described in Chapter 2, such as a system used for processing a mortgage application.

Factors in selecting input devices

The mouse and keyboard are now standardized in their functions. The main innovations have been the introduction of the wireless keyboard and mouse which help remove desk clutter. Figure 3.21 shows a wireless keyboard and mouse from Microsoft that uses the Bluetooth standard for wireless transmission of data. As the picture shows, the introduction of additional keys for managing frequent tasks such as opening a document or sending mail and of a wheel for scrolling on the mouse are now available on the more expensive input devices.

Other input devices

Other input devices that can be found in organizations include:

    document scanners
    Touchscreens
    digitizer pads and graphic tablets
    digital cameras and webcams
    microphones
    Radio Frequency Identification (RFID)
    barcode readers
    Virtual Reality devices.

Figure 3.21 icrosoft® wireless keyboard and mouse
Source: reprinted by permission from Microsoft Corporation

RFID and barcode systems are commonly found in warehouses and distribution centers (see also Chapter 12). They may also be found at the sales counter of many large shops and supermarkets where they are used to scan purchased items and automatically record their price and update stock records.

Barcode is a relatively old technology. RFID is much newer and consequently is still undergoing considerable development. Barcode requires a label to be visible to the equipment operator in order to be scanned whereas RFID utilizes radio waves to send signals between the scanning device and the tag on the product or container. This, coupled with the fact that RFID tags can store much more information than a simple barcode label, has led to its becoming the preferred technology of many organizations.

Recent studies of the technologies, however, have confirmed the speed advantage of RFID but have also shown that in some harsh operating environments barcode equipment is considerably more durable (White et al., 2007). This highlights the importance of considering the effectiveness of devices in their real-world application. It is tempting to adopt new technologies because they appear to offer new features or improved speed and capacity, yet it is vital that they are employed only when they will provide actual bottom-line and operational benefits.

Assistive technologies

Computing devices, hardware, software and communication devices are not generally designed for use by people with impaired abilities. Such impairments may be physical or mental, and be present from birth or brought about by illness, accident or old age (**www.fastuk.org**).

For instance, the quest for miniaturization and multifunctional integration often results in more compact keyboards and smaller and more complex visual displays that may be difficult for some people to operate. Microsoft's Surface is a bridge between the real world around us and the virtual world of computing and information processing but is inaccessible to non-sighted users or those with limited motor skills (**www.microsoft.com/surface/en/us/default.aspx**).

There are a number of technologies and devices that are designed to assist people to use computing devices or to access information resources that they would otherwise be unable to do (RNIB, 2008; RNID, 2008):

- Hardware
  - Reading machines that use optical character recognition (OCR) to read documents aloud
  - Braille embossers and printers
  - Braille displays
  - Large, flat screens and monitors
  - Keyboards with larger, widely spaced buttons
  - Textphones that convert speech to text.
- Software
  - Customizable graphical user interfaces
  - Screen magnifiers
  - Screen readers that read text aloud
  - Voice-to-text and voice-controlling applications (**www.nuance.com/naturallyspeaking/**).

Not only do these technologies enable more people to access the exciting, informative and labour-saving potential of the World Wide Web, but they may also enable them to compete successfully in the job market and find fulfilling employment.

Debate 3.1

Do assistive technologies allow people with disabilities to compete in the job market, or, do they enable organizations to employ people with disabilities?

Should organizations be compelled by law to introduce assistive technologies even if they don't yet employ any people with disabilities?

Introduction to network technology

Today, the Internet is the best-known form of network, but it has been widely used by businesses for only a relatively short time. In this section we will look at other forms of computer network that also have an established business use. We will explore Internet technology in the next section.

Computer network
A communication system that links two or more computers and peripheral devices to enable transfer of data between these computers

The purpose of a computer network is to transfer data between different computers or hardware devices. The client/server model introduced earlier in the chapter requires a computer network to transfer data between the client and server computers. The server may also be connected to other hardware devices such as a network printer or a back-up system using a network.

Local-area network (LAN)
A computer network that spans a limited geographic area such as a single office or building

Computer networks are constructed on different scales. Small-scale networks known as 'local-area networks (LANs)' can be set up in an office, a small business or even at home. Larger-scale networks which may span a city, a country, the world or space are known as 'wide-area networks'. These effectively link together different LANs. Wide-area communications are sometimes referred to as 'telecommunications systems'. These systems consist of both the hardware and the software necessary to set up these links. Telecommunications systems enable a business which operates from different locations to run as a single unit. This means that the same information and control structures do not need to be repeated at each company office. Instead, information can be managed centrally and control maintained from a central location. As well as improving internal communications in a company, telecommunications allow companies to collaborate, using electronic data interchange or web-based e-procurement, with partners such as suppliers.

Wide-area network
Computer networks covering a large area which connect businesses in different parts of the country or in different countries

Telecommunications systems
The systems used to transmit information between different locations

The benefits and disadvantages of computer networks tend to be common regardless of the scale of network. Advantages and disadvantages of a computer network are summarized in Table 3.6. It is apparent that there are many advantages which have led to the wide-scale adoption of both local- and wide-area networks. Although the advantages clearly outweigh the disadvantages, the problems suggested by the disadvantages need careful management and these are all reviewed in later chapters in this book.

Telecommunications channels

Telecommunications channels are the different media used to carry information between different locations. The first form of channel is traditional cables and wires, known as 'guided media'. In the second form of channel, known as 'unguided media', digital data are transmitted using different parts of the electromagnetic spectrum using satellite, microwave and radio transmitters and receivers. These are now commonly referred to as 'wireless networking'. The term wireless networking is used to refer to technologies that make access to a network possible using wireless media, i.e. without the need for wires, cables or connectors. Access is usually through a local network access point enabling access to a home network or company LAN. For example, wireless LANs are now used at home and in business because of their convenience. In a later section we look at Wi-Fi internet access, another form of wireless networking.

Guided media
Communications channels that use cables and wires

Unguided media
Communications channels which are wireless

Wireless networking
Local-area networking using wireless media

Table 3.6 Advantages and disadvantages of computer networks

Advantages	Disadvantages
1 Facilitate sharing of information	1 Organization becomes overdependent on networks for access to information and applications
2 Reduce duplication of information	
3 More rapid information transfer, including real-time information access	2 Cost of initial set-up, usage and maintenance
4 Reduce hardware requirements through sharing of devices for input, output and processing of data	3 Reduced security of information as information is exposed to increased risk of internal and external access, modification and deletion
5 Enable software to be managed centrally and reduce need for local copies of software	4 Can facilitate information overload as e-mails and documents are more easily distributed
6 Assist in information security by requiring log-in for access to certain data	
7 Enable transformation of business through e-business applications connecting with different stakeholders	
8 The Internet also provides potential to reach new international markets or new groups of customers at a relatively low cost	

Bluetooth
A wireless standard for transmission of data between devices over short ranges (less than 10 m)

Bluetooth is another wireless technology for short-range data transmission between devices. Applications of Bluetooth include wireless keyboards (Figure 3.21) and beaming data between a PDA and a desktop or a laptop and a printer at distances of up to 10 m. It has been suggested that Bluetooth represents a security risk through a process known as 'bluesnarfing'. An example often referred to is that if you so wished you could go to an airport passenger lounge and scan the diaries or contacts on passengers' laptops, phones or PDAs.

Different forms of guided media

The main types of cabling used in LANs are based on copper cabling. Data are transmitted along this by applying a voltage at one end, which is received at the other. A positive voltage represents a binary one and a negative voltage represents a binary zero. There are two main types of twisted copper cabling used in networks, known as 'twisted-pair' (often used for 10Base-T Ethernet) and 'co-axial' (used for Thin 10Base-2 Ethernet).

Integrated services digital network (ISDN)
A data communications technique for transfer of digital data using phone lines

Asymmetric digital subscriber line (ADSL)
A communications technique for making use of existing telephone lines to provide very high data transfer rates

Broadband services
Services that offer high-speed data transfer

Data transmitted digitally over phone lines can use a range of techniques. Digital telephone exchanges support an **integrated services digital network (ISDN)** standard that allows data transfer rates that are up to five times faster than the traditional POTS ('plain old telephone service'). An ISDN telephone line provides two separate 'channels', allowing simultaneous voice and data transmissions. **Asymmetric digital subscriber line (ADSL)** services make use of existing telephone lines to provide very high data transfer rates. ADSL is said to be 'asymmetric' since download data transfer rates are different (higher) from upload rates. Such high-speed services are known as '**broadband services**'. When used to access the Internet they make practical the transmission of larger volumes of data used for downloading music (for example, see On Demand Distribution (**www.ondemanddistribution.com**) which is used to feed many music download services in Europe) or streaming video (see, for example, BBCi Broadband, **www.bbc.co.uk/broadband**). Leased lines or secure virtual private networks (VPNs) with higher-speed access using the T1 standard are used by larger organizations.

Fibre-optic is a relatively new transmission medium, and consists of thousands of fibres of pure silicon dioxide. Packets are transmitted along fibre-optic cables using light or photons emitted from a light-emitting diode at one end of the cable, which is detected by a photo-sensitive cell at the other. Fibre-optic cables give very high transmission rates since the cable has very low resistance. This is well known as a method by which cable TV is delivered to homes.

Wi-Fi

Wi-Fi ('wireless fidelity')
A high-speed wireless local-area network enabling wireless access to the Internet for mobile, office and home users

Wi-Fi is the shorthand often used to describe a high-speed wireless local-area network. Wi-Fi can be deployed in an office or home environment where it removes the need for cabling and adds flexibility. However, it has attracted most attention for its potential for offering wireless access in cities and towns without the need for a fixed connection. The Intel Centrino mobile chip launched in 2003 offers facilities to make Wi-Fi access easier for laptop users.

As an example, in 2002 some airports, cafés and hotels started offering Wi-Fi 'hot spots' which allowed customers access to the Internet from their laptops or other mobile devices without the need to connect using a wire. This helped differentiate them from other services without this facility. Since then, wireless LANs have appeared everywhere. At the end of 2002, there were 4,200 Wi-Fi locations in the US, but network operators expected to install over 55,000 new hot spots in the following five years.

There was extensive media coverage of Wi-Fi when it was launched and, as is often the case with new technologies, the technology does not appear to satisfy a demand. Neil McIntosh in the *Guardian* (2003) quotes Lars Godell, a telecoms analyst at Forrester Research. In a recent research note, he said,

> It's as if the dotcom boom and bust never happened – this bubble seems ready to burst. I agree there is some need, but think there has been very pointed exaggeration of the need for internet access around the clock, and on top of that the willingness to pay for it. And that is the critical issue when you create a business plan.

He also noted that 'the usage rates of wireless Lan have been appallingly low'. He cites the case of Amsterdam's Schipol airport, through which 41 million passengers pass every year, but where there are only a dozen Wi-Fi hot-spot users a day. Other hot-spot operators confirm, in private, that they see similarly low usage numbers.

Despite the media hype about public wireless networks, it appears as if the main applications for wireless networks are at home and at work. According to IDC, people are connecting wirelessly at home rather than taking to Wi-Fi via a hot spot. In a survey of 2500 users of mobile devices, IDC found that 34 per cent of those who use Wi-Fi connect to a wireless network at home, compared with 27 per cent at work. The use of wireless LANs at work is also increasing. The DTI Benchmarking Survey (**www.ukonline-forbusiness.gov.uk/benchmarking2003**) showed that nearly a quarter of businesses were now using wireless LAN. Note that this increased usage has security limitations since with Wi-Fi encryption is limited and communications can potentially be intercepted or 'sniffed' by anyone in the vicinity with appropriate scanning software.

Telecommunications components

In addition to the clients and servers in a client/server network, there are other hardware components in a network. The most important are:

Modem
Modulator–demodulator used to convert data between digital and analogue forms when transmitting data over telephone lines

● The **modem**. The modem (modulator–demodulator) is widely used in small businesses and in the home. A modem connected to a computer allows users to send and receive data via an ordinary telephone line. A modem works by converting data between digital and analogue forms. The modem receives analogue data transmitted via a telephone line and converts this into digital data so that the computer can make use of it. Similarly, the modem converts outgoing digital data into an analogue signal before transmitting it. The speed of modems is measured

Baud
A measure of performance of a modem or similar device equivalent to one bit per second

in **baud** or bits per second (bps). The standard modem used in home computers is 56.6 kbps, equivalent to approximately 4700 characters per second. Broadband access is at much higher speeds such as 256 kbps for ISDN or over 512 kbps for ADSL. Each uses a specific type of modem. Cable modems are used for households or businesses connected to a fibre-optic cable network.

Hubs
Used to connect groups of computers to a network

- **Hubs.** Used to connect up to 20 PCs to a network in a convenient way using patch cables (which look similar to phone cables and sockets) running between the back of each PC and the hub. The hub may then be attached to a server or a backbone connection leading to the server. Switches are now commonly used as an alternative since they are cheaper.

Bridges and routers
Device used to connect networks and control the flow of data between them

- **Bridges and routers.** Used to connect different LANs and transfer data packets from one network to the next. They can be used to connect similar types of LAN. They also offer filtering services to restrict local traffic to one side of the bridge, thus reducing traffic overall. Routers can select the best route for packets to be transmitted and are also used on the Internet backbones and wide-area networks to achieve this. Although these devices used to be distinct, they are now produced as hybrids which share functions. Companies that are linked to the Internet usually use a router as a gateway to attach their internal network to the Internet. This is often combined with a **firewall**, which is intended to reduce the risk of someone from outside the company gaining unauthorized access to company data.

Firewall
Hardware used to increase security of part of a network through preventing unauthorized access from beyond the network

Repeaters
Devices used to increase efficiency of transmission over long distances

- **Repeaters.** Over a long transmission distance, signal distortion may occur. Repeaters are necessary to increase transmission distances by regenerating signals and retransmitting them.

Electronic data interchange (EDI)

Electronic data interchange (EDI)
The exchange, using digital media, of structured business information, particularly for sales transactions such as purchase orders and invoices between buyers and sellers

Electronic data interchange (EDI) is an established technique for electronic communications between businesses. It predates PCs and the World Wide Web by some margin since its use was initiated in the 1960s. One application of EDI is **electronic funds transfer (EFT)**. The idea of standardized document exchange can be traced back to the 1948 Berlin Airlift, where a standard form was required for efficient management of items flown to Berlin from many locations. This was followed by electronic transmission in the 1960s in the US transport industries. The EDIFACT (Electronic Data Interchange for Administration, Commerce and Transport) standard was later produced by a joint United Nations/European committee to enable international trading.

Electronic funds transfer (EFT)
Automated digital transmission of money between organizations and banks

EDI is perhaps best understood as a replacement of paper-based purchase orders with electronic equivalents, but its applications are wider than this. The types of document exchanged by EDI include business transactions such as orders, invoices, delivery advice and payment instructions as part of EFT. There may also be pure information transactions such as a product specification, for example engineering drawings, or price lists.

EDI has been defined thus:

> Electronic data interchange (EDI) is the computer-to-computer exchange of structured data, sent in a form that allows for automatic processing with no manual intervention. This is usually carried out over specialist EDI networks.
>
> DTI (2003)

Internet EDI
Use of EDI data standards delivered across non-proprietary IP networks

Internet EDI is still popular for exchanging data within businesses. For example, Ariba describe their Supplier Network as 'the largest transacting network in the world'. It includes 300,000 suppliers which process over $120 billion in annual spend in 70 currencies across 130 countries. Buyers and suppliers use the EDI network to exchange product/service catalogue data, purchase orders and commercial invoices. Over 23 million purchase orders and 11.5 million invoices are processed annually. Ariba supports a diverse range of standards including cXML, EDI, CIF and Punchout. The company reported $339 million in annual revenues for 2009 (EDI Basics, 2010).

Value-added network (VAN)
A secure wide-area network that uses proprietary rather than Internet technology

Internet EDI enables EDI to be implemented at lower costs since, rather than using proprietary, so-called **value-added networks (VANs)**, it uses EDI standard format documents such as that for a purchase order, but using lower-cost transmission techniques through **virtual private networks (VPNs)** or the public Internet.

Internet technology

Virtual private network (VPN)
A secure, encrypted (tunnelled) connection between two points using the Internet, typically created by ISPs for organizations wanting to conduct secure Internet trading

The Internet
The Internet refers to the physical network that links computers across the globe. It consists of the infrastructure of network servers and communication links between them that are used to hold and transport information between the client PCs and web servers

Internet service provider (ISP)
A provider providing home or business users with a connection to access the Internet. They can also host web-based applications

Backbones
High-speed communications links used to enable Internet communications within a country and internationally

The Internet is a large-scale computer network that enables communication between millions of connected computers worldwide. Information is transmitted from client PCs and other devices whose users request services from server computers that hold information and host business applications that deliver the services in response to requests. Thus, the Internet is a large-scale client/server system. According to Internet World Stats (**www.internetworldstats.com/stats.htm**), there are approaching two billion Internet users worldwide. Meanwhile Netcraft estimates there are over 200 million websites (**www.netcraft.com/survey**).

Figure 3.22 shows how client PCs within homes and businesses are connected to the Internet via local **Internet service providers (ISPs)** which, in turn, are linked to larger ISPs with connection to the major national and international infrastructure or **backbones**. In the UK, at the London Internet Exchange which is in the Docklands area of east London, a facility exists to connect multiple backbones of the major ISPs within the UK to a single high-speed link out of the UK into Europe and through to

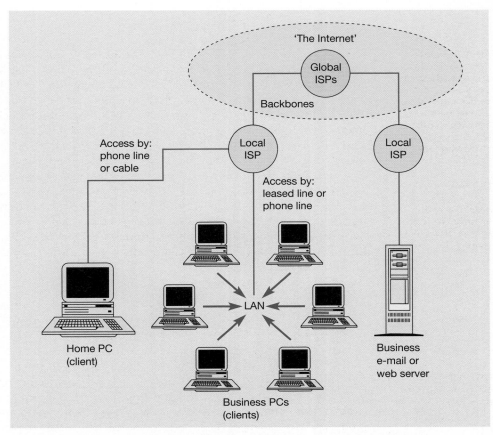

Figure 3.22 Physical and network infrastructure components of the Internet
Source: Chaffey (2004)

the US. These high-speed links can be thought of as the motorways on the 'information superhighway', while the links provided from ISPs to consumers are equivalent to slow country roads.

The development of the Internet

World Wide Web (WWW)
A method for accessing information published on the Internet. It is accessed through web browsers which display web pages and graphics downloaded from web browsers

Metcalfe's law
The value of a network grows by the square of the size of the network

The history and origin of the Internet as a business tool are surprising since it has taken a relatively long time to become an essential part of business. It started life at the end of the 1960s as the ARPAnet research and defence network in the US that linked servers used by key military and academic collaborators. It was established as a network that would be reliable even if some of the links were broken. This was achieved because data and messages sent between users were broken up into smaller packets and could follow different routes. The history of the Internet is indicated diagrammatically in Figure 3.23, or you can view a more detailed timeline via the Hobbes Internet timeline (**www.isoc.org/guest/internet/history/brief.shtml**).

It was the advent of the **World Wide Web**, which was invented by Tim Berners-Lee of CERN, that was responsible for the massive growth in business use of the Internet. The World Wide Web provides a publishing medium which makes it easy to publish and read information using a web browser and also to link to related information. The web followed what is known as **Metcalfe's law**, first stated by Bob Metcalfe, who was co-founder and formerly chief executive of networking company 3Com. He is reputed to have said in presentations made for the company,

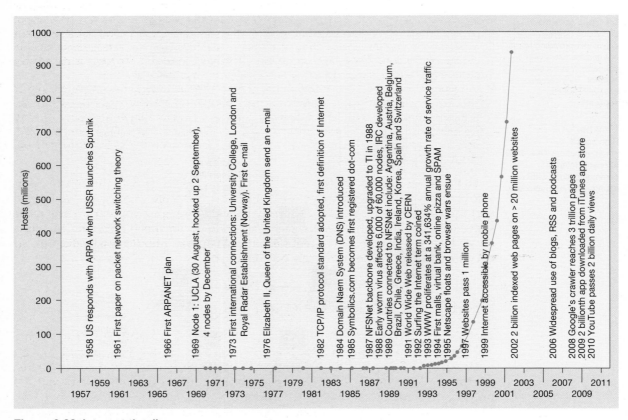

Figure 3.23 Internet timeline
Source: Chaffey (2004)

The power of the network increases exponentially by the number of computers connected to it. Therefore, every computer added to the network both uses it as a resource while adding resources in a spiral of increasing value and choice.

This 'law' is particularly relevant in the context of the Internet: it explains the rapid growth of the World Wide Web as the number of web information sources has increased. Some argue that without controls on the quality of information and how it is indexed, it may actually decline in value as it gets larger since it becomes more difficult to find good-quality information despite the advances in search engines. Metcalfe's law also shows how a community website such as a discussion board increases in value as the number of its active members increases. It also shows how the more links a website has, the number of visitors will not increase linearly since each site linking has multiple sites linking to it.

See the timeline at **www.w3.org/History.html** for a summary of the development of the web. Alternatively, read Berners-Lee (1999) for a description of the invention of the web and future plans. This shows that the first proposal for the forerunner of the World Wide Web arose because of problems with information management at CERN, a European centre for physics research, published in 'Information management: a proposal' (Berners-Lee, 1989). This document paints a familiar picture of many organizations, as the extract below shows, and is effectively a manifesto for the need for knowledge management, before the term became popular.

> CERN is a wonderful organization. It involves several thousand people, many of them very creative, all working toward common goals. Although they are nominally organized into a hierarchical management structure, this does not constrain the way people will communicate, and share information, equipment and software across groups.
>
> The actual observed working structure of the organization is a multiply connected 'web' whose interconnections evolve with time. In this environment, a new person arriving, or someone taking on a new task, is normally given a few hints as to who would be useful people to talk to. Information about what facilities exist and how to find out about them travels in the corridor gossip and occasional newsletters, and the details about what is required to be done spread in a similar way. All things considered, the result is remarkably successful, despite occasional misunderstandings and duplicated effort.
>
> A problem, however, is the high turnover of people. When two years is a typical length of stay, information is constantly being lost. The introduction of the new people demands a fair amount of their time and that of others before they have any idea of what goes on. The technical details of past projects are sometimes lost forever, or only recovered after a detective investigation in an emergency. Often, the information has been recorded, it just cannot be found.

Berners-Lee's original conception of the web was that it should be editable so that authors could readily update their own and others' documents directly through the browser. Although this is now effectively possible through a content management system accessed through browsers, public access to documents is now rare. The nearest we have to the original conception is the Wikipedia (**http://en.wikipedia.org**), an encyclopedia that anyone can freely contribute to.

What is the World Wide Web?

HTML (Hypertext Markup Language)
A standard format used to define the text and layout of web pages. HTML files usually have the extension .HTML or .HTM

The World Wide Web, or 'web' for short, provides a standard method for exchanging and publishing information on the Internet. If we take the analogy of television, then the Internet is the equivalent to the broadcasting equipment such as masts and transmitters, and the World Wide Web is equivalent to the content of different TV programmes. The medium is based on standard document formats such as **HTML (Hypertext Markup Language)**, which can be thought of as similar to a word-processing format such as that used for Microsoft Word documents. This standard has been widely adopted since:

- It offers **hyperlinks** which allow users to move readily from one document or website to another – the process known as 'surfing'.
- HTML supports a wide range of formatting, making documents easy to read on different access devices.
- Graphics and animations can be integrated into web pages.
- Interaction is possible through HTML-based forms that enable customers to supply their personal details for more information on a product, perform searches, ask questions or make comments.

It is the combination of web browsers and HTML that has proved so successful in establishing widespread business use of the Internet. The use of these tools provides a range of benefits, including:

- Ease of use since navigation between documents is enabled by clicking on hyperlinks or images. This soon becomes a very intuitive way of navigation which is similar in all websites and applications.
- It can provide a graphical environment supporting multimedia which is popular with users and gives a visual medium for advertising.
- The standardization of tools and growth in demand mean that information can be exchanged with many businesses and consumers.

Web browsers are software tools such as Microsoft Internet Explorer that we use to access the information on the WWW that is stored on **web servers**. Web servers are used to store, manage and supply the information on the WWW. The main web browsers are Microsoft Internet Explorer and Netscape Navigator or Communicator. Browsers display the text and graphics accessed from websites and provide tools for managing information from websites.

You will know what a web browser and web server are, but how do they work? Figure 3.24 shows the process by which web browsers communicate with web servers. A request from the client PC is executed whenever you type in a web address, click on a **hyperlink** or fill in an online form such as a search. This request is then sent to the ISP and routed across the Internet to the destination server using the mechanism

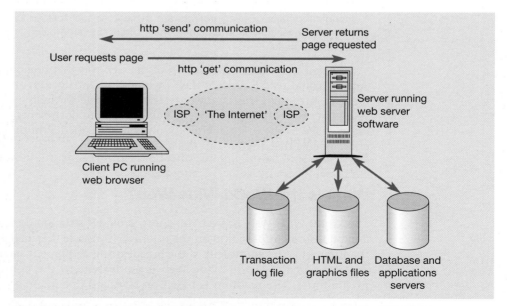

Figure 3.24 Information exchange between a web browser and web server
Source: Chaffey (2004)

Static web page
A page on the web server
that is invariant

Dynamic web page
A page that is created in
real time, often with
reference to a database
query, in response to a
user request

Transaction log file
A web server file that
records all page requests

described in the next section on protocols. The server then returns the requested web page if it is a **static web page** (fixed), or, if it requires reference to a database, such as a request for product information, it will pass the query on to a database server and will then return this to the customer as a **dynamic web page**. Information on all page requests is stored in a **transaction log file** which records the page requested, the time the request was made and the source of the enquiry. This information can be analysed to assess how users access an Internet, extranet or intranet website.

Internet standards – how does the Internet work?

One of the reasons for the success of the Internet and World Wide Web is that they are based on standard methods of exchanging data across the network which have been widely adopted by software and hardware vendors and businesses. We will briefly review Internet standards and then web standards in order to explain how the Internet works.

Internet data transfer standards

We have seen how information is requested by a user of a web browser and returned by the web server, but how does this information transfer occur over the Internet? Some of the key concepts are suggested by this definition of the Internet from the US Federal Networking Council:

> 'Internet' refers to the global information system that – (i) is logically linked together by a globally unique address space based on the Internet Protocol (IP) or its subsequent extensions/follow-ons; (ii) is able to support communications using the Transmission Control Protocol/Internet Protocol (TCP/IP) suite or its subsequent extensions/follow-ons, and/or other IP-compatible protocols; and (iii) provides, uses or makes accessible, either publicly or privately, high level services layered on the communications and related infrastructure described herein.
>
> (Leiner et al., 2000, reporting on the definition from 24 October 1995)

TCP/IP
The Transmission Control
Protocol is a transport-
layer protocol that moves
data between applications.
The Internet protocol is a
network-layer protocol that
moves data between host
computers

TCP/IP development was led by Robert Kahn and Vince Cerf in the late 1960s and early 1970s and, according to Leiner et al. (2000), four ground rules controlled Kahn's early work on this protocol. These four ground rules highlight the operation of the TCP/IP protocol:

1 Distinct networks would be able to communicate seamlessly with other networks.

2 Communications would be on a best-effort basis, that is, if a data packet didn't reach the final destination, it would be retransmitted from the source until successful receipt.

3 Black boxes would be used to connect the networks; these are now known as the 'gateways' and 'routers' produced by companies such as Cisco and 3Com. There would be no information retained by the gateways in order to keep them simple.

4 There would be no global control of transmissions; these would be governed by the requester and sender of information.

It can be seen that simplicity, speed and independence from control were at the heart of the development of the TCP/IP standards.

The data transmissions standards of the Internet, such as TCP/IP, are part of a larger set of standards produced by the International Standards Organization (ISO) known as the 'Open Systems Interconnection (OSI) model'. This defines a layered model that enables servers to communicate with other servers and clients. Data are transferred between different layers through defined rules. When implemented in software, the combined layers are referred to as a 'protocol stack'. The seven layers of the OSI model are:

- *Layer 7. Application.* The user interface program such as a web browser or e-mail reader that creates and receives messages.
- *Layer 6. Presentation.* These protocols are usually part of the operating system. They include data representation of different image, video and text formats.
- *Layer 5. Session.* This includes data transfer protocols such as SMTP, HTTP and FTP.
- *Layer 4. Transport.* This layer ensures the integrity of data transmitted. Examples include the Internet Transmission Control Protocol and Novell SPX.
- *Layer 3. Network.* Defines protocols for opening and maintaining links between servers. The best known are the Internet IP protocol and Novell IPX.
- *Layer 2. Data-link.* Defines the rules for sending and receiving information.
- *Layer 1. Physical.* Low-level description of physical transmission methods.

Layers 5 to 7 are known as the 'application layer' and are typically achieved within a single piece of application software such as the web browser. Layers 1 to 4 are part of the systems software and usually incorporate both operating system and network operating system. Through breaking the different functions of data communications into different layers, it becomes possible to integrate different software and hardware from different manufacturers into complex telecommunications networks – a key benefit of standards-based approaches.

The postal service is a good analogy for the transmission of data around the Internet using the TCP/IP protocol. Before we send mail, we always need to add a destination address. Likewise, the IP protocol acts as an addressed envelope that is used to address a message to the appropriate IP address of the receiver (Figure 3.25).

The Internet is formally a packet-switched network that uses TCP/IP as its protocol. This means that, as messages or packets of data are sent, there is no part of the network that is dedicated to them. This is the same as the fact that when your letters and parcels are sent by post they are mixed with letters and parcels from other people. The alternative type of network is the circuit-switched network such as phone systems where the line is dedicated to the user for the duration of the call. Taking the analogy further, the transmission media of the Internet such as telephone lines, satellite links and optical cables are the equivalent of the vans, trains and planes that are used to carry post. Transmission media for the Internet include analogue media such

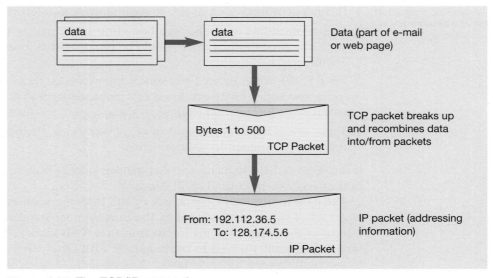

Figure 3.25 The TCP/IP protocol
Source: Chaffey (2004)

as phone lines and faster, digital media such as integrated service digital network technology (ISDN) and more recently asynchronous digital subscriber line (ADSL).

The facility for data to follow different routes on the Internet arises from one of the original requirements of the Internet. In the Cold War era, it was important that data could follow different routes if the servers and networks of a military installation were destroyed.

In addition to the transmission media, components of the network are also required to direct or route the packets or messages via the most efficient route. On the Internet these are referred to as 'routers' or 'hubs', and are manufactured by companies such as Cisco and 3Com. The routers are the equivalent of postal sorting offices which decide the best route for mail to take. They do not plan the entire route of the message, but rather they direct it to the next router that seems most appropriate given the destination and current network traffic.

IP address
The unique numerical address of a computer

Some addressing information goes at the beginning of your message; this information gives the network enough information to deliver the packet of data. The **IP address** of a receiving server is usually in the form such as 207.68.156.58, which is a numerical representation of a better-known form such as **www.microsoft.com**. Each IP address is unique to a given organization, server or client, in a similar way to postal codes referring to a small number of houses. The first number refers to the top-level domain in the network, in this case .com. The remaining numbers are used to refer to a particular organization.

Packet
Each Internet message such as an e-mail or HTTP request is broken down into smaller parts for ease of transmission

Once the Internet message is addressed, the postal analogy is not so apt since related information is not sent across the Internet in one large message. For reasons of efficiency, information sent across IP networks is broken up into separate parts called '**packets**'. The information within a packet is usually between 1 and 1500 characters long. This helps to route information most efficiently and fairly, with different packets sent by different people having equal priority. The transmission control protocol TCP performs the task of splitting up the original message into packets on despatch and reassembling it on receipt. Combining TCP and IP, you can think of an addressed IP envelope containing a TCP envelope which in turn contains part of the original message that has been split into a packet.

Internet-related standards bodies

IS managers will also monitor the creation and adoption of new standards promoted by international standards bodies. Many of these standards are related to Internet technologies, for example:

- The Internet Corporation for Assigned Names and Numbers (ICANN, **www.icann.org**)
- The Internet Society (**www.isoc.org**)
- The Internet Engineering Task Force (IETF) (**www.ietf.org**)
- The World Wide Web consortium (**www.w3.org**)
- Telecommunications Information Networking Architecture Consortium (TINA-C) (**www.tina.com**).

There may also be standards initiatives which directly affect a specific industry. For example, the World Wide Web consortium has developed and promoted data transfer using the XML standard, defined later in this section, but it has been adopted vertically in industries such as petroleum and chemicals with the support of organizations within that industry.

The HTTP protocol

HTTP, the hyptertext transfer protocol
A standard method used to transfer and process web content through client computers issuing requests from web servers which then deliver the relevant content

When the World Wide Web was developed, Tim Berners-Lee also developed a protocol, **HTTP, the hypertext transfer protocol**. This was a standard method for web browsers and servers to transfer requests for delivery of web pages and their embedded graphics. When you click on a link while viewing a website, your web browser will request information from the server computer hosting the website using the http protocol. Since this protocol is important for delivering the web pages, the letters http:// are used to prefix all web addresses. HTTP messages are divided into HTTP 'get' messages for requesting a web page and HTTP 'send' messages as shown in Figure 3.24. The web pages and graphics transferred in this way are transferred as packets, which is why web pages do not usually download smoothly, but in jumps as different groups of packets arrive.

The inventor of HTTP, Tim Berners-Lee, describes its purpose as follows (Berners-Lee, 1999):

> HTTP rules define things like which computer speaks first, and how they speak in turn. When two computers agree they can talk, they have to find a common way to represent their data so they can share it.

Uniform resource locators (URLs)

Uniform (universal) resource locator (URL)
A web address used to locate a web page on a web server

Web addresses refer to particular pages on a web server which is hosted by a company or organization. The technical name for a web address is **uniform or universal resource locator (URL)**. URLs can be thought of as a standard method of addressing, similar to post or ZIP codes, that makes it straightforward to find the name of a site.

Web addresses are usually prefixed by 'http://' to denote the http protocol explained above. Web addresses always start with 'http://', so references to websites in this book and in most promotional material from companies omit this part of the URL. Indeed, when using modern versions of web browsers, it is not necessary to type this in as part of the web page location since it is added automatically by the web browser. Although the vast majority of sites start with 'www', this is not universal, so it is necessary to specify this.

Web addresses are structured in a standard way as follows:

```
www.<domain-name>.<extension>.<filename.html>
```

Domain names

The domain name refers to the name of the web server and is usually selected to be the same as the name of the company, and the extension will indicate its type. The extension is known as the global top-level domain (gTLD). There are also some 250 country-code top-level domains (ccTLD).

Common gTLDs are:

- **.com** represents an international or American company, such as **www. travelagency.com**
- **.co.uk** represents a company based in the UK, such as **www.thomascook.co.uk**
- **.ac.uk** is a UK-based university (e.g. **www.leeds.ac.uk**) and **.edu** is a US university such as **www.mit.edu**
- **.org.uk** and **.org** are not-for-profit organizations (e.g. **www.greenpeace.org**)
- **.net** is a network provider such as **www.virgin.net**.

The 'filename.html' part of the web address refers to an individual web page, for example 'products.html' for a web page summarizing a company's products. When a web address is typed in without a filename, for example **www.bt.com**, the browser automatically assumes that the user is looking for the home page, which by convention is referred to as index.html. When creating sites, it is therefore vital to name the home page index.html. The file index.html can also be placed in sub-directories to ease access to information. For example, to access a support page a customer would type **www.bt.com/support.**

Note that gTLDs are continuously under review and in 2000 ICANN, the Internet Corporation for Assigned Names and Numbers (**www.icann.org**), granted seven new gTLDs. These became available from June 2001 and included .biz for business, .name to be used by individuals, .museum, .pro for professionals, .aero for aviation, .coop for co-operatives and .info. The new names have not been widely used by existing businesses with existing domain names, but do offer alternatives for new businesses. According to another view, existing companies such as Amazon will attempt to additionally register with the new domain such as '.biz' which will not help to increase the availability of gTLD names.

HTML (Hypertext Markup Language)

Web-page text has many of the formatting options available in a word processor. These include applying fonts, emphasis (bold, italic, underline) and placing information in tables. Formatting is possible since the web browser applies these formats according to instructions that are contained in the file that makes up the web page. This is usually written in HTML or Hypertext Markup Language. HTML is an international standard established by the World Wide Web Consortium (and published at **www.w3.org**) intended to ensure that any web page authored according to the definitions in the standard will appear the same in any web browser. HTML files can be authored in an ordinary text editor such as the Notepad program available with Microsoft Windows. Modern word processors also have an option to save formatted information in the HTML format. Alternatively, many software utilities such as Macromedia Dreamweaver and Microsoft FrontPage are available to simplify writing HTML.

An example of how HTML is used for formatting is given below. The HTML code used to construct pages has codes or instruction tags such as <B> to indicate to the browser what is displayed. The <B> tag, for example, is simply used for bold formatting of characters. A <P> is used to denote a paragraph. Each starting tag has a corresponding end tag usually marked by a '/', for example <B>Buy Now!</B>.

HTML code

```
<P> This text is <B>bold </B></P>
<P> This text is <I>italic</I></P>
<P> This text is <U>underlined</U></P>
```

Browser display

This text is **bold**
This text is *italic*
This text is <u>underlined</u>

Links, or, more strictly, hyperlinks are essential to the function of the web since these enable a user to click on a link text, graphic or button and jump to another part of the same document, a different document on the same site, or a completely different site. The link tag is identified by '<A HREF= " "></A>' tag and can be thought of as being in two parts as the example below shows. The first part <A HREF="index.htm"> is used to specify the target address or destination page to link to, in this case the home page of the current site.

HTML code

```
<A HREF="index.htm"> Go to home page </A><BR>
<A HREF="http://www.bbc.co.uk ">Go to the BBC website</A>
```

Browser display

Go to home page
Go to the BBC website

The simplicity of HTML compared to traditional programming languages makes it possible for simple web pages to be developed by non-specialists such as marketing assistants preparing an HTML e-mail newsletter for customers, particularly if a template for more complex parts of the page is already constructed. Interactive forms and online sales systems are more complex and usually require some programming expertise, although tools are provided to simplify creation of these systems.

Indexing, describing and referencing HTML documents

When the early version of HTML was designed by Tim Berners-Lee at CERN, he based it on the existing standard for representation of documents. This standard was SGML, the Standard Generalized Markup Language which was ratified by the ISO in 1986. SGML uses tags to identify the different elements of a document such as title and chapters. According to publisher O'Reilly's XML.org site it has been used

> for describing thousands of different document types in many fields of human activity, from transcriptions of ancient Irish manuscripts to the technical documentation for stealth bombers, and from patients' clinical records to musical notation. SGML is very large and complex, however, and probably overkill for most common applications.

HTML used a similar approach to identify the document and its components. For example, the tag for the title that appears at the top of the browser window is <TITLE>. While HTML has proved powerful in providing a standard method of displaying information that was easy to learn, it is largely presentational. HTML only had a limited capability for describing the data on web pages. A capability for summarizing the content of pages is an example of **metadata**. 'Meta' is a Greek prefix, which in an information management context can be summarized as providing a description or definition about a topic or item.

HTML also has a limited capability for describing documents through **HTML meta tags**. These are presented at the start of the document in the header area. As the boxed example shows, they can be used to specify a document's author, last update and type of content. This uses only some examples of meta tags; the full definition and an introduction to HTML is available from the World Wide Web consortium at **www.w3.org/MarkUp**.

Metadata
A definition of the structure and content of a collection of data or document: data about data

HTML meta tags
Standard HTML codes used to specify the content and characteristics of the document

```
<HEAD>
<TITLE>An intranet document example</TITLE>
<META name="author" content="Dave Chaffey">
<META name="keywords" content="phone directory, address book">
<META name="description" content="An online phone book">
<META name="date" content="2005-11-06T08:49:37+00:00">
</HEAD>
```

One application of meta tags is that they are used by search engines to identify the content of documents. Early search engines such as AltaVista ranked higher in their listings documents which had meta keywords that corresponded to the words typed into the search engine by its user. This led to abuse by companies who might include the name of their competitor or repeat keywords several times in the meta tags, a process known as 'search engine spamming'. As a result most search engines now attach limited importance to the keyword meta tags, in fact Google does not use them at all. However, most search engines, including Google, do attach relevance to the <TITLE> tag, so it is important that this does not just contain a company name. For example, easyJet.com uses the following title tag which incorporates the main phrases potential visitors may type into a search engine.

```
<title>easyJet.com — easyjet low cost airline, easy jet, flight,
air fares, cheap flights</title>
```

One of the problems with the use of meta tags in HTML documents is that their significance is not recognized by all document authors – some documents do not have any meta tags at all. It would be much more useful for searchers if the date meta tag were widely adopted since this would allow everyone to find the most recent documents; however, it is not widely used. Instead, search engines such as Google have to use the date the document was last published to a web server – this is often not a guide to the most recent content since the whole website is refreshed regularly, even if the content itself has not changed.

XML (eXtensible Markup Language)

XML or eXtensible Markup Language
A standard based on customized tags that enables the definition, validation and interpretation of data, and so facilitates the transfer of data within and between applications and organizations

The weaknesses with HTML described above have been acknowledged and, in an effort coordinated by the World Wide Web Consortium, the first **XML or eXtensible Markup Language** was produced in February 1998. This is not strictly a replacement for HTML since HTML and XML can coexist – they are both markup languages. To help developers use HTML and XML together, a new standard, confusingly known as XHTML, was adopted. Like HTML, XHTML and XML are also based on SGML. The key word describing XML is 'extensible'. This means that new mark up tags can be created that facilitate the searching and exchange of information. For example, product information on a web page could use the XML tags <NAME>, <DESCRIPTION>, <COLOUR> and <PRICE>. The tags can effectively act as a standard set of database field descriptions so that data can be exchanged between companies once a standard has been agreed.

Arguably an understanding of XML is more important to managers than an understanding of HTML, since it goes beyond tags to format and link pages to offer a method for exchange of data. The power of XML lies in its capability to define the elements of any type of structured data. As the examples of XML applications later in this chapter show, it has proved very important in the implementation of business-to-business e-commerce through its ability to exchange data.

An XML implementation typically consists of three parts, the XML document, a document type definition (DTD) and a stylesheet (XSL), which are usually stored as separate files. We need a simple example to understand how these relate. Let's take the example of a bookstore cataloguing different books. You will see from this example that it is equivalent to using a database such as Microsoft Access to define database fields about the books and then storing and displaying their details.

The XML document contains the data items, in this case the books and references the DTD and XSL files:

Data items: The XML document <books.xml>

```
<?xml version="1.0"?>
<!DOCTYPE Bookstore SYSTEM "books.dtd">
<?xml-stylesheet type="text/html" href="books.xsl"?>
<Bookstore>
<Book ID="101">
    <Author>Dave Chaffey</Author>
    <Title>E-business and E-commerce Management</Title>
    <Date>30 November 2003</Date>
    <ISBN>0273683780</ISBN>
    <Publisher>Pearson Education</Publisher>
</Book>
<Book ID="102">
    <Author>Dave Chaffey</Author>
    <Title>Total E-mail Marketing</Title>
    <Date>20 February 2003</Date>
    <ISBN>0750657545</ISBN>
    <Publisher>Butterworth Heinemann</Publisher>
</Book>
</Bookstore>
```

Note: The tags such as Publisher, Book and author are defined for this particular application. They are defined in a separate Data Type Definition document which is shown below.

The DTD referenced at the start of the XML document defines the data items associated with the root element, which in this case is the bookstore:

Data definition: Document Type Definition <books.dtd>

```
<!ELEMENT BookStore (Book)*>
<!ELEMENT Book (Title, Author+, Date, ISBN, Publisher)>
<!ATTLIST Book ID #REQUIRED>
<!ELEMENT Title (#PCDATA)>
<!ELEMENT Author (#PCDATA)>
<!ELEMENT Date (#PCDATA)>
<!ELEMENT ISBN (#PCDATA)>
<!ELEMENT Publisher (#PCDATA)>
```

Notes:
The Bookstore can contain many books *
Bookstore is known as the 'Root element'
+ Allows for one or more author
PCDATA stands for Parsed character data, i.e. A text string, further validation of fields could be used
REQUIRED shows that this field is essential

The XSL document uses HTML tags to instruct the browser how the data within XML files should be displayed. Separation of data from their presentation method makes this a more powerful approach than combining the two, since users can switch readily between different presentation schemes such as with and without graphics, according to their preference.

Presentation: Document Style Sheet File <books.xsl>

```
<?xml version='1.0'?>
<xsl:stylesheet xmlns:xsl="http://www.w3.org/TR/WD-xsl">
<xsl:template match="/">
    <html> <body>
    <table cellpadding="2" cellspacing="0" border="1"
    bgcolor="#FFFFD5"> <tr>
                <th>Title</th>
                <th>Author</th>
                <th>Publisher</th>
                <th>Date</th>
                <th>ISBN</th>
                </tr> <xsl:for-each select="Bookstore/Book">
            <tr><td><xsl:value-of select="Title"/></td>
                <td><xsl:value-of select="Author"/></td>
                <td><xsl:value-of select="Publisher"/></td>
                <td><xsl:value-of select="Date"/></td>
                <td><xsl:value-of select="ISBN"/></td>
            </tr> </xsl:for-each>
</table>
</body> </html>
</xsl:template>
</xsl:stylesheet>
```

Note: The style sheet uses standard HTML tags to display the data.

This style sheet would display the data as follows:

Display of data through browser

Title	Author	Publisher	Date	ISBN
E-business and E-commerce Management	Dave Chaffey	Pearson Education	30 November 2003	0273683780
Total E-mail Marketing	Dave Chaffey	Butterworth Heinemann	20 February 2003	0750657545

Examples of XML applications

Like other technology standards, the long-term success of XML will be dependent on how many organizations adopt standards for particular applications of data exchange. As well as the World Wide Web Consortium, other organizations are active in promoting it. The Dublin Core metadata initiative (DCMI) (**www.dublincore.org**), so called since it first met in Dublin, Ohio in 1995, has been active in defining different forms of metadata to support information access across the Internet. An important part of this initiative is in defining a standard method of referencing web documents and other media resources. If widely adopted this would make it much more efficient to search for a document produced by a particular author in a particular language in a particular date range. It would also make searching for documents on particular topics more reliable. A summary of the standard is shown in Table 3.7. Its most appropriate implementation for web resources is based on an element of XML known as RDF (**resource definition framework**), which is shown below, although it can be implemented in other forms. RDF is used to define attributes and express relationships between these attributes. Relationships between objects such as different fields or documents can be described using three elements or triples similar to the subject, verb and object of a simple sentence. For example: Dave Chaffey (object) is the creator (verb or property) of **www.davechaffey.com** (subject or resource), or Field 19 (object) in a database is a field of type (property) Zip code (subject).

Table 3.7 Summary of metadata for the document definition from the Dublin Core

Metadata item	Description
Contributor	An entity responsible for making contributions to the resource.
Coverage	The spatial or temporal topic of the resource, the spatial applicability of the resource, or the jurisdiction under which the resource is relevant.
Creator	An entity primarily responsible for making the resource.
Date	A point or period of time associated with an event in the lifecycle of the resource.
Description	An account of the resource.
Format	The file format, physical medium, or dimensions of the resource.
Identifier	An unambiguous reference to the resource within a given context.
Language	A language of the resource.
Publisher	An entity responsible for making the resource available.
Relation	A related resource.
Rights	Information about rights held in and over the resource.
Source	A related resource from which the described resource is derived.
Subject	The topic of the resource.
Title	A name given to the resource.
Type	The nature or genre of the resource.

Source: Dublin Core Metadata Initiative (http://dublincore.org/documents/2008/01/14/dces/)

Unfortunately, it is very difficult to move from creation of a standard such as DCMI to wide adoption of the standard. One of the first requirements is buy-in from creators or vendors of tools for managing documents and support from tools vendors of search engines services and CMS: barriers to adoption are highlighted in Activity 3.4.

It was speculated that perhaps the best application of the Dublin Core is on controlled internal environments such as intranets and extranets, where its use can be mandated, to make information resources easier to find. Organizations can stipulate use of metadata in both the creation of documents and in search engine indexing. An organization could therefore develop an index and sitemap automatically from metadata and improved information retrieval precision. An example is the EGMS metadata standard which aims to improve intergovernment searching using the UK online search engine (see **www.govtalk.gov.uk** for details).

It is now over five years since the Dublin Core elements shown in Table 3.7 were initially specified and many of the barriers to adoption appear to have been successfully overcome. They are now supported by many systems and software tools including DSpace, Fedora, OpenOffice, Microsoft Office, Adobe Acrobat, Dreamweaver and WordPress.

An example of an industry-specific XML standard is Chem eStandards, the XML standard for the chemical industry, which covers 700 data elements and 47 transactions and is sponsored by the Chemical Industry Data Exchange (CIDX, **www.cidx.org**). The open, non-proprietary standards are vendor-neutral.

The importance of XML is indicated by its incorporation by Microsoft into its BizTalk server (**www.microsoft.com/biztalk**) for B2B application integration. The BizTalk server enables different enterprise applications described in Chapter 2, such as SAP and JDEdwards, to exchange information as part of improved supply chain management. Microsoft summarizes the benefits of Biztalk as:

1 Reduced 'time to value', i.e. development time and cost of application integration
2 Easy integration with virtually any application or technology
3 Scalability to any size of application
4 Support for industry standards such as EDI, XML and Simple Object Access Protocol (SOAP)
5 Reliable document delivery including 'once only' delivery of documents, comprehensive document tracking, and logging and support for failover
6 Secure document exchange – this is not an integral feature of XML but has been built into this application
7 Automation for complex business processes
8 Management and monitoring of business processes
9 Automated trading partner management
10 Reduced complexity in development.

Another widely adopted application of XML is ebXML (**www.ebxml.org**). This standard has been coordinated by Oasis (**www.oasis-open.org**), which is an international not-for-profit consortium for promoting Internet standards. The original project was intended to define business exchange using five standards:

● business processes (support for different activities and transactions involved in buying and selling online)
● core data components
● collaboration protocol agreements
● messaging
● registries and repositories.

Oasis define three types of transactions that form business processes:

1 *Business Transaction*. A single business transaction between two partners, such as placing an order or shipping an order.
2 *Binary Collaboration*. A sequence of these business transactions, performed between two partners, each performing one role.
3 *MultiParty Collaboration*. A series of binary collaborations composed of a collection of business partners.

One application developed using ebXML is to enable different accounting packages to communicate with online order processing systems. This new standard has been recognized by 85 per cent of the accounting industry, the World Wide Web Consortium and the United Nations. In addition, over 120 national and international accounting software vendors have confirmed that they are developing interfaces. Exchequer Software Ltd (**www.exchequer.com**) is the first company to embed this new technology in its products, which means it receives orders via e-mail directly into its own accounting system. This has resulted in a reduction of 30 per cent in processing costs and a sales increase of 40 per cent. The e-business module of the accounting software can be used to provide a remotely hosted e-commerce shopping cart system with regular updates of stock details, pricing matrices, account information and transactional data, such as outstanding orders and invoices. The importance of XML standards is further suggested by Mini case study 3.1 'Ancient stone helps create e-business standard' and Activity 3.4.

Activity 3.4 — E-business standards

Purpose

To explore the different types of e-business standards and their significance for managers.

Activity

You have recently joined a medium-sized organization as an Operations Director. As part of your appointment, you have been tasked with increasing supply chain management efficiency using electronic transactions. You know that XML standards have been widely adopted by larger organizations, but there are a bewildering number of standards, standards bodies and vendors.

visit the www

1 Visit the websites of the main standards organizations such as Biztalk (**www.biztalk.org**), Oasis (**www.oasis-open.org**) and RosettaNet (**www.rosettanet.org**) and produce a diagram summarizing the different parts and purposes of the different standards.

2 Write a short justification for the adoption of XML-based standards which will form part of your business case for presentation to the management team who have no knowledge of XML.

Governments are also using XML to standard data transfer between departments. Examples of the UK government's draft schema, for example for transfer of patient records, are at **www.govtalk.gov.uk**.

Mini case study 3.1 — Ancient stone helps create e-business standard

RosettaNet is a consortium of many of the world's leading information technology, electronic components and semiconductor manufacturing companies working to create, implement and promote open e-business process standards.

RosettaNet is named after the Rosetta Stone (Figure 3.26), a slab of black basalt which was carved in Egypt in 200 BC. The same inscription (a royal decree praising Egypt's king, Ptolemy V) was written on the stone three times: once in hieroglyphic, once in demotic, and once in Greek. It was discovered in 1799 by Napoleon's troops near Rosetta in Egypt. Like XML, it was used for translation or information transfer – in this case between three different languages. Jean François Champollion, a French Egyptologist, compared the three languages and deciphered Egyptian hieroglyphics for the first time. The stone now resides in the British Museum, in London.

RosettaNet has developed Partner Interface Processes (PIPs) which are 'specialized system-to-system XML-based dialogs that define business processes between trading partners. Each PIP specification includes a business document with the vocabulary, and a business process with the choreography of the message dialog.' PIPs apply to the following core processes:

Cluster 1: *Partner Product and Service Review*. Allows information collection, maintenance and distribution for the development of trading-partner profiles and product-information subscriptions

Cluster 2: *Product Information*. Enables distribution and periodic update of product and detailed design information, including product change notices and product technical specifications

Cluster 3: *Order Management*. Supports full order management business area from price and delivery quoting through purchase order initiation, status reporting, and management. Order invoicing, payment and discrepancy notification also managed using this cluster of processes

Cluster 4: *Inventory Management*. Enables inventory management, including collaboration, replenishment, price protection, reporting and allocation of constrained product

Cluster 5: *Marketing Information Management*. Enables communication of marketing information, including campaign plans, lead information and design registration

Cluster 6: *Service and Support*. Provides post-sales technical support, service warranty and asset management capabilities

Cluster 7: *Manufacturing*. Enables the exchange of design, configuration, process, quality and other manufacturing floor information to support the 'Virtual Manufacturing' environment

A single example of a PIP from Cluster 3. Order Management is Segment 3A: Quote and Order Entry. This allows partners to exchange price and availability

Figure 3.26 The Rosetta Stone from the British Museum
Source: © Alfredo Dagli Orti/Corbis

information, quotes, purchase orders and order status, and enables partners to send requested orders, or shopping carts, to other partners. Some of the business tasks and events supported are:

PIP 3A1: Request Quote
PIP 3A2: Request Price and Availability
PIP 3A3: Request Shopping Cart Transfer
PIP 3A4: Request Purchase Order
PIP 3A5: Query Order Status
PIP 3A6: Distribute Order Status
PIP 3A7: Notify of Purchase Order Update
PIP 3A8: Request Purchase Order Change
PIP 3A9: Request Purchase Order Cancellation
PIP 3A10: Notify of Quote Acknowledgment
PIP 3A11: Notify of Authorization to Build
PIP 3A12: Notify of Authorization to Ship
PIP 3A13: Notify of Purchase Order Information
PIP 3A14: Distribute Planned Order

It can be seen that every conceivable business process has been standardized and defined in messaging between organizations based on XML.

The three examples below show the significance of RosettaNet according to this standards organization.

Intel

In 2003, Intel publicly announced plans to end EDI business processes company-wide by 2006 and rely on RosettaNet as a key enabler to its future e-business strategy. By 2004, Intel had implemented RosettaNet as the company's standard for business-to-business integration with 89 of its trading partners in 17 different countries. The company processed more than 10 per cent of its revenues and supplier purchases in 2002 using RosettaNet e-business technology standards. Intel transacted more than US$3 billion in customer orders and US$2 billion in supplier purchases on RosettaNet, increasing by approximately seven times the total amount of business processed via RosettaNet connections in one year.

In 2010, RosettaNet is part of GS1 US™, a not-for-profit member-driven organization, administers the UPC and develops worldwide standards and solutions for identification numbers, data carriers, electronic commerce, and global data synchronization. More than 200,000 GS1 US member companies now use open, global GS1 Standards to optimize their value chains and business processes.

Nokia

RosettaNet is the primary enabler for Nokia's system-to-system integration, with its demand supply network allowing the company to automate the extreme challenge of processing over 10 million components per hour. Currently, the major business groups within Nokia, including suppliers, contract manufacturers, logistics and customers, are involved in RosettaNet implementations across the globe.

Sony

In 2002, Sony centralized its vendor managed inventory system (VMI) by connecting with over 90 suppliers using the RosettaNet standard. Like Intel, Sony intends to replace EDI with RosettaNet. Sony's EDI replacement will initially cover its mass-production procurement, but in the longer term RosettaNet will replace EDI for all aspects of Sony's business.

Source: Material contained herewith is reserved by RosettaNet © 2004 www.rosettanet.org

The semantic web

The semantic web
A concept describing the use of metadata or self-description of WWW documents to enable context-understanding programs to selectively find what users want through more efficient location and exchange of data

The semantic web is a concept promoted by Tim Berners-Lee and the World Wide Web Consortium (**www.w3.org**) to improve upon the capabilities of the current World Wide Web. Semantics is the study of the meaning of words and linguistic expressions. For example, the word 'father' has the semantic elements male, human and parent and 'girl' has the elements female, human and young. The semantic web is about how to define meaning for the content of the web. As mentioned above, finding information on a particular topic through searching the web is inexact since there isn't a standard way of describing the content of web pages. The semantic web describes the use of metadata through standards such as the XML, RDF and the Dublin Core to help users find web resources more readily.

Agents
Software programs that can assist humans to perform tasks

The semantic web also refers to exchange of information through the use of software **agents** running on different computers. Agents are software programs created to assist humans in performing tasks. In this context they automatically gather information from the Internet or exchange data with other agents based on parameters supplied by the user.

The applications of the semantic web are best illustrated through examples. Berners-Lee et al. (2001) give the example of a patient seeking medical treatment for a particular condition. They envisage a patient having a personal software agent (effectively a search engine) which is used to find the best source of treatment. The personal agent will interact with the doctor's agent which will describe the symptoms and search pages from different healthcare providers which detail their services. The patient's agent will then give them the different treatment options in terms of cost, effectiveness, waiting time and location. Similarly, a personal agent could be used to find the best flight or a business agent could be used to participate in a reverse auction. Rather than visiting several websites to compare flight times and prices the user would tell the agent: 'I need the best deal from A to B, flying midweek from my nearest airport' – rather like asking travel agent staff.

Examples of the use of the semantic web and XML are contained at http://owl.mindswap.org which styles itself 'the first site on the semantic web'. An example of a page marked up using ontologies for a university researcher can be found at www.cs.rpi.edu/~hendler/. Ontologies formally define the relationships between terms. For example, a zip code is part of a location.

The wireless Internet

Wireless Application Protocol (WAP)
WAP is a technical standard for transferring information to wireless devices such as mobile phones

M-commerce (mobile commerce)
Electronic transactions or messaging conducted through mobile devices such as laptops, PDAs and mobile phones, typically with a wireless connection

3G
Third generation of mobile phone technology with high-speed data transfer enabling video calling

i-mode
A mobile access platform widely used in Japan that enables display of colour graphics and content subscription services

Wireless connection to the Internet is possible in several different forms. WAP internet access from mobile phones has now been with us for several years. In 1999 the first of a new generation of mobile phones such as the Nokia 7110 were introduced and they offered the opportunity to access the Internet. These are known as 'Wireless Application Protocol or WAP phones' or, in more common parlance, 'web-enabled' or 'Internet phones'. What these phones offer is the facility to access information on websites that has been specially tailored for display on the small screens of mobile phones. There was a tremendous amount of hype about these phones since they seemed to provide all the benefits that have been provided by the World Wide Web, but in a mobile form. Levels of product purchase by mobile phone and content access have proved very low in comparison with the Internet, even for standardized products such as books and CDs. Many **m-commerce (mobile commerce)** providers such as Sweden's M-box went into receivership. However, analysts expect that with new access platforms, such as **3G**, this will change. For example, travel is the leading e-commerce category in Europe by revenue for the fixed Internet. Users visit WAP sites to download ringtones and e-mail and access news, sport and entertainment content when they do not have PC access.

The Japanese experience with **i-mode** suggests that with a suitable access device that supports colour images, the impact of 3G could be significant. MobileCommerceWorld (2001) reports that Japanese i-mode users spend an average of 2614 yen ($21.60) each month on wireless content and m-commerce. Mobile phone ringtones and other music downloads are the most popular i-mode purchases, followed by other paid-for information such as dating services. The strength of the proposition is indicated by the fact that over 30 million Japanese use this service despite a launch less than two years previously.

In 2001 new services became available on GPRS (General Packet Radio Service). This is approximately five times faster than the GSM (Global System for Mobile Communciations) previously used for mobile phones (Table 3.8) and is an 'always-on' service which is charged according to usage. Display is still largely text-based and based on the WAP. Uptake of these services was limited due to the need for new handsets and the cost of data services. In March 2003, a completely new generation of services known as '3G' became available based on UMTS (a wireless transmission standard referred to in Table 3.8). With this, delivery of video downloads and chat becomes possible, enabling instant access or 'always-on'. In 2003, Hutchinson Telecom introduced the first 3G phone to the UK market. In the long term, such phones seem likely to transform the way we access the Internet, both as consumers and business people, since many facilities available from a desktop PC are available within a handheld unit. The specification shows the types of feature that will be available. The main features are: dual-mode 2G/3G device supporting data upload of 64 kbps and download of 384 kbps

Table 3.8 Comparison of mobile phone technologies

Generation of mobile technology	Main standards	Maximum data transfer rate (downlink)	Approximate adoption levels 2008
1G Analog cellphones of 1980s	Frequency Division Multiple Access (FDMA)	9600 bits/sec	N/A
2G Circuit switched, digital cellphones introduced in 1991	GSM (Global System for Mobile communications) Code Division Multiple Access (CDMA) TDMA ('Time Division Multiple Access')	13 kbit/s	c. 80% globally
2.5G introduced in 2001	GPRS (General Packet Radio Service (GPRS) EDGE (Enhanced Data rates for Global Evolution)	114 kbit/s	N/A
3G Packet switched introduced in 2004	UMTS (Universal Mobile Telecommunications System) W-CDMA (Wideband Code Division Multiple Access) High-Speed Downlink Packet Access (HSDPA)	14.4 Mbit/s	c. 28% in Europe and US according to Comscore
3.5G Introduced in 2008	Evolved HSPA/HPSA+	42 Mbit/s	N/A
4G Projected 2012–2015	Fourth Generation. No agreed standards	2012–2015 time scale	N/A

(used for videos), 65,536 16-bit colour display of 46 × 57 mm (132 × 162 pixels), web browsing, two cameras for picture and video, download and playing of audio and video (supports MPEG4 and WMA files), downloading and playing Java games using Java™ technology, qwerty keyboard, e-mail and word processing.

In the UK auctions for the licence to operate on these frequencies have exceeded £20 billion – such is the perceived importance of these services by the telecommunications companies (telcos). Many commentators now believe it will be difficult for the telcos to recoup this money, and this has resulted in large falls in their share prices. Charges for new 3G services and handsets will initially be several times those for GSM services and this is bound to limit the initial uptake. A new realism seems to be afoot in the telecoms industry, partly as a result of limited uptake of such services as WAP and picture messaging.

BBC (2003a) reported that John Erskine, the head of network operator O2, said:

> 3G is no longer a field of dreams adhering to the philosophy that if you built it, users will come. Now the attitudes are more pragmatic and led by market demand.

Jean François Pontal of Orange concurred, saying:

> We might suggest ways customers might like to use services but at the end of the day they will be defined and deployed by the street. The next big thing is here already, in clubs, warehouses and bedrooms.

Hutchinson, which launched the 3 network (**www.three.co.uk**) in the UK, failed to reach its target for 1 million phone sales in its 2003 launch year, so these comments seem apposite.

SMS messaging

Short-message service (SMS)
The formal name for text messaging

In addition to offering voice calls and data transfer, mobile phones have increasingly been used for e-mail and short-message service (SMS), commonly known as 'texting'. SMS is, of course, a simple form of e-mail that enables messages to be transferred between mobile phones. According to the Mobile Data Association (2010), over 3 trillion text messages were sent worldwide in 2009, bringing the total number of messages sent in 2009 in the UK to 96.8 billion (Figure 3.27). This suggests an average of over 1600 messages per person annually and a much higher figure for some users! In 2002, telecoms providers launched Picture Messaging or Multimedia Messaging Services, which it was hoped would capitalize on the interest in texting.

Sending texts is certainly popular with users: a survey in the UK by MDA (2003) showed that

- 70 per cent of mobile phone users send text messages;
- 94 per cent of 18-24-year-olds send personal texts;
- 34 per cent of those aged between 18 and 24 send 36 or more messages a week;
- 14 per cent of people send business text messages on their mobile phone.

Texting has proved useful for business in some niche applications. For example, banks now notify customers when they approach an overdraft and provide weekly statements using SMS. Text has also been used by consumer brands to market their products, particularly to a younger audience as the case studies at text agency Flytxt (**www.flytxt.com**) and TextIt, the organization promoting text messaging, (**www.text.it**) show. Texting can also be used in supply chain management applications for notifying managers of problems or deliveries.

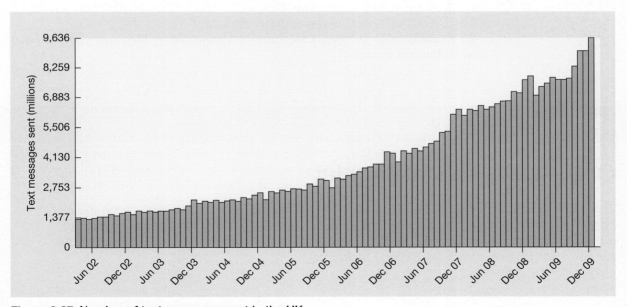

Figure 3.27 Number of text messages sent in the UK
Source: Mobile Data Association

QR Codes show England fans the way

QR Codes (from the name Quick Response Codes) are a development of barcode technology (**www.denso-wave.com/qrcode/index-e.html**). They encode data in two dimensions, unlike barcode that uses one, which enable them to contain far more data than a comparably sized barcode. At first, QR Codes had applications in industry where they were used to track component parts but are now found in almost any application where data needs to be transferred.

QR Codes may typically be read by a suitable mobile phone. As well as containing information, the QR Code may be a hyperlink that automatically directs the user's phone to a place on the World Wide Web: such a link between the physical world and the virtual world is termed a hardlink.

In 2008, the England Football Squad's shirts were fitted with QR Codes embedded in a label. Reading the code redirects you to a WAP site that provides additional content about the England Team (England, 2008).

Questions

1 What other novel applications of QR Codes could be developed?

2 Answers are limited only by the scope of imagination of the reader!

Interactive digital TV

It could be argued that interactive digital television (iDTV) is another form of wireless Internet access, although it does not use Internet-related technologies. In Europe, total digital TV penetration was expected to double from 30 per cent in 2003 to 60 per cent in 2008. Access to information on iDTV is limited in comparison with the Internet, partly because of limitations imposed by the bandwidth and the cost of publishing on a provider such as Sky. It is often referred to as a 'walled garden' arrangement. As a result, the main information providers are large retailers and banks. The government and the BBC also provide information through this channel since many households do not have Internet access, but do have iDTV. The limited range of information publishers on iDTV is in contrast to the World Wide Web which is low-cost and uses open, non-proprietary standards.

To conclude this chapter, Case study 3.3 summarizes how one company has adopted Internet standards.

Online sales soar at easyJet

This article summarizes how easyJet has exploited the Internet standards introduced in this chapter. It starts by illustrating the historical development in the use of the Internet by easyJet. It then considers different success factors. The questions are posed to the person responsible for web technologies at easyJet, Simon Pritchard.

Very few bricks and mortar companies can claim to have had a more successful e-commerce strategy than easyJet. With around 90 per cent of sales generated from its Web site, the Internet has helped easyJet make the transition from an upstart airline to Europe's leading low-cost carrier.

The European 'open skies' agreement of 1987 paved the way for easyJet's existence. This ten-year period of deregulation meant that from 1997 any airline could operate on any route within the European Union. Routes that had previously been the high-profit preserve of national flag-carrying airlines were opened up to competition from smaller, more agile and efficient airlines.

In 1995, easyJet began corporate life with two leased planes flying from Luton Airport [near London] to Glasgow and Edinburgh. The no-frills service and cost-conscious business model enabled easyJet to advertise its flights 'as affordable as a pair of jeans – £29 one way'. The company's enigmatic founder Stelios Haji-Ioannou ensured that the new business received plenty of publicity, including television documentaries on the company and numerous high-profile protests against companies whose policies meant greater costs for easyJet's customers.

1998 was a landmark year in terms of easyJet's Internet strategy. The company opened its doors to e-commerce, notching its first online seat sale in April of that year. Just 18 months later, the company sold its millionth seat online. The rate of online sales continued to increase, with the two million mark passed just five months later, and the three million mark a mere three months on from that.

In 2001 the company reported that 89.2% of its total ticket sales now took place online compared to 64.3% one year earlier. This has been aided by not advertising its call centre phone number and providing discounts for booking online (**www.theregister.co.uk/2001/05/09/easyjet_pushes_90_of_ticket/**).

EasyJet completed a merger with Go, the low-cost airline established by British Airways, in 2002. In the 12 months to June 2002, the combined airlines carried almost 14 million passengers, had a fleet of approximately 65 Boeing 737 aircraft, and had a turnover of almost £600 million (based on the most recent full year financial reports of each company).

In 2004 easyJet expanded its capabilities allowing customers to change flights or flight details online. While this was possible at call centres beforehand, moving the facility online has given it a cost and flexibility advantage over its nearest competitors that provide similar services (**http://management.silicon.com/itdirector/0,39024673,39118984,00.htm**).

In the same year it expected to see £750,000 savings from an investment of £300,000 in Customer Relationship Management software (**http://software.silicon.com/applications/0,39024653,39126581,00.htm**).

In 2007 the company improved its internal IT support services by outsourcing the Helpdesk. It was deemed essential to provide 24/7 IT support but that couldn't be achieved with their relatively small IT department (**www.silicon.com/retailandleisure/0,3800011842,39169462,00.htm**).

It also began providing a personalised flight information and booking system using 'Gadget' technology that is built into Windows Vista operating system (**http://software.silicon.com/os/0,39024651,39165546,00.htm**).

Simon Pritchard is the Web manager at easyJet, making it his responsibility to oversee the performance, usability and development of the easyJet.com Web site. A graduate of Natural Sciences at Cambridge University who spent his third year studying experimental psychology, Simon has an acute awareness of the need to understand how people think. This is strongly evident in the user experience of the easyJet site, which is straightforward

and successfully adopts the down-to-earth, common sense approach for which the company is known.

There has clearly been a decision to embrace the Internet within easyJet. How did that come about and how happy are you with that decision?

We are very happy with that decision. Around 90 per cent of all our sales are made on the Internet – it's been a very big success, it's worked very well for us. The move to the Web began before I joined the company, when every business was starting to wonder how the Internet could help it, and easyJet was no exception. Travel also looked, at least from an academic standpoint, to fit the bill quite well, particularly for a ticketless airline, in that fulfilment of the sale was no more complex than displaying a confirmation number on screen – no distribution or warehouse logistics to worry about after the sale had happened.

While easyJet was wondering what it could do with the Web, it was also enjoying a period of very rapid growth and was determined to keep costs low. The airline was based, as it still is, in easyLand in Luton Airport. The easyLand call centre was then taking 100 per cent of sales – we only sell direct to customers – and the growth of the airline was therefore bringing into question the need to re-locate to a larger facility or to establish a second call centre. There was this idea that if we could persuade our customers to book online, that would keep costs lower, leaving our call centre at pretty much its existing size, and enable us to grow the business through the Internet.

There were, of course, both advocates and sceptics within the organisation at the time. So in April 1997 a brochureware site appeared at easyJet.com, with just a few details about the airline and details of a telephone booking line. The phone number was unique to the Web site. A lot of calls started coming in on this special number, and that convinced the sceptics that this Internet thing really did have something to offer. We set about working with the then supplier of our reservations system to deliver online sales, and it's been up, up and away ever since.

To have 90 per cent of sales generated from the Internet channel is incredible, particularly for a business that was formed before e-commerce really took hold.

Obviously the fact that we're direct sell only means we are in total control of our sales channels, which probably made it easier than it has been for others to drive that figure upwards. It has still been hard work, though. We've used both carrot and stick to push our Internet sales percentage way above the Internet penetration in our markets. The carrots have been in the guise of discounts when booking online, and in making very attractive inventory available exclusively via the Web site – we were the first airline to offer Internet-only promotions. The stick has been to restrict the flights available to customers on the phone. Our 'one month rolling window', as we call it, means that if you want to book a flight more than a month in advance of travel you can only do that online. Because easyJet has a very simple pricing structure – fares are generally cheaper the earlier you book – this is a great incentive to book on the Internet.

So has a desire to make the most of the Internet changed the business model?

I wouldn't say it's changed the business model – it fits in very well with the model, and the low-cost imperative. Ultimately, selling online is much cheaper than it would be with every sale going through the call centre. And one of our sales tools – generating huge sales peaks through highly publicised promotions – really needs the Web to be effective. One of the promotions we did with a national newspaper in the early days jammed a local telephone exchange because of the number of calls that came in. A scalable Web site is much better able to cope, and is more cost-effective, than a manned call centre.

What special considerations for the airline industry need to be taken into account? Did any of them present particular challenges for easyJet, in driving so many sales online?

Possibly the biggest challenge is that often a great deal of time passes between booking online and turning up at the airport. Beyond what the site needs to communicate about the sale – fares, taxes, destination information – there is an awful lot to get across that relates to us being ticketless, what travel documents are required, when we recommend checking in, when check-in closes, and what items may or may not be carried in baggage. Over the phone, communication is always serial – the call centre agent covers each item one after the other, with an opportunity to assess whether the customer has heard and understood. Online, each point on a page is presented together at once in parallel, each competing with the other for the customer's attention. Short of adding a compulsory checkbox next to each item, it's proved to be a bit of an art to fine-tune the bits of the site we see most people taking most notice of or printing off. Although we are ticketless, people seem to want to have something with them – an aide-mémoire of where they are flying and when. We've taken a lot of time to condense and clarify on the confirmation page and email the key nuggets of information that are that bridge between the point of sale and the delivery of the service at the airport.

We liaise closely with our operational colleagues at the airport. One of the most common problems we were experiencing was passengers booking online for the wrong day. To offer customers a reasonable choice of flights and fares on routes which, when we started, we flew just once or twice a day, we would display, say, flights for the 1st, 2nd and 3rd day of the month when they had requested the 2nd. That isn't always what people are expecting, so some customers would assume all flights were for the 2nd, not noticing they were booking for the 1st. Among a range of tweaks to prevent such confusion, the easiest and perhaps most effective was to ensure that at every point in the booking process dates were presented with both the month and day of the week spelt in full. People are far more certain about the day of the week they want to travel than they are about the date. Coders tend to roll their eyes – 'a date's a date, what does it matter?' – but these small things have made quite a difference.

That brings us onto the general design goals of the Web site. Can you tell me what you wanted to achieve from the user experience when designing the site?

Branding is important, particularly with easyJet, and the colour orange is a very important part of that, whether the Web designer in me likes it or not. You need customers to arrive at the site comfortable that they've got the right web address – that the easyJet in the newspaper ad is the easyJet.com in front of them. 'High design' has never been a priority, as it seems to have been with some other companies – flash animations, glossy feel-good graphics, all that stuff are not what easyJet is about. easyJet.com is our primary sales channel and an important communications channel, and the design had to focus on these functions. We needed as broad as possible a browser base supported – exclude no-one from buying, where possible. We needed simplicity and speed. There has been a lot of focus on usability.

A key illustration of this focus, and a move copied by rivals since, relates to the first step of the booking process. Initially, the point at which you start selecting your route and get on with checking flights and fares was three clicks deep into the site. We said 'hang on a minute – this site's about selling, let's make sure the first page people see allows them to get on with buying'. Now the home page is also the first step of the booking process. There's no confusion in the mind of the user: the route selector is there, up front, almost spelling out 'start here'.

We've also insisted there are no barriers at all to checking flight times, availability and prices. No log-ins, no registration, nothing that might put people off enquiring – fares and availability are a click away, and fast. If you just want to know times and not prices, go to the booking engine; if you want to know prices, go to the booking engine. All roads lead to a no-commitment, barrier-free availability and fare request, from which customers are already halfway into buying.

Do you think now we are seeing more of a trend towards simplicity now that people actually do significant business via the Internet?

I think we're seeing an 'anti-trend' trend. People are looking round and seeing the businesses that have been successful online, and perhaps looking at some of the more spectacular failures, and drawing a few conclusions. One of those, I think, is don't follow fads – keep it simple. There's definitely a place for high design on the Web, but e-commerce is probably not where it's at. Focused strategy, careful adaptation of best practice to the specific business needs, simplicity and usability is winning through. We've kept very focused on doing what we do, keeping it simple, and not making a song and dance about it.

At one point, the fad was 'stickiness'. Web sites, apparently, had to be sticky. [Visitor duration on a sticky site is higher than a non-sticky site.] We had many debates about stickiness within easyJet. In the end, we kept the focus on a non-stick site. The faster it was, the more efficient the service to customers. Provide compelling content for those who are in the mood to browse, sure, but in general people don't want to chew up time booking their flights; they want to spend their time in Athens, Madrid, Barcelona, Amsterdam.

Are there any other key success factors?

Part of persuading people to book online is convincing them it's secure. Being a young, ticketless airline encourages the perception that we're a technically savvy company, one you can trust online. The tremendous offline brand – with easyJet regularly acting as consumer champion – has been very important in instilling confidence in customers when they are online. And once you start being seen as a successful e-tailer and pass milestones like a million seats sold online, more people are happy to take the plunge.

What about the technical issues related to security?

Safety is paramount in operating aeroplanes, and security is paramount in running an e-commerce platform. It's also important to communicate the fact to consumers. The Internet application that we started with, and the Internet application we use now, is totally integrated into the core sales system. Customer data has never been stored on the Web platform itself.

In protecting data between the Web site and the customer's computer, we continue to follow best practice – now 128-bit SSL encryption.

What challenges did the merger with Go present to you from an IT perspective? Initially the two Web sites and brands ran independently but presumably that wasn't the long term plan?

No, we decided to move to a single Web site and a single brand – easyJet. Early on, easyJet.com offered both airlines' routes on its home page, transferring the booking process over to go-fly.com when a Go route was selected. We developed full support for Go sales in the existing easyJet system, which would make easyJet.com the primary sales channel for Europe's number one low-cost airline – clearly a big milestone presenting a range of challenges.

The biggest issue was volume: taking the sales traffic of two significant European airlines and directing it through a single channel clearly led to a big jump in the transaction volume the easyJet system had to handle.

A great deal of stress testing and capacity planning went on to ensure we were ready for the volume. We knew we had a scalable architecture, and we had put that architecture to the test shortly before, with high-profile TV-advertised promotions that had run with few, if any, technical hitches. Our own internal testing loaded the system many multiples higher even than these peaks, and the results looked positive for our ability to handle the combined demands of the new airline.

We were also busy working on intranet projects – discussion forums, feedback forms, and a special news section devoted to the merger, for example. These enabled employees of the two airlines to 'meet' (virtually), to keep up to date, and let senior managers know how staff felt about what was going on.

Are you satisfied that Microsoft's platform is growing with you, is able to handle scalability issues?

Yes, absolutely. Maybe three or four years ago, if we were doing what we are doing now with Microsoft technologies, we might be thinking differently. When it was suggested we base our new system on Microsoft technologies, we weren't short of people saying 'it can't be done'. But a proof-of-concept system showed it could be, and the doubters started to fall silent. Now, as the technology improves, we are getting more and more out of the current system in our stress tests. Scalability is what we needed, and it looks as though it's going to scale very well.

What was the rationale for basing your online operations on the Windows platform?

We, as a company, have adopted a principle of using Microsoft core technologies whenever possible. That is primarily because of affordability, ease of use, and focusing resources on a single skill set. We are now in the happy situation of using Microsoft technologies at all stages of the booking process, from Web site through middleware to the core reservation database. We use XML extensively throughout the booking process, and that's been very successful.

Reference to XML leads us on to the possibility of talking about Web services. Can you tell me about future initiatives that you have planned and how you could envisage using Internet technology on an ongoing basis?

XML certainly has been one of the big technology focuses for easyJet over the past years and we've developed many of our internal systems to embrace XML. Web services are obviously a very interesting evolution, and a number of projects have been pencilled in that might involve them. But we are not generally early adopters – that can be costly. We tend to sit back, play with the technology a little, and see how it is being used. We're at that stage with .NET, I suppose. .NET has great support for Web services, and I can see other benefits – particularly in the advanced caching features now available to Web applications. So we've done plenty of prodding and poking around with .NET, but the current focus is the merger.

Presumably having a basis on XML makes life a little easier there as well with ease of interoperability.

Absolutely. Having a suite of standards-based applications will undoubtedly reduce the complexity of future development. Building enhancements should be so much simpler.

Source: Reachlive (2002) interview with Simon Pritchard of easyJet. Published online at www.reachlive.net/interviews/Q4-02/SimonrPritchard.htm

Questions

1 Assess the reasons why easyJet has been able to achieve over 90 per cent of its sales over the Internet.

2 What approaches were used in the creation of easyJet's online presence which were significant in its success?

Summary

1 The technology infrastructure of an organization is made up of the hardware, software, content and data used to deliver information services to employees, customers and partners.

2 A client/server architecture is commonly used as part of the infrastructure with networks of client computers such as PCs or Macintoshes connected to one or more server machines that provide additional resources such as applications, data storage or printers.

3 The main components of an individual computer are microprocessors, memory, permanent storage, screen and printer output devices, and mouse and keyboard input devices.

4 Computer networks are defined according to their scale (local area or wide area), the telecommunications channels (guided and unguided or wireless media) and the components such as modem, hubs and routers.

5 The World Wide Web is the primary method of information publication and service delivery on the Internet. Standards such as HTML are used for presentation of data and documents and XML is widely used for exchange of data.

6 Wireless technologies for accessing the Internet such as Wi-Fi and 3G are increasing in importance.

Exercises

Self-assessment questions

1 Explain the different components of the technology infrastructure of an organization with reference to your place of study.

2 Produce a table summarizing the main components of a basic PC, giving a short description and a typical specification for each component.

3 Distinguish between memory and storage. Which alternative options are available for memory and storage?

4 What are the main alternative output devices for a PC? Explain the options and the criteria on which the best device can be based.

5 Which Internet standards are involved when a web page is requested by a client and served from a server?

6 What are the benefits and disadvantages of client/server systems?

7 Explain the differences between HTML and XML. What are their relevance to managers?

8 Describe two alternatives approaches for wireless access to the Internet.

Essay and discussion questions

1 You are advising a small start-up company that specializes in web design on the hardware infrastructure they will require. The company will have a director, one business development manager, a head designer and four designers. Define a suitable technology infrastructure for this organization, explaining the purpose of the components and estimating their cost.

2 You have been asked to produce a report on the relevance of XML to an organization that already uses EDI for ordering raw materials from its suppliers. You should define XML, explain its advantages and disadvantages for procurement in comparison with EDI and outline specific problems with its implementation.

3 You work for an IT industry analyst. Your next assignment is the production of a report on the future adoption of public Wi-Fi networking over the next five years. Produce a structure for your report and then use existing online data sources to fill in the details of your report.

4 When launched in Europe, 3G technologies often fell behind adoption forecasts. Explain the reasons for this phenomenon and assess the future prospects for the technology over the next three years.

5 Explain the concept of the 'semantic web'. What is its future relevance to businesses?

6 Explore the concept of device convergence and its implications for an ecommerce manager of an airline or retailer.

References

BBC (2003a) Mobile bosses cautious over 3G. Jane Wakefield, *BBC News*, 24 February. Available online at: http://news.bbc.co.uk/i/hi/technology/2787787.stm.

BBC (2003b) Huge computing power goes online. *BBC News*. Available online at: http://news.bbc.co.uk/2/hi/technology/3152724.stm.

BBC (2008) Storm warning for cloud computing. Bill Thompson, BBC News, 27 May. Available online at http://news.bbc.co.uk/1/hi/technology/7421099.stm.

Berners-Lee, T. (1989) Information management: A proposal, CERN March 1989, May 1990. Internal CERN document published at: www.w3.org/History/1989/proposal.html.

Berners-Lee, T. (1999) *Weaving the Web. The Past, Present and Future of the World Wide Web by its Inventor*. Orion, London.

Berners-Lee, T., Hendler, J. and Lassila, O. (2001) The semantic web. *Scientific American*, 17 May. Published online at: www.sciam.com.

BOINC (2008) Choosing BOINCprojects. Available online at: http://boinc.berkeley.edu/projects.php.

Chaffey, D. (2004) *E-Business and E-Commerce Management*, 2nd edn. Financial Times Prentice Hall, Harlow.

DTI (2003) *Business in the Information Age – International Benchmarking Study 2002*. UK Department of Trade and Industry. Available online at: www.ukonlineforbusiness.gov.uk/benchmarking2002.

EDI Basics (2010) http://www.edibasics.co.uk/blog/2010/08/who-has-the-largest-b2b-integration-network/

England (2008) Interact with new England kit. Available online at: http://news.sky.com/skynews/home/sky-news-archive/article/20082851308970.

Hitachi (2008) Hitachi global storage technologies. Available online at: www.hitachigst.com/hdd/technolo/overview/chart18.html.

McIntosh, N. (2003) Will Wi-Fi fly? *Guardian*, Thursday 14 August. www.guardian.co.uk/online/story/0,3605,1017664,00.html.

IDC (1999) *Reinventing EDI: electronic data interchange services market review and forecast, 1998–2003*. International Data Corporation, Framlington, MA.

IDC (2002) Online travel services set to boost mobile commerce. IDC Research Press release, 23 January. www.idc.com.

Infoworld (2008) What cloud computing really means. Galen Gruman, 7 April. Available online at http://www.infoworld.com/article/08/04/07/15FE-cloud-computing-reality_1.html.

Kampas, P. (2000) Road map to the e-revolution. *Information Systems Management Journal*, Spring, 8–22.

Leiner, B., Cerf, V., Clark, D., Kahn, R., Kleinrock, L., Lynch, D., Postel, J., Roberts, J. and Wolff, S. (2000) *A Brief History of the Internet*. The Internet Society. www.isoc.org/internet-history/brief.html. Continuously updated document.

Lyman, P. and Varian, H. (2003) How much information? – online research summary. Available online at: www.sims.berkeley.edu/research/projects/how-much-info-2003/.

MDA (2003) Mobile Data Association Professional Text Messaging Report 2003. Available online at www.text.it.

MobileCommerceWorld (2001) i-Mode users spending more on content. 26 November. Press release based on data from Infocom. www.mobilecommerceworld.com.

MobileCommerceWorld (2002) British SMS records smashed in December. 24 January. Press release based on data from the Mobile Data Association. www.mobilecommerce-world.com.

Patterson, D. A., Gibson, G. and Katz, R. H. (1988) A case for redundant arrays of inexpensive disks (RAID). *Proceedings of the 1988 ACM SIGMOD International Conference on Management of Data*, pp. 109–116, June, US.

Poincaré, H. (1906) *Wissenschaft und Hypothese*. Teubner, Leipzig.

RNIB (2008) Access Technology. Available online at: www.rnib.org.uk/xpedio/groups/public/documents/publicwebsite/public_rnib002927.hcsp.

RNID (2008) Products and equipment for deaf and hard of hearing people. Available online at: www.rnid.org.uk/information_resources/productsandequipment/.

SETI (2008) Projects: SETI@Home. Available online at: www.planetary.org/programs/projects/setiathome_20080115.html.

Simon, H. A. (1955) On a class of skew distribution functions. *Biometrika*, 42, 425–40.

Telegraph (2008) 'The Grid' will see 80,000 computer network processing data from LHC. Available online at: http://news.bbc.co.uk/2/hi/technology/3152724.stm.

Von Bertalanffy, L. (1976) *General Systems Theory: Foundations, Development, Applications*. George Braziller, NY. [Final revised edition.]

Wei Choo, C. (2000) Closing the cognitive gaps: How people process information. In D. Marchand, T. Davenport and T. Dickson (eds), *Mastering Information Management*. Financial Times Prentice Hall, Harlow, pp. 245–53.

Wei Choo, C. (2001) Environmental scanning as information seeking and organizational learning. *Information Research*, 7(1). Available online at: http://InformationR.net/ ir/7-1/paper112.html.

Wei Choo, C., Deltor, D. and Turnbull, D. (2000) Information seeking on the web: An integrated model of browsing and searching. First Monday. Peer reviewed articles on the Internet, 5(2), Feburary. See http://131.193.153.231/www/issues/issue5_2/choo/index.html.

White, G. R. T., Gardiner, G., Prabhakar, G. P., and Abd Razak, A. (2007) A comparison of barcoding and RFID technologies in practice. *Journal of Information, Information Technology and Organizations*, 2, 119 – 32.

Further reading

Berners-Lee, T. (1999) *Weaving the Web. The Past, Present and Future of the World Wide Web by its Inventor*. Orion, London. A readable description of how the concept of the World Wide Web was developed, by its creator, giving his views on its future development.

visit the www

Weblinks

Acronym Finder (www.acronymfinder.com) The web's most comprehensive database of acronyms, abbreviations, and initialisms. 318,000+ definitions! Even contains an entry for 'TLA' – the Three Letter Acronym beloved of technology vendors.

EDI Basics (2010) http://www.edibasics.co.uk/blog/2010/08/who-has-the-largest-b2b-integration-network/

Free Online Dictionary of Computing (http://foldoc.doc.ic.ac.uk) A free resource hosted at Imperial College UK containing 14,000 terms.

How Stuff Works (http://computer.howstuffworks.com) The computer channel of How Stuff Works explains how different hardware components work in detail.

Internet.com (www.internet.com) A portal providing a wealth of information on Internet Standards via related sites.

Whatis.com (www.whatis.com) A reference source giving definitions and links to further information for every conceivable term related to information technology.

World Wide Web Consortium (www.w3.org) Standards setting body for HTML, XML, etc.

For multiple-choice questions and annotated weblinks relating to this chapter visit this book's website at: **www.pearsoned.co.uk/chaffey**

Part 2
STRATEGY

In Part 2 we explore different strategic approaches organizations use to manage information. Information mangement strategies are reviewed from three different perspectives: information management strategy (Chapter 4); knowledge management strategy (Chapter 5) and information systems strategy (Chapter 6).

4

Information management strategy

Objective

To describe the key elements of an information management strategy.

Learning outcomes

After reading this chapter, you will be able to:

● Justify the need for a defined information management strategy.

● Relate information management strategy to other organizational strategies.

● Describe the management issues that need to be addressed in an information management strategy.

Management issues

Typical questions facing managers related to this topic:

● Do we need an information management strategy?

● How does the information management strategy relate to IT/IS and knowledge management strategies?

● How should we structure and resource information management?

● Which management controls should be built into an information strategy?

Links to other chapters

The main related chapters are:

➤ *Chapter 1* introduces information management concepts such as the information transformation process and information lifecycle.

➤ *Chapter 4* places information management strategy within the context of IS strategy.

➤ *Chapter 6* details the development of a knowledge management strategy.

➤ *Chapter 8* explains the analysis and design involved with developing an information architecture.

➤ *Chapter 10* describes approaches for improving information quality.

➤ *Chapter 12* describes legal compliance issues for information management.

Introduction

Information management strategy is one of a series of strategies that organizations develop and implement to sustain or improve their position in their markets. These strategies include organizational or corporate strategy, marketing strategy and operations management strategy. To best understand the nature and purpose of information strategy, it is helpful to consider it in the context of the organizational strategy it should support.

Organizational strategy defines the future direction and actions of an organization or part of an organization. For example, Johnson and Scholes (2001) define organizational or corporate strategy as:

> *the direction and scope of an organization over the long-term: which achieves advantage for the organization through its configuration of resources within a changing environment to meet the needs of markets and to fulfil stakeholder expectations.*

This definition highlights these elements of strategy:

1 Strategies define the future direction of an organization.

2 Strategies are devised to achieve advantage for the organization (strategic objectives).

3 Strategies define the allocation of resources to achieve this advantage.

4 Strategies are primarily driven by the needs of the organization, but also by the needs of stakeholders such as shareholders, customers, suppliers or employees.

5 Strategies should be responsive to the dynamic environment in which an organization operates.

These elements of organizational strategy apply equally to other business strategies such as information management strategy, marketing strategy and operations management strategy which all support the organizational strategy. So an information management strategy must be aligned with the organizational objectives and involves defining how to manage information resources to support these objectives. We can define **information management strategy** as:

> *Definition of management approaches to the organization, control and application of organizational information resources through coordination of people and technology resources in order to support organizational strategy and processes.*

This definition shows that information management strategy treats the information assets of an organization as a resource which must be structured and controlled through managing people resources and technology resources. Managed together, the three resources of information, people and technology introduced in Chapter 1 must support organizational strategy.

In the first section of this chapter, we look in a little more detail at why an information strategy is needed – we see the types of problems that can occur if an effective strategy is not in place. The picture at the start of this chapter alludes to the lack of control on information. Information is often not managed as an important resource, but it is 'as free as the birds'. We then consider the relationship between an information management strategy and closely related strategies which are also commonly developed by organizations. These include knowledge management strategy, information systems or information technology strategy, and e-business strategy. This is a significant issue for today's organization since many organizations possess all of these strategies, while some only possess one or two. Yet all these strategies essentially involve the management and coordination of information, people and technology resources to support organizational strategy and improvement. In the main part of

Organizational strategy
Definition of the future direction and actions of an organization specified as approaches and allocation of resources to achieve specific objectives

Information management strategy
Definition of management approaches to the organization, control and application of organizational information resources through coordination of people and technology resources in order to support organizational strategy and processes

the chapter we explore different themes or issues that need to be addressed within an information strategy and consider some key approaches. Many of these approaches, such as the information audit and security, are covered in more detail later in the book, so these later sections are cross-referenced.

Why is an information management strategy needed?

It is said that the organizations that will be successful in the future will be those that recognize the importance of their knowledge assets. Furthermore, it will be those organizations that effectively manage those knowledge assets that will benefit from the competitive advantage that comes from being a 'knowledgeable firm'. After all,

'Knowledge is power'

Managing knowledge assets, however, is much more than the process of creating and implementing a corporate database to store existing wisdom, case histories or 'rules of thumb'.

In Chapter 1 we saw the relationship between data and information, now it is essential to understand in simple terms what knowledge is.

Data are the raw numbers or facts that an organization may possess about itself, its products, processes, services or competitors. Information is produced when those data are analysed. For example, if the numbers of customers entering a store is counted over a period of time, those data may be represented in graphical form such as a histogram. This histogram is a source of information and shows the rise and fall of demand much better than the long list of data.

Knowledge is having an understanding of the significance of that information (Kluge, Stein and Licht, 2001). For instance, the histogram may indicate that the number of customers entering the store rises sharply on Saturdays and Sundays. This may suggest that extra staff will be required on these days in order to cope with the increased business.

It is tempting to conclude that a corporate information strategy should therefore seek to increase its store of valuable knowledge by maximizing the amount of data that an organization possesses about itself and its operating environment, suppliers, customers and competitors etc.

This approach, however, gives rise to concerns over the logistics of data capture and storage.

Data and information needs – concerns about data quantity

Firstly, there are limits to the quantity of data that an organization can retain. Some organizational data can be captured or recorded with minimum effort. Transaction processing systems, for example, can capture and process vast amounts of customer-related data and this can be fed directly into corporate databases. Similarly, EDI systems, warehouse RFID and the gamut of inputs to MIS or ERP systems provide effective sources and means of data capture.

Other organizational data are not so easily captured, particularly for those organizations that do not have integrated corporate information systems. Supplier delivery performance, employee absenteeism, employee productivity, equipment uptime and customer feedback information may all have to be recorded and entered into corporate databases manually. This is not only slow and expensive but also introduces opportunities for errors to be made. These errors will affect the accuracy of any analysis that is performed and therefore reduce the value of any subsequent knowledge that is gained.

Secondly, the amount of data that can be captured about an organization and its environment is unfeasibly large. Every single operation, every employee, every product and every single key-press is an item of data that could be analysed. In order to reduce this complexity, organization could choose to limit their field of scope to those aspects of the business that are considered crucial to their operation. Supermarkets, for instance, could decide to focus on developing their knowledge of their customers.

The point at which those customers pay for their goods at the checkout would seem the most logical point at which to capture data. The existing TPS would presumably already be recording the amount of money spent, the time of purchase, and, if the customer possessed a store card or loyalty card, the system would capture some other customer demographic data. In order to maximize their knowledge of customers, though, the organization could capture data about many other factors:

- Did the customer use a trolley or a basket?
- What route did the customer follow around the store?
- Which products did they examine but not purchase?
- Did the customer walk, drive or use public transport to reach the store?
- Were there some products they could not find?
- Why did they choose to come to the store today?

Not only are some of these data very difficult to capture automatically, much of it would be extremely difficult, and annoying to the customer, to capture by person-to-person survey. As well as the practical difficulties involved in capturing these data there are practical limits to the amount of data that can be stored in an information system. Storing such an enormous quantity of data would require a correspondingly huge database.

While there is almost no limit to the number of storage devices that can be linked together to form a repository that could contain the data, there is a limit to the size and number of storage devices that an organization could afford to purchase.

For some organizations there may even be limits to the physical space that they could devote to data storage: it may be entertaining at this point to consider how much data a large supermarket could store about itself before the servers took up more space than the store! It is also important not to overlook the ongoing costs of equipment maintenance and data back-up which also increase as the volume of data capture and storage increases.

Casson and Wadeson (1996) highlight the importance of assessing the proximity of information with its intended end-user. They consider the 'economic distance' between information and users that should be minimized in order reduce the overall cost of information to the business. Organizations therefore need to balance the desire to capture more data in order to increase its knowledge assets, with the practical limitations of space, cost and complexity of capturing, storing and analysing those data.

Data and information needs – concerns over time, quality and cost

The practical problems of data and information capture and storage may be considered in terms of the three key measures of quality, cost and time.

The time taken to capture data may be a significant determinant of strategy. If it is likely that the time taken to capture the pertinent data is greater than the frequency at which the data change or are replaced then it is not logical to attempt to capture them. Also, if data can only be captured manually or require some degree of manual intervention before they are stored and analysed then it is likely that data quality compromised and any subsequent analysis flawed. This is a significant issue and poor information quality has even been said to threaten the very existence of an organization (Ballou, Madnick and Wang, 2003).

Perhaps the most difficult consideration to make is that of cost. While it is relatively simple to assess the cost of data capture and even the cost of the hardware to store those data it is much more difficult to justify how much of the easily captured data it is cost-effective to store.

We know that larger amounts of relevant data allow organizations to perform more meaningful analysis which can produce better understanding of the operating environment. Yet even if organizations focus upon the data that are easiest to capture and are most accurate and relevant there may still be a vast amount that can be captured. It is now a question of comparing the future value of those data with the cost of capturing and storing them. It is, however, almost impossible to predict what knowledge may be produced as a result of possessing a larger quantity of data. It is likely that a year's worth of customers' buying-habit data will be more useful than a week's worth, but it is unlikely that an organization could assess how much knowledge we would gain about our customers as a result. It is even less likely that we could predict how many extra sales or how much extra profit such knowledge would result, so that we could offset it against the cost of acquiring the extra data in the first place.

Organizations are therefore faced with the dilemma of recognizing that knowledge is valuable and that more data are required in order to become more knowledgeable. They are, however, unlikely to be able to predict the value of that knowledge in order to justify the expense of expanding and improving the information systems to capture the necessary data.

The information lifecycle

Information lifecycle
The sequence of activities involved in information management from creation through to permanent deletion of information

The active management of information as an organizational resource to achieve better business results involves management of the **information lifecycle**. The different elements of this lifecycle are shown in Figure 4.1. This shows that information management is a dynamic process that involves collection of information involved with business processes, organization of this information and its processing and maintenance. Management of information through its lifecycle is one of the aims of records management. All records have a lifecycle that can be characterized as creation; currency (actively referred to and updated); semi-currency (seldom referred to

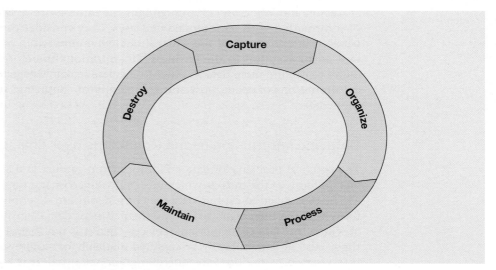

Figure 4.1 The information lifecycle

and typically placed in an archive); and finally disposal. Think of the e-mails you send and receive – these will all pass through such a lifecycle and you will have your own personal records management policy which decides how you process them through their lifecycle using your e-mail readers.

Maintenance of information involves reviewing the quality of information and updating it as appropriate. Maintenance may also include archiving information until it is no longer required. Eventually, most information is destroyed when there is no longer a need for it or there is a legal requirement to destroy it. The information policy described in Chapter 10 will set out procedures for managing the different phases of the information lifecycle.

As a further example of the information lifecycle, consider when a company acquires a new business customer via a sales representative visit. Collection of information will involve recording the customer's details; organization will involve assigning the customer to a particular group of customers, perhaps based on size or industry type; processing is analysis and dissemination of information about this customer, often relative to other customers; and maintenance involves ensuring that the customer details are up to date so they can be used to contact the customer, for marketing campaigns for example. Legal requirements may dictate that customer information be destroyed after a period of 5 or 10 years from the last sale.

The information lifecycle can also be viewed at a macro-level for all information within an organization to help develop appropriate strategies and implement approaches to collect, organize, process and maintain information. This approach is also described in Chapter 6.

To the traditional activities of the information lifecycle, Marchand et al. (2002) have added an additional activity, namely the sensing of information from the external environment. An important sensing activity is the collection of **competitive intelligence (CI)** (see Chapter 5). Through capturing and sensing this information, organizations are better placed to respond to external threats.

We saw in Chapters 2 and 3 that technology solutions for information lifecycle management are available from vendors to support the management of data as they change through time.

Competitive intelligence (CI)
A process that transforms disaggregated information into relevant, accurate and usable strategic knowledge about competitors, position, performance, capabilities and intentions

Records management
The process of managing the creation and maintenance of and access to documents and records about individuals and events related to an organization through the information lifecycle

Record
A document or an instance of an entity within a business

Records management

Records management is a term used by information management specialists to refer to the activities involved in managing structured, formal information. It refers to the process of managing records from creation through access, modification, archiving and deletion as referred to in the above section on the information lifecycle. Traditionally, the type of information referred to as a **record** is information in forms such as books, documents, photographs and microfilm. In the digital age, records include e-mails, digital images and voice-mail. Computerized records of different entities within an organization such as customers, employees and products can also be considered to be an aspect of records management. Owing to division of responsibilities within an organization the records management function is often limited to management of documents within the organization. However, the British Standards Institute (BSI, 2001) uses a broad definition – it defines records as

information created, received, and maintained as evidence and information by an organization or person, in pursuance of legal obligations or in the transaction of business

and records management as the

field of management responsible for the efficient and systematic control of the creation, receipt, maintenance, use and disposition of records, including processes for capturing and maintaining evidence of and information about business activities and transactions in the form of records.

These definitions highlight the importance of records management in legal compliance. For example, records management is important to legal issues such as the freedom of information and data protection laws described in Chapter 12. Records management is also of value since it can reduce costs through:

- better use of physical storage space and computer server resources within an organization;
- better use of staff time since information is easier to access;
- improvement of control and security of value information resources.

Formal strategies

Many organizations do not have an information management strategy or they will already have an information systems strategy which may refer to information management, so we have to ask the question 'Why is an information management strategy necessary?' One way of answering this question is to look at the problems organizations experience when there are difficulties in managing this resource. An obvious problem is protecting information from malicious or accidental events which destroy or corrupt the data.

Data quality, as already mentioned, is a further issue. A global survey from PricewaterhouseCoopers (2001) showed significant problems with data quality. Over three-quarters of 600 large organizations surveyed admitted to experiencing problems as a result of data quality and, as Figure 4.2 shows, many of these problems affect their ability to win business or deliver adequate services to their customers. Note that this survey refers to data quality, but this is only a subset of information quality issues as discussed in Chapter 10.

Perhaps the level of problems experienced by respondents is unsurprising since 60 per cent of respondents claimed not to have a formally documented board-approved strategy on data management and data quality.

There are also positive reasons for developing an information management strategy. In Chapter 1 we saw how information is essential to operating, controlling and improving individual organizational processes (see Figure 1.1) and so the performance

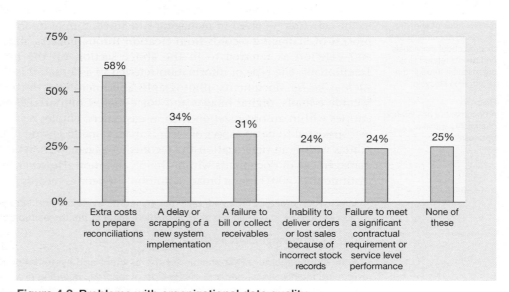

Figure 4.2 Problems with organizational data quality
Source: PricewaterhouseCoopers (2001)

of the whole business through business performance management (BPM) systems. We also saw how information can add value, reduce costs and create competitive advantage (see Figure 1.3). Many of the respondents to the PricewaterhouseCoopers survey pointed out that the value of information technology lies in its capacity to facilitate information delivery at all levels of an organization. This information can deliver competitive advantage by giving superior insights about an organization's markets through intelligence on customers and competitors and information on how to improve the performance of internal processes. This is arguably the most important reason for developing a sound information management strategy.

A further insight into the reasons for introducing an information management strategy are suggested by Liz Orna, of the Association for Information Management. Orna (1999) suggests that the following are the main benefits from having a defined information management strategy based on development of an information audit and creation of an information policy:

- It becomes possible to integrate all information activities, and to use all information quickly and effectively to make efficient business decisions.
- Promotes openness of communications throughout the company, both between and within levels.
- Will foster a culture of innovation and knowledge sharing.
- Forms a sound strategy for investment in information systems and technology.
- Ensures that awareness of opportunities and threats is communicated throughout the company, and allows timely responses to these.

There may even be occasions when an existing information system is no longer available to service the needs of an organization. Specific parts or divisions of an organization may be sold off and may need to develop their own stand-alone systems. This happened to Birds Eye Iglo Group (BEIG) when they were bought by Permira (Computing, 2008a). Finding themselves without the support of their previous owner's information systems, they had limited time in which to develop and implement their own systems.

The importance of a structured approach to information management based on a sound information management strategy is suggested by Mini case study 4.1 'Consequences of poor information management strategy'. It will be shown in this chapter that such errors are not solely due to failure with information systems strategy and execution at project level, but are also a result of insufficient attention to information management strategy.

A further information management problem, not referred to in the mini case study, is the expense of searching for external information such as market and competitive intelligence on which to base business decisions. Productivity of employees can be reduced dramatically if employees searching for information are unable to access the information they are looking for. For organizations where a high proportion of

Mini case study 4.1   Consequences of poor information management strategy

Mini case 1 – the utility company

Utility companies are fighting tooth and claw to gain and retain customers. One utility company estimated that it lost an average of 30 customers per day or more than 10,000 customers per year, because staff did not have access to the right information to handle customer queries. This was equivalent to $5.5 million in lost revenue.

Mini case 2 – the bank

Inconsistent information and structures between different systems often means that the same data have to be entered into more than one system. A study at a UK bank estimated that duplication of effort totalled more than $3.2 million per year.

Mini case 3 – the insurance company

An insurance company spent $67 million developing a replacement information system. After acquisition of another company, they found it would cost nearly the same amount to adapt the system to their new requirements. If the previous system had had an adaptive information architecture this effort and cost would have been avoided.

Mini case 4 – the insurance organization

An insurance organization at the forefront of adopting the latest technologies did not stop to examine its relevance to executives, staff or customers, making the assumption that the latest technology solutions must be relevant and useful. Information-related projects included database marketing, customer data analysis, mobile data services, customer relationship management, business retention, data mining and e-business solutions. Using a checklist of information categories with managers from fourteen business areas identified the types of information that were really important. When these were mapped to recent technology projects they showed little significant impact on critical information. The technology projects created some new information that was not useful at all, improved the usefulness of information that was not particularly relevant and even took away information that had previously been useful! Using defined information categories before would have prevented wasted cost and effort.

Source: Evernden and Evernden (2003)

employees rely on information such as professional services, overall productivity losses are potentially greater. For example a Butler Group (2006) report found that employees performing ineffective searches and wasting time looking for information can cost companies up to 10 per cent in salary expenses. Richard Edwards, senior research analyst who completed the research commented: 'Over 50 per cent of staff costs are now allocated to employees performing so-called information work. The typical information worker can now spends up to one-quarter of his or her day searching for the right information to complete a given task'.

These problems with information management imply that management control of information is lacking and this, in turn, is indicative of insufficient attention to information management strategy and policy.

In a later section of this chapter we will look in more detail at approaches to developing and implementing a coherent information strategy. Case study 4.1 will give you a flavour of the issues that an information management strategy will seek to address. Read Case study 4.1 to understand some of the main reasons why managing corporate information is a significant issue for organizations.

Case study 4.1

Ten commandments for information management

This case highlights the key issues in managing data and shows why organizations should view this as a strategic rather than a tactical issue. The insights are from four business people who are closely involved with information management. Note that the extract refers to data quality and management, but it should strictly refer to information quality and management.

Dealing with data is a time-consuming exercise. The need to respond to spam and viruses, or to comply with legislation, can give the impression that data are the enemy.

So turning data into extractable value to reduce time and costs requires a new way of thinking and working.

Companies that do not consider data quality are wasting time and huge amounts of money. *Computing* brought together a panel of experts to offer 10 tips for making a data quality project work:

Christine Craven, head of retail information at Abbey (formerly Abbey National bank; now Santander)
Tony Rodriguez, chief executive of Avellino software
Tom Scampion of Trillium Software
Nigel Turner, manager of data quality consulting at BT Exact.

1 Prepare for cultural change

Data management is not a quick-fix technology issue. It is a process; a way of thinking that will be a big challenge to many organizations.

'It's a significant lifestyle change, warns Christine Craven. Abbey saved £15.2m using a data profiling and analysis product, Avellino Discovery, in conjunction with its data warehouse.

'The response of the IT department to business-critical issues was to offer solutions that were very local, and would have been fine short-term, but would not have satisfied the needs of the business', she says.

'We then put the systems areas together with some high-up business people, and came up with a totally different solution which not only satisfied the business-critical issues, but moved information into a central store that was then available to the rest of the organization.

'That was a mindset change for IT because they were losing control.'

2 Define what you mean by data quality

Concentration on the quality of data is not an exact science. Quality is defined only by business requirements.

'No company can get 100 per cent control over data quality. That's an impossible aim', says Nigel Turner.

'We don't own all of it and we all have lots of legacies in our companies and more and more partners. Data quality is never an end-in-itself goal.'

The starting point for action has to be working out how much valuable data you hold and how you intend to use it, he suggests.

'If you built a library but forgot to create an index, people would consider that pretty crazy.'

3 Think strategy, not tactics

Our thinking about data tends to be based on tactical responses to problems. But value can only be derived from a more strategic approach, says the panel. That means understanding what you have.

'The problem is that we don't look at data management in the same way we capacity plan our hardware, network infrastructure or anything else we do in IT', says Tony Rodriguez.

'If you can manage your data using the right technologies, you can build a picture. You can find areas to start an initiative where you weren't even thinking of one.'

4 Ensure clear leadership and ownership

Craven is convinced that the key to Abbey's success is leadership.

'We have top-down support: the owner of information is a businessman, the chief operating officer, who is the number two in the company', she says.

The muscle of the highest levels of management ensures that data that do not conform to the rules are outlawed, she adds.

5 Do not allow silo thinking. Centralize policies

Most companies have little or no central vision for data management. But a centralized policy is crucial, according to the panel.

'One of the first things we did at BT was to decide on a best-of-breed toolset', says Turner.

'We then gathered together all the people in the company with knowledge and experience of that toolset into one unit. IT departments could not do their own thing and invent their own local solutions.'

6 Educate staff, or at least ensure that everyone knows their role

'The ownership of data quality is everyone's duty', says Turner.

'You have to make everyone feel responsible in some way, from the person who inputs the data at the front end right the way through to the IT systems.'

Abbey National quickly understood that data quality was a people issue.

7 Focus on business need

There is an interesting parallel with data warehousing six or seven years ago, says Rodriguez.

'The successful ones were the ones sponsored by the business. The ones that failed were those from the IT side.'

8 Learn from others and mistakes

When it started to get serious about data quality programmes, BT looked outside its own boundaries to see what other companies were doing.

'We find that those most interested are those who have had the pain of failing before', says Rodriguez. 'They are open to the idea of not wanting to fail again.'

9 Create metrics so that the value of the projects are clear

'Good data is not an objective truth', warns Tom Scampion.

'You cannot have any other metrics than fitness for purpose. Good data just supports the business.'

10 Remember the customer

Accurate information is a huge issue for customer confidence.

'The ability to recognize customers, however they communicate with you, is useful in the positive side of upselling and cross-selling – just keeping them as a customer', says Scampion.

'But it's also useful in identifying who you don't want to be using your product.'

Source: The 10 commandments for handling data, *Computing*, 1 October 2003

Questions

1 Review the ten commandments for handling information management. For each commandment devise a single sentence which would explain to a business manager why information management is important.

2 Are there any additional commandments you would use, based on your experience or understanding of information management literature?

3 In groups, agree a priority order for the ten commandments in order of strategic importance.

4 These commandments imply a need for a separate information management strategy or policy. From your experience of working in organizations or your understanding of IS strategy, do you think these issues could be managed through other organizational strategies such as corporate strategy or IS strategy?

The significant problems with information management shown in the mini case study suggest that in many organizations the strategic approach to information management is inadequate. There is not sufficient emphasis or focus on information management, since the focus is on the information technology and software applications. To help provide this focus a discrete information management strategy is developed by organizations. But this raises issues of who is responsible for information management (IM) and what their relationship is to the managers responsible for related information systems/information technology (IS/IT) strategy and knowledge management (KM) strategy. In the next section we examine the relationship between these strategies to assess how they can be reconciled.

The relationship between strategies for managing information-related resources

Information is used as a resource throughout all organizations, is essential to the operation of all business processes, and is consumed and created at all different levels of management. This makes information a potentially difficult resource to manage since it is not clear where responsibility for information management should lie. The importance of information and its distribution throughout the organization suggests that all employees will have some responsibility for information quality, but this needs to be coordinated. Furthermore, we saw in Chapter 1 that information can only be managed effectively if we can also manage the related people and technology resources. Strategies for managing information must also consider relevant technologies and the people who use information.

Responsibility for information-related resources

But where does this responsibility for coordination of the information resource lie? Is it the responsibility of the senior management team; finance (for financial and business-performance-related information); operations (for process performance and supply-chain-related information); human resources (for employee-related information); marketing (for customer-related information); legal (for managing legal culpability); or information technology?

Who the CISO reports to	2007	2008	2009	2010	Three-year change*
Chief Information Officer	38%	34%	32%	23%	- 39%
Board of Directors	21%	24%	28%	32%	+ 52%
Chief Executive Officer	32%	34%	35%	36%	+ 13%
Chief Financial Officer	11%	11%	13%	15%	+ 36%
Chief Operating Officer	9%	10%	12%	15%	+ 67%
Chief Privacy Officer	8%	8%	14%	17%	+ 113%

Figure 4.3 Reporting path for the Chief Information Security Officer showing who they report to within organization.

Source: PricewaterhouseCoopers (2010).

The PricewaterhouseCoopers Global State of Information Security Survey 2010 (PricewaterhouseCoopers (2010)) evaluated the responsibility for information security, a key aspect of information management. The results reported in Figure 4.3 showed that increasingly information security is a concern of senior managers with the CISO (Chief Information Security Officer) reporting directly to senior managers. The report also has useful insight on the source of information security breaches. For example, over half of the incidents are from current and former employees with hackers accounting for around one third of incidents.

To manage information quality, there would seem to be a need for managers in different parts of the organization who manage different processes to be responsible for it. It would also seem that overall coordination is needed as well. Senior managers in organizations also need to ask: Who ensures that information management helps support organizational strategies? Who is responsible for providing information services that deliver external information? Who produces guidelines and audits information quality? Who is responsible for knowledge management? Who protects organizational information? Who provides the technology infrastructure and applications for the diverse needs of different parts of the organization?

There is, of course, not a single, simple answer to these questions. As a consequence, approaches to business information management differ greatly between organizations. In business, the different perspectives on how information should be managed can be broadly characterized as ranging from technology-led to information-led. In the technology-led approach, information management is just one aspect of information systems or information technology management, with the main focus the creation of applications that deliver information to end-users, the maintenance of the IT infrastructure and provision of support for users of these systems. Here, technology is the resource which is the focus of strategy. In the information-led approach, the focus is not technology, but understanding the information needs of different business users and providing information services which deliver good-quality information to these users. Here information is the resource which is the focus of strategy.

Alternative relationships between strategies for managing information-related resources

Figure 4.4 summarizes some of the options for control and ownership of information management strategy. Which do you think would be most appropriate in a large organization and in a small organization? In Figure 4.4(a), IS strategy is a subset of the IM strategy and the manager labelled as chief information officer or information services manager (or IM steering group) would typically be responsible for it. In Figure 4.4(b) the roles are reversed, with IM strategy part of the IS strategy and the manager would typically be dubbed IT manager, computing services manager (or controlled through an IS/IT steering group) responsible for IS. In Figure 4.4(c) KM is dominant. In Figure 4.4(d), IM, IS and KM strategies coexist, but each is distinct with separate ownership and control of each. Some overlap between strategies is inevitable. While Figure 4.4(d) is perhaps most appealing since it emphasizes the importance of each strategy, there is a resource overhead in managing each of these strategy initiatives separately, which is only feasible in a large organization. Figure 4.4(d) also presents a problem since there will be conflicting demands of resources to deliver the strategies such as people and technical resources to create and implement different applications. This suggests that the approaches shown in Figure 4.4(a), (b) and (c) will be most effective since there is a single person or steering group responsible that will allocate and control resources in response to different business needs. These are also more manageable within a small to medium organization where a single person is likely to be responsible for IS, IM and KM strategy.

The market in which an organization operates and its culture will also determine which approach from Figure 4.4 is most appropriate. In a media organization such as EMAP (**www.emap.com**) producing consumer or business magazine publications, the emphasis will be on managing information which is at the core of the organization's product, so (a) may be most appropriate. In a fast-moving consumer goods or manufacturing company, for example a volume producer of beverages such as Britvic (Pepsi, Tango, Robinsons and J_2O brands in the UK, **www.britvic.com**), (b) may be most appropriate since the emphasis will be on delivering information systems applications to manufacture, market and distribute products. For a management consultant such as KPMG (**www.kpmg.com**), sharing knowledge of consultants operating within different market sectors and countries is strategically important, so (c) may be most appropriate.

Research insight 4.1 'How managers perceive information management' describes research that has been conducted into how different managers perceive and so control information management within their organizations. This research, summarized by Marchand et al. (2002), identified four different schools or potential approaches to business information management. First, there is the *Information Technology School* (or information systems emphasis), where the focus is on selecting appropriate technology

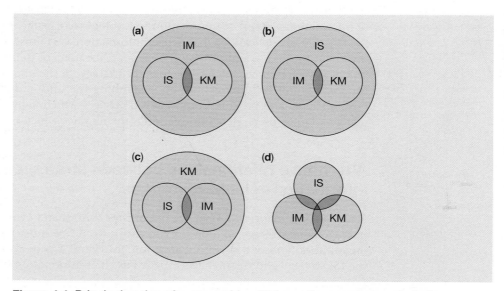

Figure 4.4 Principal options for ownership of information management strategy

to support decision making. Second, there is the *Information Management School* where the focus is on managing the information lifecycle for different types of information. Third is the *Behaviour and Control or Human Resources School* where the emphasis is on recruiting, motivating and training staff to promote good work behaviours and values. Fourth is the *Management Control School* where the management of information centres on managing people and linking their performance to business performance management (BPM).

It is evident from the Research insight that the Information Technology (Information Systems) and Information Management Schools correspond to the technology-led and information-led approaches to business information management identified earlier in this section. The Behaviour and Control and Management Control schools add different perspectives to business information management. They emphasize the importance of managing staff behaviour to promote good information management quality and highlight the importance of information in managing individual and organizational performance. Knowledge management is not explicitly identified in this framework, but we can see that it fits in most closely with the Information Management, Behaviour and Control and Management Control schools.

Different academic fields of study related to business information management also have different emphases. These naturally mirror the information-led and technology-led approaches of business. The two main fields of study are information management and IS/IT. There is also a growing amount of research conducted into knowledge management. However, as Marchand et al. (2002) note, research into Behaviour and Control and Management Control schools is more limited.

One of the key aims of Part 2 of *Business Information Management* is to integrate these different approaches since we believe that, in many previous texts, the emphasis has been on the Information Technology (Information Systems) School, with insufficient recognition of the importance of the role of the Information Management, Behaviour and Control and Management and Control Schools.

Research insight 4.1   How managers perceive information management

Marchand et al. (2002) summarize an international research project conducted at the International Institute for Management Development at Lausanne in Switzerland. The research objective was to investigate the perspectives of senior managers on the use of information, people and IT in achieving superior business performance. The study involved 1200 senior managers and over 200 senior management teams from 103 international companies as well as selected case studies.

The research posed fundamental questions such as 'How do successful companies manage their people, business information and IT practices to achieve superior performance?' and 'Why does information use in some companies lead to better business results than in other companies in the same industries?'

The authors describe three different approaches or schools of how information management was viewed within management thinking and practice. The characteristics of the four different schools are summarized in Table 4.1. This study showed that different managers viewed the three capabilities of IT practices, information management, information behaviours and values in an integrated manner rather than subscribing to an individual way of thinking. The information orientation framework is intended to provide managers with a framework which helps integrate the different concepts. The COBIT IT governance framework illustrated in Figure 6.1 is a useful framework for practitioners that helps integrate these concepts, although the emphasis is placed on the information technology school.

The study showed that different managers viewed the three capabilities of IT practices, information management, and information behaviours and values in an integrated manner rather than subscribing to an individual way of thinking.

Table 4.1 A summary of the different schools of management thinking and practice regarding information management suggested by Marchand et al. (2002)

School	Focus	Typical job titles	Strengths (+) and weaknesses (−)
Information Technology School	Selecting appropriate technology to support decision making	IT or IS Manager	+ IT applied to support operational and tactical decision making − IT less effective in supporting strategic decisions involving unstructured dynamic information − Focus on return on investment (ROI) of new systems − Limited focus on how information is used by people
Information Management School	Managing the information lifecycle for different types of information Knowledge management	Chief Information Officer (CIO), Information or Library Services Manager	+ Information viewed as a strategic resource to be managed − Information management not commonly viewed as of strategic importance, so often relegated to low-level departmental roles − Difficult to establish value of information and ROI for knowledge management initiatives
Behaviour and Control School (HR)	Improving people's information usage behaviours and values	Informal, but related to knowledge management activities sometimes instigated through human resources	+ Recognizes the importance of motivating, rewarding and managing staff to promote change to best practices − Improving information usage and behaviours not seen as a significant part of the role for HR − Limited research and dissemination of best practice on this topic
Management Control School	Using information to manage people and link their performance to business performance	Chief Executive Officer (CEO), senior managers and directors	+ Helps to link individual and business unit performance to company performance − Control viewed negatively by staff, as a way of making them 'work harder' rather than 'work smarter'

We believe that, with the current state of research in academia and practice in organizations, it is not practical, or even desirable, to produce a unified approach to business information management strategy. Instead, we have to deal with the reality that different researchers, teachers and managers place the emphasis of strategy in different places.

In Part 2 of the book, we consider how organizations develop different strategies to improve business information management. To ensure that effective information services are delivered, we believe that in medium-large organizations, three distinct, yet integrated, types of strategy need to be developed – an information management (IM) strategy (Chapter 4), a knowledge management (KM) strategy (Chapter 5) and an information systems strategy (Chapter 6). Information management (IM) strategy and knowledge management strategy (KM) are covered separately since we believe that different approaches are needed to develop and implement these strategies, which cannot be adequately described if they are grouped under the heading of 'IS strategy'. The strategic significance of IM and KM strategy is likely to be marginalized if they are considered as part of IS strategy. Additionally, as we have said, IS, IM and KM strategies are traditionally separate research disciplines, and within large organizations they are often managed with different managers responsible for each.

Information technology strategy is referred to in each chapter as part of the IS/IM/KM strategy. IT strategy is usually involved not in strategy formulation, but rather in planning the deployment of the technology infrastructure and architecture to achieve strategic goals for IS/IM/KM. Successful execution of the plans to implement IS/IM/KM also requires a suitable approach to project management, which is described in Chapter 7.

Figure 4.5 summarizes the different topics which are covered in each of the three chapters in Part 2.

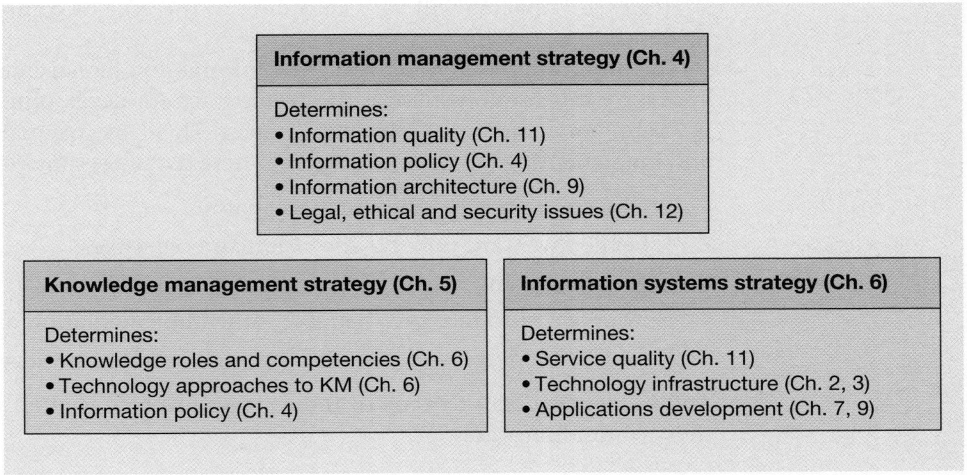

Information management strategy (Ch. 4)

Determines:
- Information quality (Ch. 11)
- Information policy (Ch. 4)
- Information architecture (Ch. 9)
- Legal, ethical and security issues (Ch. 12)

Knowledge management strategy (Ch. 5)

Determines:
- Knowledge roles and competencies (Ch. 6)
- Technology approaches to KM (Ch. 6)
- Information policy (Ch. 4)

Information systems strategy (Ch. 6)

Determines:
- Service quality (Ch. 11)
- Technology infrastructure (Ch. 2, 3)
- Applications development (Ch. 7, 9)

Figure 4.5 Different forms of strategy needed for effective business information management

Debate 4.1

A separate organizational information management strategy is not necessary – it should be integrated into IS/IT strategy.

Developing an information management strategy

What are the typical stages in creating an information management strategy? Which issues should an information management strategy address? In this section, we will seek to answer these questions.

The strategy process

It can be argued that an information management strategy plays a different role in supporting and driving organizational performance from other organizational strategies such as corporate strategy, marketing strategy or communications strategy or even information systems strategy. These other strategies are fundamental to the success of the organization and, typically, annual plans and longer-term three- to five-year strategic plans will be developed to support each strategy. Information and knowledge management strategy are viewed in many organizations as subsets of the corporate or information systems strategy – they are lower down the hierarchy of strategies. As such they may not require as much depth or frequency as other strategic plans.

Furthermore, an information strategy or knowledge management strategy is often developed in response to the types of problems with managing information suggested by Figure 4.1. So these information management strategies can be conceived of as a relatively short-term strategic initiative necessary to address a significant organizational problem or opportunity. An e-business or e-commerce strategy can be viewed in a similar way. Once an information management, knowledge management or e-business strategy has been developed and implemented and the problems or opportunities successfully addressed, these issues will sometimes assume a more minor role, as they become subsumed within the corporate or information systems strategy. Of course, the relative importance and frequency with which information strategies are updated will vary according to the type of company, as discussed with reference to Figure 4.4.

The physical process for creating the information management strategy does, however, have much in common with the approach for developing a corporate strategy, a marketing or communications or IS strategy. There are five main stages in developing and implementing any type of strategy. These five stages answer these questions:

1 'Where are we now?' – the situation analysis.
2 'Where do we want to be?' – the vision and objectives.
3 'How are we going to get there?' – the strategy.
4 'How do we introduce the changes?' – the implementation of the strategy.
5 'How are we doing?' – the monitoring and control of strategy.

Adding a little detail to each of these stages, we find that all types of strategy have these common features:

● Internal and external environment scanning or analysis is needed as part of the situation analysis. Scanning occurs both during strategy development and as a continuous process in order to respond to competitors.

● Clear statement of vision and objectives are required. Clarity is required to communicate the strategic intention both to employees and the marketplace. Objectives are also vital to act as a check as to whether the strategy is successful!

● Strategy development can be broken down into strategy option generation, evaluation and selection. An effective strategy will usually be based on reviewing a range of alternatives and selecting the best on its merits.

● After strategy development, enactment of the strategy occurs as strategy or tactics implementation.

● Control is required to monitor operational problems, check to see whether objectives have been met and adjust the operations or strategy accordingly.

In this chapter, we will not review each of the five stages separately. In Chapter 10 we describe the process of creating a plan to manage information quality which has similar stages. Instead in this chapter we will provide an overview of the issues and themes which need to be addressed in all the stages of the information management strategy. These issues are introduced in this chapter and signposts are provided to additional detail elsewhere in the book.

Information management strategy issues

In this section, we highlight the issues that need to be considered in an information management strategy by looking at three well-known frameworks for information management developed in the 1990s.

1 The Hawley Committee IM Guidelines

A comprehensive summary of strategic issues related to managing information was produced by the Hawley Committee (1995). See Research insight 4.2 'Information management guidelines from the Hawley Committee Report' for background and detail of these guidelines. The ten strategic issues identified can be summarized as follows:

1 Information relevancy
2 Organizational significance of information management
3 Legal and ethical compliance
4 Assessing information value
5 Information quality
6 Legal and ethical compliance with specific reference to information lifecycle management
7 Information management skills of employees
8 Information security including risk management
9 Maximizing value from information
10 Information systems strategy.

Research insight 4.2 **Information management guidelines from the Hawley Committee Report**

The Hawley Committee was set up in 1994 by the KPMG IMPACT Programme, a partnership of major user organizations which have been collaborating since 1989 in order to research the effective use of IS for information management through learning from each other's experience. The Committee was set up to advise on how information assets should be managed within a company. There were two broad themes. The first theme was around how information management could be used to improve operational capability and so shareholder value. Hawley (1995) gave these examples of success experienced by member organizations that had enhanced their information management:

● winning more major contracts by combining detailed information across an organization and between suppliers to achieve faster and more accurate bids;
● enhancing after-sales service by being able to identify items purchased and service history by customer;
● the use of information systems during Operation Desert Storm enabling distribution of orders to forward troops and handling of equipment stocks and combat supplies with a speed and accuracy hitherto unobtainable, facilitating one of the fastest armoured advances in military history;
● improving design of goods and components by logging and monitoring of component failures;
● identifying a new product range as a result of a review of an organization's intellectual property.

The second theme was possible business disasters caused by mismanagement of information. Example problems included:

● a major legal battle running to millions of pounds alleging wrongful use of another organization's information;
● an organization shipping product which used another's intellectual property; the cost ran into tens of millions of pounds;
● the leaking of a bank's system of screening customers for credit;
● an organization found guilty and heavily fined in a major safety case because they were unable to produce records of employee training.

A series of British Standards have now been developed to guide the management and retention of organizational records. Electronic records in particular have specific problems which must be addressed and are detailed in BIP 0089:2008 (**www.bsi-global.com/en/Shop/Publication-Detail/?pid=000000000030175177**):

The digital preservation problem
- The need for document preservation
- Defining 'long-term'
- Preservable digital documents
- Aspects of preservation
- Preservation challenges
- Preservation approaches
- Digital document preservation policy

Retention periods
- Definitions
- Principles of retention periods
- Implementation

Standards-based archival formats
- Characteristics of archival formats
- Standards bodies
- Non-digital archival format
- Digital archival formats
- Guidance for specific document categories

Storage media
- Paper
- Microfilm
- Magnetic tape
- Optical disk
- On-line storage
- Summary

Metadata
- Metadata in long-term preservation of digital documents
- The purpose of metadata
- Metadata formats
- Metadata schemas
- Custom schemas
- Data standards
- UK Government
- Metadata location
- Technical metadata
- Other relevant standards

Archive creation and maintenance
- Core concepts
- OAIS functional model

Related standards and publications
- The OAIS model
- Records management
- Document management
- Legal admissibility
- PDF/A

Source: Hawley (1995)

Since the Hawley Guidelines were produced around 15 years ago, we have to question the extent to which they are still relevant for modern organizations. Activity 4.1 explores this issue. You will find that, while the core principles remain valid, today there are different perspectives on information management. There is a new focus on these information management issues:

11 *Business performance management.* Management of organizational performance through business performance metrics systems such as the balanced scorecard. See Chapter 10.

12 *Knowledge management.* Identification of responsibility for knowledge management strategy and its implementation. See Chapter 5.

13 *Market and competitive intelligence.* There is now more prominence given to systems and responsibilities for scanning the external environment to alert managers to changes in the marketplace. See Chapter 5.

14 *Information sharing and dissemination.* Internet-based tools such as corporate information portals (Chapter 2), content management systems (Chapter 3) and e-mail alerts are now commonly used for sharing and distributing information such as that in 11, 12 and 13. See Chapters 6, 8 and 9.

15 *Legal requirements.* New practical governance laws (Sarbanes–Oxley), privacy and freedom of information acts have increased legal constraints. See Chapter 12.

Activity 4.1	Strategic issues of information management

Purpose	To evaluate the findings of the Hawley Committee in order to identify relevant issues for information management within all organizations.
Group activity	Starting with a blank piece of paper, identify at least ten strategic issues for information management and approaches to manage these issues. Different groups should consider different sizes of organization from different industry sectors. Now review the ten guidelines of the Hawley Committee and devise a two- or three-word summary of each. Which strategic issues that you identified have been omitted from the Hawley Committee Report, partly through the report being around 15 years old?

Present your answer in a table such as Table 4.2.

Table 4.2 Elements of an information management strategy

	Information management issue	Management control approach or tool
1		
2		
3		
4		
5		
6		
7		
8		
9		
10		

2 Orna's information policy and information audit

Practical Information Policies by Elizabeth Orna (1999) of the Association for Information Management is a valuable source of guidance to organizations on improving information management. At the start of the book she defines information management, saying that it is concerned with:

- How information is acquired, recorded and stored.
- Where information resources are located in the organization and who has responsibility for them.
- How information flows within the organization and between the organization and the outside world.
- How the organization uses it [information quality].
- How people who handle it apply their skills and cooperate with one another.
- How information technology supports the users of information.
- What information costs and the value it contributes.
- How effectively all these information-related activities contribute towards achievement of the organization's objectives.

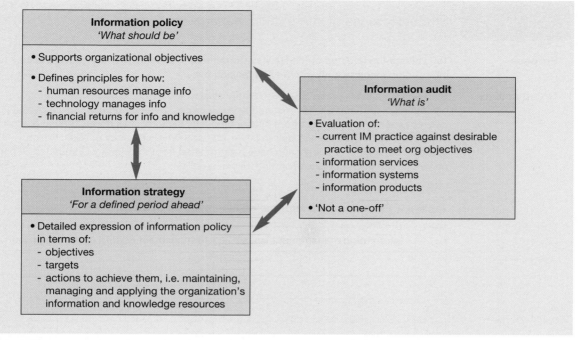

Figure 4.6 The relationship between Orna's tools for information management

This definition has elements in common with the Hawley Committee definition, such as the need for the right skills, technology and meeting objectives, but it also emphasizes the need to assess information, flows, structures and responsibilities.

Orna recommends using three main tools to assist in the creation and implementation of information management strategy. These are summarized in Figure 4.6. The **information policy** is a statement of how information management should ideally be conducted in the organization – 'what should be'. This can be considered to be a long-term document that is updated periodically. The **information strategy** is effectively an action plan for improving information management which sets objectives to improve information quality and defines the tactics in terms of revised management and employee practices to achieve these objectives. This is a shorter-term device which might have yearly or twice-yearly updates. Finally, there is the **information audit** which is used to assess the current level of information quality and management practice – 'what is'. It is also used as a situation analysis tool to support the creation of the information policy and information audit, but is further used to assess whether the information strategy goals have been achieved, so Orna recommends it is 'not a one-off' – although it may be treated as such in practice.

We explore the enactment of the information policy and information audit later in this chapter and in Chapter 10.

Information policy
A statement of an organization's approach to information management

Information strategy
A plan with a defined timeframe setting information management objectives and tactics and controls to achieve them

Information audit
An evaluation of the usage and flows of information within an organization in supporting organizational objectives

3 The Willard model of information resource management

A less well-known method of considering the aims of information management strategy, which predates Orna's book, was produced by Nick Willard (1993) in association with ASLIB. This has since become known as 'the Willard model'. It describes five elements of IRM:

1 *Identification*. The discovery of information resources and the recording of their features in an inventory.

2 *Ownership*. The establishment of responsibility for the upkeep of an information resource.

3 *Cost and value*. Assessment of the cost of an information resource and its value to the organization.

4 *Development*. The further development of an existing information resource to enhance its value to the organization.

5 *Exploitation*. The processes which may allow a resource to generate further value through conversion into an asset or a saleable commodity.

Identification of information resources is consistent with the use of the information audit to understand information holdings. Today, it would also include knowledge discovery (Chapter 5). Defining ownership or responsibility for specific resources is a key part of information management. The notion of attaching cost and value to resources was relatively novel at the time and is still being researched today, as we will see later in the chapter. Development is part of information strategy. Exploitation is in line with what the Hawley Committee were recommending when they said: 'The harnessing of information assets and their proper use for maximum benefit of the organization including legally protecting, licensing, re-using, combining, representing, publishing and destroying'.

Information management themes and approaches

In this section we will examine, in a little more detail, some of the main themes in information management strategy which we identified in the previous section. Each of these themes and approaches is covered in more detail later in the book, so this section acts as an introduction to these topics.

IM theme 1: Information value

While every organization contains vast amounts of information, the information will naturally vary in importance or value. An information management strategy forces an organization to question the value of its information. Information can be prioritized in importance and better-quality information delivered. Information value can be assessed in terms of its fitness for purpose or quality using information mapping or auditing techniques described in IM management approach 3, Information resource analysis (p. 196). Once information has been identified as valuable, plans can then be put in place to:

● protect it from deletion or modification;

● share it within a defined audience;

● improve its quality.

Lower-value information can either be improved to increase its relevance to managers or removed from detailed reports to produce summaries.

Information value is managed through the information management approaches to audit and protect information. Ward and Peppard (2002) state that 'delivering value to the business is the key rationale behind an information management strategy – to add value by exploiting information as a key business resource'. They describe two approaches for managing this value. First, they suggest the risk and value assessment approach recommended by Hawley (1995), which involves categorizing the value or importance of different types of information in three ways as described below. In reality, these tests are applied to more specific types of information than those described, and specific values are assigned to each. The three ways of valuing information described in the Hawley Report were:

1 According to market value (i.e. as a tradable asset based on the price paid for information or the value to perform the analysis);

2 The impact of its loss or occurrence of errors in the information (i.e. replacement value, damage to reputation etc.);

3 Its impact on the business (i.e. in terms of cost reduction potential or revenue generation).

The report suggested that types of information asset that could be assessed using these three criteria included:

- Market and customer information
- Product information
- Specialist knowledge
- Business process information
- Management information and plans
- Human resource information
- Supplier information
- Accountable information

While this is a useful way of categorizing different information types and highlighting the impact of theft or loss, it not clear that it is realistic to value information. Research into valuing information was conducted between 2000 and 2002 by a team from the Department of Information Science, University of Loughborough (Oppenheim et al., 2002). A survey of practice by information management experts and senior managers suggested that trying to measure the actual and potential value of information itself was 'going down a blind alley', although earlier research has modelled this in some organizations. Instead, understanding how well specific types of information were supporting organizational effectiveness dependent on their quality was seen as more effective.

Ward and Peppard (2002) also suggest that information can be classified according to its value to current strategy and future strategy. There are four categories:

1 *Strategic information.* Information is critical to business and of greatest value. This includes the information used for corporate performance management (see Chapter 1) such as objectives, performance metrics and business drivers. It also refers to external information such as competitive intelligence and market information.

2 *High-potential information.* The potential value to the business may be high, but it is not confirmed. Knowledge management could fit into this category in some organizations as they assess whether it is likely to become strategic information in future.

3 *Key operational information.* Information is essential for core processes and its value is enhanced by horizontal integration. This is the largest volume of information about sales transactions and customers. It is of limited value for future strategy, but relevant to implementing the current strategy.

4 *Support information.* Needed for supporting the operation of the business, but of little strategic value. This would include information about staff such as time sheets and holiday bookings. Management of this information is a low priority, although it still needs to be accurate and cost-effective.

This method of classifying information is similar to that used to classify investments in an information systems portfolio as described in Chapter 6. So Ward and

Peppard (2002) suggest that applications support for each of these categories should be assessed. For example, for strategic information, are the reporting systems appropriate for corporate performance management and scanning together with dissemination for competitive intelligence and marketing information?

IM theme 2: Information quality (see Chapter 10)

Information quality is determined by the suitability of information to support a decision or task. The concept of information quality was introduced in Chapter 1, where we said that it depended on its relevance, accuracy, timeliness and form. To understand these concepts further, refer to Table 4.3 and complete Activity 4.2.

Table 4.3 The three dimensions of information quality

Content dimension	
Accuracy	Information correct
Relevance	Information can support decision making
Completeness	No data items missing
Conciseness	Information is not too detailed
Scope	May be broad or narrow, internal or external to the organization
Time dimension	
Timeliness	Available when needed. Immediate or real-time information is a common requirement. Alerts are also a requirement
Currency	Information is up to date
Frequency	Information supplied at appropriate regular intervals
Time period	A time series covers the right period of time
Form dimension	
Clarity	Information readily interpreted
Detail	Both summary 'dashboard' views and detailed 'drill-down' views may be required
Order	Data sorted in a logical order and can be modified
Presentation	Tabulations and graphs
Media	Hard copy (print-outs) and soft copy (electronically stored and displayed)

Activity 4.2	Assessing information quality of online resources
Purpose	To explore the concept of information quality in the context of online information sources, which we all continuously assess for quality.
Pairs activity	Referring to the different aspects of information quality shown in Table 4.3, discuss how you assess the information quality of a website for these cases: 1 An online article about information quality. 2 A 'news and views' website for the IT or another industry. 3 A comparison website for choosing travel insurance. What are the common characteristics of information quality for each?

Although information quality is usually assessed, using characteristics such as those shown in Table 4.3, according to its availability to support specific decisions or actions, a broader notion of information quality within an organization can also be identified. Poor organizational information quality is indicated when staff, customers or other partners are surveyed and they believe that they do not have access to the type of information they need, or it isn't accurate or available when they need it, in the form that it is needed.

The classic content, time, form dimensions characterization of information shown in Table 4.3 is not exhaustive. One major omission is information accessibility. At a simple level, information may be available on a system, but not everyone has ready access to it. For example, most hospitals will now have an intranet with clinical information, but there will be a limited number of access points and times to access them. Of even greater concern, information may be available only in certain parts of an organization. This may be because of the 'silo arrangement' referred to in Chapter 2 where different information systems occur in different parts of the organization. Alternatively, it may be because staff in one area do not want to or see the need to share information. When information is held on different systems, there are also problems of information duplication: for example, it is not uncommon for information related to a customer to be held in several different databases in an organization such as a sales transactions database, a direct marketing database and a service database. This impacts the accuracy of information since there may be a problem with information consistency as data such as customer address may be held incorrectly in one database, but correctly in another. Data replication can be used to enforce consistency. One of the goals of many customer relationship management programmes is to introduce a single view of the customer to avoid these problems and to give better customer service, such as when they phone about order status. Ward and Peppard (2002) argue that a 'stable integrated information framework' is needed for these purposes to maximize the value of information. Part of this approach is creating an organizational 'information architecture' as described in Chapter 9.

To assess current information quality, information mapping is conducted (management approach 3, p. 196). To improve information quality its importance needs to be recognized through clearly defined responsibilities for information quality (management approach 2, p. 192), as is suggested in Table 4.4.

The attributes of good information quality need to be well understood by all involved in the design and review of new information systems as part of information systems development (Chapter 7) and development of information architecture (Chapter 9). This implies training for managers and specialist designers such as information architects. But information quality also needs to be the responsibility of all employees involved with capturing and using information. The assessment and improvement of information quality is the topic of Chapter 10.

IM theme 3: Information security (see Chapters 9 and 12)

Information must be safeguarded from accidental and deliberate modification or deletion by people and also natural events which may destroy the media on which it is held. Many organizations now implement a formal information security management system or information security policy to protect their information assets.

The information management strategy will mandate that there is a security policy. This may be a policy developed in-house, or adoption of a security standard such as BS7799. This standard, based upon the PDCA cycle (Deming, 1986), defines the following process:

- **Plan** – business risk analysis
- **Do** – internal controls to manage the applicable risks

Information accessibility problem
Is an online or offline information source physically accessible?

Information duplication problem
Similar types of data are repeated in databases in separate parts of the organization

Information consistency
Similar data items have different values in different databases

Single view of the customer
Information on a customer is consistent regardless of which system it is accessed through

Information security management system
An organizational process to protect information assets

- **Check** – a management review to verify effectiveness
- **Act** – action as necessary.

The standard defines ten guiding principles, which are discussed in more detail in Chapter 11:

1 Security policy
2 Security organization
3 Asset classification and control
4 Personnel security
5 Physical and environmental security
6 Communication and operations management
7 Access control
8 Systems development and maintenance
9 Business continuity planning
10 Compliance.

IM theme 4: Legal and ethical compliance (see Chapter 12)

One of the implications of living in an 'information society' is that more and more information is held about individuals on computer systems. Governments have developed many laws both to protect individuals and to give government agencies access to information which may be needed for 'law enforcement'.

In Chapter 12 we review the vast number of laws that organizations are subject to when company information is held online. It is interesting to note that for GlaxoSmithKline the importance of legal issues is such that the main information management function reports to the legal function (Case study 4.2). In this chapter we will simply give an indication of some of the ways in which laws can be breached. These include:

- sharing customer data with a third party without the customer's consent;
- sending out unsolicited e-mail to a consumer;
- an e-mail from an employee which denigrates another organization or defames an individual;
- monitoring employee access to data and online services;
- not providing online access suitable for those with visual impairment.

A further perspective on legal requirements is records management, which was introduced in Chapter 1. If we consider the information lifecycle, different actions need to be taken for legal compliance at each stage of the lifecycle:

1 *Records creation and capture*. The time and place of creation of new customer records must be logged for transparency in case of a complaint.
2 *Records access*. The modification, the person who modified it and time it was made should be recorded.
3 *Records disposal*. The information policy may need to specify how long records are kept before they are deleted for legal compliance.

Accounting scandals at the start of the new century, such as that at Enron, have given increased prominence to the accuracy of information. In 2002, the US introduced the Sarbanes–Oxley Act, which required tighter controls on the accuracy of financial information. The chief information officer is required to sign a document that confirms that the information and technology systems support the financial integrity that is being attested to by the finance officer. Equivalent laws have also been introduced in other countries.

In addition to legal breaches such as these, there are also ethical breaches, which may not contravene the 'letter of the law', but could still damage customer relationships. For example, at the time of writing, it is still legal in the UK to send out e-mails to existing business customers without their consent. However, this is not consistent with the 'permission marketing' approach outlined in Chapter 12, so it may annoy customers and damage the brand. A better ethical approach will be to send out an e-mail with a 'statement of origination' included which explains how the e-mail address was collected and the legal situation.

An increasingly important topic for many organizations is eco-friendliness, or 'green' issues, and this is beginning to affect the management of information technology in organizations. Computer equipment uses large amounts of electrical energy, the production of which often results in the production of 'greenhouse gases' and the pollution of the environment. IT hardware rapidly becomes outdated and obsolete and needs to be disposed of.

These issues are prompting IT managers to look into ways of reducing waste and energy consumption (ZDNet, 2008a). This will not only bring environmental benefit but could result in significant cost savings for the organization.

It may also become a strategic competitive advantage. Microsoft has recently been embarrassed by reports that indicate it is poor at providing recycling and disposal information for its products (ZDNet, 2008b). In the future, consumers may be dissuaded from purchasing products from non-green organizations. It would not take much time before component manufacturers found that they needed to prove their eco-friendliness before being able to supply the larger IT equipment providers.

IM theme 5: Knowledge management (see Chapter 5)

The importance of this theme depends, to a great extent, on the type of organization. For some organizations such as a management consultancy, effective knowledge management is an important contributor to business effectiveness. In these cases, a separate knowledge management strategy is likely to be developed. For others, particularly smaller organizations, it may not be necessary to have a separate knowledge management strategy since priorities will lie with information management themes we have discussed earlier, such as information value, quality and security. Instead, the information management strategy may refer to supporting knowledge management through more limited initiatives based around sharing knowledge via an intranet.

It is important to recognize that the concepts of organizational knowledge and learning organizations, though phrases that are widely used in literature, are not to be interpreted to mean that organizations are conscious or 'knowing' entities. Rather, they are collections of individuals that possess knowledge and information systems may be more useful if constructed while considering 'within whom does knowledge reside' (Simon, 1991).

IM theme 6: Technology support (see Chapters 2, 3 and 6)

Technology support to achieve the objectives of the information management strategy involves selecting relevant information systems applications and infrastructure. Projects to deliver this infrastructure will be negotiated as part of the information technology, information systems and information services strategies described in Chapters 6 and 11.

IM management approach 1: Structuring the information management function

Information management unit
An organizational unit responsible for information management strategy within an organization

The need for a separate organizational structure with a clearly defined information management remit was discussed at the start of the chapter. In essence an **information management unit** provides a focus for improving information management that everyone in the organization is aware of. The creation of this unit demonstrates a commitment by senior management to information management since they have empowered the group with the resource and responsibility to improve information management.

In a large organization, the information management unit may be a small department or team of people. In smaller organizations the information management function may be a single person who works full-time or part-time on information management. This person will work in conjunction with other managers, possibly through a working or steering group. A single person should always be ultimately responsible for information management. It will work best if this is a senior manager such as a finance director or IT manager.

The group should be monitored as to how it delivers against its objectives. The main role of the group will typically be to:

- develop and manage implementation information management strategy;
- set information-related policies such as data protection policy, employee monitoring policy;
- educate and train staff and disseminate best practice.

In the UK National Health Service, patient and treatment information is vital to service delivery. The central management team or NHS Executive first created a separate information management group to set policies and standards and disseminate best practice. However, this did not have control of budget and there was duplication of approaches in the different regions. There is now a large independent organization, the NHS Information Authority, (now NHS Connecting for Health). Its original objectives are to:

- support the effective use of national electronic health records to improve patient care through the provision of the Integrated Care Record System (ICRS);
- provide information services and knowledge for decision making for staff, patients and public;
- establish and maintain health informatics as a recognized and respected national profession;
- provide reliable and secure information infrastructure services;
- provide specialist support services for national initiatives.

From these objectives, it can be seen that it has a role in information management, knowledge management and information systems (infrastructure).

A further example of how a large organization manages its information function is provided by Case study 4.2. This illustrates how a separate information management group has been created in GlaxoSmithKline. In this case it is part of the corporate legal department. This has the benefits of emphasizing its importance and keeping it separate from the information technology grouping.

A global information management strategy at GlaxoSmithKline

Elspeth Scott is Director of Global Information and Records Management within pharmaceutical and healthcare company GlaxoSmithKline plc (www.gsk.com). In this article, Elspeth describes the formation of this new information management group, its role and objectives.

The merger of two big companies offers huge opportunities – and, of course, some attendant threats too. For me, it has provided the opportunity of a lifetime – the chance to help ensure that this new company, GlaxoSmithKline plc, manages information in such a way that it realises all the benefits that good practice can bring and mitigates the risks associated with poor management of information. In this article I'd like to talk about why I believe that the formation of a group responsible for ensuring a global approach to the management of information is important not only for our profession, but for businesses everywhere. I also want to consider how we propose to deliver value.

How did this happen?

During the integration planning phase prior to actual merger, a Taskforce, led by the VP of Corporate Compliance, was formed of people involved in information and records management in different business sectors with a view to determining how to achieve global consistency across the new company. The taskforce produced a number of recommendations around the role and remit of a new central global group which would provide global policy, standards and consultancy on the management of information and records. The resulting organisation, Global Information & Records Management (Global IRM), relates closely to the Corporate Legal Division, and reports to the VP of Corporate Compliance who in turn reports to the Chief Executive Officer. Having previously developed information policies and standards within an IT group, I find this positioning with Legal and Compliance is excellent since it affords a far higher degree of visibility and 'clout'. We are already working closely with our legal colleagues in the development of our policies and retention schedules.

Why is such a group necessary?

As ever in the world of business, cost is a key driver for change. Litigation is an increasingly expensive reality, especially in the US, with vast sums of money being spent in litigation discovery alone. Our shareholders need to be assured that we are managing information and records effectively and minimising the risks of keeping too much for too long and without the appropriate context. The Hawley Committee report put this issue firmly on the Board's agenda but we are seeing daily reports of major

companies being embarrassed by records that have been kept too long or probably should never have existed in the first place. The pharmaceutical industry is particularly heavily regulated and tends to have a good track record for managing information in those business critical areas, but that good practice needs to be extended across all parts of the business in a consistent and cohesive manner. We are increasingly seeing globalisation of the business and that includes (and indeed predicates) the adoption of common IT platforms. With the use of common technologies comes the need for a common approach to how to use these tools and consistent standards for the management of information and records. It is very important not to distinguish between paper and electronic records. As my records management colleagues keep stressing, 'a record is a record is a record' ... and one can transform into the other at the flick of a switch! Retention policies and schedules should be the same whatever the medium.

Who are we?

We are a group of 17 information and records management professionals with a remarkably high number of years of experience behind us! We were formed by the amalgamation of a small international group doing information policies, standards and good practice, with the consultancy team of a group doing best practice in records management in the US in one of the former companies. We have a global remit and do not undertake any 'hands-on' records management, but do work closely with those operational groups to develop the policies, standards, records retention schedules and educational materials.

What do we plan to deliver?

Our three-year strategic plan can be very simply described as BUILD (the policies, standards and retention schedules), IMPLEMENT (across the entire company through communication and an accompanying education programme) and MONITOR COMPLIANCE. These are logical steps which will take time and events will overlap as individual policies are rolled out. The first step, naturally, is to build a team capable of delivering the agreed objectives. That can be both a problem and an opportunity! During the integration phase, there are many other groups vying for key talent so one must move swiftly to fill one's vacancies and begin to meld a number of individuals into an effective group. In our case, that involved bringing people from the US and the UK together and beginning the process of changing the focus and mindset from 'local' to 'global'. That cannot be accomplished overnight but must be done with thoughtful career development planning and team-building activities that encourage that cultural shift.

One of the saddest things about a merger such as we have undergone, is the dislocation of the networks one has built up to get things done. People move, change roles or leave. Conversely, one of the most exciting tasks in any newly merged organisation is creating new networks. It takes time to find out who is responsible for what and indeed, it is not uncommon to find another group playing a remarkably similar role to one's own! It takes a lot of energy to go out and establish those networks but it is a critical success factor.

Policy and standards development
This includes all stages of the policy development process from initial identification of business need through discussion with key stakeholders, through drafting, gaining consensus with wider stakeholder groups/representatives, obtaining approval to rolling out to the business with appropriate marketing. The first policy to be developed is essentially an 'umbrella' policy which draws attention to four key risk areas associated with information management, namely:

- Records retention
- Information classification and protection
- Data privacy
- Copyright.

Specific policies for records retention and information classification and protection have also been drafted and are being submitted for executive level approval. It is not necessary for the Global IRM group to 'own' all these separate policies. In the case of the information classification policy, there has been joint authorship of the policy and it is likely that Group Security will 'own' the associated standards. Likewise, data privacy and copyright policies may be owned by other groups, with Global IRM supporting the education and implementation effort as part of good practice around management of the information lifecycle. The records retention policy roll out will be accompanied by a global retention schedule for the new company which will supersede the legacy schedules of the former companies. The new schedule is functionally based and aimed at category level rather than individual record series. Initially the global schedule will be based on US/European/Japanese laws and regulations but gradually the legal research from other countries will be added to ensure global applicability.

Education and training
A vital part of the role and responsibility of the Global IRM group will be communication of the emerging information policies, standards and guidelines to the business and ensuring that people know what is expected of them. People need training and guidance on consistent implementation of best practice. But how do you reach 110,000 people in widely different parts of the world? Although Global IRM can coordinate and produce educational and training materials, we cannot rely simply on provision of our web site as a central source of information. We shall have to work hard to ensure that everyone has access to training and guidance on the management of information, regardless of where they are or what language they speak. Close liaison with functional and business sector training groups will be essential to ensure effective penetration of education to ensure that our messages are being built into business specific training. A further group that may be able to help us achieve that aim but that has not been a traditional partner of information management, is Human Resources. HR has a vested interest in ensuring that the workforce is as effective as possible and the ability to manage information is becoming a core competency in today's world.

Consultancy
Our role as information management consultants is likely to be at a fairly high level for those areas of the business which already have their own information and records management expertise. For areas of the business where this expertise may be lacking, then the central group should be able either to provide appropriate assistance or to influence business managers to supply the required resources in order to comply with the policies.

Auditing
Once the policies have been rolled out and employees have been educated, then it will be time to audit and assess the impact of those policies and delivery against one of the original aims of the group, which was reduction of risk. Once again, there will be inadequate resources within the global group to conduct all such audits so this will be done in partnership with the existing audit function(s) within the company. In the meantime, we are establishing a baseline against which we can measure our success and demonstrate value to the company.

Conclusion
There are many challenges ahead for this new global team, not the least of which is simply getting people's attention at a time when the whole organisation is trying to come to terms with the new situation. However, it is enormously encouraging that information and records management is already on the agenda of the Corporate Executive Team and that the necessary policies, standards and retention schedules will be put in place. The biggest challenge of all will lie in implementation and the real test of our value will be linked to the level of penetration into the business and into the consciousness of each employee. Policies are necessary, but we are really aiming for people's hearts and minds! We want to ensure that when people create information, they automatically think about its lifecycle: what is its purpose? who needs to see this? how long must it be

kept? where should it be stored? is it sensitive/confidential? We shall be working closely with our IT colleagues to ensure that as far as possible, policies are 'hardwired' into our systems. If we make life simple, then we will encourage compliance. And if we encourage compliance we will be protecting the company from risk and helping to ensure effective use of our knowledge assets. That way we will deliver the promised value.

Source: Elspeth Scott, Director of Global Information and Records Management within GlaxoSmithKline. Article: Global information and records management, **www.managinginformation.com/ globalinformation.htm**

Questions

1   Where does information management fit within the GlaxoSmithKline organizational structure? Assess the advantages and disadvantages of this approach according to the article and your own experience.

2   What information management activities does the group complete? To what extent could these be successfully completed within an information technology department?

IM management approach 2: Responsibilities

In addition to creation of distinct overall responsibility for information management as a whole, it can be suggested that responsibilities for information management should be defined elsewhere in the organization.

Evernden and Evernden (2003) suggest that when developing an information architecture for an organization, there should be four types of responsibility or ownership:

1   *Governance responsibility*. Managers responsible for the overall directional and control of information management. Their work involves obtaining funding for projects and systems to improve information and quality and ownership for their implementation.

2   *Stewardship responsibilities*. Information stewards are responsible for quality of information and this involves activities such as information capture or creation, dissemination and deletion.

3   *Infrastructure responsibilities*. This is creating the right environment for using information. This is a more technical role involving setting up and integrating information systems, creating database structures or information architectures for website pages and protecting the information resource.

4   *Usage responsibilities*. Usage is the responsibility of the end-user of information. Beyond actually using the information, activities include assessing information for quality and highlighting problems with quality.

This list of responsibilities shows that everyone in the organization is responsible for information. As was argued in the section on information quality, it follows that all staff must be adequately educated about the importance of information and trained in using it and the supporting applications effectively. The example at the start of this chapter showed that a vast amount of money is wasted in business each year by employees wasting time in searching for online information.

Critiquing the roles and responsibilities in IM

It is perhaps useful at this point to consider the practicalities of these suggested responsibilities in managing corporate information. Recently organizations have reported the difficulty in defining and implementing clear IT strategies because too many people are involved in the process (ITPro, 2008).

Governance and stewardship

Allocating overall responsibility for information system governance would seem an appropriate and effective way of ensuring that the various information systems of an organization supported the achievement of the overall organizational strategic goals and intents, and that system developments received appropriate attention and resources.

However, assigning stewardship responsibilities to an individual presents some potential problems. Since the prime purpose of many information systems is to ensure that the right data and information reach the right people at the right time, the inclusion of an individual with responsibility to create new information would seem to remove the locus of control away from the end-user. This would slow down the process of information creation as dialogue took place between the steward and the end-users as the end-users made requests for information from the stewards, or the stewards interrogated end-users in order to understand what their information requirements might be. In either case, the quality of information that is generated suffers because it is delayed or misinterpreted.

Usage and lessons from the past

Also, assigning responsibility for determining information quality to end-users would present problems that have been known about in other business disciplines for many years. Manufacturing organizations used to employ Quality Departments whose responsibility it was to check products for quality prior to sale or use. While this did prevent many (but not all) problems from reaching the customer, many defective products required further costly rework to make them fit for purpose. It was not until the Japanese automotive manufacturers introduced the ideas of 'right first time' and 'zero defects' that Western manufacturing companies moved responsibility for quality back to the persons that made the products in the first place. Similarly, assigning responsibility for checking the quality of information to end-users is moving the responsibility for providing high-quality data away from those people who are requested to provide it in the first place.

Manufacturing companies have developed their quality management techniques largely influenced by Japanese practices. Total Quality Management (TQM) is one example that is perhaps the pinnacle of quality management to which many manufacturing organizations now aspire. It is notable that recent research into data quality in information systems is beginning to employ terms such as Total Data Quality Management (TDQM) (Xu and Koronios, 2004). This suggests that there are lessons in quality management in other types of business or in other business functions that can be employed in information system design and development. Taking account of the lessons learned elsewhere may enable system designers and developers to integrate effective and proven quality management practices.

Activity 4.3 illustrates the issue of responsibility further.

The Joint Information Systems Committee of the UK for future and higher education in its Guidelines for Developing an Information Strategy (JISC, 1995), suggests that it is important to identify clear responsibilities for information. They envisage five main roles:

1 *Information strategy committee.* A steering committee for the development of the information strategy. Involved in initial development of strategy and to monitor implementation and operation. It is recommended that the chair be very senior – Pro-Vice-Chancellor or equivalent.

2 *Information (strategy) manager/director.* This person is custodian of the information strategy and is expected to be capable in project and change management. The main tasks expected by JISC (1995) are:

<table>
<tr><td>**Activity 4.3**</td><td>**Assigning responsibilities for information ownership at the Lo-cost Airline Company**</td></tr>
</table>

Purpose

To apply the different roles for managing information within the organization suggested by Evernden and Evernden (2003).

Activity

Identify different responsibilities for information in the appropriate place on the grid of Table 4.4.

Choose your answers from finance department, marketing department, sales department, operations department, IT department, human resources department, individuals involved in business process. Some responsibilities may involve shared responsibility, e.g. for governance.

Table 4.4 Responsibilities for information management

Information category	Governance	Stewardship	Infrastructure	Usage
Customer information				
Transaction information (ticket sales)				
Logistics information (crew rostering)				

- managing the implementation of the strategy;
- maintaining and monitoring its effectiveness;
- proposing changes to it on the basis of wide consultation.

3 *Information custodians.* Responsible for maintaining standards for a defined set of information items. Responsibilities include:
  - auditing the use of the information to ensure compliance with information standards;
  - suggesting changes to the definition or parameters of the information items;
  - delegating the responsibility for information quality.

4 *Information users.* These include academic and administrative staff, students, prospective students, alumni, industry, the funding councils, research councils. JISC (1995) suggests that information users within the institution must be aware of the information strategy and how it affects them (an information policy or acceptable use policies for computing networks are used to communicate this).

5 *Information service.* This is a combination of the library and information service within the university. JISC notes that some institutions have found it desirable to merge the two main information services (library and computing) under a single managerial head (and reporting to one committee) since the difference between types of information (and forms of access to them) continues to diminish.

Chief information officer (CIO)
Manager with responsibility for information assets and/or information systems strategy

The chief information officer (CIO) role

An approach to governance that can be adopted by large organizations is having a **chief information officer (CIO)**. This concept originated in the US where many organizations have a CIO, but it has not been widely adopted elsewhere, as shown by Research insight 4.3 'The elusive CIO'. The article suggests that, despite the title, the emphasis of responsibility is often on information systems rather than information management. Laws have been introduced to increase financial accountability and accuracy such as the 2002 Sarbanes–Oxley Act in the US. The chief information officer is now required to sign a document that confirms that the information and technology systems support the financial integrity that is being attested to by the finance officer. Equivalent laws have also been introduced in other countries. Such laws can only increase the importance of the CIO role.

The influence of the CIO is also increasing within government. The UK announced the creation of a new post of government chief information officer in late 2003. The five-year ICT strategy of 2005 focused on three areas: putting the citizen in the centre, shared services, and professionalizing IT-enabled business change. Following its successful delivery, the CIO Council moved on to ICT infrastructure. The CIO has responsibility for a yearly spend of some £16 billion.

The influence of organization CIOs, though, still appears to suffer from a lack of influence and resources. Recently a gathering of security experts discussed the challenges that face modern organizational CIOs and identified that they need to take a more strategic approach to system security above firefighting individual security issues (Computing, 2008b). A key role of the CIO must be to gain the support of other executives and they will need to understand the basic business operating parameters and constraints in order to meet this objective.

Debate 4.2

Every organization should have a chief information officer whose main responsibility is management of information as a strategic resource.

Research insight 4.3   **The elusive CIO**

The poor visibility of the chief information officer in many organizations brings to mind 'The Scarlet Pimpernel', which could be adapted to:

> They seek him here, they seek him there
> Those managers seek him everywhere
> Is he in heaven or is he in hell?
> That demned elusive CIO.

> They seek him here, they seek him there
> Those managers seek him everywhere
> If you should see him, please do give a yell!
> That demned elusive CIO.

In the UK a poll of FTSE-100 companies reported in *Information World Review* (2003) found that only a handful have a bona fide information officer, while many split the role between a couple of departments, or, in some cases, across separate company divisions. *Information World Review* (2003) reported that in several cases, companies were confused by the question of whether they had someone who fitted the description of a chief information officer (CIO). They tended to say: 'Yes, we have a CIO, but he [and it is usually a he] handles IT without ever getting involved with information services.'

ICI, the chemicals group, was one of only a few to have a traditional CIO. In ICI, it is Anthony Foster who works just below board level and reports to the chief executive since the departure of the chief operating officer. The company explained that this is a senior post with a wide remit and that it has a 'dotted line' chain of command linking the CIO into decisions made on IT and information services within each of ICI's four business units.

Another with a traditional CIO role was oil company BP, although the current job title is 'group vice president (digital business)', a position which reports to the deputy group chief executive. According to BP the role exists 'so that one senior person can concentrate on all aspects of communication and information, leaving the other executives to get on with core competencies of oil exploration and production'.

The survey suggested that industrial companies in particular are run along product lines with usually just a slim executive board with no CIO or IS responsibilities linking them together at the top. Information technology has often been devolved and is handled at a much more junior level within each discrete division. BOC, the industrial gases group, and power-plant manufacturer Rolls-Royce are examples of this. The CIO role is scattered across corporate relations, R&D and IT, with no distinct chief or reporting structure. In Rolls-Royce, information is under the remit of the director of communications, who reports to the chief executive.

The survey suggests that in some other organizations, a chief knowledge officer (CKO) role has been adopted, with the CKO being responsible for information management, but also helping people work together through using knowledge. However, the situation is fluid, with BT appointing a CKO to drive a knowledge management initiative and later merging the role with that of chief information officer.

See also Mini case study 1.1 'Capital One creates value through information' in Chapter 1 for perspectives on the different roles of the CIO.

Source: Adapted from Information World Review (2003)

IM management approach 3: Information resource analysis

In this section, two information resources analysis techniques known as 'the information audit' and 'information mapping' are introduced. They are discussed further in Chapter 10, Managing information quality.

Information audit
An evaluation of the usage and flows of information within an organization

The **information audit** is a key part of developing an information strategy. Orna (1999) explains that it is necessary as a means of establishing a foundation for using information strategically. An information audit has been defined by the Aslib Information Resources Management Network, referenced in Orna (1999), as:

> a systematic examination of information use, resources and flows, with a verification by reference to both people and existing documents, in order to establish the extent to which they are contributing to an organization's objectives.

It is apparent from this definition that the information audit is a structured approach to evaluating the information resources and information flows of an organization as these resources are used (see Figure 4.6). Significantly, the definition also shows the importance of the audit in linking the organization's objectives. Swash (1997) describes the nature and purpose of the information audit, which is to identify for the organizational information resource:

● actual and potential users of information;
● the information quality requirements for these users;
● the types of information available;
● where information is held (including multiple sources);
● how the information is used and how this relates to organizational objectives;
● systems or applications used to capture, store and disseminate information;
● problems with information management that result in poor communications or wastage;
● the cost of information usage.

Information mapping

Information mapping
An approach for identifying the value of and relationships between organizational information resources

Information mapping is a well-established technique to help organizations manage information as a resource. It can still be applied in a modern organization, and there is perhaps a more urgent need for it with the ever-expanding volume of company information. The aims of using information mapping, according to Horton (1988), is to identify 'critical information resources' and those of 'marginal information value'. It can also be used to identify the need for applications to better manage these resources.

Evernden and Evernden (2003) describe the purpose of information maps as to catalogue, understand, organize and navigate the information resource. One result of the mapping process is to show what information is available and what is not.

Information mapping was refined into an information analysis toolkit known as 'Infomap' (Burk, 1988). Using this technique 'information resource entities' (IREs) are identified. These include information sources, systems and services. IREs are then plotted on an organizational information matrix with these axes:

- *Information holdings* (goods that produce revenues and reports)
- *Information handling function* (responsibilities for managing information such as library or information resource)
- *Information content* (specific content)
- *Information media* (form in which information is captured, stored or accessed such as internal mail, application, intranet, e-mail).

Evernden and Evernden (2003) suggest that there are four components to an information map.

These are summarized in Table 4.5.

Table 4.5 A summary of components of information mapping as suggested by Evernden and Evernden (2003)

Component	What it shows	Purpose
Big picture	Summary, equivalent to a world map showing main information types and links	Provides overview of main information types and the relationship between them for navigating at a finer level
Neigbourhood diagrams	Detail about a process such as a sales transaction	Summarizes information needed to support a process. Identifies redundant and omitted information
Views	Summarizes information items relevant to a particular type of person or operation	Highlight information needs of a particular person
Information value chains	A type of view showing information flows	Shows how the flow of information creates value

IM management approach 4: Information policy

Information policy
A statement of an organization's approach to information management

Creating an **information policy** is a great device for improving information management practice within an organization. It highlights the importance of information management to staff and details their responsibilities. While information policy is, for some, synonymous with information strategy, we saw in our discussion of Figure 4.6 that more typically it is a brief statement of intent of how information should be managed and used within an organization. It will support strategy at a high level, by providing a mission statement for information management, but will also give more detailed guidelines on staff responsibilities as to how they should use information.

Orna (1999) characterizes information policy as follows:

- At the level of principles
- Fairly short statements (providing principles by which future action may be conditioned)
- Each developed at one go (as a result of preparatory work)
- Meant to be robust enough to last (not detailed action plans).

This differs from the information strategy which is used to support action through a plan for a specific period (yearly, three-yearly).

Information policy exerts a strong influence on information quality, which is discussed in more detail in Chapter 10. Mini case study 4.2 gives an example of information policy for a small organization.

IM management approach 5: Risk management

Risk management is a management approach that can be applied across a range of business areas. For example, we also refer to it in Chapter 7 with respect to managing risks on information systems projects.

Mini case study 4.2 **An example information policy from an SME**

The SME is a chartered surveyors that turned to Liverpool John Moores University to conduct an information audit and create an information policy in order to improve organizational performance. The drivers or objectives for creating this information policy, which are common to many companies, include:

- To promote strong information flows between the different departments.
- To eradicate all information barriers. Promoting top-down and bottom-up communication flows.
- To keep all staff informed on the company's business plans and changes in strategic direction.
- To enhance customer relations and service quality to both existing and potential clients.
- To eradicate poor customer relations and contact management.
- To harness the high degree of tacit knowledge within the company.
- To ensure that all staff have the information and knowledge that they require to perform their role effectively.
- To help the company achieve its corporate objectives and become the market leader in this marketplace.
- To use the intranet more effectively to share information resources and knowledge.
- To continually review the effectiveness of information systems as the company grows and as information needs evolve.

Basic obligations of the information policy

1 Information resources are the property of *Company A* as a whole, not of individuals or groups within the firm.
2 Everybody in the organization is required to:
  – Know what information they require in order to do their job.
  – Be aware of the information needs of others within both their department and other functions.
  – Use information in order to enhance their knowledge to support their work.
  – Interchange information and knowledge with people both inside and outside of the organization to help the firm achieve its aims.

  – Effectively manage information resources that they are responsible for.
3 *Company A* is obliged to provide all staff with the education, training and support to enable them to do so.
4 Colleagues will apply their tacit knowledge in their role and are expected to make it available to the organisation's knowledge base if they leave *Company A*.

Policy details (extract)
Company A will:
1 Define the knowledge that it requires to achieve its goals, and identify the ways in which all staff need to use information and knowledge.
2 Audit the firm's use of information regularly to ensure effective use and transference of information and knowledge is upheld.
3 Ensure that the right information is gathered from external sources and generated inside to facilitate all staff in their roles.
4 Exploit all knowledge fully to meet the information needs of all staff, and to adapt to changes in both the environment and the company's goals.
5 Ensure that all information is delivered on time, to the right people, in the right format.
6 Identify those individuals responsible for managing information resources, and the stakeholders of such resources.
7 Promote the exchange of information between the managers of information resources and the stakeholders.
8 Develop and maintain an infrastructure of systems and information technology to support the management of information resources and information interactions within Company A and externally.
9 Use knowledge and information ethically in all of the firm's internal and external activities, so as to preserve and enhance its reputation.
10 Safeguard our resources of information – current and historical – so that they remain accessible for use at all times.

Source: Mike Swain, Liverpool John Moores University

Risk management is used to identify potential risks in a range of situations and then take actions to minimize the risks. We all unconsciously perform risk management throughout our lives. For example, when driving we will constantly assess the risk of actions taken by other drivers, assess the likelihood of danger and respond accordingly. Before we set out, when planning our route, we may also manage risks by considering which are the most dangerous routes and which are the most likely to have delays. Organizational risk management shares most in common with the second situation. Risk management involves evaluating potential risks and then developing strategies to reduce risks and learn about future risks. Risk management typically has these four steps:

1 Identify risks, including their probabilities and impacts.
2 Identify possible solutions to these risks.
3 Implement the solutions targeting the highest-impact, most likely risks.
4 Monitor the risks to learn for future risk assessment.

Information management risks were assessed by the Hawley Committee and the categories of risk and solutions identified are summarized in Table 4.6.

The Hawley Committee also suggested that a specific analysis could be conducted for different forms of information asset such as market and customer information or product information and subsets of these. Questions suggested by Hawley (1995) that should be asked are:

1 What is the monetary value of the asset to the organization?
2 What is the value or importance of the asset to the organization defined by impact of theft, damage, loss or major error on a scale of 1–5?
3 What is the value or importance of the asset to the organization defined by its potential to increase revenue or reduce costs on a scale of 1–5?

To review the elements of information management strategy reviewed in this chapter against real organizational strategies, complete Activity 4.4 and see Case Study 4.3 for insights on how GlaxoSmithKline managed the implementation of part of its information management strategy.

Table 4.6 Risk management assessment for information management

Area of risk	Solution for reducing risk
1 Accidental damage or loss (including disk corruption)	• Backup and restore procedures (see Chapter 11 for further details) • User education
2 Deliberate acts of theft, abuse, vandalism, etc.	• Security procedures such as anti-virus software, firewalls (see Chapter 11) • Employee contracts and disciplinary procedures
3 Loss of people	• Employee contracts • Succession planning
4 Inaccurate or untimely information	• Validation and verification procedures (see Chapter 11) • Staff development and training
5 External relations	• Security procedures • Contractual measures
6 Intellectual property rights (IPR)	• Employee contracts • Registration of IPR
7 Destruction of facilities	• Disaster recovery planning (see Chapter 11)
8 Legal accountability	• Protection and security • Employee training

Source: adapted from Hawley, 1995

Activity 4.4 — Evaluating information strategies at UK universities and colleges

Purpose
To explore the development of an information management strategy in one type of organization.

Activity

visit the www

Refer to case studies from JISC listed at:
www.jisc.ac.uk/search.aspx?keywords=case+studies

These have been implemented through adoption of the JISC (1995) standards. Select one or several of the institutions for which a published information management strategy exists. Now evaluate the published information strategy capabilities of the institution(s) against the elements of information strategy described in this chapter, i.e.

- IM theme 1: Information value
- IM theme 2: Information quality
- IM theme 3: Information security
- IM theme 4: Legal and ethical compliance
- IM theme 5: Knowledge management
- IM theme 6: Technology support
- IM management approach 1: Structuring the information management function
- IM management approach 2: Responsibilities
- IM management approach 3: Information resource analysis
- IM management approach 4. Information policy
- IM management approach 5. Risk management

Case study 4.3   FT

Information management at GlaxoSmithKline – the Robin Hood connection

This case gives a different perspective on information management at GlaxoSmithKline from that in Case study 4.2 which was from the Director of Global Information and Records Management. In Case study 4.3, the perspective is from a technology manager, Arif Devji, UK director of IT Infrastructure. The case looks at the introduction of a new storage management system and how buy-in and funding from different business areas were achieved.

The headquarters of pharmaceuticals giant GlaxoSmithKline (GSK) makes a bold statement, towering over the M4 motorway on the approach into Central London. And with 100,000 employees and annual pharmaceutical sales of nearly $25bn, it has a massive requirement for storing information.

That need is managed by Arif Devji, UK director of IT Infrastructure, and the prime mover behind an ambitious project called 'Sherwood'. This name comes from the lair of the English legend Robin Hood, who took from the rich to give to the poor. Mr Devji took funds from various GSK internal budgets and repaid the donors in huge IT savings.

When a new pharmaceutical product is distributed, GSK has to keep track of every consignment. If one patient experiences an adverse reaction to a drug treatment then GSK might scan through millions of records to locate and recall a particular batch of drugs. This is a global liability – a product shipped from London can be recalled by the US Food and Drug Administration. Mr Devji stresses that this places a weighty responsibility on GSK's IT services. 'We cannot say we will try our best. Lives are at stake here.'

GSK have been using RFID to track products from development onwards. The technology can be employed in the laboratory where it retains information about the contents of test tubes through to providing detailed traceability on manufactured and delivered shipments (**www.computing.co.uk/computing/news/2142928/retailers-seeing-returns-rfid**).

Despite heavy investment in storage devices, largely from Hewlett-Packard, GSK's storage needs were doubling every year. But this growth in physical capacity was undermined by inefficient usage.

Storing data on the latest technology is straightforward. But accessing it is not. The structure of data can create low utilisation of expensive equipment.

Mr Devji admits that at GSK 'our utilisation rate was quite low, around 50 per cent'. All this storage resource operated on the direct attached storage (DAS) model, with each storage unit hooked directly, but separately, into one part of GSK's IT infrastructure.

Software compatibility between different generations of storage was a further issue. 'Most of the storage hardware came from HP, but the site had grown over 10 years and we had seven suppliers in all. Nobody starts with a clean slate in IT, but backing up these different systems while keeping colleagues in other time zones happy was becoming a real problem.'

The legacy of pharmaceutical sector mergers involving SmithKline and Beecham and Glaxo Wellcome had left its mark on the diverse IT resource that GSK inherited. Mr Devji took the challenge of overhauling GSK's storage strategy as a very personal quest. 'I had to come up with a solution', he says.

GSK employs the largest sales and marketing force in the pharmaceuticals industry, and the Sherwood project had to justify itself by boosting the sales line. This was not going to be an IT-driven project. Mr Devji claims that the potential savings from Sherwood meant that GSK executives were ready to sacrifice elements of their sales and marketing budgets, rather than expecting the entire spend to come from the IT department. 'If you enable your colleagues to function well, they will trust you more', he says.

The human element loomed large in Mr Devji's plan. His IT staff had grown weary of servicing the heterogeneous storage resource at inconvenient times. 'I told them I would give them their weekends back.' Sherwood would be built around a single supplier and storage giant EMC was chosen for one reason above all, that it specialises in the storage issue to the exclusion of any other IT products.

Network-attached storage (NAS) was the new architecture. NAS keeps storage apart from other systems, but allows a host of different computers to access that storage, rather than funnelling the data via one machine as in the DAS model. One EMC Symmetrix machine, costing £750,000, replaced a host of storage devices. The utilisation issue, with one storage device being full to capacity while another had surplus space that could not be accessed in the DAS world, became a thing of the past. With NAS, software – rather than hardware – is the prime force. Data can be recalled and deposited across a range of systems and physical sites. Mr Devji's passion evidently drove Sherwood through departmental committees. 'If you are single-mindedly obsessed with doing the right thing you will win support from others and you will make it work', he says.

Sherwood has been up and running for a year. It has already produced savings of £1.3m, derived not just from storage processing, but from reductions in telephony and efficiencies in staff deployment.

Challenged to prove that these are real figures, Mr Devji does not hesitate. 'How do I know it is working? I look at my own budget. It has been cut by £700,000 in the past year and will be reduced by £300,000 in consecutive years. And our staff retention today is fantastic.'

GSK had also made significant advances in the way that information was stored and communicated when it replaced its 14 libraries with a single virtual library. Although the project will reduce headcount the main benefits will be in standardisation of information availability and the release of vital and expensive floorspace. One key area of the project was in improving staff information-retrieval skills. While specialist information management staff will remain in place GSK is investigating data mining software which will enable scientific staff to perform their own queries (**www.research-information.info/riwin03rees.html**).

Source: Michael Dempsey, Corporate profile: GlaxoSmithKline, Feather in cap for Sherwood leader, FT.com; 16 October 2002

Questions

1 Why is storage management an important business issue for GlaxoSmithKline?

2 How was buy-in for this information management project achieved from the business units? What are the benefits and drawbacks of this approach?

As a summary of the strategic issues of information management introduced in this chapter, refer to the following guidelines from Evernden and Evernden (2003). These authors provide these guidelines for use as a diagnostic for how well information is managed within an organization. They can also be considered as prerequisites for an information management strategy.

1 *There is a clear and distinct vision of information as a corporate resource.* These authors believe that a separate responsibility for corporate information and technology is a success factor for information management. Management and staff recognition of the importance of information is one of the measures for whether there is a clear and distinct vision.

2 There is an organization unit responsible for information and knowledge that is distinct from the information technology function. The authors do acknowledge that this could be a separate team or group within the IT function, but recommend that it be separate to highlight the importance of information management.

3 *There is a well-defined strategy and action plan for improving the effectiveness of information use across the organization.* The authors suggest that evidence of a well-defined strategy includes projects to improve information quality, auditing of information resources through an information map and training programmes for maximizing the use of information.

4 *Information that is vital and necessary to make key decisions is always readily and easily available.* Questions that determine whether information is 'readily and easily available' include whether additional information is needed, whether current information could be presented better and whether improvement of decision-making capability is possible.

5 *All information is available in a consistent and integrated format.* If information is from multiple sources this consistent information is unlikely to be achieved.

6 *Management believes that there is considerable value to be gained from the organization's use of information.* This is related to the first diagnostic. This is about the perception of importance of information as a management tool.

7 *Information management is seen as the responsibility of business people as well as the information technology function.* This shows whether an organization has been successful in assigning responsibility for information quality and usage to business areas. If responsibility resides in an information technology function then issues such as information security are likely to be addressed, but not information utility.

8 *Information has a key role in all business processes.* By definition and through necessity information is required to support business processes, but this comment addresses whether information is used adequately to improve the performance of these processes.

9 Financial approval is readily available for investment in the information infrastructure of the organization (as opposed to technology investments). This is really a further test for whether strategic importance is attached to information management. The authors point out that justifying investment in technology projects may be more straightforward in that there are more tangible deliverables.

10 Information is used to support innovation and creativity in product and service development, business processes and customer support. These are specific examples of the business processes in point 8, but those highlighted are those where information application is sometimes neglected.

Summary

1 Distinct information management strategy is developed in many organizations to help exploit and protect information assets. An information management strategy will include the following themes and strategies.

2 *IM theme 1:* Information value. Involves prioritization of information assets to focus on the most valuable. High-value assets must be protected and distributed and should be commercially exploited.

3 *IM theme 2:* Information quality. Information quality, which is its suitability for end-users, depends on its content-relevance, timeliness and form. Procedures need to be in place to evaluate and improve information quality.

4 *IM theme 3:* Information security. Information should be safeguarded from accidental and deliberate modification or deletion by both people and natural events. Many organizations develop an information security management system or information security policy to protect their information assets.

5 *IM theme 4:* Legal and ethical compliance. Organizations should ensure their information usage is consistent with legal and ethical norms in the countries in which they operate.

6 *IM theme 5:* Knowledge management. Strategies for capturing, developing and sharing knowledge within an organization are developed.

7 *IM theme 6:* Technology support. Technology support to achieve the objectives of the information management strategy involves deploying the information systems applications and infrastructure.

8 *IM management approach 1:* Structuring the information management function. An organizational unit focusing on managing information can be created.

9 *IM management approach 2:* Responsibilities and training. Responsibilities should be understood for governance, stewardship, infrastructure and usage.

10 *IM management approach 3:* Information resource analysis. Techniques such as information mapping and information audits can be used to support the IM themes described above.

11 *IM management approach 4:* Risk management. Threats to information are identified and plans put in place to minimize these risks.

Exercises

Self-assessment questions

1 Distinguish between information management and knowledge management.

2 Summarize the needs for a distinct information management strategy within an organization.

3 What is the typical relationship between information systems and information management strategy in an organization?

4 How can an information management strategy manage organizational information as a resource?

5 How can information quality be assessed and improved?

6 Describe different ways in which responsibilities for information management can be assigned.

7 Describe the purpose and content of an information policy.

8 What are the stages in creating an information audit?

9 Summarize approaches to information mapping.

Essay and discussion questions

1 Discuss alternative approaches to structuring the information management function within an organization.

2 Assess the most appropriate relationship between information management, knowledge management, information systems and e-business strategies within a large organization.

3 Evaluate the suitability of the Hawley (1995) recommendations for information management.

4 Which factors shape the role and responsibilities of the chief information officer in a large organization?

5 Assess different approaches to analysing the use of information as a resource in an organization.

6 You are an information management consultant. Produce a template for the elements of information strategy that could be applied in different organizations.

References

Ballou, D., Madnick, S. and Wang, R. (2003) Assuring information quality. *Journal of Management Information Systems*, 20 (3), 9–11.

BSI (2001) Information and documentation – Records management – Part 1 General. British Standard BS ISO 15489–1:2001.

Burk, C. (1988) *Infomap: A Complete Guide to Discovering Corporate Information Resources.* Prentice-Hall, Englewood Cliffs, NJ.

Butler Group (2006) *Enterprise Search and Retrieval*, Research report, October. Accessed from http://www.networkworld.com/news/2006/102006-search-cuts-productivity.html

Casson, M. and Wadeson, N. (1996) Information strategies and the theory of the firm. *International Journal of the Economics of Business*, 3 (3), 307–330.

Computing (2008a) IT Frozen Out in Birds Eye Deal. By Angelica Mari [03-04-2008] Available online at: www.computing.co.uk/computing/news/2213375/frozen-birds-eye-deal-3928474.

Computing (2008b) Security chiefs urged to embrace risk. By Phil Muncaster [03-03-2008] Available online at: www.computing.co.uk/itweek/news/2213410/security-chiefs-urged-embrace.

Deming, W. E. (1986) *Out of the Crisis*. MIT Center for Advanced Engineering Study, Cambridge, MA.

Evernden, R. and Evernden, E. (2003) *Information First. Integrating Knowledge and Information Architecture for Business Advantage*. Butterworth Heinemann, Oxford.

Hawley, R. (1995) Information as an asset: The board agenda/The Hawley Committee; a consultative document for chairmen, chief executives and boards of directors developed on behalf of the KPMG IMPACT Programme by a committee under the chairmanship of Dr Robert Hawley, chief executive of Nuclear Electric plc. – London: KPMG, 1995. [1]: A consultative report. – 30pp.; 30cm. [2]: Checklist and explanatory notes. – 16pp.; 23cm.

Horton, F. (1988) Mapping corporate information resources. *International Journal of Information Management*, 8, 249–54.

Information World Review (2003) No place for a chief information officer. By James Ashton [10-03-2003] Available online at: www.computing.co.uk/Features/1139450.

ITPro (2008) Too Many Cooks Spoil the Broth. Asavin Wattanajantra [31-01-2008] Available online at: www.itpro.co.uk/news/161316/too-many-cooks-spoil-the-broth-in-it-strategy.html.

JISC (1995) *Guidelines for Developing an Information Strategy. The Joint Information Systems Committee of the UK for Future and Higher Education.* Available online at: www.jisc.ac.uk/index.cfm?name=infostrategiesrguidelines.

Johnson, G. and Scholes, K. (2001) *Exploring Corporate Strategy,* 6th edn. Financial Times Prentice Hall, Harlow.

Kluge, J., Stein, W. and Licht, T. (2001) *Knowledge Unplugged: The McKinsey and Company Global Survey on Knowledge Management.* Palgrave, Basingstoke, UK.

Marchand, D., Kettinger, W. and Rollins, J. (2002) *Information Orientation: The Link to Business Performance.* Oxford University Press, Oxford.

Oppenheim, C., Stenson, J. and Wilson, R. (2002) A new approach to valuing information assets. *Journal of Information Science,* 29(5), 419–32.

Orna, E. (1999) *Practical Information Policies,* 2nd edn. Gower, Basingstoke.

Outsell (2001) Super Information about Information Managers. Report on study conducted by Outsell Inc. for Factiva, Dialog and KPMG.

PricewaterhouseCoopers (2010) The PricewaterhouseCoopers Global State of Information Security Survey 2010. Research report, published September.

Simon, Herber A. (1991) Bounded rationality and organizational learning. *Organizational Science,* 2, (1), 17–27.

Swash, G. (1997) The information audi. *The Journal of Managerial Psychology,* 12 (5), 312–18.

Xu, H. and Koronios, A. (2004) Understanding information quality in e-business. *Journal of Computer Information Systems,* 45 (2), 73–82.

Ward, J. and Peppard, J. (2002) *Strategic Planning for Information Systems,* 3rd edn. Wiley, Chichester.

Willard, N. (1993) Information resource management. *Aslib Information,* 21(5).

ZDNet (2008a) IT Chiefs Need More Incentive to go Green. [20-03-2008] Available online at: http://news.zdnet.co.uk/itmanagement/0,1000000308,39370689,00.htm.

ZDNet (2008b) Microsoft Nears Bottom of Greenpeace League Table. [18-03-2008] Available online at: http://news.zdnet.co.uk/hardware/0,1000000091,39369882,00.htm.

Further reading

Henczel, S. (2001) *The Information Audit: A Practical Guide.* Springer Verlag, Heidelberg. Describes an approach to completing an information audit; includes Australian case studies to illustrate the different stages of the information audit.

Orna, E. (1999) *Practical Information Policies,* 2nd edn. Gower, Basingstoke. Describes an alternative approach to completing an information audit; includes UK case studies.

Ward, J. and Peppard, J. (2002) *Strategic Planning for Information Systems,* 3rd edn. Wiley, Chichester. Chapter 10, Strategies for Information Management: Towards Knowledge Management provides an excellent overview of approaches for developing a strategic information management framework.

visit the www

Weblinks

CIO Connect (http://visitors.cio-connect.com/magazine/) Freely available magazine with case studies and articles about issues concerning CIOs in large UK organizations.

COBIT (www.isaca.org/cobit) IT governance model for control objectives for information and related technology.

IBM Systems journal (www.research.ibm.com/journal) Articles by IBM researchers including information management and knowledge management.

Information Research Online journal (http://informationr.net/ir) Published by Professor T.D. Wilson of the University of Sheffield. Main focus is information retrieval, but useful papers on knowledge and information management.

Information World Review – VNU Publishing (**www.iwr.co.uk**) European weekly. No archive at this site, but can be searched from *Computing*.

JISC Information Strategy guidelines (**www.jisc.ac.uk**) The Joint Information Systems Committee of UK for Future and Higher Education has guidelines and cases for developing information strategy in the UK.

Managing Information (**www.managinginformation.com**). ASLIB publishes the subscription magazine *Managing Information* which has partial online content and a newsletter online.

> For multiple-choice questions and annotated weblinks relating to this chapter visit this book's website at: **www.pearsoned.co.uk/chaffey**

5

Knowledge management strategy

Objective

To apply tools and models to develop knowledge management strategies.

Learning outcomes

After reading this chapter, you will be able to:

● Understand the nature of organizational knowledge.
● Assess the value of organizational knowledge.
● Identify key management issues of knowledge management.
● Select and assess the value of information systems to knowledge management.

Management issues

Typical questions facing managers related to this topic:

● How do we use knowledge to increase organizational efficiency and competitiveness?
● How can ICT support a knowledge management strategy?
● What are typical barriers to effective knowledge management?
● How should knowledge management strategy be aligned with corporate strategy?

Links to other chapters

The main related chapters are:

➤ *Chapter 1* introduces data, information and knowledge and their relationship. Also introduces information and knowledge management.
➤ *Chapter 8* describes approaches for managing change associated with the introduction of new IS, IM and KM processes.
➤ *Chapter 10* discusses techniques for evaluating and improving the quality of information and knowledge.

Introduction

Knowledge and wisdom have been valued in society for centuries, embedded in and transferred through many different social processes. The symbol of wisdom in an owl is recognizable and venerated throughout the world. However, fast-paced change in the business world led to many organizations undervaluing the role knowledge played in their organizations and did not assess the impacts of knowledge loss.

During the Second World War observers noted that the building of a second aeroplane took considerably less time than that of the first one, and the second had fewer defects than the first. This was the start of the process of 'learning by doing' and 'learning from experience' (Prusak, 1998). A realization emerged that if organizations can manage the learning process better, then they can become more efficient.

Knowledge management (KM) has developed and grown as a concept since it came to prominence in the mid-1990s when writers such as Davenport and Prusak published some of the first articles on the topic. The management of knowledge and the development of knowledge strategies have become priorities for organizations as they have realized how the application of knowledge can be key in adding value and differentiating products and services. The position of chief knowledge officer (CKO) has become a key strategic role alongside chief information officer (CIO) in many organizations.

Knowledge management strategy
Defined and coordinated plan of actions to enable core business processes using knowledge management techniques

An overview of the **knowledge management strategy** process followed in this chapter is illustrated in Figure 5.1. This process illustrates an approach to knowledge management, from understanding theories defining the nature of knowledge, then assessing knowledge assets, developing a strategic approach based on the knowledge requirements of the organizations, and implementing the strategy using a range of techniques.

The focus will be firstly to understand how knowledge supports the underlying business processes and corporate objectives and then to classify the knowledge. Knowledge gaps can then be targeted. Then strategy approaches and practical imple-

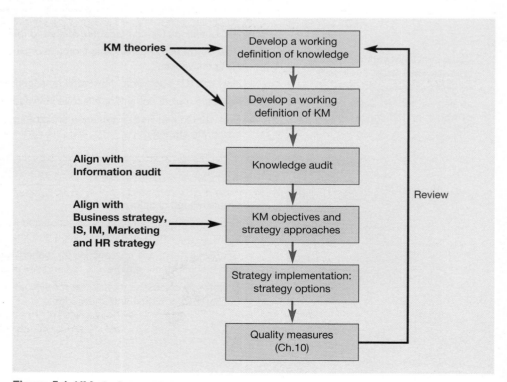

Figure 5.1 KM strategy process

mentations can be identified. A knowledge management strategy must have an element of measurement in order to feed back and improve the knowledge quality and assess return on investment (ROI). Information and knowledge quality are discussed in Chapter 10.

We have seen in previous chapters (1 and 4) how organizations develop an information orientation, using information management and information systems for competitive advantage; in this chapter we shall discuss how knowledge management enables knowledge creation, decision making and innovation. All organizations will use knowledge as the basis for action; knowledge management has relevance to businesses from the SME to the multinational.

It is important to remember that knowledge management is not new: organizations have always practised it to some degree; what has happened is that the pace of change in the economy and the competitive nature of global and national economies have meant that knowledge is now the key to competitive advantage in a way that was not apparent before.

The concept of 'knowledge workers' has emerged – Bahra (2001) distinguishes them from 'procedural workers' using the following characteristics:

- Knowledge workers are changed by the information in their environment, and they in turn seek to change others through information.
- Diversity and ad-hoc patterns are common in knowledge work. New information is sought out, reused and passed on in opportunistic ways, dependent on the changing context and interleaving of the workers' activities.
- Communications networks are highly variable, with different patterns and use of media. Teams form and disband within the space of a day.

Knowledge management has also been influenced by the emergence of decision theory and the use of information technology to enhance information quality and the decision-making process. The importance of decision making for an organization to function effectively is illustrated by the use of decision support systems by managers over the past 30 years. In Chapter 2, on page 42, we saw how the Anthony model identifies decision making at three levels: operational, tactical and strategic.

Defining knowledge

To recap from Chapter 1: the European Framework for Knowledge Management (Mekhilef et al., 2003) defines data, information, and knowledge:

- *Data*. Discrete, objective facts (numbers, symbols, figures) without context and interpretation.
- *Information*. Data which add value to the understanding of a subject, and in context, are the basis for knowledge.
- *Knowledge*. The combination of data and information, to which is added expert opinion, skills and experience, to result in a valuable asset which can be used to aid decision making. Knowledge may be explicit and/or tacit, individual and/or collective.

It is therefore important that we understand the difference between these three concepts and their relationship in an organizational context; each organization will have unique scenarios involving combinations of data, information and knowledge.

From information to knowledge and from knowledge to information

The meaning of data and information and the relationship between them is relatively straightforward, but this is not the case with defining knowledge! On a simple level, knowledge can be regarded as the next level of sophistication or business value after the transformation from data to information. However, the reverse transformation from knowledge to information also occurs. Orna (1999) says:

> Knowledge and information are separate but interacting entities; we transform one to another constantly.

For knowledge held by an individual to be communicated to others it must be converted into verbal, written or visual information. In the context of Figure 1.8, knowledge tends to be less structured and is often transmitted informally – it is less tangible than structured, formal information.

Murray (2000) describes how Professor N. Venkatraman at Boston University School of Management suggests the 'DIKAR model' of transformation of Data to Information to Knowledge to Actions to Results. He notes that the reverse transformation process 'RAKID' also occurs and this is instructive to understanding what relevant knowledge is – relevant knowledge informs business actions and results. The 'DIKAR model' is described in more detail at the start of Chapter 10 in the context of managing information quality.

Returning to our airline company example (Figure 1.7) helps explain this relationship between data, information and knowledge. In this case, the data from individual ticket sales are transformed into information about the relative performance of different routes in terms of capacity utilization (proportion of seats sold). This information might include trends from previous years, sales against budget and maps of sales for different regions. However, this information is of little value if the manager does not know how to interpret and respond to it. As Einstein put it:

> Computers are incredibly fast, accurate and stupid. – Human beings are incredibly slow, inaccurate and brilliant. – Together they are powerful beyond imagination.

Knowledge
The application of expert opinion, skills and experience to data and information for decision making

Knowledge management
The combination of strategies, techniques and tools used to capture and share knowledge within an organization

To add value to this information, managers must apply their **knowledge** to decide how to respond if the sales and seat utilization on one route are much lower than on others. Thus knowledge is the processing of information and is a skill based on previous understanding, procedures and experience. The knowledge capability can be considered to be an individual asset of managers or a collective asset for the organization as a whole – organizational knowledge. **Knowledge management (KM)** seeks to share this experience within a company.

The European Guide to Best Practice in Knowledge Management (Mekhilef et al., 2003) defines knowledge as:

> The combination of data and information to which is added expert opinion, skills and experience to result in a valuable asset which can be used to make decisions. It is the essential factor in adding meaning to information. Knowledge may be explicit and/or tacit, individual and/or collective.

To further explain knowledge we can make these observations:

- Information is of little value until we apply knowledge to act upon it – it is knowledge that enables effective decision making.

- Knowledge refers to what an organization's employees know and understand – their expertise.

- Knowledge is learnt through experience and education.

The definition of Mekhilef et al. (2003) also includes the concepts of explicit and tacit knowledge. **Explicit knowledge** refers to details of processes and procedures that have been codified or captured and recorded. Explicit knowledge can be readily detailed in procedural manuals and databases. Examples include records of meetings between sales representatives and key customers, procedures for dealing with customer service queries and management reporting processes. **Tacit knowledge** is less tangible than explicit knowledge – it refers to experience on how to react to a situation when many different variables are involved. It is more difficult to encapsulate this knowledge, which often resides in the heads of employees. Techniques for sharing this knowledge include learning stories and histories. Examples include knowing how to react when changes occur in the marketplace, such as a competitor launching a new product or a merger between two major competitors.

Knowledge management implies that an organization has adopted a structured approach to utilizing knowledge. The European Knowledge Management Framework identifies five core knowledge process activities, which are related as shown in Figure 5.2. These are:

1 *Identify knowledge.* The requirements or reasons for knowledge management are assessed and an analysis is undertaken of what knowledge is available and what knowledge is lacking (the knowledge gap).

2 *Generate (new) knowledge.* Practices are developed to create new knowledge. Heisig and Iske (2003) mention training and learning by joint problem solving at the team or individual level at the department or organizational level through research and development, establishment of expert groups which are sometimes called 'communities of practice', recruitment of experts and buying another company. Furthermore, knowledge creation is firmly linked with action and experience (Miller and Morris, 1999; Leonard and Sensiper, 1998), with action being regarded as '*the basic unit of learning activity*' (Bedny, Karowski and Bedny, 2001, p. 414).

3 *Store knowledge.* Knowledge assets are built up by finding ways of embedding knowledge in the organization of its employees. This does not necessarily mean storing it in databases, since most tacit knowledge will remain in the heads of people.

4 *Distribute knowledge.* A method must be found of transferring knowledge to particular employees of teams as they need it. Heisig and Iske (2003) identify the *Stock* method of distribution where knowledge is made available through databases and the *Flow* method where knowledge is transferred directly from person to person through collaboration, workshops or mentoring.

5 *Apply knowledge.* All the other KM activities will be wasted if the knowledge sources are not utilized.

Figure 5.2 also shows that to be successful, the five core knowledge management activities need to be aligned or integrated into the organizational business processes. KM will also involve external knowledge sharing with clients and suppliers.

A perhaps overused but common expression in business is 'our people are our most valuable asset'. This value arises principally because of the knowledge of the people. So staff along with other knowledge resources are sometimes referred to as knowledge assets or **intellectual capital (IC)**.

Knowledge management is a theme throughout this book, but is referred to in detail in Chapters 4 and 8 where issues involved in KM strategy and implementation are described. Key managerial issues with knowledge management are highlighted by the findings of a 1999 IDC survey of 255 US CIOs. The main problems noted were:

● Lack of understanding of KM and its benefits (55 per cent)

● Lack of employee time for KM (45 per cent)

● Lack of skill in KM techniques (40 per cent)

Explicit knowledge
Codified knowledge that can be readily expressed and understood, such as business procedures

Tacit knowledge
Mainly intangible knowledge that is typically intuitive and difficult to record

Intellectual capital
The knowledge assets of an organization comprising the people, structures and tools used to utilize knowledge within an organization and its stakeholders

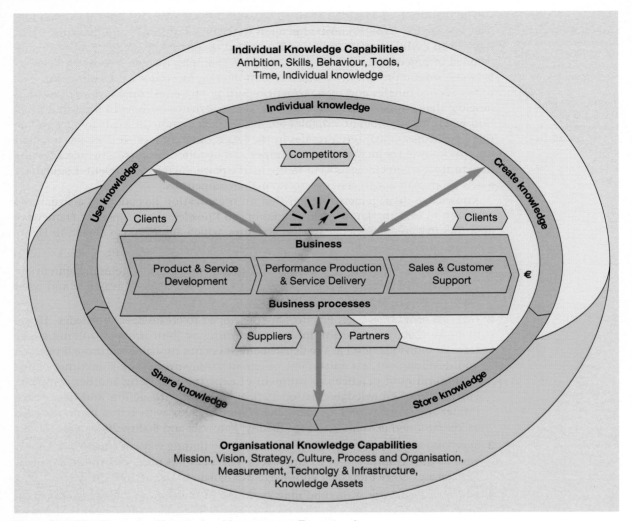

Figure 5.2 The European Knowledge Management Framework
Source: Heisig and Iske (2003)

- Lack of encouragement in the current culture for sharing (35 per cent)
- Lack of incentives/rewards to share (30 per cent)
- Lack of funding for KM initiatives (24 per cent)
- Lack of appropriate technology (18 per cent)
- Lack of commitment from senior management (15 per cent).

To summarize this introduction to knowledge management concepts, the straight-forward definitions provided by Dan Power are helpful (Power, 1999):

Knowledge refers to what one knows and understands. Knowledge is sometimes categorized as either unstructured, structured, explicit or tacit. What we know we know is explicit knowledge. Knowledge that is unstructured and understood, but not clearly expressed is implicit knowledge. If the knowledge is organized and easy to share then it is called structured knowledge. To convert implicit knowledge into explicit knowledge, it must be extracted and formatted.

Knowledge Management is the distribution, access and retrieval of unstructured information about 'human experiences' between interdependent individuals or among members of a workgroup. Knowledge management involves identifying a group of people who have a need to share knowledge, developing technological support that enables knowledge sharing, and creating a process for transferring and disseminating knowledge.

Debate 5.1

> *Distinguishing between information management and knowledge management activities within an organization is not useful since the two need to be managed as an integrated whole.*

To conclude this section, Figure 5.3 summarizes different methods of categorizing organizational information sources.

Traditionally, the model shown in Figure 5.4 is used to represent data information and knowledge. Snowden (2003) in Figure 5.5 takes a different view, focusing on the concept of wisdom as an overarching concept, focused on the role of knowledge and the context, transforming data into information that can be transferred. Snowden's model is preferable as it emphasizes the complexities of organizational processes.

Davenport and Prusak (1998) also provide a valuable discussion of knowledge:

> Knowledge is a fluid mix of framed experience, values, contextual information, and expert insight that provides a framework for evaluating and incorporating new experiences and information. It originates and is applied in the minds of knowers. In organizations, it often becomes embedded not only in documents and repositories but also in organizational routines, processes, practices, and norms.

There are many wide-ranging interpretations of what knowledge is across the fields of information technology, human resources, information systems and information management. An organization developing a knowledge management strategy must agree upon what knowledge means for its business activity, learn from academic discussion of the issue and then develop its own definition. As we shall see in the strategy section, there are many different ways in which organizations can imple-

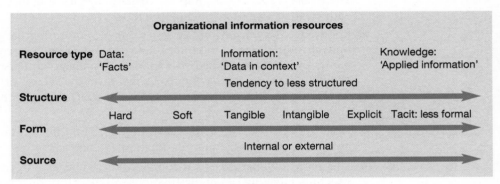

Figure 5.3 Different ways to categorize information resources

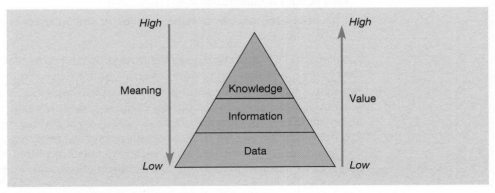

Figure 5.4 Data, information and knowledge

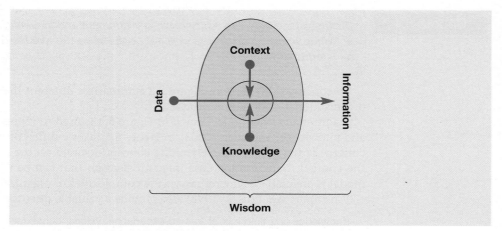

Figure 5.5 Alternative view of data, information and knowledge
Source: Snowden (2003)

ment a knowledge management strategy, and understanding the nature of knowledge in their organization is vital to devising an appropriate approach.

Using the example of the Lo-cost Airline Company we can identify some examples of data, information and knowledge in a business context:

- Data: the airline will hold vast amounts of data on customers: names, addresses, credit card information, passport numbers, dates of travel, travel destination. The airline will also gather external data about the pricing strategies of its competitors. These data are held in a database. The airline marketing manager has been briefed with creating a new fare pricing structure.

- Knowledge developed from several years of monitoring the external market and understanding how to interpret the external data on fares compared to the company's own data is applied. The marketing manager understands the context in which to use the data, having read a report on the success of a previous campaign and from a meeting with sales executives at which customer perceptions of pricing and destination choice were discussed.

- From the databases, the manager will produce information in the form of a report, grouping customers by travel destination and fare paid.

- The marketing manager then combines these elements to produce a new pricing structure, targeting certain destinations. A report (information) is sent to the chief executive to communicate the knowledge the manager has developed and to trigger actions and decisions that will enable the airline to remain competitive and enable market differentiation.

- The chief executive, overseeing all parts of the business, now has the wisdom to make a decision.

Polanyi (1967) introduced two definitions of knowledge: tacit knowledge (subjective) and explicit knowledge (objective). Tacit knowlege is knowledge of experience – simultaneously knowledge and practice. Explicit knowlege is about rationality and sequential knowledge. To recap from Chapter 1, we introduce the definitions of tacit and explicit from the European Knowledge Management Framework (Mekhilef et al., 2003). Explicit knowledge refers to details of processes and procedures that have been codified. Explicit knowledge can be readily detailed in procedural manuals and databases. Examples include records of meetings between sales representatives and key customers, procedures for dealing with customer service queries and management reporting processes. Tacit knowledge is less tangible than explicit knowledge: it refers to experience on how to react to a situation when many different variables are involved. It is more difficult to encapsulate this knowledge, which often resides in the heads of employees.

In order to understand the value that knowledge can bring to specific business processes and objectives it is vital to understand the nature of organizational knowledge and the transfer and conversion processes that take place. Nonaka and Takeuchi (1995) identify four different processes in which knowledge is created and transferred. These processes are shown in Figure 5.6. They are:

- tacit to tacit through a process of socialization;
- tacit to explicit through a process of externalization;
- explicit to tacit through a process of internalization;
- explicit to explicit through a process of combination.

We can now map the scenario from the Lo-cost Airline Company in the previous scenario into this model:

- Tacit to tacit: the marketing manager discusses and learns about latest sales trends with a sales executive.
- Tacit to explicit: another sales executive sends an e-mail putting forward their thoughts on what the new pricing structure should be.
- Explicit to tacit: the marketing manager reads and understands the reports to develop a new insight and understanding of the situation (knowledge).
- Explicit to explicit: the marketing manager combines knowledge from reports produced from the database to produce an overview of the current situation.

In order to understand the nature of knowledge in organizations and how individuals create knowledge, we should also consider several frameworks for understanding knowledge. The European Framework (Heisig and Iske, 2003) emphasizes a holistic view of knowledge management focused on both individual and organizational knowledge capabilities. Knowledge management practitioners regard the Nonaka model as a useful tool rather than a complete model; the Nonaka framework has limitations as it has been developed in a Japanese cultural context and is based on manufacturing industry experience (Snowden, 2003). Many knowledge initiatives often fail as they focus too closely on the tacit-to-explicit section of Nonaka's model.

We can also define knowledge by type in terms of function (Zak, 2002):

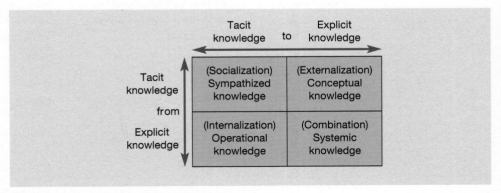

Figure 5.6 Nonaka's tacit/explicit model

Source: from *The Knowledge Creating Company: How Japanese Companies Create the Dynamics of Innovation*, Oxford University Press, New York (Nonaka, I. and Takeuchi, H. (1995), By Permission of Oxford University Press, Inc.

- Declarative knowledge (knowledge about)
- Procedural knowledge (know-how)
- Causal (know why)
- Conditional (know when)
- Relational (know with).

J.C. Spender's framework highlights a distinction between individual and social knowledge: his framework provides a 'contrast between the explicit knowledge that individuals feel they possess and the collective knowledge on which this explicit knowledge actually stands, and the interaction of the two' (Spender, 1998 in Newell et al., 2002). Spender highlights four different types of knowledge:

- Individual/explicit (conscious)
- Individual/implicit (automatic)
- Social/explicit (objectivified)
- Social/implicit (collective).

Strategically Spender has argued that collective knowledge is the most useful because this type of knowledge is the one that firms would find difficult to understand and imitate. Later in the chapter we shall introduce the concept of communities of practice developed by Brown and Duguid (2000) and Wegner et al. (2002) as part of a strategy for developing collective knowledge. However, this framework does not highlight processes for creating knowledge.

Alavi and Leidner (2001) provide a taxonomy of knowledge types that may be present in an organization:

Knowledge type	Definitions	Examples
Tacit	Knowledge is rooted in actions, experience and involvement in specific context	Best means of dealing with specific customer
Cognitive tacit	Mental models	Individual's belief on cause-effect relationships
Technical tacit	Know-how applicable to specific work	Surgery skills
Explicit	Articulated, generalized knowledge	Knowledge of major customers in a region
Individual	Created by and inherent in the individual	Insights gained from completed project
Social	Created by and inherent in collective actions of group	Norms for inter-group communication
Declarative	Know-about	What drug is appropriate for an illness
Procedural	Know-how	How to administer a particular drug
Causal	Know-why	Understanding when to prescribe the drug
Conditional	Know-when	Understanding how the drug interacts with other drugs
Relational	Know-with	Best practices, business frameworks, project experiences, engineering drawings, market reports
Pragmatic	Useful knowledge for an organization	Understanding why the drug works

Frank Blackler (1995) has developed 'five images' of knowledge which draw together views of knowledge from different writers:

● Embrained knowledge is dependent on conceptual skills and cognitive abilities.

● Embodied knowledge is action-oriented and is likely to be only partly explicit.

● Encultured knowledge refers to the process of achieving shared understandings.

● Embedded knowledge is knowledge which resides in systemic routines.

● Encoded knowledge is information conveyed by signs and symbols.

Understanding and applying these three different views of knowledge from Nonaka, Spender and Blackler in the context of their own organization is vital for managers devising a knowledge management programme. These views of knowledge should be used to interpret the results of knowledge audits and assessment techniques such as the ASHEN model (see later in the chapter) and will then inform strategy choices.

Managers should, however, also be aware of the factors that inhibit the creation and transfer of knowledge among their employees. Szulanski (1996) discusses the notion of 'internal stickiness' and identifies 'absorptive capacity', 'causal ambiguity' and 'source–sender relationship' as significant determinants of the success of knowledge transfer between individuals.

Defining knowledge management

Kelleher and Levene (2001), introducing knowledge management in the British Standards Institute's *Guide to Good Practice in Knowledge Management*, uses a definition developed by Royal Dutch/Shell:

> The <u>capabilities</u> by which communities within an <u>organization</u> <u>capture</u> the knowledge that is critical to them, <u>constantly improve it</u> and <u>make it available</u> in the most effective manner to those people who need it, so that they can <u>exploit it creatively</u> to add value as part of their work.

As with definitions of knowledge, it is also vital that organizations develop a definition of knowledge management in relation to their own particular scenarios. By looking at the keywords highlighted in the Shell definition we can see how Shell uses KM processes to add value to its business processes.

The European Framework for Knowledge Management was introduced in Chapter 1 and is shown in Figure 5.2. The framework enables a holistic view to be taken of the business processes, knowledge processes and capabilities required to support knowledge management.

The framework offers a perspective on knowledge management that places organizational business processes at the core. A knowledge management strategy must be based around business objectives. Businesses must understand how knowledge adds value to business performance. Knowledge management is also characterized by the inclusion of clients, competitors, suppliers and partners in the process: the emphasis is on inclusion of all players in the value chain.

The five core processes developed in the European Framework have been developed from analysis of more than 100 knowledge management frameworks. We will now briefly consider each of these core processes (Heisig and Iske, 2003):

1 *Identify knowledge*: people need to think about what they want to achieve and the knowledge required to make it happen. If knowledge is lacking, a knowledge gap has been identified.

2 *Create knowledge*: new knowledge is created by training, learning by doing and problem solving – creating new knowledge for products and services. Innovation is vital to this process.

3 *Store knowledge*: knowledge assets form the knowledge base of an organization. These assets may be stored in documents or databases or memorized as tacit knowledge.

4 *Share knowledge*: distribution to the right people at the right time. The stock approach is when knowledge is shared via documents and databases; a flow approach is when knowledge is shared person-to-person.

5 *Use knowledge*: applying what we know, used in the business processes.

The final layer, individual and organizational capabilities, is focused upon making sure that employees have the right mix of capabilities to use the core knowledge processes successfully in their business processes and that the organization develops an environment to encourage this.

Many organizations mistakenly assume that KM is about the use of information technology and that technology could replace the skill and judgement of an experienced human worker. Technology does, however, aid in the exchange of information and knowledge within and outside the organization (Davenport and Prusak, 1998). It is therefore crucial that the chief knowledge officer or business manager responsible for knowledge management strategy understand the relationship between knowledge and technology. Harry Scarborough (Bahra, 2001) notes that:

> Knowledge management tends to be treated mainly as an issue for information systems experts. The schemes they produce are predominantly on the supply side, focusing on data and communications systems and processes for making people's tacit knowledge explicit and available for the rest of the organization. As a result, knowledge is treated as a commodity and often confused with data.

Davenport and Cronin (2000) have identified three approaches to knowledge management and problems of 'semantic drift' (misuse of language and conflicting definitions of words) when the term is used. The distinctions that are raised are important to make sure that knowledge management initiatives do not simply become information management initiatives. The three approaches are:

- Knowledge management is information management by another name. A conflation of knowledge management with the organization of knowledge, the traditional label for the coding and classification of recorded material (content).

- Knowledge management is the management of know-how: processes and **ontologies**. The emphasis is on the discovery and extraction of value when existing processes and resources are anatomized and recompiled.

- Knowledge management optimizes the conditions for adaptive co-evolution. The key is the interplay of tacit and explicit knowledge.

Ontology
An explicit formal specification of how to represent the objects, concepts and other entities that are assumed to exist in some area of interest and the relationships that hold between them. This term is sometimes used by knowledge managers when dealing with organizational relationships

Commitment to key knowledge principles from the top level of organizations is vital. PricewaterhouseCoopers (2003) identifies the following best practices to enable knowledge management:

- Build executive-level enthusiasm for leveraging organizational knowledge to foster innovation and learning.

- Eliminate organizational barriers that inhibit knowledge sharing.

- Demonstrate organizational commitment to learning and leveraging knowledge.

- Develop a process for identifying organizational knowledge.

- Connect employees through technology and opportunities for personal interaction.

- Make knowledge quickly and easily accessible across the enterprise to support value creation.

In many organizations knowledge management may be owned by IT, HR, finance or marketing departments. The subject is, however, interdisciplinary and wide-ranging. Figure 5.7 illustrates how different management disciplines interact within the concept of knowledge management.

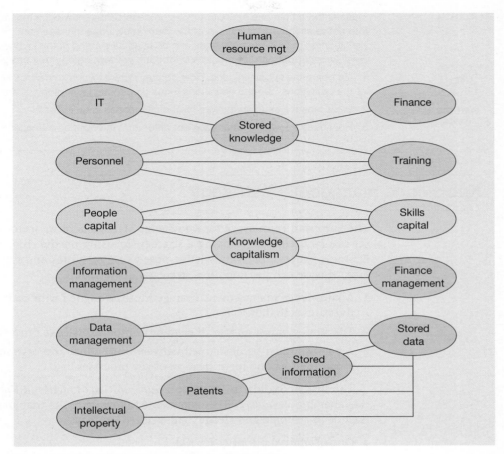

Figure 5.7 Knowledge management relationships
Source: Bahra (2001)

Research insight 5.1   Deadly sins of knowledge management

These are:

1 Not developing a working definition of knowledge
2 Emphasizing knowledge stock to the detriment of knowledge flow
3 Viewing knowledge as existing outside the heads of individuals
4 Not understanding that a fundamental intermediate purpose of managing knowledge is to create shared context
5 Paying little heed to the role and importance of tacit knowledge
6 Disentangling knowledge from its uses
7 Downplaying thinking and reasoning
8 Focusing on the past and the present and not the future
9 Failing to recognize the importance of experimentation
10 Substituting technological contact for human interface
11 Seeking to develop direct measures of knowledge

Source: from *California Management Review*, Vol.40, No.3 (Fahey and Prusak 1998), Copyright 1988, by The Regents of the University of California. Reprinted from the California Management Review, Vol. 40, No.3. By permission of The Regents.

Activity 5.1	Defining knowledge management

Purpose   To illustrate the differing views of knowledge management.

Activity   There is more than one set of practices or ideas about knowledge management. Use the Internet to search for definitions of the term 'knowledge management'. Find at least five definitions. The following websites can be used as starting points: **www.gurteen.com, www.knowledgeboard.com, www.brint.com, www.googleguide.com/glossary.html**

visit the www

1 Compare the five definitions. How do they differ? Which key words or phrases appear in the definitions? Do the definitions focus on people, technology or processes?
2 What reasons can you think of for the differences in definition?
3 How does knowledge management differ from information management?

Knowledge management strategy

The European Framework for Knowledge Management we introduced earlier in chapter can be used in developing a strategy, focusing on the three layers: value-adding business process, core knowledge-processing activities and critical success factors. From this we can develop three strategy imperatives:

1 A knowledge management strategy must be aligned with corporate business objectives and activities.
2 The strategy must enable all elements of the knowledge processing lifecycle.
3 A balance must be developed between individual and organizational capabilities according to 1 and identification of key processes in 2.

The British Standards Institute's *Guide to Good Practice in Knowledge Management* (Kelleher and Levene, 2001) suggests the following topics that an organization should include in a simple knowledge management strategy:

● Organizational priorities for KM
● KM mission and vision
● KM operating plan (including objectives and perceived benefits)
● KM budget
● Plan for KM technical infrastructure
● Plans for KM communities of practice
● Proposed KM metrics and proposed knowledge-sharing incentives and rewards
● Plans for KM training
● Plan for communication of KM strategy to all internal and external stakeholders
● Plan for integrating KM and organizational strategy.

When devising a KM strategy it is vital that the evidence gathered and analysed in the initial evaluation stages of KM strategy development be used to understand how organizational knowledge meets business objectives and future needs and opportunities. The KPMG knowledge management survey (Kok et al., 2003) highlights that strategic knowledge management objectives can only be achieved when they are internally linked to clearly defined business processes.

Organizations must ask themselves the following questions about the nature of their business in relation to knowledge assets required:

- What are the core aspects of our business?
- How is the industry we operate in changing?
- What are our competitors doing to differentiate themselves in the marketplace?

The start of the knowledge management strategy process will make use of traditional strategy tools such as SWOT (Strengths, Weaknesses, Opportunities, Threats) analysis and PEST (Political, Economic, Social and Technology) analysis to assess the general business environment. A knowledge-based SWOT analysis can be used to map knowledge resources available against the four headings. This type of SWOT will ask the following types of question:

- What areas of our business benefit from applied, valued knowledge?
- What areas of our business lack knowledge?
- Are there opportunities to exploit knowledge?
- What (competitive) threats are there to knowledge being lost or losing value?

Research insight 5.2   **How important is knowledge management to business?**

A regular survey on knowledge management among the top 500 organizations in the UK, France, Germany and the Netherlands is carried out by KPMG (Kok et al., 2003). The survey highlights three key challenges for the future deployment of knowledge management:

1 Taking advantage of unexploited business opportunities
2 Extending KM across customers, suppliers and partners
3 Assuring successful implementation.

The survey also highlighted the business case for knowledge management: 80 per cent of respondents considered knowledge to be a strategic asset and 78 per cent of respondents believed they were missing out on business opportunities by failing to exploit available knowledge successfully. In terms of benefits 50 per cent reported clear financial benefits and return; in terms of non-financial benefits 73 per cent experienced quality improvement, 68 per cent increased teamwork, 64 per cent increased speed and responsiveness and 55 per cent better decision making by frontline workers.

A 2001 survey by the management consultants McKinsey found that 'successful companies build a corporate environment that fosters a desire for knowledge among their employees and that ensures its continual application, distribution and creation' (Hauschild et al., 2001). Companies that were successful at knowledge management set ambitious goals for product development and process innovation.

The knowledge audit

Knowledge audit
Systematic, formal assessment of organizational knowledge assets, processes and flows

Before an organization can define the focus, scope and nature of its knowledge management strategy a comprehensive assessment must be made of capabilities and knowledge processes in relation to core business activities. A **knowledge audit** is a systematic process of identifying knowledge assets and their relationship across an organization. It will offer a formalized way of documenting the assessment of the current organizational knowledge base.

The European Framework (Mekhilef et al., 2003) offers this definition:

A systematic review typically, based on questionnaires, interviews or narrative techniques of the knowledge within an organization. Often also includes a systematic mapping of knowledge interactions and flows within and between organizations, teams and individuals.

What is the difference between an information audit and a knowledge audit? These two processes may often be carried out at the same time and may often overlap; however, the two processes should have different outputs. An information audit, as we have seen in Chapter 4 (and will see again in Chapter 10), will focus on assets that an organization has in terms of recorded and documented information. The key difference is that an information audit is likely to be more focused on information 'objects' whereas the knowledge audit is people-centred, focused on employee knowhow and knowledge flow.

The information gained from a knowledge audit will then be used at all points in the knowledge management strategy, from selecting strategy options to defining performance metrics to assessing the success of the knowledge management programme.

A team will need to be assembled to carry out the audit, bringing together a mix of skills. Table 5.1 lists the people who will need to be considered, depending on the objectives of the audit.

The frequency of organizational knowledge audits will depend on the plans put in place in the knowledge strategy, in terms of assessing progress and key business events that fundamentally impact on the organization's knowledge processes. For example, a merger between two organizations will have a large impact on organizational structure, internal networks and sharing issues.

Table 5.1 Knowledge audit roles

Title	Skills/Competencies
Senior manager	Vision – linking knowledge management objectives to business objectives
Business strategist	Planning and goal setting
Human resource manager	Assessment of employee skills and competencies
Corporate information manager/Librarian	Organization of internal and external information assets
Information systems/IT analyst	Development of information systems to support business processes and IT platform implementation
Chief knowledge officer/Knowledge manager	Organizationally independent analyst, understands how KM works across the organization

The knowledge audit process is shown in Figure 5.8.

Define audit objectives

The objectives for the knowledge audit will focus on what the organization needs to know in order to develop a business-focused strategy. Particular business problems already apparent may offer some guidance in the priority of the objectives. Stages in reaching the objectives could include:

● Assess factors that inhibit knowledge sharing.
● Assess factors that encourage or promote knowledge sharing.

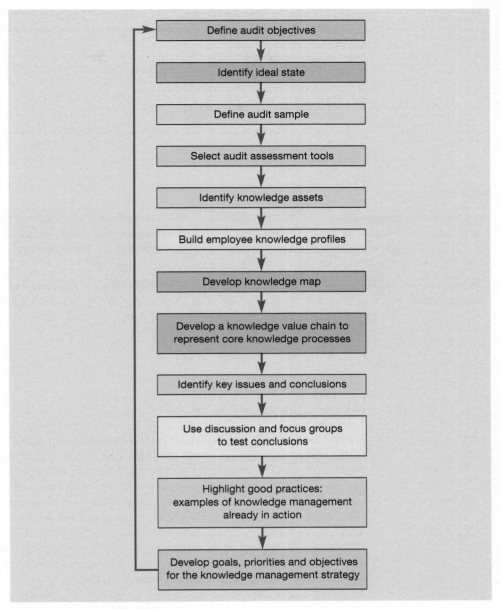

Figure 5.8 Knowledge audit process

- Identify knowledge bottlenecks.
- Identify sources of knowledge creation and innovation.
- Map informal networks and patterns of knowledge sharing across the organization.
- Map knowledge flows from external sources and networks.
- Assess the impact of customer or supplier knowledge.

Identify ideal state

In order to develop a benchmark for the gap analysis stage, organizations must develop a document that assesses the overall business strategy, the desired knowledge processes, assets and capabilities. Analysis of activities of competitors or business partners will also provide important information. This process will also form a crucial part of the strategic planning process. Key business objectives will be broken down and linked related to:

- knowledge assets linked to value-adding business processes;
- knowledge-processing activities;
- individual and organizational capabilities.

Business objectives should be mapped against relevant categories of knowledge as an indication of desired knowledge outcomes. The example in Table 5.2 uses the categories of knowledge introduced earlier.

Table 5.2 Ideal state

Business objectives	Declarative knowledge (knowledge about)	Procedural knowledge (know-how)	Conditional knowledge (know when)	Causal knowledge (know why)	Relational knowledge (know with)
To improve market share	Knowledge about the changes in the overall market sector in which the company operates	Knowledge about how to target new customers	Knowledge about when to launch a new product or service	Knowledge as to why market share has fallen	Knowledge from comparing current sales and stock information

Define audit sample

Several factors may impact upon the size of the audit sample chosen. Knowledge audits can be complex and time-consuming and may require high levels of intensive resourcing. Ideally, knowledge audits should be organization-wide, otherwise many key relationships and knowledge processes can be overlooked. Owing to the organic and fluid nature of modern organizations, many key processes may no longer take place across easily recognizable hierarchical structures. Another view of a knowledge audit will be to focus on products and services rather than organizational units.

The sample will need to reflect all levels of the organization where employees apply knowledge to business processes; in most modern organizations this means that all employees should be considered for inclusion.

After a knowledge audit has been undertaken, knowledge managers now experienced in the process may be able to undertake local small-scale knowledge audits on a regular basis; for example, after a major product or service launch.

Select audit assessment tools

As with all forms of research methodology, the research tools chosen will reflect the objectives of the research. It is likely that a knowledge audit will need to use a mix of tools to develop a balanced view of the organization. Audit tools will include:

- Questionnaires to capture large volumes of data
- Interviews to explore issues in greater depth
- Focus groups to explore issues in greater depth and understand relationships
- Narrative techniques to explore knowledge that is context-dependent, to overcome the problem of people only knowing what they need to know when they need to know it (techniques include narrative databases, storytelling and post-implementation reviews).

| Activity 5.2 | Using the ASHEN model |

Purpose To illustrate the use of the ASHEN model to understand knowledge assets.

Activity Choose either the organizational unit you work in or the cohort of students you belong to. Think of a task you have undertaken and completed as a group.

1 Identify three knowledge disclosure points (KDP)

[a] _____

[b] _____

[c] _____

2 Ask the ASHEN questions for each KDP and complete Table 5.3.

3 Reflect upon how the ASHEN model is useful in the knowledge audit process.

Table 5.3

	KDP 1	KDP 2	KDP 3
Artefacts			
Skills			
Heuristics			
Experience			
Natural talent			

The ASHEN model has been devised by IBM (Snowden, 2003) and offers a holistic view of knowledge assessment in order to make sense of the data and information gained from using the above tools. The ASHEN model focuses on what Snowden describes as 'knowledge disclosure points'. These are any events or activities that reveal knowledge through use:

- decisions
- problem resolution
- solution creation
- judgement
- learning points.

Using the example of the Lo-cost Airline Company scenario introduced earlier, a knowledge disclosure point would be when the airline marketing manager uses judgement to make a decision about the pricing structure.

These are then used to create the context in which the ASHEN questions can be asked. ASHEN breaks down into these categories:

- *Artefacts*. Anything made by people, processes, documents, tools in which knowledge is embedded.
- *Skills*. Abilities that can be trained and measured without ambiguity – but remember the time issue.
- *Heuristics*. Rules of thumb, the outcome of experience, the main repository of knowledge, mostly unarticulated.
- *Experience*. Accumulated experience of failure and success which allows the right pattern to be triggered in the right context.
- *Natural talent*. Some people are just better at doing things than other people – and they are often not the people you expect.

The results of the ASHEN process will then feed into the development of inventories of knowledge assets, employee profiles and value chain analysis.

Build profiles of employees

Profiles of employees can be built from the information gathered from the knowledge audit. A picture can be built of the competencies, skills and know-how of staff.

The following questions are examples of how questionnaires will be used to build the profiles:

- What are your core areas of expertise?
- Which projects have you worked on?
- Have you authored any documentation in the last year?
- Where have you previously worked?
- What training courses have you attended in the last year?
- What areas are you interested in but not currently working on?
- Would you grade yourself as an expert in any of the organizational IT systems?

As well as nominating themselves, experts can be recognized by looking at recommendations by other employees in their unit or team, by managers and from documentation published (internally or externally).

The profile could also include a Belbin (2003) team profile, generated from a self-diagnostic questionnaire. Belbin roles can be categorized as:

- *action-oriented roles* – shaper, implementer and completer finisher;
- *people-oriented roles* – coordinator, team worker and resource investigator;
- *cerebral roles* – plant, monitor evaluator and specialist.

Learning styles can also be categorized using a self-diagnostic test developed by Honey and Mumford (1986). The following categories of learner are used:

- *Activists*: people who learn by doing.
- *Reflectors*: people who learn by observing and thinking about what happened.
- *Pragmatists*: people who like to understand theories behind actions. Require models, concepts and facts.
- *Theorists*: people who need to understand how to put learning into practice.

Develop a knowledge map

If the knowledge audit is small-scale, it may be easy for the knowledge audit team to develop knowledge maps using basic drawing software. The map will indicate relationships and flow of knowledge between individuals. Displaying this information visually will offer different views of where knowledge resides within the organization and will enable strengths and weaknesses to be highlighted. Developing a **knowledge map** will help an organization understand the characteristics of knowledge. This will inform the selection of viable knowledge strategy options.

> A knowledge map is a navigation aid to explicit and tacit knowledge, illustrating how knowledge flows through the organization. The knowledge map portrays the sources, flows, constraints and terminations of knowledge within an organization. Knowledge mapping helps to understand the relationships between knowledge stores and dynamics.
>
> (Grey, 1999)

The knowledge map can also be used as a practical tool by employees to navigate organizational knowledge as part of normal organizational business activity. If we think of an organization as a knowledge market, the knowledge map enables the matching of knowledge buyers to knowledge sellers; this process also involves intermediaries as knowledge brokers. Knowledge maps are then developed into usable IT-based tools, often hosted on organizational intranets (see Expertise databases and corporate yellow pages, p. 246).

Knowledge management practitioners have found that basic mapping processes can be used to derive greater insight if they are applied in the context of the formal discipline of social network analysis. Social network analysis has been developed by social scientists in order to understand and visually represent social relationships in terms of information and knowledge flow.

> Social Network Analysis [SNA] is the mapping and measuring of relationships and flows between people, groups, organizations, computers or other information/knowledge processing entities. The nodes in the network are the people and groups while the links show relationships or flows between the nodes. SNA provides both a visual and a mathematical analysis of human relationships.
>
> (Krebs, 2002)

Figure 5.9 illustrates a simple example of social network or 'kite network'. The actors are identified in the network as nodes, with colours (see key Figure 5.10) indicating the organizational units they belong to. The network indicates three popular measures:

- *Degrees*: number of direct connections a node has. In Figure 5.9 John has the most direct connections.
- *Betweenness*: how nodes are located between the important constituencies. Nodes act in broker roles. In Figure 5.9, Sue takes this role.
- *Closeness*: access to all the nodes on the network. In Figure 5.9, Simon and Claire are the closest to everyone else, directly and indirectly.

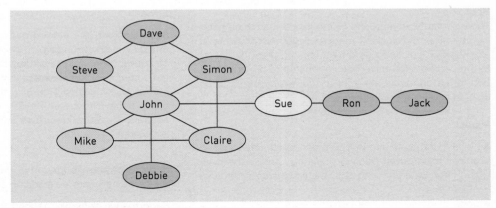

Figure 5.9 Kite network map

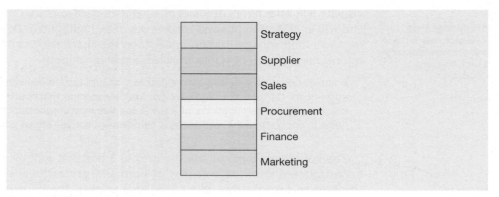

Figure 5.10 Kite map key

From the network single points of failure can also be identified, illustrating places where the network can be isolated. Nodes that connect their group to others are known as 'boundary spanners'; these nodes are well positioned to become innovators, as they have access to ideas and information flowing in other clusters. Peripheral players such as Ron and Jack on the edge of a network would be regarded by many as not very important. However, peripheral nodes are often connected to networks that are not currently mapped. Ron and Jack are therefore very important as fresh sources of knowledge not available inside the company (Krebs, 2002).

Case study 5.1

Using social network analysis as part of a knowledge audit

A real-life case study: large banking organization going through a major restructuring and rebranding following a turbulent few years. Study represents the first instance of a number of mergers of old hierarchical departments. The resource manager is looking to this exercise to make sure that lessons get learned about the complexities of such change and how to cope with it. The case shows the key stages in using social network analysis: mapping, measuring and modelling.

Scenario

Three separate workgroups distributed across three different locations have been merged together following an extensive organization-wide restructuring plan. Two of the former workgroups have been relocated to a single location in London while the rest of the new workgroup are located in offices in Glasgow.

Issues

- Need to integrate informal communication networks.
- Integrate informal decision-making, problem-solving and information-sharing activities to reduce emergence of factions.
- Loss of personnel has led to a loss of not just their knowledge and skills but their networks of relationships within and outside the groups.

Approach

- *Map*: Uncover the hidden patterns of communication that drive workgroup performance.
- *Measure*: Measure the extent of certain properties of the communication networks that affect performance.
- *Model*: Use knowledge of how the people in the workgroup behave to create models of the groups and use scenario-based planning to improve performance of knowledge networks.

Two types of knowledge networks

Work-based networks are made up of two types of network:

- *Performance networks*: related to the core tasks of the group (information seeking, decision making, problem solving).

- *Facilitating network*: relating to the factors that provide the necessary conditions for the performance network to exist.

Methodology

The following questions about performance networks were asked to groups of employees:

- *Information seeking*: How frequently do you acquire information from the following people necessary to do your work?
- *Decision making*: From whom do you seek inputs and decisions before making a key decision?
- *Problem solving*: Who do you typically turn to for help in thinking through a new or challenging problem at work?

All answered on a scale of 0–5 where: 0 = Never, 1 = Yearly, 2 = Quarterly, 3 = Monthly, 4 = Weekly, 5 = Daily.

The following questions about facilitating networks were asked to groups of employees:

- *Awareness*: I am aware of this person's skills and experience.
- *Accessibility*: When I need information or advice, this person is generally accessible to me within a sufficient amount of time to help me solve my problem.

Both rated on a scale of 1 to 5, with 1 being the lowest and 5 being the highest.

- *Communication*: How frequently do you communicate with the following people on work related matters?

Answered on a scale of 0–5 where: 0 = Never, 1 = Yearly, 2 = Quarterly, 3 = Monthly, 4 = Weekly, 5 = Daily.

SNA outputs: maps

Maps are used to improve the building of understanding of the group as a collection of networks. *Example map*: Figure 5.11.

Map explanation: This map shows who people perceive when they need information or advice, who is generally accessible to them within a sufficient amount of time to help them solve their problem. The size of the node is based on the percentage of the network that perceive that individual as being accessible. While this may or may not actually be the case on an individual basis the perception of not being able to access the skills and talents of others will have an effect on the level of satisfaction. Also, the low accessibility of Node 4 is worrying considering that he is at the centre of the formal reporting structures. It also reflects a general pattern of low accessibility of former Group employees. This will be highlighted in greater detail later on when discussing the density of interactions between former groupings.

Interpretation of metrics

- *Avg. Distance*: How accessible people are overall. This figure of less than 2 means that on average people in the network will perceive themselves to have good access to at least one person who will perceive that they have good access to any of the members in the network. This is good to know as even if you cannot access a particular person's skills someone in your network will.
- *Max Distance*: This indicates that there are people within the network who will be inaccessible to each.

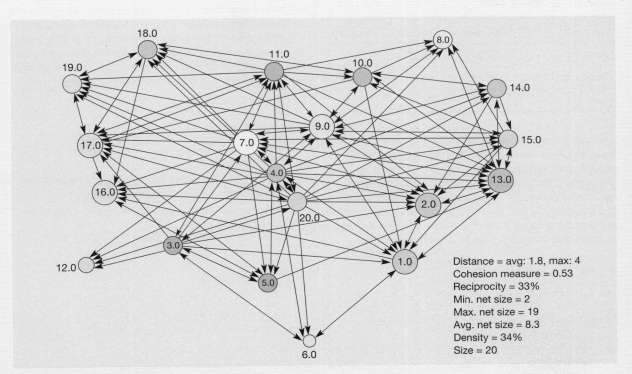

Distance = avg: 1.8, max: 4
Cohesion measure = 0.53
Reciprocity = 33%
Min. net size = 2
Max. net size = 19
Avg. net size = 8.3
Density = 34%
Size = 20

Figure 5.11 Case study social network analysis

- *Cohesion Measure*: A standard network cohesion measure that ranges from 0 to 1. A value of 0.53 indicates a moderate level of overall cohesion.
- *Reciprocity*: Only a third of the ties are reciprocated in that only a third of the people are perceived as being accessible by those they perceive as being accessible to them.
- *Density:* The density of the network is a measure of number of potential ties that actually exist and the measure of the average percentage of the network that an individual perceives as being accessible by them. A value of 34 per cent indicates there may be problems of accessibility across the network as a whole.
- *Avg. Network Size*: Same kind of indicator as density, but using a measure of the number of people as opposed to the percentage of the network.
- *Max. Net Size*: There is one person in the network who perceives that everyone else in the network is accessible to them.
- *Min. Net Size*: There are people within the network who perceive that only 2 people in the network are available to them with enough time to aid their decision making and problem solving.

SNA outputs: group density tables

In addition to diagrams and maps, group density tables can be used to highlight overall patterns of relationships within networks containing identified sub-groups. These provide valuable high-level context that enables managers to understand the extent of the problem of intra-group communication.

Case study density table

	Group 1	Group 2	Group 3
Group 1	50%	36%	36%
Group 2	20%	68%	36%
Group 3	24%	22%	80%

Group density table explanation: The table shows the level of perceived support both for people within the groups and between people in the different previous groupings. The table should be read as the percentage of the total potential links that actually exist from people in the Group in the first column that perceive the people in the Group indicated in the row above as being accessible to them with sufficient time to solve their problems. The

values in the diagonal indicate level of perceived accessibility within the former groupings.

Interpretation of group density table

The density measures provide an indication of the level of cohesion within the groups and the strength of the links between groups. The table above reflects what would have been expected for recently merged groups. Group 3 is the group that has remained located in the same Glasgow office and has highest internal cohesion. The other two groups which have been consolidated into a single location and the people in the two groups show much lower levels of perception of accessibility within and outside of the group. The main takeaway for managers from this table should be 1) people in group 1 are not perceived as being accessible to others, and 2) people in group 3 do perceive those outside of their group as being accessible to them.

Summary of issues

The following issues emerged:

- There is lack of integration of the key networks surveyed.
- This provides the information to plan more effective strategies to manage the group.
- The ability of the network to perform is based on suitability of the structure to the nature of the tasks it must perform.

Modelling and planning

Using the information on the current state of the network combined with a mixture of communication theories and insights, it is possible to create models of how the group will evolve over time, in different scenarios. Sessions were conducted with managers and employees to create a variety of models of behaviour for members of the group. These were used to create a network-based computational model that can be used to explore how the network is likely to respond in different scenarios.

Source: Andy Swarbrick, Network Consulting

Questions

1 How can social networks analysis add value to the bank's knowledge management strategy?

2 Discuss the difference between performance and facilitation networks.

Develop a knowledge value chain to represent core knowledge processes

From the audit process an inventory will be produced, mapping knowledge assets against knowledge categories and value-adding activities against business processes. Using a model of knowledge, a value chain will be used to explain the different ways in which knowledge can be used to add value to business processes. The knowledge value chain will indicate where knowledge is combined and the nature of the knowledge used in processes. Knowledge may be discussed in terms of one of the three frameworks introduced earlier in the chapter.

The value chain model in Figure 5.12 is a framework that can be used to map knowledge processes against business processes.

A further categorization (Zak, 2002) can also be used to analyse the value of knowledge:

- *Core knowledge*: minimum required 'just to play the game'. Will not offer long-term advantage. Commonly held by all members of an industry sector.

- *Advanced knowledge*: enables a firm to be competitively viable, showing differentiation between competitors.

- *Innovation knowledge*: enables a firm to lead its industry and competitors. Will often challenge the nature of industry activities or market activity.

These categories can also be mapped onto a value chain, illustrated in Figure 5.13.

The split between tacit and explicit can be mapped against business activities, services or products. Figure 5.14 offers a view of how activities can be mapped against

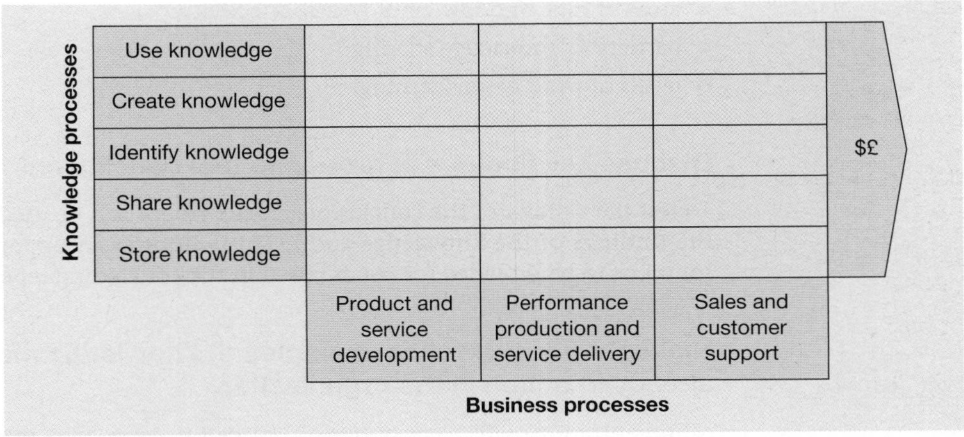

Figure 5.12 Knowledge value chain

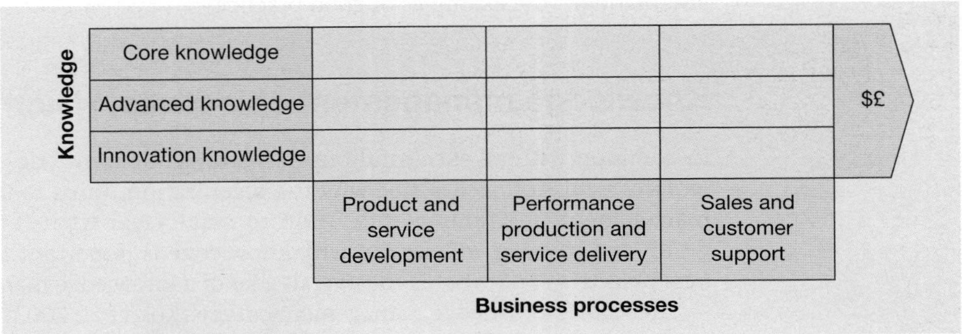

Figure 5.13 Knowledge value chain: types of knowledge

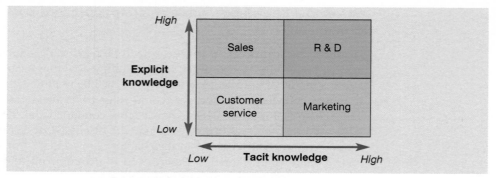

Figure 5.14 Mapping activities against knowledge

high or low levels of tacit and explicit knowledge. This view can be used to understand the knowledge processes that should be used to support these areas.

Determine key issues and conclusions

As with an information audit, analysis will be undertaken to assess the audit findings against the desired state. Gaps will then be analysed and developed into a set of strategic issues related to knowledge management:

● key knowledge assets available;
● employee skills and competencies;
● areas of high and low employee connectivity;
● barriers to knowledge sharing;
● levels of work-based learning.

Discuss key findings in groups to test conclusions

To test the validity of the conclusions, focus groups can be used to assess and validate the findings of the knowledge audit. This will offer an opportunity for innovative solutions to be provided for issues raised in the concluding reports.

Highlight good practice examples of knowledge management already in action in the organization

All organizations will have systems in place for knowledge management which may not be labelled, will have grown organically and may not have been previously analysed. A good starting point for knowledge management programmes is to share and highlight the examples of good practice.

Knowledge management objectives, vision and mission

In common with all successful business strategies, knowledge management strategy requires a mission to describe why the organization wants to undertake a knowledge management programme and vision to make clear what it wants to do. The KM vision and mission will set out why knowledge is important to organizational business objectives and what is the overall goal of a knowledge management strategy.

The KPMG knowledge management survey (Kok et al, 2003) highlights key knowledge management objectives:

1 realizing synergies between units (83 per cent);

2 achieving higher added value for customers (74 per cent);

3 improving quality in operational and functional processes (70 per cent);

4 reducing costs (67 per cent);

5 accelerating innovation (63 per cent);

6 boosting revenues for new market development (37 per cent);

7 reducing exposure to specific business risks (26 per cent).

Using information and the visual representations derived from the knowledge audit we can develop knowledge management objectives based around business need and evidence of knowledge-based activities. Two gaps will have been identified:

- knowledge gap: what the organization must know and what the organization knows;
- strategic gap: what the organization must do and what the organization can do.

This enables a link to be made with overall business strategy and knowledge management strategy.

Activity 5.3	Defining knowledge management objectives

Purpose   To identify knowledge management objectives related to business objectives.

Activity   This example will use the Lo-cost Airline Company. In Table 5.4, translate the key business objectives into knowledge management objectives. As an example the first objective has been completed.

Business objectives	Knowledge management objectives
Provide the lowest fares in the industry	Continuously develop, share internally and apply knowledge about customer pricing structure
Efficient cost-management	
Provide friendly efficient service related to customer need	
Annual increase of passenger traffic of 5 per cent	
Identify and develop new flight routes	
Generation of 90 per cent of all sales over the Internet	

Strategy selection

We can identify different approaches that can be taken to develop a knowledge management strategy.

Codification versus personalization

Hansen et al. (1999) identified two different knowledge management strategies: codification and personalization.

In a codification strategy knowledge is carefully organized and stored in databases, where it can be easily used by anyone in the organization. The features of this approach are:

- reuse of knowledge assets;
- a structured approach to created explicit knowledge objects;
- high investment in IT;
- highly IT-literate workforce;
- reward systems for contributing to document databases.

In a personalization strategy the focus is upon the person who developed the knowledge and sharing through person-to-person contacts. The use of ICT in this scenario will be to help people communicate knowledge rather than store it. The features of this approach are:

- expert economics: highly customized solutions;
- moderate investment in IT;
- key competencies for staff are skills in dealing with ambiguity and problem solving;

Activity 5.4	Assessing knowledge management strategy approaches

Purpose   To match differing knowledge management approaches to different business categories.

Activity   For various organizational sectors use Table 5.5 to suggest a KM strategy mix. Make sure you can justify each selection.

Table 5.5

	Codification	Personalization
Internet banking		
Computer games		
Airline		
Online bookseller		
Car manufacturer		
Pharmaceutical		
Health service		
Local government		

- one-to-one mentoring;
- rewards for sharing directly with others.

The selection of one of these strategy options will depend on the relationship an organization has with its client groups, the business models used and the competencies of the people employed by the organization. An organization will not wholly follow one of the strategies but will place a strong degree of emphasis. Hansen et al. (1999) suggest the mix should be 80 per cent to 20 per cent (either way). An organization will assess the approach in terms of core areas of business activity.

The example of an Internet bank (such as Smile, **www.smile.co.uk**) that provides a support services centre can used to illustrate this. We can ask the following questions to assess the two strategy options:

- Does the company offer standardized products and services?
- Are the products and services mature or innovative?
- What types of knowledge do employees rely on to solve problems?

Focusing on how the business creates value for customers, we can see that the company will receive thousands of calls from customers with problems requiring the knowledge and expertise of the call centre staff. Business activity is focused upon efficient reuse of knowledge about how the Internet banking systems work and how previous problems have been solved. The key for the business is a reliable system that provides structured solutions that can be reused. Reuse of knowledge will save time and associated costs and allow more calls to be taken in a day. Customers will gain knowledge of tried and tested solutions. The emphasis in this example is upon codification.

Explorer versus exploiter

Using the ideas of Zak (2002), we can focus upon the gaps that will be identified by the knowledge audit process. An organization may discover that to execute its business strategy it requires a level of knowledge processing to close its internal knowledge gap. Many competitors will be operating at a higher level of knowledge across many more knowledge positions. The company therefore needs to close the external knowledge gap. The required strategic position of these companies is to become explorers – creators or acquirers of the knowledge needed to become and remain competitive.

Conversely, organizations may find themselves with evidence that knowledge resources and capabilities significantly exceed the requirements of the competitive position. The company therefore needs to further exploit the current knowledge platform. In this situation the company will take the strategic position of an exploiter.

As with codification and personalization, the two are not mutually exclusive – organizations will need to find the right mix. Exploitation and exploration will take place in different parts of an organization. For example, research and development will be focused on exploring – creating new products. However, a sales department will be focused on exploiting current knowledge resources. In the light of these strategy options, organizations can create new knowledge maps that indicate the spread of exploiters and explorers and their relationships.

The two approaches should not operate in isolation, so that they can reinforce each other. The knowledge created and acquired by the exploration process must be applied and exploited.

Aggressive versus conservative

Zak (2002) builds upon the explorer-versus-exploiter equation. Firms that are oriented towards exploiting internal knowledge exhibit the most conservative strategy, while unbounded innovators (exploring and exploiting beyond organizational boundaries) represent the most aggressive strategy. An aggressive strategy will be required in highly knowledge-intensive industries and where there are large knowledge gaps with competitors.

The combination of the internal/external, exploiter/explorer, aggressive/conservative approach is represented in Figure 5.15.

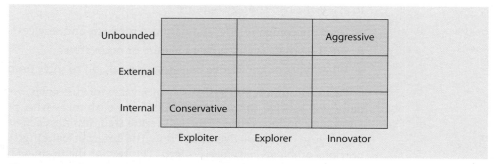

Figure 5.15 Aggressive vs conservative strategy

Source: from *Developing a knowledge strategy*. In C. Choo and N. Bontis (eds) *The Strategic Management of Intellectual Capital and Organizational Knowledge*, Oxford University Press (Zak, M 2002), By permission of Oxford University Press, Inc.

Technocratic versus economic versus behavioural

Earl (2001) has developed further definitions of schools of knowledge management, developing a taxonomy of knowledge management. The schools draw on many of the aspects introduced, but use a technocratic/economic/behavioural broad categorization, with further splits. We can also see the different types of companies that use the different approaches (Table 5.6).

Table 5.6 Technocratic versus economic versus behavioural

School / Attribute	Technocratic			Economic	Behavioural		
	Systems	Cartographic	Engineering	Commercial	Organizational	Spatial	Strategic
Focus	Technology	Maps	Processes	Income	Networks	Space	Mindset
Aim	Knowledge bases	Knowledge directories	Knowledge flows	Knowledge assets	Knowledge pooling	Knowledge exchange	Knowledge capabilities
Unit	Domain	Enterprise	Activity	Know-how	Communities	Place	Business
Example	Xerox, Shorko films	Bain and Co, AT & T	HP, Frinto-Lay	Dow Chemical, IBM	BP, Amoco Shell	Skandia British Airways	Skandia Unilever
Critical success factors	Content validation Incentives to provide content	Culture/ incentives to share knowledge Network to connect people	Knowledge learning and information Unrestricted distribution	Specialist teams Institutionalized process	Sociable culture Knowledge intermediaries	Design for purpose Encouragement	Rhetoric artefacts
Principal IT contribution	Knowledge-based systems	Profiles and directories on intranets	Shared databases	Intellectual assets register and processing system	Groupware and intranets	Access and representational tools	Eclectic
'Philosophy'	Codification	Connectivity	Capability	Commercialization	Collaboration	Contactivity	Consciousness

Knowledge management strategy at the UK Department of Trade and Industry (DTI)

How the DTI, a central UK government department, developed a knowledge management strategy in 2003–04. This illustrates the mix of strategy approaches and how the business strategy was linked. (The DTI was succeeded by the Department for Business, Innovation and Skills.)

The DTI strategy

One of the key recommendations of the DTI Reviews was that the Department needed much greater strategic focus in order to achieve its aims.

DTI's ambition was Prosperity for All, by raising productivity and competitiveness by supporting successful business, ensuring fair markets and promoting world-class science and innovation. The strategy provided a longer-term direction for achieving this. It sharpened our focus on where we could make the greatest difference moving forward.

The strategy set clear priorities for the next five years and described how we would deliver on these commitments. These policy priorities were based on the best available economic evidence of where DTI could make the greatest contribution to raising UK productivity.

The DTI Knowledge Management Strategy

DTI's Change and Knowledge Management Unit (CKMU) had the role of supporting performance improvement in DTI and driving forward the change agenda arising from the reviews of the Department, working closely with the rest of the Department and the Board. It was part of the Human Resource and Change Management function. Its priorities were to:

- Identify and embed new ways of working in the department
- Promote appropriate behaviours, including forward thinking
- Promote the sharing of knowledge and good practice
- Promote measurement, benchmarking and evaluation.

We were working to deliver a number of current projects in each of these areas. Related to all of these were two further cross-cutting priorities:

- Improving the DTI's internal communications
- Acting as programme manager for the Departmental Change Plan, reporting to the Executive Board.

New ways of working

CKMU was working to provide the necessary infrastructure to embed project and programme management in the DTI. Key components included helping senior managers understand their role in promoting project working; ensuring that the supporting systems for financial and staff resourcing and management were in place; and making available training, mentoring and coaching for project managers and their teams.

We were also aiming to improve the effectiveness of meetings at DTI – to ensure they were well focused and time bound, output driven, and delivered desired results. CKMU was drawing up a strategy for implementing a programme of facilitation awareness and training across the department, in consultation with staff who had already been trained as facilitators through a pilot project during 2001/02.

Behaviours

DTI was implementing three core commitments – reach out, value people, be courageous – which articulate the behaviours needed in DTI if we were to be effective in delivering on our vision 'prosperity for all'. These commitments reflected the wider focus on enhancing performance through a shared purpose, developing strong external partnerships, and providing a supportive environment for all staff, and were an integral part of the DTI's change programme. CKMU had been working with the support of the Board to engage staff and senior leaders in making the commitments a reality.

futurefocus@dti promoted shared thinking about future challenges, supported the development of realistic policies and strategies to help realize the DTI's vision. Developed partnership with business, it provided a neutral environment in which to explore how forces driving change might play out in the future and what the consequences might be for government and its customers. Supported by professional facilitators, futurefocus@dti delivered customized workshops focused on achieving participants' specific requirements whether framing strategies, testing policy options, developing business plans or simply opening up thinking.

Enhanced change capabilities and desired behaviours

The DTI was also aiming to improve the effectiveness of meetings and awaydays to ensure they were well focused and time bound, and delivered desired results. CKMU was working on a strategy to take this forward. CKMU were also building up a database of internally trained facilitators to support the delivery and design of others' awaydays, and enhancing the awareness of the benefits of facilitation and offering training interventions throughout the year, building on the successful pilot run in 2001/02.

knowhow@dti

CKMU had been working to improve the way DTI uses and shares its knowledge since 1999. Our major project in 2003–04 was the development of knowhow@dti, a directory of staff skills, interests and experiences that would help users find and learn from others across the Department who have valuable knowledge that could help us save time and develop better results.

Knowledge implementation and strategy

We were implementing a number of projects as part of DTI's knowledge strategy, particularly around improving the DTI's use of evidence in policy making, and strengthening the link between HR policies and practices and knowledge retention.

Our previous work on storytelling was also being taken forward in the context of our change programme. We also completed an evaluation of an earlier project on supporting communities of practice.

Measurement and evaluation of change

CKMU was working with others in DTI to establish a range of performance indicators to measure the progress achieved through the Departmental change plan. These were focused on change in key business processes within the Department, complementing externally focused meas-ures of stakeholder perceptions and the achievement of DTI's business goals underpinning the prosperity for all vision. Our approach was based on the development of existing measures in our staff surveys, external benchmarking, as well as the use of externally developed tools such as the Organizational Culture Inventory survey. This work would feed into the balanced scorecard approach being implemented as part of the DTI's new business planning process.

Project objectives

To continually track the impact of the change programme by surveying DTI staff on a regular basis with respect to their attitudes to working in the Department and the evolving culture.

Project outcomes

A benchmarked and valid statement of the development of the Department towards the desired vision as generated by the DTI reviews.

Sources: Department of Trade of Industry Strategy web pages (www.dti.gov.uk/ckmu/unit.html)

Questions

1 Which approach(es) to knowledge management can you identify?

2 How did the DTI's knowledge management strategy link to the overall strategy?

Strategy options: knowledge management in action

We will now assess the strategy options that can be used in practice to implement the approaches defined on the knowledge management strategy.

Communities of practice

If an organization decides it will develop a knowledge management strategy around the personalization approach (described earlier in the chapter), an understanding of how communities can be developed and managed is vital.

Learning makes organizational knowledge assets usable. Knowledge relates to a 'knower' – we treat information as being more independent but knowledge will be associated with someone. For example, we will ask 'where is that information?' but not 'who knows that?'. Learning in organizations is vital to knowledge creation, sharing and transfer. There is a new emphasis on people. Learning in practice (e.g. in work-based situations, not classroom learning) involves becoming a member of a 'community of practice'.

We can break learning into two categories: 'learning about' and 'learning to be' (Brown and Duguid, 2000). For example, we can learn about a subject such as a medical condition by using the Internet; however, this is different from learning to be a doctor. Learning to be is not based on the accumulation of information, compared to learning about. Through practice we learn to be, by assimilating information. Communities of practice are vital to an organizational knowledge management strategy that sees learning processes beyond the limits of formalized training.

One of the originators of the communities of practice concept, Etienne Wegner (Wegner et al. 2002), has developed the following description:

> Communities of practice are groups of people who share a concern, a set of problems, or a passion about a topic, and how they deepen their knowledge and expertise in this area by interacting on a ongoing basis. These people don't necessarily work together, but they meet because they find value in their interactions. As they spend time together they typically share information, sight and advice. They help each other share problems.

Communities of practice have always existed in organizations; as knowledge becomes increasingly crucial to competitive advantage the role they play is more important and requires management. If we return to the definition of knowledge management from Royal Dutch/Shell earlier in the chapter, communities are highlighted as a vital component. The development of communities of practice requires an open, empowered organizational culture. In this cultural environment communities will not only grow from 'top-down' knowledge management programmes, they will grow organically from employee initiation.

Figure 5.16 illustrates how communities of practice differ from other forms of organizational structures; it illustrates:

- *formal departments*: clear defined boundaries, permanent, structured around organizational goals;
- *operational units*: clear defined boundaries, permanent, structured around ongoing operations and processes;
- *project teams*: clear boundaries, though may work across departments and operational units, limited lifespan, structured around project goals;
- *communities of practice*: fuzzy boundaries, delineated across the organization. Organic evolution.

We can use a model developed by Wegner et al. (2002) for the development of communities of practice. Balance must be developed between these three elements:

- *Domain*. What issues do we care about? How will the community relate to the organizational overall strategy and knowledge management strategy?
- *Community*. What roles will people play? How will people meet and connect? What activities will take place?
- *Practice*. What knowledge will be shared? What leaning activities will take place? What can be standardized?

Community of practice
A group (often interdisciplinary) linked by shared interest in a subject area; the group will organically evolve over time in terms of membership and scope. The purpose will be to learn and share

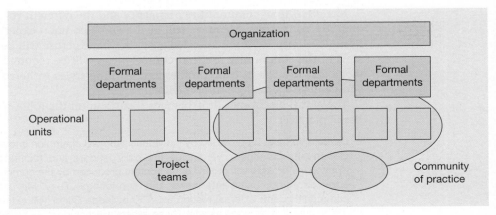

Figure 5.16 Communities of practice

The following categories can be used to classify communities of practice (American Productivity and Quality Center, 2000):

- *Helping communities*: employees help each other to solve problems.
- *Best-practice communities*: developing, validating and disseminating best practice.
- *Knowledge-stewarding communities*: organize, upgrade and distribute the knowledge.
- *Innovation communities:* foster unexpected ideas and practices. Intentionally mix boundaries to gain new perspectives.

We can use as examples two organizations, the Lo-cost Airline Company and a central government department (Treasury/Ministry of Finance), to illustrate how the communities can develop in practice.

The Lo-cost Airline Company:

- Helping communities: a community to help sales staff understand a new electronic booking system.
- Best-practice communities: a community based on service quality measures.
- Knowledge-stewarding communities: a community based on competitive intelligence reports about the airline sector. Organizes and distributes key reports.
- Innovation communities: a community to develop a new queuing system for airport check-in procedures. Involves company staff and airport managers from outside the company.

Central government, department (Treasury, – Ministry, of Finance):

- Helping communities: a community to help staff use a new financial management software package.
- Best-practice communities: a community based on best practice in accounting procedures.
- Knowledge-stewarding communities: a community based on the topic of child poverty, drawing together data, reports, presentations and policy documents stored across organizational repositories.
- Innovation communities: a community to develop new ways of assessing national economic performance. Involves government officials and academics.

The other important decision to be made relating to how a community of practice will be practically implemented will be whether the focus is on social connections or virtual – should ICT applications be used to collaborate electronically? The use of technology and mix with social interactions will be defined by the nature of the issues and the complexity of the community. The different communities can also be related to the codification (ICT) and personalization (social) strategy examples used earlier. Table 5.7 lists characteristics that must be understood.

Membership of communities of practice and the different roles of the members are vital to their success. Members will be drawn based upon expertise profiles that have been developed from the knowledge audit. The expertise will be matched against the aims of the community. General competencies will be required from all community members. The Belbin team profiles and learning styles gathered from the knowledge audit will also aid selection of members.

The global electronics firm Siemens focuses upon the following roles in communities of practice:

> Leadership must be provided by individuals who will champion and sponsor the community. Community managers will act as the daily leaders and facilitators of the community. Knowledge brokers will organize the content produced by the community in terms of knowledge captured, using interviews and debriefings. They will provide links with other communities and external resources. A Knowledge Editor will extract, codify and summarize to create knowledge assets. These assets will include case studies and how to guides
>
> (Jubert, 1999)

Table 5.7 Communities: ICT and Social networks

	ICT networks	Social networks
Practical implementation	Discussion forums, collaboration tools, often hosted on intranets	Meetings, workshops, seminars
Relationships	Can be standardized, harder to develop trust and understanding	Fluid – can be weak or strong
Geography	Can be global	More likely to be local
Boundaries	Organizational	Internal and external
Example	British Telecom: Jasper system. Intranet-based system, based on user profiles, alerting members to new discussions and documents	Daimler Chrysler: Austauschgruppe. 240 experts develop new directions in research

Several strategies can be developed to implement communities of practice:

● Support communities that already exist.
● Start with a large number of communities.
● Pilot, then roll out on large scale.
● Pilot, then gradually roll out.

The selection of these implementation options may depend on the knowledge-sharing culture already in existence in the organization, the nature of the knowledge activities from the knowledge audit and the representations of relationships and connections from a knowledge map or social network analysis.

Competitive intelligence

Competitive intelligence can be seen as a tactic used by organizations to improve the knowledge of issues relating to competition in the company's operating environment. Developing a balanced knowledge management programme includes requirements related to knowledge of competitive threats. Competitive intelligence focuses upon competitive threats and the transferring of market share from the competitors' bottom line. It is a systematic programme for gathering, analysing and managing information that can affect an organization's plans, decisions and operations.

Miller (2001) has identified four phases of the competitive intelligence cycle:

1 Identification of key decision makers and their intelligence needs
2 Collection of information
3 Analysis of information and upgrading it to intelligence
4 Dissemination of intelligence to decision makers.

The following illustrates how competitive intelligence relates to information and knowledge management:

● Information management helps us understand what has happened.
● Competitive intelligence helps us understand what is likely to happen externally and what our options are.
● Knowledge management helps us change what is likely to happen, internally and externally, through innovation, reinvention and repositioning.

In relation to the explicit/tacit split that is used to define knowledge in competitive intelligence the distinction will be made between primary (e.g. interviews with customers) and secondary sources (e.g. news sources on the web). The relationship between competitive intelligence and knowledge is illustrated in Figure 5.17.

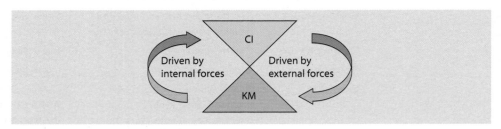

Figure 5.17 CI and KM relationship

The internal focus of knowledge management and external focus of competitive intelligence mean that a synthesis of the two will ensure that a holistic business strategy is developed. The knowledge culture and processes developed in a knowledge management strategy will enable the successful application of knowledge generated by a competitive intelligence programme. The goal of both is that business should be a continuous series of decisions conveying wisdom in evaluating options for organizations.

Nicholas Speh, a knowledge manager at Shell, describes the relationship between the two concepts in the context of his company:

> Knowledge management facilitates the here and now, focusing on capturing, sharing and emphasising the role of people, culture and process. Competitive intelligence is more focused on the future on possibilities, helping to shape decision making, and emphasising trends patterns, and what is currently uncertain or unknown. Where knowledge management hopes to improve job performance, competitive intelligence hopes to lead to faster and better action.
>
> (Bahra, 2001)

There are tensions between knowledge management and competitive intelligence. The emphasis on openness and knowledge sharing related to knowledge management may cause problems; advantage may be given away if intellectual assets are benefiting competitors. In this scenario knowledge is not being managed effectively.

Story and narrative management

Focusing upon the use of stories and narrative as a tactic for sharing knowledge and experience is a recent innovation that has become a formal knowledge management discipline. Storytelling is a way to enable the sharing and transfer of knowledge using the power of the medium to offer perspectives on topics that could otherwise be missed in using formal procedures to turn tacit knowledge into explicit knowledge.

The European Guide to Good Practice defines narrative as:

> Techniques employed in KM environments to describe complicated issues, explain events, communicate lessons learned, or bring about cultural change. The techniques can involve story telling, narrative databases, or after action reviews (retrospective accounts of significant events in an organization's recent past, described in the voices of people who took part in them).
>
> (Mekhilef et al., 2003)

Stories can be important for the following reasons:

1 They can be used as a way for a company to obtain information about its customers, their needs and the contexts of use for their products.

2 They can be a useful way to share information within a company.

3 They can be used to help explain how and why products and services might be used.

4 Stories about products, services and practices can be shared by customers.

The most valuable tacit knowledge is context-dependent, so we will use this knowledge only when we need to use it; for example, this knowledge may not be apparent by simply asking someone to write down what they know about our customers' characteristics. However, asking someone to recount an event as a story may draw out different knowledge perspectives and learning.

An overview of how the storytelling process can be used is illustrated in Figure 5.18.

A narrative database uses only original material and searches this material based on questions. The database will be indexed and then searched on a free text basis. Observing the patterns of use can determine where investment in best practice might be best focused. The database can be of great value to new staff entering an organization to understand the culture and nature of organizational knowledge processes.

Storytelling and narrative techniques have been used by organizations such as the World Bank, the Department of Trade and Industry (DTI) and IBM.

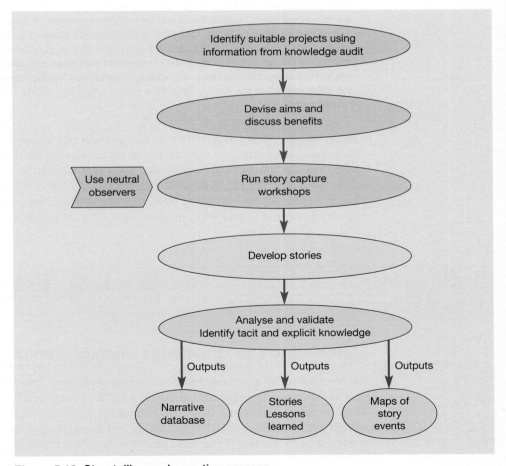

Figure 5.18 Storytelling and narrative process

The DTI used storytelling to evaluate the process of producing the 'Opportunity for all' competitiveness White Paper in 2001. The process of producing a White Paper (major government policy statement) is not standardized: there is not a 'right' or a 'wrong' way to produce one. The process also happens infrequently. This meant that the DTI was struggling to learn and apply knowledge from previous White Paper experiences.

The DTI was attracted to the storytelling approach due to the following benefits they identified (DTI, 2001):

- *Relevance*: storytelling puts learning in context through specific examples.
- *Flexibility*: storytelling provides some key learning points but preserves flexibility around their application.
- *Richness*: stories have the potential to transfer tacit and codified knowledge.
- *Transferability*: storytelling is a natural form of human communication.

The DTI developed workshops at which discussion was based around memorable events over a time line; anecdotes and positive and negative experiences were noted. Stories were then generated as metaphorical tales (imaginatively but not literally applicable to describe the event). The output of the process was a 'survival pack for anyone undertaking future projects, the pack includes a map, stories, skill cards. The stories were written so that on every alternate page there was a real world description of what the metaphorical tale sought to illustrate' (DTI, 2001).

IBM uses the following process for storytelling workshops:

> As the storytellers tell their story, they are observed by trained observers who identify decisions, judgements, problems resolved or unresolved and chart these together with associated information flows. Once the storytelling has come to a conclusion, the observers present their model for validation and the whole group charts for each decision/judgement/problem resolution cluster what knowledge was used and what was its nature: tacit in the form of skills possessed by individuals (experiences, intuition, relationships, understanding etc.); explicit in the form of artefacts (pricing models, quality control procedures, rules, research etc.).
>
> (Bahra, 2001)

Storytelling and use of narrative techniques will not be applicable to every organization because of different organizational cultures. An understanding of the culture of the organization from the knowledge audit and evaluation of strategy approaches will be used to assess the value of storytelling. Organizations focused upon a personalization approach will be more open to using storytelling. Gaps in organizational knowledge related to problems in learning from past projects are often the projects for starting the process.

Using information and communications technologies (ICT) to enable knowledge management

Matching ICT to knowledge management requirements

The strategy selection of a codification or personalization approach will heavily influence the amount an organization invests in ICT to support knowledge management. The information gathered from the knowledge audit and use of the ASHEN model will inform the choice of ICT applications and infrastructure required. An assessment can made as to where ICT can be deployed to enable knowledge processes.

In the strategy section of this chapter we learned that the development of the codification strategy approach (people to documents) will focus on using databases to structure and codify documents, whereas the personalization approach will focus on the use of ICT as a communication tool.

ICTs cannot manage knowledge on their own, but they can provide access to the right mix of data and information to enable workers to extract, create, share and transfer knowledge. As knowledge is highly dependent on context (understanding when to apply knowledge), ICT systems used must concentrate on supplying the 'right information to the right people at the right time'. Prusak (1998) states that 'if you're implementing new technology just for the purpose of knowledge management, it may be waste of money'.

As we have already discussed in Chapter 1, information overload is a major problem for the modern organization and a major barrier to gaining the expected benefits from information and communication technologies (ICT). Any ICT solutions that are deployed to enable knowledge management must be considered in terms of having a positive impact in reducing information overload and not adding to it.

Intranets and extranets

The concept of intranets and extranets was introduced in Chapter 2.

Intranet
A closed internal network based on Internet and World Wide Web technologies

The development of corporate intranets has often been the initial focus of the ICT element of a knowledge strategy. Intranets are the central element because they offer opportunities for collaboration across a single platform and the possibilities of creating a centralized and structured point of access to a wide range of knowledge. Owing to the complex knowledge needs of employees, intranets can often be underused when they fail to meet the needs of employees effectively. We will focus on how a structured information architecture can improve the effectiveness of intranets in Chapter 9. The key to a successful intranet that will support knowledge management objectives is to focus on core knowledge processes that can take place across an internal web-based platform.

Intranets will have two main functions in an organization:

● To support process-based activity related to business activities, e.g. accounting, stock management, expense submission.

● To support organizational communication and group work.

It is the second category that relates to knowledge management: connecting people to knowledge across the organization. An organizational intranet will often host collaboration tools, knowledge maps and expertise databases.

Observation of intranet evolution has shown that there are often three stages of development for intranets:

1 *Static*. Basic web pages stored on a web server. Information publishing is centrally controlled. Employees browse and search for information but do not interact. Content is refreshed on an irregular basis. The danger at this stage is that the intranet will become a silo of underused information, and employees will not trust the intranet as a tool to assist in knowledge work.

2 *Interaction*. The intranet develops into a dynamic environment developing around the knowledge needs of employees. Publishing becomes a regular process that many employees are involved with. Discussion boards and bulletin boards are introduced. Employees start to develop trust in using the intranet to share and locate knowledge.

3 *Collaborative electronic work space*. The intranet becomes a 'self-service' environment where all employees are empowered to share knowledge via publishing mechanisms and collaborative tools. It becomes the starting point for discovering explicit knowledge. All core business processes will take place across the intranet platform.

Extranet
An area of an internal network open to authenticated customers and partners based on Internet and World Wide Web technologies

Extranets are extensions of intranets to create secure electronic networks. They will be used by organizations to share information and knowledge with customers, suppliers and partners. Extranets will be vital for organizations that need to focus on external knowledge and create communities of practice beyond normal organizational boundaries; they can be used in sharing knowledge across a supply chain.

The problems facing extranets are often the same as those facing intranets but with the added layer of complexity of having to understand the knowledge of potentially different groups of users.

The data derived from the knowledge audit can be used to inform intranet and extranet design, ensuring that several views of organizational knowledge are represented. Structuring the design around traditional organizational units alone will not enable knowledge processes across organizational boundaries. Focus should be placed on offering different routes to knowledge alongside more traditional views, using knowledge maps to link disparate sources.

Expertise databases and corporate yellow pages

In order to gain value from the employee profiles gathered from the knowledge audit, organizations need to use this information to enable expertise location across the organization. This is done by creating a searchable and browsable database system based around the profiles. The objective of an expertise database is to enable the internal knowledge markets, matching knowledge buyers to knowledge sellers. The systems are often known as 'corporate yellow pages', as the database can extend the format of an organizational telephone directory.

The success of expertise databases is dependent on the type of culture developed within the organization: does a culture of trust exist for employees to feel willing to share expertise? The key to developing a culture where an expertise database can enable cross-departmental knowledge exchange is ensuring that employees volunteer knowledge and are not conscripted into any processes. All employees must feel that there is some benefit to them in having their profile held in the database. These issues will be discussed further on in this chapter related to incentives and rewards for knowledge management.

The structure of the database must also be considered: what information should be included related to key knowledge management objectives? An expertise profile could include the following elements (White, 2000):

- Educational courses
- Professional accreditation
- Previous employers
- Work undertaken
- Membership of networks
- Publications
- Areas of interests
- External interests.

An expertise database will need to have a common language and organizationally agreed definitions for describing the elements that make up the profiles that make up the database.

Collaborative tools

Usually delivered across an organizational intranet, collaborative tools (introduced in Chapter 2) allow person-to-person contact across electronic networks. Collaborative tools can be used to support communities of practice. They can be divided into two categories:

1 *synchronous collaborative tools*: remote sharing, presentation, chat, electronic white-boarding, voting, video and audio;

2 *asynchronous collaborative tools or groupware*: allow users to deposit, comment upon, and act upon information provided by others. Discussion software and message boards.

Selection of these tools will be based on the following factors:

- *Time*: when does the collaboration take place – at the same time or at different times?
- *Information richness*: types of content – text, video, audio.
- *Social presence*: how the tools help people connect socially – body language, tone of voice.
- *Capture*: does a record of the collaboration need to be kept?

Use of these tools requires a culture of openness, sharing and discussion. Online collaborative tools require the following elements to support knowledge management:

- *Clear links to the knowledge management strategy*: which knowledge processes can be enabled by the collaboration tools.
- *Policies and procedures*: rules and conditions of membership. Will cover issues such as archiving old discussions, when to close down a discussion and the common language to be used (e.g. foreign languages and technical languages).
- *Defined roles*: owners, editors and experts.

Many online communities using online collaboration tools establish a baseline for participation. The following example is adapted from Emint (**www.emint.org.uk**), a specialist collaboration forum for people who manage online communities:

- A good community needs at least five 'loud voices'.
- A 'loud voice' may be an expert or 'guru'.
- There will be at least 30 active members for each loud voice.
- Experts and gurus are accredited by respectful references from loud voices, so:
- gurus can accredit each other.

Communities will need to agree definition of experts and gurus. Experts or gurus may be defined by the nature of the knowledge provided from postings, previous work experience or education. Active members may be defined by regularity of visits or postings to the community.

Corporate portals

Portals offer a customized gateway to organizational information systems, aggregating content that is already available, displaying it in personalized layers. An example on the Internet is MyYahoo. Corporate portals will offer the employee a customized view of key internal and external content resources. Specialist portal software will be purchased, configured to interface with organizational information systems. A corporate portal will often be used as the 'front door' for the organization's intranet.

Key components of corporate portals can include the following (Claudio and Gordon, 2003):

- presentation layer – allows the user to personalize
- taxonomy (browsable classified hierarchical structure, e.g. Yahoo classification)
- search engine
- selected external information from the web;

and connections to:

- collaboration tools
- intranet applications or intranet web pages
- content management systems (publishing)
- document management systems
- CRM systems
- ERP systems
- financial systems
- HR systems
- Data warehouses.

Corporate portals can be an important element of an ICT strategy to support knowledge management because they aim to eliminate information overload by allowing employees to customize an interface to see the information that is relevant to them and in different combinations. Information used in context will enable better application of knowledge.

The business case for a corporate portal will focus on employees being provided with the right combinations of information, so that the employee will have a better view of a situation or issue, offering new insight and knowledge or enabling decisions to be made. See Chapters 2 and 8 for more coverage.

Customer relationship management (CRM) systems

CRM systems were introduced in Chapter 2. CRM tools used in e-business offer new perspectives on customer relationships. In an online environment customers are willing to surrender a greater depth and range of data than in a traditional business environment in exchange for the personalization that e-business can offer and the benefits such as convenience and competitive pricing.

Using CRM offers the opportunity of enhanced knowledge of customer needs and perception of services. CRM processes will be focused upon sales, service and marketing functions. Knowledge can be gained of:

- customer behaviour;
- product use;
- quality of service;
- customer preference and brand loyalty;
- how business processes relate and their design;
- skills and competencies of staff related to delivering products and services

Figure 5.19 illustrates how IT systems should support the utilization of customer knowledge.

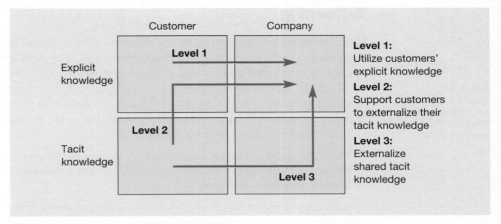

Figure 5.19 IT and customer knowledge
Source: Nonaka et al. (2000)

A knowledge management strategy can link with CRM in terms of

- linking to other forms of explicit knowledge in the organization (e.g. in document management systems;
- expertise location and management – successful resolution of a customer problem;
- collaboration and learning – working in communities to gain new insights into customer relationships.

Document management/Content management systems

Organizational knowledge will be codified in many forms of document, such as manuals, e-mails, reports, memos, correspondence and minutes of meetings. Documents may differ in format and structure. Document management systems are software-based systems that control the lifecycle of a document: capture, storage, distribution and collaboration. Document management systems will capture and store documents in a structured file system, allowing users to browse or retrieve documents. Versions of documents will be tracked and this will allow employees to collaborate in the evolution of the document.

The structure of document management systems is vital to their efficient support of knowledge management objectives, the structure being based on information architecture. (This will be covered in Chapter 9.) As we have seen with intranet design, the structure of document management systems will be informed by the knowledge audit, ensuring not only that traditional departmental structures are replicated, but enabling the knowledge communities to work across organizational boundaries.

A document management system will act as the corporate memory of explicit knowledge in an organization. If an organization is focused upon a codification approach to knowledge management, heavy investment in document management will be made. The document management system must be linked to objectives, communicating to all employees the type of knowledge they should organize and store in the system.

E-learning

In this chapter we have explored the notion that the process of learning is central to acquiring, creating and transferring knowledge. The first emphasis on learning should be as a social process and series of interactions between people (communities of practice); however, e-learning is a way that ICT can support and enhance the learning process. E-learning will typically be delivered across an organizational intranet or extranet, using web-based software, via a web browser.

E-learning
The use of electronic networks and software to deliver training or facilitate learning processes

Cisco Systems (2003) define e-learning as:

> Electronic learning. Internet-based learning, which can include content delivery in multiple formats, management of the learning experience, and a networked community of students, content developers, and experts.

Although a major benefit will be a reduction in costs of training, e-learning will also offer the following benefits, focused on value to knowledge management:

- E-learning can be integrated with other organizational processes to create a 'just-in-time' learning environment; learning can take place during the business processes.
- Richness: the use of a range of media (e.g. audio and video) can offer an interactive experience.
- Empowerment: employees are empowered to learn on their own.
- E-learning can be developed around business needs, responding to rapid change and shorter product cycles.
- Flexibility: e-learning can be personalized to individual needs.
- Collaboration: learning can be developed as a community experience involving sharing.
- Access to expertise: experts on certain subjects can offer feedback and advice online.

E-learning will be delivered using a learning management system (LMS), a database system that will manage and administer learning. The system will allow the creation of modules and courses, access to materials, tests, exams and usage data. Example of LMS in the academic sector include Blackboard (**www.blackboard.com**) and WebCT (**www.webct.com**). A learning management system will need to integrate with content management systems in order to develop a standardized information architecture.

Roles and competencies

The skills and competencies specifically focused on KM must be considered when implementing a knowledge management programme. Information and knowledge consultants TFPL (2003) describe the importance of competencies:

> Competencies are the heart of corporate capability. Many organizations now use competency frameworks as the foundation to define and assess the capability they need within their workforce and to develop learning programmes to fill 'gaps'. In a networked collaborative environment, knowledge and information competencies need to be incorporated into the corporate competency framework.

When assessing capabilities for knowledge management, the following capabilities need to be considered (TFPL, 2003):

- strategic and business;
- management;
- intellectual and learning;
- communication and interpersonal;
- information management and IT.

These competencies are represented diagrammatically in more detail in Figure 5.20.

Employees will require different mixes of these competencies depending on the nature of the organizational knowledge strategy.

As knowledge management has developed as a management discipline, two new organizational roles have emerged: chief knowledge officer (CKO) and knowledge manager. **Chief knowledge officers** are typically created to leverage knowledge into tangible business benefits, the CKO position having originated from the chief information officer (CIO), which is primarily technology driven. A CKO is more likely to view technology as an enabler for an effective knowledge management system (Bonner, 2000). In terms of the European framework introduced earlier in the chapter, a CKO will focus on the links between core knowledge processes, business activities and critical success factors, in particular organizational knowledge capabilities.

Asllani and Luthans (2003) define a knowledge manager's role as to 'plan, organize, and coordinate a mix of knowledge, information, and data, and people or knowledge workers who own the expertise'.

A **knowledge manager** in comparison to a CKO will be closely involved in planning and coordinating the core knowledge processes (identification, generation, storage, distribution and application), ensuring that they are related to business processes and outcomes. A knowledge manager will also assess and oversee the development of individual capabilities, setting the conditions for interaction between employees. Depending on the nature of the organizational knowledge strategy, a knowledge manager will also focus on using and applying ICT to enable knowledge management.

Chief knowledge officer
The organizational knowledge management champion, who will provide the KM vision and strategy

Knowledge manager
Manager who will implement the knowledge management strategy

Activity 5.5	Knowledge management roles and competencies

Purpose To identify differing knowledge management roles and skills.

Activity Local government

Scenario: you are responsible for recruiting staff in local government. Senior management has identified key knowledge management objectives and an outline knowledge strategy related to their business strategy and wish to employ several staff to develop and implement a strategy for knowledge management. A decision has been made to recruit a knowledge manager and a chief knowledge officer (CKO). Your task as recruitment manager is to write a job advert for the posts.

Using the information and concepts introduced above and examples from the Internet, devise the job adverts for the two posts. Include:

1 an outline of what the posts involve in the organization's context;
2 skills and competencies required for each post.

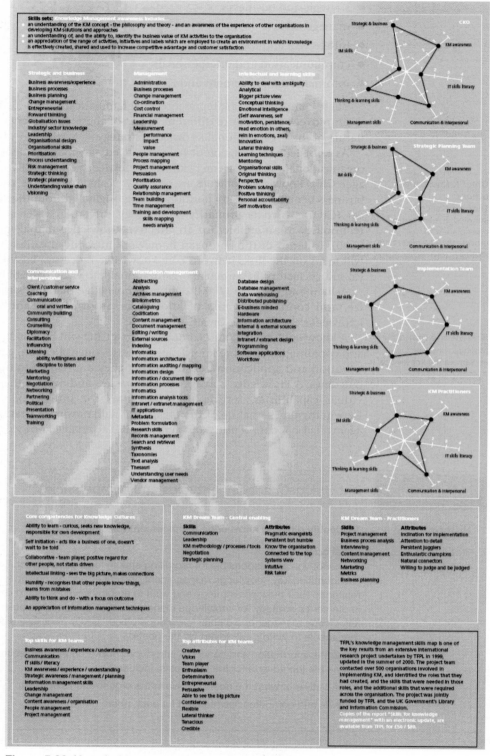

Figure 5.20 Knowledge management competencies
Source: TPFL, www.TFPL.com

Creating a knowledge-sharing culture: rewards and incentives for knowledge management

One of the biggest challenges in deriving business value from organizational knowledge management strategy is how to ensure that knowledge sharing becomes part of organizational culture. The key to the development of a knowledge-sharing culture is trust and openness. Developing this cultural aspect of knowledge management is the most challenging for managers, as many attitudes to knowledge can be deeply ingrained in organizational culture. When assessing the culture of an organization, the following questions should be considered:

- *History*. Does the organization have a history of secrecy? Are there particular events that have compounded these problems?
- *Size*. Does geographical scope inhibit knowledge sharing? Are organizational units too large or too small?
- *Technology*. Does use of ICT inhibit or encourage knowledge sharing? Are there many levels of access to electronic resources? Does ICT increase information overload?
- *Leadership*. Do senior managers openly discuss issues and encourage communication from all levels of the organization?

Two approaches can be taken when creating a knowledge-sharing culture, using rewards and incentives. Here a knowledge management strategy must be aligned with human resource strategies. The first approach will focus upon tangible rewards, which are explicit, in that employees clearly receive something in return for the knowledge they have shared.

The most common reward systems in any organization are economic: employees will receive rewards in the form of increased salary, bonus payments and stock options. These rewards may be tied to skills gained, assessment of knowledge sharing being part of an annual appraisal process. The following examples can be used to illustrate:

- At British Telecom, financial rewards were offered to employees who shared knowledge in the form of new ideas for technological innovation in BT's product and services. The best ideas were selected and rewarded.
- At Siemens, any valuable contributions to the 'Sharenet' community on the intranet receive bonus points similar to an air miles system. The points can be deemed for prizes that develop knowledge, e.g. conference attendance or training courses. This system rewards contributors and reuse, encouraging knowledge sharing and application (Gerndt, 2000).

The other form of tangible reward is the reciprocal access gained to information and knowledge; people understand that if they share they will be offered something in return. Organizations that are externally focused in their knowledge management strategy will develop this culture beyond traditional boundaries. For example, a large grocery retailer will be heavily focused upon management of supply chains – it is therefore beneficial to develop a knowledge-sharing culture with its supply chain partners.

Intangible rewards are hard to define, but must be given equal consideration. Employees will enjoy seeing the positive results of their knowledge sharing. The positive results will include enhanced reputation and personal satisfaction. Staff surveys of employees' attitudes can act as indictors as to whether this type of knowledge culture exists or is developing.

Debate: can a standard be developed for knowledge management?

Purpose

To discuss the advantages and disadvantages of standards for knowledge management.

Activity

visit the www

Read the following position statement from the British Standards Institute (BSI) on Knowledge Management published on the BSI website: **https://www.bspsl.com/secure/ bsrkm/state.pdf**.

Summarize the advantages and disadvantages of a standards-based approach to knowledge management by filling in Table 5.8.

Table 5.8

Advantages	Disadvantages

Summary

1 Knowledge has become a crucial element in the competitive business environment.

2 The key stages of developing a knowledge management strategy are: definitions, audit, objectives, strategy approaches, implementation and quality measures.

3 There are a number of ways to define knowledge: a distinction between tacit and explicit knowledge can be made. Developing a working definition of knowledge is vital to the success of a knowledge management strategy.

4 Knowledge management can be broken down into five processes: store, identify, share, create and use can be applied to business processes. Individual and organizational capabilities will impact upon how knowledge is managed in organizations.

5 All organizations must develop a working definition of knowledge management before developing a knowledge management strategy.

6 A knowledge audit enables an organization to understand knowledge assets, processes and flows. The audit data can be matched against an ideal state so that a knowledge gap analysis can be undertaken. An inventory of knowledge assets, knowledge maps and profiles of employees is the tangible output.

7 Using evidence from a knowledge audit, organizations take different approaches to knowledge management depending on the relationship between knowledge and key business processes.

8   The main approaches are codification versus personalization, exploiter versus explorer, aggressive versus conservative and technocratic versus behavioural.

9   Communities of practice are ways in which employees share knowledge and learn across organizational boundaries.

10 Competitive intelligence relates closely to knowledge management and develops a link to developing knowledge about the external competitive environment.

11 Identifying and developing the right skills for the different roles in knowledge management will have an important impact on the success of a knowledge management strategy.

Exercises

Self-assessment questions

1   What are the four stages in the tacit/explicit knowledge creation model developed by Nonaka?

2   Define knowledge management.

3   How can the data from a knowledge audit be visually represented?

4   Differentiate between the codification and personalization approaches to knowledge management.

5   How does competitive intelligence relate to knowledge management?

6   Define the four stages of the competitive intelligence lifecycle.

7   Define communities of practice.

8   Outline the role of three examples of ICT enabling knowledge management.

Essay and discussion questions

1   Discuss definitions of knowledge using examples from organizations.

2   Describe the role the knowledge audit plays in developing a knowledge management strategy.

3   What role can ICT play in enabling knowledge management?

4   Why is learning important to knowledge management?

5   Discuss the incentives that can be used to develop a knowledge management culture.

6   Outline possible reasons for failure in a knowledge management programme.

7   What does knowledge management tell us about the importance of learning to organizations?

References

Alavi, M. and Leidner, D. (2001) Knowledge management and knowledge management systems: Conceptual foundations and research issues. *MIS Quarterly*, 25(1), 107–53.

American Productivity and Quality Center (2000) Communities of Practice Report. Available online at: www.knowledgeboard.com.

Asllani, A. and Luthans, F. (2003) What knowledge managers really do: An empirical and comparative analysis, *Knowledge Management*, 7(3), 53–66.

Bahra, N. (2001) *Competitive Knowledge Management*. Palgrave, Basingstoke.

Bedny, G., Karwowski, W. and Bedny, M. (2001) The principle of unity of cognition and behaviour: Implications of activity theory for the study of human work. *International Journal of Cognitive Ergonomics*, 5(4), 401–20.

Belbin, M. (2003) Belbin team roles. Available online at: www.belbin.com/belbin-team-roles.htm.

Blackler, F. (1995) Knowledge, knowledge work and organizations: An overview and interpretation. *Organization Studies*, 16(6), 1021–46.

Bonner, D. (2000) Enter the chief knowledge officer. *Training and Development*, 54(2), 36–41.

Brown, J. S. and Duguid, D. (2000) *The Social Life of Information*. Harvard Business School Press, Cambridge, MA.

Cisco Systems (2003) E-learning overview. Available online at: www.cisco.com/warp/public/10/wwtraining/elearning/.

Claudio, J. and Gordon, C. (2003) *Realizing the Promise of Corporate Portals: Leveraging Knowledge for Business Success*. Butterworth-Heinemann, Oxford.

Davenport, E. and Cronin, B. (2000) Knowledge management: Semantic drift or conceptual drift. Association for Library and Information Science Education Conference, Toronto, January. Available online at: www.alise.org/conferences/conf00rDavenport-Croninrpaper.htm.

Davenport, H. and Prusak, L. (1998) *Working Knowledge: How Organizations Manage what they Know*. Harvard Business School Press, Cambridge, MA.

Department of Trade and Industry (2001) Tales of the unexpected – the journey of a white paper. Available online at: www.dti.gov.uk/ckmu/tales.pdf.

Earl, M. (2001) Knowledge management strategies: Towards a taxonomy. *Journal of Management Information Systems*, 18(1), 215–33.

Fahey, L. and Prusack, L. (1998) The eleven deadliest sins of knowledge management, *California Management Review*, 40(3) (Spring), 265–76.

Gerndt, U. (2000) Serving the community. *Knowledge Management*, 3(9) June.

Grey, D. (1999) Knowledge mapping: A practical overview. *SWS Journal*. Available online at http://smithweaversmith.com/knowledg2.htm.

Hansen, M., Nohria, N. and Tierney, T. (1999) What's your strategy for managing knowledge? *Harvard Business Review*, March–April, 106–16.

Hauschild, S., Licht, T. and Stein, W. (2001) Creating a knowledge culture. *McKinsey Quarterly*, Winter, 74–81.

Heisig, P. and Iske, P. (2003) European Guide to Good Practice in Knowledge Management: Final Draft for European Framework on Knowledge Management. Available online at: www.knowledgeboard.com.

Honey, P. and Mumford, A. (1986) *The Manual of Learning Styles*, 3rd edn. P. Honey, Maidenhead.

Jubert, A. (1999) Communities of practice. *Knowledge Management*, 3(2), October.

Kelleher, D. and Levene, S. (2001) *Knowledge Management: A Guide to Good Practice*, BSI, London.

Kok, G., Jangedijk, S. and Troost, J. (2003) Insights from KPMG's European Knowledge Management Survey 2002/2003. Available online at: www.kpmg.nl/kas.

Krebs, V. (2002) Introduction to Social Network Analysis. Available online at: www.orgnet.com/sna.html.

Leonard, D. and Sensiper, S. (1998) The Role of Tacit Knowledge in Group Innovation. *California Management Review*, 40(3), 112–132.

Mekhilef, M., Olesen, A. J. and Kelleher, D. (2003) European Guide to Good Practice in Knowledge Management – Chapter 1 – Terminology. Available online at: www.knowledgeboard.com.

Miller, J. (2001) *Millennium Intelligence: Understanding and Conducting Competitive Intelligence in the Digital Age*. Cyber Age Books, Medford, NJ.

Miller, W. L. and Morris, L. (1999) *Fourth Generation R&D: Managing Knowledge, Technology and Innovation*, Wiley, Chichester.

Murray, P. (2000) How smarter companies get results from KM. In D. Marchand, T. Davenport and T. Dickson (eds), *Mastering Information Management*. Financial Times Prentice Hall, Harlow, pp. 187–92.

Newell, S., Robertson, M., Scarbrough, H. and Swan, J. (2002) *Managing Knowledge Work*. Palgrave, Basingstoke.

Nonaka, I. and Takeuchi, H. (1995) *The Knowledge Creating Company: How Japanese Create the Dynamics of Innovation*. Oxford University Press, New York.

Nonaka, I., Reinmoeller, P. and Senoo, D. (2000) Integrated IT systems to capitalise on market knowledge. In G. Krogh, I. Nonaka, and T. Nishiguchi (eds), *Knowledge Creation: A Source of Value*. Palgrave, Basingstoke.

Orna, E. (1999) *Practical Information Policies*, 2nd edn. Gower, Basingstoke.

Polanyi, M. (1967) *The Tacit Dimension*. Doubleday, New York.

Power, D. (1999) Decision Support Systems Glossary. DSS Resources, World Wide Web. Available online at: http://DSSResources.COM/glossary/.

PricewaterhouseCoopers (2003) PWC global best practices. Available online at: www.globalbestpractices.com/bestrpractices.

Prusak, L. (1998) Where did knowledge management come from? *Knowledge Directions*, 1 (Fall), 90–6.

Snowden, D. (2003) Complex Knowledge. Gurteen Knowledge Conference, London, June. Available online at: www.gurteen.com.

Szulanski, G. (1996) Exploring internal stickiness: impediments to the Transfer of best practice within the firm. *Strategic Management Journal*, 17, 27–43.

TFPL (2003) Knowledge and Information Management Competency Dictionary. Available online at: www.tfpl.com/resources/competencyrdictionary.cfm.

Wegner, E., McDermott, R. and Snyder, W. M. (2002) *Cultivating Communities of Practice: A Guide to Managing Knowledge*. Harvard Business School Press, Cambridge, MA.

White, M. (2000) Building an expertise database. Available online at: www.intranetfocus.com/km/expertise.html.

Zak, M. (2002) Developing a knowledge strategy. In C. Cho and N. Bontis (eds), *The Strategic Management of Intellectual Capital and Organizational Knowledge*. Oxford University Press, Oxford, pp. 255–76.

Further reading

Burden, P. (2000) *Knowledge Management: The Bibliography*. American Society for Information Science and Technology.

Garvey, B. and Williamson, B. (2002) *Beyond Knowledge Management: Dialogue, Creativity and the Corporate Curriculum*. Prentice Hall, Harlow.

Journal of Knowledge Management. Emerald.

Knowledge Management Magazine. www.kmmagazine.com. Ark Group.

Nonaka, I. (1991) The knowledge creating company. *Harvard Business Review*, November–December, 96–104.

Nonaka, I. and Takeuchi, H. (1995) *The Knowledge Creating Company: How Japanese Create the Dynamics of Innovation*. Oxford University Press, New York.

Snowden, D. (2002) Complex acts of knowing: Paradox and descriptive self awareness. *Journal of Knowledge Management*, 6(2), 100–11.

visit the www

Weblinks

American Productivity and Quality Centre (http://www.apqc.org/km/)

Brint (www.brint.com)

David Skyrme (www.skyrme.com)

Destination KM (www.destinationkm.com/)

Electronic Journal of Knowledge Management (www.ejkm.com/)

Knowledge Management in the Federal (US) Government (www.km.gov/)

Knowledge Management Research Center (www.cio.com)

Steve Denning's website (www.stevedenning.com)

Know-Org Discussion list (www.jiscmail.ac.uk)

For multiple-choice questions and annotated weblinks relating to this chapter visit this book's website at: **www.pearsoned.co.uk/chaffey**

6

Information systems strategy

Objective

To assess alternative approaches to developing information systems (IS) strategies.

Learning outcomes

After reading this chapter, you should be able to:

● Describe approaches for developing IS strategy.

● Assess the suitability of tools for selection and generation of IS strategy.

● Evaluate approaches by which IS can support and impact business strategy.

● Explain how IS strategy can support information management and knowledge management strategies.

Management issues

Typical questions facing managers related to this topic:

● How should we align IS strategy with business strategy?

● How are information and knowledge management strategies to be integrated with IS strategy?

● Who should be responsible for IS strategy within an organization?

● How can organizations evaluate and control the effectiveness of IS strategy?

Links to other chapters

➤ *Chapter 4* explores approaches to creating an information management strategy.

➤ *Chapter 5* describes approaches to creating a knowledge management strategy.

➤ *Chapter 7* describes how the IS strategy is implemented through individual IS projects.

➤ *Chapter 11* considers approaches to resourcing IS such as outsourcing and help-desk management.

Introduction

Information systems (IS) strategy development is fundamentally concerned with defining how information systems will be used to support and impact an organization's strategy. 'Support' implies creation of strategic alignment of IS with organizational strategy. 'Impact' implies a role for IS in generating new opportunities for an organization to gain competitive advantage. A definition of IS strategy which covers both these facets is that of Doherty et al. (1999), who describe IS strategy development as:

> the process of identifying a portfolio of computer-based applications to be implemented, which is both highly aligned with corporate strategy and has the ability to create an advantage over competitors.

The definition above also shows that one outcome of IS strategy development is identification of a suitable range of information management applications in order to achieve both business alignment and impact.

The need for a long-term strategy which integrates information management, information technology and systems implementation is suggested by Wilson (1989), who stated:

> An information systems strategy brings together the business aims of the company, an understanding of the information needed to support those aims, and the implementation of computer systems to provide that information. It is a plan for the development of systems towards some future vision of the role of information systems in the organization.

As within any strategy, IS is about deploying resources to best effect. The analogy with the beehive is that strategy implementation must create a consistent, reliable infrastructure which supports the whole organization. This chapter examines approaches to developing IS strategy and reviews the analytical tools available to managers for defining IS strategy. Approaches to defining IS strategy have exercised researchers for decades, so this chapter makes reference to the development of different models for IS strategy development over the past 30 years. To ensure an applied approach, this chapter is based around a process-led view of IS strategy. We start with a definition of IS strategy and further clarification of the relationships between organization strategy and IS strategy. We then look at alternative strategic approaches to IS strategy development based around four different stages of developing an IS strategy. The chapter is structured around a four-stage generic strategy process model where we will seek to answer these questions:

1 *Strategic evaluation.* What is the current status of IS strategy and implementation within the organization and the use of information systems within the broader competitive environment?

2 *Strategic objectives.* What specifically is an organization seeking to achieve through IS strategy development?

3 *Strategy definition.* Which strategic approaches and analytical tools are available to help us formulate the IS strategy?

4 *Strategy implementation.* How should the strategy best be executed through IS projects to help achieve objectives? This is covered in Chapter 7 of *Business Information Management.*

Within each stage of IS strategy development we will review approaches and tools used to assist in achieving the goals of each stage.

What is IS strategy?

The relationship between information management strategy, knowledge management strategy and information systems strategy was introduced in Chapter 4 and see Figure 4.5, p. 177. It was emphasized that each strategy must:

1 help support the future direction of an organization;
2 achieve advantage for the organization (strategic objectives);
3 define the allocation of resources to achieve this advantage;
4 be primarily driven by the needs of the organization, but also by the needs of stakeholders such as shareholders, customers, suppliers or employees;
5 be responsive to the dynamic environment in which the organization operates.

Information systems strategy
The formulation of approaches and planning needed to deploy information systems resources to support organizational strategy

Applications portfolio
The mix of software applications used in an organization or departments

Strategic information systems planning (SISP)
Term used to refer to IS strategy formulation and planning

For the **information systems strategy**, the emphasis is on delivering an **applications portfolio** of appropriate software tools and systems that support 1 and 2 above. Furthermore, the IS strategy also determines the quality of services delivered to end-users. As explained further in Chapter 11, service quality ensures that information and applications are available across organization networks without interruption, and support can be provided to users through a help-desk system.

Historically, research into how IS strategy can support and impact organizational strategy has been referred to in a variety of ways, including information systems planning (ISP), information systems strategic planning (ISSP) and, more frequently, **strategic information systems planning (SISP)**. Each of these definitions refers to planning rather than strategy; Ward and Peppard (2002) suggest this originates since the IS strategy is commonly developed as a plan to support implementation of the business strategy.

Ward and Peppard (2002) suggest that IS strategy must consider both IS/IT strategy formulation and IS/IT planning. IS/IT strategy formulation involves exploration of the opportunities to deploy IS, given analysis of the competitive environment and the need for alignment with business strategy. IS/IT planning is an implementation plan to achieve the IS strategy. Ward and Peppard (2002) identify the following as key outputs of the IS strategy process:

1 *IS/IT management strategy.* An overall IS strategy for the organization, describing the current situation, vision and rationale for IS-related change and plans.
2 *Business IS strategies.* In larger organizations, these specify how each business unit will use IS/IT to deliver its business objectives. This will be defined at the level of applications portfolios for the business and relevant information architectures.
3 *IT strategy.* Policies for the management of specific hardware and software resources comprising the IT infrastructure. This usually also includes the provision of end-user support services such as the IT help-desk.

Regardless of the terminology used, the goals of IS strategy are common. For example, Earl (1996) in a review of the SISP literature, suggests that SISP should target the following areas:

1 aligning investment in IS with business goals;
2 exploiting IT for competitive advantage;
3 directing efficient and effective management of IS resources;
4 developing technology policies and architectures.

Earl suggests that the first two areas are *information systems* strategy, with the next focusing on *information management* strategy and the final area on *information technology* strategy.

IT governance

IT governance
Management of the
processes to direct and
control the enterprise's use
of IT in order to achieve
the enterprise's goals by
adding value while
balancing risk versus
return over IT and its
processes

Another perspective on the reasons why a sound IS strategy is needed, which also helps define the elements of a successful IS strategy, is provided by COBIT. COBIT is the widely adopted IT governance model for Control Objectives for Information and related Technology introduced in Chapters 1 and 4. COBIT (2000) defines IT governance as:

> a structure of relationships and processes to direct and control the enterprise [use of IT] in order to achieve the enterprise's goals by adding value while balancing risk versus return over IT and its processes

The IT Governance Institute (ITGI) – **www.itgi.org** – describe IT Governance as:

> IT governance is the responsibility of the board of directors and executive management. It is an integral part of enterprise governance and consists of the leadership and organisational structures and processes that ensure that the organisation's IT1 sustains and extends the organisation's strategies and objectives.

Note that the emphasis is not on the technology but on managing business relationships and processes, controlling risk and achieving return on investment. COBIT, now developed to version 4.1, identifies the key elements of IT Governance as:

- **Strategic alignment** focuses on ensuring the linkage of business and IT plans, on defining, maintaining and validating the IT value proposition, and on aligning IT operations with enterprise operations.
- **Value delivery** is about executing the value proposition throughout the delivery cycle, ensuring that IT delivers the promised benefits against the strategy, concentrating on optimizing costs and proving the intrinsic value of IT.
- **Resource management** is about the optimal investment in, and the proper management of, critical IT resources: processes, people, applications, infrastructure and information. Key issues relate to the optimization of knowledge and infrastructure.
- **Risk management** requires risk awareness by senior corporate officers, a clear understanding of the enterprise's appetite for risk, transparency about the significant risks to the enterprise, and embedding of risk management responsibilities into the organization.
- **Performance measurement** tracks and monitors strategy implementation, project completion, resource usage, process performance and service delivery, using, for example, balanced scorecards that translate strategy into action to achieve goals measurable beyond conventional accounting.

These factors again emphasize the need for IS strategy to support and be aligned with organizational strategy. COBIT also emphasizes the need for control structures to ensure that this alignment occurs. COBIT 4.1 supports IT Governance by providing a framework that ensures that:

- IT is aligned with the business;
- IT enables the business and maximizes benefits;
- IT resources are used responsibly;
- IT risks are managed appropriately.

Figure 6.1 summarizes the framework developed by COBIT in order to help organizations achieve a comprehensive and consistent approach to IT governance. It can be seen that although this is an IT governance framework, a strong emphasis is placed on managing information quality and how IT and people resources are used to manage this. As such, this framework has the benefit that it unifies the schools of Information Technology, Information Management, Behaviour and Control and Management Control referred to in Table 4.1. In Chapters 10 and 11 we discuss further the relevance of the COBIT framework for management of information quality and information service quality.

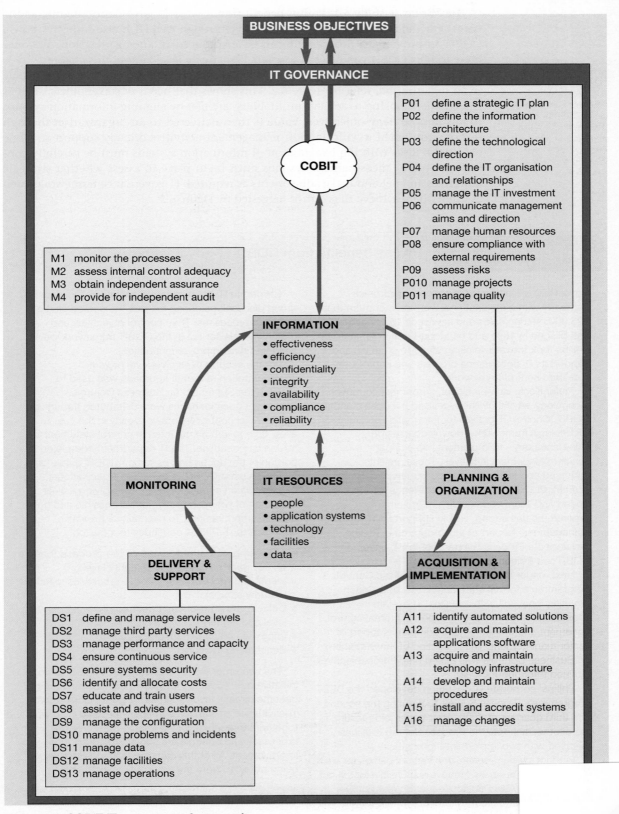

Figure 6.1 COBIT IT governance framework

Source: COBIT (2000), from Information Systems Audit and Control Association (ISACA), www.isaca.org/cobit

The Mini case study 6.1 'Philips benefit from COBIT IT governance' highlights the types of benefit an organization can achieve through COBIT. It also indicates how a COBIT improvement programme can be introduced in an organization. We refer more to how COBIT can be used to assess IS maturity level later in this chapter.

To summarize this section on how information systems strategy can deliver value to an organization, refer to Figure 6.2. This shows that needs of stakeholders, such as shareholders looking to achieve profitability, are met by aligning information systems to business strategy objectives. Value is then delivered to an organization through information when its information management activities directly support strategic objectives. Risks with implementation of information systems must be carefully controlled. Finally, measurement systems must be in place to assess whether strategic objectives are met and make adjustments as required. IT governance frameworks such as COBIT help achieve the control suggested by Figure 6.2.

Mini case study 6.1 | Philips benefits from COBIT IT governance

Royal Philips Electronics is a global electronics company with a multinational workforce of more than 225,000 offering sales and service in 150 countries. Established in 1891 and headquartered in Amsterdam, Philips took forward-thinking steps to organise and support its IT governance process and improve its IT-related control framework.

Pieter Kock, vice-president, corporate information technology, says that Philips utilised the open standard COBIT (Control Objectives for Information and related Technology) framework – downloadable from **www.isaca.org** – to implement two company-wide senior management initiatives. These projects were endorsed and led by the Philips Supervisory Board:

First, the BEST (Business Excellence through Speed and Teamwork) quality improvement programme has strong, visible support from senior management. As part of this programme, Philips developed a Process Survey Tool for IT, based on the COBIT 3rd Edition model.

Next, under the Statement on Business Controls programme a formal statement is issued by each organisational unit within Philips. These are consolidated into the annual report's internal control statement and therefore have complete support of senior management. The IT section of the Statement on Business Controls was based on control objectives outlined throughout COBIT.

Philips' corporate IT operation developed the BEST programme's Process Survey Tool during the second and third quarters of 2000. After undergoing testing in ten pilot workshops, the Process Survey Tool was released with two implementation paths:

Product division – where one contact person for each division and/or business group is responsible for roll-out.

Region (i.e. Asia Pacific, East and West Europe, Latin America and North America) – where roll-out will be facilitated country by country.

Corporate IT or trained representatives facilitated group discussions during roll-out and scored all the pertinent processes. Then control objectives and maturity levels set out in the COBIT framework were used to define improvement actions.

For the second executive-level project implementation, a formal approach was used to develop the Statement on Business Controls. Statement questionnaires were distributed throughout the financial controllers network early in the year to allow time to submit the internal control statement by its January deadline. The IT department completed its portion of the document, based on COBIT guidance.

Philips used COBIT to establish organisational capabilities on a maturity level basis, giving a clear indication of where improvement is possible and how to effect improvement. To maintain its proactive approach to IT, Philips continues to focus on:

- Assessing actual outcomes of the process (based on key goal indicators and maturity levels)
- Identifying problem areas (for IT processes with low maturity scores)
- Defining best practices ('defined process' maturity level and higher)
- Improving management processes and actions
- Benchmarking scores

The two programmes make up a ground-breaking initiative by Philips as they allow business functions to become directly involved in the IT governance debate. The initiative also enables the business and IT to work together more effectively to ensure that business processes and controls are subject to continuous improvement. All of this can only lead to better value being obtained from the group's IT investments.

Source: Information Systems Audit and Control Association (ISACA). http://www.isaca.org/Knowledge-Center/cobit/Pages/Royal-Philips-Electronics.aspx

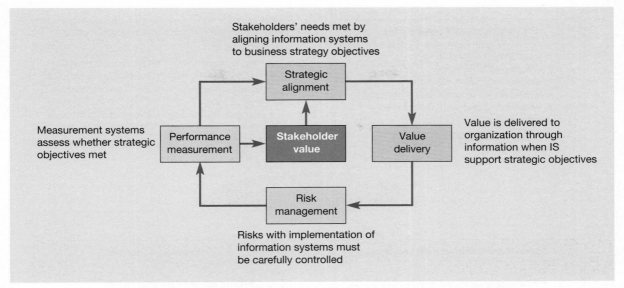

Figure 6.2 A model for controlling the contribution of information systems to an organization

Information systems strategy activities

We have said that the information systems strategy should support organizational strategy, but which specific activities are involved? These activities are used to manage the different business information management resources introduced at the end of Chapter 1. These resources include information resources, technology resources such as applications and infrastructure, and the people resources that use the other resources. Activities conducted by these people resources, which are specified and controlled through the IS strategy, have been usefully grouped into four different types of services by Ward and Peppard (2002):

1 strategy and planning services;
2 applications development services;
3 application and technical management services;
4 technology, delivery and maintenance services.

This can be adapted to recognize the importance of information services, as shown in Figure 6.3. It can be seen that these activities will be performed by IS staff who are either employees of the organization or subcontracted from a third-party organization as part of an **IS outsourcing** agreement (see Chapter 11).

IS outsourcing
Information systems are outsourced to a third party organization

To place these IS services and activities into the context of the types of information technology hardware, software and standards, look at Figure 6.4. The fundamental services are the applications at the top such as NELHS (**www.nelh.nhs.uk**), the National Electronic Library, a digital library for NHS staff, patients and the public, and HER (the electronic health record which will give a complete case history for each patient). There are also the applications required by any organization such as those for HR, procurement (e-commerce) and finance. Other services which are supplied by NHS IA are managed services such as voice, e-mail and video communications infrastructure, generic tools such as e-mail and office packages; core services such as training, support and call-centre; access and security and the physical network. The NHS IA also sets policies and standards on information quality (for clinical and management information), interoperability between health trusts (e-GIF – e-government interoperability framework) and privacy issues.

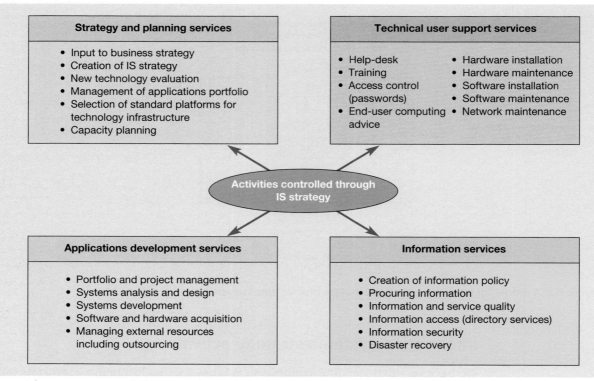

Strategy and planning services

- Input to business strategy
- Creation of IS strategy
- New technology evaluation
- Management of applications portfolio
- Selection of standard platforms for technology infrastructure
- Capacity planning

Technical user support services

- Help-desk
- Training
- Access control (passwords)
- End-user computing advice
- Hardware installation
- Hardware maintenance
- Software installation
- Software maintenance
- Network maintenance

Activities controlled through IS strategy

Applications development services

- Portfolio and project management
- Systems analysis and design
- Systems development
- Software and hardware acquisition
- Managing external resources including outsourcing

Information services

- Creation of information policy
- Procuring information
- Information and service quality
- Information access (directory services)
- Information security
- Disaster recovery

Figure 6.3 Information systems services and activities

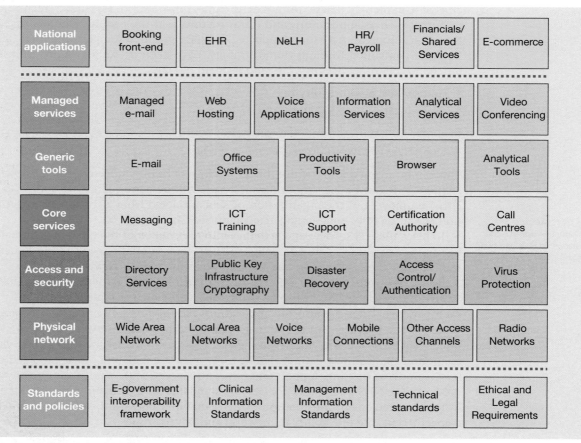

National applications	Booking front-end	EHR	NeLH	HR/Payroll	Financials/Shared Services	E-commerce
Managed services	Managed e-mail	Web Hosting	Voice Applications	Information Services	Analytical Services	Video Conferencing
Generic tools	E-mail	Office Systems	Productivity Tools	Browser		Analytical Tools
Core services	Messaging	ICT Training	ICT Support	Certification Authority		Call Centres
Access and security	Directory Services	Public Key Infrastructure Cryptography	Disaster Recovery	Access Control/Authentication		Virus Protection
Physical network	Wide Area Network	Local Area Networks	Voice Networks	Mobile Connections	Other Access Channels	Radio Networks
Standards and policies	E-government interoperability framework	Clinical Information Standards	Management Information Standards	Technical standards		Ethical and Legal Requirements

Figure 6.4 Information systems activities for the National Health Service Information Authority

Source: www.nhsia.nhs.gov.uk

Defining a process for IS strategy development

Strategy development process
A framework for approaching strategy development in a series of logical steps

In order for IS strategy development to be effective, organizations have to develop an effective **strategy development process**. The process will be effective if it can generate, as its output, an IS strategy which is aligned with the business strategy. The IS strategy development process should have these characteristics:

- *Achieves alignment of IS strategy with business strategy while identifying competitive opportunities available through IS.* These are the two core goals of any IS strategy, as explained at the start of this chapter.
- *Simplicity through well-defined stages.* The process should possess clearly defined, repeatable steps or stages that can be performed in a logical order. Such simplicity can help senior business managers work together with technical IT managers to develop the strategy.
- *Continuous process with evaluation and improvement built in.* It should be recognized that the strategy development process is a repeatable process that will have strengths and weaknesses which should be evaluated at the end of each planning cycle and adjustments made accordingly.
- *Flexibility.* The process should enable changes within the business environment to be reflected in updated IS plans.

Long-term vs short-term scope of IS strategy

Long-term IS strategy
Specifies broad strategic approaches over a three- to five-year period

Short-term strategy
Details of strategy over a six- to twelve-month period

Larger organizations may create IS strategies on different timescales. There will be a **long-term IS strategy** that looks forward three to five years and a **short-term strategy** that considers the detailed strategy for the next 6 to 12 months. It might be thought that creating a long-term IS strategy would not be practical or worthwhile since both technologies and the market in which an organization operates vary so rapidly. However, a long-term strategy is useful for several reasons. First, there will be future indications of future technologies or standards that other companies or sectors are starting to adopt. For example, some companies such as book retailers implemented e-commerce in the mid-1990s. For others, it was not practical to implement e-commerce at this time if demand from customers in the market was lower, or simply insufficient funds were available to develop an e-commerce facility. In this case it makes sense to have a longer-term strategy for staged implementation of e-commerce (Table 6.1). This enables investment in information systems to be staged over a longer period. Of course, the market or cost of technology may change such that some

Table 6.1 **Example of a staged strategy for introduction of e-commerce**

Phase	Business application(s)
Year 1: Basic internal and external communications	Simple company intranet, Internet e-mail and customer-facing website
Year 2: Buy-side e-commerce – main suppliers	E-procurement system with top 10 suppliers
Year 3: Sell-side e-commerce – smaller customers- and buy-side e-commerce – smaller suppliers	Introduce simple transactional site for smaller customers Roll out e-procurement to smaller suppliers
Year 4: Sell-side e-commerce – larger customers	New customer relationship management system
Year 5: Mobile commerce	Online orders from mobile platforms Alerts from suppliers

applications may need to be introduced earlier or even scrapped if other companies are not seeing benefits from similar applications.

For some government-funded organizations, there may be long-term targets which need to be met. For example, in the UK, the government mandated as part of an 'e-government' initiative that there should be electronic delivery of all services by 2005. These are described at the Cabinet Office E-envoy site (**http://archive.cabinetoffice.gov.uk/ e-envoy/index-content.htm**). Mini case study 6.2 'Test Valley Council IS Strategy 2002– 2005' indicates the need for, and nature of, a longer-term IS strategy at one council.

Top-down vs bottom-up IS strategy

Top-down method of IS strategy definition
The IS applications portfolio is determined by alignment with corporate objectives

Bottom-up method of IS strategy definition
The selection of the IS applications portfolio partially or completely determines the emphasis of IS strategy and how it impacts corporate objectives

We can also identify two approaches to the IS strategy process which, although distinct, are not mutually exclusive. These are frequently referred to in the subsequent coverage of alternative models that have been developed to describe IS strategy. First, a **top-down method of IS strategy definition** starts with the business objectives and then assesses which information systems can be used to help achieve these objectives. For example, if the Lo-cost Airline Company has a business objective of increasing the volume of repeat business through developing or enhancing a customer loyalty scheme, then IS such as customer relationship management systems can be developed or enhanced to help create this. Secondly, a **bottom-up method of IS strategy definition** can occur. Here the selection of the IS applications portfolio partially or completely determines the emphasis of IS strategy and how it impacts corporate objectives. For example, if different managers in the Lo-cost Airline Company, such as the marketing manager, HR manager and e-commerce manager, were to request different systems according to their own departmental or functional needs, then this helps determine IS strategy.

Debate 6.1

There is no need for a long-term (3- to 5-year) IS strategy. A short term (1-year) strategy is all that is necessary.

Mini case study 6.2 | **Test Valley Council IS strategy 2002–2005**

Test Valley Borough Council is responsible for all services in the Borough of Test Valley which covers 250 square miles of western Hampshire, in the south of the UK. In 2002, it developed an IS strategy in response to new government policy.

The introduction to the Council's IS strategy stated:

Information Technology, I.T., is used by the Test Valley Borough Council services to help them to deliver services to their customers efficiently and effectively. The Council is increasing its use and dependency of information systems. Over the next three years there will be an increasing dependency on IT to conform to the government's e-Government targets of electronic delivery of all services by 2005. New technology and new ways of working are constantly developing and the authority needs a strategy to manage these changes.

An example of the implementation of online services is shown in Figure 6.5.

The need for the IS strategy is explained as follows:

An I.S. strategy is a way of smoothly directing the decisions that the Council makes in its use of new technology. This will improve the services that we provide to our customers; the public, the Councillors and each other. The strategy has to address the present position and problems, the increasing dependence on IT by services, plan for the 'foreseeable' technology, and allow for developments that may have not been thought of yet. There is certainty that change and new developments will take place. A function of the I.S. strategy is to apply controls that will facilitate the management of these changes.

Parties involved with development of the IS strategy:

Figure 6.5 Online payment services at Test Valley Borough Council

Source: www.testvalley.gov.uk

(a) *The Executive*. Was made up of ten Test Valley councillors. The Committee met every two weeks and deliberated on all matters of policy and expense.

(b) *The Information & Communications Board*. This was chaired by a member of the Test Valley directorate, and included membership of the Electronic Services Project Manager, the Assistant to the Chief Executive, the Audit Section, the head of IT Services, the head of revenues services, the head of Administration service, the ex-chairman of the UAG and two councillors.

(c) *The Management Team*. This was composed of the members of the directorate and the head of service for each of the 12 services that make up the Test Valley management. The Management Team met weekly.

(d) *The User Advisory Group (UAG)*. Comprised senior officers from each of the Test Valley services. The task of UAG members was to ensure a planned and co-ordinated approach to IS at the Authority, by reflecting the needs and plans of their department and by feeding corporate IS decisions back to their department.

(e) *IS Working Groups*. Special interest subgroups were formed as needed to investigate a particular aspect of information technology which was of interest.

(f) *The IT Service management and staff*. This group was involved in the daily implementation of the IS Strategy as it applied to the installed equipment and software base. IT Service staff provided day-to-day support to the users of IT systems and equipment.

(g) *Internal Audit Section*. The Internal Audit Section was responsible for appraising the Council's operations. Officers had to inform the Internal Audit

Section of planned purchases and developments of information systems so that it had the opportunity to advise on internal controls and the achievement of economy, efficiency and effectiveness.

The I.S. Strategy had three major components:

- *Technology* – including operating systems, network and mobile technology.
- *Standards* – standards that are driven by legislation, working trends or best practice. These include applications.
- *Security* – to ensure information is safe, accurate and recoverable.

Examples of different elements of this IS Strategy are shown in Figure 6.6.

Timescale for annual budget development.

Although the IS strategy covered a three year period, it was amended each year according to changes in legislation and government requirements. A separate budget was then developed each year.

6 months: Initial discussion of IS strategy with User Steering Group

4 months: Presentation of preliminary IS Strategy to the Management Team

4 months: Presentation of preliminary IS Strategy the Information & Communications Board

2 months: Budget finalization through Overview & Scrutiny Committee

1 month: Budget sign-off by the Council Executive

Source: Test Valley Council IS Strategy published at: www.testvalley.gov.uk/TestValley/council.nsf/pages/Informat103716.html?OpenDocument&Start=1&Count=1000&ExpandView. Strategy being updated, September 2004

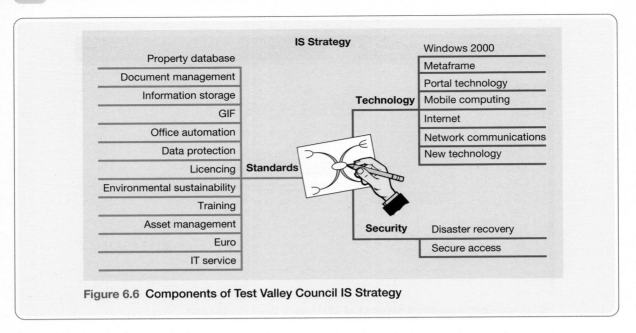

Figure 6.6 Components of Test Valley Council IS Strategy

The IS strategy development process that organizations use tends to evolve alongside the development of the organization. Earl (1996) summarizes research conducted in the 1980s and 1990s into approaches to developing information systems strategy, in this case described as Strategic Information Systems Planning (SISP). A summary of the approaches used for an IS strategy process, based on detailed studies in over 20 large UK-based organizations is shown in Table 6.2. The range of approaches is still informative since it still reflects the reality in many organizations. The five main approaches to the IS strategy development process summarized in Table 6.2 are:

- *Business-led approach.* IS strategy is led by the business and based on business plans or strategies which are analysed to identify where IS are required. This is a top-down approach. Difficulties can arise with this approach where the business strategy is not formalized, or where the business strategy is dynamic since the development of the IS strategy in this approach is typically an annual activity related to budget setting.

- *Method-driven approach.* In this approach, a formal method such as IBM's Business System Planning (BSP) method or other proprietary methods devised by IS consultants is used to develop IS strategy based on best practice. This is also a top-down approach. This approach is often taken to substantiate the IS strategy, but this may not be successful if there is a 'disconnect' between the method and the senior management team. Such formal IS strategy development tools are no longer widely used, but rather formal methodologies tend to be used now for management of specific projects (e.g. the PRINCE 2 project management approach or the Dynamic Systems Development Method) or for analysis and design (e.g. SSADM, Structured Systems Analysis and Design Method or OMT, Object Modelling Technique, described in Chapter 7).

- *Administrative approach.* This is a resource-based approach which is typically 'bottom-up'. Different IS applications and technologies vie for attention, with the result that strategic focus may be lost. However, a steering committee, often co-opting members of different business functions such as finance, marketing and operations, is often used to ensure that the portfolio of applications is prioritized and the process is transparent and repeatable. Earl's study also suggested that some applications able to deliver competitive advantage could be identified through the

Table 6.2 SISP Approaches

	Business-led	Method-driven	Administrative	Technological	Organizational
Emphasis	The business	Technique	Resources	Models	Learning
Basis	Business plans	Best practice	Procedure	Rigour	Partnership
Ends	Plan	Strategy	Portfolio		Themes
Methods	Ours	Best	None	Engineering	Any way
Nature	Business	Top-down	Bottom-up	Blueprints	Interactive
Influencer	IS planner	Consultants	Committees	Method	Teams
Relation to business strategy	Fix points	Derive	Criteria	Objectives	Look at business
Priority setting	The board	Method recommends	Central committee	Compromise	Emerge
IS role	Driver	Initiator	Bureaucrat	Architect	Team member

Source: from *An organizational approach to IS strategy-making. In M. Earl (ed.) Information Management: The Organizational Dimension*. Oxford University Press (Earl, M. 1996) p.142, By permission of Oxford University

process of submitting proposals for new IS applications. A survey of CIOs at US companies found that market-leading companies tended to involve business units more actively in the determination of the IS budget (PRTM, 2003).

- *Technological approach.* This approach tends to focus on technical plans as outputs, such as business process models, standards, information audits and data models and IT architectures. As would be expected, it is difficult for business managers to become involved when discussion tends to focus on the technical merit of different approaches, rather than their relevance to the business.

- *Organizational approach.* The organizational approach is often a response to failure in the other approaches. This approach aims to engender collaboration between the business and IS managers. It aims to focus on major themes – opportunities or problems the business may face. Earl gives examples of major themes such as a food company focusing on delivering high levels of service quality, an insurance company focusing on reducing administrative costs and a chemical company focusing on new product development. Each business problem involves both management and IS working together not only to define the strategy but also to implement it successfully. This approach also marks a move away from long-term planning to incremental improvements as they are required.

Earl reports that many organizations had used more than one approach. This suggests the difficulty in selecting an effective approach. Indeed, common problems with the IS strategy development process were identified. Of 65 concerns cited, these were most common:

1 *Resource constraints.* This includes lack of time from IS specialists and also members of the senior management team.

2 *Not fully implemented.* There were often problems with strategy implementation, even when it was felt that the strategy itself was sound.

3 *Lack of top-management acceptance.* This was often felt to be due to poor understanding of IS and its relevance to the business.

4 *Length of time involved.* The duration of strategy development was long in relation to changes in the business environment.

5 *Poor user–IS relationships.* These are often poor due to a long history of poor relationships, so they are difficult to resolve.

Complete Activity 6.1 to evaluate the strengths and weaknesses of the different approaches to development of IS strategy.

Activity 6.1 — **Evaluating different approaches to the IS strategy development process**

Purpose

To evaluate the advantages for different approaches to IS strategy development.

Activity

For a large organization such as the Lo-cost Airline Company and a smaller organization, identify for each of the five approaches to SISP presented above:

1 Its advantages.

2 Its disadvantages.

3 Possible organizational reasons for using this approach.

4 The desirability of this process relative to the others (produce a ranking for the different types of organization).

A more extensive study of the SISP process of 163 US-based organizations was undertaken by Lederer and Sethi (1992). This builds on a previous study by Lederer and Mendelow (1987). Problems with the strategy development process were grouped under three headings which it can be seen are common with those of Earl (1996). The three main areas are:

1 *Leadership issues.* The most significant problem across all companies was securing top management commitment for implementing the IS strategy plan This suggests that top management either did not have sufficient involvement with the plan or lacked confidence in whether it could be implemented by the team available. Such problems still result from lack of personal familiarity with IT by some senior managers.

   Further leadership problems were highlighted by the 1987 study, which still ring true over 20 years later:

   ● Lack of top-management awareness of the impact of IS/IT and how it offered strategic advantage – 'computers were viewed more from an operational context'.

   ● There was a credibility gap between IT industry 'hype' and what IT can actually deliver in terms of return on investment.

   ● Information was not viewed as a business resource to be managed for long-term benefit.

   ● There is often a short-term focus which leads to neglect of long-term planning.

2 *Implementation issues.* The second most significant problem was that implementation of the IS projects and data architecture required substantial further analysis. This shows that even after development of the IS strategy, significant additional input from managers is required to plan individual applications. This is not surprising, but it reflects a frustration that even when in-depth IS strategy analysis is conducted using a method such as IBM's Business Systems Planning, which covers areas such as enterprise analysis, and information modelling, further analysis which appears to duplicate effort, is required.

3 *Resource issues.* Many businesses perceived the planning exercise as taking a long time of weeks or even months. Identifying team members with the right skills to prepare the plan was also thought to be difficult.

These problems are also reflected in the five main success factors for SISP, which the study suggested were:

1 top-management involvement;
2 top-management support;
3 business strategy available;
4 study business before technology;
5 good IS management.

Responsibilities and controls for IS strategy

To control the different IS-related strategies shown in Figure 6.3, clearly defined responsibilities are needed. But where do these responsibilities lie? Deciding on these responsibilities and controls is critical to the effectiveness of business information management within any organization. It will determine the extent of problems such as those noted by Earl (1996) which are described above, i.e. insufficient resources, insufficient senior management buy-in, poor IS–user relationships and poor implementation of strategy.

A common approach in organizations is to have a single person responsible for information systems. The role is usually referred to as IS manager, IT manager or chief information officer (CIO), as explained in Chapter 4. In larger organizations this person may have been in charge of a sizeable IS or IT department with staff involved in IS planning, managing a help-desk, developing applications and maintaining applications, hardware and the network. The nature of the challenging role of IS manager is shown by Case study 6.1, which shows the approaches used by the car manufacturer Renault. With the trend to outsourcing described in Chapter 11, many IS departments have shrunk in size, with the role changing to one of managing different suppliers.

Case study 6.1   FT

Jean-Pierre Corniou of Renault shows how to bring business technology out into the open

In this case, the chief information officer of Renault talks about his experiences in managing IT at Renault. It illustrates the challenges involved with managing 1,400 applications in a large company and shows the management skills needed by the CIO.

'The key word for me is transparency. IT is about delivering services to end users, but the lack of visibility and transparency of IT is a problem in large companies. That can lead to a lack of confidence in the CIO, and can make it difficult for the CEO to understand the need for investment in products and the quality of service. My job is to bring transparency to IT.

Frankly, my job consists of being a bilingual guy: I speak both the language of business and of technology. I have to make IT understandable to everyone in the company. This is a challenge for all CIOs in large companies.

Renault, like other companies, started investing in IT in the middle 60s. It was pioneering work – there were just a few people in IT, working on large systems of great complexity.

People inside IT still have that pioneering attitude, of the era when IT was seen as secret, and complex, and they still consider IT to be a very specific environment to work in. But we need to open up, to build transparency, to build the confidence and trust of all stakeholders in the company.

One of my first major decisions at Renault was to build a team dedicated to marketing and communications. This has been questioned by my boss – why are you going to market IT? My answer was clear: because we spend a lot of money on it.

At Renault, this represents 1.7 per cent of turnover. We want to be sure that everyone in the company, starting with Louis Schweitzer [Renault's chief executive], is fully aware of the content of these expenses.

Costs like fax, e-mail, mobile phones and so on – the IT department is not totally responsible for IT costs, it's also to do with the behaviour of users.

These are things that users see as more or less free, and we need to make sure they understand their value.

We have invested lots of money in applications like ERP [enterprise resource planning] and websites, and when we analysed the level of utilisation of these products and tools, we were very surprised to see how much money had been spent on products that people were not using.

Very often, in large companies, there is a lack of training. We are not spending enough money training people to use products. At the end of a project, we are exhausted. We have spent months and years developing something, we want to move on to a new theatre of action – but the end user has not been trained.

So before investing in any new applications, the key driver is to use what already exists. We are running 1,400 different systems. Before starting anything new, I ask are you sure we are using what we have already?

My vision is to design, build, sell and maintain cars. Everything I do is directly linked to this, to the urgent need to increase turnover, margins and brand image. Every single investment and expense in the IT field has to be driven by this vision of the automotive business. What I have brought is a deep sense that the IT guy has to be totally business driven and results driven, not technology driven.

It's not so easy in this market, with the forces coming from the vendors. I fear hypes, I fear fashion, I fear sometimes consultants and vendors.

Because very often the push for new technology is a push to increase their revenues. I don't blame them for this, but really the CIO of a large company has to be the dam, the filter, between the vendor, and the reality of the business needs.

One of my challenges is to calm down the hype, and find out the real value of technology. We are in an industry where every decision is directly linked to cost reduction.

That's one of the reasons why I insist that being bilingual is so important. If you want to have credibility in the business community you have to know business.

I spend a lot of time in plants, in discussions with foremen in the field, trying to understand how they use technology to increase their efficiency.

I spend lots of time in commercial departments too, to understand the key business processes.

When I entered Renault, coming from the steel industry, I had to understand the complexity of the car industry. It's very complex, believe me. I spent days and nights trying to understand the business.

Also, you have to be operational immediately. I arrived in March 2000, and by July I had to propose to the executive committee a reorganisation of my organisation.

Bringing IT to the business community means the CIO has to be embedded in the day to day life of the organisation, and of course, to have a seat on the board. I consider myself more a business guy than an IT guy. I never studied IT.

I spend part of my time understanding the major trends in the future of IT, and trying to explain to my colleagues the extent to which IT can improve performance. It is very important to build an efficient network with my peers.

The CIO has not to be a foreigner in his own company. Communications, and learning to communicate, are very important. You have to be warm – IT appears cold, but you have to be open, and curious. That's very important.

In the automotive industry, a key factor is the digitalisation of the design process. This is fundamental to our business. You want to reduce the time to market, and the improvement of the quality and reliability, and you want better analysis of the life cycle of our products.

We are pretty advanced in this field.

The Megane family was designed and produced in 29 months, which is a very good result in the industry. In the future, to reduce the design and production time is not the real challenge, but to increase the reliability of the production schedule. It's very important to have a fully reliable planning process.

We have managed to match Renault and Nissan because we are using technology. Like e-mail, and of course videoconferencing. When you are working with a team of partners who are 12,000 kilometres away, you have to increase the communications.

For example, I and my Nissan counterpart have weekly videoconferencing, for two hours every Tuesday morning. And two days per month we meet together physically.

Renault is becoming a more and more international company with the Renault Nissan adventure. It's very important to be able to connect. This is a key factor in our progress. We have decided to build a single common network, which we will implement worldwide.

Virtual working, by videoconferencing, is becoming more important. I consider it very important to develop the software environment to increase the virtualisation of the two companies. And of course we speak English – unfortunately.'

Biography

Born: June 17, 1950 in Vichy, France

Education: Graduate of the Ecole Nationale d'Administration and holds a postgraduate degree in Economics

Career: Deputy director of employee affairs at Compagnie Generale des Eaux, deputy managing director of ANPE, director of information systems at Usinor. Joined Renault in 2000.

Source: Fiona Harvey, Bringing business technology out into the open – Jean-Pierre Corniou of Renault, FT.com; 16 September 2003

Questions

1 What does Jean-Pierre see as the challenges of integrating IT into the organization?

2 Summarize the strategic approaches used in Renault to integrate IT with the organization.

3 From the way Jean-Pierre describes his approach to integrating IT, produce a checklist of the attributes needed by a CIO or information systems manager. Add to the list.

Management sponsor for IS strategy
A senior manager who chairs the steering committee for IS strategy development and execution

Although the IS/IT manager/CIO will often develop the IS strategy, other members of the organization are needed to input to the strategy, review it and authorize investment. We have also seen that involvement of other parts of the business within the IS strategy development process is essential. Ward and Peppard (2002) suggest that a **management sponsor for IS strategy** should be involved throughout the strategy development process. They are preferably a director or senior manager who will chair the IS strategy steering committee and will ultimately approve the budget and plan. It is apparent that the involvement of a non-IT person in this role will help reassure others involved in the planning process of the management commitment to the IS strategy. It can be suggested that the steering committee should not only have a role in defining IS strategy for part of the year, but that it should also have a role in monitoring the execution of the IS strategy. The management sponsor is also effective in this role.

Approaches to achieving commitment to IS are similar to those described in Chapter 4 for information management. Techniques for achieving management control include:

1 *Appointing IS/IT director to the board*. This provides a mechanism for IS to impact strategy. The IS/IT director can actively influence business strategy and explain the contribution that IT can make. If there is not a specific IS/IT director on the board, then IT is less likely to be viewed as an opportunity.

2 *Other board member ultimately responsible for IS/IT*. This is often the finance director, particularly in organizations where IS is viewed as a cost. There is a danger here that IS may be marginalized, since the finance director will not have much time to devote to IT. If, however, there is a good relationship with the senior IS/IT manager, then this work can be subcontracted effectively, while still achieving an influence on strategy. Other possible board members who may be responsible for IS/IT include operations managers or marketing managers, particularly in organizations where IS/IT is important in communicating and directly transacting with customers such as a 'dot-com'.

3 *Steering committee or special working group*. An IS/IT steering group may be set up to define IS strategy and control IS expenditure and projects. Since different areas of the business will request new applications, there needs to be an independent means of reviewing these. Typically, the main board will not have time to review these investments. The steering group will typically include a director from the main board, plus the IS manager and different functional departmental heads or business unit leaders.

4 *Business unit leader*. In some organizations, there may be no board-level control of IS – instead each business unit will manage their own IS function. In this instance, it is unlikely that the business unit is responsible for all types of IS service presented in Figure 6.3. For example, technical user support services and information services may be controlled centrally, but applications selection may be controlled by the business unit.

The approaches presented above are not necessarily alternatives; indeed it is common to have hybrid approaches such as each of 2, 3 and 4 in operation in a large organization. To consider further the advantages and disadvantages of each approach, complete Activity 6.2.

Activity 6.2	**Where should ultimate responsibility for IS lie?**
Purpose	To review alternatives for IS responsibility within an organization.
Activity	For each of the four different alternatives for IS responsibility outlined above, list the advantages and disadvantages. Which do you think is the best solution for most organizations? To what extent do you think the best solution varies according to type of organization?

As an illustration of the range of people involved in IS strategy development, a typical university may involve these types of groups:

- *Computer Users Advisory Group*: web-based forum, advising ISSC on IS strategy and the management of services.
- *Administrative Information Systems Group*: overseeing information systems in MIS (management information systems) and administrative sections; making recommendations to ISSC. These are sometimes also referred to as 'Academic Information Systems' – used for recording, review and dissemination of marks.
- *Telecommunications Review Group*: steering the development of voice telecommunications, and advising ISSC.
- *Website Steering Group*: steering the overall development of the university's web pages and making recommendations to ISSC.
- *Information Systems Strategy Committee (ISSC)* (Council and Senate): recommendations on and monitoring of overall information systems strategy; detailed budgeting within the budget envelope; monitoring quality and reliability of central services.
- *Vice-Chancellor's Advisory Group* – receive strategy.
- *Budget Sub-Committee*: receiving plan and budget, and set budget as part of overall university budget planning.
- *Strategy and Finance Committee:* approve budget.

Within the IT industry, there is much discussion about the importance of the IS/IT manager/CIO within organizations. Research insight 6.1 'Does IS have a voice?' shows that there is quite a variation in how IS is perceived within organizations. Mini case study 6.3 'The incredible shrinking CIO' suggests that the way that CIOs are perceived certainly doesn't seem to be improving.

Research insight 6.1   **Does IS have a voice?**

IT recruitment consultancy Computer People surveyed 500 UK company directors and 500 senior IT managers to explore how the IS/IT function is perceived within organizations. The main findings were as follows:

How company directors perceive IT managers
The research suggested that company directors see IT directors as 'advisory figures, rather than people who are qualified to make important decisions on spending, according to recent research'.

How IT managers perceive company attitudes to IT
The survey found that IT-related issues were a low priority (80 per cent agreed) and this was attributed to senior managers not being able to comprehend the long-term implications of technology issues (41 per cent agreed).

IT managers as board members
IT managers were unlikely to become board members. Less than a third of UK companies had an IT director on the board. Of the IT managers surveyed, only 5 per cent thought that they had a very good chance of being promoted to the board within the next couple of years.

Source: *IT Week* (2003)

Mini case study 6.3	The incredible shrinking CIO

CIO (2003) describes the case of Williams-Sonoma (**www.williams-sonoma-inc.com**), a company selling housewares, kitchen accessories and food.

In early 2002, Jim Brownell, the CIO, sat on the executive committee, reported directly to the CEO, and oversaw a strategic, multi-million-dollar replacement of the retailer's merchandising and warehousing system. But when a new CEO took over, he decided he wanted his own CIO. So in October 2002 the 25-year IT veteran looked for a comparable position elsewhere. He couldn't find one.

CIO (2003) reports Brownell as saying:

When I looked at opportunities in CIO-land, they were unappealing. The cycle of CIOs reporting to CFOs (Chief Financial Officers) is coming back, and it's not pleasing. I heard the same story in every interview: 'We're looking for a new CIO because IT projects never deliver on time and they cost more than we expect and they don't deliver what we want. All our systems need to be replaced. Oh, and we're reducing the amount of money we're allocating for IT'.

In the end, Brownell accepted a job as senior vice-president and general manager of Escalate, a California software vendor, rather than settle for a lesser CIO job. He says: 'Quite honestly, I don't know why anyone would want the CIO job today'.

The results of surveys summarized in *CIO* (2003) suggest this isn't an isolated case:

- 22 per cent of CIOs in 2003 – as opposed to 11 per cent in 2002 – are now reporting to CFOs
- IT budgets declined or were flat for four consecutive quarters (through Q2 2003)
- 7 out of 10 companies are currently outsourcing some type of IT operation
- Average large-company CIO pay dropped 16 per cent from $434,000 in 2001 to $363,000 in 2003.

This decline in influence has continued through the first decade of the millennium. However, there are many who believe that as the global economy moves out of recession, there may be a resurgence in the power of the CIO. The demand to use technology to drive progress may permit CIOs to return to the boardroom.

For a counterpoint to this article looking at the CIO role in European companies, see the Research insight 4.3, p. 195 – The elusive CIO.

Source: *CIO* (2003) and FT.com (2010)

The stages of IS strategy development

In the remainder of this chapter, we will consider the issues that need to be addressed in an IS strategy by considering the four classical stages of strategy development shown in Figure 6.7. This strategy development process model provides a framework that gives a logical sequence in which to perform typical activities in creation and execution of an IS strategy.

The four-stage strategy development model has these characteristics:

1 Continuous internal and external environment scanning or analysis is required to assess internal strengths and weaknesses and external opportunities and threats.

2 Clear statement of objectives is needed against which to measure future performance, and a vision of the future direction of the organization is required.

3 Strategy development can be broken down into formulation of different strategic options and then selection.

4 After strategy development, enactment of the strategy occurs as strategy implementation.

5 Control is required to detect problems and adjust the strategy accordingly.

In the following section, we will look at how different issues are addressed at these four stages of strategy development. For each stage, we will look at the different analytical tools or models that have been developed to help organizations describe their current situation, or to develop strategy.

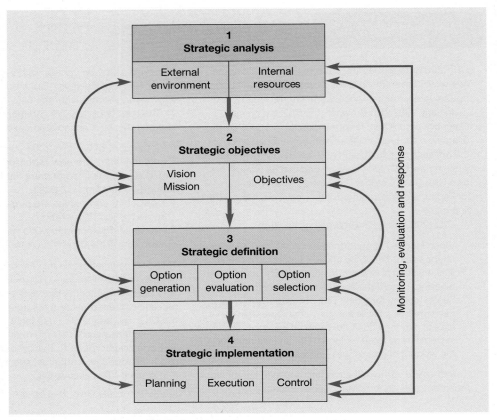

Figure 6.7 A generic IS strategy development process model
Source: Chaffey (2002), Figure 5.3

Simple models of strategic analysis

Organizational strategy is usually determined by the internal desires and intents of the owners or board of directors. As the business matures, it is increasingly affected by other internal and external factors that conspire to mediate the primary strategy.

External factors can be initiated by customers, suppliers, local and global communities.

Internal factors may arise from many stakeholder groups such as managers, front-line employees, trade unions and even material and immaterial resource constraints such as money, time, space and knowledge. Other internal pressures may arise from competing departmental and functional objectives and the competing objectives and wishes of individual managers.

The factors that may affect an organization are commonly grouped into six types; Political, Economic, Sociological, Technical, Legal and Environmental:

Political
- Changes to the company's internal management can lead to political struggles within the company.
- Changes to the country's foreign policy may prevent an organization forming or growing alliances with organizations in other countries.

Economic
- The method of costing within an organization could require a change in the accounting practices and procedures.

32222

- The host country of an organization may join a federation of countries, such as the EU, and adopt a new currency.

Sociological
- Customers and suppliers may require business to be done electronically.
- Similarly, as employees become more technically adept and aware of the benefits that virtual environments can provide, so the expectation to communicate with others using electronic means increases.

Technical
- Advances in communication and computing technologies may offer improvements in organizational efficiency and effectiveness which competitors are taking advantage of.
- The expectation and ability to work from home, connected to the office via a VPN, may also drive considerable changes.

Legal
- Legislation such as Sarbanes–Oxley can initiate changes to the way in which an organization presents itself and reports to society.
- Alterations to the organization's rules and operating procedures may initiate changes in the way that the management systems operate.

Environment
- This could be pressure from the particular environment or sector in which the organization operates or could be from the physical environment in which the organization is located.
- Alternatively, the company's commitment to their Corporate Social Responsibility or the addition of an environmental management policy such as ISO 14001 or EMAS can affect the way that they dispose of redundant equipment.

It is interesting to note that the PESTLE framework evolved from PEST through the recognition and addition of the factors Legal and Environmental. Recently the PESTLE framework has evolved further with the addition of Ethical factors, the framework now being known by the acronym STEEPLE. This new factor may also affect an organization's strategy:

Ethical
- It may be tempting for an organization to gather information about the purchasing habits and preferences of its customers, for example on which days of the week do they shop and whether they purchase anti-ageing products. While this information may be used benignly by the organization, there may be some resentment from customers that they are being 'spied upon' and data about them are being stored somewhere.

Alternatively, influencing factors can also be categorized according to whether they are Strengths, Weaknesses, Opportunities and Threats (SWOT):

Strengths
- What is the organization particularly good at? They may wish to focus on this core ability and perhaps expand it.

Weaknesses
- Where is the organization performing less well, or, alternatively, in what areas are their competitors more capable?

Opportunities
- What could the organization do to gain further market share or competitive advantage?

Threats
- What are the competitors doing that may erode their competitive advantage?

External stakeholders are often most easy to identify, such as customers, although the nature of the pressures that they impose upon an organization may not always be so obvious.

The objectives of cost, quality and delivery, discussed in Chapter 4, are perhaps the most significant measures for any organization. Even non-profit organizations need to control their internal costs so that they can provide maximum benefit for investors or donators.

Automotive manufacturing companies in the 1990s came under considerable pressure to improve their performance in the areas of cost, quality and delivery. Project management theory identifies the 'iron triangle' of cost, quality and time to be the most important factors to consider.

Slack (2001) identifies the five factors of quality, speed, dependability, flexibility and cost as the significant measurable performance objectives for any organization. Although these encompass quality and cost, they do not immediately reflect the key objective of time. The objectives of dependability and flexibility, however, are components of time in terms of on-time delivery.

Collectively these five objectives contribute to the organization's overall competitive advantage. While poor performance in any one of the objectives will not necessarily lead to a loss of competitive advantage, it is generally recognized that performing less well than competitors in quality, for example, will have a deleterious effect upon the other objectives which are dependent upon it.

For larger organizations, particularly those that have a global presence, the many factors that can affect their information systems strategy can lead to paradoxical situations.

On the one hand it is desirable for an organization to have a standardized information system utilizing common software and hardware. Commonality of equipment leads to lower purchasing costs by having greater buying power, consistent training for experts and users, easier fault-finding, and simpler system expansion and development.

However, there is often a need to tailor the information systems to suit the needs of subgroups of the organization. Just as McDonald's presents the common global image of the Golden Arches and a menu that is instantly recognizable, it tailors many of its products to suit the local markets. Similarly, some organizations may need to tailor their systems in some countries to recognize that the employees speak a different language, or use a different alphabet, or deal in another currency.

This approach, where there is a desire to achieve as much standardization as possible coupled with a need to tailor the information system to meet local conditions, is termed asymmetry.

Deciding on the degree of localization is a difficult challenge for managers; while it has been established that local preferences are significant, it is often difficult to balance localization costs against the likely increase or conversion rate through localization. In a survey published in *Multilingual* (2008), the importance of localization was seen as important, with 88 per cent of managers at multinational companies stating that localization is a key issue and 76 per cent of them saying that it is important specifically for international customer satisfaction. Yet over half of these respondents also admitted that they allocate only between 1 and 5 per cent of their overall budget for localization.

An indication of the importance of localization in different cultures has been completed by Nitish et al. (2006) for the German, Indian and Chinese cultures, assessing localized websites in terms not only of content, but also cultural values such as collectivism, individualism, uncertainty avoidance and masculinity. The survey suggests that, without cultural adaptation, confidence or flow falls, so resulting in lower purchase intent.

Singh and Pereira (2005) provide an evaluation framework for the level of localization:

1 *Standardized websites (not localized)*. A single site serves all customer segments (domestic and international).

2 *Semi-localized websites*. A single site serves all customers; however, contact information about foreign subsidiaries is available for international customers. Many sites fall into this category.

3 *Localized websites*. Country-specific websites with language translation for international customers, wherever relevant. 3M (**www.3m.com**) has adapted the websites for many countries to local language versions. It initially focused on the major websites.

4 *Highly-localized websites*. Country-specific websites with language translation; they also include other localization efforts in terms of time, date, zip code, currency formats, etc. Dell (**www.dell.com**) provides highly localized websites.

5 *Culturally customized websites*. Websites reflecting complete 'immersion' in the culture of target customer segments; as such, targeting a particular country may mean providing multiple websites for that country depending on the dominant cultures present. Durex (**www.durex.com**) is a good example of a culturally customized website.

Strategic situation analysis

Situation analysis assesses the current status of an organization with respect to a particular strategy. It asks 'Where are we now?' Situation analysis includes not only the status of the organization itself, the internal business environment, but also the external business environment. Analysis of changes within the external business environment is vital in order to identify possible threats to an organization, but also to recognize opportunities.

For the development of an IS strategy, situation analysis focuses on the internal environment and the micro- and macro-environment – these areas were introduced in Chapter 3 (see Figure 3.2, p. 95):

1 *Internal organizational environment*. This includes different characteristics of the organization which affect its strategy. These are summarized well by the McKinsey 7S model (Waterman et al., 1980) which refers to an organization's strategy, structure, systems, staff, style, skills and superordinate goals.

2 *Internal IS environment*. This reviews the sophistication of IS usage within an organization, including the current portfolio of applications and the IT infrastructure.

3 *External micro-environment (IS perspective)*. This reviews the IS capabilities and information needs of an organization's external stakeholders, including customers, suppliers, other partners and competitors.

4 *External macro-environment (IS perspective)*. The social, legal, economic, political and technological developments of the environment. These may place constraints on IS strategy, for example legal barriers, but may also create opportunities as new technologies are introduced.

We will now examine tools and techniques for assessing each of these types of environment in more detail. We will concentrate on specific tools that are used to assess an organization's adoption and utilization of information systems and its e-business capabilities.

1 Internal organizational environment

An organization's internal environment includes the different characteristics which form its identity and character. These characteristics must be acknowledged within IS strategy. IS strategy must support these characteristics and must be feasible within this context.

IS analytical tool 1: The 7S model

A useful framework for assessing the linkage between the internal organizational environment and IS is the McKinsey 7S model (Waterman et al., 1980) which refers to an organization's strategy, structure, systems, staff, style, skills and superordinate goals. We will now briefly look at each of the seven Ss to see how they may impinge on IS strategy in the context of the Lo-cost Airline Company.

- *Strategy*. The organization's strategy – its plan for allocation of resources to achieve its objective is the most significant input to the IS strategy from an organization's internal environment. For the Lo-cost Airline Company, IS strategy must support major strategic initiatives such as the development of new services or entry into new markets.

- *Structure*. Structural changes to a business are now commonplace as new strategies are adopted or mergers and acquisitions with other companies. In such cases, the IS strategy may need to focus on accommodating these changes. For the Lo-cost Airline Company, the IS strategy must manage support for the staff at the different operating locations in a cost-effective manner while maintaining a good quality of service.

- *Systems*. This applies to operating procedures or business processes rather than information systems. Changes to either of these will need to be supported by changes to information systems.

- *Style*. The style of a company or its culture does not typically directly affect information systems. In some instances, though, it may cause barriers to implementation of IS-related strategies that may require some changes in style. For instance, a knowledge management or e-business initiative within the Lo-cost Airline Company may require some changes to the style or culture of the organization. If a company is relatively conservative, this may cause difficulties with the introduction of a new system. 'Style' also refers to the managerial style and this may also be relevant.

- *Staff*. With the introduction of new IS, we need to question whether the appropriate mix of staff is available.

- *Skills*. Are the correct skills available internally? What training is required? Do we need to outsource some services?

- *Superordinate goals*. This refers to the higher goals of the company that may be encapsulated in the mission statement. The IS strategy should naturally support these goals.

Many of these characteristics of the organization's internal environment will not change significantly through time, but some will as a result of changes in business strategy and this may influence the IS strategy. Consequently, these will need to be reviewed. Typically, a much more important input to the IS strategy is the business strategy and its objectives. Note also that the seven Ss model can also usefully be applied to consider the development of the internal IS environment through the stages of growth model described in the next section.

2 Internal IS environment

Analysis of the internal IS involves the sophistication of IS usage within an organization, including the current portfolio of applications and the IT infrastructure. The gap analysis approach is an effective approach to assessing the internal IS environment. **Gap analysis** involves identification of the broad requirements from information systems by comparing the current systems and information availability to what is required by users. The information audit referred to in Chapters 4 and 10 is a form of gap analysis that is particularly relevant here, since this will highlight the need for specific types of information to support users in their work. Analysis of business processes will also identify areas where information systems can increase process efficiency and effectiveness.

Gap analysis
Identification of the requirements from information systems by comparing the current systems and information availability to what is required by users

IS analytical tool 2: Stages of growth models

IS stages of growth models provide a simple framework for assessing how developed an organization is in its application of information systems and can be used to identify gaps in provision through comparison of a current stage of IS development to a future stage of maturity. They are also useful because they enable companies to compare the sophistication of their IS strategy to other organizations' and can be used to identify future IS requirements. The best-known model is a six-stage model developed by Nolan (1979). The model has been criticized as it has dated in its reference to IS organization and structure because it was developed in the 1970s. The terminology is dated because the information systems function at this time was often fulfilled by a DP or 'data processing' department and this term features strongly in the model.

IS stages of growth model
A six-stage evolutionary model of how IS can be applied within a businesss

The model has also proved difficult to validate, i.e. to demonstrate that, in reality, organizations pass through these stages. However, the model remains particularly valid for small and medium-sized businesses and start-up organizations since these pass through similar stages. Analysis using the model can be used to raise issues about who controls IS strategy and how closely IS strategy is linked to business needs. Furthermore, the model can be applied to adoption of new information systems concepts by larger organizations.

The relationship of the six stages of the model is illustrated in Figure 6.8. It is evident that, through time, an organization's approach to managing information systems will evolve to a level of maturity where it is embedded into the strategic planning process of the business. Nolan suggested that IS management is initially focused on the technology in the initiation, contagion and control stages. A transformation occurs at this point, with more emphasis on managing the organization's data resources.

The characteristics of the six stages are as follows:

1 *Initiation*. The first use of applications within an organization. Characterized by lack of senior management interest, operational or simple office systems and transactional systems to reduce costs.

2 *Contagion*. Widespread use of applications as benefits are sought from automation and information management. Characterized by rapid growth in use of application with enthusiasm from departmental managers; overall control is limited.

3 *Control*. This stage is a reaction against excessive and uncontrolled expenditures of time and money on computer systems from the contagion stage. It is characterized by the introduction of plans, methodologies and expenditure controls, often resulting in an applications backlog.

4 *Integration*. This is a reaction against the use of departmental applications and data silos arising from earlier poor control. Traditionally characterized by use of databases, today by the use of middleware and enterprise resource planning systems. Control continues to improve at this stage.

5 *Data administration*. A change of emphasis to information management rather than focus on technology and applications. Databases and document or content management systems are introduced to help achieve this.

6 *Maturity*. Information systems are put in place that reflect the real information needs of the organization. Characterized by planning and development of IS closely linked to business strategy.

Evolution and growth of IS occurs in four different areas in Figure 6.8. These are:

1 *Applications portfolio*. This broadens from initial accounting systems focus to operational transaction-based systems and decision-support-style applications which may be deployed in different departments.

2 *DP organization*. Moving from a centralized arrangement focusing on the DP department to a more devolved approach.

3 *DP planning and control*. From an internal focus to an external focus.

4 *User-awareness*. From a reactive situation where the business departments accept new systems to a more proactive arrangement where 'the business' drives the adoption of new applications.

Earl (1989) has extended the application of Nolan's original model by suggesting that organizations will pass through similar stages of evolution for different types of technology such as relational database management, personal computing and office automation. We can suggest that such evolution occurs for the range of management and IS concepts. More recent management and IS concepts are illustrated in Figure 6.9.

The 7S framework described in the previous section can also usefully be applied to the stages of growth of IT utilization and management. This approach was used by Galliers and Sutherland (1991), who investigated its applicability through interviews with managers at four Scottish Perth-based companies. Their findings are summarized in Table 6.3. The authors suggest that any organization is likely to display characteristics across different elements of the stages within its approach to IS. However, they believe that the model is useful in assessing progression, with organizations needing to address some earlier elements before resolving later issues. Through considering the status of the seven Ss in an organization, managers can reflect on areas of weakness and identify a roadmap for improving IS support.

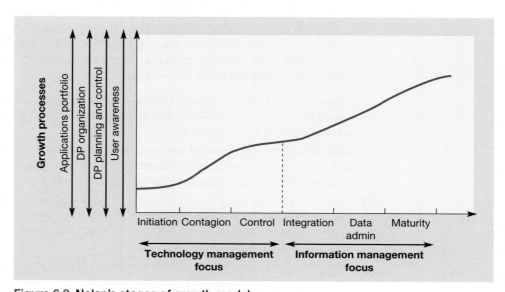

Figure 6.8 Nolan's stages of growth model
Source: Galliers and Sutherland (1991)

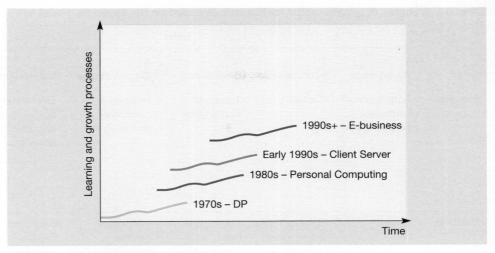

Figure 6.9 Stages in adoption of different models
Source: Galliers and Sutherland (1991)

The model is dated in its use of terminology such as 'DP manager', which would no longer be applied. The data processing department was commonly referred to in the 1970s and 1980s to describe the functional area responsible for management of what is now referred to as information systems and applications development. It is interesting to note that the term focuses on the processing of data rather than the application of information. Despite this, many small and medium-sized businesses or those that have not had the need to computerize will be able to identify with the characteristics of stages 1 and 2, so the model remains applicable.

Another weakness of the model is that outsourcing of IS services is not referred to. Outsourcing has an impact on many of the IS characteristics in Table 6.3. It could be argued that the outsourced staff will work within existing or partially modified structures, fill similar staff roles and adopt existing styles. However, since the goals for outsourcing include advancing IS management, it should result in a 'quantum leap' forward to more advanced stages in terms of strategy, structure, systems, staff, style, skills and superordinate goals.

Maturity models

Maturity models
Enable auditing of IS capabilities for comparison on a standard scale

Maturity models are closely related to stages of growth models. The distinction is that, in an IS context, they provide a means to audit the sophistication of IS usage within an organization. Organizations can then compare their stage of development on a standard scale to other organizations (benchmarking). One of the best-known maturity models is the *Capability Maturity Model for Software* from Carnegie Mellon University (Carnegie Mellon, 2001). This model, which has been revised throughout the 1990s and into the new millennium, challenges organizations to review their process of systems development. It provides a framework for managers to assess the current sophistication of their process for systems development. There are five stages to the model. These are described by the institute as:

1 *Initial.* The software process is characterized as ad hoc, and occasionally even chaotic. Few processes are defined, and success depends on individual effort and heroics.

2 *Repeatable.* Basic project management processes are established to track cost, schedule, and functionality. The necessary process discipline is in place to repeat earlier successes on projects with similar applications.

Table 6.3 A stages of growth model for IS services based on the seven Ss model

	Stage					
	1 Ad-hocracy	2 Foundations	3 Centralized	4 Cooperation	5 Entrepreneurial	6 Harmonious
Strategy	Acquisition of hardware, software, etc.	IT audit	Top-down IS planning	Integration, coordination and control	Environmental scanning and opportunity seeking	Maintain comparative strategic advantage Monitor futures Interactive planning
Structure	None	IS subordinate to finance or accounting	Centralized data processing	Information centres Information services unit	Separate coalitions with different SBUs	Centrally coordinated coalitions
Systems	Unconnected, mainly manual IS, plus financial systems	Many applications, but many gaps, large backlog	Centralized, but uncontrolled end-user computing	Decentralized approach with some controls Integrated office systems, limited DSS	Decentralized with central control and coordination Lack of internal and external data integration	Internally integrated and externally integrated systems
Staff	Programmers	Systems analysts DP manager	IS manager, data analysts and database administrators	Information resources manager/CIO, business analysts	Corporate business/IS planners (one role)	IS director/ member on board of directors
Style	Unaware	'Don't bother me'	Delegation	Democratic	Individualistic	Business team
Skills	Technical	Systems development methodology	IS believes it knows what the business wants. Project management	Organizational integration IS knows how the business works Users know how IS works	Knowledgeable users in some IS areas	Skills are at the appropriate level and continuously developed
Super-ordinate goals	Obfuscation	Confusion	Senior management concerned, IS defensive	Cooperation	Opportunistic, entrepreneurial, intrapreneurial	Interactive planning

Source: Adapted from Galliers and Sutherland (1991)

3 *Defined.* The software process for both management and engineering activities is documented, standardized, and integrated into a standard software process for the organization. All projects use an approved, tailored version of the organization's standard software process for developing and maintaining software.

4 *Managed.* Detailed measures of the software process and product quality are collected. Both the software process and products are quantitatively understood and controlled.

5 *Optimizing*. Continuous process improvement is enabled by quantitative feedback from the process and from piloting innovative ideas and technologies.

Predictability, effectiveness, and control of an organization's software processes are believed to improve as the organization moves up these five levels. While not rigorous, the empirical evidence to date supports this belief.

Published maturity levels (**www.sei.cmu.edu/pars/pars.aspx**) show that today many large specialist organizations such as NASA and information systems consultants have achieved the higher levels. However, many smaller companies have processes that are still at stage 1 or 2.

The Carnegie Mellon Capability Maturity Model is relevant for large organizations which develop and maintain their own systems in-house; it is less relevant for smaller organizations that do not conduct in-house development. A more relevant maturity model for all organizations is COBIT. COBIT, Control Objectives for Information and related Technology, introduced in Chapter 1, defines a framework for auditing information and technology resources in an organization. COBIT (2000) suggests an IT governance model which has six maturity levels. The IT Governance Institute, which manages the COBIT standard, defines the six levels as follows:

- *Level 0 Non-existent*. There is a complete lack of any recognizable IT governance process.

- *Level 1 Initial/Ad-hoc*. There is evidence that the organization has recognized that IT governance issues exist and need to be addressed. There are, however, no standardized processes, but instead there are ad-hoc approaches applied on an individual or case-by-case basis.

- *Level 2 Repeatable but intuitive*. There is global awareness of IT governance issues. IT governance activities and performance indicators are under development, which include IT planning, delivery and monitoring processes.

- *Level 3 Defined process*. The need to act with respect to IT governance is understood and accepted. A baseline set of IT governance indicators is developed, where linkages between outcome measures and performance drivers are defined, documented and integrated into strategic and operational planning and monitoring processes.

- *Level 4 Managed and measurable*. There is full understanding of IT governance issues at all levels, supported by formal training. There is a clear understanding of who the customer is and responsibilities are defined and monitored through service-level agreements. Responsibilities are clear and process ownership is established. IT processes are aligned with the business and with the IT strategy. Improvement in IT processes is based primarily upon a quantitative understanding and it is possible to monitor and measure compliance with procedures and process metrics.

- *Level 5 Optimized*. There is advanced and forward-looking understanding of IT governance issues and solutions. Training and communication are supported by leading-edge concepts and techniques. Processes have been refined to a level of external best practice, based on results of continuous improvement and maturity modelling with other organizations.

You can see from the six levels that an organization can use maturity models and stages of growth models to assess its progress according to how clearly it defines its IT responsibilities, processes, control through metrics, alignment with business strategy and continuous improvement. Such a framework has the benefit that it can act as a trusted template for developing and implementing IS strategy. Of course, much work remains to be done to develop the actual IS strategy, since generic frameworks such as COBIT do not address the reality of an individual organization in terms of its structures, culture, staff skills, the markets it operates in and the range of technologies currently in place.

Activity 6.3   Stage of growth and maturity models of IS strategy

Purpose   To assess the relevance of IS stages of growth and maturity models.

Activity   Discuss the relevance of the different IS stages of growth models and IT maturity models presented in this section, from the 1970s and 1980s to the 'e-business era'.

How relevant are these models to:

(a) A small start-up organization?

(b) A large, mature organization?

One approach is to look at the relevance to the Lo-cost Airline Company as it grew from (a) to (b).

E-business adoption stages model

When assessing the current use of ICT within a company it is instructive to analyse the extent to which an organization has implemented e-business services or applications that are available through using Internet technologies. In an early model focusing on sell-side website development, Quelch and Klein (1996) developed a five-stage model referring to the development of sell-side e-commerce. For existing companies the stages are:

1 *Image and product information*. A basic 'brochureware' website with no interactivity.

2 *Information collection*. Interactivity is introduced.

3 *Customer support and service*.

4 *Internal support and service*.

5 *Transactions*.

Considering sell-side e-commerce, Chaffey et al. (2003) suggest that there are six choices for a company deciding on which marketing services to offer via an online presence:

- *Level 0*. No website or presence on the web.

- *Level 1*. Basic web presence. Company places an entry in a website listing company names, such as **www.yell.co.uk,** to make people searching the web aware of the existence of the company and its products. There is no website at this stage.

- *Level 2*. Simple static informational website. Contains basic company and product information – sometimes referred to as 'brochureware'.

- *Level 3*. Simple interactive site. Users are able to search the site and make queries to retrieve information such as product availability and pricing. Queries by e-mail may also be supported.

- *Level 4*. Interactive site supporting transactions with users. The functions offered will vary according to company. They will be usually limited to online buying. Other functions might include an interactive customer service help-desk which is linked into direct marketing objectives.

- *Level 5*. Fully interactive site supporting the whole buying process. Provides relationship marketing with individual customers and facilitating the full range of marketing exchanges.

Research by Arnott and Bridgewater (2002) assesses the stages of sell-side e-commerce adoption reached by different businesses. They tested whether companies of different sectors and sizes and located in different countries had reached one of three stages. These were informational (information only – stage 2 above), facilitating (relationship building – stage 3 above) or transactional (online exchange – stage 4 above).

They found that a majority of firms were still using the Internet for information provision. The main factors affecting the stage adopted was the size of the company and whether the Internet was being used to support international sales – sophistication was greater in both of these cases.

For buy-side e-commerce, the corresponding levels of product sourcing applications can be identified:

- *Level I.* No use of the web for product sourcing and no electronic integration with suppliers.
- *Level II.* Review and selection from competing suppliers using intermediary websites, B2B exchanges and supplier websites. Orders placed by conventional means.
- *Level III.* Orders placed electronically through EDI, via intermediary sites, exchanges or supplier sites. No integration between organization's systems and suppliers' systems. Rekeying of orders into procurement or accounting systems necessary.
- *Level IV.* Orders placed electronically with integration of company's procurement systems.
- *Level V.* Orders placed electronically with full integration of company's procurement, manufacturing requirements planning and stock control systems.

A staged model which focuses on these buy-side applications of e-commerce based on the results of an international benchmarking study (DTI, 2000) is shown in Figure 6.10. It likens the process of adoption to moving up the steps of a ladder. Companies start off using e-mail to communicate internally and with suppliers (step 1) before moving to offering product information and availability checking (step 2), online ordering (step 3), online payment (step 4), online progress tracking (step 5); finally, when the e-business is achieved, all stages are integrated (step 6).

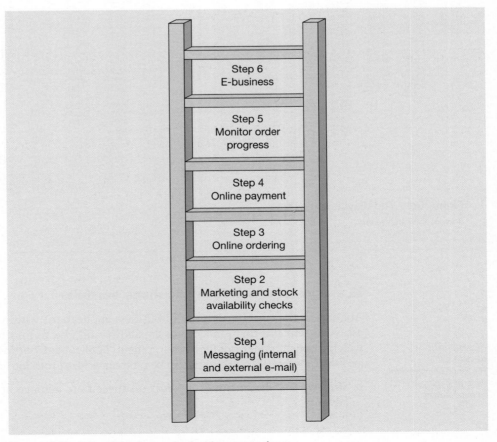

Figure 6.10 Adoption steps of e-business services

Activity 6.4 shows how we can use the Internet Archive to track the evolution of web services for different organizations.

Activity 6.4	Time travel using the Wayback machine

Purpose

To illustrate the stages of growth model for e-business by reviewing different company websites.

Activity

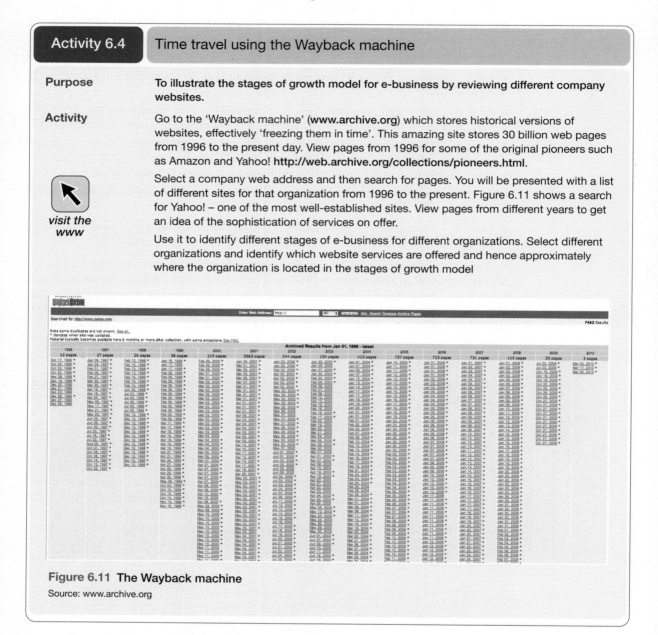

visit the www

Go to the 'Wayback machine' (**www.archive.org**) which stores historical versions of websites, effectively 'freezing them in time'. This amazing site stores 30 billion web pages from 1996 to the present day. View pages from 1996 for some of the original pioneers such as Amazon and Yahoo! **http://web.archive.org/collections/pioneers.html**.

Select a company web address and then search for pages. You will be presented with a list of different sites for that organization from 1996 to the present. Figure 6.11 shows a search for Yahoo! – one of the most well-established sites. View pages from different years to get an idea of the sophistication of services on offer.

Use it to identify different stages of e-business for different organizations. Select different organizations and identify which website services are offered and hence approximately where the organization is located in the stages of growth model

Figure 6.11 The Wayback machine

Source: www.archive.org

IS analytical tool 3: IS applications portfolio

IS applications portfolio
The range of information systems deployed within an organization

Analysis of the current portfolio of business applications within a business is used to assess current information systems capability and also to inform future strategies. A widely applied framework for assessing the **IS applications portfolio** is that of McFarlan and McKenney (1993). This enables IS to be categorized into four categories:

- *Strategic IS* – the business depends on these IS to achieve or sustain competitive advantage.

- *Turnaround IS* – the application does not currently deliver significant competitive benefits, but it has the potential to positively affect the business's competitive position.
- *Factory IS.* Currently of competitive importance, but less relevant in the future.
- *Support IS.* No significant competitive advantages are derived from these IS, although they may be important for operational purposes.

We return to strategies for managing the portfolio later in this chapter, in the section on IS strategy, since this tool is also essential to identifying relevant applications to deploy in the business.

IS analytical tool 4: Internal value chain analysis

Value chain
A model that considers how supply chain activities can add value to products and services delivered to the customer

Michael Porter's **value chain** is a well-established concept for considering key activities that an organization can perform or manage with the intention of adding value for the customer as products and services move from conception to delivery to the customer (Porter, 1980). The value chain is a model that describes different value-adding activities that connect a company's supply side with its demand side. We can identify an internal value chain within the boundaries of an organization and an external value chain where activities are performed by partners.

Through analysing the different parts of the value chain, managers can redesign internal and external processes to improve their efficiency and effectiveness. Value can be added to the customer or the next point in the value chain by reducing cost and adding value:

- within each element of the value chain such as the procurement, manufacture, sales or distribution process;
- at the interface between elements of the value chain such as between sales and distribution.

In equation form:

$$\text{Value} = (\text{Benefit of each value chain activity} - \text{its cost}) + (\text{Benefit of each interface between value chain activities} - \text{its cost})$$

Information naturally has a role both in linking the elements of the value chain and, in some cases, itself adding value or reducing costs. Examples of information flows through the value chain include demand levels from customers, inventory and stock levels, and the availability and pricing of raw materials. Figure 6.12(a) distinguishes between primary activities that contribute directly to getting goods and services to the customer (such as inbound logistics, including procurement, manufacturing, marketing and delivery to buyers, support and servicing after sale) and support activities which provide the inputs and infrastructure that allow the primary activities to take place. Support activities include finance, human resources and information systems.

Figure 6.12(a) has been re-evaluated recently since it can be suggested that there are some key weaknesses in the traditional value chain model:

- It is most applicable to manufacturing of physical products as opposed to services.
- It is a one-way chain involved with pushing products to the customer – it does not highlight the importance of understanding customer needs through market research and responsiveness through innovation and new product development.
- It does not emphasize the importance of value networks or relationships with third parties.

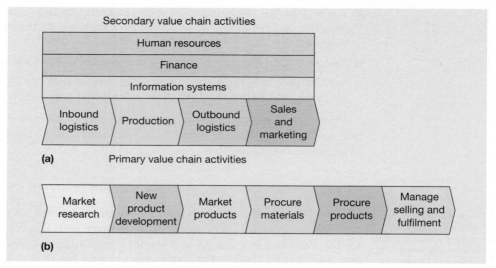

Figure 6.12 Two alternative models of the value chain: (a) traditional value chain model (b) revised value chain model

Source: Chaffey (2004) Figure 6.4

A revised form of the value chain has been suggested by Deise et al. (2000); an adaptation of this model is presented in Figure 6.12(b). This value chain starts with the market research process, emphasizing the importance of real-time environment scanning made possible through electronic communications links with distributors and customers. For example, leading e-tailers (online retailers) now monitor, on an hourly basis, how customers are responding to promotional offers on their website and review competitors' offers and then revise theirs accordingly. As new product development occurs, the marketing strategy will be refined and at the same time steps can be taken to obtain the resources and production processes necessary to create, store and distribute the new product. Through analysis of the value chain and looking at how electronic communications can be used to speed up the process, man-ufacturers have been able to significantly reduce time-to-market from conception of a new product idea through to launch on the market. For example, car manufacturers have reduced time-to-market from over 5 years to 18 months. At the same time the use of technology increases value chain efficiency, for example it enables customers to specify their needs through a website or a kiosk in a car dealership, and then the car will be manufactured to order.

3 External micro-environment

This reviews the IS capabilities and information needs of the external stakeholders of an organization, including customers, suppliers, other partners and competitors.

IS analytical tool 5: Porter's five competitive forces model

Michael Porter's classic 1980s model of the five main competitive forces that impact a company provides a useful framework for reviewing the impact of micro-environ-ment forces on an organization. The model is presented in Figure 6.13. It is widely used for strategic analysis, but can also be applied to assess the impact of new tech-nologies on an environment. For example, Porter (2001) has applied it to assess the impact of the Internet on industry. Refer to this paper and complete Activity 6.5 to assess the impact of the Internet on an industry.

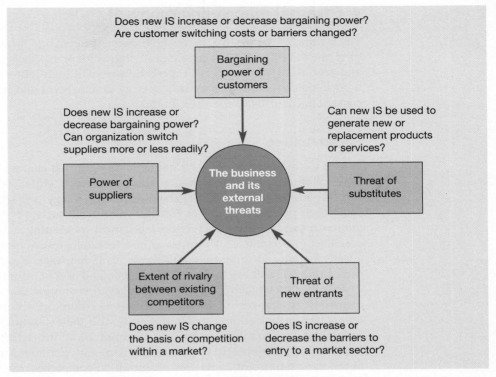

Figure 6.13 Five forces model with questions that can be asked to assess the impact of information systems or e-commerce

Activity 6.5	Evaluating the impact of the Internet on the five competitive forces

Purpose	Using Porter's five forces model to assess the impact of a technology on an industry.
Activity	Select an industry or market such as the chemical industry, electronics industry, retail books or banking markets.
	For each of Porter's five forces, assess whether the Internet has, on balance, *increased* or *decreased* the power of each of the five forces. Questions that should be asked by an organization with respect to IS or e-commerce for each of the five competitive forces have been added to Figure 6.13 to assist. Explain your reasoning, and the impact this will have on the organization at the centre.

External value chain analysis

The internal value chain analysis described in the previous section can be extended to include the industry-wide value chain. Different tiers of suppliers, distributors and customers are included in this analysis. Information flows between different value chain members can be evaluated to review how processes can be improved through information quality, i.e. provision of more detailed data, more accurate data or more timely data. Through using EDI (see Chapter 3), supermarkets were able to share information with suppliers and operate a system of vendor-managed inventory (Chapter 2) which reduced the need for stockholding in-house.

4 External macro-environment

The features of the external macro-environment for an organization are often referred to as the SLEPT or PEST factors. SLEPT stands for Social, Legal, Economic, Political and Technological factors. In this section we will highlight the SLEPT factors that need to be considered as part of IS strategy development and refer to where they are covered in more detail elsewhere in the book.

Social factors

From a technology standpoint it might be thought that changes in society have a relatively limited impact. However, as society develops, ethical considerations change and this affects how people feel about using technology and also their willingness to share their personal details. In fact, pressures from society have prompted governments to produce data protection legislation in keeping with changed ethics as described in Chapter 12. However, as new technologies are introduced, legislation is always introduced some time afterwards, so IS managers need to be aware of how their customers will react to new technologies and uses of information.

A further social factor, related to changes in economic development in different countries, is changes in the use of different communications technologies. This affects how organizations can communicate with their stakeholders, so it follows that companies have to monitor adoption of communications technology by stakeholders as part of the development of their IS and corporate communications strategies. Some of the most significant digital devices by which companies may choose to communicate with their stakeholders are shown in Figure 6.14 (e.g. digital television, broadband internet, DAB digital radio, 3G handset mobile phone). See also the 'technological' section below.

Figure 6.15 is an example of the impact of the adoption of these technologies on IS strategy; all UK councils were tasked with providing online access to their services by 2005. With student access to mobile phones approaching 100 per cent in developed countries, many educational institutions now have to provide facilities for academics, administrators and student bodies to contact students by phone. In 2003, some UK schools started using text messaging to remind students to attend classes!

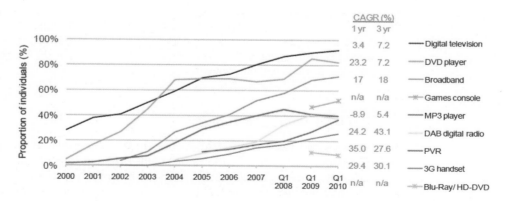

Figure 6.14 Trend in the UK adult adoption (i.e. claimed ownership) of digital devices 2000–2010

Source: Ofcom (2010)

From a commercial point of view, Chaffey (2004) points out that companies need to monitor not only adoption, but also degrees of usage of these different technologies. Decisions on investments in e-commerce technology are influenced by the proportion of customers that:

1 have access to the channel;
2 are influenced by using the channel;
3 purchase using the channel.

Although access levels to new digital devices may be high, the levels of purchase may be lower, depending on the nature of the product. Think of the car market: car purchases are in low single figures in most developed countries, yet that doesn't mean that investment in the Internet is unimportant for car manufacturers. Research shows that the majority of new car purchasers in these categories now use the Internet to decide on model and place of purchase, i.e. they are influenced by the channel. This has led to significant IS and marketing investments in technology to support car sales by companies such as BMW and Audi.

It is also necessary to evaluate adoption by different customer groups. Reference to Ipsos MORI data (**http://www.ipsos-mori.com/researchspecialisms/ipsosmediact/what wedo/technology.aspx**) shows that in the UK, over three-quarters of social group AB have access to Internet technology while it is less for the social group DE. This will also affect the decision to invest in technology. For any new technology, or indeed any product, a similar pattern of adoption by different groups has been noticed. This diffusion–adoption process (represented by the bell curve in Figure 6.15) was identified by Rogers (1983) who classified those trialling new products as innovators, early adopters, early majority, late majority, and laggards. Company adoption of new technology also follows a pattern as explained in the 'technological' section below.

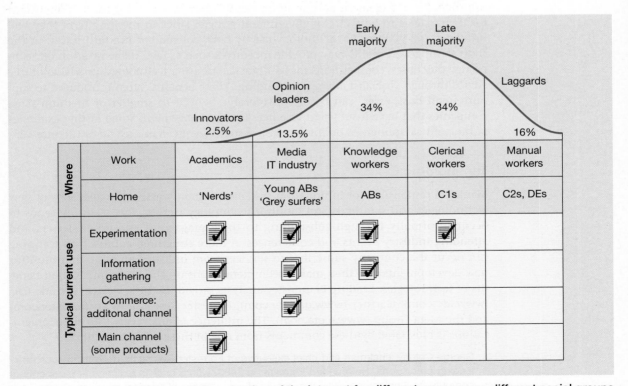

Figure 6.15 Snapshot example of the adoption of the Internet for different uses across different social groups (example – typical for 5 to 10 years after the invention of the World Wide Web in developed countries)

Legal constraints

Legal constraints on information systems are mainly driven by society's wish to protect personal information. Data protection laws have been developed in many countries and it falls to the IS manager to implement secure systems that comply with these laws. Governments have also introduced laws to protect corporate data from malicious acts of deletion. A further trend is the wish of governments to monitor data and voice traffic as a way of limiting criminal or terrorist activities.

Given the importance of developing systems and information management policies that are consistent with the law, these issues are described in more detail in Chapter 12.

Economic

The economic standing of different countries will also determine the degree of use of different communications technologies referred to under 'social factors'. Managers developing e-commerce strategies in multinational companies will monitor how the economic environment in different countries could affect adoption of web-based services they may decide to offer as part of IS strategy. Online information services such as ClickZ (**www.clickz.com/stats**) which provide a digest of reports on adoption of new technologies in different countries can be accessed to help achieve this.

Political

National governments and international organizations will enact policies that can influence IS strategy. In the latter part of the twentieth century, governments, realizing the importance of information management to the competitiveness of their companies, developed policies to encourage adoption of technology, best practice in information management and, more recently, Internet technologies. It is important for IS managers to be aware of government policies since in the long term they will influence the patterns of technology use by both consumers and businesses. In the short term, governments may provide incentives such as favourable taxation on technology purchases, competitions for best practice in using technology, provision of free advice through specialist advisers or training. These benefits, often introduced to support small businesses, can be of considerable benefit to smaller or medium-sized companies that have insufficient resources for IS management. Some further examples of the political influences on information systems are given at the end of Chapter 12.

Technological

Managers responsible for information systems constantly assess the relevance of new technologies and standards and monitor technology trends. This scanning tends to occur informally through subscribing to trade magazines and e-newsletters and attending industry events and conferences. A more structured approach to scanning can occur if a company subscribes to services from industry analysts that monitor new developments and then make recommendations on the likely impact and benefits of technologies. Leading IS industry analysts providing these services include IDC (**www.idc.com**), Gartner (**www.gartner.com**), Forrester Research (**www.forrester.com**) and the Meta Group (**www.meta.com**). The influence of analysts within these organizations is illustrated by these comments from one of these analysts in 2002:

> George Colony, chairman and chief executive of Forrester Research, delights in such challenging predictions. He founded Forrester in 1983, with a brief to examine new aspects of computer technology and how they would affect business. 'Our main quality is courage, not being afraid of making decisive statements, as long as we can back them up', he says. So,

in typically trenchant style, he dismisses Microsoft's latest operating system, Windows XP, as unfit for corporate use. 'It is not ready for prime time. Too many bugs. It would be a big mistake for any large corporations to adopt it', he says.

It is no wonder that, according to Mr Colony, Bill Gates hates him, though Microsoft continues to be a client. He shrugs: 'People can keep old versions of Windows. One of my main pieces of advice to companies is that if a technology works, keep it. Doesn't matter if it is rats on wheels that makes it work.'

Mr Colony divides executives into ties, turtlenecks and T-shirts: directors, marketing departments and technology workers. As the bubble burst, the first two categories retreated from technology. They need to come back, he argues, to marry business acumen with the possibilities technology opens up. The T-shirts will also have to change, he says.

'I am astounded by the lack of vision of the technologists. The PC arrived and the IT department fought it. The internet arrived and the IT department fought it. Companies need the whole view, both the business strategy vision and the technical savvy.'

Inside Track article: An optimist's vision of tomorrow's technology: interview George Colony,
Forrester Research, Financial Times (Fiona Harvey, 2002)

So, emerging technologies need to be assessed for relevance for an organization. If technology looks as if it has potential applications then a continuum of choice is available, from:

- ignoring the technology or applications, perhaps because it is too expensive, untried and hence there is a risk whether it will deliver real benefits, or the benefits are not likely to outweigh the costs;
- evaluating the technique and then taking a decision on whether to adopt it according to the evaluation;
- enthusiastically adopting the technique without a detailed evaluation since the combination of hype and the manager's experience convinces the manager that the technique should be adopted.

This behaviour can be summarized as:

- Cautious, 'wait and see' approach.
- Intermediate approach. Sometimes known as 'fast-follower'.
- Risk-taking, 'early adopter' approach.

Of course, this is a simple risk-against-reward decision. The risk for an early-adopting organization is that being at the leading edge of using new technologies is often also referred to as the 'bleeding edge' owing to the risk of failure. New technologies will have bugs, may not integrate well with the existing systems, or the benefits may not live up to their promise. Balanced against this, the rewards are high – adoption of a new technology may offer improvements to operational effectiveness (such as reduced costs or shorter cycle times) or can provide a competitive advantage. However, trends in technology such as greater interoperability between systems and adoption of web services mean that the advantages may be short-lived. Porter (2001) makes the assertion that gaining real competitive advantage is difficult since copying of approaches is so rapid. He gives the example of the drugstore CVS being able to roll out a complex Internet-based procurement system in just 60 days. Given this, the best balance of risk against reward may be to use a 'fast-follower' approach where use of technology by early adopters is monitored, with rapid deployment by followers if the early adopters gain benefits through using the new technology. An example of this approach is provided by the European low-cost airline Ryanair.com. This was not the earliest adopter of transactional e-commerce for passenger ticket sales, with other companies such as easyJet and British Airways offering this facility earlier. However, once the success of the other companies became apparent, the e-commerce service was rolled out rapidly, and today Ryanair.com, like easyJet, achieves over 90 per cent of its ticket sales online.

Strategic objective setting

Objective setting for information systems strategy does not only involve setting specific IS objectives, rather it involves reviewing how organizational objectives will be achieved through the information systems strategies. So the objectives for IS strategy are derived from the business objectives. This helps to achieve alignment of IS strategy with organizational strategy.

As with any type of business strategy, setting clear objectives is vital since objectives provide a mechanism for control; they provide direction and, with appropriate feedback and review, ensure adjustments can be made if the objectives are not met. COBIT (2000) explains the need for control of IS/IT concentrating on value as follows:

> … the business goal of adding value, while balancing risk versus return ensures delivery of information to the business … is enabled by creating and maintaining a system of process and control excellence appropriate for the business that directs and monitors the business value delivery of IT.

In this section we will review two widely used techniques for IS objective setting, critical success factors and the balanced scorecard. We will see, through the mini case on the development of an IT-based balanced scorecard, that more detailed specific IT objectives can be set.

Critical success factors (CSFs)

Critical success factors (CSFs)
A performance measure which must be achieved in order for business objectives to be met

Key performance indicator (KPI)
A specific measure used to determine the progress in achieving critical success factors

The use of **critical success factors (CSFs)** is valuable in helping to align new systems with business objectives. Critical success factors are those factors that determine whether business objectives will be achieved. **Key performance indicators (KPIs)** are then used to set targets for CSFs and assess whether these have been achieved. An example of this approach is provided by Dell Computer. Specific business objectives that were aimed at increasing customer loyalty were identified by the 'Dell Customer Experience Council', which had researched key loyalty drivers, identified measures to track these and put in place an action plan to improve loyalty (Table 6.4). IS applications support to help achieve these metrics could then be put in place as part of the IS strategy.

Suggestions for typical IS-specific CSFs and KPIs used by organizations are provided by COBIT (2000), the IT governance model for Control Objectives for Information and related Technology introduced in Chapter 1. COBIT uses three levels of objective-setting IS/IT performance measures. This highlights a common problem with discussions of CSFs and KPIs: different labels and different levels of indicators are used for them in different organizations, case studies and literature. One of the benefits of COBIT is that it helps achieve standardization, enabling different organizations and different parts of organizations to compare the performance of their IT processes.

At the highest level, COBIT (2000) defines general critical success factors for IS strategy which were introduced in this chapter in the section on 'What is IS strategy?'. It describes these CSFs as 'the most important management-oriented implementation guidelines to achieve control over and within its IT processes'. These are not traditional CSFs, but rather they seem to encapsulate best practice or the mission of IT; examples include 'IT governance activities are defined with a clear purpose, documented and implemented, based on enterprise needs and with unambiguous accountabilities' and 'Management practices are implemented to increase efficient and optimal use of resources and increase the effectiveness of IT processes'.

At the next level, COBIT defines more specific critical success factors, which it labels 'Key Goal Indicators'. COBIT defines the Key Goal Indicators as 'measures that

Table 6.4 Relationship between loyalty drivers and measures to assess their success at Dell Computer

Business objective	Critical success factor and KPI
1 Improve order fulfilment	• *Ship to target.* KPI: percentage of systems that ship on time exactly as the customer specified
2 Increase product performance	• *Initial field incident rate.* KPI: frequency of problems experienced by customers
3 Enhance post-sale service and support	• *On-time, first-time fix.* KPI: percentage of problems fixed on the first visit by a service representative who arrives at the time promised

Source: Based on example related in Reicheld and Schefter (2000)

tell managers – after the fact – whether an IT process has achieved its business requirements'. The specific Goal Indicators used by COBIT include:

● Enhanced performance and cost management
● Improved return on major IT investments
● Improved time-to-market
● Increased quality, innovation and risk management
● Appropriately integrated and standardized business processes
● Reaching new and satisfying existing customers
● Meeting requirements and expectations of the customer of the process on budget and on time
● Adherence to laws, regulations, industry standards and contractual commitments
● Creation of new service delivery channels.

At the lowest level, COBIT defines KPIs as 'the lead indicators that define measures of how well the IT process is performing in enabling the goal to be reached'. From the COBIT (2000) list of suggested KPIs, we can identify these KPIs for IS strategy as those that are most widely used by organizations:

1 *Improved cost-efficiency of IT processes* (for example, cost per head of delivering IS applications and the return on investment of individual applications).
2 *Increased utilization of IT infrastructure* (for example, proportion of staff using applications).
3 *Increased satisfaction of stakeholders* (through surveys of satisfaction levels and number of complaints).
4 *Improved productivity of staff* (this includes both IS staff, e.g. number of support calls answered, and business staff, e.g. calls resolution times in a call centre).
5 *Increased availability of knowledge and information for managing the enterprise.* (This tends to be an intangible measure, i.e. types of information available, but COBIT recommends assessing standard attributes of information quality, i.e. effectiveness, efficiency, confidentiality, integrity, availability, compliance, reliability.)

It can be seen that these COBIT KPIs provide a means of identifying value delivery through IS by highlighting productivity, costs, returns and satisfaction levels achieved. Meanwhile, Key Goal Indicators play a useful role in linking the IT-specific KPIs to business requirements from IS.

The balanced scorecard

Balanced scorecard
A framework for setting and monitoring business performance. Metrics are structured according to customer issues, internal efficiency measures, financial measures and innovation

In Chapter 10 we refer in more detail to the balanced scorecard, a widely used method of goal setting in corporate planning. The scorecard has proved popular over the past decade since it refers not only to traditional financial measures of performance, but also three other areas – customer concerns, internal process measures, and learning and growth. Each of these areas can be readily applied to directing and controlling IS strategy.

The balanced scorecard is increasingly used for objective setting for IS strategy, both in the sense of the *balanced business scorecard* for the whole organization, which may contain some IS-specific metrics, such as information quality or availability and staff IT skills, but also a *balanced IS/IT scorecard* which is dedicated to specific IS performance objectives and measures. Van der Zee and de Jong (1999) suggest that the balanced scorecard is a useful tool for alignment of organizational and IS objectives. They say:

> the continuously growing importance of IT requires organizations to integrate IT decisions with their common planning and decision-making processes at all organizational levels.

They suggest that it is inappropriate to attempt to align distinct business and IT management cycles – instead the balanced scorecard is seen as a suitable method of achieving integration.

Strategy definition

IS strategy definition
Setting relative investment priorities for applications, support services and infrastructure

The strategy definition part of the IS strategy specifies which resources will be deployed to achieve the organization's objectives. It also specifies how those resources will be delivered through different organizational structures, responsibilities and control mechanisms. The strategy will be based on analysis of the internal and external environment described earlier in the chapter, which will identify gaps in information provision, and it must also support the organization's strategic objectives.

The fundamental IS resource is the applications portfolio, or the mix of different applications software and the information they deliver to support the business. The other types of services shown in Figure 6.3 are also specified through IS strategy definition. So the nature of the end-user support services, information support services, will be defined as well as the work needed to create applications. Furthermore, changes to the technology infrastructure and information architecture will be necessary to support the new applications portfolio and changes to services delivered. So definition of the IS strategy involves setting relative investment priorities for applications, support services and infrastructure. The infrastructure includes both hardware and network architecture, but also information architecture.

As we have noted throughout this chapter, the creation of a strong alignment between information systems and organizational objectives has consistently been reported as one of the key concerns of IS management and IS strategy. However, strategic alignment is one of two contrasting but mutually compatible approaches that may be adopted when organizations generate IS strategy. The two broad strategic approaches are the business alignment and business impacting approaches.

Business alignment
An approach to IS strategy where innovative approaches to deploying applications are used to gain competitive advantage by influencing an organization's strategy

With the business alignment approach to IS strategy definition, the selection of the application portfolio is driven primarily by the business objectives and information needs. Enterprise resource planning for support, e.g. financial applications, is an example of this technology.

As was mentioned earlier in the chapter, business alignment is effectively a top-down method of IS strategy definition – it starts with the business objectives and assesses which information systems can be used to support these business objectives.

Note that some commentators have questioned the commonly used distinction between 'IS' and 'the business' and the emphasis of IS strategy on aligning IS with the business. *Computer Weekly* (2003) reported the comments of Jean-Louis Previdi, director of research at analyst group Meta, which show the danger of this approach. He said:

> IT directors need to change business perceptions of IT as a cost centre or face having their IT departments outsourced.

He told IT directors to manage the expectations of the whole enterprise and stop trying to align IT with the business, adding:

> A chief financial officer will never say he is aligning finance with the business ... 'IT is the business.
>   CIOs are change agents for the enterprise and should speak in terms of value, accountability, finance and return on investment across the whole business.

Business impacting
An approach to IS strategy where innovative approaches to deploying applications are used to gain competitive advantage by influencing an organization's strategy – typically a bottom-up approach to IS strategy generation

The **business impacting** approach involves identification of innovative applications for information systems which can potentially deliver competitive advantage since other competitors in the sector are less likely to use them. This often implies the early adoption of relatively new technologies. The identification and adoption of Internet technologies for customer relationship management in the late 1990s is an example of the type of applications that can be selected through an impacting approach. A business-impacting approach is often part of a bottom-up method of IS strategy definition such as the administrative approach of Earl (1996), summarized in Table 6.2.

Debate 6.2

> *Business-alignment and business-impacting IS strategies cannot be followed simultaneously.*

IS portfolio management

IS portfolio management
A structured approach to the selection and management of IS projects

We noted at the start of this IS strategy definition section that specifying the best combination or portfolio of IS applications to support and impact organizational objectives is a key part of IS strategy. **IS portfolio management** is a relatively new concept in the IS world, although IS managers have talked about the mix of applications in their portfolio for some time. *Information Week* (2003) defines this term as 'Ensuring that the right projects are done and that projects are done right'. This shows the dual meaning of the term. First, it refers to the selection of appropriate IS projects, namely those that are likely to deliver the best return on investment and support the organizational needs. Secondly, it refers to managing a range of IS development projects during implementation. This is a project management function that is explored further in Chapter 7. Mini case study 6.5 'IS portfolio management' shows how software tools are now becoming available to support this process. Figure 6.16 shows an example of software use to manage IS portfolios.

A common method of categorizing and evaluating which information systems should be given priority is the McFarlan modified grid shown in Ward and Peppard (2002) see Figure 6.17. This model recognizes that the information systems used by a single company will not fit into a single quadrant on such a matrix, but rather there will be a portfolio of IS, some of which may lie in different quadrants.

The four quadrants and questions suggested by Ward and Peppard to assess whether an application lies in the quadrant are:

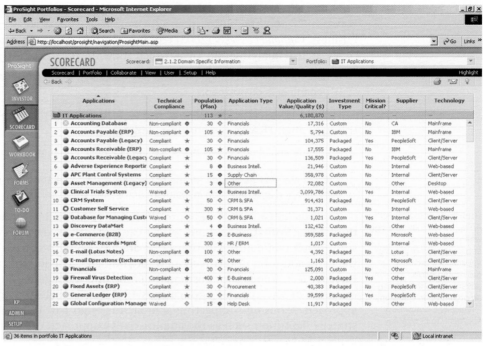

Figure 6.16 Example of a prioritized portfolio from Prosight Portfolio management software

Source: ProSight

Mini case study 6.4	IS portfolio management	

The problem

It is a familiar problem for any large IT department: too many projects, too few resources and not enough time.

The solution

The answer could lie in IT portfolio management, a technique that aims to help organisations decide which projects are worth backing – and which are not.

IT portfolio management has only been around for a couple of years, but it has already attracted much interest, analysts say. Meta Group claims more than 42 per cent of US companies are implementing IT portfolio management at some level.

But what is it? Put simply, IT portfolio management helps businesses prioritise and manage IT assets, people and projects. It seeks to apply to IT projects the same objective management that fund managers apply to financial investment. 'The concept of looking at IT investment like a portfolio of [financial] investments has some merit', says Barbara Gomolski, analyst at the Gartner Group.

Users

It is no accident that some of the biggest fans of IT portfolio management are large financial services companies. In fund management, each investment decision is weighed against its impact on the portfolio in terms of performance. But when it comes to IT projects, this discipline is often lacking.

Standard Chartered Bank, the emerging markets bank, found itself in this situation. 'The approach for putting forward a business case for approval was well established, but then the projects tended to get approved on a stand-alone basis', says Tim Carroll, programme director at the bank.

Critics argue that IT portfolio management is simply a fancy name for project management. But Mr Carroll says it goes much further. 'Portfolio management lets you look across the whole enterprise and shows you how and where you are deploying your project engineers, or a particular type of programmer skill', he says. 'It gives you a lot of data to enable better management discussions [about projects] to then take place. It also gives you a consistent lifecycle of activity for managing your projects, which is very important.'

The bank is using IT portfolio management software from Niku, a specialist vendor, to manage its group technology division, which supports 29,000 people in 50 offices around the world.

In much the same way that fund managers use software to monitor the performance of their investment portfolio, the Niku software helps Standard Chartered monitor its various 'business change' projects, as Mr Carroll calls the bank's IT-based initiatives.

It is no coincidence that interest in IT portfolio management coincides with an era of IT budget cuts. Rakesh Kumar, vice president for technology research at the Meta Group, gives the example of a UK retail bank whose IT department had to cut its budget by 4 per cent over three years. Using IT portfolio management, the bank could look across its projects in different business areas, evaluate their contribution to the bank and allocate resources accordingly.

The traditional way to handle budget cuts is for each manager to make a case for their pet project. But politics often get in the way and the axe falls heaviest on the weakest.

Portfolio management provides an objective way of assessing competing demands and, in the case of the UK bank, it meant the cuts were not as bad as many feared. 'It stopped them doing a mass cull of jobs', says Mr Kumar.

Benefits

One of the selling points for IT portfolio management is that it helps businesses align their IT project goals with corporate objectives. Just as a financial portfolio should match the investment objectives of the investor, so too should a company's portfolio of IT projects.

A challenge for many companies is choosing when and where to invest in technologies. A recent Giga Research report on IT portfolio management in financial firms, explores this by classifying different technologies as leading-edge, fast-follower or conservative. Technologies that Giga considers leading-edge include web services and running Linux on the mainframe; examples in the fast-follower category include J2EE servers and portals; mature technologies well established in financial services include high-end Unix servers and IBM's MQSeries messaging product.

Not everyone wants to be a technology leader, but companies that never adopt leading-edge technologies risk being branded as too conservative. This can be a big risk in industries that undergo rapid change. Giga gives the example of Merrill Lynch, which in the 1990s was penalised by customers and investors because it was slow to introduce online share dealing. But in a slow-changing industry like insurance, it is more acceptable to be at the conservative end of the technology spectrum. Whatever the industry, analysts agree that IT portfolio management is a promising technique. 'It provides a tighter link between IT and what the business is doing', says Ms Gomolski of Gartner.

Payback

Ironically for a technique borrowed from the investment industry, there is little evidence that an IT portfolio management tool can deliver a quantifiable return on the often high investment. Ms Gomolski says it can cost over $300,000 to deploy a commercial tool.

Standard Chartered believes IT portfolio management has already proved its worth by encouraging people to break ambitious projects into manageable chunks. 'The portfolio approach inevitably drives people to split up large-scale projects into stages', says Mr Carroll. 'That gives us options on the future and for us that is a far bigger gain.'

Source: Geoffrey Nairn, Bringing the rigour of financial investing to IT, FT.com; 1 October 2003

- *Strategic.* Applications that are critical to sustaining future business strategy.
  Test: Results in a clear competitive advantage for the business? Enables the achievement of specific business objectives and/or critical success factors?
- *Key operational.* The organization currently depends on these applications for success (mission-critical).
  Test: Overcomes known business inefficiencies?
- *Support.* These applications are valuable to the organization but not critical to its success.
  Test: Does it improve the productivity of the business and so reduce long-term business costs? Does it enable the organization to meet statutory requirements?
- *High potential.* These applications may be important to the future success of the organization.
  Test: Likely to provide future benefits, not yet quantified?

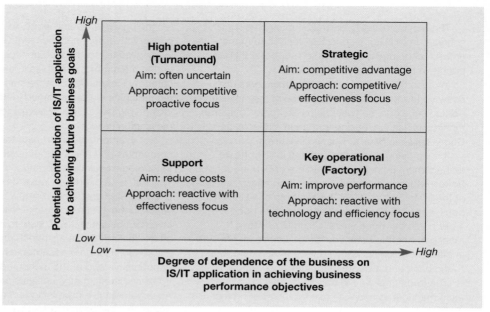

Figure 6.17 Applications portfolio
Source: Ward and Peppard (2002)

A similar approach for assessing e-business investments has been recommended by Pete Solvik, Cisco Systems' senior VP and CIO at the turn of the century. These categories help define the degree of innovation in Internet technology investment and the risk against reward. Solvik (1999) recommends categorizing possible investments into the following categories:

- *New fundamentals*. Focus on cost savings and increased efficiency in low-risk areas of the existing business. An example is an intranet that offers training, HR functions or expense report processing. Key metrics for measuring success are increased productivity and reduced internal expenses, increasing the ratio of customer-facing employees to internal employees. These projects are closest to the Support approach of Ward and Peppard (2002). Low-risk, relatively low-reward.

- *Operational excellence*. Focus on re-engineering existing business-critical processes using Internet technologies. These are medium-risk since typically they are more expensive and affect a mission-critical process. However, reversion to existing methods can occur. An example is Cisco's Virtual Manufacturing Network, an extranet that links the company's 30 manufacturing suppliers. Key metrics are increasing efficiency, decreased cycle time and increased employee access to business-critical information. These projects are closest to the Key operational approach of Ward and Peppard. Medium-risk, medium-reward.

- *Rational experimentation*. Focus on exploration of new business models on a small scale. These are low–medium risk depending on the investment made. Solvik gives the example of Dell Computer Corp.'s B2B marketplace. This hosted auctions for hardware and peripherals from Dell and from other manufacturers. It has now been discontinued. Solvik recommends that companies should use experimentation to identify the best potential applications of new technology. These projects are closest to the High potential approach of Ward and Peppard. Medium-risk, medium-reward.

- *Breakthrough strategies*. High-risk and potentially high-reward projects that fundamentally transform a company's go-to-market strategy. These are typically high-risk and high-reward projects where the company transforms its method of service delivery or product purchase. These are also closest to the High-potential approach of Ward and Peppard. High-risk, high-reward.

IS investment appraisal

IS investment appraisal is part of portfolio management. It involves assessing the investments in systems and calculating return on investment. This evaluation can be conducted for individual applications, or as part of IS strategy development as at organizational level.

IS investment appraisal
Evaluation of the return on investment on IS strategy at firm or application level

IS services strategy

The IS strategy will also define the level of end-user support services such as help-desk, training and support for problems with hardware and software. The details of approaches to supporting end-user computing and managing IS services internally and through outsourcing are described in more detail in Chapter 11. In this chapter, we will consider the location of IS, which is a key strategic decision related to IS services strategy.

IS location refers to both where the IS services are physically located and where they are managed or controlled.

IS location
Refers to both where the IS services are physically located and where they are managed or controlled

The issue of IS location is a key issue for medium-to-large organizations, particularly those with several offices or physical locations where staff are based. In such an organization, IS must be organized and located in such a way as to ensure full integration of business and IS strategies while at the same time providing full services and support for the specific IS needs of each separate business location.

King (1983) is one researcher who has focused on the IS location issue. He showed that there were two approaches to management of IS services through location, which lie on a continuum. First, in the **centralized IS location approach**, all elements of IS are at a single point within the organization. Second, in the **decentralized IS location approach**, all aspects of IS management are distributed at other points in the organization. When decentralization exists, there will be staff located within different parts of the organization who have autonomy to make their own decisions about IS. These could be general managers such as finance managers or marketing managers, or the staff may be IS/IT professionals.

Centralized IS location approach
All IS services and support are managed and located centrally

Decentralized IS location approach
All aspects of IS management are distributed at other points in the organization

Of course, most organizations will not have centralized or decentralized all their IS services, rather they will have decentralized some elements – a hybrid approach will be used. Referring back to Figure 6.3, we can see that any of these IS services can be centralized or decentralized:

1 *IS strategy and planning.* Typical activities: creation of strategy and selection of applications, technology infrastructure and information architecture.
2 *Technical user support.* Typical activities: help-desk support of users, advice and trouble-shooting technical problems.
3 *Application development.* Typical activities: building new applications or configuring, integrating and implementing packaged activities.
4 *Information management.* Typical activities: creating information management policies, controlling information quality and protecting information.

For each of these activities, there will typically be a planning and controlling function and a service delivery function. Either of these can be separately centralized or decentralized. For example, for technical user support, it is most efficient to manage the service centrally, but some localized support is likely to be required on different sites.

Each activity must be assessed to see whether it is most efficient and effective to conduct it centrally or in a distributed sense. Typical efficiency measures are service delivery levels or customer satisfaction and the cost of delivering service. Typically, effectiveness is assessed according to how well the service matches the business or customer needs; in other words, does it meet company objectives? It will be apparent that in making IS location decisions there will be a tension between centralization, which will typically improve control and minimize costs (more efficient and more effective according to some measures), and decentralization, which will tend to give a better quality of service (more efficient and more effective according to other measures).

For a large organization, such as the Lo-cost Airline Company which will be geographically distributed (i.e. have different sites in different parts of the country and in different countries) and may be functionally separated (e.g. customer service and sales is conducted from a different location from the central office where strategic activities and finance activities are conducted), it will be more practical and more cost-effective to decentralize some activities than others.

IS services outsourcing
Different information systems functions are performed by a third party over a contract period, for example hardware and software purchase and maintenance, application development and IT help-desk services

The practice of **IS services outsourcing** is closely related to IS location. Use of a third party to deliver IS support services will often provide a mechanism to increase IS centralization. Since outsourcing is a major topic, it is considered in detail in Chapter 11.

IS infrastructure strategy

It is also the role of the IS strategy to define the future technical infrastructure of the organization. By 'infrastructure' we mean the combination of systems software, networking communications and hardware platforms which were described in Chapters 2 and 3. One of the reasons for having a long-term IS strategy should be to anticipate future demands for new infrastructure arising from changes in:

- *Business applications requirements* – the infrastructure should support business demands for new applications.
- *Technology* – new technologies may give opportunity for new applications, or a means of reducing IS running costs.

Scalable
Infrastructure will operate under different capacities

- *Information storage and access requirements* – the infrastructure should be **scalable** to accommodate additional requirements and capacity loadings caused by a growth in customers, entry into new markets or mergers with other companies.
- *Legislation* – changes to laws on privacy and data protection may require changes to the way data is stored.

It is clear that flexibility in infrastructure is the key to supporting these changing requirements. Case study 6.2 is an example of an infrastructure project arising out of IS strategy to provide this flexibility.

Supermarket Tesco sets out its infrastructure strategy

Illustrates the role and importance of IS strategy in determining the IT infrastructure which can respond to changed business needs. It shows how a new technology was introduced to increase the flexibility in comparison to the previous legacy systems.

Expansion in a competitive environment relies on being able to respond to new challenges as quickly as possible.

Retail giant Tesco, which is opening new stores in the UK as well as expanding overseas, needed to be able to rapidly build new applications to help maintain its competitive edge.

Its legacy back-end servers were based on old Unix-based systems, and weren't flexible enough to handle the rapid creation of new applications.

In 2001, the company's board made a strategic decision to develop a new architecture for building and hosting web-based software.

It set out a strategy to build a back-end hosting architecture that would become the central platform for all of Tesco's applications to plug into.

What were the business objectives of the project?

The primary objective for Tesco was to web-enable its application infrastructure, cutting time to market for the development and deployment of new applications.

'We made a board-level decision to put in an entirely new application architecture for building and hosting applications', said infrastructure programme manager Steve Butler.

The platform would help Tesco maintain its competitive edge by bringing new tools to market faster.

'Speed and reactivity are key in the retail market', said Butler.

What were the key milestones in the implementation?

Planning for the system began in 2001, but development began in earnest in February 2002, with the majority of the work being done by software consultancy 1E.

'A number of phases were mapped out, beginning with the creation of a new Microsoft .Net-based development environment in April 2002', said programme manager Nigel Chubb. This was followed up with the design and delivery of a live environment.

By September, the foundation infrastructure was in place and ready for handling new applications.

'Over the Christmas period, all system development was frozen as we dealt with our busiest retail period, but by February we were able to take operational control of the platform from 1E', said Chubb

'The key deliverable from 1E was that once they had built the system for us, we had to be able to take control and move forward by ourselves', he said.

What technology was used?

The foundation of the infrastructure is a build and management platform, almost entirely based on Microsoft products, upon which all new applications are rolled out.

On the front-end, Microsoft Internet Information Server handles the presentation layer; Microsoft's .Net framework is used for the development environment; and Microsoft SQL Server provides the back-end database.

'Another component that is bolted on top of the build and management platform is an enterprise application integration layer that handles requests to and from our legacy systems', said Butler.

How did you manage the business change and people issues involved?

Chubb says it was crucial to have high-level support for the change in architecture. 'You need that level of buy-in from above to ensure success', he said.

An obvious challenge was migrating the in-house developers' skills to an entirely new development platform. 'We needed to build their confidence that this new platform could work, in order to help incent them to shift their skills', said Chubb.

Another challenge was shifting from the current application development time of one to two years, to being able to deliver new tools in as little as four or five months.

A crucial step in achieving all of this was successfully delivering the new platform and demonstrating that it could actually work as promised. 'This was a major confidence booster for the developers', said Chubb.

What results were achieved?

Tesco has created a flexible, scalable, web-based environment for building and hosting new applications, making it far more capable of rapidly adjusting to business change.

'The project was delivered on time and on budget, which was a great success considering the scale of the work being done', said Butler.

The platform has given the company the power to develop new applications in-house, or to simply purchase off the shelf software and roll it out.

'The system has cut our time to market significantly, cutting development time from years to months', said Butler.

In September 2002, the firm rolled out Customer Service Desk (CSD), its first new application, across a number of its stores.

CSD is a till-based application for dealing with customer satisfaction issues electronically, removing the previous inefficient paper-based system and substantially improving the process for both customers and store staff.

Since then, it has been able to roll out a number of additional tools, improving a wide range of processes in the firm's stores and distribution centres.

What were the lessons learnt?

'You should definitely create the development environment first, providing a strong foundation for application rollout', said Chubb.

Butler adds that it's crucial to concentrate on the business requirements and to build the system accordingly.

And both agree that working with a partner that has knowledge and experience in this type of rollout is a must.

What were the business benefits and return on investment?

As the platform forms a core infrastructure for applications, it wasn't being produced to generate a return, says Butler.

'This was seen as a very strategic project and it was recognised that the business benefit would come from the applications that would be rolled out on top of this,' he said.

Tesco now has a platform that is capable of generating powerful new tools rapidly and rolling them out quickly to stores across the world.

How do you plan to build on the project further?

'Our focus during 2002 was building and piloting the system. In 2003, we're dealing with an aggressive rollout of the new applications we've already created', said Butler.

Tesco has created a number of applications, which are in various stages of deployment across the group's 780 stores, as well as into its international operations in Korea, Thailand and central Europe.

One of the most important tools is the Mobile Shelf Edge System (MSES), a PDA-based tool that enables store staff to handle stock management on the shop floor by connecting them to the stock system across a radio frequency network.

MSES is being rolled out across the UK, while a new PeopleSoft-based human resources system is being deployed in Thailand.

Butler says the firm has plans for an e-learning system, as well as investigating a number of other potential projects.

Computing says:

As IT becomes increasingly fundamental to businesses, the ability to rapidly develop new applications and bring them live is critical to achieving corporate objectives. Tesco recognised that their previous infrastructure could hold them back, and proactively introduced new technology as a foundation for its future competitiveness.

Source: James Watson, Project of the Year Awards: Tesco, *Computing*, 23 July 2003. www.computing.co.uk/Analysis/1142526

> **Question**
>
> To what extent do you think the success of this infrastructure project reflects a sound approach to IS strategy development within Tesco? Use the case to demonstrate how Tesco managed this project as part of its IS strategy.

Strategic failure

A lack of a strategic plan or the presence of an inadequate strategy is unlikely to result in the collapse of a substantial organization, though it may contribute toward its longer-term downfall. However, the consequences of having a poor informatic strategy can manifest in catastrophic operational problems (ZDNet, 2007):

- In 1983 an undetected software bug in the Soviet early warning system wrongly indicated that the US had launched a missile attack.
- An error in a single line of code caused one of America's largest providers of telecom services to shut down, resulting in 75 million unanswered phone calls.
- Whilst attempting to convert a piece of 64-bit data into 16-bit the guidance system computer on board the satellite launching rocket Ariane 5 shut down. Back-up systems also failed from the same fault and the £4 billion vehicle was blown up.
- Wiring on two parts of the Airbus A380 failed to match up after it was discovered that the organizations responsible for engineering each part were using different versions of the computer aided design (CAD) software.

- A new computer management system was installed in the Child Support Agency (CSA) at the same time as the organization was undergoing substantial reforms. The new computer system and the new work systems failed to integrate, resulting in long-term operational difficulties and numerous people being incorrectly paid.
- The anticipated problems over the year 2000 date change (The Millennium Bug) amounted to little except for the estimated £400 billion that it cost to fix.
- In 2006, faults with laptop batteries, power supplies and other computer equipment were estimated to have cost Sony in excess of £20 million.
- While the system of obtaining a UK passport was being revised, Siemens were installing a new computerized system. Insufficient testing and training caused hundreds of people to miss holidays and millions to be paid in compensation and staff overtime.
- A small networking device at Los Angeles International Airport brought the entire operation to a standstill for 8 hours as it broadcast incorrect data throughout the system.

Summary

1 The purpose of information systems strategy development is to define how resources including information resources, software applications, human resources and technology infrastructure will be used to support and impact an organization's strategy.

2 Information systems strategy is at the core of business information management, but is supported by more detailed information and knowledge management strategies.

3 A measurable, repeatable and continuous process for IS strategy development is essential for an organization to maximize investments in information technology.

4 Michael Earl, summarized in Earl (1996), has identified these approaches to the IS strategy process or Strategic Information Systems Planning (SISP) which are still evident in IS strategy development: business-led, method-driven, administrative approach, technological approach, organizational approach.

5 IS strategy development has four main parts – strategic situation analysis, objective setting, strategy definition and strategy implementation.

6 Strategic situation analysis involves analysis of the internal status of, and external influences on, an organization environment from a business and technology perspective.

7 Strategic objective setting involves setting specific goals for how IS can contribute to an organization.

8 Strategy definition identifies the major strategic priorities for IS by assessing how the applications portfolio can align with organizational objectives.

Exercises

Self-assessment questions

1 Summarize the purpose of IS strategy development. What are the characteristics and outcomes of successful IS strategy development?

2 Distinguish between and relate IS strategy to IT strategy, information management strategy and knowledge management strategy.

3 Describe the characteristics of Michael Earl's alternative approaches to the IS strategy process: business-led, method-driven, administrative approach, technological approach, organizational approach. Evaluate the advantages and disadvantages of each.

4 What internal analysis should be conducted as part of IS strategic environment analysis?

5 What analysis of an organization's external business environment should be conducted as part of IS strategic environment analysis?

6 Evaluate different approaches for aligning IS strategy with business strategy and using it to impact business strategy.

7 Explain the concept of portfolio management.

8 Explain the differences between these types of IS investments: strategic, key operational, high potential and support.

Essay and discussion questions

1 Assess the barriers to and facilitators for creating a successful information systems strategy process.

2 Suggest approaches that managers can use to ensure that IS strategy is aligned with business strategy, but can also impact business strategy where appropriate.

3 Assess alternative approaches to selection of IS applications portfolio.

4 What should be the involvement of senior management in determining and executing information systems strategy in a large organization?

5 Assess the relevance of approaches developed for IS strategic planning for assisting in e-business strategy and implementation.

6 Much of the research into success factors for developing information systems strategy dates from the 1980s and 1990s. To what extent do you think lessons have been learnt? What might the reasons be for changes in IS implementation?

References

Arnott, D. and Bridgewater, S. (2002) Internet, interaction and implications for marketing, *Marketing Intelligence and Planning*, 20(2), 86–95.

Carnegie Mellon (2001) Research Report. CMMISM for Systems Engineering/Software Engineering/Integrated Product and Process Development, Version 1.02, Staged Representation (CMMI-SE/SW/IPPD, V1.02, Staged). Available online at: www.sei. cmu.edu/pub/documents/00.reports/pdf/00tr030.pdf. See also: www.sei.cmu.edu/cmm/ cmm.html.

Chaffey, D. (2002) *Business and E-Commerce Management*. Financial Times Prentice Hall, Harlow.

Chaffey, D. (2004) *E-Business and E-Commerce Management*, 2nd edn. Financial Times Prentice Hall, Harlow.

Chaffey, D., Mayer, R., Johnston, K. and Ellis-Chadwick, F. (2003) *Internet Marketing: Strategy, Implementation and Practice*, 2nd edn. Financial Times Prentice Hall, Harlow.

CIO (2003) The incredible shrinking CIO. 15 October. www.cio.com/archive/101503/ shrinking.html.

COBIT (2000) Executive Summary of COBIT. Released by the COBIT Steering Committee and the IT Governance Institute. Available online at: www.isaca.org/cobit.

Computer Weekly (2003) Meta: Stop trying to align IT with the business.

Deise, M., Nowikow, C., King, P. and Wright, A. (2000) *Executive's Guide to E-Business. From Tactics to Strategy*. Wiley, New York.

Doherty, N., Marples, C. and Suhaimi, A. (1999) The relative success of alternative approaches to strategic information systems planning: *An empirical analysis*. *International Journal of Information Management*, 9, 263–83.

DTI (2000) Business in the Information Age – International Benchmarking Study 2000. UK Department of Trade and Industry.

Earl, M. (1989) *Management Strategies for Information Technology*. Prentice Hall, Hemel Hempstead.

Earl, M. (1996) An organizational approach to IS strategy-making. In M. Earl (ed.), *Information Management: The Organizational Dimension*. Oxford University Press, Oxford, pp. 136–70.

Financial Times (2002) Inside Track article: An optimist's vision of tomorrow's technology: Interview George Colony, Forrester Research, by Fiona Harvey, 2 April. Available online by subscription at: www.ft.com/ftit.

Galbraith, J. (1977) *Organization Design*. Addison-Wesley, Reading, MA.

Galliers, R. and Sutherland, A. (1991) Information systems management and strategy formulation: The stages of growth model revisited. *Journal of Information Systems*, 1(2), 89–114.

Information Week (2003) Getting the IT mix right. 27 October. Available online at: www.informationweek.com/story/showArticle.jhtml?articleID=15600182.

IT Week (2003) Boardrooms ignore IT input. By David Neal [24-10-2003]. www.itweek.co.uk/News/1145603.

King, J. L. (1983) Centralised versus decentralised computing: Organizational considerations and management options. *Computing Survey*, 15(4), 319–49.

Lederer, A. and Mendelow, A. (1987) Information resource planning: Overcoming difficulties in identifying top management objectives. *MIS Quarterly*, 11(3), 389–99.

Lederer, A. and Sethi, V. (1992) Meeting the challenges of information systems planning. *Long-range Planning*, 25(2), 60–80.

McFarlan, F. and McKenney, J. (1993) *Corporate Information Systems Management*. Prentice Hall, London.

Multilingual (2008) Localizing a localizer's website: The challenge. Jan/Feb, 30–33.

Nitish, S., Fassott, G., Zhao, H. and Boughton, P. (2006) A cross-cultural analysis of German, Chinese and Indian consumers' perception of web site adaptation. *Journal of Consumer Behaviour*, 5, 56–68.

Nolan, R. (1979) Managing the crisis in data processing. *Harvard Business Review*, March–April, 115–26.

Ofcom (2010) The Communications Market 2010. Research report published at: http://stakeholders.ofcom.org.uk/market-data-research/market-data/communications-market-reports/.

Porter, M. (1980) *Competitive Strategy*. Free Press, New York.

Porter, M. (2001) *Strategy and the Internet*. Harvard Business Review, March, 62–78.

PRTM (2003) Optimizing Business Performance: Using IT for Competitive Advantage. www2.darwinmag.com/learn/research/surveyreport.cfm?id=57.

Quelch, J. and Klein, L. (1996) The Internet and international marketing. *Sloan Management Review*, Spring, 60–75.

Reicheld, F. and Schefter, P. (2000) E-loyalty, your secret weapon on the web. *Harvard Business Review,* July–August, 105–13.

Rogers, E. (1983) *Diffusion of Innovation,* 3rd edn. Free Press, New York.

Singh, N. and Pereira, A. (2005) *The Culturally Customized Web Site, Customizing Web Sites for the Global Marketplace.* Butterworth-Heinemann, Oxford, UK.

Slack, N. (2001) *Operations Management*, 3rd edn. Pearson, London.

Solvik, P. (1999) Building an Internet Company. CIO E-Business Research Center. www.cio.com/research/ec/edit/122099rexpo.html.

Van der Zee, J. and de Jong, B. (1999) Alignment is not enough: Integrating business and information technology management with the balanced business scorecard. *Journal of Management Information Systems*, 16(2), 137–57.

Ward, J. and Peppard, J. (2002) *Strategic Planning for Information Systems*, 3rd edn. Wiley, Chichester.

Waterman, R. H., Peters, T. J. and Phillips, J. R. (1980) Structure is not organization. *McKinsey Quarterly*. In-house journal. McKinsey & Co., New York.

Wilson, T. D. (1989) The implementation of information systems strategies in UK companies: aims and barriers to success. *International Journal of Information Management*, 9, 245–58.

ZDNet (2007) The Top 10 IT Disasters of All Time. Colin Barker, 22 November. Available online at: http://resources.zdnet.co.uk/articles/0,1000001991,39290976,00.htm.

Further reading

Galliers, R. and Leidner, D. (eds) *Strategic Information Management.* Butterworth Heinemann, Oxford. This book is a collection of classic IS strategy-related papers.

Ward, J. and Peppard, J. (2002) *Strategic Planning for Information Systems*, 3rd edn. Wiley, Chichester. Covers concepts introduced in this chapter in more detail, for example, value chain analysis (Chapter 5), managing the applications portfolio (Chapter 7), managing investments (Chapter 9).

visit the www

Weblinks

CIO Connect (http://visitors.cio-connect.com/magazine/) Freely available magazine with case studies and articles about issues concerning CIOs in large UK organizations.

CIO Magazine Leadership and Management Research Center (www.cio.com) Strategy guidance from US trade magazine.

COBIT (www.isaca.org/cobit) IT governance model for Control Objectives for Information and related Technology.

Computing (www.computing.co.uk) Management issues relevant to IT managers. See also other IT trade press publications featured in Chapter 1 web links.

Intellect (www.intellectuk.org) Intellect is the trade body for the UK based information technology, telecommunications and electronics industry. Guidelines.

JISC infoNet (www.jiscinfonet.ac.uk) The UK Joint Information Systems Committee Centre of Expertise in the Planning and Implementation of Information Systems in Further and Higher Education. Contains a range of case studies and practical guidelines on information strategy, but also include aspects of IS strategy.

Knowledge Brief Networked (www.kbnetworked.com) UK best-practice organization for IS and e-business procurement. Includes case studies and guidelines.

National Computer Centre (www.ncc.co.uk) Free IT adviser articles and IT Manager year book cover topical issues of IS strategy.

Silicon (www.silicon.com) UK portal providing news on IT industry developers.

> For multiple-choice questions, and annotated weblinks relating to this chapter visit this book's website at: www.pearsoned.co.uk/chaffey

Part 3
IMPLEMENTATION

In Part 3 we consider best practice in building information management solutions and introducing them into organizations. Chapter 7 shows how projects can be managed to minimize the risk of failure; Chapter 8 shows how the change associated with introducing new systems can be managed and Chapter 9 describes practical approaches to creating an information architecture.

7

Managing systems development

Objective

To assess appropriate controls for managing the risks inherent in information systems development projects.

Learning outcomes

After reading this chapter, you will be able to:

● Identify the typical stages in an information systems project.

● Identify the risks associated with typical phases of a project.

● Understand approaches used by project managers to control projects.

Management issues

Typical questions facing managers related to this topic:

● How can we avoid the high reported failure rates for IS implementations?

● Which specific risks are related to management of information management projects?

Links to other chapters

The main related chapters are:

➤ *Chapter 2* introduces the types of applications implemented during projects described in this chapter. It also discusses the criteria involved in selection of packaged software.

➤ *Chapter 6* on IS strategy explains approaches that organizations use to select the portfolio of applications that they develop.

➤ *Chapter 8* reviews how the change associated with introduction of new systems and new ways of working is managed.

➤ *Chapter 11* discusses outsourcing, where systems development and other IS services are completed by a third party.

Introduction

Managing projects to implement information systems is challenging. Look at Table 7.1, which shows examples of high-profile project management failures from UK public-service organizations over a 10-year period. Specific examples of project failures within commercial organizations are less commonly made publicly available since companies are not open to the same public scrutiny and naturally do not want to publicize their failures. However, if we look at surveys of project failures across commercial organizations, it seems that failure is also commonplace here. This is in stark contrast to traditional construction projects where problems can occur, but major setbacks are much less common.

A survey of 134 large organizations from the UK, the US and other countries shows both the importance of project management, and its challenges (KPMG, 2002). The research showed that 56 per cent of organizations had experienced failed IT projects in the previous 12 months. The average loss incurred by the businesses surveyed was £8 million per project, with the largest single project failure costing £133 million.

Table 7.1 Examples of UK public service projects

Project	Application	Project issue
Inland Revenue EDS IT outsourcing	IT services originally provided by IT department of 2,250 employees, and an annual budget of some £250 million	Ten-year outsourcing contract started in 1994. In 2000, estimated that new work will account for about a quarter of the forecast £2 billion revenue spend on the EDS contract
New NHS Number	Consistent access to patient records across the country	The NHS Executive set a target for all NHS systems to use the New NHS Number from April 1995. This target was not met a decade later, and the roll-out was suspended in 2010. The project became part of the £12bn Connecting for Health programme in 2005
National Air Traffic Services Ltd (NATS)	Air traffic control centre, Swanwick	Originally due to open in late 1996, but eventually opened only in January 2002, some £150 million over the £475m budget
Passport agency	Computerized passport processing system	Large backlogs of up to 50 days in issuing passports. £12 million additional costs due to resolving failures
Libra	Infrastructure and application to support magistrates courts	Initial contract was for £184 million over 10.5 years. In 2001 the contract costs were revised to £557 million over 14.5 years
Inland Revenue	Online tax submission service	Only 39,000 taxpayers used the service for 1999–2000, compared to a target of 315,000. Did not reach 50 per cent submission target by 2005

Implementation of specific types of information system indicate worse problems. In 2000, it was reported that around 70 per cent of CRM projects failed in terms of delivering a return on investment or completion on time.

Since the projects in Table 7.1 relate to a period of over 10 years, does this suggest that we are not getting any better at project management? An information source that can help answer this question is the Standish Group CHAOS research. This is a long-term tracking survey which has reported on tens of thousands of projects run in small, medium and large companies in the US from 1994 to the present day. The results from this research (looking at the years 2000 to 2008) are summarized in Figure 7.1. This shows that in 2008 less than a third of projects were deemed to have succeeded. For more recent examples of project failures see Clarety (2010), which summarizes the latest Standish report; this is available to subscribers only.

This chapter explores the reasons for systems project failures and possible approaches to overcome these problems. We don't look in detail at the theory and concepts of project management planning, rather we review approaches that management teams can take to increase the probability of project success. All of the projects referred to in Table 7.1 used established project management methodologies. This suggests that the reasons for failure do not lie solely with the project manager, but that a range of managers and employees involved with the project were culpable. At the start of the chapter we introduce the range of different types of information systems project, since they can vary widely in terms of scale and application. We then look at the special characteristics of information systems development projects, including their goals, typical stages and approaches used to control and manage these projects. The main part of the chapter is an exploration of specific management issues with the different phases in a systems development project and approaches to minimize the risks.

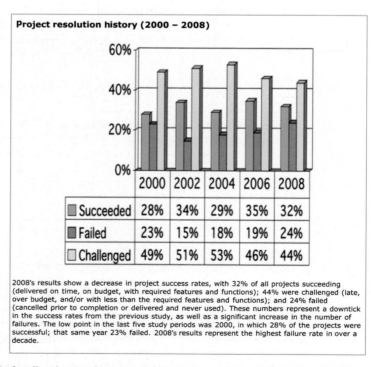

Project resolution history (2000 – 2008)

	2000	2002	2004	2006	2008
▪ Succeeded	28%	34%	29%	35%	32%
▪ Failed	23%	15%	18%	19%	24%
☐ Challenged	49%	51%	53%	46%	44%

2008's results show a decrease in project success rates, with 32% of all projects succeeding (delivered on time, on budget, with required features and functions); 44% were challenged (late, over budget, and/or with less than the required features and functions); and 24% failed (cancelled prior to completion or delivered and never used). These numbers represent a downtick in the success rates from the previous study, as well as a significant increase in the number of failures. The low point in the last five study periods was 2000, in which 28% of the projects were successful; that same year 23% failed. 2008's results represent the highest failure rate in over a decade.

Figure 7.1 Application project success rates from Standish Group CHAOS research
Source: Standish Group (2010)

Types of information systems project

The approaches to information systems development described in this chapter can be applied to three main types of implementation related to business information management. These are:

1 *Operational applications.* The 'mission-critical' systems needed to support the manufacture, sale and servicing of products. The ticketing system of the Lo-cost Airline Company is an example of an operational application.

2 *Information and knowledge management applications.* Systems used to capture, store and disseminate information within an organization. These typically include decision support systems for tactical or strategic decision making, but they could be operational. The employee intranet at the Lo-cost Airline Company is an example of an information and knowledge management application built using a content management system (Chapter 2). A customer relationship management (CRM) system also fits into this category, although it could also be categorized as operational. A CRM system involves capturing and maintaining information about customers which is used to analyse their characteristics and preferences and then devise product or campaign offers for them which are communicated to them through a range of media such as post, e-mail or face-to-face. Management control systems to improve organizational performance such as a system to implement a balanced scorecard or Six Sigma (see Chapter 10) are also information management applications. We examine the special issues with managing these types of projects at the end of this chapter.

3 *Infrastructure development.* These are projects or elements of projects where the technology supporting applications is developed. This could include introducing new hardware, upgrading network communications or deployment of a new office suite. If the Lo-cost Airline Company moved to installing Linux on all its server machines with an open-source version of its office applications such as word processing, this would be an example of an infrastructure development.

In some cases, large-scale projects can involve all three elements. This scenario is likely when major mergers occur and systems integration is required. For example, when the Royal Bank of Scotland and NatWest merged, it was necessary to merge around 100 systems from the former with 446 from the latter. This was a massive

---

Mini case study 7.1   **The UK National Health Service project to develop an integrated care records service (ICRS)**

In 2002 a new approach to providing information services for the UK National Health Service was proposed by the NHS Information Authority (now NHS Connecting for Health). In the proposal document, it was explained as follows:

> The major change proposed is to move away from the concept of a number of separate information systems based primarily around organizational structures to a situation in which professionals are provided access to the one integrated service. The services will include access to records and the functionality needed to support clinical practice.

The stakeholders affected by this new information system are:

- 'service users, where a modern IT-enabled NHS will directly and visibly impact on how they interact with the care system and on their experience as consumers of care services
- health and care professionals involved with direct patient and service user care, who will have safe, fast, modern IT to support them routinely in their work
- managers, researchers and other professionals not involved in direct patient care to have ready access to high quality, confidential, information.'

undertaking involving over 4,000 IT staff, but was achieved four months ahead of schedule in October 2002 (*IT Week*, 2003a). A further example of a project involving all elements is the Libra system for UK Magistrates' Courts Committees. This included development of a standard national application to support court work such as case management, accounting and administration – to replace the five existing systems in the organization. It also included development of a national IT infrastructure including desktop PCs, printers, networks and full online support. Mini case study 7.1 on the NHS shows a further example of a major project with a range of project elements.

Project management goals

The goals of projects to implement IS are evident from the examples of failures illustrated in Table 7.1 and Figure 7.1. In order of increasing severity for the organization, a failed information systems project is indicated by:

1 *'Overrun'* – project completed, but overruns in terms of cost or time targets. The completed system does, however, deliver benefits as expected. 'Challenged' according to the Standish Group.

2 *'Scrapping'* – project not completed – a decision is taken to scrap or end the project before completion. 'Failed' according to the Standish Group.

3 *'Neglect'* – project completed, but does not meet user or business needs. The project may also have overrun cost or time constraints. If the system does not meet user or business needs, its usage will be limited and it is probable that a replacement system will need to be developed or that users will have to revert to using previous systems. The project is unlikely to deliver a return on investment in this case. 'Challenged' according to the Standish Group.

You will notice that ending a project before completion (2) is not the worst outcome since less expenditure will result than for a delayed project which is completed eventually, but does not deliver the anticipated benefits to the user or the business. An implication of this is that management controls are necessary to review projects during development and assess whether continuation is worthwhile. This controlling role cannot usually be performed by the project manager alone because they are too close to the project and are unlikely to want to end the project because they will see this as failure. This control needs to be an independent group of people drawn from both the business and the system developers.

Royer (2003) gives examples of projects that continued despite many indications pointing to failure. Her research suggests that this is the result of the project champions becoming too close to their project and developing a collective belief in the project that makes it difficult to 'kill'. She suggests independent review with 'stage gate' controls at each stage of the project which must be passed before the project proceeds, or even an 'exit champion' to counter the 'project champion'!

It follows that for an IS project to be entirely successful, it should be delivered on time, within budget and should meet the business or user needs. However, these three criteria are often not of equal weighting. Owing to costs of IT projects together with their failure rates, meeting business requirements is usually given the greatest importance. The KPMG (2002) survey showed that the most important measures of success were:

- Meeting business case requirements (46 per cent)
- On-time delivery (21 per cent)
- Within-budget delivery (9 per cent)
- Equal weighting to all three measures (24 per cent).

In managing applications developments projects, there is a delicate balance between meeting constraints for application quality and project management constraints, which is shown graphically in Figure 7.2.

If the application needs more features or characteristics to meet the needs of the business or users than were originally envisaged at the outset, then more project resources are needed to achieve this. These project resources may include more people time to build the system or additional software or hardware to make the performance of the system acceptable. An alternative is to compromise on new features needed by the system, by removing or reducing the level of other features.

System requirements
Define how an IS will be used within the business through detailed specification of the features

Meeting the business or user needs is dependent on meeting the **system requirements** or the features of the information system. Figure 7.3 gives an indication of what still happens on many 'challenged' IS projects. The management may require something utilitarian to meet the business needs ('the people carrier'). The user's requirements may be more sophisticated and may be overspecified since they will be using the system day-by-day ('the sports car'). The designers like to produce a technically elegant system, but in doing so, it may not meet the requirements of the system in terms of features or performance ('the concept car'). If the requirements are not controlled during the project and are interpreted differently by the different people involved, then we may end up with a delivered system which is quite different from what was originally intended, so that it meets few of the original requirements ('the golf buggy')! It is the role of the project manager to reconcile the interpretation of requirements from the business, users, designers and developers.

In reality, the constraints on IS projects shown in Figure 7.2 are not fixed. Although attempts are made to estimate goals for finish time and delivery of project, these are subject to considerable error. This is because these in turn are based on estimates of the features of the system. As we will see later in this chapter, it is particularly difficult to specify features in detail at the outset of a project and this is the fundamental reason why information systems projects are subject to failure. Efforts to improve the success rate of projects must therefore focus on methods of early, clear specification of the system features or requirements.

Requirements creep
Incremental changes to the specification of an IS project during implementation

Another success factor in project management is control of changes in requirements. It is inevitable that the requirements or features will change during a project as business users identify new opportunities for features which improve the performance of the business, or alternatively proposed features prove to be unnecessary. Gradual changes in specification are known amongst the project team as '**requirements creep**'. These changes are gradual or incremental since often there will be many small changes to system specification such as output information requirements

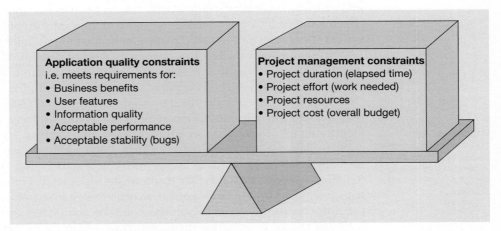

Figure 7.2 Constraints on IS project management

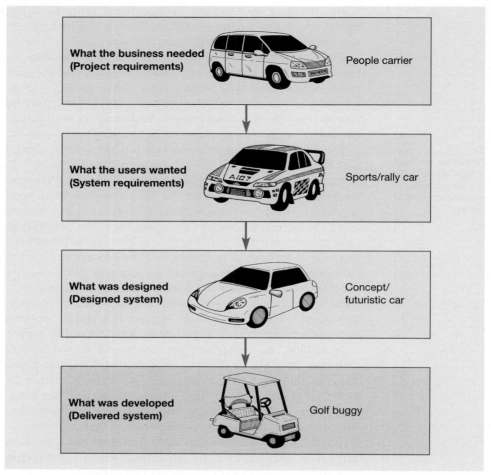

Figure 7.3 **Different interpretations of requirements during a systems development project**

and how they are visualized together with changes to the navigation of systems. One project one of the authors was involved in, for the development of a system to process mortgage applications for a bank, generated hundreds of changes in requirements every week during the peak of development. Successful project management must acknowledge that requirements changes will occur and develop strategies to control them. In a later section we look at how prototyping and the Dynamic Systems Development Method (DSDM) can be used to minimize this problem.

With requirements subject to change, flexibility is required to balance the constraints shown in Figure 7.2. A sound method of accommodating requirements changes during the projects is required, as described later in the chapter.

Requirements creep is identified by Matta and Ashkenas (2003) as one of the major risks to project management. They refer to this as the 'white-space risk' caused by not identifying all project tasks in advance. They also identify 'integration risk' where separate activities are completed as estimated, but additional work is required to integrate these sub-projects. For example, one project activity may be to develop and test functions to access a database for customer details. A related but separate activity, perhaps performed by a separate person, may be to design the on-screen form to display this information. Both of these tasks could be completed on time, but additional work is required to integrate them, which may identify further problems that need

Integration risk
Potential project overruns caused by additional work involved with integrating the output from separate activities

fixing. It follows that project plans should allow sufficient time for integration and testing of separate modules.

To summarize this section on project goals, we will use the definition of project management from COBIT. COBIT is the widely adopted IT governance model for Control Objectives for Information and related Technology. This definition is also helpful since it highlights some of the success factors in project management which we will cover later in this chapter. Project management is one of the key processes COBIT identifies for the effective governance of IT. It defines its control objective PO10 (COBIT, 2001) as follows: managing projects should:

Satisfy the business requirement:

> to set priorities and to deliver on time and within budget

and is enabled by

> the organization identifying and prioritising projects in line with the operational plan and the adoption and application of sound project management techniques for each project undertaken and takes into consideration:

- business management sponsorship for projects
- program management
- project management capabilities
- user involvement
- task breakdown, milestone definition and phase approvals
- allocation of responsibilities
- rigorous tracking of milestones and deliverables
- cost and manpower budgets, balancing internal and external resources
- quality assurance plans and methods
- program and project risk assessments
- transition from development to operations.

Approaches to building information management applications

Approaches to systems development selected by organizations cover a range of methods of building applications introduced in Chapter 2. These methods of systems build include:

Bespoke development
Information system development specifically for purpose

1 *Bespoke development.* With a **bespoke development**, the application is developed from scratch through programming of a solution.

Packaged implementation
Standard software is installed with limited configuration required

2 *Off-the-shelf.* In a **packaged implementation**, a standard existing system is purchased from a solution vendor and installed on servers and clients located within an organization. Alternatively, free or low-cost open-source software (Chapter 2) may be used. An office application or a simple accounting package is an example of an off-the-shelf packaged implementation. The criteria used to select appropriate software are discussed in Chapter 2.

Hosted solution
Standard software which is managed externally on the supplier's server

3 *Hosted solution (packaged).* With a **hosted solution**, a standard system is used, but it is not managed within the company, but by using a third-party applications service provider or web services approach (Chapter 2).

Tailored development
The standard solution requires major configuration or integration of different modules

4 *Tailored development.* In a **tailored development**, an off-the-shelf system or hosted solution is tailored to an organization's needs. This form of project is often based on integrating components from one or several vendors.

Building systems from scratch is still surprisingly common. The Standish Group (2001) survey showed the following breakdown amongst participants in relatively small projects of less than six months and involving around six people:

- developed from scratch using traditional languages and methods (33 per cent);
- purchased application and modified (15 per cent);
- developed from scratch using an object model (13 per cent);
- developed some components and purchased others (13 per cent);
- purchased application and modified extensively (12 per cent);
- purchased components and assembled the application (9 per cent);
- purchased application and performed no modifications (5 per cent).

This survey shows that for enterprise applications, in most cases some development is still common, although mixed approaches where a packaged application or components are purchased are widespread. The survey was completed before hosted applications became important.

The implications of choosing standard or packaged software are more far-reaching than at first appears, since selection of standard software for operational purposes often implies that a company must adapt its practices and processes to match the software. With increasing amounts of tailoring it becomes possible to tailor the software to match the processes.

For each of these build methods there is an option of choice of developer of the system that undertakes programming or configuration. Possible developers include:

- an internal development team that is part of an IT department;
- an internal group of end-users for small-scale systems;
- an external **systems integrator** – effectively the development work and/or the project management is outsourced.

Activity 7.1 reviews the best option for system build according to the type of project involved.

Systems integrator
A specialist company which manages IS projects requiring a range of different software modules and data migration from legacy systems

---

Activity 7.1	**Choices in systems build**

Purpose

To illustrate the management decisions required at project initiation for the type of solution and the developer of the solution. It is intended to reinforce learning from Chapter 2 where the different approaches to obtaining software applications were introduced.

Activity

Referring to the cells in Table 7.2, select the most appropriate combination of build method and type of developer for the following types of information management system in the Lo-cost Airline Company:

1 Operational application for managing staff rosters (which staff will be used on which route?).
2 Operational enterprise resource planning application integrating ticket sales with the accounting systems and procurement.
3 Spreadsheet-based information management application for assessing the effectiveness of marketing campaigns in maximizing capacity utilization (number of seats sold).
4 Infrastructure development involving migrating all staff at head office to a Linux-based operating system and office application.
5 System to scan in-bound and out-bound e-mails for viruses and spam.
6 Company intranet for a small to medium-sized organization.

Table 7.2 Approaches to IS systems development

		In-house: IT department	In-house: end-users	External: systems integrator
Build method	Bespoke			
	Installed package from vendor or open source			
	Hosted solution			
	Tailored standard package			

You should justify your choice for each type of system explaining the advantages and disadvantages of the type of system chosen.

Debate 7.1

A totally bespoke approach to procuring software applications is never required due to options for tailoring and integrating standard packages.

Traditionally, discussion of approaches to information systems development has tended to concentrate on development of operational applications using a bespoke development approach. In this chapter we recognize that there are a range of different types of IS projects and a range of development approaches. Common features of the range of project types are described together with issues specific to some types of projects and development methods. A typical example of a major modern IS development project is illustrated in Mini case study 7.2 'Alstom replaces legacy systems with enterprise resource planning system'.

Mini case study 7.2   Alstom replaces legacy systems with enterprise resource planning system

Alstom provides systems for supporting energy and transport. This project was to support the UK gas turbine part of Alstom's business. The project involved the introduction of a new enterprise resource planning (ERP) system to replace 15 critical legacy systems and many peripheral applications and connect satellite offices across the globe into a single, integrated system. The project was instigated following an IT strategy review in 2001, where it was realised that a major project was needed to provide a single integrated system based on SAP R/3. In the words of Project Director Lee Cridland: 'we realised that our vision of creating a single, integrated system was simply not feasible with our legacy infrastructure. The SAP solution is not only easier to run and manage, but has also improved our ability to collaborate with our employees and external partners on a global scale'.

The first phase of the project, completed in 2003, migrated the company's old logistics and finance systems to SAP R/3. The previous legacy systems

were a 12 year old OMAC 2000 manufacturing system and Oracle Financials. The first phase involved connecting 750 users at its Lincoln head office, as well as providing access to a limited number of international sites. The next two phases, which were implemented through 2003 and 2004, involved replacing the remaining legacy systems for pre-point of order and post-point despatch processes, including its customer service module, and extending the ERP system to a further 1000 users. Lastly, the system was rolled out to about 20 global locations.

According to Cridland, the project was financially justified on reduced IT support costs alone and Alstom expects to make a 200 per cent return on investment over the seven to ten year life of the system.

Alstom employed NovaSoft, an IT services company or 'systems integrator' to implement the project.

Source: Turbine company sets its SAP R/3 project rolling, James Watson, *IT Week*, 13 February 2003. www.itweek.co.uk/News/1138744

The project management process

Regardless of the type of project, project managers use a standard approach to plan and control projects. The project management process involves five main stages, which involve answering these questions:

1 *Estimation.* What work is involved? Estimation involves identifying what activities are involved in the project, sometimes referred to as a work breakdown structure (WBS).

2 *Resource allocation.* Who will complete the work? After the initial WBS, appropriate people resources are allocated to the tasks. Some of the issues with building up the right skills mix for a project are shown in Research insight 7.1 'Balanced resourcing for IS projects'.

3 *Schedule/plan.* When will the work be completed? Following resource allocation, the amount of time for each task can be determined according to the availability and skills of the people assigned to the tasks. There are two different concepts. **Effort time** is the total amount of work that needs to occur to complete a task. **Elapsed time** indicates how long in time (such as calendar days) the task will take and is dependent on the number of people working on the task, and their skills. Scheduling also involves identifying **milestones**, which mark the end of significant stages in the project such as agreeing the requirements specification or sign-off of the complete project. Milestones usually have clearly defined **deliverables** associated with them which are assessed for suitability.

4 *Budgeting.* What is the project cost? Once estimation, resource allocation and budgeting have been completed, a budget or costing can be drawn up for the project. This will identify the costs of people resources and hardware and software requirements. The costs involved are discussed in more detail in the section on initiation.

5 *Monitoring and control.* How is the project progressing? Monitoring involves assessing whether the project is going to plan once it has started. Control is taking corrective action as the project deviates from the plan. In particular, the project manager or project control team will want to hit milestones and review the deliverables to check whether they meet requirements.

Effort time
Total amount of work to complete a task, usually expressed in days

Elapsed time
Length of time, or duration, required to complete task

Milestone
A control point in the project marking the completion of a major project phase

Deliverable
An outcome from a phase of the project such as a specification or a version of the software

---

Research insight 7.1	Balanced resourcing for IS projects

IT Week (2003b) reported on a survey of IT directors by London's Brunel University Fluid Business Team which found that only one in five project teams was assembled with staff who had the most relevant skills. Instead, the research suggested, firms were resourcing projects with staff who simply happened to be available or those who were cheapest to employ.

But failure to ensure staff have the right skills increases the risk that projects will be unsuccessful, said Professor Rob Macredie, head of Brunel University's Department of Information Systems and Computing, who gave this example:

A firm might be looking for someone with Java skills for a software development project for example, but not everyone with Java skills would work well on that team. Finding the right mix of people has its cost, but it's worthwhile.

He suggests that as part of the project closedown review (see later in this chapter), the question of whether the skills mix for the project was right should be assessed. He also pointed out that simply hiring contractors for a project for short-term cost or resource gains does not help develop in-company skills. He suggests that someone from the company must be on the team and that skills transfer should be one of the project objectives.

Planning tools to support the project management process

Many managers use software tools to support project management by reviewing project status against the five stages above, such as schedule and budget. Microsoft Project is now the de facto standard for project management: 70 per cent of respondents to the KPMG (2002) survey used Microsoft Project, with 34 per cent using web-based tools which support collaboration better. Such tools are designed to assist with the five stages of the project management process identified above. Different project views are used for different stages to help visualize the tasks, resources and plans.

The most widely used view for creating and reviewing projects is the Gantt chart. The chart is named after Henry Gantt (1861–1919) who developed the concept while working on projects for the construction of US Navy ships during the First World War. Simply put, the Gantt chart is a horizontal bar chart or timeline showing the relationship of different tasks in a project through time, as shown in Figure 7.4. Sub-tasks such as those making up a requirements-gathering phase can be 'nested' or 'rolled up' to summarize the main high-level tasks in the project such as analysis and design.

To view the dependency between tasks, the network diagram is commonly used. This clearly shows the sequence between activities and the order in which they need to happen (Figure 7.5). For example, 'evaluate requirements' must occur before 'specification'. The characteristics of each activity are also summarized, including start date, finish date, effort time and resources. This view is important since it highlights the critical path on a project. The critical path is a sequence of activities on the project which if delayed will cause the whole project to slip. Managers monitor and control activities on the critical path closely since they affect the success of the whole project. Managers commonly talk about activities or tasks being 'on the critical path'. In Figure 7.5, the activity 'Define user requirements' is on the critical path. Any delay to this and the whole project will be delayed since it requires more effort than the corresponding tasks.

Other views list resources (Figure 7.6) and summarize the budget.

The different project visualization tools are applied as follows to the different elements of the project management process:

Project views
Alternative methods of visualizing the project tasks, resources and plans

Gantt chart
A bar chart with project activities and milestones listed down the left-hand side and dates shown across the top, and activity duration shown as horizontal bars

Network diagram
A graphic showing different project activities and the dependencies between them

Critical path
A sequence of activities which, if delayed, will delay the whole project

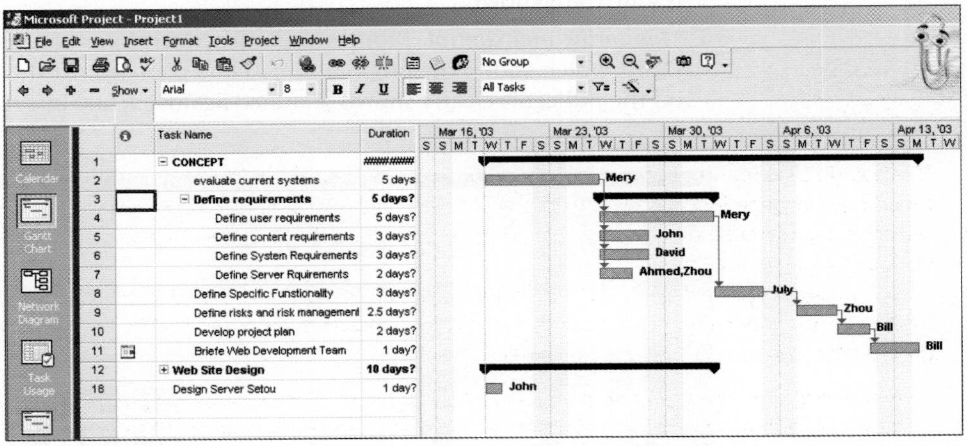

Figure 7.4 A Gantt chart from Microsoft® Project showing the task breakdown for a simple project

Source: Reprinted by permission from Microsoft Corporation

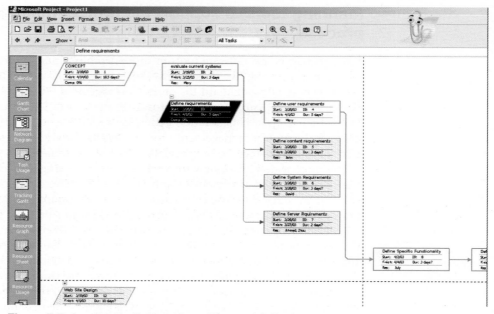

Figure 7.5 A network diagram from Microsoft® Project
Source: Reprinted by permission from Microsoft Corporation

1 *Estimation.* The Gantt view is used to type in the different tasks and estimates of how long different activities will take.

2 *Resource allocation.* Resources can also be allocated to activities using the Gantt view, but the resources are created first showing the cost and availability in the resource view (Figure 7.6).

3 *Schedule/plan.* Scheduling the sequence of tasks and their dependencies can be performed either in the Gantt chart view or in the network diagram view.

4 *Budgeting.* Budgeting for the human resources of a project effectively occurs automatically using project management software since the hourly rates of each resource are known.

5 *Monitoring and control.* Monitoring and control are conducted using a tracking Gantt which shows the original or baseline plan against the actual status. Slippage on the project is clearly shown. Planned against actual budgets can also be viewed.

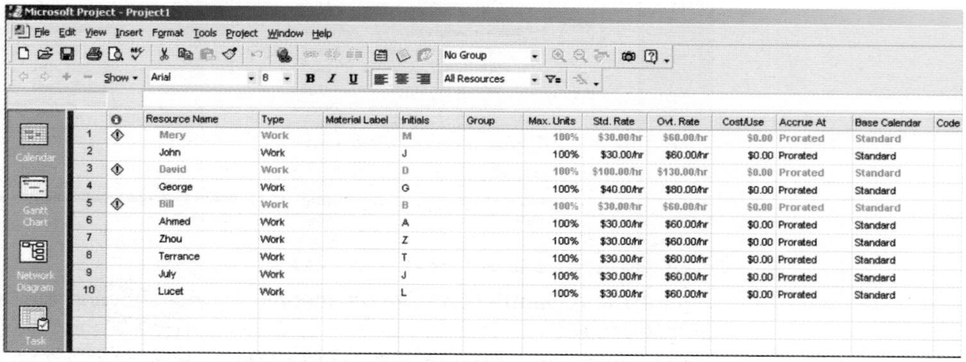

		O	Resource Name	Type	Material Label	Initials	Group	Max. Units	Std. Rate	Ovt. Rate	Cost/Use	Accrue At	Base Calendar	Code
	1	◈	Mery	Work		M		100%	$30.00/hr	$60.00/hr	$0.00	Prorated	Standard	
	2		John	Work		J		100%	$30.00/hr	$60.00/hr	$0.00	Prorated	Standard	
	3	◈	David	Work		D		100%	$100.00/hr	$130.00/hr	$0.00	Prorated	Standard	
	4		George	Work		G		100%	$40.00/hr	$80.00/hr	$0.00	Prorated	Standard	
	5	◈	Bill	Work		B		100%	$30.00/hr	$60.00/hr	$0.00	Prorated	Standard	
	6		Ahmed	Work		A		100%	$30.00/hr	$60.00/hr	$0.00	Prorated	Standard	
	7		Zhou	Work		Z		100%	$30.00/hr	$60.00/hr	$0.00	Prorated	Standard	
	8		Terrance	Work		T		100%	$30.00/hr	$60.00/hr	$0.00	Prorated	Standard	
	9		July	Work		J		100%	$30.00/hr	$60.00/hr	$0.00	Prorated	Standard	
	10		Lucet	Work		L		100%	$30.00/hr	$60.00/hr	$0.00	Prorated	Standard	

Figure 7.6 Resource view from Microsoft® Project
Source: Reprinted by permission from Microsoft Corporation

Methodologies to support the project management process

Project management methodologies
Guidelines defining a standard process for the project management process

Project management methodologies are guidelines defining a standard approach to the five main elements of the project management process. A range of established methodologies are available, which tend to vary in popularity in different countries. In the UK, PRINCE2 is an established methodology used on many public service projects. Elsewhere in Europe, standard methods include Euromethod. It will be evident from the summary in this section that there is a range of methodologies, with different strengths and weaknesses. They also have fundamental differences in the emphasis of approach. Some focus on the analysis and design techniques, others are more technology focused, others are centred on users' needs, others are focused on risk-reduction of the project management process, and others focus more on addressing change management. A KPMG (2002) survey showed that although several methodologies exist, the majority of companies still used home-grown methodologies (81 per cent) or a range of other methodologies (15 per cent). This reflects the different focuses and strengths and weaknesses of the different approaches. A further reason for the use of in-house approaches is that project management methodologies such as PRINCE2 are proscriptive and can actually add to the overhead of running a project. Also, they may not fit in with the structure and culture of many organizations.

The PRINCE2 methodology

PRINCE2 is a process-based approach for project management, sponsored by the UK Office of Government Commerce, developed from its earlier incarnation to incorporate many of the success factors for project management described in this chapter. Each PRINCE2 process has defined inputs and outputs and activities to be carried out to achieve its objectives. The PRINCE2 methodology has these characteristics, which are shared by many project management methodologies:

- Project divided into manageable stages enabling regular progress monitoring.
- Responsibilities and roles within the project clearly defined. These can be adjusted to suit the size and complexity of the project.
- Project planning is product-based, which means that the project plans are focused on delivering results, not simply planning activities.
- The project is driven by the business case which describes the organization's justification and commitment for the deliverable. This business case is regularly reviewed during the project to allow for changes in the business case during the lifecycle of the project.
- The methodology encourages the involvement of management and stakeholders as appropriate during the project, enabling good communication between the project team and the rest of the organization.

Figure 7.7 illustrates some of the main processes within a PRINCE2 project. It can be seen that the main processes control the start (start-up and initiation), middle (directing a project, control and managing stage boundaries) and end (closing a project through reviewing learnings for the future). The relationship with other projects and corporate controls is also shown.

Project tolerance
A project control mechanism used to escalate an issue to management attention when the actual project deviates from planned by a pre-agreed amount

PRINCE2 incorporates the concept of **project tolerance** for control and monitoring of projects. Tolerances can be set up to build control into a project while also giving some degree of flexibility. For example, a project or phase of a project may be given a tolerance of ±5 per cent on project cost or time. When the tolerance is exceeded the project manager needs to report back to the managing team to discuss approaches to overcome deviation from the original project parameters. PRINCE2 actually incorpo-

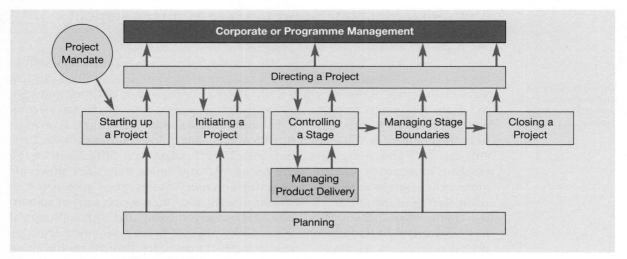

Figure 7.7 The PRINCE2 methodology process model

rates six types of project tolerance that can all be set at different levels. As well as cost and time, these include risk score, scope (number or cost of features), quality (unmet requirements and errors) and benefits (business requirements not met).

Case study 7.1 (p. 333) discusses issues with PRINCE2 implementation in a local council.

Euromethod

This is a project management method arising out of a European Community project to improve standards of project management in its constituent countries. It was developed in the mid-1990s and the specification is available at: **http://projekte.fast.de/Euromethod/.** The approach has not been as widely adopted as other methodologies and is now marketed under the Information Services Procurement Library. The new name highlights the strengths of this methodology – it focuses on issues involved with procuring IS services from third parties.

British standard 6079

BS 6079 has been published to provide guidance on all types of project. It describes a range of project management procedures, techniques and tools and gives general guidance on the planning and execution of projects. It has not been widely used for IS project management, but is widely used in other projects such as in the construction industry.

The Dynamic Systems Development Method (DSDM)

This is a project management methodology specifically developed to support a prototyping approach to information systems development. It is described in a later section once the concept of prototyping has been introduced. It has been widely adopted in Europe.

COBIT IT governance framework

The COBIT IT governance model for Control Objectives for Information and related Technology is a broad framework to assist in effective management of IT. It includes project management as one of the key processes for effective IT governance and is useful at a high level since it specifies key IS project management activities such as risk management, test plans and training plans (see COBIT, 2000). Companies that have adopted COBIT, such as Ernst and Young and Philips Electronics, are audited to verify that their IS projects contain these elements.

Systems analysis and design methodologies

Soft systems methodology (SSM)
A systems analysis methodology that determines requirements needed from a system and identifies changes to the organization and processes needed

In addition to the specific project management methodologies outlined above, there are also other methodologies concerned with the details of analysing the user and business needs of systems and creating systems design. These are systems analysis and design methodologies. For example, soft systems methodology (SSM) emphasizes the human involvement in systems and models their behaviour as part of systems analysis in a way that is understandable by non-technical experts. This technique is particularly useful for identifying requirements from a system and also anticipating reactions to change. Its premise is that it is difficult to specifically define the needs of the users and business since there are many political, cultural and interpersonal interactions within a business that may not be recognized by methodologies which take a strict process review of business. As such it is a useful approach that complements analysis and design within any systems development process. SSM originates from Peter Checkland's (1981) work to adapt systems theory into a methodology which can be applied to organizational problem situations. We outline the main stages of SSM below since although this is not a project management methodology, it has been influential in determining approaches to systems development over the past 29 years.

SSM is divided into seven distinct stages. These are:

1 *Determining the problem situation.* Research into the problem area, such as how does the current process work, what is its purpose, who are the key players?

2 *Defining the problem situation through Rich Pictures.* A visual technique used to help understanding of the problem by non-technical staff.

3 *Defining the problem situation through root definitions.* This considers the problem from a range of perspectives. Considering these helps to understand and define the problem and also highlights some of the change management issues referred to in the next chapter. Checkland describes a root definition as a *'concise, tightly constructed description of a human activity system which states what the system is',* i.e. it helps illustrate 'what' the system must do. Root definitions are created using the CATWOE checklist technique. CATWOE refers to:

- *Clients or customers* – the person(s) who benefit from, or are affected by, the outputs of the system and its activities that are under consideration. The root definition also expresses the purpose of the system for its customers.
- *Actors* – those who carry out the activities within the system.
- *Transformation* – the changes which take place either within or because of the system (this lies at the heart of the root definition).
- *Weltanschauung or worldview* – this refers to how the system is viewed from different individuals' viewpoints; sometimes this term is described as 'assumptions made about the system'.
- *Owner* – the person(s) to whom the system is answerable: the sponsor, controller or someone who could cause the system to cease.
- *Environment* – that which surrounds and influences the operation of the system but which has no control over it.

4 *Build conceptual models.* These are produced for each of the root definitions to start to define 'how' the new system should work. The conceptual models show the activities and processes that need to occur to meet the CATWOE elements.

5 *Comparison of the conceptual models with the real world*. This is an iterative process that compares the results from steps 4 and 2 to identify similarities and differences in order to make the conceptual model more accurate.

6 *Identify feasible and desirable changes*. The approaches needed to improve the current situation are defined.

7 Finally, *Recommendations* for taking action to improve the problem situation are defined. These suggest how the changes from step 6 will be implemented.

A further systems analysis and design technique that is widely used is the Systems Analysis and Design Method (SSADM), which is a methodology that defines the methods of analysis and design that should occur in a large-scale software development project. It is used extensively in the UK, particularly in government and public organizations.

Systems Analysis and Design Method (SSADM)
A methodology that defines the methods of analysis and design that should occur in a large-scale software development project. It is used extensively in the UK, particularly in government and public organizations

Systems Analysis and Design Method (SSADM)

Although not originally developed as a project management methodology, it can be used to help manage projects since it defines the activities that need to occur at different stages in the project. It recommends the technical approaches needed for requirements analysis, business systems options, requirements specification, logical systems specification, logical design and the physical design. It complements the approaches of PRINCE2 and DSDM, specifying the details of the analysis and design phases of the project which are referred to later in this chapter.

The European Foundation for Quality Management (EFQM)

The European Foundation for Quality Management (EFQM, **www.efqm.org**) was founded in 1988 by the CEOs of 14 major European companies (Bosch, BT, Bull, Ciba-Geigy, Dassault, Electrolux, Fiat, KLM, Nestlé, Olivetti, Philips, Renault, Sulzer, Volkswagen) with the endorsement of the European Commission. It now has 800 member organizations. The EFQM Excellence model is not a project management methodology, but rather it defines systems for organizational improvement. It emphasizes the importance of defined, repeatable processes which manage risks and are results-oriented – the project management process is one such process.

Organizing to support the project management process

Project management office (PMO)
A function in larger organizations for coordinating projects

Larger organizations are increasingly turning to a programme office or project management office (PMO). These are established to standardize project practices and learn from past projects with the aim of producing consistent, repeatable results. They can also have an active project management role and indeed are now seen to be more effective than the traditional approach of an executive committee. One reason for this is that responsibilities are clearer. Project managers within the PMO are directly responsible for projects and the KPMG (2002) survey reported that 58 per cent of mature PMOs reported direct to the CEO compared to only 30 per cent in immature PMOs. The respondents to the survey also felt that the executive committee approach was least effective in preventing failed projects.

Respondents to the KPMG (2002) survey believed that the most important functions of the PMO are:

● tracking and reporting (of the performance of different projects);
● coordination (of resources used by different projects);
● standards (for the elements of the project management process described above);
● governance (or management);

- risk management (encouraging the use of this approach);
- portfolio management (selecting projects from candidate projects);
- business requirements planning (planning for future projects to support business objectives).

Case study 7.1

Reading Council implements the PRINCE2 project management methodology

This case discusses the implications of the introduction of a new project management method for an organization. Although it is based on local government, the issues are common to any organization as they introduce new methods of managing systems and services. It highlights many of the issues with managing change that are discussed in more detail in the next chapter.

In 2002 the Reading Borough Council based in South-East England was working to comply with the e-Government agenda. This initiative from Central Government required local Councils to provide for all customer-facing processes to be electronically enabled by 2005 unless there was a legal or operational reason not to do so. This was a massive cross-cutting programme of work seeking to 'join up' services at local, regional, national, and European level. It was designed to drive through changes to deliver more efficient, cost-effective customer-facing transactions, and by so doing reduce the costs of bureaucracy and release funds for direct service delivery.

In such a rapidly changing local government environment, driven by the need to provide cost-effective quality services under a 'Best Value' regime, John Barnfield, IT Programme and Service Delivery Manager, believed that, based on Reading Borough Council's experience, it was essential to have a framework of coordinated control at programme and project level to successfully deliver business change. Otherwise too much will be left to chance.

It was this background of continuing change which promoted the gradual move towards the acceptance of using both PRINCE2 and MSP within the Council. John Barnfield observed that 'we did not put everything in place that was needed nor did we slavishly follow the processes all the time. Introducing PRINCE2 and MSP is about fundamental culture and business change within the organisation and this simply doesn't happen quickly'.

Below, in John Barnfield's own words are some of the lessons learned by Reading Borough Council on how to introduce PRINCE2 and MSP into an organisation.

'Corporate Managers will be cautious of any proposed corporate-wide change and will need to be convinced before committing resources. Nothing is going to change without their agreement and support. It is therefore essential that this is addressed. Corporate Management presentations and briefings are an essential part of gaining

their support. You may even find that people's perceptions of PRINCE2 and MSP are factually wrong and will need to be corrected before you gain their support for the change, but you will not be aware of who these people are! Our experiences highlighted that some early doubters became accepted users of the methodologies once misunderstandings and early fears were identified and corrected.

Lengthy, detailed presentations about the methodologies are inappropriate at senior level. Concentrate on the benefits for them and how they will be directly affected. Suggest a 'pilot' project or programme of their choice to test the methodologies in use. MSP does fit very well alongside existing Corporate Management, and actually can help manage workloads at this level.

Securing agreement to run pilots is a way of convincing any remaining 'doubters' and has the advantage of working through the practical issues. By doing this you are proving suitability in your own working environment and providing an example set of working project and programme documentation for others.

Gaining senior level support gives the corporate 'stamp' to the change. Have in mind a clear plan of how you want things to proceed before any presentations, and set realistic timescales. Have answers to the following questions:

- What is PRINCE2 and MSP and why do we need them?
- Do they need to be introduced together?
- What will be the benefits and when will they be realised?
- What's wrong with what we do now?
- Who else uses it and what type of projects and programmes do they run?
- What other Local Government sites use PRINCE2 and MSP?
- Is PRINCE2 suitable for all types of project?
- Is MSP suitable for all types of programmes?
- What impact will it have on me as a Director/ Manager?

- What will it cost and how long will it take?
- What do you expect from us?
- How will the Organisation need to change?

Once the necessary commitment has been obtained to introduce the methodology, it is wise to consider the implementation itself as a staged project, perhaps introducing the methodology on new projects only.

Use every opportunity available to sell the benefits: e.g. Newsletters, Intranet, Standards, Corporate & Directorate presentations etc. Seek to use communication channels appropriate to the staff you are trying to get the message to. If everyone bins the corporate newsletter you won't do much good promoting through that mechanism.

Recognise you may need to change opinions within your organisation (asking what else they are going to use if PRINCE2 and MSP is not used is a useful question).

You need 'Champions' prepared to drive the implementation forward, preferably not all from I.T. Tenacity and enthusiasm are two important qualities. Identify who is successful in business change and bring them onboard. Every organisation has them, and they are usually easy to spot since major changes involve the same names time and time again.

Remember change frightens people and they need to understand what you are doing, why you are doing it and how it affects them.

Follow the 'dripping tap' principle – keep feeding the organisation and before you realise it the new processes start to become part of the culture.

Be realistic in your expectations. Change like this does not happen overnight however well you promote it. Culture change can take 3–5 years.

Remember the process can be wonderful and still deliver a project or programme which 'fails'. Set expectations to recognise that success is in avoiding the waste of resources and in the delivery of projects and programmes to time, cost and quality.

Do not expect everyone to have the same enthusiasm for the approach. Recognise many people will initially see this as another demand on their already heavy workload. Again you need to sell the long-term benefits of a standard way of working, and their individual roles within the process.

People will have already run successful projects, but not in this way. Show them it need not conflict with their existing processes, and offers one overall approach which can be understood by all.'

Source: www.ogc.gov.uk/prince/downloads/templatercase.htm

Questions

1 What were the background and the benefits to Reading Borough Council of implementing a structured project management methodology such as PRINCE2?

2 What are the main barriers to introducing a project management methodology such as PRINCE2 into an organization?

3 Evaluate the article identifying success factors for:
   (a) Moving to a project management methodology such as PRINCE2.
   (b) Any systems development management project.

The systems development process

Regardless of the type of information management system being implemented, common activities need to occur at the beginning, middle and end of each project. Dividing each information systems development project into parts naturally follows from completing the work breakdown structure during estimation. For information systems development there is a well-established series of stages in completing a project. If project managers or organizations can develop a consistent, repeatable approach to completing each stage, then this will help increase the likelihood of successful project completion.

The purpose and characteristics of each stage of the systems development process are summarized in Table 7.3. Throughout the project controls are built in at the end of each stage to assess the progress of the project and to decide whether to proceed. We will see that the development stages don't all follow sequentially. For example, it is more efficient to do some initial design work during the analysis phase.

We will consider the work involved at each stage and the success factors in the final part of this chapter.

Table 7.3 Summary of the typical phases in a systems development project

Development stage	Purpose	Inputs	Process	Output
1 Initiation *Why and how is the system to be developed?*	Start-up phase	Business case for the system	Assess feasibility Project planning	Feasibility analysis Project plan Decision to proceed
2 Analysis *What should the system do?*	Define requirements of the organization and system users	Business case and the requirements from users	Determine requirements from users and documentation	Requirements document Test plan Decision to proceed
3 Design *How will the system deliver requirements?*	Specify how the system will be configured	Requirements document	Evaluation of design options for creation and integration of system components	Design document of information architecture, software process and systems architecture Decision to proceed
4 Development *Programming and configuring the system*	Implement the design	Design document	Bespoke solutions: programming system Off-the-shelf or tailored systems: configuration of inputs to and outputs from the system or integration of different system components	The different physical components of the system Deployment plan Decision to proceed
5 Implementation *Installing and testing the system Changeover from old to new system*	System deployed into organization	System components Test plan	Migrating data, testing the system and managing the changeover to the live system	Live system signed off by business as satisfactorily meeting the users' and business requirements Project closedown report Decision to proceed
6 Maintenance *Monitoring and revising the system*	To keep the system running smoothly and enhance it	Signed-off system	Monitoring the system and enhancing it as bugs and opportunities arise	Upgrades or patches to system

The waterfall model of systems development

Traditionally, when information systems were developed through the 1950s to the 1970s, each of the six stages of systems development in Table 7.3 were conducted sequentially as shown in Figure 7.8. Some overlap between stages did naturally occur, however. For example, during initiation, some preliminary analysis and design may occur. It is also inevitable that, during the project, previous stages will be revisited, as shown by the reverse arrows in Figure 7.8. The most common problem is that testing will identify errors and new requirements which mean that analysis, design and development will need to be repeated for some modules of the system. In the waterfall model, each stage could take months or even years to complete. Often,

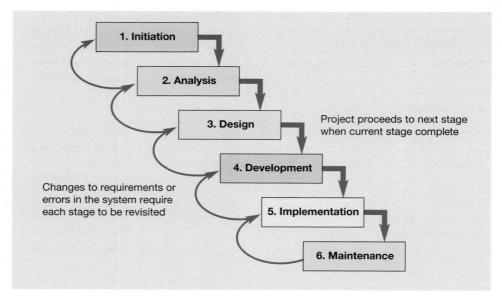

Figure 7.8 The traditional 'waterfall model' of information systems development

progression would occur from one stage to the next without a review occurring – hence the description 'waterfall model'.

Consider the problems that will arise from such an approach:

1 *Limited flexibility for changed requirements.* The waterfall concept is based around an in-depth analysis where requirements are specified in a detailed requirements specification. These requirements are then signed off. But, each stage after analysis is likely to identify different new requirements. Furthermore, the situation the business is in may change. It is difficult to implement these changed requirements since capacity for change is not built in. As a consequence, projects developed a sequential stage approach which was not likely to meet the business requirements well.

2 *Disconnect between development team and users in the business.* The main involvement of the business users is at the analysis and implementation stage. In between, the developers and users are virtually isolated for months or years until the development team effectively throws the system over the fence to the users and says 'test this'. Discussion of requirements for clarification tends not to occur, and suggestions for improvements by the development team cannot be incorporated.

3 *Protracted development times.* The lack of interaction between the business and the developers removes the sense of urgency from the project. Worse still, when the system was evaluated by the users at the implementation stage, major problems would often be identified, which meant that the project had, in effect, to go back to the start and repeat the stages.

Prototyping
An iterative process in which website users suggest modifications before further prototypes and the live version of the site are developed

RAD (Rapid Application Development)
An approach to information systems development that includes incremental development using prototypes

Prototyping

Prototyping is a common approach to developing information systems which is used to counter the problems of the waterfall model. The essence of prototyping is that it is:

● *Rapid* – Prototyping is part of a systems development approach known as **RAD (Rapid Application Development)** since the time from inception to completion is reduced to months rather than years. More rapid development is achieved through reducing the length of time of the analysis, design and build stages by combining them, in conjunction with the use of graphical software tools with which applications can be built quickly from pre-assembled components.

Prototype
A preliminary version of part or all of an information system reviewed by its users and business sponsors

- *Simple* – Skeleton applications are produced as **prototypes** that do not contain all the functions of a system but are a framework which gives a good indication to users of the information available and the look and feel of an application. They can then comment on it and say, for example, 'this information is missing' or 'we like that feature, but it would be nice to do that also' or 'that feature isn't necessary, it's not what we meant'. The prototype may initially be storyboarded as a 'paper prototype' but is usually produced as a series of screens that can be interacted with, but are not connected to a database.

- *Iterative* – Prototypes are produced often at a frequency of once every few days or weeks so that the comments from the last review can be fed into the evolving system.

- *Incremental* – Each prototype incorporates the feedback from the previous review, so each version of the application has a limited number of new features.

- *User-centred* – Users are involved at all stages of development, in describing the existing system, reviewing the prototypes and testing the system.

The stages involved with prototyping are first to identify the user requirements in outline and then rapidly develop a working prototype which the users operate to check that the software proposed is in line with their needs. Once the first prototype has been produced, there are several alternatives:

- Iterate and produce further refinements, which often occurs throughout the specification stage – when a satisfactory version has been produced other alternatives may follow.

- Develop module prototypes – prototype key views of the data from a workflow system or Lotus Notes or important data entry dialogues.

- Throw away the prototype and develop a more robust version of the software for the production version. This is often prudent, since in rapid prototyping some corners have to be cut so it may not be optimized for performance or may not have exception-handling features.

A frequent general problem with prototyping is to do 'demonstration prototyping' rather than 'hands-on' prototyping. Often prototypes are merely shown by developers to clients for general feedback and not used 'hands-on' until after several iterations of the prototype when many more features are integrated. This causes delays because problems that could have been trapped earlier will only become apparent at a late stage.

The prototyping approach is now ubiquitous since it reduces the risk of major design, functional or informational errors during the construction of the application that may be costly and time-consuming to fix at a later stage in development. Such errors should be identified early on and then corrected. The iterative approach is intended to be rapid and a site can be produced in a period of months or weeks.

Prototyping includes all the key stages in system development as shown in Figure 7.9. Repeated iterations of the analysis, design, develop, test and review stages occur during prototyping.

So, the approach to prototyping should be considered carefully. Preece et al. (2002) identify three different types of prototyping:

- *Throwaway or low-fidelity prototyping.* This is self-explanatory; the prototype is not kept as the basis for the final system. Storyboarding or use of visual tools such as Visual Basic or Macromedia Director would fall into these categories.

- *Evolutionary prototyping or high-fidelity prototyping.* Here the prototype is not discarded, but acts as the basis for the next iteration of the system.

- *Incremental prototyping.* This can be combined with evolutionary prototyping. It is where modules of the system are prototyped until each is complete, until eventually the whole system becomes complete through integration of different prototypes.

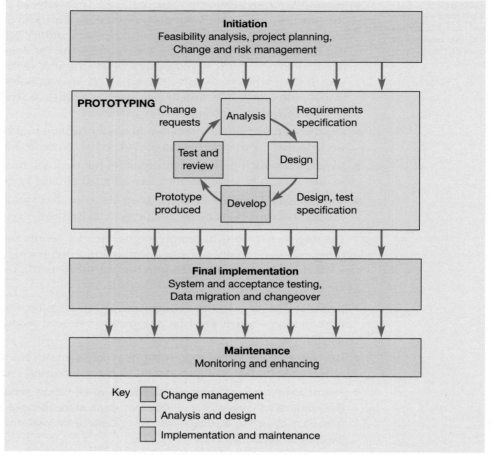

Figure 7.9 The role of prototyping within an information systems development project
Source: Chaffey (2004)

Agile software development

Agile development
An iterative approach to developing software and website functionality with the emphasis on face-to-face communications to elicit, define and test requirements. Each iteration is effectively a mini-software project including stages of planning, requirements analysis, design, coding, testing, and documentation

Scrum
Scrum is a methodology that supports agile software development based on 15–30-day sprints to implement features from a product backlog. 'Scrum' refers to a daily project status meeting during the sprint

Today, the concept of prototyping has been extended across the whole lifecycle for developing website functionality or software applications where it is known as **agile software development**. The goal of agile development is to be able to create stable releases more frequently than traditional development methodologies, i.e. new functionality will be introduced through several releases each month rather than a more significant release every few weeks, months or even years. The approach is sometimes known as 'permanent beta'. Another difference with agile development is the emphasis on face-to-face communication to define requirements rather than detailed requirements specifications.

Scrum is a methodology that supports agile software development. Scrum involves stakeholders including the *Scrum Master* who is effectively a project manager, the *Product Owner* who represents the stakeholders such as the business owners and customers and the *Scrum Team* which includes the developers.

Scrum is based on focused sprints of a 15-30-day period where the team creates an increment of potentiallly releasable software. Potential functionality for each sprint is agreed at a *sprint planning meeting* from the *product backlog*, a prioritized set of high-level requirements. The sprint planning meeting is itself iterative, with the Product Owner stating their requirements from the product backlog and the technical team then determining how much of this they can commit to completing during the forthcoming sprint. The term 'scrum' refers to a daily project status meeting during the sprint. See **www.softhouse.se/uploades/scrum_eng_webb.pdf** for an overview of the process.

The principles of agile development are encapsulated in the *Agile Manifesto* (**http://agilemanifesto.org/**) which was agreed in 2001 by proponents of previous rapid development methodologies, including the Dynamic Systems Development Methodology and Extreme Programming. The Agile Manifesto is useful in illustrating the principles of agile programming which it contrasts with traditional approaches. The text of the manifesto is:

> We are uncovering better ways of developing software by doing it and helping others do it.
>
> Through this work we have come to value:
>
> - Individuals and interactions over processes and tools
> - Working software over comprehensive documentation
> - Customer collaboration over contract negotiation
> - Responding to change over following a plan

The Dynamic Systems Development Method (DSDM)

Prototyping and RAD are not system development or project management methodologies; instead they describe an approach to information systems development. To provide a structured, consistent approach to prototyping and RAD, the Dynamic Systems Development Method (DSDM) consortium was formed by vendors and practitioners in 1994 to define a more structured and repeatable approach to RAD based on the principles summarized in Table 7.4. The consortium states (**www.dsdm.org**):

> A fundamental assumption of the DSDM approach is that nothing is built perfectly first time, but that 80% of the solution can be produced in 20% of the time that it would take to produce the total solution. A basic problem with less agile approaches is the expectation that potential system users can predict what all their requirements will be at some distant point in time. This problem is compounded by the fact that the mere existence of a new system affects the users' requirements because the methods of working have changed.

DSDM has proved a popular approach and is used by large businesses (Prudential financial services, Safeways supermarket, British Airways), system integrators (IBM, Perot Systems, Electronic Data Systems (EDS)) and government agencies. It is estimated that 20,000 systems developers have been trained in RAD.

The DSDM systems development framework

The DSDM consortium describe their approach to systems development as a framework rather than a method. This framework is based around the main project activities shown in Figure 7.10. In total there are five main activities in a DSDM project:

1 *Pre-project*. Ensures that only realistic projects start and that they are planned correctly. The feasibility study typically lasts no longer than a few weeks since later stages are more effective at defining detailed requirements. A separate business study reviews the impact of the new system on relevant business processes and their information needs.

   Outputs: Feasibility study, business study

2 *Functional model iteration*. The main purpose of the functional model iteration is on refining the business needs of the system, such as the process support and information requirements identified during the business study.

   Output: Functional model of new system.

3 *Design and build iteration*. System is engineered for testing by users – the major

Table 7.4 Principles of the Dynamic Systems Development Method

	Principles	Comments
I	Active user involvement is imperative	Users are active participants in the development process. If users are not closely involved throughout the development lifecycle, delays will occur and users may feel that the final solution is imposed by the developers and/or management.
II	The team must be empowered to make decisions	DSDM teams consist of both developers and users. They must be able to make decisions as requirements are refined and possibly changed. They must be able to agree that certain levels of functionality, usability, etc. are acceptable without frequent recourse to higher-level management.
III	The focus is on frequent delivery of products	A product-based approach is more flexible than an activity-based one. The work of a DSDM team is concentrated on products that can be delivered in an agreed period of time. By keeping each period of time short, the team can easily decide which activities are necessary and sufficient to achieve the right products. Note: Products include interim development products, not just delivered systems.
IV	Fitness for business purpose is the essential criterion for acceptance of deliverables	The focus of DSDM is on delivering the essential business requirements within the required time. Allowance is made for changing business needs within that timeframe.
V	Iterative and incremental development is necessary to converge on an accurate business solution	DSDM allows systems to grow incrementally. Therefore the developers can make full use of feedback from the users. Moreover, partial solutions can be delivered to satisfy immediate business needs. Rework is built into the DSDM process; thus, the development can proceed more quickly during iteration.
VI	All changes during development are reversible	To control the evolution of all products, everything must be in a known state at all times. Backtracking is a feature of DSDM. However, in some circumstances it may be easier to reconstruct than to backtrack. This depends on the nature of the change and the environment in which it was made.
VII	Requirements are baselined at a high level	Baselining high-level requirements means 'freezing' and agreeing the purpose and scope of the system at a level that allows for detailed investigation of what the requirements imply. Further, more detailed baselines can be established later in the development, although the scope should not change significantly.
VIII	Testing is integrated throughout the lifecycle	Testing is not treated as a separate activity. As the system is developed incrementally, it is also tested and reviewed by both developers and users incrementally to ensure that the development is not only moving forward in the right business direction but is technically sound.
IX	Collaboration and cooperation between all stakeholders is essential	The nature of DSDM projects means that low-level requirements are not necessarily fixed when the project is begun. The short-term direction that a project takes must be quickly decided without recourse to restrictive change control procedures. The stakeholders include not only the business and development staff within the project, but also other staff such as service delivery or resource managers.

Source: DSDM (www.dsdm.org)

product is the 'tested system'. Figure 7.10 doesn't show testing as a separate activity since testing is happening throughout both the functional model iteration and the design and build iteration.

Output: Tested system.

Both the functional model iteration and the design and build iteration consist of cycles of four activities:

(i)   Identify what is to be produced (analysis).
(ii) Agree how and when to do it (design and project control).
(iii) Create the product (development).
(iv) Check that it has been produced correctly (review through reviewing documents or a prototype or testing part of the system).

Most development work occurs in the two iteration phases where prototypes are incrementally built towards the tested system. Note that all prototypes in DSDM use the incremental/evolutionary prototyping approach described in the previous section. All prototypes are intended to evolve into the final system and are built to be robust enough for operational use and to satisfy any relevant non-functional requirements, such as performance.

4   *Implementation.* The implementation phase covers the cutover (transition) from the development and test environment to the operational environment. This includes training the users who have not been part of the project team. This phase may involve iterations where the system is being rolled out to users at different organizational locations over a period of time. An increment review document is produced to review the success of the project.

Outputs: Delivered system, increment review document.

5   *Post-project.* Intended to keep the delivered solution operating effectively. Uses a

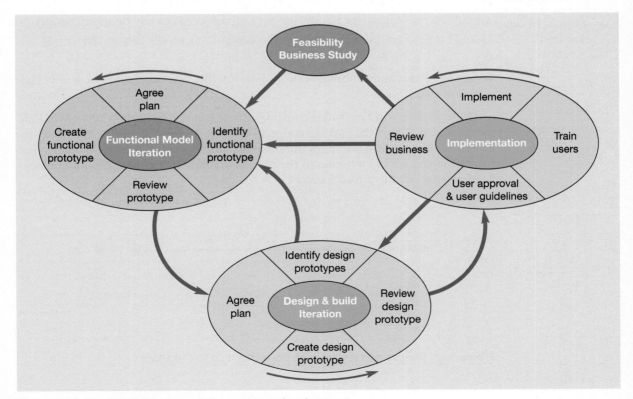

Figure 7.10 The DSDM framework for systems development
Source: DSDM

similar iterative and incremental approach to the initial development. Non-urgent fixes and enhancements may be batched up and implemented using DSDM techniques. Each new release involves a pass through each of the four stages above, starting with the feasibility and business study.

Timeboxing

The **timebox** is a key concept within DSDM. These are designed to build in flexibility in handling requirements. There is an overall timebox for each project, with shorter timeboxes of two to six weeks nested within the overall timescale.

The DSDM recommends that each timebox will typically pass through three phases, as shown in Figure 7.11. These are:

1 *Investigation* – a quick pass to see whether the team is taking the right direction.

2 *Refinement* – to build on the comments resulting from the review at the end of investigation.

3 *Consolidation* – the final part of the timebox to tie up any loose ends.

Within DSDM, the nested timeboxes are the focus for monitoring and control activities. Prioritization of the importance of different tasks is the key to this approach. Each timebox has an immovable end date and a prioritized set of requirements assigned to it which are updated and reviewed as prototyping progresses. Since timeboxes are fixed, the deliverables from the timebox are variable according to the amount of time left. Essential work required to produce the deliverables must be done, but less critical work can be omitted or deferred. Prioritization is done by applying the MoSCoW rules for assessing the importance of an activity or requirement:

M ust haves – fundamental to the project's success (Priority 1)

o

S hould haves – important but the project's success does not rely on these (Priority 2)

C ould haves – can easily be left out without impacting on the project (Priority 3)

o

W on't have this time round – can be left out this time and done at a later date (Priority 4).

Through reviewing priorities continuously it is possible to omit less critical elements and it is this that assists teams to deliver on time. It can be seen that the MoSCoW rules are also useful for minimizing requirements creep since many requirements changes are often tweaks to the user interface or data visualization that are not fundamental not the project's success.

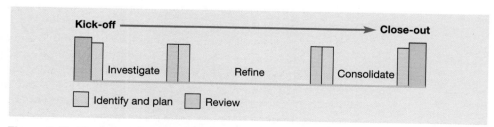

Figure 7.11 Phases and review controls within a DSDM timebox

Further systems development methodologies

Even in the early 1990s there were estimated to be in excess of one thousand variations of information systems development methodologies (Jayaratna, 1994) and this profusion of approaches has been termed 'the methodology jungle' (Avison and Fitzgerald, 1995).

Some attempts have been made to identify the most significant methodologies. Wynekoop and Russo (1997), for example, examined those that had received most attention and discussion in research journals. Yet even this approach yielded nine popular approaches and identified many others of note.

It is this surfeit of methodologies that many say has contributed to the difficulties that organizations encounter when improving their information systems. Not only is the task itself extremely complex, but even the process of choosing which methodology to adopt is a veritable minefield.

Research conducted by Gareth White and Aneka Buckley at the University of the West of England explores the use of information system development methodologies in an international bank and finds that they are rarely used effectively. Group policy suggests that a specific method is used but this is not often observed because the recommended approach does not cater for the specific requirements of the development projects, which may differ in terms of resource, scope and complexity. When specific methods are used they are also often inadequately documented. Project personnel's prior experience of systems development was also found to significantly affect their choice of and adherence to a methodology.

Other systems development methodologies that are commonly found include the following.

Structured Analysis and Structured Design (SASD)

There are a number of variants of what are often referred to generically as structured techniques (Flynn, 1992). Beynon-Davis (1993) define structured analyis as 'an attempt to separate the logical from the physical description of information systems', and structured design as 'the discipline of building hierarchical systems of modular software'.

Structured design is concerned with the selection and organization of program modules and interfaces that would solve a predefined problem; however, it makes no contribution to defining that problem. This implies that while this methodology may be beneficial, the benefits can be wasted if the initial problem was inaccurate or poorly defined, thus producing a system which does not meet real user's needs.

Jackson Systems Development (JSD)

Jackson (1983) argues that systems design is an extension of program design and that the same techniques can be usefully applied to both. JSD is an extension of Jackson Structured Programming (JSP).

JSD has a slightly different approach to other methodologies in that it attempts to solve the 'hidden path problem', which highlights the need to justify that the delivered system has met the requirements initially specified. Traditionally this is carried out in the testing phase. However, there is uncertainty about whether these tests are complete, and when testing is possible it often takes place after the system is completed and is often too late to repair any damage. Elliott and Starkings (1998) outline the three generic stages of JSD as follows:

    (1) The modelling stage
       – entity action
       – entity structure
    (2) The network stage
       – initial model
       – function
       – system timing
    (3) The implementation stage
       – physical system specification

Merise

Merise is the most widely used methodology for developing information systems in France. It is important to discuss this methodology owing to the context of the research carried out. The approach has three cycles: the decision cycle, which relates to various decision mechanisms; the lifecycle, which reflects the chronological process of a Merise project from start to finish; and the abstraction cycle, which describes the various models for process and data in each three stages. Merise's benefits include participation of end-users and senior management as well as data processing professionals in its decision cycle.

Structured Analysis, Design and Implementation of Information Systems (STRADIS)

STRADIS follows the typical phases of initial and detailed investigation followed by analysis and design that are found in most other systems development methodologies. However, it does not specifically address the implementation phase.

Yourdon Systems Model (YSM)

YSM is similar to STRADIS; however, the top-down design used in STRADIS is not always appropriate. It is for this reason that a 'middle-up' approach called event partitioning is used, whereby the analyst begins by drawing a top-level context diagram indicating system boundaries; following interviews with users, a list of events in the environment to which the system must respond is constructed. YSM follows three phases: the feasibility study, looking at the present system and its environment; constructing the essential model, which aims to describe the essence of a software system in terms of requirements and data needed; and implementation modelling, which aims to incorporate those feature found in the customer's statement of requirements.

End-user development

There are many system development approaches that take note of the requirements of the users and operators. These are generically termed end-user methodologies. Information system experts and developers tend to act like consultants to the projects, while end-users take a greater degree of control of events than they normally do in other approaches.

Research insight 7.2	**Rapid results teams**

Matta and Ashkenas (2003) describe an approach similar to DSDM, 'rapid results initiatives using rapid results teams'. They give the example of the implementation of a large-scale customer relationship management (CRM) or salesforce automation system (Chapter 2) that is intended to double sales revenue over a period of two years. With a traditional project management approach, separate teams might include those set up to (1) research and implement appropriate software packages, (2) analyse the way in which customers interact with the company in order to improve this process, (3) develop training programmes for the sales and service staff. With this approach, each of these teams might succeed in achieving its objectives, but without the assurance that the overall project will be successful. For instance, a common failing of such projects is that the method of working may be so different for sales staff that they do not use the new system all the time, or indeed at all, since they perceive it as hindering their selling activities. This is an integration risk that is not identified until it is too late.

Instead, Matta and Ashkenas (2003) suggest that a single team should be set up to achieve rapid results in a smaller-scale pilot. In this case a small number of sales staff in one region could be involved in all aspects of developing and testing the system. Similar activities to those described above would occur, but the risk with sales staff and other problems would be identified and overcome because of the smaller-scale nature of the project. Further 'rapid results initiatives' can then occur for other regions or the system can be rolled out across the company with reduced risks, using the learnings from the initial project. The authors distinguish traditional 'horizontal' activities which occur in parallel – for example, the analysis, software implementation and training – from the 'vertical' activities or pilot projects which are intended to integrate the horizontal activities.

Case study 7.2

Information systems development in the Police Force

This case study discusses the latest development of the information system used in the Command and Control Room of a Police Force in the UK. Although the new system is extremely powerful, it is plagued by fundamental operational issues. It highlights the importance of recognizing the needs of users and other operational conditions during the development of computer-based information systems.

The Command and Control Room is where crimes and disturbances are reported and all other requests for Police assistance are received. Contact is typically made in the form of 999 calls from the general public but other messages may be received in the form of e-mail, SMS text messages and radio messages from Police Officers and other public services.

There are a number of staff that work in the Command and Control Room and use the information system. Each member of staff is responsible for receiving all calls from a discrete area of the region that the Police Force covers.

Each person uses several pieces of hardware to operate the information system, shown in Figure 7.12:

Screen 1 (left) allows the operator to access multiple functions:
- Radio System
- Telephone System
- Closed Circuit Television (CCTV)
- Helicopter Cameras
- Audio Setup Function

Screen 2 (centre) also allows the operator to access multiple functions:
- Database to recorded incident details (Date, Time, Names etc.)
- Access to Intelligence Databases (known offenders, etc.)
- Staff Rotas including a list of all active Police Officers
- Access to several databases containing general Force information

Screen 3 (right) provides access to one function:
- Real-time map displaying Police Officer positions

Screens 1 and 3 are operated by touch. On Screen 1, for example, the operator touches the button labelled 'Radio' to access the radio function.

All three screens use different fonts, font sizes and colour schemes. Although each screen is clear and easy to read, some operators find it difficult to switch quickly between reading dark text on a light background to light text on a dark background.

The mouse allows operators to navigate around Screen 2 and the keyboard allows them to update the database of incident details.

The headset allows the operator to listen to incoming telephone or radio messages and to provide important information to Officers, such as directions to an incident taken from the real-time map on Screen 3.

Underneath the desk is a footpedal which allows the operator to switch the headset from send (talk) to receive (listen) while they are typing or using the touchscreens.

Quite often an operator will be using Screen 1 to view CCTV and switch radio channels, using Screen 2 to update the incident records, viewing Screen 3 and giving directions to an incident while simultaneously communicating with a Patrol Car radio message arriving in their left ear and a helicopter radio message arriving in their right ear.

The Control Room operators have identified a number of problems with the system, most of which are encountered on a daily basis:

- It is not possible to access CCTV footage while changing radio channels. Screen 1 has to be switched from the page that lists the Radio functions and the page that shows the CCTV pictures.
- When searching the intelligence databases, dates, people's names and addresses have to be entered exact. For example, searching for John will not identify anyone with the name Jon. This can add significantly to the time taken to provide vital information to Police Officers.

- Occasionally the touchscreens will 'freeze' and the system has to be switched off and rebooted in order to continue to work.
- It is not possible to alter the positions of the screens or the footpedals. This causes great difficulties for those operators that are either very short or very tall.
- The screen that is used most often is Screen 1, yet this is positioned to the left of the workstation. The majority of operators are right-handed and have to stretch to across their body to use the screen. This has resulted in some repetitive strain injuries.
- Some operators have begun to use their left hand to use Screen 1 to avoid strain and injury. Unfortunately, they are less able to press the buttons accurately with their left hand and this has slowed their pace of work. The Command and Control Room has a back-up Control Room in the event that there is a power failure. This back-up facility is located several miles away. Despite the distance between the facilities, recent modifications to the national grid by the local utilities companies have resulted in both of them now being connected to the same power supply. If a lightning strike causes power to be lost in the main Command and Control Room then power will also be lost in the back-up Control Room.

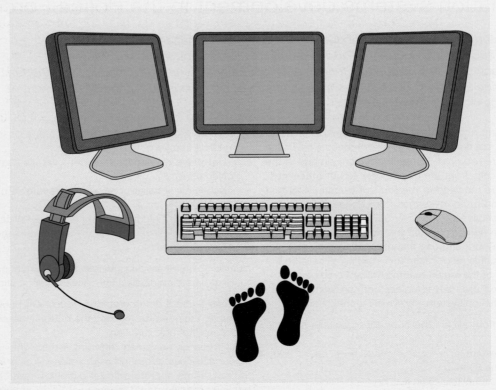

Figure 7.12 Police Force Command and Control Room

Questions

1 Which specific systems development methodology could have been adopted to ensure that many of the current problems were minimized or eliminated prior to system implementation?

2 How many of the problems are computer-related issues such as hardware or software faults?

3 How could the system have been developed so that these problems were solved before implementation?

4 How could the system be improved to make it easier for the operators to use?

Risk management

Risk management
Assessing potential reasons for failure for projects and developing strategies to reduce risks

Risk management is a valuable approach to help reduce the likelihood of project problems. It is typically used in the start-up phases of information systems development projects. Its purpose is to identify potential risks which may prevent the project from achieving its goals and then ensure that actions are taken to minimize these risks.

The risk management process involves these stages:

1 Identify risks, including their probabilities and impacts. Risks can be categorized in a matrix, as is shown in Figure 7.13.

2 Identify possible solutions to these risks.

3 Implement the solutions targeting the highest-impact, most likely risks.

4 Monitor the risks to learn for future risk assessment.

Figure 7.14 illustrates typical risks for IS projects and recommended solutions according to the UK Office of Government Commerce, while mini case study 7.3 'Dell begs ToryDems to Keep NHS IT project' illustrates risks in NHS IT projects.

In the final part of this chapter we look at specific risks that can occur for different activities or phases within the systems development lifecycle and appropriate solutions to minimize these risks.

Writing in the *Software Magazine*, the Standish Group suggested a series of success factors for an applications development project. These are summarized in Table 7.5 with each success factor ranked according to importance.

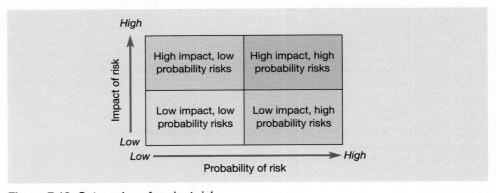

Figure 7.13 **Categories of project risk**

RISKS (failure causes)	Impact on project
Design and definition failures • Required outputs not described with sufficient clarity – no scope definition prior to authorisation • Over-ambition – sweeping into a single project all "good ideas – all deliverables in one chunk" • Project seen as an IT project, not part of wider process to deliver business objectives • End-goal too distant with too few review points to confirm business case	Projects have little understanding of what they have to do to "succeed" and far too many stakeholders to satisfy. Without clear definition of interim success or assessment of what is achievable, projects drift into long term activities which become uncontrolled and uncontrollable. *Ultimately, failure is designed in.*
Decision making failures • Prime responsibility rests with committees • Consensus must be achieved on all issues • No single individual in authority – project manager makes decisions in absence of sponsor	Key issues are logged but remain unresolved as all people with an interest are consulted. Outcomes of consultation will be blurred in order not to trigger opposition and veto. Projects are not given clear direction – key actions are not taken or are inconsistent. *Ultimately, a failed project evolves.*
Project discipline failures • Project documentation replaces project management • Milestones are too distant – slippage is not managed • Weak arrangements to identify and evaluate risks and allocate them to managers with authority • Requirements changes not reflected in "immutable" deadlines • Contingency planning is weak or unrealistic • Project beyond the experience and capability of the Project Manager	Plans are constructed based on deadlines which are pre-determined; few people actually believe they reflect reality so slippage or the impact of change is not taken seriously. Prospect of failure is not allowed to be acknowledged so few preparations are made for problems which do arise. *Ultimately, the project moves, unacknowledged, into failure, costs escalate.*
Supplier management failures • Project has little understanding of supplier commercial imperatives (e.g. in fixed price contracts) • Supplier not selected on basis of VFM • Projects are launched without an agreed contractual completion date, acceptance criteria and cost limit • Insufficient transparency of management information between client and supplier • Suppliers managed to limit cost rather than risk – no validation of suppliers assumptions	The key early part of the project is confused by contractual debate and positioning – often leaving both sides disappointed. This mistrust is then exacerbated by misunderstanding of supplier and project motivations creating further disputes and resort to contract – leading to a culture of secrecy and "sides". *Ultimately, the project focuses its energies on blame for failure.*
People failure • Disconnect between project and those who own the need • Culture in project teams to explain away real risks, and to hide not address problems • Needs of users not understood due to secrecy or haste during definition and design phase • Too few senior people with real authority	Project staff develop what they believe to be "developable" and avoid asking for guidance – given the risk of veto and delay. Requirement "owners" fail to understand what is feasible and therefore request deliverables and change which are impracticable in the given timescales or budget. *Ultimately, the project delivers failure.*

Figure 7.14 Typical risks for IS projects and recommended solutions

Source: UK Office of Government Commerce 'Why projects fail guide'
(www.ogc.gov.uk/sdtoolkit/reference/ogcrlibrary/bpbriefings/itrprojects.pdf)

Mini case study 7.3   Dell begs ToryDems to keep NHS IT project

Dell is urging the coalition government not to cut the world's most expensive civilian IT project – the NHS's National Programme for IT.

Parts of the £12.7bn scheme are in the firing line for cuts, not just because of the absurd cost but also because of its unpopularity with doctors and patients.

Harry Greenspun, Dell's chief medical officer, warned PublicTechnology.net there was a danger the baby was being thrown out with the bath water. He said there was a need to make the technology easier to use and manage, but there were still benefits to be had from increasing computer use in the health service.

But a new health minister, Simon Burns, has been given responsibility for the over-budget project.

Doctors are losing faith in summary care records in particular. The Local Medical Committee has proposed several motions, which if passed will go on to the British Medical Association conference in the summer.

The major complaint is that the Summary Care Record scheme was pushed out across the country before any evaluation of the trials was undertaken. Also controversial was the decision to make people opt out of the service.

One motion says simply: 'That conference deplores the way the SCR is being rolled out.'

They also call for a proper evaluation of the medico-legal implications of records containing wrong information – doctors have previously said that they do not trust SCRs enough to rely on them for patient data.

The BMA said in March that the roll-out should be stopped.

The SCR seems a likely candidate for cuts, because only a few hundred practices have started uploading records but people have heard of it, so there will be a political benefit to canning it. The bigger question is whether the amputation of SCR is enough to save the rest of the project.

When the NPfIT launched we were promised it would be different to other government IT projects. We were assured there would be one responsible owner; there isn't. Richard Granger quit in 2007.

We were told there would be lots of competing suppliers; there aren't. iSoft needed a government bail-out and Fujitsu and Accenture both decided to walk away.

Source: John Oates, The Register,
http://www.TheRegister.co.uk/2010/05/21/dell_nhs_pork/

Table 7.5 Success factors in applications development projects

Success factor	Ranking	Commentary
Executive support	18	An executive sponsor or champion is important to getting an organization behind a project.
User involvement	16	User involvement is essential, both in defining the requirements and demonstrating the value of the system to other users.
Experienced project manager	14	The Standish Group survey shows that 97% of successful projects have an experienced project manager.
Clear business objectives	12	Not the most important factor since the three factors above can help success even if the objectives aren't clear from the outset.
Minimized scope	10	Reduced requirements scope helps make the project more manageable. The authors note that minimizing the length of time between milestones can also help, as can focused micro-projects each with a small team of four people or fewer and clear deliverables.
Standard software infrastructure	8	If the infrastructure such as operating system, system development tools or database is varying, then this will increase the chance of failure. Integration of modules is easier when the software infrastructure is stable.
Firm basic requirements	6	If the base-level requirements can be fixed early on to minimize requirements. The Standish Group recommend: 'Creating minimal, obtainable base requirements and then developing those features will reduce the effect of change. Delivering minimal features allows users and executive sponsors to see quick results. As a result, project managers are better prepared to articulate the needs and priorities of the next project phase.'
Formal methodology	6	CHAOS research shows that 46% of successful projects use a formal project management methodology, compared with 30% of challenged and failed projects. This provides a realistic picture of the project and resources committed to it. And it results in steps and procedures the team can reproduce and reuse.
Reliable estimates	5	Reliable estimates are based on a detailed estimation process which is realistic about work volumes from the start rather than time-constrained.
Other criteria	5	These factors include small milestones, proper planning, competent staff, and ownership.

Source: From *Software Magazine* (2001), with commentary added

Debate 7.2

Limited improvements in project success rates have occurred over the past decade. This can be attributed to poor project management skills.

Key activities in systems development

In the final part of this chapter we summarize the work that needs to be completed during each phase of the systems development lifecycle during prototyping. Specific techniques and tools used to assist each stage are described. Specific risks associated with different types of projects and solutions to these problems are identified.

Systems initiation phase

Initiation phase
The first phase of a systems development project. It establishes project feasibility and produces a plan

The **initiation** or start-up **phase** is the first phase in an information systems development project. Its aims are to evaluate whether the project is feasible and to prepare a project plan.

Key activities of systems initiation

1 Produce feasibility study

Feasibility study
A report assessing the viability of the system

A **feasibility study** evaluates the need for and impact of the system and considers different alternatives for acquiring software. There are four main types of feasibility that may be evaluated. These are summarized in Table 7.6.

In DSDM, a business study is produced as well as a feasibility study. A collaborative technique is recommended for production using a series of facilitated workshops attended by key staff who pool their knowledge and try to achieve consensus on the priorities of the development. The result of these workshops is the 'business area definition' which identifies the business processes involved and associated information but also the classes (or types) of users who will be affected in any way by the introduction of the system. This is equivalent to operational and organizational feasibility. This information enables a more accurate project plan to be constructed and assists in identifying project risks.

2 Project plan

As explained at the start of the chapter, the project plan defines the:

- activities involved in the project (the work breakdown structure);
- human and technical resources to complete these tasks;
- schedule or time framework;
- risk management plan;
- budget.

Table 7.6 Different aspects of feasibility evaluated in the feasibility report

Feasibility type	Purpose	Issues considered
Economic	Costs of benefits of different solutions	• Cost–benefit analysis
Technical	Outline the best technical solution	• Make-or-buy decision • Produce shortlist of software, suppliers and systems integrators • Integration with existing systems
Operational	Determine impact on business processes	• Assess how well processes are supported by new system • Identify outline requirements
Organizational	Assess fit with organizational structure and culture	• Outline approach for introducing new system into organization

Typical problems of the initiation phase

A common problem with the initiation phase is that insufficient time is devoted to it since team members are keen to proceed with the work; they are swept up with enthusiasm for the project. Goals for the project and plans to achieve them are likely to be unrealistic. This may mean that the costs of the project may exceed its budget. If insufficient gathering of requirements occurs, this means that the activities and so the budget and timescale are underestimated. Organizational, operational and technical risks may also not be identified, which will all cause problems at later stages in the project.

Systems analysis phase

Systems analysis
Determination of
information system
requirements

Systems analysis determines the business and user requirements of an information system. Fact-finding techniques are used to ascertain the user's needs and these are summarized using a range of documentation and diagramming methods.

Key activities of systems analysis

The key activities of systems analysis involve different methods of eliciting and summarizing the requirements for the new system from the business. The main methods below are presented in a logical order for conducting these activities.

1 Focus groups

These can have a similar format to the 'business area definition' that occurs at the initiation phase of a DSDM project. Focus groups or brainstorming is useful at an initial stage in the project to identify major organizational and process issues which the project should address, and these can then be followed up in more detail with the other requirements-gathering techniques.

2 Documentation

A range of documentation may be available from existing systems. This may include previous requirements specifications, user guides, procedure manuals or help systems. Pre-existing good-quality documentation may make documenting the requirements of the new system quicker since many of the requirements will be shared.

3 Surveys

Questionnaires are sent to potential users of the system and users of the existing system. These also provide a structured method of requirements gathering. It is possible to determine key features by asking respondents closed questions, such as selecting from a list, or asking more general open questions, such as 'What are the three best and worst features of the current system?' Surveys work best if performed before interviews since key findings can be followed up in more detail at the interview stage.

4 Observation

This involves assessing how users of the current system work when completing different activities. It is an essential technique for identifying inefficiencies in a system. Today, most users will already be using a computerized information system, so automated tools can be used for logging keystrokes, or tracking eye movements, which is particularly useful for systems requiring interaction with web pages. It is less clear at which point observation should occur in the sequence of requirements determination activities. It will often occur in parallel with other activities.

5 Interviews

Interviews are a more structured form of collecting requirements than focus groups. They give an individual time to reflect on their needs and describe problems with the existing system. Detailed requirements are collected so it makes sense if interviews happen towards the end of requirements gathering. Some interviews with managers may be useful at an earlier stage in requirements determination. Interviews work best if they are semi-structured, with a prepared script of questions which must be answered but flexibility for other concerns to be described.

6 Prototyping

Prototyping of new systems through paper or on-screen prototypes will in itself elicit requirements. Advocates of rapid applications development argue that not too much time should be spent on other techniques of requirements elicitation since potential users of a system often change their mind, or identify new requirements when prototypes are viewed. Techniques such as DSDM therefore incorporate prototyping into systems development as soon as the initiation phase is complete.

7 Producing the requirements specification

The requirements specification will detail how the system should support its users and business processes. It will include:

- Business requirements – what are the required business outcomes of developing the new system?
- Summary of system users and their general requirements.
- Process support requirements – which work activities will the system support?
- Data output requirements – what information will be available to users and managers of the system?
- Data input requirements – what information will be captured for the system, what will its source be (other systems and manual data entry)?
- Data visualization requirements – how will data be entered and viewed by users?

Typical problems

Assuming requirements for a new system without conducting sufficient analysis is a common problem, particularly for small-scale systems. It is important to use the full range of techniques described above and involve a representative range of people to ensure that this phase produces realistic estimates.

Systems design phase

The **systems design phase** defines how the system will function. A 'divide and conquer' approach to design is used. Design is broken down into two phases. The first is a **systems design** which defines the overall structure of the system – which modules will be created to deliver the system requirements. Systems design involves breaking down the whole information system into subsystems and how they will interact with other subsystems. The second phase is the **module design** which specifies how each subsystem will work and how it in turn will be divided into further subsystems or objects.

Key activities in systems design

The key activities during system design that happen as part of system design and module design are:

- *Software architecture* – defines how different modules will work at the level of program code. System modules or objects will be broken down further into individual program functions or methods.

- *Hardware architecture* – defines the need for different hardware components or infrastructure of the system.

- *Information architecture* – this specifies the data inputs and information outputs of the system and defines the most efficient methods for capturing, storing and modifying the data. Database design is part of the information architecture.

- *Security design* – defines how the information will be protected. This relates to information architecture in that certain data items will usually have access to different classes of users.

- *User interface design* – defines the different screens that users will interact with, including menu options, data entry forms and other navigation elements.

Typical problems and solutions

Although the design phase is based on the requirements specification document, there is a lot of overlap between analysis and design phases. Designers may find that the requirements specification does not prescribe in enough detail what is needed from the system, or they will make additional suggestions for improvements. At this point, it will be necessary to consult the users of the system for clarification. This may cause major delays if the channels of communication between the designers, the analysts and the users are not established. One of the benefits of prototyping and methods such as DSDM is that they recognize and enable the need for continued consulting with the users.

As with many of the phases of the system development lifecycle, insufficient time may be spent on the design phase. This may require more rework at a later stage.

Systems development phase

At the **systems development phase** the physical system is created by technical staff. Systems development involves creation of the system through programming, database management and configuration.

Key activities in systems development

The main activities in the systems development phase are:

1 Programming individual system modules and fixing errors or 'bugs' in the system.
2 Creating the database structures and data manipulation functions such as database triggers and stored procedures.
3 Creating the user interface for access through web browsers.
4 Testing the database, programs and interface.
5 Writing system documentation for the users and future developers.

Typical problems and solutions

The main difficulty with the development phase is the introduction of bugs or errors into the system by developers. The problem is that developing a major system requires tens or hundreds or millions of lines of code. Each line represents an opportunity to include an error which can potentially 'bring the system down'. Even experienced programmers may produce around ten defects per thousand lines of code.

To remove such defects from the system, developers are encouraged to test each module by using test harnesses which simulate the loads and range of data on each module. A relatively new approach is **Extreme Programming (XP)**. One aspect of this is that programming is completed in pairs with a view to producing more effective, maintainable and less error-prone code. Although this may appear expensive, consider that the proponents of this model estimate that the people costs of software development projects are typically 20 times higher than the hardware costs. Much of this cost is involved in detecting and removing errors. Paired programming is one aspect of Extreme Programming which is a method similar to DSDM and covers the planning–design–coding–testing lifecycle phases as described at **www.extremeprogramming.org/rules.html**.

Systems implementation phase

Systems implementation involves introducing the system into the business. This starts with providing test versions of the system and then, once test results are satisfactory, rolling out the system to business users and managing the **changeover** from the old system to the new system. Migration or changeover from a previous information system to a new system is particularly important for mission-critical e-business systems where errors in management of changeover will result in a negative customer experience or disruption to the supply chain.

Key activities in systems implementation

1 Changeover

The alternatives for migrating from different versions of a system are summarized in Table 7.7.

2 Data migration

Data migration
Transfer of data from old systems to new systems

For an e-commerce system for a bank, for example, data migration would involve transferring or exporting data on existing customers and importing them to the new system. It is sometimes also referred to as 'populating the database'. Alternatively a middleware layer may be set up such that the new system accesses customers from the original legacy database.

3 Testing

End-user testing always occurs before a system becomes live. Its purpose is threefold – first to check that it meets the business or process requirements, second to check the software for ease of use, and third to check for bugs caused by inexperienced system users. With iterative development methods, the need for extensive end-user testing at the end of a project should be reduced.

Typical problems and solutions

There are many cases of systems failing at the changeover. Failure at this stage may be due to unexpected problems when the system goes live which were not tested in the test environment. For example, the load on a live system could be higher than that in the test environment. A further problem is that there is a reluctance to delay the 'go-live' date despite the system not being fully tested.

Table 7.7 Advantages and disadvantages of the different methods of implementation

Method	Main advantages	Main disadvantages
1 Immediate cutover Straight from old system to new system on a single date	Rapid, lowest cost	High risk. Major disruption if serious errors with system
2 Parallel running Old system and new system run side by side for a period	Lower risk than immediate cutover	Slower and higher-cost than immediate cutover
3 Phased implementation Different modules of the system are introduced sequentially	Good compromise between methods 1 and 2	Difficult to achieve technically owing to interdependencies between modules
4 Pilot system Trial implementation occurs before widespread deployment	Essential for multinational or national roll-outs	Has to be used in combination with the other methods

Even changes that are widely recognized as being considerable improvements for everyone, such as moving from a DOS-based (one that is text based) information system to a Graphical User Interface (GUI) (one that uses a mouse to point-and-click), can be problematic for some employees. Migrating from a DOS-based to a GUI accounting software package in one non-profit organization led to increased employee fear of change. Even though the change would result in user-customizable displays and fewer key-strokes (less work) for the staff, the change was perceived as being a significant technical leap that would take a great deal of training and practice before they would reach the levels of productivity that they achieved with the existing system (White et al. 2009).

Systems maintenance phase

Systems maintenance involves managing the system once it is live. Problems with the system must be fixed. Since there is also time to reflect on the project overall, some organizations will look to learn from their experiences on the project through a project close-down review.

Key activities in systems maintenance

A key activity is responding to errors as they are found. If serious, the problems will have to be solved immediately through issuing a 'patch' release to the system; otherwise they will be recorded for a later release. A system is required for promptly reporting and reviewing errors.

A formal review may occur after the end of projects; this is the post-implementation review. It assesses the success of the systems development project and lessons are recorded for future projects. Reviews that are 'event-driven' or 'time-driven' may also take place.

Event-driven reviews take place when there is a specific incident or something happens. An event could be a system failure such as an item of hardware failing. This would trigger a review of the element or area of the system that failed and implement a solution. Additionally, the review would try to identify any other areas of the system where a similar failure could take place and the solution is also implemented there. For example, if a hard disk fails it may be replaced with one that has a longer mean time between failures (MTBF). This type of hard disk may be replaced throughout the system so that failures are less likely to occur in the future.

Time-driven reviews occur at predetermined intervals after the system is live. Initially there may be daily reviews of system performance against parameters that were derived at the system design stage. If the system fails to perform within those parameters then further investigation and corrective action will be taken. The frequency at which these reviews take place is usually extended after a period of time operating within expected parameters. Reviews are gradually undertaken less frequently, first weekly, then monthly and finally annually.

Typical problems and solutions

Problems with the maintenance phase tend to be a consequence of maintenance not being part of the overall project, so processes for reporting, reviewing, fixing and notifying problems may not be in place. A project close-down review is often omitted in organizations that do not have a project quality management system in place since it all too easy to move on to the next project and sweep problems with the project 'under the carpet'.

Specific risks related to Internet and content-based projects

The approaches to project management described in this chapter have been primarily developed for operational systems and infrastructure projects. The approaches and methodologies largely predate the increase in use of Internet technologies to deliver information through intranets, extranets and public-facing websites. Projects to implement such facilities encounter many of the problems traditionally experienced when completing projects when planning and control are inadequate. However, it is pertinent to ask whether new project-related risks are introduced with these types of system. At the end of Chapter 8 we look at specific problems in change management associated with such projects, taking the example of a company portal, CRM systems and business intelligence systems. It can be argued that many of the problems that such projects face do not arise early in the project at the stage of analysis or design, but are involved with encouraging user adoption at implementation. Many of these approaches such as intranets or extranets are novel and so will be unfamiliar to their users. This may lead to problems with acceptance on implementation. Of course, as we have said in this chapter, involving users throughout the project in specifying requirements and prototyping early versions of the systems can help gain greater acceptance.

Such projects naturally have similar stages of development to traditional information systems development stages described earlier in this chapter. Similar success factors are also required, such as management buy-in, user involvement and careful project control. Specific issues for this type of project include:

- *Initiation* – education to explain the purpose of the intranet and the importance of updating it is particularly important. Care must taken in calculating the return on investment with information-based projects.

- *Analysis and design* – specialist methods of mapping the information requirements are used, as described in Chapter 9 on information architectures.

- *Development* – the design phase is relatively limited compared to most bespoke applications since a content management system, existing CRM application or e-commerce server will be used to set up structures for data storage. Development of the web-based user interface needs specific skills, which differ somewhat from those of non-web-based applications. These issues are also covered in Chapter 9.

- *Implementation* – a lot of work will be required to populate the system with information. Since much of the information will already be available, methods of integrating with other systems, such as exporting the information from other systems and then importing this information, may be necessary.

- *Maintenance* – the maintenance phase is particularly important in these types of projects since content needs to be kept up to date. Responsibilities and update mechanisms for this are required. The usage of different information types in web-based systems can be readily tracked and evaluated to check the relevance of information. Controls need to be in place to maintain the quality of information, and these controls are referred to in Chapter 10 which is devoted to managing information quality. Responsibilities for updating content on intranets and extranets need to be established, with controls which ensure that updating occurs as existing information becomes out of date. The COBIT (2000) IT governance guidelines on project management are useful in this context in that they acknowledge the need for controls to improve information quality.

Summary

Goals of project management for information systems. To deliver a product that meets the business and user needs and is delivered within time and budget constraints.

1 *Types of projects.* These include operational applications, information and knowledge management projects and infrastructure. Projects may include at least one of these.

2 *Approaches to building IS.* Range from bespoke applications developed from scratch to off-the-shelf or packaged solutions installed in a company or externally hosted which offer varying options for tailoring or configuration. They may be created in-house, or using a systems integrator.

3 *The project management process.* The standard approach includes estimation, resource allocation, scheduling or planning, budgeting and monitoring and control of deliverables at key milestones.

4 *The systems development process.* A series of controlled stages for building information systems. The traditional approach to systems development was the sequential waterfall model, but this has been superseded by iterative, rapid applications development methods such as DSDM.

5 *Risk management.* A project management technique that involves identification and assessment of likely sources of project failure and approaches to manage these risks.

6 *Systems initiation phase.* The start-up stage in a project which involves developing a feasibility study and project plan.

7 *Systems analysis phase.* What the system should do. Involves determination of requirements through techniques such as surveys, interviews and observation and definition of requirements using a requirements specification and related documents.

8 *Systems design phase.* How will the system work? Involves specification of software, hardware and information architecture.

9 *Systems development phase.* A physical system is created through programming, database management and configuration of inputs and outputs.

10 *Systems implementation phase.* Introduction of the system to the organization. Involves data migration, testing and changeover to the live system.

11 *Systems maintenance phase.* Monitoring and control of the system once it is live.

Exercises

Self-assessment questions

1 What are the characteristics of a failed information systems project?

2 Describe the alternatives for sourcing a new information system.

3 What are the benefits of the different approaches to sourcing a new system?

4 Summarize the tools that a project manager uses to control a project from its inception to its completion.

5 Contrast the traditional waterfall model and rapid application development approach to systems development.

6 Describe the activities that must occur at the start of a project, before detailed analysis occurs.

7 Distinguish between analysis and design activities.

8 Summarize the activities that need to occur between when the system design of a new project is complete and the system sign-off.

Essay and discussion questions

1 Explore the reasons why information management projects continue to exhibit a high rate of failure.

2 Evaluate the relative risks involved at each stage of a systems development project (or within the different activities of a rapid applications development project) and suggest techniques that can be used to control these risks.

3 Where should the responsibility for IS project management lie within a large organization? Assess the alternatives.

4 How do the success factors for the completion of an information systems project vary for:

(a) a transactional information system such as a customer relationship management system and

(b) a knowledge-based system such as a corporate information portal to promote knowledge sharing?

5 Summarize the characteristics of an effective project office or project management office (PMO) within a large organization.

6 Assess the advantages and disadvantages of using a structured project management method such as PRINCE2 within a large organization and a small organization.

References

Avison, D. and Fitzgerald, G. (1995) *Information Systems Development: Methodologies, Techniques and Tools*, 2nd edn. McGraw-Hill International, Glasgow, UK.

Beynon-Davis, P. (1993) *Information Systems Development*, 2nd edn. The Macmillan Press, Basingstoke.

Chaffey, D. (2004) *E-Business and E-Commerce Management*, 2nd edn. Financial Times Prentice Hall, Harlow.

Checkland, P. B. (1981) *Systems Thinking, Systems Practice*. Wiley, Chichester.

Clarety (2010) A summary of project failure rates in 2009. Source: Clarety Blog, www.claretyconsulting.com/it/comments/project-and-programme-failure-rates/2009-06-27/.

COBIT (2000) Executive Summary of COBIT. Released by the COBIT Steering Committee and the IT Governance Institute. Available online at: www.isaca.org/cobit.

COBIT (2001) Control Objectives. COBIT, 3rd edn. Released by the COBIT Steering Committee and the IT Governance Institute. Available online at: www.isacf.org/cobit.

Elliott, G. and Starkings, S. (1998) *Business Information Technology: Systems, Theory and Practice*. Addison Wesley Longman, New York.

Flynn, D. J. (1992) *Information Systems Requirements: Determination and Analysis*. McGraw-Hill, Maidenhead, UK.

IT Week (2003a) RBS completes 'largest ever' IT project, Andy McCue, 5 March. www.itweek.co.uk/News/1139214.

IT Week (2003b) Team tactics cut project risks, Madeline Bennett, 24 October. Available online at: www.itweek.co.uk.

Jackson, M. (1983) *Systems Development*. Prentice Hall, Hemel Hempstead, UK.

Jayaratna, N. (1994) *Understanding and Evaluating Methodologies: NIMSAD, a Systematic Framework*. McGraw-Hill, Maidenhead, UK.

KPMG (2002) KPMG Assurance surveys. Program Management Survey, October. www.kpmg.co.uk/kpmg/uk/services/audit/surveys.cfm.

Matta, N. and Ashkenas, R. (2003) Why good projects fail anyway. *Harvard Business Review*, September, 1–8.

Preece, J., Rogers, Y. and Sharp, H. (2002) *Interaction Design*. Wiley, New York.

Royer, I. (2003) Why projects are so hard to kill. *Harvard Business Review*, September, 5–12.

Software Magazine (2001) Collaboration: Development & Management Collaborating on Project Success. February/March. Authors: Jim Johnson, Karen D. Boucher, Kyle Connors and James Robinson. www.softwaremag.com/archive2001feb/Collaborative Mgt.html.

Standish Group (2010) Extreme CHAOS report.

White, G. R. T., Samson, P., Thomas, A. and Rowland-Jones, R. (2009) The implementation of a quality management system in the not-for-profit sector. *The TQM Journal*, 21(3), 273–83.

Wynekoop, J. L. and Russo, N. L. (1997) Studying systems development methodologies: An examination of research methods. *Information Systems Journal*, 7, 47–65.

Further reading

Matta, N. and Ashkenas, R. (2003) Why good projects fail anyway. *Harvard Business Review*, September, 1–8. A good review of project management risks and solutions to reduce them.

Stapleton, J. (2002) DSDM: *A Framework for Business Centred Development*. Addison Wesley, Reading, MA. A professional's book on DSDM that gives an overview of the stages involved in DSDM.

visit the www

Weblinks

Dynamic Systems Development Method Consortium (www.dsdm.org) An outline of the approach is provided for non-members, with detailed definitions available for paying members.

JISC Project management infokit (www.jiscinfonet.ac.uk).

Knowledge Brief Networked (www.kbnetworked.com) UK best-practice organization for IS and e-business procurement. Includes case studies and guidelines on project management.

Project Management Institute (www.pmi.org) Leading professional body with a selection of topical articles on issues in project management from the institute's journal. Selected free articles.

Project Management Today magazine (www.pmtoday.co.uk).

Project Smart (www.projectsmart.co.uk) A collection of resources from Duncan Haughey, a practising PRINCE2 project manager.

Software Project Management links page (www.comp.glam.ac.uk/staff/dwfarthi/proj-man.htm) A comprehensive collection of links on software project management produced by Dave Farthing of the University of Glamorgan.

Successful delivery toolkit (www.ogc.gov.uk/sdtoolkit/reference/deliverylifecycle/impplans/projrmgmt.html) Produced by the UK Office of Government Commerce.

For multiple-choice questions, and annotated weblinks relating to this chapter visit this book's website at: **www.pearsoned.co.uk/chaffey**

8

Managing change

Objective

To identify the typical reactions to change associated with the introduction of new information management initiatives and approaches to manage them.

Learning outcomes

After reading this chapter, you will be able to:

● Identify models of response to change associated with information management initiatives.
● Assess the suitability of responses to organizational change associated with the introduction of new information management approaches.

Management issues

Typical questions facing managers related to this topic:

● Are there typical responses of individuals to organizational change which can be anticipated and controlled?
● What are the success factors for managing change associated with major information management implementations?

Links to other chapters

The main related chapters are:

➤ *Chapter 7* describes the development and implementation of new systems from a project management perspective.
➤ *Chapter 10* describes the human issues in managing information quality which are also related to change management.

Introduction

The implementation of every new business information management solution will significantly affect individual employees and the dynamics of the teams. If this human impact is not recognized and managed then resistance to change will occur and the initiative may fail or not deliver the results expected. Many information systems texts explain approaches to managing the systems development lifecycle and techniques used by business analysts for systems analysis and design, as outlined in Chapter 7. However, they do not tend to consider in any depth how the individual user of new applications or information management approaches will feel about them and how this will affect their behaviour. The reality is that people in business do not have the chameleon-like ability to change in response to their environment. So, we believe that it is important for the perceptions and reactions of employees to information management initiatives and management techniques for controlling these reactions to be studied.

Improving organizational performance through business information management often involves new approaches to working and the need to manage the associated change. Approaches to managing changes to organizational processes and structures and their impact on organizational staff and culture are known as **change management**. Approaches to managing change associated with information management initiatives are the subject of this chapter.

Change management
Managing process, structural, technical, staff and culture change within an organization

The high failure rates for information systems projects mentioned in the previous chapter are often a consequence of managers' neglect of how users will react to new ways of working. The need to manage change not only applies to new information systems, but is critically important to all business information management initiatives, whether it is the introduction of a new enterprise resource planning system, an intranet facility for knowledge management, conducting an information audit or implementation of a policy to improve data quality.

The introduction of new information systems requires their users to learn how to use new systems, but more significantly they may require new methods of working. The changes experienced by staff tend to be greatest for large-scale projects which are intended to achieve **business transformation**. For example, the introduction of an e-business system to support online sales or online procurement may introduce major changes for staff working in these areas. Both types of system represent a potential threat to existing staff. Some staff may have been working face-to-face with customers or suppliers for many years and they are now asked to use technology which decreases the human element of contact. They may consider that this reduces the efficiency of the work, they may feel that their jobs are less interesting or even that their jobs are under threat.

Business transformation
Significant changes to organizational processes implemented to improve organizational performance

In this chapter we start by considering different forms of change and models for how change occurs. We will relate different forms of change to the introduction of different forms of information management application. We then look at approaches that organizations can take to manage change, again relating this to specific issues of information management. Finally, we take five examples of change management associated with new information systems to illustrate typical problems of managing change associated with particular types of information management application.

Different types of change

Incremental change
Relatively small adjustments required by an organization in response to its business environment

Discontinuous change
Change involving a major transformation in an industry

Viewed at a large scale across an entire industry, change takes one of two forms. **Incremental change** involves relatively small adjustments required by changes in the business environment. Organizations scan their environment and make adjustments according to the introduction of new products from competitors, new laws or long-term changes in customer behaviour such as the increasing spending power of teenagers. In the airline industry, incremental change involves the introduction of new routes, takeover or merger between airlines or the overall increase in air travel. Organizations also make changes to improve the efficiency of their processes. **Discontinuous change** or transformational change involves a more significant change in the business environment which changes the basis for competition. For example, in the airline industry, the law that deregulated the industry in Europe in the 1980s, opening up the market to new entrants, was a discontinuous change. The rapid reduction in passenger flights caused by the 11 September 2001 attacks on New York is another example of a discontinuous change. The introduction of a low-cost 600-seater supersonic airliner would be likely to lead to another discontinuous change.

Organizational change
Includes both incremental and discontinuous change to organizations

How do the types of change, described above at industry level, affect organizations and individuals within these organizations? **Organizational change** mirrors that at industry level. It can occur on a continuous or incremental basis or on a discontinuous basis. Such change occurs as management teams respond to changes in the environment by modifying their strategies and the character of their organizations. The McKinsey 7Ss model introduced in Chapter 6 suggests the types of organizational change that occur. There are the three 'hard Ss' referred to by McKinsey as strategy, structure and systems and the four soft 'Ss' of skills, shared values, staff and style. In the context of information systems projects, modifications to any of these may be required as part of the implementation of the new approach. For new systems which involve incremental change, skills, systems and staff will be impacted while with systems that involve discontinuous change such as an e-business initiative, any of the seven Ss may be involved.

Nadler et al. (1995) developed a useful way of classifying types of organizational change. This uses the concepts of incremental and discontinuous change together with anticipatory or reactive change. **Anticipatory change** occurs when an organization makes proactive changes in order to improve its efficiency or to create an advantage within the competitive environment. **Reactive change** is a direct response to a change in the external environment. The different forms of change are combined in Figure 8.1 to create four types of organizational change:

Anticipatory change
An organization initiates change without an immediate need to respond

Reactive change
A direct response by an organization to a change in the organization's environment

1 *Tuning.* This is an incremental form of change when there is no immediate need for change. It can be categorized as 'doing things better'. New procedures or policies may be used to improve process efficiency, i.e. to reduce time to market or reduce costs of doing business. As we saw in Chapters 2 and 4, information systems are often used for this purpose.

2 *Adaptation.* Also an incremental form of change, but in this case it is in response to an external threat or opportunity. It can also be categorized as 'doing things better'. For example, a competitor may introduce a new product or there may be a merger between two rivals. A response is required, but it does not involve a significant change in the basis for competition.

3 *Re-orientation.* A significant change or transformation to the organization is initiated due to discontinuous change. There is not an immediate need for change, but the change is in anticipation of change. When IBM was one of the first organizations to introduce the concept of 'e-business' in the mid-1990s, this was a

re-orientation in the way it delivered its service (with an increased focus on consultancy services rather than hardware and software) which helped to spark a wider change in the way businesses worked.

4 *Re-creation*. In re-creation, the senior management team of an organization decides that a fundamental change to the way it operates is required to compete effectively. In the airline industry, established airlines have had to establish change programmes to respond to the low-cost carriers, for example by emphasizing service quality or introducing rival low-cost services. Both re-orientation and re-creation can be categorized as 'doing things differently'. The challenge of managing change will be greatest for the discontinuous forms of change shown in Figure 8.1.

Debate 8.1

Information systems projects are always used to support incremental change rather than discontinuous change.

Different scales of managing change in information management initiatives

What forms of change shown in Figure 8.1 are typically involved in information management? Are information management initiatives typically about doing things better or doing things differently? From a strategic viewpoint we can state generally that information management systems are a tuning response. They are not typically directly driven by marketplace changes; rather they are intended to improve performance through increasing efficiency as part of continuous improvement. Introducing a new accounting system or human resources management system or customer relationship management system are good examples of this type of response to change. The change issues involved with introducing such systems will typically not include structural change or re-definition of roles. However, the individual and team will be affected by the system and will need to be encouraged to adopt the system.

Business process management

Business process management
An approach supported by software tools intended to increase process efficiency by improving information flows between people as they perform business tasks

So, some forms of information management initiative such as the introduction of a human resources management system are simply about improving efficiency – they involve incremental change. The practice of improving the efficiency of business processes with the assistance of information systems is an important activity in many organizations, as is shown by Case study 8.1 (p. 369). It can be seen that the label in vogue at the time of writing is 'business process management' (BPM). This encompasses different scales of improving business process as introduced above.

	Incremental	**Discontinuous**
Anticipatory	Tuning	Re-orientation
Reactive	Adaptation	Re-creation

Figure 8.1 Characterization of organizational change
Source: Nadler et al. (1995)

The BPM concept has been defined by Gartner (2003) as follows:

> BPM is a methodology, as well a collection of tools that enables enterprises to specify step-by-step business processes. Proper analysis and design of BPM flows require a strong understanding of the atomic business steps that must be performed to complete a business process. As BPM executes a business process, these atomic steps will often correspond to well-known business activities, such as checking credit ratings, updating customer accounts and checking inventory status. In effect, the BPM process flow is often just a sequence of well-known services, executed in a coordinated fashion.

> Classic document workflow, which was BPM's predecessor, focused on humans performing the services. Fueled by the power of application integration, BPM focuses on human and automated agents doing the work to deliver the services.

Discontinuous process change

Although BPM often refers to continuous, incremental change, other forms of information-management-related applications such as e-ticketing for an airline will be associated with discontinuous change – with low-cost airlines such as easyJet and Ryanair now selling over 80 per cent of their tickets online, this has had a fairly significant impact on the airline industry. The introduction of e-business applications or enterprise resource planning systems described in Chapter 2 is also often related to transformational change programmes.

In the early-to-mid 1990s organization-wide transformational change was advocated under the label of 'business process re-engineering (BPR)'. It was popularized through the pronouncements of Hammer and Champy (1993) and Davenport (1993). The essence of BPR is the assertion that business processes, organizational structures, team structures and employee responsibilities can be fundamentally altered to improve business performance. Hammer and Champy (1993) defined BPR as:

Business process re-engineering (BPR) Identifying radical new ways of carrying out business operations, often enabled by new IT capabilities

> the fundamental rethinking and radical redesign of business processes to achieve dramatic improvements in critical, contemporary measures of performance, such as cost, quality, service, and speed.

The key words from this definition that encapsulate the BPR concept are:

● *Fundamental rethinking* – re-engineering usually refers to changing of significant business processes such as customer service, sales order processing or manufacturing.

● *Radical redesign* – re-engineering is not involved with minor, incremental change or automation of existing ways of working. It involves a complete rethinking about the way business processes operate.

● *Dramatic improvements* – the aim of BPR is to achieve improvements measured in tens or hundreds of percent. With automation of existing processes, only single-figure improvements may be possible.

● *Critical contemporary measures of performance* – this point refers to the importance of measuring how well the processes operate in terms of the four important measures of cost, quality, service and speed.

Willcocks and Smith (1995) characterize the typical changes that arise in an organization with process innovation as:

● work units change from functional departments to process teams;
● jobs change from simple tasks to multidimensional work;
● people's roles change from controlled to empowered;
● focus of performance changes from activities to results;
● values change from protective to productive.

In *Re-engineering the Corporation* Hammer and Champy (1993) have a chapter giving examples of how IS can act as a catalyst for change. These technologies are familiar from applications of e-business such as those described in Chapter 2 and include tracking technology, decision support tools, telecommunications networks, teleconferencing and shared databases. Hammer and Champy label these as 'disruptive technologies'; they can force companies to reconsider their processes and find new ways of operating. It is arguable, though, whether technology is commonly disruptive in the sense of achieving major changes such as those in the re-orientation and re-creation categories of Figure 8.1.

Many re-engineering projects were launched in the 1990s and failed owing to their ambitious scale and the problems of managing large information systems projects. Furthermore, BPR was also often linked to downsizing in many organizations, leading to an outflow of staff and knowledge from businesses. As a result BPR as a concept has fallen out of favour and more caution in achieving change is advocated.

Less radical approaches to organizational transformation are referred to as '**business process improvement (BPI)**' or by Davenport (1993) as 'business process innovation'. Taking the example of a major e-business initiative for supply chain management, an organization would have to decide on the scope of change. For instance, do all supply chain activities need to be revised simultaneously or can certain activities such as procurement or outbound logistics be targeted initially? Modern thinking would suggest that the latter approach is preferable.

If a less radical approach is adopted, care should be taken not to fall into the trap of simply using technology to automate existing processes which are sub-optimal – in plain words, using information technology 'to do bad things faster'. This approach of using technology to support existing procedures and practices is known as **business process automation**. Although benefits can be achieved through this approach, the improvements may not be sufficient to generate a return on investment.

The three approaches are summarized in Table 8.1.

A staged approach to the introduction of BPR has been suggested by Davenport (1993). This can also be applied to e-business change. He suggests stages that can be applied to e-business as follows:

- *Identify the process for innovation* – these are the major business processes from the organization's value chain which add most to the value for the customer or achieve the largest efficiency benefits for the company. Examples include customer relationship management, logistics and procurement.

- *Identify the change levers* – these can encourage and help achieve change. The main change levers are innovative technology and, as we have seen, the organization's culture and structure.

- *Develop the process vision* – this involves communication of the reasons for changes and what can be achieved in order to help achieve buy-in throughout the organization.

Business process improvement (BPI) Optimizing existing processes, typically coupled with enhancements in information technology

Business process automation (BPA) Automating existing ways of working manually through information technology

Table 8.1 Alternative terms for using IS to enhance company performance

Term	Involves	Intention	Risk of failure
Business process re-engineering	Fundamental redesign of all main company processes through organization-wide initiatives	Large gains in performance (>100%?)	Highest
Business process improvement	Targets key processes in sequence for redesign	(<50%)	Medium
Business process automation	Automating existing process Often uses workflow software (Chapter 2)	(<20%)	Lowest

- *Understand the existing processes* – current business processes are documented. This allows the performance of existing business processes to be benchmarked and so provides a means for measuring the extent to which a re-engineered process has improved business performance.

- *Design and prototype the new process* – the vision is translated into practical new processes which the organization is able to operate. Prototyping the new process operates on two levels. First, simulation and modelling tools can be used to check the logical operation of the process. Second, assuming that the simulation model shows no significant problems, the new process can be given a full operational trial. Needless to say, the implementation must be handled sensitively if it is to be accepted by all parties.

Cope and Waddell (2001) have assessed approaches that managers in manufacturing industry in Australia use to introduce e-commerce services. They tested for different stages of transformation, from fine-tuning through incremental adjustment and modular transformation to corporate transformation. They found that in this particular industry, at the time of the survey, a relatively conservative approach of 'fine-tuning' was predominant.

Case study 8.1   FT

Business process management

This case gives a modern perspective on approaches to improving business processes using information systems. It summarizes the tools, benefits and some of the problems associated with business process management.

With competition becoming seemingly tougher every quarter, companies are starting to experiment with a series of interlinked technologies that allow them to optimise their business processes and to react quickly when market conditions change.

These technologies are collectively known as business process management (BPM). They include tools for business process modelling, workflow management, process monitoring, enterprise application integration and managing organisational change, all of which greatly help information to flow through organisations by co-ordinating and sometimes supplementing companies' key enterprise software packages, such as application suites supplied by SAP, Oracle and Siebel.

A furniture manufacturer, for example, could plan how it wants its customer orders processed, from initial confirmation to cash in the bank, using a process modelling tool that designs each stage in the order's evolution.

This tool then helps the manufacturer to create "workflow" software that automatically routes the customer order – and all the work associated with it – to the right people and places, in the right order. The workflow application takes decisions on how to advance the order, using pre-defined business rules. It closely monitors the order's progress, and if the order gets held up or seems to

encounter problems, it sends an alert in real time to the appropriate manager.

BPM has obvious advantages. Remodelled processes are usually more effective than their predecessors, generating immediate cost savings and competitive advantages. MSB International, an agency supplying workers on temporary contracts to companies, used BPM tools from Metastorm to revamp its contract processing. Previously, each new contract took an hour of a salesperson's time to process after it was agreed. Now the work takes five minutes and is far less prone to error.

Rob Marston, infrastructure manager at MSB, says the business benefit is "astounding". The software cost £50,000 and generated a return of £100,000 within a year by making sales people more effective, he says.

Just as importantly, BPM can help businesses change processes more quickly, perhaps with only minor changes to workflow rules, which minimises maintenance costs. "Hardly a week goes by when we don't change our business processes", says Mr Marston. "The board recently changed some authorisation procedures, and that took about ten minutes to implement. It sounds small, but in the old days, that would have taken a week."

BPM can help align IT infrastructures more closely with business needs. "It helps to break down the traditional barriers between the business way of describing a process and the IT way of implementing a process. That makes it more likely that developers can deliver what the business is asking them to deliver", says Derek Payne, fulfilment technology manager at Leica Microsystems, an optical product manufacturer.

BPM can also help organisations collaborate by aligning their business processes more closely. As web services technologies start to make information flows between organisations easier, supply chains should become shorter and more effective. "This helps to enhance the ability to work outside your own environment with trading partners", says Mr Payne.

Lastly, by defining processes carefully, BPM clears the way for the radical outsourcing of entire business processes, such as manufacturing or accounting. "The success of BPM will come less from allowing business processes to be redesigned, and more from making it easier to source parts of the business process offshore", predicts Will Cappelli, a research fellow at Forrester Research.

Mr Cappelli sees BPM as a Trojan horse for big IT services companies, enabling them to sell business process outsourcing (BPO) to corporations. BPO is the fastest-growing service in their market, and Mr Cappelli expects IT companies to absorb best-of-breed BPM experts such as Metastorm and Sterling Commerce to support this push.

Nevertheless, BPM is no walkover. As a complex set of technologies that do not always work together easily, it requires great effort and discipline to implement. "The hardest part is understanding the business processes," warns Mr Marston. "Initially, we tried to analyse everything about each process, but either the analysis was wrong, or the business had changed by the time it was implemented. So now we evolve our processes continually."

A big danger is that over-enthusiastic companies may use BPM to create too many new business processes, says David Stephenson, European managing director of supply chain specialist Yantra. "You can create a proliferation of business processes, and the simplification of your business processes gets lost as a result. You have to

keep a tight control over the design process", Mr Stephenson warns.

BPM technologies are also not as sophisticated as some vendors claim. "Many people are going to be sucked into an idea that sounds very seductive until they get into the detail", warns Rakesh Kumar, a vice president of technology research at analyst Meta Group. "Integration between technologies is a critical problem. Even if you have the technology problems solved, mapping internal business processes to core IT processes is another problem."

Gartner, the IT consultancy, said in a research note in December 2002 that corporate satisfaction with BPM is already high and is continuing to rise – making it a rarity in the IT world. Gartner urged clients to adopt BPM, predicting that it would deliver them a 10 to 15 per cent return on their investment over the following two years. BPM "will hold the key to creating new revenue opportunities and shortening product creation processes", it added.

Nevertheless, BPM is no panacea. Businesses must educate their staff and trading partners carefully about the changes it will bring to the business, or resistance to change – whether conscious or not – will emerge.

Source: Douglas Hayward, Smoothing the workflow, FT.com; 15 May 2003

Questions

1 How does the article suggest that business thinking and practice has evolved since the exhortations for business process re-engineering in the 1990s?

2 Summarize the benefits for BPM discussed in the article.

3 Discuss the need for a concept such as BPM when all new information systems and information management initiatives are ultimately driven by process improvement.

To summarize this section and apply the forms of change shown in Figure 8.1 to different types of information management initiatives, complete Activity 8.1.

Activity 8.1	The magnitude of change and information management applications
Purpose	To explore the extent of change involved with different information management applications.
Activity	Consider the type of change which is associated with these different forms of business information management initiatives for the Lo-cost Airline Company relative to the framework shown in Figure 8.1:

1 Introduction of new human resources management application.
2 Introduction of online ticket sales system.
3 Introduction of enterprise resource planning application for managing operational management of airline routes used by both managers and staff delivering service.
4 Knowledge management programme for improving knowledge-sharing capabilities of managers at company headquarters.
5 An information management initiative based on an information audit of information used by managers within the head office.
6 The introduction of an online customer service facility for employees and customers to improve response to inbound customer enquiries following a survey that showed competitors delivered superior service quality.

Tip Note that while the framework of Figure 8.1 is useful for evaluating the extent of change, it may not always be clearly distinguished whether change is anticipatory or reactive, for instance, so there are no clear-cut solutions to this activity. However, it is worthwhile in that broad differences in the extent of change and the impact on staff and organizational structure are evident.

Models of change

Change
The transition between two dynamic states

Models of organizational and social change are well established. Lewin (1951), one of the first people to study social and organizational change, pointed out that change occurs as a transition between two dynamic states. Each of these situations is itself dynamic since incremental change occurs repeatedly to achieve continuous change. Kurt Lewin referred to this as 'stable quasi-stationary equilibrium'. When change is managed intentionally, Lewin recommended that three stages be involved:

1 *Unfreeze* or unlock from the present position or behaviour by creating a climate of change through education, training and motivation of future participants.
2 *Move* quickly from the present state to the new state by developing and implementing the new way of working.
3 *Refreeze* by making the system an accepted part of the way the organization works.

Lewin believed that change management was not limited to approaches to achieve the new state, but also covered ensuring that *behaviour did not revert to a particular state*. This is a particularly important point in relation to information management since improved practices may not last. For example, staff may be trained and motivated to improve data entry quality as described in Chapter 10, but this may be short-lived if there are not incentives and checks to ensure that they continue their new behaviour. Similarly, web-based information and knowledge management initiatives which may be partly based on intranets have often failed because information is not kept up to date and usage falls. Staff have been educated to achieve awareness of the new system and trained in how to use it, but sufficient attention has not been given to making this change persist. We return to approaches to managing this change later in the chapter.

Individual responses to change

When people experience change, whether it be personal or work-related, they experience a variety of emotions. It is useful for both the individuals affected by change and the change managers to be aware of the transitions that occur during the change process. These personal transition phases or responses to change are summarized in Figure 8.2. Research by Adams et al. (1976) suggests that an individual will pass through all of these experiences during change. Through managing the process, they may be able to reduce the magnitude of the feelings or accelerate parts of the process.

The main elements of transition summarized in Figure 8.2 are:

1 *Awareness/shock.* Often, people have little warning of change, so the initial reaction is shock, rapidly followed by anxiety or even panic. Clearly the degree of shock will be dependent on the desirability of the transition and how well the individual is prepared for it. In a business change management context, both can be controlled to some extent.

2 *Denial.* This involves denying or underplaying negative consequences of change and often turning attention to other issues. Resistance to change is high at this stage.

3 *Depression.* This happens once the individual realizes that the change is not reversible. Depression is not merely passive – the feeling of dissatisfaction may lead to anger and disputing the need for change.

4 *Letting go.* At this point the individual experiences the need to 'move on' and start to dissociate him- or herself from the previous situation.

5 *Testing.* The individual starts to experiment with the new situation. Acceptance may increase, but anger can still be aroused as problems are encountered.

6 *Consolidation.* The individual builds on positive aspects of change and minimizes the negative aspects of change.

7 *Acceptance.* The final acceptance occurs when the new situation is seen as 'normal'.

In a later section we review how change managers can use this understanding of individuals' response to change to help manage the transition.

Resistance to change
Staff actively or passively demonstrate opposition to new working practices

Individuals commonly exhibit **resistance to change** when confronted by change. There are many understandable reasons for people to resist the technological change that arises from new approaches to information management within an organization. These include:

● limited perspectives and lack of understanding;

● threats to power and influence of managers (loss of control);

● perception that costs of the new system outweigh the benefits;

● fear of failure, inadequacy or redundancy.

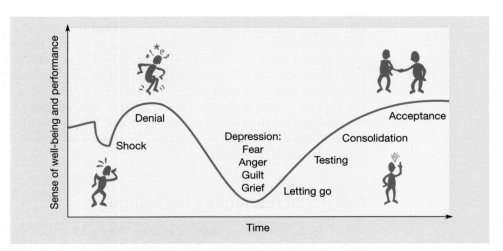

Figure 8.2 Transition curve indicating the reaction of staff through time from when change is first suggested

Dependent on the individual's reaction to change, resistance to change may be exhibited. Direct sabotage of new systems is not typically possible unless one has system administrator access, but indirect sabotage may occur. This is best characterized as 'systems avoidance'. This is a significant problem for many different forms of information management initiative. It typically involves bypassing a new system by continuing with an obsolete, parallel or personal system. For example, a business-to-business sales representative or account manager, faced with introduction of a sales force automation system (part of a customer relationship management system) in which they have to record all meetings and phone contacts with potential customers, may decide not to use it for various reasons. They could be a traditionalist who feels selling is about people not technology, alternatively they may feel they don't have time, or perhaps the system is more efficient than their previous method. Instead, the sales person may continue to use a manual paper-based system, a personal system they have used at other companies or may simply not record the details of sales visits. Clearly it is important for change managers to understand the reasons to resistance to change. This is a particularly difficult problem to manage and many CRM projects have foundered for this reason. One of the difficulties here is that change in user behaviour from several decades of previous experience may be required. Providing a new system without any support or with training only is insufficient to change behaviour. In a later section we will look at approaches that are used to manage this type of change. An associated reaction is criticism of the system, which if vocal can recruit other employees into systems avoidance.

To summarize the ways in which resistance to change may manifest itself, the following may be evident:

- *Aggression* – in which there may be physical sabotage of the system, deliberate entry of erroneous data or abuse of systems staff.
- *Projection* – where the system is wrongly blamed for difficulties encountered while using it.
- *Avoidance* – withdrawal from or avoidance of interaction with the system, non-input of data, reports and enquiries ignored, or use of manual substitutes for the system.
- *Criticism* – concerns about the system are actively voiced, although they may not be justified.

Organizational culture and change

Organizational culture should also be considered when reviewing how change is managed within an organization. The type of culture is dependent on the attitudes, values and beliefs held by members of an organization and how the organization views itself in relationship to its competitors, its customers and other external factors. Culture is also influenced by the social relationships between different areas of the business and the type of management control structure used. For instance, the culture in an organization with a strong hierarchical structure tends to be more formal than in organizations with a flatter organizational structure. In smaller organizations and start-ups, culture is likely to be strongly influenced by the personal beliefs of the owner of the business as they and other members of the management team will try to instil these beliefs in the organization. As organizations grow, the resulting culture is still likely to reflect the original roots of the company, although managers will seek to change the culture to be in line with their ideals and strategy.

Capacity to respond to change is partly dependent on an organization's culture. Schein (1992) argues that a consideration of culture helps identify success factors for managing change. He provides a threefold classification of culture that helps to identify what needs to be done:

Systems avoidance
End-users of a system show resistance to change through non-use or reduced use of a system

Organizational culture
The values and beliefs shared by members of an organization

1 *Assumptions* are the invisible core elements of an organization's culture such as a shared collective vision within the organization. One of the challenges in change management is to question core assumptions where appropriate, especially if they seem to be obstructing change.

2 *Values* are preferences that guide behaviour, such as attitudes towards dress codes and punctuality within an organization or ethics within a society. Often such values are transmitted by word of mouth rather than being enshrined in written documents or policy statements. As with organizational assumptions, values are hard to change, especially when the views that embody them are firmly held. With respect to the management of information quality that is discussed in Chapter 10, individual and shared values influence perceptions on the importance of, and care taken with, information quality. Some organizations have a culture that is more formal or quality-oriented that will be more amenable to introducing changes to improve quality.

3 *Artefacts* are tangible material elements of cultural elements. These will be identifiable from the language used in the policies, procedures and acronyms of the organization, and the spoken word and dialects of the society. In some ways they are also the easiest to change. Policies such as information policies can be created or rewritten, but it is the organization's and staff's values and assumptions that will determine how they are perceived and consequently acted upon.

The implications of organizational culture for information systems implementation are important. While the 'artefacts' associated with information systems developments may be clear, it is the 'assumptions' and 'values' that will ultimately determine the success of the implementation and it is to these that the change management process must be largely directed.

Boddy et al. (2001) summarize four different types of cultural orientation that may be identified in different companies. These differ according to the extent to which the company is inward-looking or outward-looking, in other words to what extent it is affected by its environment. They also reflect whether the company is structured and formal or whether it has a more flexible, dynamic, informal character. The four cultural types of cultural orientation are:

1 *Survival (outward-looking, flexible)* – the external environment plays a significant role (an open system) in determining company strategy. The company is likely to be driven by customer demands and will be an innovator. It may have a relatively flat structure.

2 *Productivity (outward-looking, ordered)* – interfaces with the external environment are well structured and the company is typically sales-driven and is likely to have a hierarchical structure.

3 *Human relations (inward-looking, flexible)* – this is the organization as family, with interpersonal relations more important than reporting channels, a flatter structure, and staff development and empowerment are thought of as important by managers.

4 *Stability (inward-looking, ordered)* – the environment is essentially ignored, with managers concentrating on internal efficiency and again managed through a hierarchical structure.

Complete Activity 8.2 to consider how these different types of culture may affect the ease with which a company can introduce improvements to knowledge management.

Models of technology acceptance

One aspect of change that is often overlooked is that of the employee's perception of the technology that is being adopted or adapted. Many theories and models have been developed that measure or interpret people's attitudes and opinions and may be used to determine an organization's readiness for change and the likelihood of success of any change initiative.

What is sometimes difficult to determine is which model to use in a particular case. Some models for instance, focus upon the individual's beliefs or attitudes towards technology and others upon the social aspects of change. Developed from research into the adoption of information systems in social care in the UK, Table 8.2 summarizes the most prominent models and indicates the primary determinants that each one explores. The matrix may be used to aid the selection of an appropriate assessment tool and comprises:

TRA	Theory of Reasoned Action – Fishbein (1967); Ajzen and Fishbein (1973); Fishbein and Ajzen (1975)
TPB	Theory of Planned Behavior – Ajzen (1985); Ajzen (1991)
TAM	Technology Acceptance Model – Davis (1986); Davis (1989)
TAM2	Extended Technology Acceptance Model – Venkatesh and Davis, (2000)
TAM & TPB	Combined TAM and TPB Model Taylor and Todd, (1995)
PC UTIL	PC Utilization – Thompson et al. (1991)
IDT	Innovation Diffusion Theory – Lazarsfeld et al. (1949); Rogers (1962); Rogers and Shoemaker (1971); Rogers (1995)
SCT	Social Cognitive Theory – Albert Bandura (1977, 1986, 1989, 2001)
UTAUT	Unified Theory of Acceptance and Use of Technology – Venkatesh et al. (2003)

Table 8.2 Technology acceptance matrix

Determinants to test	Model								
	TRA	TPB	TAM	TAM2	TAM & TPB	PC UTIL	IDT	SCT	UTAUT
Predict intention	✓	✓	✓	✓	✓		✓		✓
Predict/determine use	✓	✓	✓	✓	✓	✓	✓	✓	✓
Technology known	✓	✓	✓	✓	✓	✓	✓	✓	✓
Technology not known			✓	✓			✓		✓
Beliefs	✓	✓							
Attitudes	✓	✓	✓		✓	✓			
Performance expectancy			✓	✓	✓	✓	✓	✓	✓
Effort expectancy			✓	✓	✓	✓	✓		✓
Social influence	✓	✓		✓	✓	✓	✓		✓
Facilitating conditions		✓			✓	✓	✓		✓
Age		✓							✓
Gender		✓	✓	✓					✓
Voluntary use	✓	✓	✓	✓		✓	✓		✓
Mandatory use			✓	✓					✓
Experience	✓	✓	✓	✓	✓	✓	✓		✓

Source: Abid Mohammed and Gareth White, University of the West of England, 2008

Activity 8.2	The constraints of culture on implementing a new knowledge management approach
Purpose	To identify different approaches to introducing information management policies that may be appropriate according to different types of organization culture.
Activity	Evaluate which of the four general categories of organizational cultural orientation summarized by Boddy et al. (2001) are likely to be most amenable to introduction of a knowledge management initiative which focuses on competitive intelligence (i.e. sensing the actions of competitors from information gained by staff and published external sources – see Chapter 6 on information systems strategy). *Tip* Take each type of cultural orientation as characterizing an individual company. First rank them according to the ease with which you think a competitive intelligence initiative could be introduced.

Approaches to managing change

Hayes (2002) notes that for external forces of change, it may be difficult for those in an organization to manage and control the impact of change – the deterministic view. On the other hand, the voluntarist view is that managers can make an important difference to managing the impact of change. In the case of information systems management, it is clear that much can be done to reduce the impact of change, although some negative aspects of change will remain. Change management is conducted by change agents who are the managers responsible for controlling change. In the context of business information management, the change agent could be the project manager responsible for implementing an information system, the CIO responsible for implementation of an ERP system, an e-business manager responsible for increasing adoption of e-business by an organization, or an information manager introducing an information quality programme. Since such information management projects will also involve senior managers and departmental managers who communicate to staff the benefits of change, these more general managers can also be considered change agents.

Change agents
Managers involved in controlling change transitions

There are many process models for achieving change. These naturally tend to mirror the process models for implementing information systems described in the previous chapter. Information systems projects are simply one type of change management project. For example, Jay and Smith (1996) identify four phases in their change model:

1 *Initial orientation*. In the orientation phase, it is necessary that there be a clear understanding of the reasons for bringing about change. This would include a cost–benefit analysis and specific terms of reference for the project. A change strategy must be developed that includes an indication of how quality would be measured, the project milestones, and how objectives would be measured and the change project organized. A skilled change team should be established and committed change sponsors identified. In an information systems development project, as described in Chapter 7, this stage corresponds to the project start-up phase.

2 *Preparation*. The preparation phase will involve an analysis of the environment within which the change is to take place. This includes an identification of the critical success factors for change along with a threat analysis. A work-plan for the change process that includes detailed tasks and timings must also be developed. The change direction must be announced to those affected and there should be an

emphasis on maximizing communication effectiveness. It is necessary to communicate the future position to a wider audience and the need to make the change and its potential consequences must be clearly specified. The final step in this phase is to provide direction, particularly through strong communication of the goals and how they will be achieved. Hayes (2002) notes the importance of diagnosis at this stage to evaluate the differences, particularly from a staff perspective, between the initial state and the final state. This diagnosis is used to build a case or vision for change which can be communicated to staff. In an information systems development project, as described in Chapter 7, this stage corresponds to the initiation phase, but it continues through analysis, design and implementation.

3 *Change implementation.* In the third phase, Jay and Smith suggest that the changes be implemented by piloting the change, introducing the new procedures, conducting training and finally rolling out the change. In cases where a new information system is being rolled out to the whole organization at the same time, choosing a pilot department or site may be difficult. However, the organizational aspects as they relate to reporting relationships, job definitions, training schedules, working procedures and reward systems must be still be defined and communicated. Appropriate training should be completed and the implementation must be carried out using a roll-out plan. In an information systems development project, as described in Chapter 7, it is unclear where the change implementation phase starts. From the perspective of those staff involved in prototyping it could start at the analysis stage, for those involved in testing it is at a later stage, and from the end-users of the system it is when the system becomes live.

4 *A supportive phase.* In the final phase, the change must be stabilized. This means that management must openly commit itself to the change and fine-tune or adjust procedures where necessary. Measuring acceptance and new behaviour and producing a formal report can be used to evaluate the effectiveness of the change. There must be prevention of a relapse, such as an attempt to revert to old systems and practices or even bypassing the new system altogether. Conducting regular review meetings along with continual training and procedure reviews can help this. In an information systems development project, as described in Chapter 7, this stage corresponds to the post-implementation phase.

Hayes (2002) has summarized how change managers can facilitate progress through the overall change process and progress through the transitions an individual makes during change shown in Figure 8.2. He notes the following general implications of the transition model for change managers:

- The overall shape of the transition curve will take different forms – individual stages may be longer or shorter and the degree of mood change at each stage can vary considerably.
- There will often be a time lag between the announcement of a change and a reaction to it. It is possible to mistake initial shock and denial for acceptance of the change.
- Different people and different parts of the organization will pass through the change cycle at different rates and in different ways.
- Change managers will typically be out of step with other staff since they are involved earlier and deeper.
- The cycle cannot be avoided, but there is much that change managers can do to facilitate people's progress through it.

Hayes (2002) also gives specific advice about how change managers can facilitate change through each transition in Figure 8.2. This advice is summarized in Table 8.3 together with typical implications for information management initiatives and applications. It can be seen that in column 3 the different transition stages can be broadly mapped onto the stages of a systems development project as described in the previous chapter.

Table 8.3 Facilitating progress through transition

Transition phase	Typical actions by change managers	Implications for information management applications
1 Shock/awareness	Create a climate of receptivity to change. Announcement sufficiently in advance to involve senior managers.	Pre-announcement and involvement are readily practicable for information management. Announcement and ownership by a senior manager are still important, even if project is not of strategic importance.
2 Denial	Diagnosis of the reason for denial is important. Gently support the staff through denial. Repeat message of reason for change and justify. Find ways to get staff involved in change early.	Involvement is typically a requirement of information management projects, so this is usually practical for some staff; for others, communication of the benefits and progress of the project and the implications for them should be considered.
3 Depression	Providing support and listening are required at this stage rather than ignoring complaints.	This stage tends not to be marked for information management-related change projects.
4 Letting go	Continued explanation of the benefits of the new system without denigrating the past approach. Setting targets associated with the new system.	Around this stage, prototypes of the new system will be available which will help with the process of letting go since tangible evidence of the new system and, hopefully, its benefits will be available.
5 Testing	Testing is encouraged by encouraging experimentation without blame where problems occur.	Testing corresponds to the testing phase of the system or adoption of the new system dependent on involvement. Positive or negative feedback on the new system should be encouraged, discussed and acted upon where appropriate.
6 Consolidation	This is facilitated by reviewing performance and learning and recognizing, rewarding and communicating benefits.	Improvements achieved through the system should be assessed and communicated.
7 Reflection and learning	This is achieved through structured learning about the change through reviews and encouraging unstructured learning such as feedback about the system.	Post-implementation reviews can occur at this stage. The use of a structured system to log problems with the system or process can also help.

Source: The middle column is based on a summary of the commentary in Hayes (2002)

Soft systems methodology

The soft systems methodology (SSM) introduced in the previous chapter is also a useful tool for understanding responses to organizational change. The methodology was specifically developed for understanding social or human systems and implications of their transformation. SSM considers business processes as 'human activity systems' and seeks to define the current problem, different solutions and gauge reactions to the new system. It identifies different stakeholders in the system, such as clients, actors who conduct activities and the owner of the system, and their reactions.

Stakeholder involvement in change management

To manage change associated with the introduction of new approaches to information management, it is useful to understand the role of different stakeholders within an organization and beyond. Stakeholders vary in importance in terms of their seniority and their ability to affect change, but the needs and contributions of all stakeholders should be considered. There are three main types of stakeholders:

● *System sponsors* are the backers of the system or change in approach. They tend to be senior managers whose role is to be budget holders for the change initiative or responsible for a successful outcome or both. They are committed to the change and want to achieve success. The sponsors will try to fire up staff with their enthusiasm and stress why introducing the approach is important to the business and its workers.

● *System owners* are departmental or process managers in the organization who will use the system to support their areas of the business. For an enterprise system there could be several system owners, for example a marketing director could be responsible for the CRM component of an e-business system while the operations director is responsible for the supply chain management part of the system.

● *System users* are staff in the different areas of the business who are actively involved in using the system to support their day-to-day work. This could be a buyer in procurement, a production line manager in a factory or an accountant in the finance department.

Amongst system users, two additional types of stakeholders are often identified who are helpful in influencing the perceptions of other users. These are:

● *Legitimizers* who support the need for the system and are respected since they are experienced in their job, regarded as the experts by fellow workers or simply popular.

● *Opinion leaders* whom others watch to see whether they accept new ideas and changes. They usually have little formal power, but are often (but not always) regarded as good ideas people who are receptive to change. If such people are critical of the system then this can spread resistance to change.

Of course, legitimizers and opinion leaders will be likely also to be initially resistant to change and therefore need to be identified and involved early in the change management project since their support is important.

Leadership qualities

The need for senior management involvement is a common theme in discussion of success factors for change management. For example, Schein (1992) concluded that three variables are critical to the success of any large-scale organizational change:

1 the degree to which the leaders can break from previous ways of working;
2 the significance and comprehensiveness of the change;
3 the extent to which the head of the organization is actively involved in the change process.

Note that points 1 and 3 both involve the roles of senior management. In the context of point 2, e-business is a significant and comprehensive change that suggests that active senior management involvement is essential. One of the difficulties is that senior management may be at best unfamiliar with use of the information technology, or at worst technophobic.

If the senior management team has the vision to realize the impact of improvements in information management and related technologies, they are more likely to commit the resources and sponsor the changes required for success. Note also Schein's point that the head of organization needs to be actively involved. It is not a matter of simply communicating change at the start, but 'seeing the project through' by actively monitoring change by talking to staff and communicating progress on the initiative. Through this approach the importance of the project is emphasized – otherwise it will be relegated as 'something to be left to the IT department'. If managers are cynical, treating technology as a support function rather than a major change lever, then not only will they be unlikely to invest sufficiently in e-business, but they will not drive the initiative with sufficient enthusiasm and this will be apparent to staff.

Kotter (1995) distinguishes between the capabilities of managers as managers and as leaders. He sees management simply as the ability to set and accomplish plans through control and problem solving. While this is a capability required by system sponsors and system owners, leadership is more important, he suggests, to successful change management. He suggests that leadership in a change management context involves:

- articulating the vision in ways that are understandable by the people affected by change (he says this is often 'undercommunicated by a factor of 10 (or 100 or even 1000)';
- involving people in deciding how to achieve the management vision, thereby giving them some sense of control;
- supporting people to achieve the vision by being a role model and providing coaching and feedback;
- providing focus by identifying short-term wins;
- recognizing and rewarding success.

Cope and Waddell (2001) have assessed the role of leadership style in e-commerce implementations. They assessed the most common approaches to e-commerce implementation, distinguishing between these approaches:

- *Collaborative* – widespread participation of employees occurs to define the changes required and techniques to achieve them.
- *Consultative* – management takes the final decision, after calling on some employees for input.
- *Directive* – the management team takes the decisions, with the employees generally trusting them to do so and generally informed.
- *Coercive* – the management team takes the decision with very limited recourse to employees.

Of these approaches, the consultative approach was, as might be expected, most common, but other statements used in the research suggested that there were elements of other approaches.

Yet, while it is often stated that 'senior-management involvement' is essential, often this involvement appears to be limited in scope – senior managers perhaps give verbal backing to a project, but little more. Kotter (1995) provides eight practical steps of leadership that can be applied both by senior managers and by other less senior change agents:

1 Establish a sense of urgency.
2 Form a powerful coalition (a change team).
3 Create a vision which is imaginable, desirable, feasible, focused, flexible, communicable.
4 Communicate the vision.
5 Empower others to act on the vision.
6 Plan for and create short-term wins.

7 Consolidate the change and produce more change.

8 Institutionalize new approaches by demonstrating the benefits.

An example of a leader who possessed many of these characteristics of leadership was Jack Welch, CEO of General Electric from 1981 to 2001, who was actively involved in the move to e-business and the adoption of the Six Sigma method of process control. He actively owned such projects and communicated forcefully the importance of these initiatives. To stress the importance of e-business he instituted 'management boot camps' to increase managerial participation in e-business and also created a system of mentoring where younger, technically literate staff passed on their knowledge to 600 more senior managers. The talent of Jack Welch for communicating his vision is indicated by this extract from one of his last AGM speeches for General Electric (Welch, 2001):

> Last year I told you I believed e-Business was neither "old economy" nor "new economy", but simply new technology. I'm more sure of that today. If we needed confirmation that this technology was made for us, we got it. GE was named last year "e-Business of the Year" by InternetWeek magazine and awarded the same title last week by WORTH magazine.
>
> Digitization is, in fact, a game changer for GE. And, with competition cutting back because of the economy, this is the time for GE to widen the digital gap, to further improve our competitive position. We will do that by increasing our spending on information technology by 10% to 15% this year despite the weak economy.

Employee motivation

We have seen that employees commonly exhibit resistance to change. For change agents to know how to motivate employees, it is useful for change agents to 'get inside the minds' of their employees and understand what the problems are. Kotter and Schlesinger (1979) have identified four reasons for resistance to change. The obvious reason is *parochial self-interest*. Employees will understandably resist change if they expect to lose something of value to them. Resistance to change can arise simply through *lack of trust, arising from misunderstanding*. Kotter and Schlesinger also acknowledge that some stakeholders will make *different assessments* – they will evaluate the benefits and costs of change differently from their managers. They may consider that the change will not improve their performance or the organization's profitability. Finally, stakeholders may have a low tolerance for change, often leading to fear and anxiety. This may be due to an individual, an organization's culture or previous exposure to change – they be unfamiliar with it, or over-familiar with it!

Kotter and Schlesinger (1979) then go on to list six methods of dealing with resistance to change which can usefully be applied to any change project. Here we will apply them to the example of the sales force automation (SFA) system. The six methods are:

1 *Education and persuasion.* This is covered separately in the section that follows on education and training. In the context of the SFA, education and persuasion would have to appeal to *parochial self-interest* – it would be important to demonstrate that the new system would not damage the capacity of sales staff to earn money. It would also be necessary to demonstrate that the system will benefit the organization as a whole to minimize *different assessments*. This shows that when an organization selects a new system, the managers have to convince not only themselves of the need for the new system, but also their employees! Kotler and Schlesinger note that the approach used should not only use rational persuasion based on a reasoned argument. Some element of 'buzz' should be introduced to get staff excited about the change.

2 *Participation and involvement*. Kotler and Schlesinger say that participation and involvement can *'excite, motivate and help create a shared perception of the need for change'*. Participation and involvement in creation of an information system involves assistance in specification. It is not practical because of the time taken to interview or observe everyone about their current working practices which is perhaps the most effective way to achieve involvement. It could be argued that for the SFA system it would be useful to involve as many people as possible in interview and in particular the opinion leaders and legitimizers. Furthermore, everyone should be surveyed using a questionnaire to show that their view is important (even if this is a relatively ineffectual method of identifying system requirements).

3 *Facilitation and support*. These are required to counter resistance to change arising from fear and anxiety. For the SFA system, line managers would be important in supporting members of the sales team as they started to use the new system, through listening to problems or frustrations (emotional support) and seeking to resolve problems where possible (practical support). It would also be important that an internal expert on applying the system be available on each team, or available via a central help-desk. It would be important that the help-desk be internal and not outsourced to the original supplier who wouldn't have knowledge of the specific issues of the company adopting the system.

4 *Negotiation and agreement*. Negotiating and agreeing rewards for change is the main approach here. Clearly, rewards should not always be used, but they will be most helpful when resistance to change is high. For the SFA system, managers might find it useful to meet representatives of the sales force to discuss or negotiate and agree changes to the remuneration system. Small additional bonuses are used for sales made by Independent Financial Advisers where the application for a product is made online since this will ultimately save money through electronic purchasing and encourage adoption of the new online channel.

5 *Manipulation and co-option*. Manipulation is covert, i.e. it involves deliberate biasing of messages to try to persuade others. This manipulation may be on a one-to-one basis from line managers to staff or from senior managers. Co-opting involves getting the involvement of a key figure, even if they have relatively little to directly contribute to the change project. In the SFA example, a sales person who is perceived as a trouble-maker or project saboteur could be co-opted to the project team to deflect their criticism by increasing their involvement.

6 *Direction and a reliance on explicit and implicit coercion*. Coercion involves the change managers effectively forcing new behaviour through granting or withdrawing outcomes valued by employees. In the SFA case, coercion could be achieved by writing into the employees' performance-related contract the need to use the system regularly. Alternatively, bonuses could be reduced if the system is not used. While such measures are likely to be effective, their use has to be carefully considered since exerting such control is likely to cause resentment.

From these guidelines on managing change it is apparent that the explanation of benefits and giving specific examples of improvements are important. Hayes (2002) recommends that **valued outcomes** be evaluated to help understand the levers that will help facilitate change. A valued outcome is a benefit that occurs to employees during their employment, such as pay or favourable working conditions. In addition to these, John Hayes lists the following in his book: interesting or meaningful work, autonomy, opportunity for competition or collaboration, opportunities to be creative, power and influence, belonging or involvement, security, working with considerate supervisors, satisfaction, challenge, achievement, recognition, status, openness or sharing, and using knowledge and skills. He suggests that the availability of these types of valued outcomes should be evaluated before and after change and ranked in impor-

Valued outcomes
A valued outcome is a benefit that occurs to employees during their employment, such as pay or favourable working conditions

tance. This can be used to identify how to communicate the benefits arising from change and understand and counter the benefits lost or reduced through change.

Motivation of employees is strongly dependent on the capability of the change managers to communicate effectively. Hayes (2002) discusses the importance of perception of change agents by employees in their communications. He suggests that it is important that change agents are not seen to be communicating one-way, i.e. from managers to staff. It is important that the change agents are also seen to be listening and acting on information from the employees. He says:

> The change managers may attempt to perform in a way that gives the impression to others that they are committed to a shared approach to change; however, they may actually give off signals, verbal and non-verbal, that contradict this intended impression.

Hayes recommends that four characteristics of communications should be reviewed as part of employee motivation:

1 *Directionality*. We have already suggested that it is important that communication be a two-way process. Furthermore, there is a danger in large organizations, where information is filtered when it is passed from top to bottom or bottom to top, that the final recipients may not receive all the information they need. For example, the drive and vision of change from senior managers will not be effectively communicated from the top if it is delivered by less enthused or poorly regarded junior managers. In the reverse direction, negative comments from staff regarding change may not reach senior managers.

2 *Role*. We saw in a previous section that some types of employee such as legitimizers and opinion leaders have a great capacity to influence. It is important that they are identified and involved actively at all stages of the change process. On the other hand, there is a danger of excluding some types of roles such as relatively new employees who may respond negatively to the change processs.

3 *Content*. The information itself transmitted in communication is, of course, key to effective communication. Sufficient detail must be contained with communications to justify change, but at the same time the message should be kept straightforward and clear. Consideration also needs to be made to how good news and bad news should be communicated. External information is often of value in supporting the case for change, but is often under-utilized.

4 *Channel*. Information on change can be delivered verbally, via paper memos, e-mail, phone, or even mobile text messages. Choosing the appropriate range of channels is key here. Verbal communications on a one-to-one basis or larger-scale meetings are likely to be most effective in communicating the vision and need for change. Further details can be provided in written communications. E-mails are useful in keeping a group of people informed about a project and soliciting feedback. Text messaging is of limited value owing to space constraints, but can be used for brief updates. Texting has been used to inform people that they are redundant and is probably not the best channel for receiving this news!

An example of a good approach to communicating change to employees is provided by RS Components which, when first introducing the e-commerce site **www.rswww.com** as part of its new electronic sales channel, set aside an area of the staff canteen and set up a stand staffed by members of the electronic commerce team. Other staff were then encouraged to learn about using the Internet and the services that the website would provide. By this means all staff understood the purpose of using the Internet and were more supportive of it. Additionally, it helped support the adoption of an in-company intranet. More formal education and training which explains the purpose of the Internet marketing strategy and provides practical training for those involved was also necessary.

Debate 8.2

Motivating employees to change their behaviour as part of an information-man-agement-related change project is critical to success. Senior management ownership and involvement is unimportant.

Changing job design

The Job Characteristics model developed by Hackman and Oldham (1980) provides a useful framework for designing jobs that provide a good experience to improve staff motivation. These issues in job design should be considered by change agents since improvements to job design can be achieved and then emphasized in communications. The five intrinsic characteristics of a job are:

1 *Skill variety*, which is dependent on the extent to which a job involves a range of skills.
2 *Task identity*, how well the work is defined relative to other tasks or whether an employee sees a job through 'from start to finish'.
3 *Task significance* or the importance of the work.
4 *Autonomy* or freedom in completing work.
5 *Feedback* from employer.

To enhance these psychological characteristics Hackman and Oldham (1980) suggest that the following approaches can be used:

● *Task combination* – by combining tasks employees see more of the whole task. This often occurs in BPR projects and ERP systems which involve increasing the range of tasks completed by one person.
● *Natural work groups* – groupware (Chapter 2) can be used to support work groups which may often be created through BPR.
● *Establish customer relations* – this helps enhance the significance of the task to the individual if they are working directly with customers or have information about how customers perceive the company, its product and the level of service.
● *Vertical loading* – this involves employees taking responsibility for tasks perhaps previously completed by supervisors. With the automation enabled by information systems, staff can concentrate on value-adding activities. For example, e-procurement may enable members of a purchasing department to spend more time negotiating favourable agreements with suppliers rather than processing invoices.
● *Opening feedback channel* – this also involves providing staff with information from internal or external customers: in this case, information about levels of customer satisfaction.

Education and training

'Education' in a change context refers to the communication of reasons for change and updates on progress. The opportunity for feedback should be part of this. 'Training' in a change context refers to instruction on how an employee will be expected to work in the future. For information systems projects, training is clearly about how to use new software. For information management projects where new information sources are provided, perhaps through an intranet, the training is less on which buttons to push, but rather on the types of information available and how they can be applied to improve work performance. Training may also be needed to improve data quality, as described in Chapter 10. It would appear that many information-management-related projects fail to achieve the right balance between education and training. There is either insufficient training to be able to use new software tools correctly, or the tools training is available and there is insufficient education about the reason for using new software tools. The authors of this book have been involved in, or observed, the implementation of many systems ranging from banks, to retailers, to government departments, to systems for engineers, marketers and sales staff. We have seen that insufficient education and training is a common occurrence which leads to resistance to change and under-utilization of the new tools. It is not clear why insufficient attention is paid to education and training, but it appears that essentially it is a fear that the time taken in education and training will itself cause disruption, loss of productivity and so resentment. With the example of sales force automation and CRM tools for sales staff, introduced earlier in the chapter, sales staff are usually on performance-related pay dependent on the number of sales they make. So their managers will realize that they will resent time spent in education and training since they will perceive it as time lost when they could be making sales.

From this discussion of managing employee motivation, we can conclude the following:

- A range of techniques can be deployed and these must carefully balance the need for 'the carrot and the stick'.
- The literature stresses the need for two-way communication and dialogue using a range of different communication channels.
- Staff motivation is dependent on organization culture and existing job characteristics. It may be difficult to modify these underlying drivers of employee satisfaction during an individual change project.
- For information management projects it is important that education not be limited to training how to use the new systems, but also explain the reasons for their introduction and the implications for the individual and their teams.

To conclude this section on managing change, complete Activity 8.3.

Activity 8.3	Managing e-commerce-related change at the Lo-cost Airline Company
Purpose	To apply some of the concepts of change management introduced in this chapter.
Activity	This activity 'winds back the clock' to the time when the Lo-cost Airline Company did not have an online sales facility. Using the models of employee response to change and change management introduced in this chapter, explain how change could be managed for the introduction of the system described in the section below.
Background	The project to introduce online ticket sales involved not only customers using the system, but the staff in the call-centre who took orders over the phone. They were migrated to a web-based system delivered over the intranet which for efficiency was the same as that used by customers. The new system was initially slower to use for staff who were familiar with a traditional text-based application – both for searching for flights and for entering customer and booking details. The main staff affected by the introduction of the new system were the hundreds of call-centre staff and their team leaders (each team of 25 has a single leader).

Research insight 8.1	The role of Human Resources Departments

Changing an information system has been shown to have far-reaching effects beyond merely the technology that is used and the data that are captured and stored. An organization's culture may be affected, job roles and responsibilities may change and people may become demotivated. Management skills and techniques as well as employee education and training are key factors that determine the success, or otherwise, of any change programme.

Cotran et al. (2005) found that the successful implementation of an Enterprise Resource Planning (ERP) system in a global organization was achieved by involving Human Resources at an early stage to manage the effect of the resultant changes to working conditions.

Maguire and Redman (2007) examined the approach taken by a major public service organization towards information system development. They found that the Human Resources function was not involved to any great degree and that the 'softer' management skills were being ignored.

Specific examples of change management in BIM

In the final section of this chapter, we take four examples of different applications of business information management. We have selected examples of large-scale information management applications which are often challenging in achieving adoption of the new approach. We focus on issues of change management, but also refer to specific technical or management issues which may arise with the introduction of these new approaches to information management.

For each example we use a standard format, describing the nature of the business information management solution (what is it?), its benefits, typical risks and change management issues and finally a review of possible solutions or success factors. All of these solutions have been introduced elsewhere in the book, so cross-references are provided if you want to refer to where the approach is introduced or explained further.

Corporate information portal
Organizational information resources are made accessible via an intranet using structured and non-structured approaches

Intranet
A network within a single company which enables access to company information using the familiar tools of the Internet such as web browsers. Only staff within the company can access the intranet, which will be password-protected

Extranet
Formed by extending the intranet beyond a company to customers, suppliers, collaborators or even competitors. This is again password-protected to prevent access by all Internet users

1 The corporate information portal

What is it?

Corporate information portals were introduced in Chapter 2. A **corporate information portal** provides a primary gateway to organizational information and a method of sharing knowledge among staff. Typically, the corporate portal provides structured access to information stored in HTML web pages and is more commonly known by its user as 'the company **intranet**'. A corporate or enterprise portal will also consolidate many existing separate intranets into a single access point – If some of the information on the portal is also made available to third parties such as channel partners, then it is known as an '**extranet**'. Documents held on file servers in other standard formats such as those for spreadsheets, word processors and Adobe Acrobat may also be available.

The types of information available through a corporate portal include relatively static information such as a company phone directory, procedures and policies as well as more dynamic information such as company news. Providing dynamic information on the marketplace (competitive intelligence, Chapter 5) and on company performance is also common in more sophisticated portals. E-mail is often used to alert intranet users to information relevant to them. Instant messaging may also be used to provide real-time information sharing. To visualize what a corporate information portal looks like, think of a personalized consumer portal such as MyYahoo! (**http://my.yahoo.com**), but containing access to company information. E-mail or instant messaging may also be used to deliver information. HSBC, one of the largest financial services organizations in the world, has worked with Yahoo! to use instant messaging to assist its Global E-business team to communicate with cross-functional teams around the world. To see an actual example of a corporate portal, see Figure 8.3. In Chapter 2 it was mentioned that other applications may be accessed via the intranet – it can also become the main access point for employees to launch applications to manage information.

Figure 8.3 A corporate portal

Source: Nasa, http://www.hq.nasa.gov/pao/portal/

What are the benefits?

The benefits of corporate information portals and intranets, summarized from Chapter 2, include:

1 Improved information sharing
2 Enhanced communications and information sharing (communications)
3 Increased consistency of information
4 Increased accuracy of information
5 Reduced or eliminated processing
6 Easier organizational publishing.

In terms of the attributes of information quality explored in Chapter 11, the benefits are that relevant information can be found more readily, for example using the search facility. Information is relevant since it can be tailored or filtered to the individual or their work processes and alerts can be sent by e-mail. The information is more likely to be accurate since it is stored in a central place where it can be better controlled, which should mean that it is more likely to be up to date. First and perhaps foremost, it provides accessibility – information that was previously stored in printed manuals or was available in a separate system to which another department had access is available online, to use an over-used expression, 'at the click of a mouse'! The online storage and ease of access also have implications for cost reduction – less time is spent finding information and storing it in printed form.

Problems of change management

The difficulties with implementing intranets can be divided into the technical challenges of implementation such as creating the information architecture, which is described in Chapter 9, and problems with encouraging initial adoption and continued usage both by employees who actively supply information and those who use it passively. It is relatively easy to raise awareness of the launch of an intranet or of new content on the intranet. What seems to be more difficult is to maintain information update and usage. These problems of achieving initial adoption and continued usage are explored in this section.

Approaches to managing change

McFarland (2001) summarizes approaches to introducing an intranet, based on an interview with Heidi Collins, author of *Corporate Portals*. These are some of the approaches recommended to maximize information quality, user involvement and engagement:

1 *'Cover all your bases'*. This refers to using a cross-discipline project team which may be composed of managers from library or information services, human resources, IT and functional departments such as finance, operations and marketing. It is also suggested that sufficient analysis be done to identify current information needs (i.e. an information audit, Chapter 10), using interviews and surveys.

2 *Avoid generalization.* It is recommended that content should be themed for particular types of employee, not for an average employee. It is recommended that the system have phased implementation for one 'community' at a time, such as finance, sales or HR. This has a higher impact on users in each area and also enables the project to be broken down more readily.

3 *Keep current.* McFarland (2001) says: '*Intranets buckle under the burden of useless, outdated information*'. She recommends using software that uses automatic content expiration dates that automatically remove content when it is no longer applicable. Another approach is to make individuals responsible for particular types of content.

Staff responsibilities are reinforced formally by making this content updating part of their performance evaluation. Sometimes staff are incentivized to contribute content, as shown by the Siemens ShareNet portal. In this case, knowledge sharing amongst engineers and sales people was a key objective of the portal. Initially, in an approach called 'Bonus On Top', country managers were awarded a bonus according to the sharing of knowledge within their sales team. However, this did not directly reward individuals, so the company moved to using a more effective scheme known as 'ShareNet Shares'. This scheme was similar to Air Miles, with staff receiving bonuses for entering knowledge into the library (30 points), answering urgent requests for information (50 points) on the portal, and rating others' contributions to the portal (10 points). The points could then be exchanged for gifts such as mobile phones or textbooks. The top 50 points earners were invited to a conference in New York about improving ShareNet further!

4   *Measurement.* It is useful to get feedback on the level of usage of the intranet. Data on usage can be obtained from web log files which will show the types of content accessed and when. McFarland (2001) suggests that for the average corporate intranet, only 5 to 10 per cent of the organization will use it on a regular basis, but organizations that have an intranet that is supporting employees well with their information needs will be used by 70 to 80 per cent of employees daily. The opportunity for informal feedback through regular surveys of intranet users is also useful, particularly during initial introduction of the intranet. Many organizations set the default home page of their employees' web browsers in order to maximize exposure and potential use.

Many of the approaches to managing change described above also apply to extranets. In Chapter 2, five questions were asked when assessing the success of an extranet which could also be applied to corporate information portals.

To conclude this section, read Mini case study 8.1 and complete Activity 8.4.

Mini case study 8.1	**IT and change in small to medium businesses**

Small to medium-sized businesses (SMBs, also known as small to medium-sized enterprises, SMEs) have utilized technology to remain competitive with larger organizations, particularly in the adoption of web-based commerce. This is, however, a paradoxical situation whereby it is usually the SMBs that are too small to support a dedicated staff of web experts with sufficient expertise to ensure that any IT infrastructure is suitably robust and secure.

Alternatively, there are facilities to host IT services remotely, leaving them to focus on their core skills.

Careful selection of suitable providers is paramount and the hosting company should act as an extension of the organization, an accountable partner.

Source: Gary Chen, Yankee Group, http://i.i.com.com/cnwk.1d/html/itp/ThePlanet-YG_CapEx-Free-Hosting.pdf

Activity 8.4	Keeping a portal alive

Purpose   To review management controls that can be used to keep intranet content up to date.

Activity   You are an owner-manager of a business of 250 staff which produces office furniture. The intranet gives access to a staff directory, the latest product information and sales figures. Identify approaches that could be used to control the quality of information for each of these three types of information. After identification of different approaches, summarize generic controls which could be applied to any intranet.

2 Sell-side e-commerce

What is it?

Sell-side e-commerce
E-commerce transactions
between a supplier
organization and its
customers possibly
through intermediaries

We saw in Chapter 2 that 'sell-side e-commerce' refers to e-commerce transactions between a supplier organization and its customers, which may be other businesses (B2B) or consumers (B2C). We saw that these transactions may be financial, i.e. when a sale occurs, but they may also be informational such as information requests or support enquiries.

What are the benefits?

The benefits to the selling organization of adopting sell-side e-commerce are summarized in Table 8.4. It can be seen that there are some strategic benefits, such as the ability to enter international markets, or sell to different types of customers more readily and add value to service through better information about produce usage and service. For existing markets, e-commerce enables companies to deliver their products and services more cost-effectively.

Given these benefits to sell-side e-commerce, companies have enthusiastically embraced it. An international benchmarking study analysing the adoption of e-commerce by the UK Department of Trade and Industry (DTI, 2002) showed that in many developing countries, over 80 per cent of businesses of all sizes have some form of access to the Internet. However, this is not the entire story. Not all employees will have access to the Internet and it will not be used to support processes. Companies wishing to participate in B2B e-commerce with their customers need to analyse how common particular activities are. They then need to promote a change in behaviour in their customer base, if they are to achieve the benefits of sell-side e-commerce referred to above. Table 8.5 shows that the adoption of specific online purchasing activities such as identifying suppliers and automated reordering is much lower.

For consumer e-commerce, a similar picture exists, with levels of Internet access now exceeding 50 per cent in many developed countries, but there are lower levels of product selection and purchase online. Figure 8.4 shows that for some products such

Table 8.4 Typical tangible and intangible benefits from sell-side e-commerce

Tangible benefits	Intangible benefits
• Increased sales from new sales leads giving rise to increased revenue from: – new customers, new markets – existing customers (repeat-selling) – existing customers (cross-selling) • Marketing cost reductions from: – reduced time in customer service – online sales – reduced printing and distribution costs of marketing communications	• Adding value to products through supporting information, applications and customer service • Corporate image communication • Enhance brand • More rapid, more responsive marketing communications including PR • Faster product development lifecycle enabling faster response to market needs • Learning for the future • Meeting customer expectations to have a website • Identifying new channel partners, supporting existing partners better • Better management of marketing information and customer information • Feedback from customers on products

Table 8.5 Variation in adoption of different types of sell-side e-commerce transactions

E-business service	Percentage adoption across all businesses									
Online activity	Australia	Canada	France	Germany	Italy	Ireland	Japan	Sweden	UK	USA
Identify suppliers	42	41	40	39	42	42	13	42	54	51
Check availability of supplies	37	35	26	29	16	40	19	49	49	42
Track order progress	26	31	27	30	19	25	7	40	35	41
Make payments	40	21	7	29	19	23	8	38	19	19
Use after-sales support	42	38	29	35	30	38	10	62	47	52
Automatic reordering through shared systems	10	16	23	19	9	13	3	7	9	11
Collaborative product design and development	16	15	10	28	20	14	6	24	15	20
Collaborative demand planning and forecasting	6	10	9	15	11	6	3	17	7	10

Source: DTI (2002)

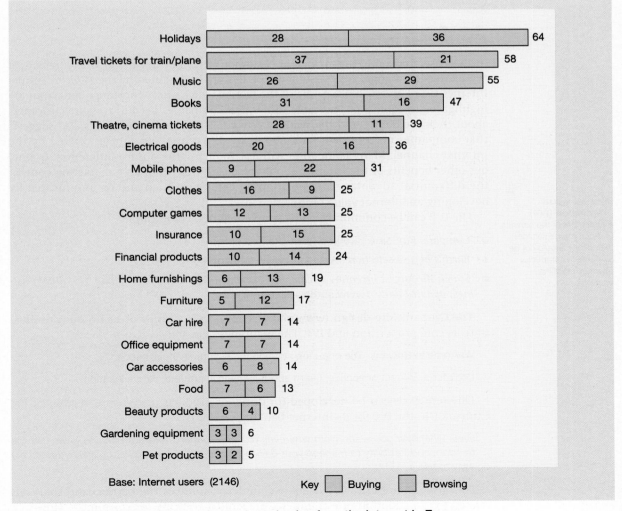

Figure 8.4 Survey results for browsing and purchasing from the Internet in Europe

Source: European Interactive Advertising Association (2004)

as books there is a relatively high ratio of browsers to buyers, but for others such as furniture and financial products, it is much lower. Of course, this is dependent on the nature of the product. Such e-commerce retailers need to find methods for changing behaviour and converting browsers to buyers.

Problems of change management

The problems of change management for sell-side e-commerce are similar to those of corporate portals and intranets, but this time it is an external audience that must be influenced to encourage a change in behaviour from previous ways of working. There is a similar problem of encouraging continued usage and participation in the use of online information resources and applications.

When sell-side e-commerce systems are introduced into a company there are also problems of conflict with other parties who also communicate with customers. For instance, sales representatives and distributors may feel that their role is being usurped. Customer-service staff in contact centres also have to be trained to manage enquiries from customers through a range of channels. However, in this coverage we concentrate on influencing customers, which is a different type of change management from the employee-related change management issues covered by other examples in this chapter.

Approaches to managing change

In this case, managing the change of customer behaviour must start with a review of the barriers to change. For consumers, barriers are highlighted by the *Which?* Annual Internet User Survey (2002). Some of the factors which affect consumer behaviour are highlighted in Table 8.6. This table shows that companies need to reassure customers about their credibility and the security offered. The question on prices also suggests that companies need to be clearer about the differential advantages offered by the Internet channel. Many companies will not want to offer a price differential online, but other benefits of the Internet should be clearly stated. In an e-marketing context the differential advantage and positioning can be clarified and communicated by developing an **Internet value proposition (IVP)**.

Internet value proposition (IVP)
A statement of the benefits of e-commerce services that ideally should not be available in competitor offerings or offline offerings

The IVP can be communicated by simple taglines. For example:

- *'Compare. Buy. Save'*, Kelkoo (**www.kelkoo.com**)
- *'Earth's biggest selection'*, Amazon (**www.amazon.com**)
- *'Search the largest inventory of cars and trucks on the Internet. More than 1.5 million listings, updated daily'* (**www.autotrader.com**).

The Citibank site design (**www.citibank.com**) uses a range of techniques to illustrate its core proposition and IVP. The main messages are:

Welcome to Citibank: The one-stop solution for all your financial needs.

Look for a product or service; Learn about a financial product; Find a location.

Different IVPs can be developed for different products or different segments. For Citibank UK, the IVP for its Internet banking service is:

Bank whenever you want, from wherever you are. Citibank Internet Banking gives you the freedom and flexibility to manage your day-to-day finances. It's secure, convenient and very easy to use.

For business-to-business sell-side e-commerce, some of the barriers and solutions related to the adoption of e-commerce are similar to those for consumers. However, overall, encouraging B2B e-commerce seems to be more challenging. The proportion of business transactions conducted online is lower than for many consumer products, as is suggested by a comparison of Figure 8.4 and Table 8.6. Inspection of Figure 8.5 shows some of the reasons businesses report for not adopting online technologies. Amongst the non-users fear of fraud and confidentiality breaches are relatively high, so it is important to reassure about these factors. Skills and costs are other factors. It can be seen that a similar form of research could be usefully employed to understand non-adoption of corporate information portals, but based around attributes of information quality.

There are additional complications in migrating businesses online which result in differences in the buying process between organizational or industrial buying and consumer buying. In a business context the decision to use a particular supplier, or select a product, is often not made by a single individual, but rather by a buying

Table 8.6 Perceptions about online shopping in the UK adult population

Is shopping on the Internet cheaper than in the high street shops?			
Agree 46%	Disagree 28%	Don't know 24%	Not applicable 1%
It is not safe to use a credit card to buy things on the Internet			
Agree 44%	Disagree 28%	Don't know 21%	Not applicable 6%
I would feel safer online knowing that the website carried some form of independent certification			
66%	22%	9%	2%

Source: *Which?* (2002)

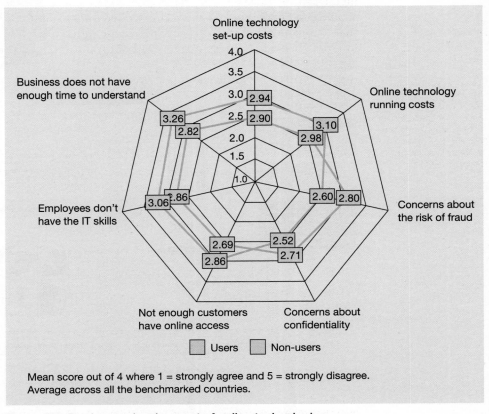

Mean score out of 4 where 1 = strongly agree and 5 = strongly disagree. Average across all the benchmarked countries.

Figure 8.5 Barriers to development of online technologies
Source: DTI (2002)

group or, in marketing parlance, the 'decision-making unit'. Typical members are users, influencers, buyers, deciders and gatekeepers. So, for a business customer to adopt e-commerce services involves persuading not one person, but several people. Also, the nature of purchases will vary considerably, with some regular purchases, some modified re-buys and potentially large-volume purchases of non-standard products. These differences appear to have resulted in a lower overall adoption of e-business for online trade.

If we look at an example of one company, the difficulty in encouraging adoption is indicated. RS Components (**www.rswww.com**) has had an award-winning transactional website since the mid-1990s. Yet, inspection of their annual report suggests that in its European markets, the proportion of sales achieved online is just 10 per cent (although it is higher in new markets it has entered such as Japan). This shows that there is a level of inertia in business, with businesses apparently happy with their existing methods of purchase from RS Components, whether it be by phone, mail order or visiting one of the local trade counters for items as they are required. To encourage switching to the Internet channel, RS Components puts on education workshops which are intended to demonstrate, through case studies and return-on-investment calculations, the benefits of migrating to online purchases. It also clearly emphasizes the benefits of online purchases on its websites, devoting a lot of space to this (Figure 8.6). The company also has an area of its site devoted to encouraging the adoption of e-procurement for purchasing managers.

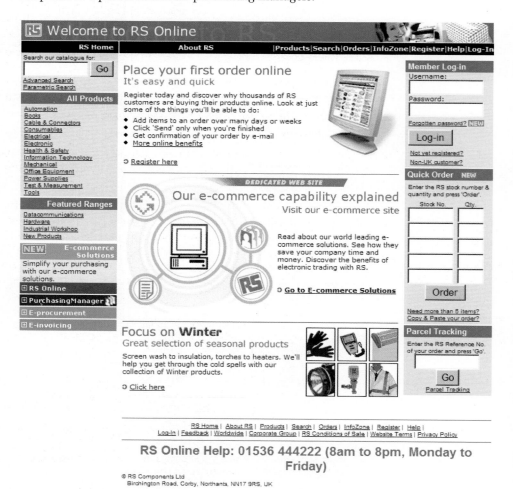

Figure 8.6 RS Components transactional website

Source: www.rswww.com

3 Customer relationship management

What is it?

Customer relationship management (CRM) systems
A system used to automate the process of marketing and delivering services to customers

Customer relationship management (CRM) systems were introduced in Chapter 2. They are used to support the marketing and delivery of services to customers. In the context of The Lo-cost Airline Company, a CRM system would include tools for helping customers select the best flight, purchasing tickets, answering pre-flight queries and support in any post-flight queries such as problems with baggage. A CRM system may also be used for marketing relevant, personalized offers direct to customers through direct mail (post) or e-mail. Essentially, CRM systems manage all interactions with a customer and its employees. Many CRM systems are delivered through a web interface, meaning that customers can effectively serve themselves (web self-service, Chapter 2). At a higher level, CRM systems enable customers to become more 'customer-centric'. The meaning of this is suggested by the elements that Siebel (2002) suggests are at the core of a CRM strategy:

- *Effective customer segmentation* – organizations can market to, sell to and serve customers more effectively by targeting their unique needs and preferences and understanding their relative value. Customers are grouped according to their needs and value and different offerings are delivered to each. CRM also enables marketing communications to be tailored on an individual level according to past products purchased, for example. These facilities are provided by the marketing module of a CRM system (Figure 8.7). The analytic capabilities are also used to determine the effectiveness of marketing and adjust it.

- *Integrated multi-channel strategy* – customers require services to be delivered over a range of channels such as phone, web, e-mail, face-to-face or by mail (Figure 8.7). These channels all need to deliver the same experience to the customer and, from the company's perspective, support each other in achieving sales and customer satisfaction.

- *Well-defined integrated customer-focused business processes.*

- *The right skills and mindsets.*

- *The right technology* and in particular a consistent, up-to-date picture of all *information and contacts related to a customer* (characteristics and sales, service, campaign contacts), sometimes referred to as 'a single view of the customer'.

Single view of the customer
All staff using different channels can access comprehensive, consistent, up-to-date information about a customer, thus enabling their queries to be answered adequately

Siebel Systems is one of the largest providers of CRM systems and was integrated with Oracle in 2006. It now has 5,000 customers and 4.6 million users worldwide (http://crmondemand.oracle.com/en/index.htm). These are typically large organizations. In 2003 it introduced with IBM, Siebel On Demand, a web services application that is intended for smaller customers at a rate of tens of dollars per month per employee. Salesforce.com and Microsoft are competitors in this on-demand approach

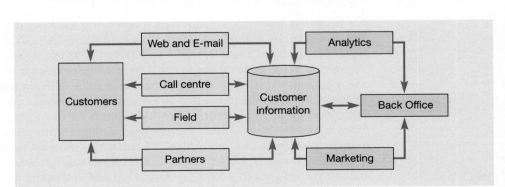

Figure 8.7 Main components of a typical CRM system
Source: Siebel (2002)

to CRM supply. Siebel is used as the case study tools vendor company for this section since it is representative of the difficulties of change management associated with all CRM systems. Siebel (2002) had reported that the overall size of the CRM market was estimated at \$23 billion. Of these projects 87 per cent would be customer CRM implementations and only 13 per cent using packaged implementations such as Siebel's. Intriguingly, more recent figures place the market size as somewhere around \$15 billion (**http://www.crmforecast.com/saasresearch.htm**).

What are the benefits?

CRM systems offer a range of benefits which are dependent on the different modules of a CRM system adopted. A CRM module for web-based sales will result in large cost-savings since the customers serve themselves. A CRM module that supports employees in a contact centre (inbound communications) should increase customer satisfaction because queries should be answered more quickly since the customer details are readily available. A CRM module to support sales representatives or account managers meeting face-to-face with customers should make them more effective since customer needs and orders can be better tracked. A CRM module to support outbound marketing communications, i.e. direct mail and e-mail campaigns, should result in lower costs and higher responses since the offers and information can be targeted to the right people, so reducing wastage.

In a survey of its customers (Siebel, 2002), the following benefits were reported by adopters of CRM (potential sources of these benefits added in brackets):

- 8 per cent increase in revenue [through better targeting of customers in marketing campaigns, giving a greater response, selling more products to existing customers (up-selling and cross-selling) and reducing customer attrition].

- 18 per cent increase in employee productivity [customer contacts can be handled more rapidly since information is rapidly provided and processes partly automated].

- 18 per cent increase in customer satisfaction [this again arises since information is more readily to hand and fulfilment should be improved, i.e. the customer is more likely to receive the product or service they ordered on-time]. Increasing customer satisfaction has been shown to reduce attrition and increase customer retention.

- 13 per cent increase in customer retention [arising from increased satisfaction and better targeted communications].

- 13 per cent decrease in operating costs [resulting from fewer staff needed to serve customers, manage processes and provide better targeted communications with less wastage].

Problems of change management

It is fair to say that CRM systems have a reputation for being difficult to implement – 70 per cent failure of implementations is a figure often quoted. Many vendors of CRM systems experienced a fall in revenues in 2001 to 2002 as the purchase of such systems was put on hold partly due to uncertainty with implementations. The actual failure rate is difficult to establish. ZDNet (2002) summarizes different research undertaken by analysts – Butler Group found that 70 per cent of CRM implementations fail. A Gartner study found that 55 per cent of all CRM projects failed to meet customers' expectations. A 2001 Bain & Company survey of 451 senior executives found that CRM ranked in the bottom three categories among 25 popular software tools evaluated for customer satisfaction. However, ZDNet (2002) reports on another survey (not by a well-known IT analyst) that showed that 'only 35 percent of CRM implementations, when considered over their entire life, can be considered failures'. It reported that, in contrast, 45 per cent of CRM implementations were producing a payback. Despite this latter report, it seems clear that it is difficult to achieve success in CRM implementations!

Approaches to managing change

Gartner (quoted in Siebel, 2003) estimates 'that 75 percent of the challenge of building better relationships with customers is contingent on change management rather than technology'. It explains that part of the problem with change is that up to 30 per cent of employees may be directly affected by a large-scale CRM implementation, such as in a financial services company with many customer-facing staff in call-centres and in branches that use technology to assist in customer interactions. This suggests that one of the difficulties with this type of system is caused by the scope of change – it is broad. One approach to better control the change is to have an overall CRM project with sub-projects for the different modules described above, which each have their own plans for how to manage change.

Siebel, one of the leading providers of CRM systems, has recognized that managing change is a key project risk in CRM implementations and that consequently this may lead to reduced adoption by companies that do not think the risk/reward balance is right. Siebel has produced literature (Siebel, 2003) to explain to its customers and prospects approaches for reducing the risk arising from managing change.

Siebel (2003) identifies six 'levers of change management'. These are approaches to manage change that you will recognize as similar to those introduced earlier in the chapter. We will apply each to a CRM implementation:

1 *Compensation and rewards.* In a CRM context, performance evaluation and improved structures need to be created which promote behaviour that is 'customer-centric', i.e. it helps to understand the customer better and deliver better service. For example, customer satisfaction might be added as an evaluation criterion for employee performance, in addition to the more traditional measures such as number of sales achieved or number of service calls resolved. Staff may also be incentivized to improve data quality. For example, a bank ran a competition to identify the member of call-centre staff who collected the most customer e-mail addresses since this field in the database had poor coverage. Similar sales representatives can be incentivized to record details of customer visits more accurately.

2 *Boss behaviour.* This is described as the actions, attitudes and decisions of a supervisor, manager or executive, i.e. different levels of manager. A method is not suggested as to how an organization could assess or improve the extent to which managers support the change associated with the introduction of the CRM system. It is incumbent on managers to be aware of their role in supporting change. A top-down approach where the most senior managers actively support change and encourage this attitude in the managers that report to them seems to be the most practical approach. This can then be cascaded down the different levels of a large organization. Performance review and evaluation can again be used to control behaviour.

3 *Policies and processes.* Changes to policies and processes required by a new system need to be identified early, defined clearly and communicated to staff. Perhaps many of the problems arising with CRM systems result from a failure to acknowledge that the CRM implementation is not 'just a new software tool', but also 'a new way of working'. The changes to sales processes need to be documented and the implications for staff explained. In a CRM system, examples of staff activities which need to be redefined, provided by Siebel (2003), are initiating and closing sales opportunities, addressing customer complaints and managing partnership relationships.

4 *Training.* New skills are clearly required by employees to execute the new business processes with the new software. But Siebel (2003) notes that many CRM projects do not provide employees with sufficient training or at least training that targets the right needs. Formal training in using the software is not the only approach. Mentoring in the workplace by more skilled staff is another approach that is mentioned. Adequate help systems built into the software and available on the web systems and access to help-desk staff who understand the organization's issues are also important.

5 *Communication.* The emphasis is placed on communication having sufficient frequency and depth. It should not be limited to an initial communication about a new system, but should keep staff informed throughout the implementation, including the phase when the system becomes live and problems are often encountered. Frequent communications can be achieved using many media. Siebel (2003) mentions a mix of non-verbal and verbal communications, including 'employee portals, e-mails, broadcast voicemails, newsletters, memos, videos, luncheons or breakfasts, meetings and speeches'! It suggests that non-verbal communications are sometimes neglected, but are useful to communicate the importance of the new system. Finally, the importance of two-way communication is emphasized. Meetings should also solicit feedback from employees on their concerns and how they can support and facilitate change.

6 *Organizational structure.* Siebel (2003) notes that the existing structure must support open communications to promote change. The structure must also be suitable to encourage collaboration which supports the ultimate goal of serving the customer better. Through making minor adjustments to reporting lines and how teams collaborate, this is a signal which communicates that senior managers expect the members of the organization to work together to achieve change.

Cross-departmental collaboration during implementation is a further issue with CRM projects. It is often unclear where ownership of the project lies. Is it the marketing department, the operations department (for customer service), the IT department, customer information manager or a member of senior management? To resolve this problem, it is important that one clear owner of the project be established and that they are at director level. A change or project team involving the different stakeholders needs to meet regularly to manage change and control the project. Siebel (2003) notes that

> the influence of top executives is required to overcome the cultural resistance, organizational inertia, political battles, disagreements and other similar challenges that crop-up when considerable cross-organizational change takes place. Since resistance attributed to internal factors plagues CRM projects and frequently contributes to their failure, strong executive sponsorship and commitment to enforce change in the face of criticisms and organizational discomfort is an imperative.

ZDNet (2002) offers four guidelines for success in managing change associated with CRM. These emphasize the importance of focus on customer-centricity (the deployed system must actually enhance the experience for the customer); engaging line staff (consistent with the guidelines above); being willing to change the organization (structures, processes and reporting, again consistent with the guidelines above) and setting measurable goals (this is not normally mentioned as part of change initiatives, but is, of course, important for implementation of any new approach).

4 Business intelligence

What is it?

Business intelligence
Software used to analyse and improve business processes through the provision of analysis and reporting capabilities

Data mining
Software is used to identify relationships within data items in a database

'Business intelligence (BI)' refers to a category of software or approach to information management used by managers to understand and improve the performance of their processes. At its simplest, 'business intelligence software' is a modern term for business reporting software. This software counters information overload to deliver relevant, timely information to managers' desktops and into their hands. At its most complex, it offers sophisticated analysis tools for identifying patterns and relationships within data – an approach known as '**data mining**'. Such information tools have been previously known as 'decision support systems' (DSS).

Data mining is commonly used within marketing applications, marketing-related examples of data mining techniques including:

- *Identifying associations* – a shopping basket analysis by a chemist revealed an association of shoppers who purchase condoms and foot powder. It is not clear how this information can be used!

- *Identifying sequences* – shows the sequence in which actions taken by customers occur, e.g. path or clickstream analysis of a website.

- *Classifications* – patterns, e.g. identifying groups of website users who display similar visitor patterns.

- *Clustering* – finding groups of facts that were previously unknown. Customers who purchase a particular product can be grouped according to their characteristics. Potential customers who share these characteristics can then be identified.

- *Forecasting* – using sales histories to forecast future sales.

Data warehouses
Large database systems containing detailed company data on sales transactions which are analysed to assist in improving the marketing and financial performance of companies

Data mining is often performed on data stored in **data warehouses**. Data warehouses are large database systems (often measured in gigabytes or terabytes (1 terabyte = 1,000 billion bytes)) containing detailed company data on sales transactions which are analysed to assist in improving the marketing and financial performance of companies. Data warehouses are usually separated from the operational databases of an organization, as is shown in Figure 8.8. Data are transferred from the operational system(s) into the data warehouse every night, week or month depending on the analysis requirements. Detailed database queries can then be performed without slowing down the operational systems. Figure 8.8 shows that the results obtained from the data warehouse can be accessed by a specialist piece of software from vendors such as Cognos or Business Objects, or increasingly though a web browser as part of the intranet.

William Inmon is often known as 'the father of the data warehouse'; he defines a data warehouse as:

A subject oriented, integrated, time variant, and non-volatile collection of data in support of management's decision making process.

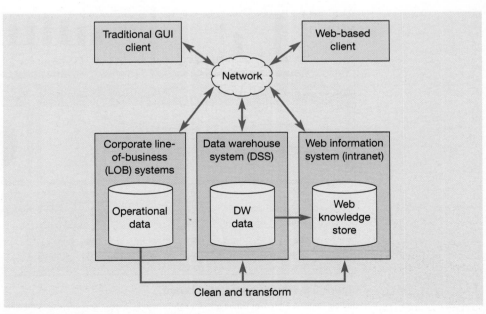

Figure 8.8 **Architecture of a data warehouse**
Source: Bocij et al. (2003)

It is worth considering each of the characteristics of the definition in more detail:

- *'subject oriented'*. Examples of subjects that are commonly held in data warehouses for analysis are customer and product.
- *'integrated'*. An important principle of data warehouses is that information be collected from diverse sources within an organization and brought together to enable integrated analysis.
- *'non-volatile'*. Data are transferred from operational information systems such as sales order processing systems into a data warehouse where the information is static – it is not updated. This is to prevent degradation of the performance of the operational systems.
- *'in support of management's decision making process'*. This final point emphasizes the purpose of the data warehouse.

Data warehouses form a category of business intelligence software that has been adopted by many companies for analysis of transactions to help improve their competitiveness. A good example is where retailer Boots analyses the transactions of its loyalty card users, amounting to over 500,000 product transactions each day. Such has been their popularity that the term 'data warehouse' has to a great extent displaced 'EIS' in software purchases for strategic and tactical decision making.

What are the benefits?

The benefits of business intelligence software centre on providing improved quality of information for managers to assist them in assessing and improving the performance of business processes. Broadly speaking, two levels of BI use can be identified. First, it is used at a tactical level by managers and analysts looking to improve the efficiency of their processes. Secondly, business intelligence software is used by more senior managers for reporting and analysis. Such systems were formerly labelled

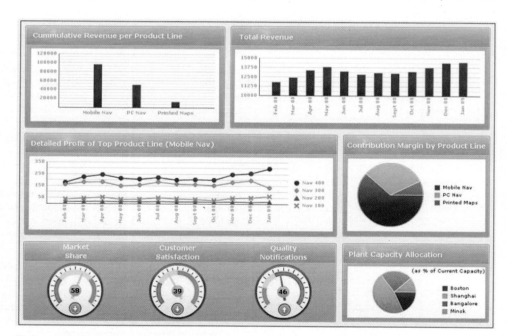

Figure 8.9 Performance dashboard

Source: SAP AG, http://m.zdnet.com.au/sap-business-suite-7-screenshots-339296904.htm

'executive information systems' (EIS). There is an overlap here with the **corporate performance management** systems described in Chapter 10. Such systems are used by senior managers to monitor the performance of the parts of the business they are responsible for. Typically a **performance dashboard** such as that in Figure 8.9 will be available, with different summaries of key performance indicators and drivers from which more detailed information can be obtained. Such facilities are now often available through the corporate information portal facility described earlier in the chapter. Such systems offer managers the facility to track actual performance against targets across the business, including finance, sales and production. When variance from target is identified, drill-down can be used to help identify the source of the problem.

It can be seen from the figure that the main benefit provided to managers by the information is easy access to relevant, timely information. Such systems provide managers with summary information in a visual form that is rapid to interpret. They can also be linked to alerts via e-mail or SMS when variance exceeds a given threshold.

Case study 8.2 discusses data analysis methods.

Corporate performance management
A process for improving the performance of organizations based on performance metrics

Performance dashboard
A summary of complex information about the effectiveness of organizational performance using a combination of tables, charts and graphics

Case study 8.2

A discussion of data analysis methods

Fair Isaac, a global provider of decision management solutions, outlines four major areas of analytic techniques and may utilise them in combination:

Exploratory data analysis
Predictive modelling
Optimization
Decision analysis

Exploratory data analysis
Seeks to establish relationships in the data to gain insight. Within this exploration, no specific outcome is assumed. An example of this group of techniques would be cluster analysis, used to develop a strategic marketing segmentation. Other techniques in this category are factor and principal component analyses.

Predictive modelling
Seeks to identify and mathematically represent underlying relationships in historical data, in order to explain the data and make predictions or classifications about new data. Predictive models are frequently used as ways to summarize large quantities of data as well as to increase the value of data. In the financial services, telecommunications, direct marketing and e-commerce industries, they are commonly used as inputs to decisions. An example would be the use of logistic regression to classify prospects as good or bad credit risks. Other techniques in this category are boosting, collaborative filtering, discrete choice modelling, discriminant analysis, INFORM, log-linear models, neural networks, pattern recognition, regression, support vector machines, survival analysis and tree modelling methods. Expert systems and RFM also fit in this category, but are different in that they can be derived judgmentally without historical data.

Optimization techniques
These seek to efficiently and effectively search across a set of possible solutions to a problem (either constrained or unconstrained) with the goal of maximizing or minimizing a particular mathematical function. Techniques in this category are genetic algorithms, linear programming and non-linear programming. Several of the predictive modelling and decision analysis techniques rely on optimization techniques to reach their results.

Decision analysis
By modelling the decision itself, it allows for the optimal decision to be identified. The purpose of decision analysis is to assist decision makers in making better decisions in complex situations, usually under uncertainty. Components of decision analysis include graphical decision models, multiple objective decision analysis, sequential decisions and utility theory. Since decision analysis delivers the most value when coupled with active, continuous learning from observations, the need for well-planned or designed data is critical in the building of a robust decision model.

Source: Fair Isaac Corporation, Whitepaper, A Discussion of Data Analysis, April 2006

Problems of change management

Case study 8.3 'Fighting the flood of data' gives an indication of the benefits and problems of introducing business intelligence systems. Some of the problems referred to in the case include using different BI tools in different areas of the business, using tools for data mining in such a way that they don't support the business, lack of focused objectives, and insufficient data cleansing (Chapter 10). These data warehouse projects, which were common in the mid-1990s, reported similar failure rates to CRM projects. A report prepared in 1998 by analysts IDC, at a time when many data warehouse projects were undertaken, identified these problems:

1 Raising users' expectations higher than you can deliver.
2 Letting the project scope become unmanageable.
3 Underusing the warehouse.
4 Letting management interest.
5 Not fully developing business requirements.

A further 1998 report, by the Meta group, identified these failings:

35–40 per cent: data quality;

30–35 per cent: transforming/scrubbing legacy data, managing end-user expectations;

20–25 per cent: managing management expectations, business rule analysis, managing metadata (data about data);

15–20 per cent: database performance tuning/scaling, ROI justification;

10–15 per cent: time to load/refresh data;

5–10 per cent: security, maintenance.

It seems that a particular problem with data mining is that, because of its exploratory nature, it is unclear what the goals should be, since the general aim could be stated as 'to find hidden patterns in the data which can be used to improve performance'. This also makes it difficult to put a value on the return on investment for these types of projects.

Approaches to managing change

In contrast to the systems described earlier in this section, where the change management issues are around encouraging adoption of new systems and new approaches by employees, it is the behaviour of managers and often senior managers that needs to be influenced in adoption of BI systems. Managing human change associated with these systems can be divided into the issues of encouraging change in senior managers to use these systems and ensuring that technical staff involved in data warehousing projects are managed to ensure that their efforts deliver business benefits.

When corporate performance management systems are introduced, a key issue is how senior managers react to them. One would hope that the days are gone when senior managers would boast that they don't know how to switch on their computer or send an e-mail. Yet, still one hears this story. More commonly one meets managers whose mindset is to drive organizational performance through the management information (MI) packs. Of course, it may be more efficient for senior managers to review such MI at meetings, without recourse to a PC, and to leave the drilling down to their juniors. In 1979 John Rockart wrote about different attitudes or approaches to MI (Rockart, 1979). The four different attitudes still seem apposite. In the first approach, MI is simply seen as a by-product of operational reporting. In such cases, information may not be aggregated sufficiently to take decisions, indeed the right types of information may not be available. Executives will often see performance analysis as a task to be delegated to less senior managers. The second attitude arises from the intangible nature of information that is part of strategic decision making. Rockart characterizes this through this statement:

> Top executives' activities are dynamic and ever changing, so one cannot predetermine exactly what information will be needed to deal with changing events at any point in time. These executives, therefore, must be dependent on future-oriented, rapidly assembled, most often subjective and informal information delivered by word-of-mouth from trusted advisers.

The third approach is the 'key indicator approach' which is becoming pervasive today and is supported by tools such as performance dashboards. At the time that Rockart wrote his article indicators were mainly limited to financial variables, but today's approach is to use the balanced scorecard approach (Chapter 10) which considers customer- and employee-related aspects of business performance in addition to financial metrics. The fourth approach is a holistic approach known as the 'total study'; it is based on a detailed analysis of managers' information needs and provides key performance indicators with the facility to drill down to find more detailed information.

As with all information systems, training of senior managers in how to use the software is required. But one of the aims of modern business intelligence systems is that the software can be configured to readily show key reports – this role is typically performed by members of the management reporting team, so there needs to be careful analysis of information requirements. Perhaps a more important training need, given the volume of data available from these systems, is to develop information analysis skills, although it might be difficult to suggest that this is a training need for senior managers. Simple guidelines can help in making better use of, and creating better, performance dashboards. *Harvard Management Update* (1998) presents guidelines for information analysis by managers. The main guideline is to identify the 'metrics that matter'. Although dashboards already provide a summary of information, there can still be quite a depth of information across several screens. Typical reports generated by Excel can run to many pages. Managers need to question the value of every data item using the metrics tests described in Chapter 10. The article suggests that questions that should be asked to assess the value of metrics include: Does the metric directly support the organizational objectives (i.e. is it a performance driver)? Does focus on this metric alone cause a problem? The article gives the example of a fast-food vendor that focused on 'chicken efficiency' – how much had to be thrown away. To improve this metric, staff cooked chickens on demand, which resulted in a long queue of dissatisfied customers, but the metric was improved. Are we checking leading (future) indicators (such as employee and staff satisfaction) as well as lagging indicators (sales and financial performance)? It is important not only to look backwards, to be reactive to variations between targeted and actual performance, but also to look forwards, to be able to forecast to help control future direction.

The reports on problems with data warehouses described in the previous section suggest that a common problem is setting managers' expectations too high about what is possible through a data warehouse. Communication to employees on the objectives of the project and capability of the software seems important to avoid promising a 'holy grail' of information management. Additionally, Case study 8.3 suggests that there is a trend away from using data warehouses which use a separate repository of data extracted from operational data as shown in Figure 8.8. Instead, data are analysed directly from the operational database(s). The reports also indicate the importance of identifying data quality as a risk factor in such projects, and putting in place measures to control this, as described in Chapter 10.

Data warehouse specialist David Kelly identified 10 critical factors in implementing a data warehouse (Kelly, 1997). These are a mix of technical approaches and issues. The 10 factors together with our explanation are:

1 *Information*. To state the obvious, a capability must be available to produce relevant information from the system which is essentially a data repository. This implies clear objectives and careful analysis to identify relevant information.

2 *Ease of access*. The system must be readily available and easy to use by managers as well as technical staff. Some data analysis tools can be described as 'designed by statisticians, for statisticians'.

3 *Data standards*. Corporate standards are required so that values such as currency and dates are uniform across the organization. Methods of calculating derived values must be consistent also.

4 *Dedicated resource*. The resources of the system need to be dedicated to data analysis and data mining. It is not clear why this is the case.

5 *Adequate performance*. With advances in technology, this is less of a problem today.

6 *Corporate sponsorship*. As we have seen for other systems, senior management ownership is important since data warehouse projects were typically high-cost, cross-enterprise projects requiring collaboration by a range of staff.

7 *Operationally stable*. The system needs to be reliable and secure.

8 *Agreed infrastructure*. At the time, Kelly felt it was essential that the infrastructure be distinct from decision support.

9 *New user culture*. Since the data warehouse may require new user processes the culture must be right in order to accept these changes.

10 *Source data*. The relevant data must be available through integration with other systems.

Kelly goes on to discuss specific issues of managing user perception. Problems specific to a data warehouse project include the ownership of data. Since data in a data warehouse will be from many sources, this needs to be clearly established and managed by a cross-functional team. He also mentions the culture and skills of members of the team. There is a particular risk with data-mining teams that the project analysts will be mathematicians and statisticians who will be interested in the theories of patterns within the data. While of intrinsic interest, this will not help achieve return on investment on the project! Kelly suggests that team members need these attributes: customer-orientation (to their customers in the business), flexibility to change in project direction, good political skills, good communication skills, capability of teamwork, capability of taking a broad and enterprise-wide perspective. He places excellent analytical skills as the last prerequisite!

To conclude this section on issues of managing change for different information managagement applications, complete Activity 8.5 to identify common issues.

Activity 8.5	Summarizing common themes in change management for BIM

Purpose of activity	To summarize the common approaches to managing change in information management applications described in this chapter.
Activity	Review the sections in the last part of this chapter, from Corporate information portals to Business intelligence, and summarize (a) common problems of managing change when introducing information systems and (b) common approaches to maximize the chances of success.

Case study 8.3

Fighting the flood of data

This case highlights the continuing importance of business intelligence software. It looks at some of the drivers for adoption and possible technical problems with introducing it. It does not confront the people-related issues of managing change when such systems are introduced. This issue is addressed as one of the questions that follows.

In the face of an economic downturn, one might have expected companies to cut back on IT projects across the board. Spending on business intelligence tools, however, remains healthy. According to Forrester Research, the analyst group, as many as 44 per cent of companies are considering investing in business intelligence software. This puts growth in business intelligence ahead of that in customer relationship management (CRM), enterprise resource planning (ERP) and integration technologies.

Business intelligence software helps companies analyse and manage information across their operations, whether it is sales data produced by an electronic point of sale (EPOS) system, information from distributors, statistics from a website or traffic from a call centre.

As IT departments improve the connections between business systems, the amount of data reaching managers can increase dramatically.

Areas such as supply chain management, ERP and production systems are showing a trend towards real-time data gathering. This holds out the potential for far quicker and more accurate decision-making. But there is also a danger: managers risk being overwhelmed by the sheer volume of information they receive. Rather than better decision-making, the result can be executive paralysis.

'It can happen that instead of reacting to the information they receive, managers are swamped', says Roy Bernard, strategy director of The Aspect Group, a consultancy that builds information systems. The best way to avoid this, Mr Bernard suggests, is to start with smaller projects, extending their scope as managers become more familiar with the technology.

Often, though, companies introduce business intelligence systems without thinking first about the questions they want to answer. They are not helped by the sheer quantity of information that is available. The number of analysis tools on offer sometimes makes matters worse.

Adopting a single set of business intelligence tools is a good start. Forrester Research found that more than 80 per cent of companies operate multiple business intelligence tools. This can lead to inconsistencies and 'several versions of the truth'. Instead of making decisions, managers spend time arguing about which set of data to use.

Yet a centralised approach can be equally unhelpful when business intelligence specialists fail to communicate with the managers who ultimately carry out decisions.

'Companies have fallen down in the past by using too wide a range of tools', says David Metcalfe, Forrester's analyst for business intelligence in Europe. 'But we also have situations where the statistical whizz-kids use data-mining techniques to find interesting mathematical issues to solve, but which bear no resemblance to the problems the business managers face. That is a huge disconnect.'

First, then, a company needs to make sure that its business intelligence tools are attempting to answer the right questions. This is not only the case where business intelligence is handled by a dedicated team. Systems such as 'executive dashboards', which display data in one place for senior managers, are little use unless they provide the right information. A business will not become more responsive just because managers have more data at their fingertips. The reverse can even be true.

'Companies gather information about their customers and accumulate massive amounts of data without thinking about what it enables them to do', cautions Mike Lucas, technology manager at systems integrator Compuware. 'They can become flooded with information, and that clogs up innovative decision-making.'

And even the right information will not fulfil its promise unless it is put into context. Raw sales data is more meaningful when set alongside information about current marketing campaigns; and data on repair times achieved by a field service force makes more sense if managers know the age of the appliances they are fixing.

In the past, companies would set up major data warehousing projects just to gather the raw numbers for analysis. Such projects are both costly and time-consuming. Instead, the latest generation of business intelligence tools draws information directly from a company's IT systems, then presents it in a consistent, usually web-based, format.

Direct feeds of data from operational systems such as customer ordering software or ERP are much more likely to be up-to-date and accurate. This is important, because data cleaning is expensive. Forrester estimates that as much as 60 per cent of the cost of a business intelligence project lies in data cleaning.

The need for a large, up-front investment in data warehousing is also reduced if companies focus business intelligence projects on finding answers to specific questions, such as 'How can we cut purchasing costs?' or 'How can we persuade existing customers to buy more?'. Where business intelligence projects are well defined and managed, the rewards can be significant.

Source: Fighting the flood of data, Stephen Pritchard, FT.com; 7 May 2003

Questions

1 What are the typical problems in introducing business intelligence tools that are described in the case study?

2 What additional people-related problems do you think may arise when business intelligence systems are introduced for end-users? Assess these problems, which are not directly considered in the article, based on the concepts of managing change introduced earlier in this chapter.

Summary

1 Managing change associated with information management initiatives is important since often users will be faced with new ways of working and new software tools. The response to change must be managed to ensure that the new system is adopted by staff to achieve the return on investment.

2 Across an industry, change occurs at two scales – *incremental change* involving small adjustments to improve efficiency and respond to normal changes in its environment and *discontinuous change* which is caused by a significant change in the business environment.

3 Information management initiatives may support either incremental or discontinuous change.

4 Models of supporting organizational change illustrate the need to manage the transition from one dynamic state to the next. Change management does not end when a project has been completed since otherwise behaviour may revert to an original state.

5 There is a well-established transition model of human response to change with stages of awareness or shock, denial, depression, letting go, testing, consolidation and acceptance.

6 Associated with these reactions, individuals exhibit resistance to change which in an information systems context may involve not using the system or actively voicing concerns about it.

7 Organizational culture may also affect the ability of individuals to react to change.

8 Structured approaches to managing change involve identifying change agents who work out the best way to manage the transitions from one state to another, including the human response.

9 Identification of key staff in managing change is important since these will influence others. The role of senior managers is critical in communicating the vision for change and then supporting it through their actions. Team members who legitimize systems and opinion leaders also need to be involved to support change.

10 Approaches to motivating staff need to be reviewed. The approaches we looked at include education and persuasion, participation and involvement, facilitation and support, negotiation and agreement, manipulation and co-option, direction and a reliance on explicit and implicit coercion. Training and changes to job design are also important approaches.

11 In the final section of the chapter we considered approaches to managing change for four information management initiatives that are often subject to problems of change. These are the corporate information portal, sell-side e-commerce, customer relationship management and business intelligence.

Exercises

Self-assessment questions

1 Relate the concepts of incremental change and discontinuous change to information systems implementation.

2 Summarize the transition model of individuals' reaction to change and describe approaches to counter or minimize these reactions in an information systems implementation.

3 What are the signs of resistance to change exhibited by employees in the context of an information system implementation and how can they be countered?

4 Why should organizational culture be considered when managing a change programme?

5 Describe the typical approaches taken by a change agent to minimize problems of change on an information management project.

6 Who are the different stakeholders involved in change and how do they need to be managed?

7 How can staff be motivated to encourage new behaviours and minimize resistance to change?

8 What are the most typical problems in managing change for information management projects and how can they be minimized?

Essay and discussion questions

1 Summarize how different models of organizational and individual responses to change can be applied to minimize problems of change management in an information-management-related change project.

2 Write an essay on how different types of stakeholder in a change project can be involved and managed to assist in successful completion of the change project.

3 How should change be managed for successful implementation of different forms of knowledge management initiative?

4 Assess the change management issues and approaches to accommodate them that would be required for introduction of:

   (a) an electronic procurement system into an organization's purchasing department;
   (b) a new accounting system with business intelligence reporting capabilities into a finance department;
   (c) a human resources extranet giving employees access to self-service applications for all human-resources-related interactions traditionally performed directly with the human resources department.

5 Discuss how information systems are used to support different forms of incremental change and discontinuous change and the different change management issues that arise in each.

6 Produce a change management plan for introducing one of the following types of information management initiatives at a university:

- customer relationship management system used for managing student recruitment;
- an intranet for staff;
- an intranet for students.

References

Adams, J., Hayes, J. and Hopson, B. (1976) *Transitions: Understanding and Managing Personal Change*. Martin Robertson, London.

Ajzen, I. (1985) From intentions to actions: A theory of planned behavior. In J. Kuhl and J. Beckmann (eds), *Action Control: From Cognition to Behaviour*. Springer series in social psychology. Springer, Berlin, pp. 11–39.

Ajzen, I. (1991) The theory of planned behavior. *Organizational Behavior and Human Decision Processes*, 50(2), 179–211.

Ajzen, I. and Fishbein, M. (1973) Attitudinal and normative variables as predictors of specific behavior. *Journal of Personality and Social Psychology*, 27(1), 41–57.

Bandura, A. (1977) Self-efficacy: Toward a unifying theory of behavioral change. *Psychology Review*, 84, 977, 191–215.

Bandura, A. (1986) *Social Foundations of Thought and Action: A Social Cognitive Theory*. Prentice-Hall, Englewood Cliffs, NJ.

Bandura, A. (1989) 'Human agency in social cognitive theory.' *American Psychologist*, 44, 1989, 1175–84.

Bandura, A. (2001) 'Social cognitive theory: An agentive perspective.' *Annual Review of Psychology*, 52 (1), 2001, 1–26.

Bocij, P., Chaffey, D., Greasley, A. and Hickie, S. (2003) *Business Information Systems: Technology, Development and Management*, 2nd edn. Financial Times Prentice Hall, Harlow.

Boddy, D., Boonstra, A. and Kennedy, G. (2001) *Managing the Information Revolution. An Organizational Perspective*. Financial Times Prentice Hall, Harlow, UK.

Cope, O. and Waddell, D. (2001) An audit of leadership styles in e-commerce. *Managerial Auditing Journal*, 16(9), 523–9.

Cotran, K., Buchmeiser, U., Seguin, J. and Pelster, B. (2005) HR's role in implementing JTI's global ERP system. *Strategic HR Review*, 4(5), 24–7.

Davenport, T. H. (1993) *Process Innovation: Re-engineering Work through Information Technology*. Harvard Business School Press, Boston, MA.

Davis, F. D. (1986) A technology acceptance model for empirically testing new end-user information systems: Theory and results. Doctoral dissertation, Sloan School of Management, Massachusetts Institute of Technology.

Davis, F. D. (1989). Perceived usefulness, perceived ease of use, and user acceptance of information technology. *MIS Quarterly*, 13(3), 319–39.

DTI (2002) *Business in the Information Age – International Benchmarking Study 2001*. UK Department of Trade and Industry. Latest version available online at: www.ukonlinefor-business.gov.uk/benchmarking2002.

Fishbein, M. (1967) Attitude and the prediction of behavior. In M. Fishbein (ed.), *Readings in Attitude Theory and Measurement*, pp. 477–92. Wiley, New York.

Fishbein, M. and Ajzen, I. (1975) *Belief, Attitude, Intention, and Behavior: An Introduction to Theory and Research*. Addison-Wesley, Reading, MA.

Gartner (2003) Gartner Application Integration and Middleware Strategies Research, Note T-19-4751, J. Sinur, D. McCoy and J. Thompson, 14 April. The Gartner Group (www.gartner.com).

Hackman, J. and Oldham, G. (1980) *Work Redesign*. Addison-Wesley, Reading, MA.

Hammer, M. and Champy, J. (1993) *Re-engineering the Corporation: A Manifesto for Business Revolution*. HarperCollins, New York.

Harvard Management Update (1998) *Using measurement to boost your unit's performance. Harvard Management Update*, 3(10).

Hayes, J. (2002) *The Theory and Practice of Change Management*. Palgrave, Basingstoke.

Jay, K. E. and Smith, D. C. (1996) A generic change model for the effective implementation of information systems. *South African Journal of Business Management*, September, 27(3).

Kelly, D. (1997) *Data Warehousing in Action*. Wiley, Chichester.

Kotter, J. (1995) Leading change: Why transformation efforts fail. *Harvard Business Review*, March–April.

Kotter, J. and Schlesinger, L. (1979) Choosing strategies for change. *Harvard Business Review*, March–April.

Lazarsfeld, P. F., Berelson, B. and Gaudet, H. (1949) *The People's Choice: How the Voter Makes up His Mind in a Presidential Campaign*. Columbia University Press, New York.

Lewin, K. (1951) *Field Theory in Social Science*. Harper and Row, New York.

Maguire, S. and Redman, T. (2007) The role of human resource management in information systems development. *Management Decision*, 45(2), 252–64.

McFarland, J. (2001) Corporate portals. *Harvard Management Communication Letter*, June, 3–5.

Nadler, D., Shaw, R. and Walton, E. (1995) *Discontinuous Change*. Jossey-Bass, San Francisco, p. 24.

Rockart, J. (1979) Chief executives define their own information needs. *Harvard Business Review,* March–April.

Rogers, E. M. (1962) *Diffusion of Innovations*. The Free Press, New York.

Rogers, E. M. (1995) *Diffusion of Innovations*, 4th edn. The Free Press, New York.

Rogers, E. M. and Shoemaker, F. F. (1971) *Communication of Innovations: A Cross-Cultural Approach*, 2nd edn. The Free Press, New York.

Schein, E. (1992) *Organizational Culture and Leadership*. Jossey-Bass, San Francisco.

Siebel (2002) Annual report. www.siebel.com.

Siebel (2003) Applied change management: a key ingredient for CRM success. Siebel White Paper, Siebel resource center. www.siebel.com.

Taylor, S. and Todd, P. A. (1995) Assessing IT usage: The role of prior experience. *MIS Quarterly*, 19(2), 561–70.

Thompson, R. L., Higgins, C. A. and Howell, J. M. (1991) Personal computing: Toward a conceptual model of utilization. *MIS Quarterly*, 15(1), 124–43.

Venkatesh, V. and Davis, F. D. (2000) A theoretical extension of the technology acceptance model: Four longitudinal field studies. *Management Science*, 45(2), 186–204.

Venkatesh,V., Morris, M. G., Davis, G. B. and Davis, F. D. (2003) User acceptance of information technology: Toward a unified view. *MIS Quarterly*, 27 (3), 425–78.

Welch, J. (2001) CEO of GE, speech to Annual Shareholders Meeting. Atlanta, GA, 25 April.

Which? (2002) Annual Internet User Survey. Consumer Association. www.which.net/surveys/survey2002.pdf.

Willcocks, L. and Smith, G. (1995) IT enabled business process reengineering: Organizational and human resource dimension. *Strategic Information Systems*, 4(3), 279–301.

ZDNet (2002) CRM failures: don't blame the tools, Adrian Mello, 18 December. http://techupdate.zdnet.com/techupdate/stories/main/0,14179,2902068,00.htm.

Further reading

Hayes, J. (2002) *The Theory and Practice of Change Management*. Palgrave, Basingstoke. Provides a clear introduction to change management theory and approaches to manage organizational change.

visit the www

Weblinks

Intelligent Enterprise Magazine (**www.intelligententerprise.com**) Portal for professionals providing news and articles on data warehousing and other information management topics.

IT Toolbox (**http://businessintelligence.ittoolbox.com**) A collection of resources on business intelligence.

SAS (**www.sas.com/apps/whitepapers/whitepaper.jsp**) An extensive collection of vendor-oriented white papers on business intelligence.

Traffick (**www.traffick.com**) A guide to public, search and corporate portals and suppliers.

For multiple-choice questions, and annotated weblinks relating to this chapter visit this book's website at: www.pearsoned.co.uk/chaffey

9
Building an information architecture

Objective

To understand success factors for building an effective information architecture.

Learning outcomes

After reading this chapter, you will be able to:
- ● Identify the parts of an information architecture strategy.
- ● Review information architecture techniques and tools.
- ● Understand the success factors for design of information architecture for a range of information environments.
- ● Assess the factors contributing to an effective information architecture.

Management issues

Typical questions facing managers related to this topic:
- ● How do I match information architecture to business processes?
- ● Which information modelling tool do I select?
- ● How do we design information architecture for an intranet?
- ● How can our information systems interoperate?
- ● How can I develop information security policies?

Links to other chapters

The main related chapters are:
- ➤ *Chapter 2* explains the types of software and the role in information management; some of the software introduced here is used to develop information architecture (e.g. databases).
- ➤ *Chapter 3* explains the role of key technologies for information management, many of which are developed further in the current chapter in the context of information architecture.
- ➤ *Chapter 4* outlines the key strategic approaches to managing information; information architecture will be informed by information management strategy.
- ➤ *Chapter 10* on managing information quality. Effective information architecture is one part of effective management of information quality. Chapter 10 develops quality issues in detail, drawing on quality issues raised in the current chapter (e.g. data dictionaries).

Introduction

Systems development lifecycle (SDLC)
A model representing sequential stages for systems development

Information architecture
Definition and structure of organizational information related to information systems

The **systems development lifecycle (SDLC)** illustrates the process of system development broken down into key phases. The model known as 'the waterfall SDLC' was introduced in Chapter 7 and is illustrated in Figure 9.1. This illustrates how the chapter will use the SDLC waterfall model to outline the key processes in building an **information architecture**. The strategy chapters (4, 5 and 6) have discussed how strategic priorities for information systems and information and knowledge management will be related to business objectives. In Chapter 7 the planning processes for information systems have been discussed. This chapter will now focus on the analysis design, implementation and maintenance of information architectures.

Definitions

In order to implement the priorities defined in the strategies outlined in the previous chapters we must use defined information requirements. The aim will be to translate them into usable information systems. Coherent information architecture will provide the framework and structure to make information systems a usable reality.

First, we will define the term 'architecture'. The Institute of Electrical and Electronics Engineers (IEEE, 2000) defines the term as:

> the fundamental organization of a system embodied in its components, their relationships to each other and to the environment, and the principles guiding its design and evolution where:
>
> - fundamental organization means essential, unifying concepts and principles
> - system includes application, system, platform, system of systems, enterprise, product line
> - environment is developmental, operational, programmatic, … [the] context of the system.

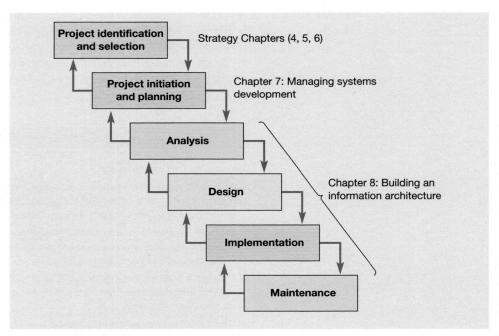

Figure 9.1 Systems development lifecycle
Source: Adapted from Hoffer et al. (2002)

IEEE (2000) explains the term in Standard 1471 Recommended Practice for Architectural Description of Software-Intensive Systems. In this standard the IEEE states that explicitly 'architected' systems seem to turn out 'faster, better and cheaper' and that 'architecture is recognised as a critical element in the successful development and evolution of software intensive systems'.

The positioning of information architecture in relation to the overall enterprise architecture is illustrated in Figure 9.2. We have already discussed the key issues related to enterprise architecture in terms of hardware, software and technologies in Chapters 2 and 3. The UK Office of Government Commerce (2004) describes enterprise architecture thus:

> In simple terms, an enterprise architecture identifies the main components of the organization or a sub-set of it (such as its information systems), and the ways in which these components work together in order to achieve defined business objectives. The components will include staff, business processes, technology, information, financial and other resources.

The Butler Group (2004) makes a useful comment about enterprise architecture that can also be applied to information architecture: 'nobody would dream of starting to build a house without the necessary plans'.

The term 'information architecture' was first used in the 1960s by Richard Wurman who became interested in how information related to urban environments could be gathered, organized and presented in meaningful ways to architects and urban planners. Wurman formally defined architecture as the science and art of creating 'an instruction for organized space' (Hourican, 2002).

We can liken information architecture to a honeycomb: the workers (bees) using information as a core asset (honey and eggs) within a defined structure (hexagonal cells). The *Oxford English Dictionary* definition of honeycomb states that 'the shape and arrangement of the cells secures the greatest possible economy at once of space and of material'; this analogy can also be drawn with information architecture: well-designed information architecture will lead to efficient and effective use of information, allowing organizations to match information to people who need it.

Information architecture will be used by information system designers and information managers to design information systems that facilitate task completion, developing consistent procedures and rules for organizing and structuring information.

The Asilomar Institute for Information Architecture is focused on information architecture from a web design perspective and defines it (AIFIA, 2003) as:

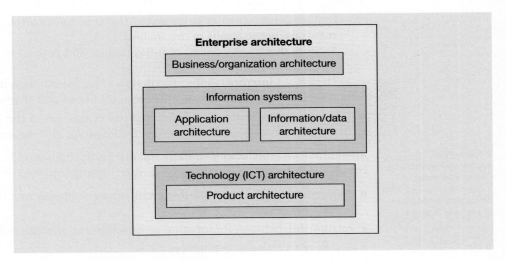

Figure 9.2 Enterprise architecture

- The structural design of shared environments
- The art and science of organizing websites, intranets, online communities and software to support usability and fundability.

This definition is useful, but the definition we will use for information architecture will be broader, looking at the context of a wider range of information systems.

Information architecture

Strategic analysis, as explained in Chapters 4, 5 and 6, enables us to establish strategic priorities for information systems and information management. Strategic priorities will have emerged, focused upon key business processes that must be supported by information systems and the key information resources that must be managed. The key benefits of information architecture will be:

- reduction in the costs of finding information;
- improved efficiency of the information-based organizational process;
- new value derived from information through reuse.

The information architecture process is defined in Figure 9.3, which outlines the key building blocks of organizational information architecture:

- The information architecture is driven by the information systems, information management and knowledge management strategies. Key features of the organization's information can be identified in terms of strategic importance.
- The requirements of the information architecture must then be developed around understanding key business processes and user actions and behaviours.
- The requirements must then be analysed in terms of three key aspects:
  - *Systems analysis*: assessing what new systems need to do in relation to requirements. This chapter looks at systems from the perspective of databases, intranets and websites.
  - *Security analysis*: what the key information assets are, what the implications are of their security being compromised, and areas of security vulnerability.
  - *Interoperability analysis*: understanding which systems need to interact across the organization and with partner organizations, plus the common standards and information structures required.
- Design of the information architecture can be broken down into three components:
  - System design: the design of systems around information architecture requirements using the results of the analysis.
  - Security design: the design of infrastructure and policies to protect information assets and systems.
  - Design for interoperability: the design of an information architecture that can be applied across a range of software applications and IT platforms.
- Implementation, maintenance, testing and evaluation of the information systems that use the information architecture, feeding back into the analysis stage.

Information architecture strategy
Overall information architecture framework for an organization related to higher-level strategies

An **information architecture strategy** will discuss the high-level frameworks required to coordinate information architecture across an organization. The strategy will include:

- objectives of how information architecture supports organizational strategies already defined;
- relationship between information architecture and the different systems required;
- details of technology integration;
- Procedures for applying common data and information definitions across the organization.

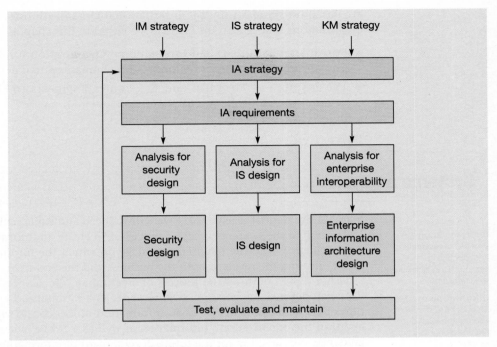

Figure 9.3 Information architecture process

Some organizations will also develop an information architecture policy, a document that will set out the key principles that will be used to create, manage and develop an organizational information architecture. The State of Arizona (2003a) publishes its Data/Information Architecture Policy on the web. The policy has the core following components:

1 scope;
2 general principles;
3 listing of target technologies;
4 data/information architecture standards:
  (a) data modelling
  (b) classification of data
  (c) database access;
5 implementation (security).

Standards for information architecture

In order to improve consistency and information flow across boundaries, standards have been developed, nationally and internationally. Developing a standardized approach to common aspects of information architecture allows the information architect to concentrate on the key aspects of designing systems around business and user needs. A common approach also allows system developers to work across organizational boundaries. As we shall also see later in the chapter, interoperability has become vital to organizations using the Internet and the World Wide Web to conduct business. There is a requirement to have common ways to share, receive and view information from a variety of platforms in a standard interface (e.g. a web browser).

The standards referred to in this chapter come from a variety of organizations – one organization does not control the many information architecture standards. Many standards set by national organizations such as the British Standards Institute are based on standards by the International Organization for Standarization. The organizations that govern the standards covered in this chapter include:

- British Standards (BSI) and International Organization for Standarization (ISO): user documentation, information security, human-centred design processes.
- The Institute of Electrical and Electronics Engineers (IEEE): for architectural description of software-intensive systems.
- W3C: XML, RDF.

Systems analysis

Systems analysis
Process of researching and identifying organizational and user requirements

Information model
A conceptual model of information related to organizational functions or processes

Many of the standards (e.g. XML) were introduced and explained in Chapter 3.

The aim of the systems analysis process is to create an information model derived from evidence from the requirements stage on which the information design can be based, meeting the needs of both the business and the end-user.

Fisher (2003) outlines the process of creating an information model moving from 'less well defined information requirements to a rationalized and optimized definition of these needs. It is why as an information model consists of an "as is" view (an audit) of the organization's information as well as a "to be" view (a blueprint) giving guidance and direction for the future development of information systems.'

Fisher (2003) also outlines a static view that is 'information-centric' and a dynamic approach that is 'business-process-centric'.

- Static view: focuses upon structures of information elements:
  - logical data model (shows relationships)
  - data standards
  - metadata
  - taxonomy or classification.
- Dynamic view: focuses upon processes and how information is created, managed and used:
  - a business processes model
  - an information process model or information workflow model
  - a data flow model (transitions and states of information during the lifecycle).

An information model will take a different form depending on the system the information architecture is being developed for. For example, later in the chapter we will use a data flow diagram (DFD) as a way of modelling for database design. We will now move through the key elements of systems analysis in turn.

Identifying information architecture requirements

The starting point of the systems analysis process is the identification of requirements through research or investigation. The research framework for systems analysis should take the following factors into account: context, content and users (Rosenfeld and Morville, 2002).

- Context is focused upon business goals, funding, politics, culture, technology and human resources.
- Content is focused upon data and information types, content objects, volume and structure.
- Users focuses upon audiences, tasks, needs, information behaviour, experience and vocabularies.

Using the results from the information and knowledge audits

The results of information and knowledge audits will have produced the following outputs which can be used in the information architecture building process:

- Categorization of key information types and formats used or required for organizational processes.
- Gap analysis to enable a distinction to be made between information and knowledge currently available and new information and knowledge required.
- Relationship between information types.
- Maps of information and knowledge flows.
- Information linked in key people involved in information and knowledge creation, use, communication and storage across the organization.

Information audits are discussed in more detail in the Chapters 4 and 10.

Identifying stakeholders

Stakeholder
An individual or group with an interest in the success of an information system or an individual or group that will be affected by the outcome of the information system. A stakeholder has a vested interest in the information system

Before undertaking information gathering using techniques such as interviews, key **stakeholders** related to the information architecture must be identified. Stakeholders will be identified in the information audit process. Typical stakeholders are listed in Table 9.1. In order to understand the different contexts the stakeholders operate in, it will be important to differentiate between internal and external stakeholders as their needs and expectations may need to be managed in different ways. The process of stakeholder analysis will take place looking at groups of stakeholders and developing criteria for selection to make sure they are indicative of the organizational and external environment.

In Chapter 8 (Managing change) the following types of stakeholders were identified:

- System sponsors
- System owners
- System users

(Refer back to Chapter 8 for fuller definitions if you need.)

Table 9.1 Information architecture stakeholders

Internal stakeholders	External stakeholders
Client	Service provider
Acquirer	Vendor
Owner	Subcontractor
User	Planner
Operator	Customer
Architect	
System engineer	
Developer	
Designer	
Builder	
Maintainer	

Questionnaires

Questionnaire
A structured set of
questions used to derive
information based on
research objectives

The use of **questionnaires** is a common method of research in the systems analysis process. The structure and ordering of the questions is important. Representative and informative results can then be fed into the systems analysis process. Questionnaires can be efficient methods of data collection when the researcher knows exactly what is required and how to measure the variables. A questionnaire might be delivered personally, in electronic form or remotely by mail. The systems researcher should bear in mind the importance of clarity and explanation if they cannot be personally present when the questionnaires are completed.

Questionnaires must be developed with the respondent as the focus:

- making clear that their input is valuable and is playing a part in the development process;
- avoiding long questions that make the questionnaire too long to complete;
- avoiding questions that lead towards or suggest one particular answer.

Open questions will be asked where a more detailed response is required and the type of answer cannot be codified in advance. An example of an open-ended question would be asking a user: 'What don't you like about the current information system used for this process?'

Closed questions will in contrast ask the respondent to make choices from a set of alternatives provided by the researcher. An example would be a question asking the user to rank information types in terms of relevance to a process. Closed questions have the advantage of allowing the respondent to make fast decisions. If the results of the questionnaire are to be analysed using a statistical package, closed questions make the coding of data easier.

Interviews

Interview
A series of questions
(orally delivered) by one or
more people (the
interviewer) in which the
responses of the
interviewee are recorded

As an analysis technique, **interviews** will be an important part of the research process, often following after questionnaires. Interviews must be coordinated and planned in the same way as questionnaires: a relevant and representational stakeholder sample must be selected, questions must be balanced and sequenced carefully and the results must then be recorded and presented in a meaningful format that will feed into the next stage of the analysis process.

Activity 9.1	Researching requirements at the Lo-cost Airline Company: questionnaire
Purpose	Develop a set of questions for a questionnaire as part of the systems analysis processes for the redevelopment of the company intranet at the Lo-cost Airline Company.
Activity	As the information manager at the Lo-cost Airline Company you have been given a brief to redevelop the company intranet which has been identified as having low levels of use and is not being used to support key business processes. 1 As part of the start of the analysis process you need to develop a questionnaire: write down ten questions, a mix of five open and five closed, that will form part of the systems analysis process. 2 Now place the questions into a logical sequence. 3 Write a single paragraph explaining the questionnaire to a company employee.

Interviews can be broken into three categories:

- Fully structured. All questions and their order are decided upon in advance and the interviewer does not deviate during the course of the interview.
- Semi-structured. Some questions are decided upon in advance, with some room for the interviewer to respond and add supplementary questions.
- Open. The interviewer comes to the interviewee with a series of topics for discussion.

The benefits of interviews are:

- There is a high chance of obtaining useful information owing to the interactive nature of interviews.
- The interviewer has a clear commitment from the interviewee to enter into a dialogue.
- Questions can be followed up.
- Ambiguities can be probed.

Possible problems with interviews include:

- The time taken to complete an interview is much longer than for a questionnaire, and only a smaller sample can be interviewed.
- Time taken to record and process the information is longer than for questionnaires.
- High costs in terms of commitment of staff time.
- Problems of bias from the perspective of the interviewer. (Is the interviewer the system owner or developer and therefore sensitive to criticism?)

Observation

A common method of understanding information used by organizations is observing how users process and handle information using current information systems (these may be paper or electronic). By establishing this process it is possible to understand user actions in relation to information in the context of information system use.

In order for the observation to be representative the sample and methods must be validated in advance. The following questions must be asked of the users who will be observed:

- Will the users know they are being observed for the stated purpose – how might this affect the results?
- Is the sample chosen representative of the user population?
- Will the users be carrying out their own day-to-day tasks or tasks chosen specifically for the research?

The results will need to be recorded, which could be done using a grid to record certain user behaviours. Some organizations may also make use of video cameras to record the observation.

Audit of documentation

This process should have taken place during the information audit. An assessment of documentation already in use in an organization will offer important evidence of data types required for capture and storage and the type of information output required. The types of documentation that will be audited include:

- Existing guides and manuals for information systems.
- Forms (paper or electronic) currently used to capture information.

- Documentation that is available about information systems such as website or intranet use statistics, search statistics, types of query, numbers and types of system inputs and outputs (e.g. data entry, report production).
- Documentation intended for publication on web-based systems.
- Security policies and guidelines currently in use.

Logical
In the information systems context, a logical representation is an abstraction of the real situation developed in order to give the user a view of how the system must be organized and structured

CASE management tools
Computer-aided software engineering tools provide an automated process for graphical representation of systems development. The purpose of CASE tools is to simplify and manage the analysis and design stages of systems development if a level of complexity is reached

Reverse-design
Taking a physical database design from a database application and presenting it as a logical model

Information flow diagram
A simple high-level diagram illustrating information flows

Systems diagrams

The following sections illustrate how we can complete the systems analysis stage using diagrams to represent data, information, objects and relationships and how they interact. This stage of systems analysis is a logical representation rather than the physical one that we will look at in the design section of this chapter.

These diagrams are often created using CASE management tools. These tools may be used for developing entity relationship diagrams (ERDs), for example (introduced later in the chapter). Microsoft provides basic CASE tools in their Access database software (the views of relationships between tables). It also provides a tool called 'Visio' that can be used to create information models, which includes the ability to reverse-design a database. An example of Visio is shown in Figure 9.4. Database software company Oracle also provides a CASE management tool called 'Oracle Designer'.

Information flow diagrams

The first stage of modelling the information derived from the initial research stages of the systems analysis process is the development of an information flow diagram. Working at a high level (broad overview), the diagrams have an information focus. The diagram will illustrate source and destination (which could be a department or category of user). An arrow will illustrate the information flow, with a description explaining and describing the information that is travelling from the source to the destination. Figure 9.5 illustrates the key for an information flow diagram. Figure 9.6 illustrates a simple information flow.

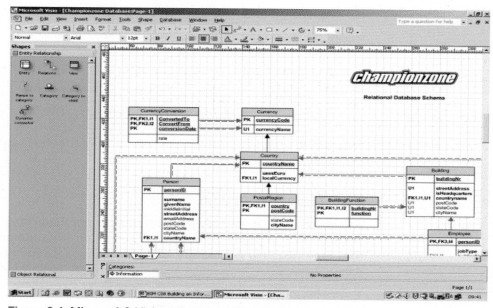

Figure 9.4 Microsoft® Visio software: entity relationship diagram
Source: Reprinted by permission from Microsoft Corporation

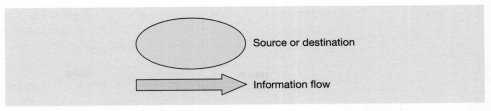

Figure 9.5 Information flow diagram key

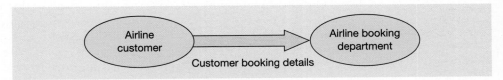

Figure 9.6 Simple information flow illustration

We will now create an information flow diagram for the Lo-cost Airline Company illustrating the information flows that take place, from a passenger booking a flight to arriving at their destination. This diagram would give a systems analyst designing a new booking information system a picture of the information inputs and outputs and the internal and external actors involved in the information flows.

On the diagram we can notice the following aspects:

- The sources that produce the information, e.g. the passenger
- The destinations of information, e.g. the airline company
- The connections between sources and destinations
- The information that flows between sources, e.g the catering department is connected to the airline crew.

Activity 9.2	Understanding an information flow diagram

Purpose To convert information from the information flow diagram into a table.

Activity From the information flow diagram (Figure 9.7) convert the information into Table 9.2, the first line of which has been completed already. A table like this would often be used as the start of the information diagram process.

Table 9.2

Source/producer	Flow	Destination
Passenger	Booking information	Booking department

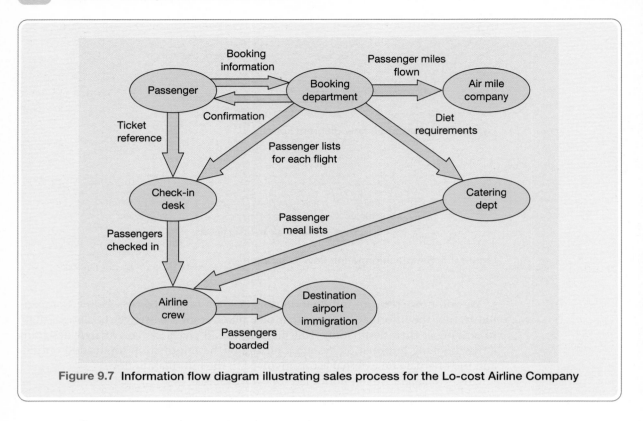

Figure 9.7 Information flow diagram illustrating sales process for the Lo-cost Airline Company

Data flow diagrams

Information flow diagrams give a useful high-level view as a starting point in the systems analysis process; however, we need to break down and define the processes, inputs and outputs in more detail in order to inform the physical design process correctly. A **data flow diagram** (DFD) enables us to take a process focus as opposed to the information focus in the information flow diagram. Returning to the State of Arizona Data/Information Architecture Policy (2003a) and the section on data modelling standards, DFDs are part of a defined process that takes place in information architecture development.

Hoffer et al. (2002) describe data flow as 'data in motion, moving from one place to another. A data flow could represent data on a customer order form or a payroll check. A data flow could also represent the results of a query to a database, the contents of a printed report, or data on a data entry computer display form.'

Figure 9.8 illustrates the symbols that are used in data flow diagrams. The symbols are explained in further detail below:

Data flow diagram
A graphical representation in the form of a diagram illustrating external sources, flows, processes and data stores

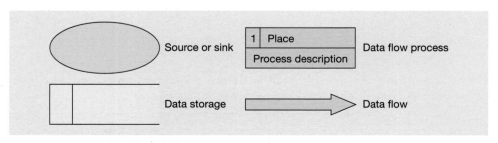

Figure 9.8 Data flow diagram key

- *Sources and sinks*. These are information sources that are the origin and/or the receiver of data. A source provides and a sink receives. These are external entities and exist outside of the system boundary.
- *Process*. Illustrates the actions performed on data so that they are transformed, stored or distributed in order to facilitate another process. A process will have a number in the top left-hand corner, a place (a physical location) in the top right-hand corner and a process description in the bottom part of the box.
- *Data store*. A representation of physical storage place for data. It can receive or output data.

Table 9.3 outlines rules (Hoffer et al., 2002) that govern data flow diagramming.

Table 9.3 DFD rules

Process
A No processes can have only outputs. It would be making data from nothing (a miracle). If an object has only outputs then it must be a source.
B No process can have only inputs – a black hole. If an object has only inputs, then it must be a sink.
C A process has a verb label.

Data store
D Data cannot move directly from one data store to another data store. Data must be moved by a process.
E Data cannot move directly from an outside source to a data store. Data must be moved by a process that receives data from the source and places data into the data store.
F Data cannot move directly to an outside sink from a data store. Data must be moved by a process.

Source/sink
H Data cannot move directly from a source to a sink. It must be moved by a process if the data are of any concern to our system. Otherwise the data flow is not shown on the DFD.
I A source/sink has a noun phrase label.

Data flow
J A data flow has only one direction of flow between symbols. It may flow in both directions between a process and a data store to show a read before an update. The latter is usually indicated, however, by two separate arrows since these happen at different times.
K A fork in a data flow means that exactly the same data goes from a common location to two or more different processes, data stores, or sources/sinks (this usually indicates different copies if same data are going to the different locations).
L A join in a data flow means that exactly the same data come from any two or more processes, data stores or sources/sinks to a common location.
M A data flow cannot go directly back to the same process it leaves. There must be at least one other process that handles the data flow, produces some other data flow, and returns the original data to the beginning of the process.
N A data flow to a data store means update (delete or change).
O A data flow from a data store means retrieve or use.
P A data flow has a noun phrase label. More than one data flow noun phrase can appear on a single arrow as long as all of the flows on the same arrow move together as one passage.

In developing a DFD we can again use a table (9.4) to understand what the components will be before constructing the diagram. The table would be filled out (one example from the Lo-cost Airline Company has been filled in), listing all the processes and the inputs and outputs (and indicating whether they are from sources or data stores). When describing these components the systems analyst will need to make sure that they follow the rules above in selecting the right words or phrases.

Figures 9.9 and 9.10 illustrate a level-one data flow diagram. This is a simple high-level version of processes that the Lo-cost Airline Company carries out when processing a passenger booking. In this level-one example the process numbers go from one to seven. The process of building this diagram can be progressed by creating a series of mini-DFDs and then linking them together. Note that on the diagram none of the flows overlap each other, in order to develop the diagram clearly; a data store (labelled 1) has been included twice.

Entity relationship diagrams

Entity
An entity is a self-contained piece of data that can be referenced as a unit

Entity relationship diagramming (ERD) is an approach to model the relationships between data conceptually. The ERD model will then lead into the normalization process of physically designing a database. Beynon-Davies (2004) describes an **entity**

Table 9.4 Data flow diagram components

Processes	Process inputs	Process outputs	Data stores	Source (external)	Sink (external)
Issue ticket reference	Passenger details	reference no	Passenger database	None	Passenger

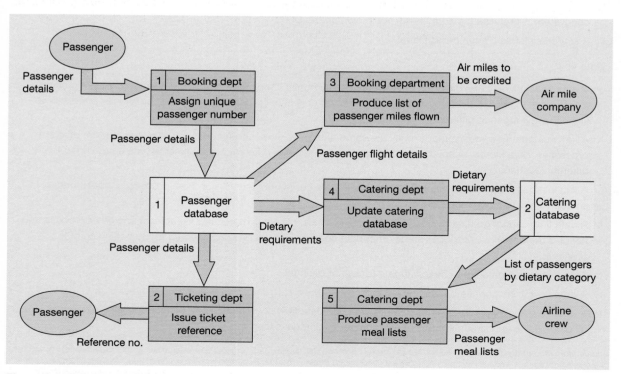

Figure 9.9 Data flow diagram

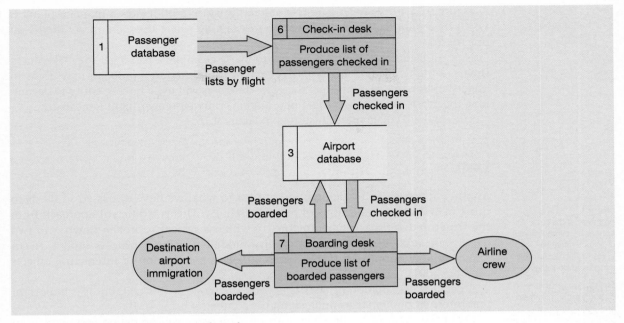

Figure 9.10 Data flow diagram continued

as 'a thing that an organization recognizes as being capable of an independent existence and can be uniquely identified' and a relationship as 'some association between entities'. In an ERD an entity can have more than one relationship. In this section we will again use the generic example of the Lo-cost Airline Company as an illustration.

Figure 9.11 illustrates the symbols used in **entity relationship diagrams**. We will now look at the different ways that ERD can represent relationships. Once the entities have been identified, specific data for each entity need to be written down. For example, we will note the example attributes for the entities in Table 9.5; from this attribute data relationships will start to emerge, e.g. between flight numbers.

Entity relationship diagram
A graphical representation that displays, entities, relationships and attributes

Table 9.5 Attributes for entities

Passenger	Flights
Name	Flight number
Address	Time
Passport numbers	Date
Flight numbers	From
Sex	Destination

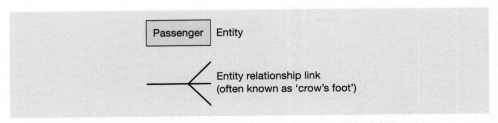

Passenger | Entity

Entity relationship link
(often known as 'crow's foot')

Figure 9.11 Entity relationship diagram key for the Lo-cost Airline Company

Figure 9.12 illustrates a one-to-one relationship: a pilot flies a plane, a plane is flown by a pilot. In Figure 9.13 we see an example where there are many flights on one route.

Now, in Figure 9.14 we have a many-to-many example: a passenger may take many flights, a flight will take many passengers. In this situation a problem may occur in understanding the relationship – therefore designers will use a linking entity to decompose the relations. In Figure 9.15 a new linking entity passenger/flight is created.

The final ERD diagram is illustrated in Figure 9.16.

UML

Object
A person, a thing, or concept. Building blocks of object-oriented systems. Objects know things and do things

Object-oriented
A programming method that uses objects as building blocks in software applications

Another approach to modelling, in contrast to what we have discussed so far, is to think of systems as collections of reusable **objects**. This is a different approach from the structured approach taken before, in which a system is broken down into two parts: data modelling and functionality modelled using a process model. In an **object-oriented** approach systems are defined as a collection of interacting objects (Ambler, 2001).

A detailed explanation of UML is beyond the scope of this text, but it is important that information managers understand the context of using UML.

Using the example of the Lo-cost Airline Company, we can define passenger as an object; it knows things: name, address, passport number; and it does things: requests a reservation, checks in, boards a flight. Other objects for the Lo-cost Airline Company would include aircraft, route and flight.

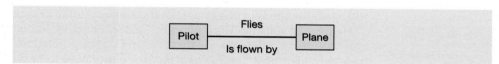

Figure 9.12 Entity relationship diagram for the Lo-cost Airline Company: one-to-one

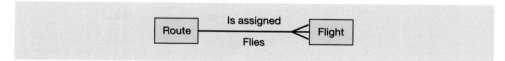

Figure 9.13 Entity relationship diagram for the Lo-cost Airline Company: one-to-many

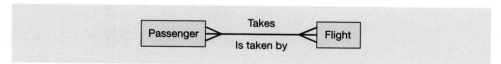

Figure 9.14 Entity relationship diagram for the Lo-cost Airline Company: many-to-many

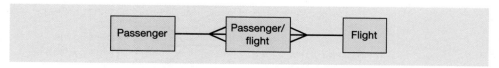

Figure 9.15 Entity relationship diagram for the Lo-cost Airline Company: decomposition

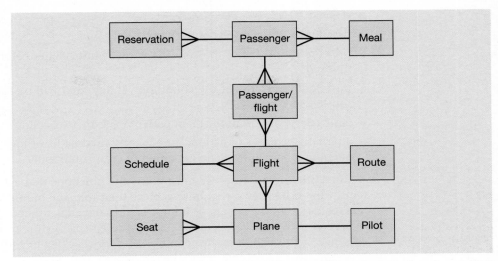

Figure 9.16 Entity relationship diagram for the Lo-cost Airline Company

Unified modeling language (UML)
UML is a visual modelling methodology covering the notation and ways of specifying, modelling and documenting object-oriented systems

The **unified modelling language (UML)** was developed to provide a common approach for modelling object-oriented systems. The goal of UML is to describe systems in terms of object-oriented diagrams. We will look at use case diagrams and using CRC cards from the UML methodology in this chapter.

Use case analysis

Use case analysis
A view of describing the sequence of actions and functionality a system should deliver facilitating the work of actors

Use case analysis is part of the unified modelling language (UML). Eriksson and Pneker (1998) describes the use case view as follows: 'the desired usage of the system is described as a number of use cases in the use case view, where a use case is a generic description of a usage of the system (a function requested)'. Ambler (2001) describes a use case as 'a sequence of actions that provide a measurable value to the user'.

Actors

Actor
Someone or something (person, organization or external system) that interacts with the system

A use case diagram will show a number of **actors** and their connection to use cases that the system offers. Actors represent roles in system use rather than individuals. Actors will be identified from assessments of who uses systems, what tasks they undertake and the processes identified. An actor will be communicating with the system by sending or receiving information. The key to consistent selection of actors is to remember that actors are used to model roles, not the physical real-world people, organization or systems.

Two types of actor can be ranked (Eriksson and Pneker, 1998):

- Primary actor: uses the main functionality of the system, e.g. adds information, produces reports.
- Secondary actor: uses secondary functions of the system, e.g. maintains and backs up the system.

The main focus of the use case diagram should be the primary actor.

Use cases

A use case should be documented before diagramming takes place, listing in a table key aspects of the case. Ambler (2001) suggests that the following aspects should be documented:

- name;
- description: an overview of the case;
- pre-conditions: list of the conditions that must be met before a use case may be invoked;
- post-conditions: list of the conditions, if any, that will be true once the use case finishes successfully;
- basic course of action: the main path of logic an actor follows through a use case;
- alternative courses of action: infrequently used paths of logic that result from an alternative way to work, an exception or error condition.

In identifying use cases we must assess the functions that actors require from systems, what tasks they carry out to achieve their role, the information they provide to and require from the system. It is important to remember that actors may be involved in several use cases. For example, taking the Lo-cost Airline Company example the passenger actors will be involved in use cases for checking in and meal booking.

Use case diagramming

Figure 9.18 illustrates a use case diagram for the Lo-cost Airline Company; Figure 9.17 is a legend illustrating the components. In this diagram we can see several use cases related to actors by lines of communication. You should notice that the diagram is not time-ordered in terms of sequencing the use cases.

Although this information is important, it will be added to later sequences of the systems analysis. Also note that every actor must be involved with at least one case and every case with at least one actor.

Card sorting

Card sorting is a way in which users can become actively involved in the development process of information architecture. Two different examples will be introduced in terms of web design and object-oriented design. The active involvement of users, developers and analysts in the process increases the feeling of stakeholders being involved in the project and actively (in a physical sense) contributing to the design process.

Card sorting for web classification

Web classification
The process of arranging a way of organizing objects on websites in a consistent manner

Web classification systems are one of the most problematic areas in web design: websites are frequently designed from the perspective of the designer rather than the information user, leading to labels, subject grouping and categories that are not intuitive. A website or intranet that is designed around an employee view of the

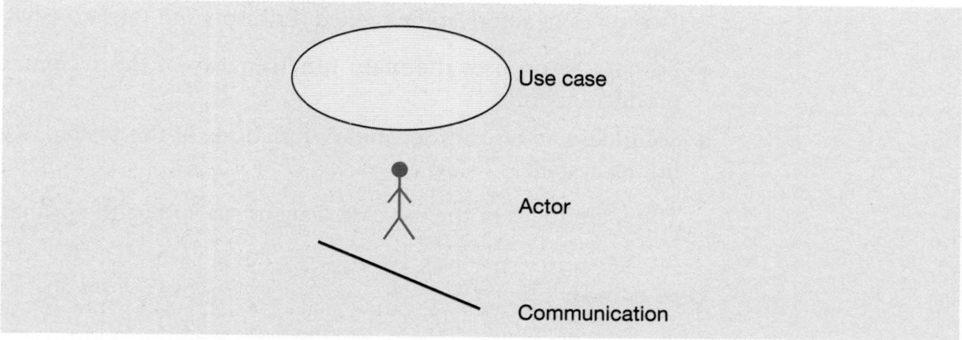

Figure 9.17 Use case legend

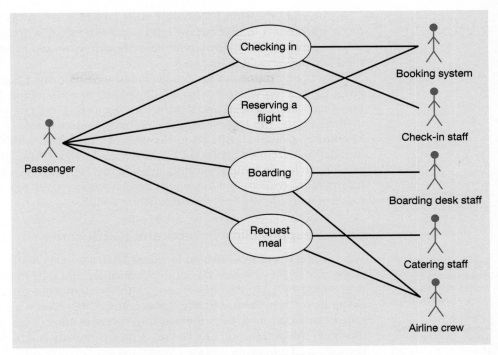

Figure 9.18 Use case diagram for the Lo-cost Airline Company

organization (e.g. mirroring the organization's structural hierarchy) might not be a view of the organization that a user will understand. Web classification should categorize web objects (e.g. documents, links) in order to facilitate information task completion or information goals the user has set.

Robertson (2003a) identifies the following questions when using card sorting to aid the process of modelling web classification systems:

● Do the users want to see the information grouped by: subject, process, business group, or type of information?
● What are the most important items to put on the main menu?
● How many menu items should there be, and how deep should the menu structure go?
● How similar or different are the needs of the users throughout the organization?

Selected groups of users (from stakeholder analysis) will be given index cards with the following written on them, depending on the aim of the card sorting process:

● Types of documents
● Organizational key words and concepts
● Document titles
● Descriptions of documents
● Navigation labels.

Robertson (2003a) suggests that card-sorting sessions must have at least four participants, in order to stimulate debate and discussion. The cards should be numbered to aid the analysis process after the card-sorting session has taken place.

The user groups will then be given one or several of the following tasks:

● Group together cards that they feel relate to each other.
● Select cards that accurately reflect a given topic or area.
● Organize cards in terms of hierarchy – from high-level terms (broad) to low-level terms.

At the end of session the analyst must take the cards away and map the results into a spreadsheet to find out the most popular terms, descriptions and relationships. If two or more different groups are used the results should be compared and reasons for differences should be analysed.

Once the classification list has been developed a further feedback session can be given to the users who participated, illustrating how the results have been developed into a navigation scheme and structure for organizing web content.

To illustrate, the Lo-cost Airline Company could use this card-sorting process to develop an overall classification for their intranet. This would involve all the key intranet user groups working on a card-sorting exercise. Before the exercise the information architect would develop a list based on analysis of existing company information, drawing out key words and concepts related to tasks and information needs of users (drawn from the information audit).

Class Responsibility Collaborator (CRC) cards

Domain model
Representation of business concepts relevant to problem space

CRC card
A collection of physical index cards used in sessions with users and key system stakeholders to model classes

When using the object-oriented language UML a **domain model** is needed to act as a glossary of terms to enable classes to be identified and used in meaningful ways. CRC cards, used by UML developers, are a similar method to the previous web design example. A **Class Responsibility Collaborator (CRC) card** is a collection of standard index cards that have been divided into three sections (Ambler, 2001). Figure 9.19 illustrates the card layout. The Lo-cost Airline Company will now be used to illustrate the CRC card modelling process.

The three sections on the card are:

- Classes: collections of similar objects
- Responsibilities: anything a class knows or does
- Collaborators: a request to do something.

Developing the card in the context of the Lo-cost Airline Company in Figure 9.20, the three sections can be explained in more detail:

- Classes. The example used is the term 'passenger' to describe a class. Classes can be found from the process of identifying actors (discussed in the previous section on use case analysis). Classes may also emerge from looking at definitions of business concepts defined by your organization, e.g. How are customers defined?
- Responsibility. For the example we know that we need to write down all the information the passenger knows that will be used in the airline's business processes. A passenger will also do things such as check in or board the plane.
- Collaborator. In the example we know that the passenger needs to collaborate with the flight class to get information about which flight they booked on, so that they can check in.

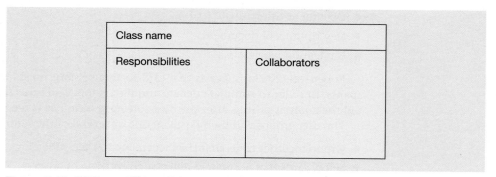

Figure 9.19 CRC card illustration

Passenger	
Passport number Name Provides personal information Reserves flight Checks in Boards the plane Address Phone number	Flight

Figure 9.20 CRC card for the Lo-cost Airline Company

Figure 9.21 illustrates that classes can be broken down further into:

- Actor classes: people or organizations that interact with the system. In the example there is now an actor class Passenger <<Actor>>.
- Business classes: places, things, concepts that describe the organization's activities. Business classes are generally not indicated. On the diagram: the class labelled 'passenger'.
- User interface classes: screens, menus, reports. In the example the interface is labelled: Checked in list <<UI>>. This could be a report generated from a database viewed on screen and then printed out.

The final CRC diagram (Figure 9.22) illustrates how to alter the responsibilities and collaborators in light of making the subdivision of classes.

Potential cards will be filled out before a CRC modelling session; at the session the participants will then be asked to comment in terms of their own context and perception of the system. The facilitator will prompt the participants to comment on, amend and create the new classes, responsibilities and collaborators.

Analysis for interoperability

When assessing the information used by an organization in the context of developing an information architecture for interoperability, the systems analyst must aim to draw a picture of information systems interacting across the organization and outside

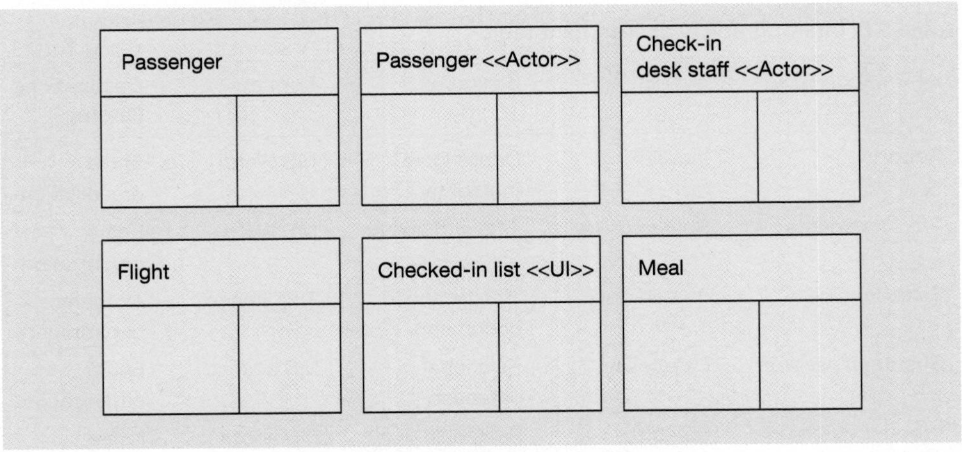

Interoperability
The ability of computer systems to work together, conforming to common standards

Figure 9.21 Lo-cost Airline Company CRC cards: types of class

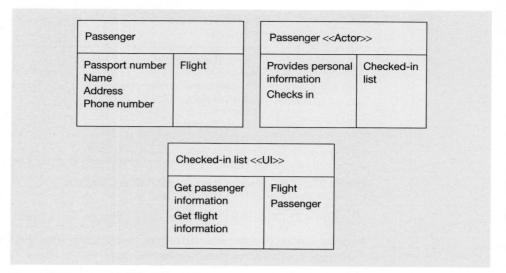

Figure 9.22 Lo-cost Airline Company: example CRCs with responsibilities and collaborators added

the borders of the organization. Interoperability will be important for the following reasons:

- improving efficiency in reuse of information;
- avoiding mistakes from duplication;
- implementing enterprise search engines that search across a wide range of information systems, e.g. understanding which documents should be indexed.

The analysis process must map how information needs to flow between different information systems, the current formats the information is held in and the nature of the information. Table 9.6 can be used to understand information in the context of interoperability. It is important to make the distinction between structured and unstructured information: databases are examples of highly structured information compared to a Microsoft Word document stored by an employee on a file server, which is unstructured.

From this table the process of mapping information into interchange formats (such as XML) with common structural standards (e.g. DTDs and schemas) can take place. (These issues are discussed later in the chapter in the section of interoperability design.)

Table 9.6 Interoperability assessment table

Information type	System	Structure	Format	Destinations (internal)	Destinations (external)
Reports	Intranet	Dublin Core metadata	MS Word	Entire organization	
Product sheets	Shared drive	Title and author	MS Word	Entire organization	Customers
Sales invoice	Shared drive	Title (scanned document)	TIFF image	Accounts department	Customers
Customer records	Database	Relational database	MS access	Entire organization	
Product catalogue	Database	Relational database	MS access	Entire organization	Partner organizations

Security analysis

Introduction to information security

Information security is defined by the US National Security Telecommunications and Information Security Committee as the 'protection of information and the systems and hardware that use, store, and transmit that information' (Whitman and Mattord, 2003). Security is a vital final part of building information architecture, ensuring that information assets that the information architecture makes available to users are protected. Pipkin (2000) notes that security is a series of trade-offs: 'the greater the level of security required, the more administration and controls that are required, and the greater the tendency to reduce the ease of use. These trade-offs must be evaluated in the same way as any business asset and process.'

Legal issues such as privacy legislation require levels of security for personal information. In the UK, for example, the British Standard for Information Security is recommended for all organizations to comply with the security provisions of the 1998 Data Protection Act. (Legal issues relating to security are covered in more detail in Chapter 12.)

The key features of information security are:

- *Availability*. Making sure information is available to those who need it and that they can use the information when appropriate.
- *Confidentiality*. Making sure information access is available only to those who require it. The opposite side to availability.
- *Authenticity and integrity*. Safeguarding the accuracy of information – is it the same as the original? Has it been altered or corrupted?

An information security system will have the following components:

- Data and information assets. Listing of the key assets to be protected.
- Hardware.
- Software.
- Policies and procedures.

Standards: British Standard for Information Security BS7799

The Plan, Do, Check, Act model (PDCA) is a core part of the British Standard for Information Security (British Standards Institute, 2002) and is illustrated in Figure 9.23.

The PDCA model offers a clear process for security management systems to be developed. The key components are explained below:

- *Plan*. Establish policy, objectives, targets, processes and procedures relevant to managing risk and improving information security to deliver results in accordance with an organization's overall policies and objectives.
- *Do*. Implement and operate the security policy, controls, processes and procedures.
- *Check*. Assess and, where applicable, measure process performance against security policy, objectives and practical experience and report the results to management for review.
- *Act*. Take corrective and preventive actions, based on the results of the management review, to achieve continual improvement.

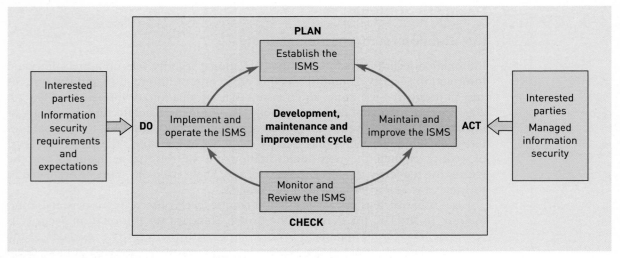

Figure 9.23 PDCA model for Information Security Management Systems (ISMS)
Source: BSI, BS 7799-2: 2002, Figure 1

The security analysis process will include an investigation of any existing documentation relating to security. This will include assessing any security policies in place, documented security breaches and incidents and information from information security controls already in place.

The core component of the security analysis stage is risk analysis: identifying, assessing and evaluating levels of risk relating to information held by an organization. The security analysis requires an assessment of the following areas:

- *Information assets* – what are the key resources we are trying to protect? What are they worth? What security level can they be assigned?
- *Threat assessment* – a common list of threats to information security would include:
  - human errors: inadvertent acts, which could be internally by employees or externally by service providers
  - system failure: a technical failure of software or hardware
  - natural disasters: fire, flood, etc.
  - malicious acts: deliberate acts of sabotage.
- *Impact assessment* – what are the implications of our information assets being compromised? Impacts could include:
  - system downtime
  - information confidentiality breach
  - information destruction or corruption.
- *Security weakness assessment* – in what ways may our systems become compromised? For example:
  - design flaws
  - social engineering (obtaining security information by deception).

The evidence from this analysis will lead to the development of controls to ensure that the security objectives are met. The controls will be dealt with in the security design section of this chapter.

Design

Database design

The process of database design requires the information architect to define the structure of a database. A database will contain tables, records and fields. Bocij et al. (2003) state that the functions of a database are to 'enter, modify, report and retrieve information'. An introduction to database software was given in Chapter 2. This section offers an overview of the key issues relating to database design; in order to fully explore the issues in this section a specialist database design textbook should also be consulted.

In a relational database, tables are related to each other using a set of rules. Each relation must have a primary key, a field that will act as a unique identifier for each record in a table. A primary key must be unique and cannot be null. Primary keys can be selected from candidate keys that all have the capacity of a unique identifier. A secondary key is used to link to a primary key in another table. In Figure 9.24 we can see an example of primary key (employee ID) defined in Microsoft Access, in a database for employee expenses. Figure 9.25 illustrates the links between the primary and secondary keys and the relationships defined in Microsoft Access.

Normalization

The process of normalization is used to optimize the database to minimize redundancy or duplication of information. The aim of normalization is to reduce data redundancy and create well-formed relations in the database design. The process of normalization will draw upon the information and data models introduced in the analysis stage of the chapter.

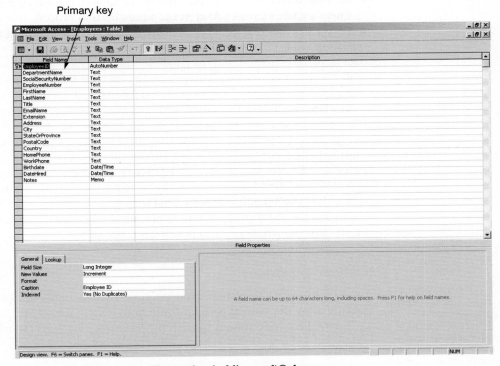

Figure 9.24 Primary key illustration in Microsoft® Access

Source: Reprinted by permission from Microsoft Corporation

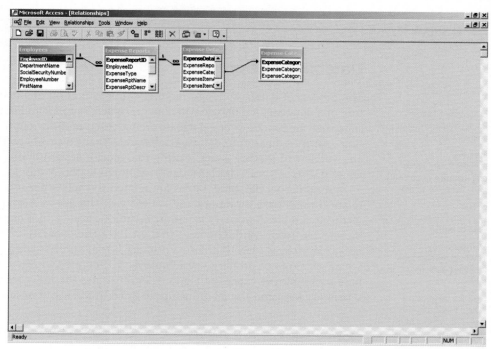

Figure 9.25 Relationships in Microsoft® Access
Source: Reprinted by permission from Microsoft Corporation

The normalization process will start with unnormalized data. Data in unnormalized form consists of a single relation with all the attributes, and can be represented in tabular form. This form may also be called 'ONF' (zero normal form). At this stage no consideration has been given to how the data in the table relate.

There are five normal forms in the normalization process; however, in practice only the first three are used by most database designers. The process of the first normal form repeating groups of data will be identified. Repeating groups can cause problems when data have to be entered into the database. Taking the Lo-cost Airline Company example: if all the passenger and flight data were in one table it would not be possible to enter a new passenger into the table without also having to add a flight.

The first normal form requires the removal of repeating groups of data, and the identification of a primary key. All key attributes must be dependent on the primary key.

The second normal form states that there must be no partial dependencies, which means that no attribute can be dependent on only a portion of the primary key. The process will assess the dependent attributes. Any attributes that are not functionally dependent on the whole key are removed to a new relation, and the part of the key on which they are dependent is copied to the new relation, becoming the primary key.

Finally, the third normal form is produced when each non-key attribute 'depends on the key, the whole key and nothing but the key'.

Data dictionaries

Data dictionary
Special type of metadata definition used in databases, acting as a catalogue of all data elements, containing their names and structures and information about their usage

In order to ensure consistent database design across an organization, or many organizations using the same types of information, we will use a **data dictionary**.

A data dictionary should contain the following elements (Mattila, 2001):

● Data element definitions

● Table definitions

● Database schema (graphical representation of the whole table).

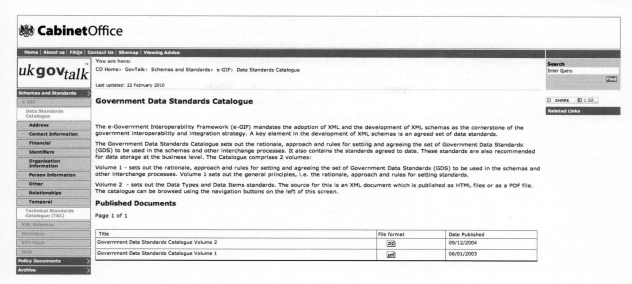

Figure 9.26 UK Government Data Standards Catalogue

Source: http://www.cabinetoffice.gov.uk/govtalk/schemasstandards/e-gif/datastandards.aspx

An example of a data dictionary in action is the UK Government Data Standards Catalogue (Figure 9.26).

Data dictionaries are also discussed in Chapter 10: Managing information quality.

Case study 9.1

FT

Remote database administrators and vendors

In today's digital world, information resides in databases. The ability of your business to manage that information can mean the difference between life and death. At the local hospital, everything from your lab results and X-rays, to full medical records are stored in a database. At the bank, all your financial records and transactions are stored in a database. At a retail store, store inventory to point of sale information is all housed in a database. Like or not, we live in a digital world, and businesses need this information to survive.

The amount of data being stored in databases is growing at an alarming rate each year. Compound that with the fact that in today's global economy the database that holds this information needs to be available 7 days a week, 24 hours a day. This is putting an incredible strain on organizations' internal resources (Database Administrators) to deal with it all.

Accelerating this problem even more is the fact that database administrators – specialized resource needed to maintain databases – are hard to hire, hard to retain, and even harder to keep up to speed with the constantly changing technology landscape.

Recognizing this fact, the only way many organizations can ease this strain is to seek outside help. Historically companies seeking outside help would go out and hire a consultant to come in on a time and material basis, to fill these critical needs. When you hire a consultant this way, you pay for 8 hours of work, even if you don't have 8 hours of work for them to do. The consultants hired in this manner would come to your physical work site to perform all services rendered.

Anyone who has ever done this knows first hand what an expensive way this is to solve the problem. It's even more expensive when you want that high priced expert to work off hours. Often times, working off-hour shifts is a requirement of the job of the DBA. Think about it, you would not want your point of sale application coming down when customers are placing an order in the store.

To fill this critical need, a new generation of database administration vendors exists. This new generation of vendors uses the power of the Internet in ways that were not possible 10 years ago to make these high-end database administration resources available remotely, whenever and wherever they are needed. This service is known as remote database administration (RDBA). Since they are coming in remote, you only use these high-end experts to solve you problems for the amount of time they are actually needed. Unlike the traditional model where you are obligated to use the consultant for a full day's work each and every time you use them.

Things to consider when choosing a remote database administration vendor

There are a number of diverse situations where experience has shown us it makes sense for a company to engage a remote database administration vendor to either augment your existing team or outsource your database administration needs. In these situations, there is a very high likelihood you will receive significant benefit from such a relationship. Some of the key reasons include:

- The database is critical to your business
- You are a geographically diverse organization

- Upcoming database upgrades
- Unable to deal with all the vendor patches
- Performance issues
- Need to implement new database features
- Recently inherited database your internal staff is not equipped to support
- Trouble hiring and retaining DBAs

Source: Michael J Corey, Ntirety, Choosing a Remote DBA instead of a full-time consultant, Nov 2007

Questions

1 Why may it be important for many organizations to employ RDBAs?

2 Why may it be preferable to hire an RDBA vendor instead of employing trained staff directly?

Web design

From the analysis stage we will develop conceptual blueprints for web pages that reflect the evidence gained from research and information auditing. The key terms, labels and concepts that need to be consistently applied to web pages from this logical stage will now be developed into usable physical designs.

The difference between websites and intranets

The concepts of websites and intranets were introduced in Chapter 2. To recap: when referring to a website, this means a public site available on the World Wide Web, whereas an intranet can be combination of an internal websites, e-mail and hosted applications.

When designing for web-based information systems it is important to make a distinction between intranets and websites. Although in terms of technology both run on the same type of platform – HTML pages are viewed through a web browser, delivered from a web server – there are many differences to consider. White (2001) states that intranets do not benefit from the intensive use of graphics, tend to be broad rather than deep, and have to cope with a wide range of formats, many of which have not been explicitly written for web publishing.

Different structures will be used to control and manage these two areas. Websites are often maintained by small teams of specialists with responsibility for content creation and management. These teams are often based in marketing or communications departments. Intranets are, as we observed in Chapter 5, vital in encouraging the sharing of information and knowledge. They are therefore more devolved in their structure, allowing as many staff as possible to contribute, offering a true picture of corporate knowledge.

Robertson (2003b) summarizes a comparison between intranets and websites. See Table 9.7.

Table 9.7 Websites and intranets compared

Aspect	Corporate website	Intranet
Business goals	Communicate information; support marketing; sell products	Broad goals, including: communicate information accurately, improve staff efficiency
Audience	External users: wide range of skills and experience; limited understanding of organization	Internal users: good understanding of organization; wide range of information needs
Familiarity	Infrequent users: not familiar with site or organization	Frequent users: familiar with site and organization
Efficiency	Secondary issue for the site, unless frequently used by visitors	Primary goal of the site: to improve staff efficiency
Browsers and platforms	Many and varied	Consistent (SOE: standard operating environment)
Size	Small to medium	Medium to extremely large
Content and structure	Narrow, structured around key products and services	Broad, varied information types and content
Content updates	Weekly or monthly	Daily
Presentation	Appearance very important for promotion and sales	Consistency more important than appearance
Authoring models	Often centralized	Typically decentralized
Metadata	Support the needs of Internet search engines	Support the needs of staff and site management
Integration with other systems	Limited, often only e-commerce systems	Extensive, core part of site functionality
Legal liability	Liable for every word published	Reduced legal exposure
Accessibility and usability	Very important	Very important

Analysis for web design: web blueprint

As with database design, it is important to assess the information gained from the analysis stage and model the information concepts logically before starting the physical design process. Information from the requirements research and information flow diagrams stages will offer an overview of the types of information needed by the users in the context of the business. The next stage is to translate this into a **web blueprint** offering a high-level view of the website. A web blueprint is a form of sitemap view of a website.

Web blueprint
An overview sitemap indicating pages, types and page components and their relationship to the home page

Many web designers may move straight from the requirements into using a tool such as Macromedia Dreamweaver and start creating pages in HTML (for an overview of HTML refer back to Chapter 3) – this is a mistake as two stages are being missed out. Figure 9.27 gives an overview of the key web design processes covered in this chapter. The conceptual blueprint stage offers a bridge between the logical and physical stages of web design.

Rosenfeld and Morville (2002) describe a blueprint as 'showing the relationships between pages and other components'. For example, blueprints offer a way to show how users will find information in the site using search and browse methods (search and browse are explained later in the web design section of this chapter). The blueprint will not show how all the pages in the site relate to each other in exact detail.

As with the other information and data diagrams we have used to model in this chapter we can use a tool such as Microsoft Visio to illustrate the blueprint using common symbols. The example used in this section is the development of a university intranet. Figure 9.28 is a blueprint working at high level illustrating how the intranet pages and components conceptually relate. There is also a key on the diagram.

The blueprint is depicting:

- An entrance point to the site, normally called a 'gateway'.
- Related pages grouped together using a dotted boundary.
- Pages that introduce two distinct divisions of the university: the faculties and non-academic departments.
- How these then relate to similar sets of pages for each division, first, at directory level, then further sub-sites around generic topics. Similar sets of pages are illustrated by the black shadow on the diagram.
- Components of the news and search and browse pages, e.g. the home page taking news headlines from the more detailed university news page.
- The legend, which also includes the 'to be created' symbol to track development progress.

Page design and wireframes

Wireframe
Also know as 'schematic', a way of illustrating the layout of an individual web page

Wireframes are a recognized form of design used by web designers to lay out a web page before using web editing tools to start the page creation process. Wodke (2002) describes a wireframe (sometimes known as a 'schematic') as 'a basic outline of an individual page, drawn to indicate the elements of a page, their relationships, and their relative importance'. A wireframe will be created for all types of similar page groups, identified at the blueprint stage. As with the other information and data diagrams developed in this chapter, we can use a tool such as Microsoft Visio to illustrate the blueprint using common symbols.

At the wireframe stage, emphasis is not placed on use of colour or graphics, which will be developed in conjunction with branding or marketing teams and graphic designers and integrated into the site towards the end of the wireframe process. The focus of a wireframe is still architecture and structure rather than visuals. Rosenfeld and Morville (2002) point out that wireframes should be collaborative, but should be controlled by information architects rather than graphic designers. This is an important management issue that web managers must carefully consider when selecting teams for web-based projects.

The aim of a wireframe will be to:

- integrate consistently available components on the web page (e.g. navigation, search boxes);
- order and group key types of components together;
- develop a design that will focus the user on to core messages and content;
- make correct use of white space to structure the page;
- develop a page structure that can be easily reused by other web designers.

Wodke (2002) offers the following processes for developing a wireframe:

1   Start with a box in the middle of your sheet of paper.
2   Add the global elements.
3   Add unique elements in order of importance.
4   Add dynamic elements (if any).
5   Add text and graphics.
6   Add numbered notes to explain the elements.

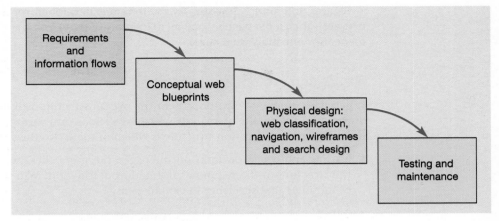

Figure 9.27 Web design processes

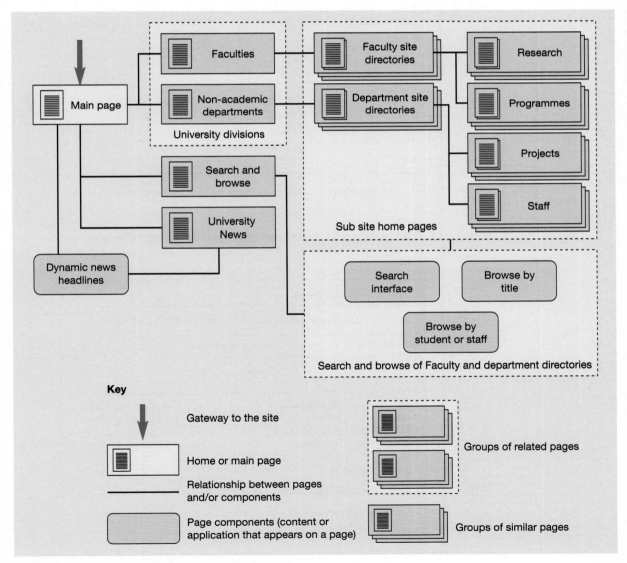

Figure 9.28 Web blueprint for a university intranet

Figures 9.29 and 9.30 show two wireframes developed for a university intranet, first with the global elements (available on every page) and then with the unique elements (for one individual page).

Navigation systems

When designing a navigation system the overall structure will need to be developed, drawing on the results of analysis processes such as card sorting. The first decision to make regarding navigation structure is which of these two the structure will be:

● Narrow and deep: few links on the pages, but more clicks required to move down the structure to the required information destination. Will work best on websites or intranets that specialize in certain areas.

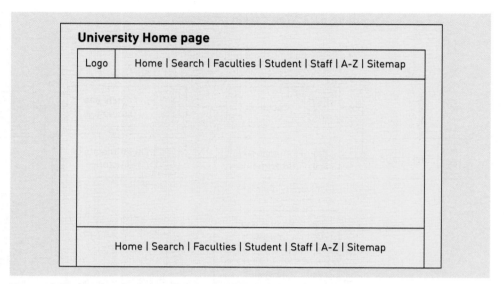

Figure 9.29 Basic wireframe for a university intranet with global elements

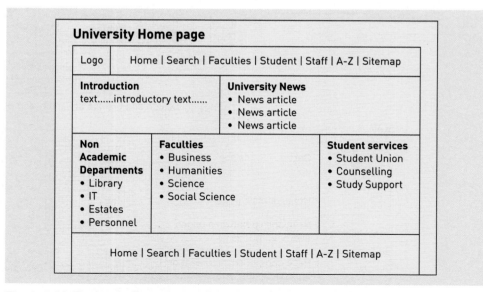

Figure 9.30 Basic wireframe for a university intranet with global elements and unique elements

- Broad and shallow: more links on pages, fewer clicks to information destination. Will work best when websites or intranets offer a wide range of information that can be clustered into groups of links. Intranets are generally said to work better with broad and shallow structure as they need to offer a gateway to the entire organization.

The two types of structure are illustrated in Figures 9.31 and 9.32.

Rosenfeld and Morville (2002) introduce the concept of global, local and contextual navigation as a way of breaking down navigation into subsystems. They are illustrated in Figure 9.33 as diagrams and then in a real-life example from the UK HM Treasury website (Figures 9.34 and 9.35).

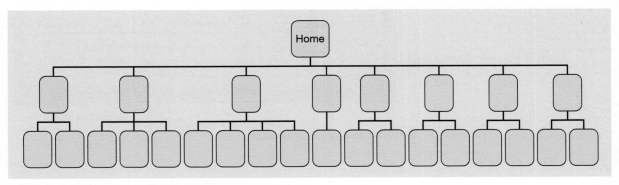

Figure 9.31 Broad and shallow navigation

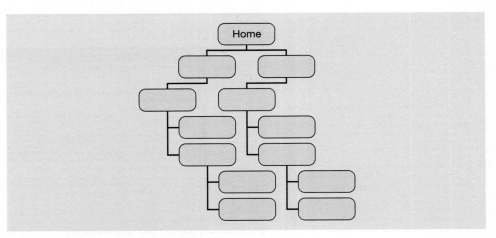

Figure 9.32 Narrow and deep navigation

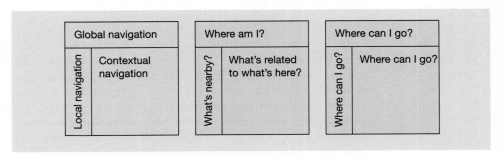

Figure 9.33 Global, local and contextual navigation

Source: Rosenfeld and Morville (2002)

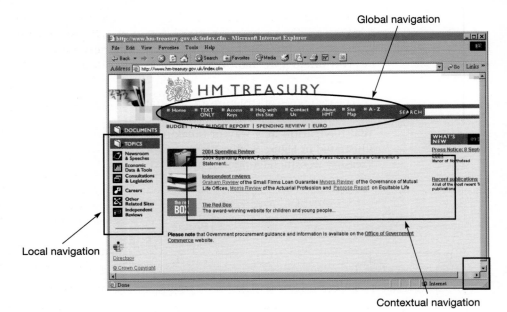

Figure 9.34 Website: navigation illustration

Source: www.hm-treasury.gov.uk

Figure 9.35 Navigation: deeper structure

Source: www.hm-treasury.gov.uk

Jacob Nielsen (2000) introduces the concept of breadcrumbs as a way of showing users where they are in the site hierarchy. The term is taken from the way breadcrumbs were followed by Hansel and Gretel (in the fairy tale) to reach their destination. Breadcrumbs help users understand the context of a page; they are simple and do not take up too much space on the page, leaving space for the core page content. Breadcrumbs are the markers by which users can explore a site along an increasingly specific path. An example of breadcrumbs for the university intranet example we have used in this chapter would be:

Intranet Home > Faculties > Science > Chemistry

The item that is not linked (not underlined) indicates to the user where they are in the hierarchy. Figure 9.36 illustrates breadcrumbs in action on a website.

Search versus browse

When designing for the web environment it is important to understand the focus that will be placed on the search tools used to locate information. The important question to ask is how many of your users will have a preference for using a search engine when visiting the website or intranet.

Intranets generally grow rapidly and the volume of content will increase, making information location difficult. Usability expert Jacob Nielsen states that for intranets 'a high end search engine is an absolute necessity' (Nielsen, 2000). A high-end search engine will have high-quality, detailed indexing and advanced search features.

User Interface Engineering (2001) conducted research to assess whether search-dominant users existed, that is, users who will always go to the search box first when using a website or intranet. Thirty different users were observed, performing 121 different shopping tasks. The results of the survey had the following findings:

- 20 per cent of participants were link-dominant (chose links exclusively).
- None of the users were search-dominant (chose search engines exclusively).
- For 21 per cent of the sites, every single user who visited only used search. It seems that these sites were search-dominant, not the users.
- 32 per cent of the sites were link-dominant.
- 47 per cent were not dominant to search or links.

This research implies that there is something inherent in the site's design that causes users to choose the search engine or the links, not a hard-and-fast preference of the user. The authors made the following valuable conclusion:

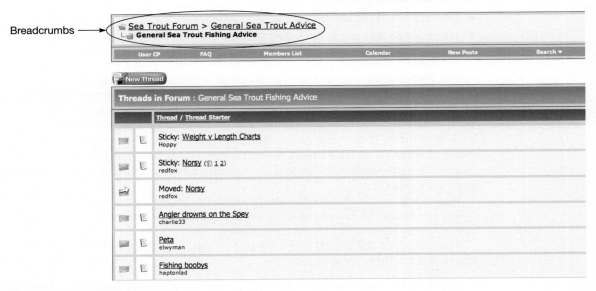

Figure 9.36 Breadcrumb example

Source: http://www.seatroutforum.com/forumdisplay.php?f=2

we noticed that one of the factors that predicted whether users would initially start with search or with the links was the type of product being sold on the site. Certain types of products lend themselves better to being searched. For example, users typically go to the search engine to find a specific book or CD, however they tend to use the links to find a particular item of clothing. We believe that the nature of the content on the site can play a huge role in whether it is a search- or link-dominant site... Depending on the specific content on their site, teams might want to focus specifically on either the search engine or the links, but not necessarily both.

From this study we can see that learning about the type of content a site has is vital in assessing the role of search tools and navigation systems: a focus needs to be made on one or the other. The resulting home page therefore may be link-rich, with many different options for users to start exploring the site, or a simple page with the search box as the main focus for the user. Investments will therefore be made into:

- the research and development of detailed classification and structure; or
- high-end search tools.

Using search technologies

The selection, configuration and design of search tools are key factors in successful web design. Search tools can range from the free-service Microsoft services available with Windows Vista and the Windows 2008 server to highly customizable and search software such as Verity (**www.verity.com**). The website Searchtools.com illustrates the range of search tools that can be purchased for websites and intranets: over 200 are listed.

The issues to consider when selecting search tools are:

- How many documents do we have to index? Are there enough to merit the use of a search engine?
- What type of documents do we want to index? For example, HTML, Word, Acrobat/PDF?
- What type of searches will be carried out? Full text? Key words?
- Will the search engine index and search metadata? What metadata standard will be used?
- Will the search engine index titles?
- How often will the site be indexed?
- Will users be able to use advanced features or refine the results?
- What information will be presented with the results?

The above aspects will determine levels of configuration of the search tools: the greater the number of configurations used the longer the development time in developing the search solution. For example, if you want to search on key words on every document on a 20,000-page intranet, key words must be added to the metadata of each document. It may not be possible to do this manually – therefore a specialist piece of software must be used to assign key words to each document by being 'taught' to meta-tag documents with certain characteristics. This is a time-consuming and costly process.

Figures 9.37 and 9.38 illustrate advanced search options on a website. Note ways the search can be refined in terms of the key types of information content that the organization produces and how the results are presented.

The design of the search interface and results page is an important aspect: the design must address these issues:

- Where will users type in their search query? A dedicated page? A box on the home page?
- Can the user search by content type? By date?
- What results will the user see?

The importance and use of these options will depend on the results gathered from the analysis stage of the process, understanding user requirements, relative to the information content and business requirements.

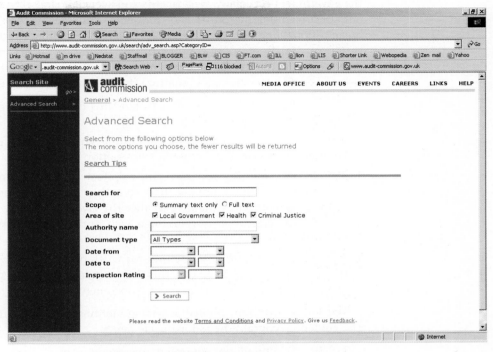

Figure 9.37 Advanced search design example
Source: www.audit-commission.gov.uk

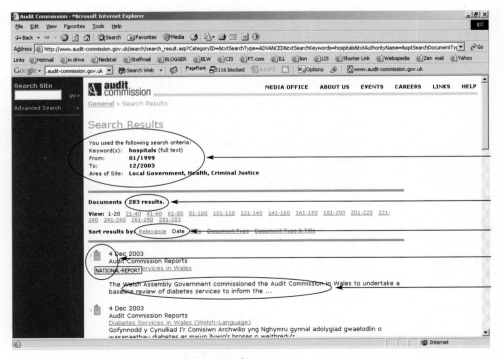

Figure 9.38 Search results design example
Source: www.audit-commission.gov.uk

Organizational standard and guidelines

In large organizations the development, management and maintenance of websites and intranets may be distributed across many parts of an organization. For example, the government has many departments and agencies; large firms may maintain different sites for different countries or products or market sectors; on an intranet each organizational unit may have the ability to publish. In order to ensure consistent application of design standards and organizational style an organization will publish documentation for web designers, editors and authors to follow in order to communicate and enforce the standards required. The documentation will come in many forms:

- A manual stipulating the technical standards that must be followed, e.g. versions of HTML used, metadata standards used.
- A manual stipulating the physical design requirements, e.g. position of search boxes, standard labels to be used on navigation bars.
- Templates containing core navigational elements already embedded in the page that cannot be edited, leaving the web author to add the content to certain areas of the page without being able to alter the layout. Templates can be used in web content management systems or a web authoring tool such as Macromedia Dreamweaver.
- Style guides containing guidelines for written content, how certain documents should be written and laid out; this will include examples of grammar, fonts, paragraphs and headlines allowed on web documents.

The UK government publishes web guidelines for all government departments. The guidelines contain the following elements:

1 An illustrated handbook for web management teams
2 A website starter kit containing templates
3 A framework for senior managers
4 A quality framework for website design based around the international standards ISO 13407: Human-centred design processes for interactive systems (1999) and ISO TR 18529: Ergonomics of human system interaction – Human-centred lifecycle process descriptions (2000)
5 Guidelines for UK government websites.

Examples of UK government templates (home page and sitemap) are in Figures 9.39 and 9.40. Note the areas where the layout is mandated (e.g. the navigation elements) and where the web designer, editor or author will add and amend their own content.

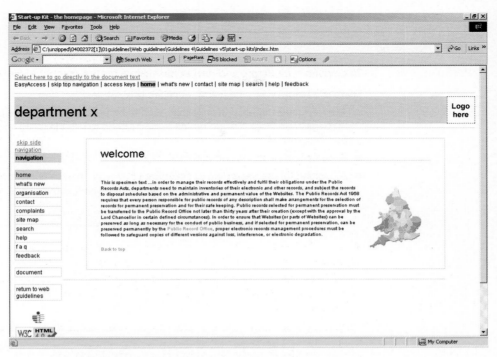

Figure 9.39 UK government template example: home page

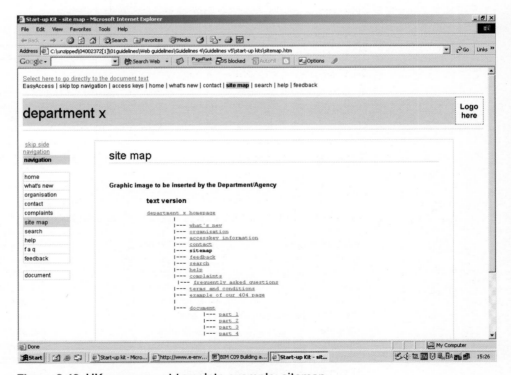

Figure 9.40 UK government template example: sitemap

Activity 9.3   Intranet design at the Lo-cost Airline Company

Purpose   To develop a wireframe and navigation system for the Lo-cost Airline Company intranet.

Activity   There is a blank wireframe below – in each box suggest:

- The navigation labels and links that need to be applied to the home page (from the list of 30 pages supplied). You do not necessarily need to include all 30 links. They are in no particular order.
- The position for logos and graphics.
- A position for the search box. Think about how you need to apply the analysis and design principles you have learnt in the chapter. Think about global, local and contextual navigation.

Intranet pages
Home
Company news
Search
Sales
Weekly message from the chairman
Human resources
Company share price
IT support
Paris branch
London branch

Berlin branch
Brussels branch
Rome branch
Flight tracking
Business strategy
Latest sales reports
Accounts
Airline industry news
Holiday/leave booking system
Sales figures
E-commerce sales database

Customer complaints
Marketing
Pilot information
Cabin crew information
Plane servicing
Catering
Language options
Company discussion forum
New employee starter pack
Staff directory

Uses of metadata on web pages

The concept of metadata and the Dublin Core version was introduced in Chapter 3. Using the example of the UK government again, we can see the application of the Dublin Core metadata standard in the form of an adapted version called the 'e-government meta-data standard' (e-GMS). The standard has been adapted to meet the information needs of UK government departments and agencies. An example from a UK government website is given in the box. Note that in the subject category e-GMS tag the terms used are taken from the Government Category list, a form of taxonomy that we will discuss later in the chapter.

Taken from: www.ukonline.gov.uk

```
<!- retrieve html content for region 0 ->
<!-meta tags-><meta name="eGMS.Title" lang="en"
content="Homepage">
<meta name="eGMS.Description" lang="en" content="ukonline - the
easy way to government information & services online. The main
point of entry to UK government websites. ">
<meta name="eGMS.Date.Created" lang="en" content="2003-09-
11T11:17:49-00:00">
<meta name="eGMS.Date.Expires" lang="en" content="">
<meta name="eGMS.Identifier" lang="en" content="100001">
<meta name="eGMS.Subject.Category" lang="en" content="Science,
technology and innovation|Information technology|Internet
Government, politics and public administration
Government, politics and public administration|Public adminis
tration|Modernising government|e-Government ">
<meta name="eGMS.Type" lang="en" content="Web guidance|Home page
">
<meta name="eGMS.Coverage.Spatial" lang="en" content="United
Kingdom">
<meta name="eGMS.Coverage.Temporal" lang="en" content="">
<meta name="eGMS.Audience" lang="en" content="">
<meta name="eGMS.Contributor" lang="en" content="">
<meta name="eGMS.Publisher" lang="en" content="UK Government
Cabinet Office,
Office of the e-Envoy,
Stockley House,
130 Wilton Road,
London,
SW1V 1LQ,
UK.
editor@ukonline.gov.uk">
<meta name="eGMS.Language" content="en">
<meta name="eGMS.Subject.Keyword" lang="en" content="uk online,
ukonline, portal, govt, egovernment, government, e-government,">
<!-meta tags end->
```

Activity 9.4	Creating Dublin Core metadata using an online generator

Purpose	**To apply and edit Dublin Core metadata using an online metadata generator.**
Activity	Access the sample Intranet page for the Lo-cost Airline Company that has been added as a link to the student resources for the chapter at **www.pearsoned.co.uk/chaffey**. Look at the page, make notes about the content and print the page out for the reference. Copy the address from the browser address bar (right mouse click > copy or control and C).

visit the www

Now go the URL: **www.ukoln.ac.uk/metadata/dcdot/**. At the input box add the URL you have copied by right mouse click   paste or control and V pressed together. Make sure the RDF box is not checked. Submit the URL. You will receive a page of results with Dublin Core tags already generated. As the process is automated some of the tags require further editing. In the boxes below the generated code, edit or add extra information to make the tags more relevant to the Lo-cost Airline Company. Refer to the tag descriptions at **http://dublincore.org/documents/dces/** if you are unsure what to include in each tag.

Submit and view the final results.

Designing for interoperability

In order for information to be reused in a number of environments, both internally and externally, common information architecture must be defined that allows the reuse of information across a wide range of platforms and across organizational boundaries.

Taxonomy, thesauri and controlled vocabularies

The approaches in this section will often be used in the following applications or information environments:

- websites or intranets;
- search portals;
- electronic document management systems;
- electronic record management systems;
- content management systems.

The following three concepts are ways that information architecture will be applied to aid the browsing and search of organizational information: by creating a controlled vocabulary to define organizational activites, a taxonomy (classification scheme) to develop a hierarchy, or a thesaurus to identify relationships to aid retrieval. Pidcock (2003) states that these three have the following in common:

- They are approaches to help structure, classify and/or represent the concepts and relationships pertaining to some subject matter of interest to some community.
- They are intended to enable a community to come to agreement and to commit to use the same terms in the same way.
- There is a set of terms that some community agrees to use to refer to these concepts and relationships.

Controlled vocabulary
A list of equivalent terms, often enumerated

A **controlled vocabulary** is defined by Rosenfeld and Morville (2002) as 'a list of defined terms in the form of a synonym ring, or a list of preferred terms in the form of authority files'. A synonym ring connects a set of words that are defined as equivalent for the purposes of retrieval. The synonym ring for the university intranet example we have been using in this chapter could include the words teacher, lecturer, teaching staff and module leader. A controlled vocabulary can therefore be used to aid users when they are searching: if a page or document is indexed only on the word 'lecturer' but the user searches on 'teacher', the results will still return pages containing 'lecturer'. In this situation the term 'lecturer' would be called the 'preferred term' and the term 'teacher' would be the 'variant term'. An authority file will be a list of preferred or accepted terms.

Fast et al. (2002) outline the ways that equivalent or alternative terms can be used:

- synonyms (two words with the same meaning, like 'jeans' and 'dungarees');
- homonyms (words that sound the same, but have different meanings, like 'bank' the financial institution and 'bank' the side of a stream or river);
- common misspellings;
- changes in content (e.g. countries that change their name or have various spellings);
- identifying 'best bets' or the most popular pages associated with a certain term;
- connecting a woman's married name to her maiden name;
- connecting abbreviations to the full word (e.g. NY and New York, the chemical symbol Si with the element silicon).

Taxonomy
A browsable hierarchy of organizational classification terms

'**Taxonomy**' is a term which has been taken from the life sciences, where plants and animals and other life forms are classified into hierarchical and related groups. Gilchrist (2003) states that the number of large corporate enterprises developing taxonomies had risen to 80 per cent by 2003 from a figure of 20 per cent three years previously. Taxonomies have risen in importance on intranets where large numbers of documents need to classified for search and retrieval. The scale of the problem of users being unable to find the information they need is illustrated at companies such as BT and Microsoft which are estimated to have between 2 and 3 million documents on their intranet.

Why are taxonomies important? Wylie (2003) states that they are a crucial element of effective knowledge management. Taxonomies are the response to the following challenges:

- the level of information overload and information complexity;
- the implementation of enterprise portals using content management systems that require content tagging in order to customize information;
- the growth of B2B e-commerce and the emergence of web services, which require agreed information architectures so that relevant information can be shared between systems and people in a timely manner;
- the need to be more innovative by making connections between related concepts across different disciplines.

Gilchrist (2003) defines a taxonomy as 'an enterprise-wide master file of the vocabularies and their structures, used or for use, across the enterprise, and from which navigation and search support are most prominent'. Rosenfeld and Morville (2002) refer to taxonomies as classification schemes that may be a front-end browsable hierarchy like Yahoo! (**www.yahoo.com**) and a back-end tool used by information architects, authors and indexers for organizing and tagging documents.

The UK government has created a high-level taxonomy called 'The Government Category List' to offer a coherent way for citizens to browse government information on

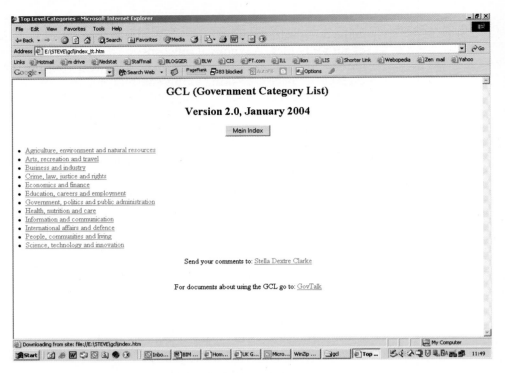

Figure 9.41 UK Government Category List: top level
Source: HMSO

cross-government portals. Figures 9.41 and 9.42 illustrate the category list in web format (HTML) at high and low levels. Figure 9.43 also illustrates the government category list in specialist taxonomy-building software called Wordmap (**www.wordmap.com**).

Thesauri are often the most valuable but are also the most complex of these three concepts – they are difficult to develop without specialist software to manage the relationships. A **thesaurus** will be used to index documents for browsing and will work as a search tool, matching terms to documents for users and offering terms to search with. A thesaurus may therefore work in the background matching terms for users or as a tool as part of the search interface, helping users define their search terms. Figure 9.44 illustrates a search thesaurus in action at the Social Science Information Gateway.

In a thesaurus the following formats are used to express the relationships:

BT Broader term
NT Narrower term
RT Related term
U   Use
UF Used for

Thesaurus
A more developed and complex controlled vocabulary, showing relationships in terms of hierarchy, equivalence and association

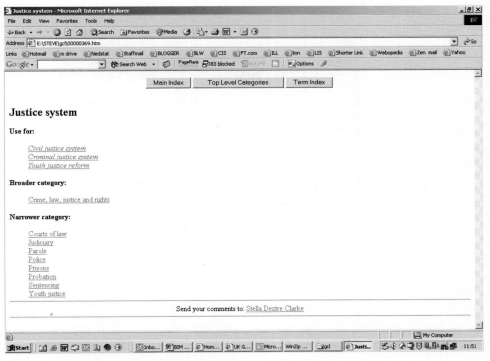

Figure 9.42 Government Category List
Source: HMSO

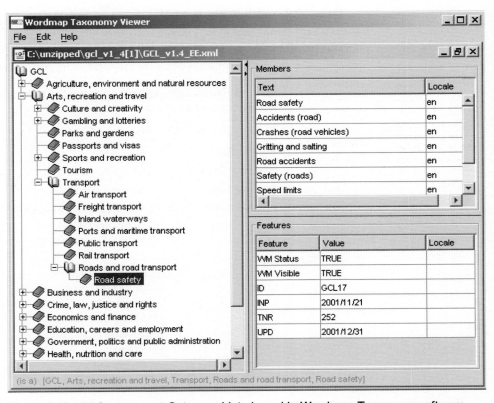

Figure 9.43 UK Government Category List viewed in Wordmap Taxonomy software
Source: HMSO

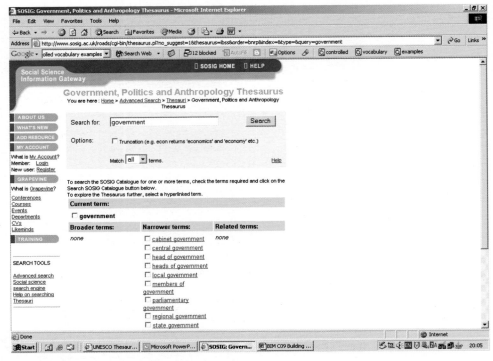

Figure 9.44 Searching using a thesaurus

Source: www.sosig.ac.uk/roads/cgi-bin/thesauras.pl

Tables 9.8 and 9.9 illustrate the terms in use (taken from the US Library of Congress Global Legal Information Network Thesaurus). The term selected is 'computer security', shown in context in Table 9.8 and then the full record is in Table 9.9.

Table 9.8 Thesaurus example showing the term 'computer security' in context

Term	Crime prevention
Record Type	Main Term
Narrower Term	Computer security
Broader Term	National security
Related Term	Administration of justice
	Computer crimes
	Criminal investigation
	Criminal law
	Criminal offenders
	Detention
	Informants
	Intelligence services
	Juvenile delinquency
	Police
	Public welfare

Table 9.9 Thesaurus example showing the full record for the term 'computer security'

Term	Computer security
Scope	Note Refers to protecting computer hardware, software, databases, systems, networks, websites, or associated communications equipment or programs from unauthorized or malicious access, copying, misuse, disclosure, modifications, damage, or destruction
Used For	Access restrictions for computers Computer access controls Computer hackers Computer hacking Computer privacy Computer systems security Cyber security Data protection in computers Data security Database protection Electronic systems security Firewalls in computing Hackers and hacking (computers) Security for computers Security measures for computers Security of computer networks Security of computer systems Security of computers Website protection
Record Type	Main Term
Broader Term	Computers Crime prevention National security
Related Term	Automation Communications Computer crimes Copyright Criminal law Databases Electronic commerce Internet National defense Secrecy Technology Terrorism

Case study 9.2

Sainsbury's: getting connected with a taxonomy

Sainsbury's was in the process of re-platforming its core IT systems and as part of this activity has moved from a company intranet to a portal. The portal is called Connect. Having chosen the software for Connect we moved rapidly through implementation and this meant that we needed to design a taxonomy to be available for use in the system before launch – a very tall order.

Sainsbury's approach

Thinking about the information assets of Sainsbury's I decided that there were two ways of identifying categories by:

- analysing the document population in the old intranet and brainstorming concepts in workshop sessions
- with a small group of colleagues who could be considered as representative of the whole business.

There were advantages and disadvantages either way but neither was perfect. Documents had to be classified or they could not be migrated from the old intranet to the portal and the classification terms had to be loaded to the software before the migration commenced. We were therefore looking for a rapid, but workable, solution.

Analysing the document population

How do you analyse a document population to design and apply a taxonomy? Again there are two choices

- the first is manual using people to analyse and construct a hierarchy of terms
- the second is to use technology.

A manual approach is slower and subject to the vagaries of human judgement and inconsistency. The automated approach is faster but the output is less accurate and benefits from human intervention to refine and improve the language, structure and application. In one study the automated approach produced taxonomic accuracy of 65%.

Looking at the document population in the old intranet, I realised that it was not representative of the business. Sainsbury's had chosen, as so many organisations do, to grow its intranet organically. In the early days of the technology intranets were seen largely as a communications tool and nothing more. Many organisations set up intranets on the basis of try it and see. The expectation was that free and unfettered use would stimulate enthusiasm and growth of content leading to critical mass. But if you don't have a strategic plan and development of the intranet is piecemeal, then activities within the organisation could well be under-represented in the document population giving a distorted view of what is important or significant to the organisation. I concluded that we didn't have to choose between the manual and automated approach as analysing the document population of the intranet would not give us a comprehensive picture.

Workshop sessions

Because of the tight deadline and the lack of critical mass in the existing document population we were pointed in the direction of the brainstorm approach and I decided to organise some workshops. Champions were identified for each part of the business and they were asked to select a representative group of colleagues who had a depth of knowledge about the business, what it does and how it operates. I organised two sessions for each major operating area, the first to brainstorm and the second to review the output. Occasionally a third session was required but mostly two were sufficient having warned the group that they would not be let out of the room until we had negotiated an agreed set of terms! We used a large white board and looked at a high-level view of activities and processes and what information was required to support the process then we extrapolated a set of terms. There were four rules; no acronyms, no jargon, no names of departments and at all times use plain English. I then took the output away, analysed for conflict, contradiction and logic and produced a prototype hierarchy for review at the second workshop.

The pitfalls of organisational hierarchy

It seems as though there is a deep human instinct to think in terms of organisational hierarchy. Belonging to a structure or group of people gives you a strong sense of identity and it is easy to think about work like this so naturally you start to organise information in this way. But for information retrieval purposes across a large and diverse organisation, arranging and labelling information according to departmental names is not an effective way of facilitating searching for information for two reasons:

- Continuous change is a feature of modern corporate life, divisions and departments are frequently reorganised and restructured. More and more work is project based, staffed by multi-disciplinary teams that are formed and disbanded sometimes very rapidly.
- Employees do not necessarily know what departments or teams do.

So the shifting sands of organisational hierarchy cannot be relied on for finding information. Also these days entrepreneurial behaviour and innovation are valued. The objective is to devise solutions, which answer the problem and do it rapidly and at least cost. To do this it is often advantageous to think 'outside the box' looking for ideas, experience and opportunities in other parts of the business. If you classify information by department it tends to reinforce 'silo' thinking.

Breadth and depth

Having harvested a language, the next task was to model a hierarchy. One of the frequently asked questions at recent professional meetings has been how many terms do I need in my taxonomy and how broad and deep should the hierarchy of terms be? The simple answer is as big as it needs to be in relation to the number of documents or information objects being categorised and the nature of the documents or information objects to which it is being applied.

At Sainsbury's we have developed a taxonomy that is six broad at the top level and a maximum of four deep. The top level reflects what the supermarket business does, how it does it and what it needs to know about to operate a successful retailing business. The six top-level concepts include:

- Business Direction and Performance – every company needs to know what are its policies and strategies, in other words what direction the company is going in. Sainsbury's needs to know how well it's doing. Knowledge about performance is critical. Performance includes measuring, monitoring and evaluating projects, programmes and financial activities. We want to know how we did perform (retrospection), how we are performing (current) and how we want to perform in the future.
- Business Support – every company has supporting and enabling functions, such as running buildings and organising people, which are essential to supporting the business.
- Our Customers – knowledge about our customers is critical to making the business profitable and understanding what direction the company should be going in. This is where the analysis is done to understand what are customers' needs and to plan and develop ways of engaging the customer through branding, format and segmentation.
- Our Products and Services – Sainsbury's needs to know what it's selling to its customers. What are the products and services, the type and content? How do we develop them? Products and services include the spectrum of tangible products, such as tins on shelves, through to more intangible products such as mortgages through Sainsbury's Bank.

- Suppliers and Supplying – a core function is the ability to deliver products to the point of contact with the customer. Supplying includes relationships with suppliers and all the activities around the warehousing and movement of products.
- Selling – another core function is how Sainsbury's organises and displays its products and services to achieve sales at the point of contact with the customer, which is not necessarily in store. Included are operations in stores, Sainsbury's to You (online sales) and Sainsbury's Bank to name a few.

From design to implementation

The final stage in the design process was to take a sample of documents and test the taxonomy. How easy was it to classify a document using the taxonomy? Given the time constraints it wasn't possible to test a large number of documents but obviously the larger the sample of documents and the larger the number of users testing the model the more useful the findings will be. The results were reassuring and we proceeded to load the taxonomy in to the portal software.

Owners of information in the old company intranet were required to migrate content to the portal and they were the first group of users to be trained in the migration labs on how to use the taxonomy. The usual reaction was to ask where their department name was to be found. The second reaction was to ask why they couldn't select more than one category to classify their documents with – the confetti approach to taxonomy. Classification is definitely not a substitute for indexing.

A group of about 350 regular content publishers were the key audience and thereafter all portal users, which meant the majority of colleagues. The portal has not been in operation long enough for us to be able to fully evaluate the taxonomy. Over the coming months I will be monitoring how documents are classified and this will help us to fine tune the language and add new terms where required. Since the taxonomy was built as an abstract model I will even be looking to see if there are any terms that are not being used and they will be removed. Our catchphrase as ever will be simplicity and practicality.

Source: Reproduced by kind permission of Sainsbury's Supermarkets Ltd

Questions

1 Why have Sainsbury's chosen to use a taxonomy?
2 List the benefits that a taxonomy has offered Sainsbury's.
3 Identify the stages in the taxonomy development at Sainsbury's.

Using Extensible Markup Language – XML

An overview of the XML language was introduced in Chapter 3 relating to technologies used for information management. In this chapter we will develop further the concept of using XML as a way of developing interoperability between information systems. XML is a vital component of interoperable information architectures. By agreeing to a given DTD or schema, a group of developers has accepted a set of rules about document vocabulary and structure that enable information consistency. By agreeing XML rules relating to business areas, industries and information types, such as e-business XML (ebXML), standards for using XML have emerged to enable application of XML (an agreed standard itself).

XML schemas

XML schemas
A set of rules in XML language for specifying the structures of XML document types. Documents that reference schemas must conform to the rules specified

In Chapter 3 we introduced the concept of using DTDs for validating the structure of XML documents. However, there is another way of validating XML document structure that offers more flexibility and intergrates better with the XML language: the **XML schema**. Dick (2001) points out that DTDs have drawbacks: they are the only part of the XML family of standards that do not themselves use XML document syntax, therefore applications and tools must be able to process both XML document and XML DTD syntax. This prevents XML being a universal XML data exchange format.

XML schemas provide data-oriented data types in addition to the more document-oriented data types XML DTDs support, allowing support for data-specific types like decimal, integer, date and time. Schemas are defined by use of the XSD tag and are saved as .XSD files which are referenced at the start of XML files.

The example in the box is a snippet of a schema developed for addresses and personal information developed by the UK government. In this example integer values can be specified, as can lengths of data types.

```
<xsd:simpleType name="StreetReferenceTypeType">
<xsd:restriction base="xsd:integer">
                    <xsd:enumeration value="1"/>
                    <xsd:enumeration value="2"/>
                    <xsd:enumeration value="3"/>
                    <xsd:enumeration value="4"/>
</xsd:restriction>
</xsd:simpleType>
<xsd:simpleType name="LocalityType">
<xsd:restriction base="xsd:string">
                        <xsd:minLength value="1"/>
                        <xsd:maxLength value="35"/>
</xsd:restriction>
```

Uses of XML

We can use an example of XML in the public sector. The UK government faces a problem that many large diverse organizations face: large numbers of departments and sectors have developed their own information architecture and a number of different IT platforms. The UK government's strategy for e-government set out to achieve 100 per cent availability of all government services by the end of 2005. In order for many departments to deliver these services they must work together and share data and information. For example, the delivery of the online child benefit service requires data to be shared between HM Revenue & Customs (tax department) and the Department for Work and Pensions (responsible for social benefits). Sharing data such as address information will be problematic if the standards for how the address information is written are not agreed, e.g. should the first name be used? How should the postcode be written?

The e-government interoperability framework (e-GIF) (Office of the E-envoy, 2003b) is the UK government initiative to develop information architecture across UK government:

> The main thrust of the framework is to adopt the Internet and World Wide Web specifications for all government systems. Throughout this section use of the term 'system' is taken to include its interfaces. There is a strategic decision to adopt XML and XSL as the core standards for data integration and management of presentational data. This includes the definition and central provision of XML schemas for use throughout the public sector. The e-GIF only adopts specifications that are well supported in the market place. It is a pragmatic strategy that aims to reduce cost and risk for government systems whilst aligning them to the global Internet revolution.

The e-GIF project website contains schemas that are to be used by departments when they wish to share certain types of information related to processes that are carried out jointly or outputs can be reused.

Government accounting requires departments to provide the central department managing the data with updated information about their occupation of property. Originally it was believed that this could be accomplished electronically, but in practice incompatibility problems between databases made the creation of linkages extremely difficult. Instead, information exchange has taken place using a variety of non-electronic methods, including face-to-face liaison meetings between local departmental and Office of Goverment Commerce (OGC) representatives. The Electronic Property Information Mapping System (e-PIMS) has been developed to provide users with online access to OGC's database, which will enable them to update their own property information and to view the central civil estate as a whole on an electronic map (Office of the E-envoy, 2002).

By using XML schemas as a common way of structuring the property data, the following benefits can be seen:

- Data only need to be manually entered once.
- Data can be reused on other government systems.
- There are no constraints on the technical architecture, database products or methods of data representation within the user's environment.
- This will allow third-party suppliers to provide updates to e-PIMS via e-mail or the Internet.

RSS

Really Simple Syndication (RSS)
A version of XML and RDF that offers a standardized way of syndicating news headlines (or similar types of content) across the World Wide Web

The concept of RDF was introduced in Chapter 3 as a way of describing resources using the XML language. As XML has developed into a common standard for data markup and exchange, organizations saw the value of developing a common way to use XML to mark up news or information that can be 'chunked' into headline and stories. **RSS (Really Simple Syndication)** is a specified version of RDF written in such a way that other applications can use the content to display in the way the user requires. For example, by taking the RSS from the *Guardian* online weblog (**www.guardian.co.uk/news/blog**) a user can read the headlines and stories alongside headlines from other RSS-enabled websites, or a system developer could develop an XSL style sheet to format the content for an organization's intranet. One of the major uses of RSS is taking content from weblogs (or blogs). The process using RSS from the

Guardian online weblog is illustrated in Figures 9.45 and 9.46 and the view from a newsreader in Figure 9.47.

The *Guardian* now offers an 'Open Platform' (**www.guardian.co.uk/open-platform**) service to share content with other websites and so extend its reach through affiliation.

Table 9.10 shows the core tags in the RSS 2.0 specification (Harvard Law, 2003). Other optional tags are then used such as language and copyright.

Table 9.10 RSS core tags

Element	Description	Example
title	The name of the channel. It's how people refer to your service. If you have an HTML website that contains the same information as your RSS file, the title of your channel should be the same as the title of your website.	GoUpstate.com News Headlines
link	The URL to the HTML website corresponding to the channel.	www.goupstate.com
description	Phrase or sentence describing the channel.	The latest news from

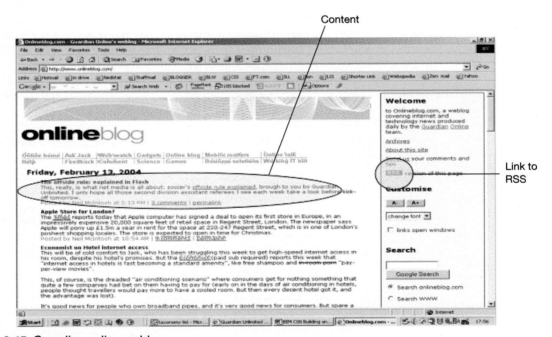

Figure 9.45 *Guardian* online weblog

Source: from www.guardian.co.uk, Copyright Guardian News & Media Ltd 2004

Content marked up in RSS

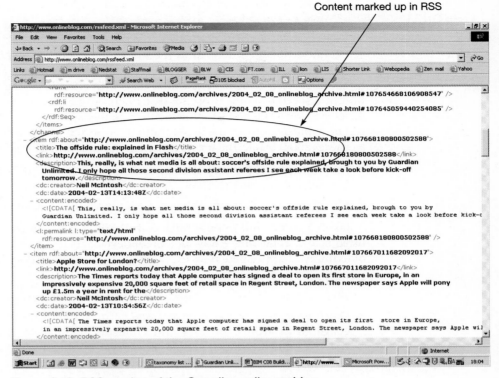

Figure 9.46 RSS version of the *Guardian* online weblog

Source: from www.guardian.co.uk, Copyright Guardian News & Media Ltd 2004

Headline   News item

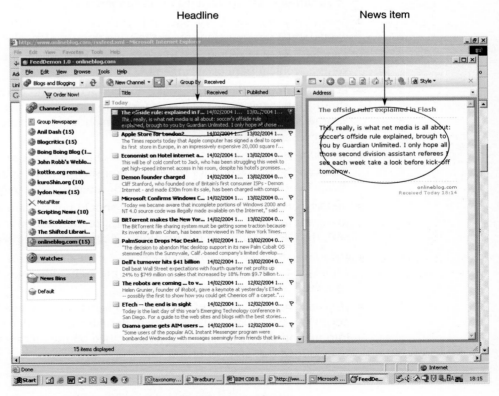

Figure 9.47 RSS displayed in FeedDemon software

Source: from www.guardian.co.uk; www.feeddemon.com, Copyright Guardian News & Media Ltd 2004

Usability

Usability
The ability of systems to meet the defined needs of users

The term 'usability' is defined in the British Standard/ISO Standard Human-centred Design Processes for Interactive Systems as the 'extent to which a product can be used by specified users to achieve specified goals with effectiveness, efficiency and satisfaction in a specified context of use' (BSI,1999). Any information architecture must be developed with the aim of implementing usable systems; the principles of usability can be applied to any of the types of information system discussed in this chapter.

Badre (2002) breaks the measurement of usability into two components:

- Ease of learning: the time it takes users to learn how to do a job using the system compared to another method.

- Ease of use: the minimum number of actions required to complete a task successfully.

Jakob Nielsen (n.d.), a usability consultant, has developed usability heuristics, listed below. They offer a way for system developers to assess a wide range of aspects of usability. Heuristics are rules of thumb or a procedure that seeks a solution.

- *Visibility of system status.* The system should always keep users informed about what is going on, through appropriate feedback within a reasonable time.

- *Match between system and the real world.* The system should speak the user's language, with words, phrases and concepts familiar to the user, rather than system-oriented terms. It should follow real-world conventions, making information appear in a natural and logical order.

- *User control and freedom.* Users often choose system functions by mistake and will need a clearly marked 'emergency exit' to leave the unwanted state without having to go through an extended dialogue. Support undo and redo.

- *Consistency and standards.* Users should not have to wonder whether different words, situations or actions mean the same thing. Follow platform conventions.

- *Error prevention.* Even better than good error messages is a careful design which prevents a problem from occurring in the first place.

- *Recognition rather than recall.* Make objects, actions and options visible. The user should not have to remember information from one part of the dialogue to another. Instructions for use of the system should be visible or easily retrievable whenever appropriate.

- *Flexibility and efficiency of use.* Accelerators – unseen by the novice user – may often speed up the interaction for the expert user such that the system can cater to both inexperienced and experienced users. Allow users to tailor frequent actions.

- *Aesthetic and minimalist design.* Dialogues should not contain information which is irrelevant or rarely needed. Every extra unit of information in a dialogue competes with the relevant units of information and diminishes their relative visibility.

- *Help users recognize, diagnose and recover from errors.* Error messages should be expressed in plain language (no codes), precisely indicate the problem, and constructively suggest a solution.

- *Help and documentation.* Even though it is better if the system can be used without documentation, it may be necessary to provide help and documentation. Any such information should be easy to search, focused on the user's task, list concrete steps to be carried out, and not be too large.

Source: www.useit.com/papers/heuristic

Testing is a vital part of any assessment of information architecture, assessing whether the system developed is meeting the needs of the user. The implementation process of an information system should include a usability evaluation report that documents the usability tests carried out and actions required. The BSI standard 13407 (BSI, 1999) outlines the core components of a usability evaluation report:

1 Executive summary
2 Product evaluated
3 Objectives of evaluation
4 Context of use
5 Measurement plan
  (a) Users identified
  (b) Methods
  (c) Sequence of activities
6 Results
  (a) General
  (b) Video analysis
  (c) User interface design
  (d) Workflow and process
  (e) Training requirements
  (f) User perception questionnaires
7 Recommendations.

The results of the testing process will be used to improve the current system and will feed back into the start of the systems analysis process.

Activity 9.5	Jakob Nielsen's ten usability heuristics

Purpose To apply a set of usability rules to two websites.

Activity

visit the www

Select two websites from large organizations (public or private sector). Think of a task to complete on the site or a targeted piece of information to find on the site. Using the ten heuristics introduced earlier, mark each website out of five for each heuristic and total a score for both websites (Table 9.11). Some suggested URLs: **www.dwp.gov.uk, www.ibm.com, www.dell.com, www.easyjet.com, www.livjm.ac.uk**

Heuristic	Website 1 (score out of five)	Website 2 (score out of five)

Security design

The security design process will focus on the correct controls being in place to manage the security issues that have been identified in the analysis stage. Security design is broken down into two categories: the logical design and physical design. Whitman and Mattord (2003) describe logical security design as blueprints that examine and implement key policies and the physical design as the technology required to support the blueprints.

Who should be responsible for security? If we return again to the policies of the State of Arizona (2003b), they clearly state who is responsible for security. The policy establishes that:

- Budget units are responsible for providing security protections commensurate with the risk and magnitude of harm resulting from unauthorized access, use, disclosure, modification to, or destruction of either (1) information collected or maintained by or on behalf of the budget unit or (2) information systems used by a budget unit or by a contractor of a budget unit or other organization on behalf of the budget unit.

- Budget units shall ensure that networks, hardware systems, and software application systems operate effectively and provide appropriate confidentiality, integrity, and availability, through the use of cost-effective management, personnel, operational, and technical controls.

- Budget units shall ensure that adequate security is provided for all information collected, processed, transmitted, stored, or disseminated in budget unit software application systems.

- Budget units are responsible for ensuring that information security management processes are integrated with budget unit strategic and operational planning processes.

Security design: logical

Security policies

The SANS institute (2004) explains the differences between policies, standards and guidelines:

> A policy is typically a document that outlines specific requirements or rules that must be met. In the information/network security realm, policies are usually point-specific, covering a single area. For example, an 'Acceptable Use' policy would cover the rules and regulations for appropriate use of the computing facilities. A standard is typically collections of system-specific or procedural-specific requirements that must be met by everyone. A guideline is typically a collection of system-specific or procedural-specific 'suggestions' for best practice.

Whitman and Mattord (2003) describe a security policy as providing 'the rules for the protection of information assets of the organization'; Barman (2002) adds that they are the high-level plans that describe the goals of the security procedures.

To illustrate the range and depth of security policies that can be developed, visit the SANS institute website where over 30 policies and templates are available for download; they range from encryption policies to wireless communication policies (**www.sans.org**).

A high-level information security policy document will be developed, overviewing all the security issues, and then smaller, issue-based polices will be developed, based around use of certain applications or services; e.g. e-mail, Internet.

The overall information security policy document should contain the following elements (BSI, 2000):

1   A definition of information security, its overall objectives and scope and the importance of security as an enabling mechanism for information sharing.

2   A statement of management intent, supporting the goals and principles of information security.

3   A brief explanation of the security policies, principles, standards and compliance requirements of particular importance to the organization, for example:
    (a) compliance with legislative and contractual requirements;
    (b) security education requirements;
    (c) prevention and detection of viruses and other malicious software;
    (d) business continuity management;
    (e) consequences of security policy violations;
    (f) a definition of general and specific responsibilities for information security management, including reporting security incidents;
    (g) references to documentation which may support the policy, e.g. more detailed security policies and procedures.

Acceptable use policies

Often the high-level security policy will be used and read only by senior management and stakeholders involved with security on a day-to-day basis as part of their work; other employees will be given the smaller issues-based policies that are relevant to them. Often employees will be given an acceptable use policy to agree to the first time they are issued with authentication to use the organizational IT systems and network. The purpose of an **acceptable use policy** is to summarize the overall policy for users, outlining the responsibilities the user has to information security in the organization. An acceptable use will cover the following areas:

Acceptable use policy
Specified rules for using information systems and networks from a user perspective

- account and password responsibilities;
- definition of unacceptable use of systems and network;
- allowable use of systems and network;
- user responsibilities;
- organizational responsibilities;
- legal obligations stated in contracts of employment.

Security design: physical

The physical design process focuses upon the technology required, supporting the information security objectives and policies; solutions will be developed in terms of hardware and software.

The physical design will cover the following areas:

- Deployment of firewalls (hardware and software used to protect internal networks)
    - How many?
    - Where will they be placed physically?
    - What traffic will they be configured to block?
    - Software selected
- Intrusion detection systems (IDS) – alerting systems for information security breaches
    - Types of breaches detected
    - Software selected

- Encryption technologies (ways of scrambling data using defined data 'keys')
  - Levels of encryption (complexity of message scrambling)
  - Use internally
  - Use externally – messages sent and received
- Access control devices
  - Biometrics (e.g. fingerprints)
  - Swipe cards
- Wireless access devices
  - Software
  - Hardware allowed to access network
- Remote access
  - Software
  - Hardware allowed to access network.

The level and use of the above technologies will be related to levels of risk assessment in the planning stage.

Summary

1 Information architecture provides the structure that makes information systems a usable reality.

2 Information architecture strategies and policies will be developed drawing upon IM, KM and IS strategies.

3 Systems analysis must research user requirements and identify stakeholders.

4 Object orientation is an alternative to structure and process models.

5 Card sorting can provide a method for allowing users to be actively involved in the modelling process.

6 Normalization is part of the design process, simplifying entities and making sure duplicate data are removed.

7 The difference between websites and intranets must be understood by web designers.

8 Page design can be represented using a wireframe.

9 Taxonomy, thesauri and controlled vocabularies enable interoperability through defined language and relationships between terms.

10 Security analysis will asses the information assets, the risks and associated vulnerabilities.

11 Information security can be broken into logical and physical categories. Logical concerns blueprints and policies. Physical concerns the implementation using technology.

Exercises

Self-assessment questions

1 List and define the first three forms of normalization.

2 Explain the purpose of a DFD.

3 What are the key components of systems analysis?

4 How can web designers illustrate website design concepts?

5 What does a use case diagram represent?

6 What value does XML have to information architects?

7 Define interoperability.

8 Explain what a taxonomy is.

Essay and discussion questions

1 Explain the importance of the systems analysis phase in developing information architecture.

2 Discuss the difference between information flow diagrams and data flow diagrams.

3 Explain the value of card sorting in the system analysis stage.

4 What value does the BS7799 Standard for information security have in helping improve information security?

5 Discuss how a wireframe can aid the web design process.

6 Explain why usability is important to information architecture.

7 Compare and contrast taxonomies and thesauri.

8 You have been asked to develop an information system to capture information about employee holiday entitlements. Outline the key stages in developing the information architecture for the system.

9 You have been asked to develop an organizational intranet for a company that currently only shares information using file servers. Outline the key stages in developing the information architecture for the intranet.

References

AIFIA (Asilomar Institute for Information Architecture) (2003) About AIFIA. Available online at: http://aifia.org/pg/aboutraifia.php.

Ambler, S. (2001) *The Object Primer: The Application Developer's Guide to Object Orientation and the UML*, 2nd edn. Cambridge University Press, Cambridge.

Badre, A. (2002) *Shaping Web Usability: Interaction Design in Context*. Addison-Wesley, Harlow.

Barman, S. (2002) *Writing Information Security Policies*. New Riders, Indianapolis.

Beynon-Davies, P. (2004) *Database Systems*, 3rd edn. Palgrave, Basingstoke.

Bocij, P., Chaffey, D., Greasley, A. and Hickie, S. (2003) *Business Information Systems: Technology, Development and Management for the E-Business*. Financial Times Prentice Hall, Harlow.

British Standards Institute (1999) BS 13407 Human-centred Design Processes for Interactive Systems. BSI, London.

British Standards Institute (2000) BS7799 Information Technology Code of Practice for Information Security Management. BSI, London.

British Standards Institute (2002) BS7799 Information Security Management Systems. BSI, London.

Butler Group (2004) Enterprise architecture. An end-to-end approach for realigning IT with business aims. Butler Group, Hull, England.

Dick, K. (2001) *XML: A Manager's Guide*. Addison-Wesley, Harlow.

Eriksson, H. and Pneker, M. (1998) *The UML Toolkit*. Wiley, New York.

Fast, K., Leise, F. and Steckel, M. (2002) What is a controlled vocabulary? Boxes and arrows. Available online at: www.boxesandarrows.com/archives/whatrisrarcontrolledrvocabulary.php.

Fisher, M. (2003) Developing an information model for information and knowledge based organizations. In A. Gilchrist and B. Mahon (eds), *Information Architecture: Designing Information Environments for Purpose*. Facet, London.

Gilchrist, A. (2003) The taxonomy. In A. Gilchrist and B. Mahon (eds), *Information Architecture: Designing Information Environments for Purpose*. Facet, London.

Harvard Law (2003) RSS 2.0 specification. Available online at: http://blogs.law.harvard.edu/tech/rss.

Hoffer, J., George, J. and Valacich, J. (2002) *Modern Systems Analysis and Design*, 3rd edn. Prentice Hall, Harlow.

Hourican, R. (2002) Information architectures – what are they? *Business Information Review*, 19(3), 16–22.

IEEE (2000) IEEE 1471-2000 Standard for Architectural Description. Institute for Enterprise Architecture Developments. Available online at: www.enterprise-architecture.info/Images/Documents/IEEE%201471-2000.pdf.

Mattila, S. (2001) Data dictionary – what should be in it. University of Canberra. Available online at: www.canberra.edu.au/~sam/whp/datadict.html.

Nielsen, J. (2000) *Designing Web Usability*. New Riders, Indianapolis.

Nielsen, J. (n.d.) Ten usability heuristics. Useit.com. Available online at: www.useit.com/papers/heuristic/heuristicrlist.html.

Office of the E-envoy (2002) e-PIMS Fact Sheet – Large Scale Data Interchange with e-PIMS via XML. Available online at: www.govtalk.gov.uk/schemasstandards/xmlschemaDocument.asp.

Office of the E-envoy (2003a) Web guidelines. Available online at: www.e-envoy.gov.uk/Resources/WebGuidelines/fs/en.

Office of the E-envoy (2003b) E-government interoperability framework version 5.1. Available online at: www.govtalk.gov.uk/documents/e-gifrv5rpart1r2003-04-25.doc.

Office of Government Commerce (2004) Enterprise architectures. Available online at: www.ogc.gov.uk/sdtoolkit/reference/deliverylifecycle/setdir/enterpriserarch.html.

Pidcock, W. (2003) *What are the differences between a vocabulary, a taxonomy, a thesaurus, an ontology, and a meta-model?* Meta Model.com. Available online at: www.metamodel.com.

Pipkin, D. L. (2000) *Information Security: Protecting the Global Enterprise*. Prentice Hall, London.

Robertson, J. (2003a) *Information design using card sorting. Step Two*. Available online at: www.steptwo.com.au/papers/cardsorting/index.html.

Robertson, J. (2003b) *World apart: the difference between intranets and websites*. KM column, March. Available online at: www.steptwo.com.au/papers/kmcr intranetvsweb.

Rosenfeld, L. and Morville, P. (2002) *Information Architecture for the World Wide Web*, 2nd edn. O'Reilly, Sebastopol, CA.

SANS Institute (2004) Security Policies Project. Available online at: www.sans.org/resources/policies/.

State of Arizona (2003a) Data/information architecture policy. Available online at: http://gita.state.az.us/policiesrstandards/html/p740rdatarinformationrarchitecturer policy.htm.

State of Arizona (2003b) IT Security Policy. Available online at: http://gita.state.az.us/policiesrstandards/html/p800ritrsecurtiyrpolicy.htm.

User Interface Engineering (2001) Are there users who always search? Available online at: www.uie.com/articles/alwaysrsearch.htm.

White, M. (2001) Content management systems for intranets. *Vine: The Journal of Information and Knowledge Management Systems*, 31(3).

Whitman, M. E. and Mattord, H. J. (2003) *Principles of Information Security*. Course Technology, Boston, MA.

Wodke, C. (2002) *Information Architecture: Blueprints for the Web*. New Riders, Indianapolis.

Wylie, J. (2003) *Taxonomies: Frameworks for Corporate Knowledge: The Shape of Things to come?* Ark Group, London.

Further reading

Deane, S. and Henderson, R. (2003) *XML Made Simple*. Made Simple Books, Oxford.

Fleming, J. (1998) *Web Navigation: Designing the User Experience*. O'Reilly, Sebastopol, CA.

Holmes, M. (2002) *Web Usability and Navigation: A Beginner's Guide*. McGraw-Hill, Berkeley, CA.

Hylton, A. (2002) The role of the knowledge audit in corporate intranet design. IT Toolbox. Available online at: http://km.ittoolbox.com/documents/document. asp?i=2101.

International Journal of Human-Computer Studies. Elsevier.

Neilsen, J. and Tahir, M. (2002) *Homepage Usability: 50 Websites Deconstructed*. New Riders, Indianapolis.

Rob, P. and Coronel, C. (2004) *Database Design, Implementation and Management*, 5th edn. Course Technology, Boston, MA.

Williamson, H. (2001) *XML: The Complete Reference*. McGraw-Hill, Berkeley, CA.

Wurman, R. S. (2001) *Information Anxiety 2*. Que, Indianapolis.

Weblinks

visit the www

About.com:databases (http://databases.about.com/) References sources and how-to guides.

Boxes and Arrows (www.boxesandarrows.com/) Peer-written journal discussing information architecture issues.

DB Forums (www.dbforums.com/) A discussion forum for discussing database issues.

Gerry McGovern.com (www.gerrymcgovern.com) Content management consultant, contains a weekly column containing articles on web content issues.

Intranet Focus Ltd (www.intranetfocus.com) Intranet consultancy contains articles and links.

Lycos tutorial (howto.lycos.com/) Understand database basics.

Microsoft Visio (www.microsoft.com/office/visio/) Software tool for drawing information models and diagrams.

Oracle Designer (http://otn.oracle.com/products/designer/index.html) CASE tool available with Oracle database management software.

SearchOracle.com (http://searchoracle.techtarget.com/) News and tips on databases.

Security Focus (www.securityfocus.com/) Security professional community.

W3C (www.w3c.org) International organization governing World Wide Web standards for XML and RDF.

Webopeadia (www.webopedia.com/) Online dictionary for computer and Internet terms. Use to define terms you have not heard before, e.g. normalization.

Yahoo! Directory (http://dir.yahoo. com/ComputersrandrInternet/software/databases/) Software>databases. Database resource links.

Multimedia resources

Nielsen Norman Group (2003) Paper prototyping: a how-to training video. Order from **www.nngroup.com/reports/prototyping/** (DVD).

For multiple-choice questions, and annotated weblinks relating to this chapter visit this book's website at: **www.pearsoned.co.uk/chaffey**

Part 4
MANAGEMENT

In Part 4 we review approaches to manage information to improve its contribution to an organization while also guarding against problems caused by managing information within an organization. Chapter 10 shows how information quality can be improved; Chapter 11 shows how information services can be delivered and Chapter 12 shows which legal and ethical issues must be considered.

10

Managing information quality

Objective

To review approaches for evaluating and improving organizational information quality.

Learning outcomes

After reading this chapter, you will be able to:

● Assess approaches for managing information quality.

● Understand the relationship between data quality, information quality and knowledge quality.

● Define the purpose and process of an information audit.

Management issues

Typical questions facing managers related to this topic:

● How do we highlight the importance of information quality to employees?

● What approaches should we use for managing information quality?

● Who is responsible for information quality?

Links to other chapters

The main related chapters are:

➤ *Chapter 1* the concept of information quality is introduced.

➤ *Chapter 4* the role of the information audit and information policy in information management strategy is introduced.

Introduction

How much importance is attached to managing the quality of an organization's information resources? In many organizations, which lack an information strategy, it appears as if the importance of information quality is not recognized – there are many other much more visible and pressing challenges. For commercial organizations, increasing profitability through increasing sales and reducing costs gives rise to many other management challenges. Strategies need to be developed, plans created and tactics executed. For not-for-profit organizations, delivering services to satisfy their customers and to meet targets set by the organizations and people that fund them gives rise to a further set of management challenges.

With the work required for all these business challenges it is natural that the strategic management of information resources is not at the front of managers' minds in organizations which have not developed an information orientation (Chapter 1). Yet the availability and use of quality information contribute directly to the capacity of managers to develop strategies, create plans and execute tactics. Without good-quality, relevant information, without the right information, in the right place at the right time, managers will not be able to make the best informed decisions. Sometimes there will be too much information, sometimes not enough and sometimes information quality will be poor. The capabilities of information technology can make information more challenging since it is possible to collect a tremendous amount of information, but some will still be incomplete or missing.

To solve these types of information management problems the first stage is to recognize the existence of a problem and develop an information strategy to provide a framework to improve information management practices as described in Chapter 4. The current chapter follows on from Chapter 4 – it describes the details of implementing and managing an information strategy. The main focus in this chapter is managing the quality of information. We describe a process to evaluate the current quality of information and related data and knowledge in an organization and then improve the quality of these resources. One aspect of quality is identifying defects, errors or abnormalities in data. Unfortunately, it is often not as easy to identify errors in data as identifying the 'odd-one-out' in the image on the opening page of this chapter. Furthermore, information quality is not only concerned with errors, it is also about achieving relevance for its recipients and this is an intangible concept. This makes assessing and improving information quality a difficult challenge.

The process of improving information quality described in this chapter is summarized in Figure 10.1. The first stage is to understand the characteristics of good-quality information. We introduce the attributes of information quality such as relevance, timeliness and accuracy using the 'DIKAR' model which was introduced in Chapter 5. The second step to improve information quality is to conduct an information audit, which was introduced in Chapter 4. The information audit is used to identify the information types within an organization and it assesses how well the information resources and information practices support organizational objectives. We see through examples how it is used to understand the specific information requirements of an organization and identify the gap between what is required and what is currently available. The third and fourth stages described in this chapter are the creation and implementation of an information quality policy to improve information quality as indicated from the information audit. Note that a description of a broader information policy including reference to topics such as security was described in Chapter 4. The final stage is to create a control mechanism which ensures that information quality is monitored on an ongoing basis and continuously improved. In the coverage in this chapter, separate sections on the attributes of information quality and the

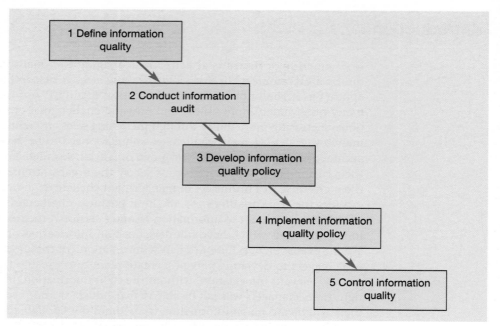

Figure 10.1 A process for improving information quality

information audit will be followed by a single section on information quality policy which will cover information quality policy creation, implementation and control.

We have selected information quality rather than the information audit or information policy as the main focus of this chapter for two reasons. First, the main emphasis of the information audit, as described by authors such as Orna (1999), Swash (1997) and Henczel (2001), is on an analysis of the information resources rather than the management actions that are needed to make better use of these resources. Furthermore, the development of the information audit concept was initially conducted by experts in library and information services managing external data sources such as books, trade magazines and market reports. While this is an important part of information management, the issues involved with managing internal company databases such as customer databases and product inventory are not emphasized sufficiently. For example, the case studies in Henczel (2001) mainly concern provision of information services by a library and there is scant reference to improving data quality in her book. Instead we also need to consider specific practical issues which need to be managed on an ongoing basis, such as data quality and the quality of business intelligence metrics and metrics for corporate performance management. Second, we believe that the practical issues in managing *data* quality on which good *information* quality is based are not sufficiently emphasized in the information audit process. In this chapter we review, in some detail, the characteristics of data quality and how to improve data quality. Third, an important part of improving data quality, information quality and knowledge quality is the information behaviours of organizations' employees. This is also not sufficiently emphasized in the information audit or information policies in our opinion. This is not to say that the information audit is not a valuable tool in improving information quality practices in organizations. It undoubtedly is a valuable and underused tool. The fact that it is not widely known by managers and academics who are not information management specialists suggests that its scope is perhaps too narrow. Through focusing on information quality, other aspects such as managing data quality and metrics for corporate performance management which are more widely known and used can be included.

Define information quality

In Chapter 1 we introduced the notion of information quality. We said that quality is essentially 'fitness for purpose'. Lillrank (2003) reviews the definition of information quality in detail. He says that there are four types of quality definition: (1) conformity to requirements, (2) meeting or exceeding customer expectations, (3) cost of quality and (4) value for money. 'Fitness for purpose' is equivalent to the first two definitions. The other two definitions introduce other aspects of quality. 'Excellence' implies the importance of relative quality – information quality will be excellent if it is superior relative to competitors'. Quality in terms of cost also needs to be considered. Good-quality information may be available within an organization, but if it is not used it is not cost-effective.

Definitions of data quality may be further refined and enhanced. Miller (1996), for example, identifies ten dimensions of information quality and states that these attributes may be benchmarked to improve the effectiveness of information systems:

1 *Relevance.* Is the information useful for the recipient or does it meet their needs?

2 *Accuracy.* Fundamentally this means information that does not contain errors. However, the cost of producing error-free information increases with the quantity and complexity of the underlying data. It may therefore be necessary to achieve a cost-effective level of accuracy.

3 *Timeliness.* Business conditions change rapidly and it is necessary to provide information that is up to date. Once again the need to ensure high-quality information may introduce error-checking operations that delay the provision of information to users.

4 *Completeness.* While it is desirable to possess all the relevant information about a business process or a customer, this must again be balanced with the cost of obtaining and storing such a huge quantity of data (see Chapter 4).

5 *Coherence.* Information that is not easily understood can lead to a lack of coherence since it may not be assimilated.

6 *Format.* The way that information is presented to users is of great importance. The way that costs are presented by an Accounting Department on a balance sheet can differ greatly from the way that costs are presented on the Maintenance Department's budget spreadsheet. Information needs to be provided in a manner that suits the user.

7 *Accessibility.* Users should be able to get hold of information as quickly and easily as possible, or as quickly and easily as is technically feasible or affordable.

8 *Compatibility.* Relates to the way that new information fits or complements existing information. This may be affected by the format in which documents are produced, or the language that is used to describe the information that they contain.

9 *Security.* Information must be held safely within an information system. It must be protected from accidental and deliberate damage and theft.

10 *Validity.* Information may be regarded as valid, or true, when it represents what is actually happening in the real world. This may be partially achieved by ensuring that it is relevant, accurate, timely and complete.

At a practical level, information quality can therefore be assessed according to how well it supports the work of different individuals in an organization to complete their tasks and help them make decisions. It appears that many e-businesses suffer from poor information quality because they have proceeded to implement their e-systems without adequately considering a strategy for ensuring that high-quality data and information are captured and shared (Xu and Koronios, 2004). Information quality can also be assessed at an organizational level, by how well it supports the operation of processes and helps in achieving organizational objectives. The Ministry of Defence (MoD) recognizes the importance of high-quality information and has committed £100 million to improve the IT systems that troops use in battle. The project was scheduled to begin in 2010 and, echoing the characteristics of high-quality information listed above, will use 'near real-time data' presented to 'the people that really need it' in 'the right usable format' (*Computing*, 2008).

It follows that to assess and improve information quality at an organization level we need to understand the range of tasks and decisions supported by an organization, or, to approach the problem another way, we need to assess quality for all the different types of information resources used in an organization. These include those sourced internally and externally and information which can be characterized as 'hard' and 'soft'. It also includes the quality of data and knowledge. In the next section, we examine the relationship between these concepts.

The DIKAR and RAKID models

DIKAR model
Describes the transformation of Data to Information to Knowledge, leading to Actions and Results

The 'DIKAR model' provides a useful tool for understanding the attributes of information quality. The model is shown in diagrammatic form in Figure 10.2. 'DIKAR' describes the transformation of Data to Information to Knowledge leading to Actions taken by managers which deliver Results. It is similar to the examples of the data-to-information transformation process we introduced in Chapter 1.

This is a simple but powerful model which unifies the concepts of data, information and knowledge since, according to Murray (2000), it highlights the role of knowledge in actions by managers that produce business results. He says that often knowledge managers concentrate too much on the typical 'left-to-right' approach. They make the mistake of 'going with the flow', of concentrating on the supply of knowledge rather than the desired results. Instead he suggests that it is better to follow the results-driven approach, sometimes known as the 'RAKID model' indicated in Figure 10.2. That is, to start with the results and then deduce the knowledge required needed to achieve them. He says that the knowledge should be considered in two categories: 'knowledge as a body of information (which can be readily processed by suitable IT and resides at the "data/information" end of the flow) and knowledge as know-how (which requires good people management and is found at the "action" end)'. This approach is similar to that advocated in information audits, as we will see later in this chapter. For example, Orna (1999) describes how the information audit should start by considering how the objectives of an organization (i.e. the Results in Figure 10.2) and its processes are supported by Knowledge and in turn how the Knowledge is supported by Information.

RAKID model
The reverse of the DIKAR model, used as approach to inform data, information and knowledge requirements from their ability to deliver business results

We have added an indication of the attributes or characteristics of quality needed for each element of the DIKAR/RAKID model in Figure 10.2. The figure shows that to achieve information quality within an organization we need to understand and manage both data quality and knowledge quality. The quality of each type of element in the DIKAR model is dependent on the quality of the elements to the left from which it is formed. So information quality is dependent on data quality, knowledge quality is dependent on data quality and information quality, action quality is based on data quality, information quality and knowledge quality, and the quality of results is dependent on data quality, information quality, knowledge quality, and action quality!

Information quality is dependent on data quality assessed through attributes such as accuracy, completeness, validity and consistency, as described later in this section. Knowledge quality is dependent on information quality assessed through attributes such as relevance, presentation and timeliness. Knowledge quality is also dependent

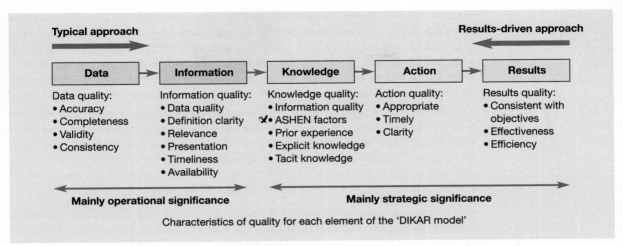

Figure 10.2 The 'DIKAR' model of the transformation of Data to Information to Knowledge, leading to Actions and Results, with quality of each element of the model highlighted

Source: Adapted from Murray (2000)

on the experience of managers and their access to tacit and explicit knowledge. The quality of actions and results is dependent on the capabilities of managers to create, analyse and action performance-management metrics. It can be argued that the management of data quality and to a lesser extent information quality is mainly of operational significance. Knowledge quality, action quality and results quality are of greater strategic importance since these will directly affect the performance of the organization. We will now examine in more detail the meaning of quality in the context of each element of the DIKAR model.

Data quality

Inherent information quality
The degree to which data accurately define real-world objects

Data quality is described by English (1999) as **inherent information quality**. He defines this as the degree to which data accurately reflect the real-world object that the data represent, whether this is information about a person, a business event or other types of object. Data quality or inherent information quality refers to the quality of source data that is used to build information resources used by managers. It is perhaps easiest to think of data quality in the context of a database. Data quality can be assessed by referring to the different entities that form the tables in a database. For the Lo-cost Airline Company, for example, different entities might include customer, bookings, employee, supplier, routes and schedules. For each of these entities we can assess data quality according to different attributes or fields according to these characteristics. For example, for a geographic location for a customer defined by a postcode or zip code, the aspects of data quality are as follows:

1 *Accuracy*. Accuracy means that the data correctly define the event or object which they describe. For a postcode – accuracy means does the postcode actually describe where the person lives? Data could be inaccurate if the customer has moved address since the data were collected, i.e. the data are out of date.

2 *Completeness*. Completeness refers to whether all the data are present. A company could profile its postcode or zip code field for completeness. It may find that these are recorded for only 80 per cent of customers. This means that is difficult to identify where a fifth of customers live, which is important for targeting relevant communications to them which are often based on the lifestyle of people living in a particular area.

3 *Validity*. Validity means that the data fall between acceptable ranges defined by the business. For a postcode there will be a standard format in every country that is required for valid data. Validity does not necessarily mean that the data are accurate. For example, customer birth dates must be within a defined range such as from 1900 to the present day, but are inaccurate if the birth dates are not correct for some reason. Validity is sometimes defined as congruence with business rules.

4 *Consistency*. Consistency means that the data elements are consistently defined and understood. With a UK postcode, for example, some people entering the postcode 'DE22 1GB' may not realize that a full postcode is required and may have entered just 'DE22' – the postal area. Consistency is particularly important where different sources of information are used in an analysis. For example, are customer enquiries measured in a similar way in different countries?

It is easier to evaluate data quality if different forms of data quality are identified. For example, Molineux (2002) identifies five levels of data in reference to customer data, but these can be applied to other forms of data such as accounting data. The five levels of data are:

1 *Demographic*. Characteristics of an individual customer such as age, sex, date of birth, address and phone number. This is largely static, but when a customer moves, contact details will require updating – this is a major challenge in customer data quality.

2 *Transactional*. Information about business events or interactions involving tomers. This includes purchases and contacts via phone or e-mail.

3 *Behavioural*. Information about how a customer interacts with the company. This includes clickstream data obtained from web and e-mail.

4 *Relationship*. For consumers it may be useful to know relationships between family members such as husband and wife, mother and daughter. For business customers, it is useful to know the relationship between different people in the business.

5 *Derived*. Data collected by analysis tools such as customer profitability or lifetime value, customer growth potential and propensity to purchase. Derived data are strictly information since they are produced by information processing. These data are of particular concern in data protection since it may be necessary to make customers aware of them.

We will see in a later section how checks can be performed when data are entered into a system to help improve data quality. For example, a test could be performed for real postcodes, and users would be prompted if the field did not contain a valid postcode.

The importance of data quality is stressed by information quality consultant Larry English who has estimated that the potential cost of poor data quality could be as high as 10–25 per cent of total revenues based on quality-cost analyses performed with organizations (English, 1999). These costs include duplication of work required by data correction and data cleansing, maintaining duplicate data sources and opportunities lost through inadequate data for processes. If information quality is poor, business processes will be inefficient or fail and wrong decisions will be made. Think of the columns in newspapers cataloguing customer complaints such as banks that overcharge, or retailers who sell faulty products but fail to act on customer complaints. The majority of these problems are a result of poor information quality. They have a direct cost in terms of staff time to solve these problems, but also an indirect cost because of the bad publicity generated and the likelihood that they will not get further business from these customers. Surveys of why customers select new suppliers for a range of products repeatedly show that poor customer service is the main reason for switching suppliers; this is often a consequence of inefficient processes and poor information quality delivering poor customer service.

Confirmation that customer dissatisfaction is one of the main reasons for ensuring good-quality information is confirmed by the results of a survey summarized in Figure 10.3. The figure shows that the time spent to correct or reconcile data and lost credibility of a system amongst staff are other problems. Specific savings that are available through improved data quality are evident in Mini case study 10.1 'Abbey Bank cuts costs through improving data quality'.

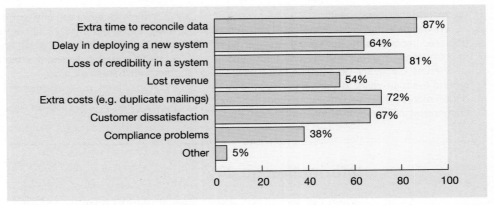

Figure 10.3 Problems due to poor-quality data based on 286 respondents who could select multiple answers
Source: Data Warehousing Institute (2002)

| Mini case study 10.1 | **Abbey Bank cuts costs through improving data quality** |

Abbey Bank treats data as a critical corporate asset and has a board-level-agreed strategy and method for managing it. The bank has created a 'data superstore' (data warehouse) that can be accessed by any authorised user or application within the bank. It is used in strategic marketing planning, for example, and in the bank's many customer and sales initiatives. Management positions with clear responsibilities for information quality have been created.

Abbey Bank uses a software tool from data quality provider Trillium Software whose company slogan is 'Know your data, know your business'. Their software 'Discovery' was used by Abbey Bank to better understand its data and ensure marketing, customer service and other operations are supported with high-quality, accurate and complete customer information and business intelligence from a central enterprise data warehouse. Discovery enables the bank to better understand the data structure within the warehouse and other databases and to pinpoint issues for resolution. By doing so, the bank has been able to cost-effectively raise data quality levels. It has also cut the time it takes to analyse the accuracy of customer data by 90 per cent, easing pressure on IT resources and improving marketing efficiency since more relevant communications can be delivered to customers.

Discovery builds data from various sources within the organisation into a central database server based on 'associative technology'. Associative technology combines traditional database functionality with support for ad-hoc analysis and allows easier and more flexible interrogation of the information. Using a browser-like interface, staff can navigate the data and drill down to examine potential problems.

Abbey Bank breaks down the estimated Net Present Value of savings assisted by Trillium Software Discovery (so far) as follows:

- More efficient integration of Abbey Bank data into the central data architecture delivered £1 million (US$1.5m) NPV.
- Migrating databases into the central data architecture can now be achieved faster and with more accuracy. The total benefit is estimated at £2.5 million ($4m) NPV.
- Data-cleansing activities, assisted by analysis provided by Avellino Discovery, have netted the bank £1.7 million ($2.7m) in savings.
- More accurate bad debt provisioning and credit scoring have led to well over £10 million ($16m) in NPV benefits.

Comments provided by staff to Trillium Software show the impact of the system and named roles responsible for data quality.

Ed Wrazen, VP, EMEA operations of Trillium Software commented, 'Quality, timely and cost-effective data and information for management decision-making and operational effectiveness is a competitive business asset.'

'We estimate that Trillium Software Discovery has delivered benefits to the bank worth some £15.2m', said Christine Craven, Head of Retail Information.

'Without Discovery, we estimate that it would take around five man-years to manually check the 29 million records that need migrating [from the data warehouse] into a new customer database', said Christine. 'With Discovery automating much of the process, we estimate this activity will instead take around three man-months.'

Jean Knight, head of information quality, says the old system took 40 hours to analyse one field in five million records. The bank is introducing new software that takes just three hours to complete the same task.

'We can actually see and resolve issues now rather than making assumptions about the data. This highlighted some human errors, such as missing dates of birth', she said, adding that the technology paid for itself within three months.

(Abbey Bank now operates as Santander.)

Source: Based on Trillium Software (www.trilliumsoftware.com)

Information quality

When organizations create a formal plan to improve information quality it is useful to separate information quality attributes into two categories: data quality attributes and information quality attributes. As the examples below show, this gives us a better understanding of the level of information quality and also helps us identify problems with information quality and propose solutions. We saw in the previous section that data quality has been described by Larry English as inherent information quality.

Pragmatic information quality
The degree to which information quality is of value to those who use it and the organization as a whole

The other element of information quality which we consider in this section is known as **pragmatic information quality**. This is described by English as the degree of usefulness and value that data have to support the enterprise processes. He notes that information that is of high inherent information quality could be of low-value pragmatic information quality.

English (1999) suggests that information quality is dependent on (f indicates 'is a function of') the quality of data, i.e. correct values, the clarity of definition of meaning and how understandable the form or presentation is to its user. He expresses this as follows:

$$\text{Information quality} = f(\text{Data quality} + \text{Definition} + \text{Presentation})$$

Pragmatic information quality concerns the value of information for its different users. The attributes of pragmatic information quality effectively prompt the question: are users of the information satisfied with it for their purposes? Continuing with the example of geographical data, we can use the postcode or zip field to understand the distribution of our customers in a country. For example, a marketing manager at the Lo-cost Airline Company may be trying to understand whether there is potential for increasing their market share in different parts of the country. To do this they will need to know not only the postcodes for their customers, but also the total annual sales for customers and an estimate of total sales in a region. This can be approximated by modelling the populations of different regions together with estimates of total expenditure on low-cost flights in the regions.

The attributes of pragmatic information quality are:

1 *Relevance.* A vital aspect of information quality – it must directly support a decision that needs to be taken or a task that needs to be performed. Relevance relates closely to knowledge quality. Identifying relevant data is a key method of countering information overload.

2 *Presentation.* The data must be presented in a form that makes them easily understandable. This is dependent on the type of information. For geographically related

information, presentation of regional variations on maps may be most appropriate. For other applications, tabulations, spreadsheet pivot tables or different forms of graph may be the best format. The information must be of the correct level of detail, as explained below.

3 *Timeliness*. Information needs to be up to date for most applications. How current the data need to be depends on the problem. To analyse market share information across a country, data up to a year old might be acceptable. But to analyse data about promotions on flights it is important that the data be made available as soon as possible so that learnings can be incorporated into future marketing campaigns. If information takes a month to collate, then its relevance will decrease. Xu et al. (2003) note the conflict between timeliness and accuracy for accountants. They say that if only five or six days are available for producing end-of-month reports then accuracy decreases as estimates rather than exact figures may have to be provided.

4 *Availability*. Information that is of high quality in terms of relevance, presentation and timeliness may still be of low quality from the perspective of a manager who is unable to access it because it is held elsewhere in the organization or they do not have access to it.

For business performance metrics there are additional frameworks for evaluating the quality of information, such as 'SMART'. This is described in the subsection below on 'Assessing the quality of business performance metrics' which is in the section 'Actions and results quality – performance management systems'. Note that the section on human factors in information quality also covers other significant elements of information quality related to behaviours and values that people in organizations place on information.

Real time
Information is available for analysis almost immediately events or transactions occur

One of the capabilities of modern information systems is to deliver information in **real time** – it is available for review as soon as the transaction occurs. Electronic ordering systems in supermarkets use real-time information tools to give real-time information on sales and e-commerce site managers have real-time 'web analytics' on where their website visitors come from, which pages they visit and which products they buy. Figure 10.4 shows real-time information from one of the authors' websites delivered through a web analytics tool based on an application service provider (see Chapter 2).

Relevance is also dependent on *detail* – if information is too detailed at the transaction level, such as that in Figure 10.4, then the 'big picture' is unclear. Alternatively, sometimes more detailed information is needed to inform a decision – particularly to identify the reasons for a management problem. To see the big picture, information systems need the capability to aggregate data, which is sometimes known as 'roll-up'. Figure 10.5 shows similar data to the previous figure, but this time aggregated data on number of pages viewed through the whole year.

Drill-down
An information system provides the capability to visualize more detailed information

For other applications, more detailed information is required. For example, a web analytics tool such as Yahoo! Web Analytics can be used to see the source of visitors to a website. Figure 10.4 shows that for this site a number of visitors were referred from Google. The capability to find more detailed information is known as '**drill-down**'. We can drill down further to see particular key phrases that are typed in by visitors, as shown in Figure 10.6. This detailed information can be used to adjust the key phrases on the site to attract more visitors or to inform development of new content that visitors are interested in. Another example of drill-down for the Lo-cost Airline Company might involve a manager noticing a dip in sales in one country relative to another, and they might then want to investigate whether this problem was worse on particular routes. To do this they would have to drill down to look at whether sales on all routes were down or whether there was a problem with a particular route. Alternatively, they might drill down to see whether the problem was worse in some sales channels such as phone or Internet.

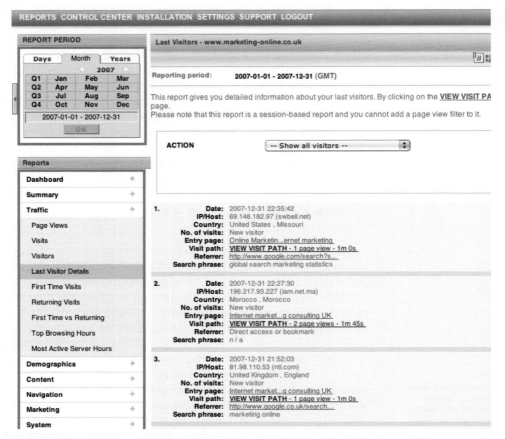

Figure 10.4 Real-time information about pages recently viewed on a website

Source: Data for Marketing Online (www.marketing-online.co.uk) visualized using Yahoo! Web Analytics

The four attributes of information quality presented above are particularly relevant when reviewing the value of hard data such as operational statistics which have been transformed into data. But how relevant are they for assessing the quality of soft information used to form and express knowledge? Let's illustrate this through considering five different types of information used by a business-to-business hardware manufacture such as Tektronix (**www.tektronix.com**), Le Croy (**www.lecroy.com**) or Agilent (**www.agilent.com**) who supply the billion-euro market in oscilloscopes for testing electronic circuits produced by companies such as Intel, Nokia and Sony:

1 An analyst report about international trends in adoption of technologies by organizations. This might be used by an IT manager to inform them about which technologies they should be considering. For example, Gartner releases an annual 'Must Do' CIO Resolutions report summarized in the press releases section of Gartner.com.

2 Competitive intelligence about this billion-dollar market sector to determine new product releases and sales to major customer accounts.

3 A verbal or written report from a sales representative to their sales manager of a visit to discuss future sales prospects with an important customer.

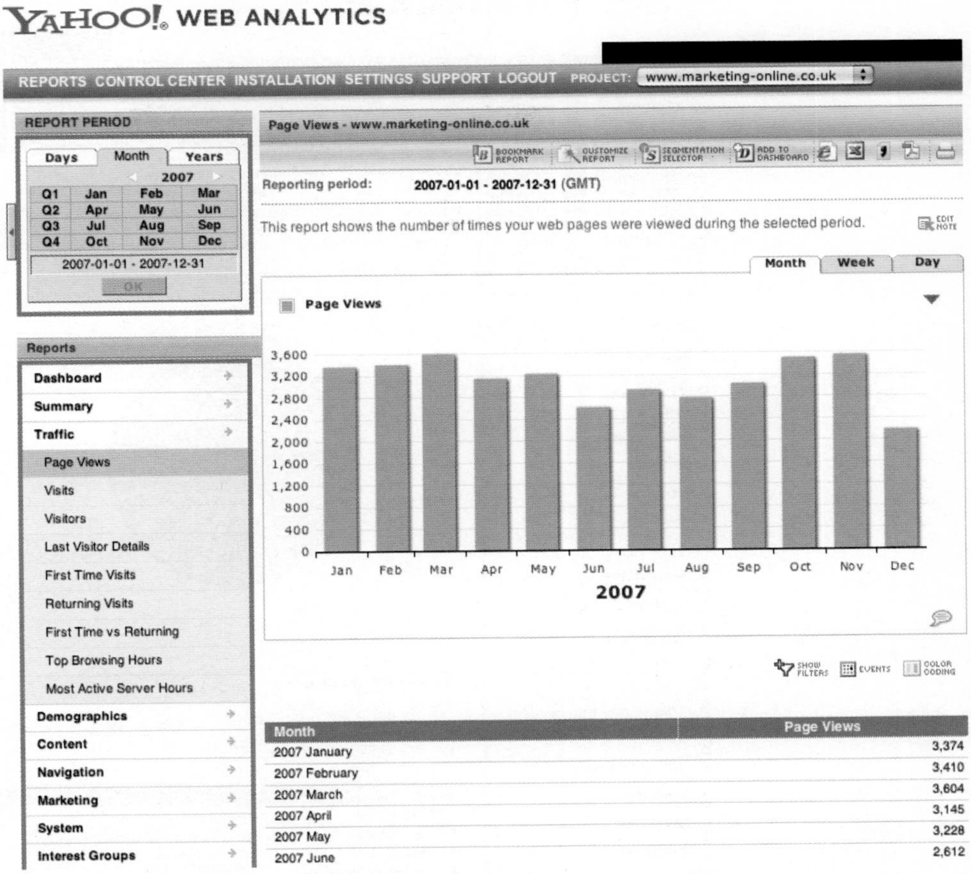

YAHOO! WEB ANALYTICS

Figure 10.5 Aggregated or rolled up information on pages viewed on a website
Source: Data for Marketing Online (www.marketing-online.co.uk) visualized using Yahoo! Web Analytics

4 An extranet page summarizing product specifications, benefits and prices for a hardware manufacturer for access by its distributors.

5 A rented list of e-mail addresses available from trade magazines for different industries of potential customers for a hardware company to create awareness and encourage trial of their products.

The first three examples are soft information which is used to communicate and create knowledge and the last two are hard information used for operational purposes. It can be seen that in all cases, the pragmatic aspects of information quality such as relevance, presentation or understandability and timeliness are still important. Note that inherent aspects of information quality (i.e. data quality), in particular accuracy, completeness and validity, are also important, even for the soft information.

Consider an analyst's report. This will not be speculation, but will be based on a research study of adoption of technology. Here information quality will be dependent on the research methodology and in particular the chosen sample size and sample frame. You are probably familiar with these concepts from research methods modules. In brief, the sample size is the number of respondents to the survey. Although this is often the main factor used to assess the validity of research, the sample frame is crucial. In this example, the sample frame would include the countries used in the

Sample size
The number of respondents to a survey

Sample frame
An assessment of the characteristics of a survey determining whether the sample is representative

Figure 10.6 Drill-down to search key phrases used to reach a website

Source: Data for Marketing Online (www.marketing-online.co.uk) visualized using Yahoo! Web Analytics

survey, the type of managers interviewed and the characteristics of the companies they work for, such as size and industry sector. These are also aspects of data quality.

To reflect on the relationship between data quality and information quality, complete Activity 10.1 which applies the concept of information quality to a specific problem.

COBIT information quality requirements

The COBIT governance model for Control Objectives for Information and related Technology introduced in Chapters 1 and 6 places a strong emphasis on managing information quality. COBIT refers to certain criteria for what it describes as business requirements for information. It groups these requirements in three areas. It uses 'quality requirements' to refer to negative aspects of data quality such as incomplete or inaccurate data, but also some aspects of information quality such as presentation.

| Activity 10.1 | Evaluation of information quality |

Purpose   To understand the distinction between the different aspects of information quality.

Activity   You are a manager responsible for recruiting international students to your university. You want to use external information sources to assess the performance of your college or university in comparison to other institutions and the national average in student recruiting.

visit the www

1   Using the attributes of inherent and pragmatic information quality, define your information quality requirements for the information or metrics used to assess performance.

2   Using the Internet, identify different sources of published data about international student numbers available on the Internet. Assess each data source in terms of information quality and research methodology.

It uses 'fiduciary requirements' to highlight the importance of compliance with laws and regulations such as those for data protection and financial transparency which are described in Chapter 12. Also part of the fiduciary requirements is information that supports the 'effectiveness and efficiency' of operations. Finally, it uses 'security requirements' to highlight the importance of confidentiality, integrity and availability. This three-way division of information quality requirements into quality requirements, fiduciary and security requirements is broader than some traditional assessments of information quality which tend to neglect the fiduciary and security aspects. COBIT further divides the business requirements of information quality into the seven categories shown in Table 10.1. In the third column, the quality requirements are related to the information on flight capacity used in Chapter 1 to illustrate whether the marketing and scheduling of flights for the airline has been effective. It can be argued that the COBIT framework is less useful from an information management perspective than traditional frameworks of quality. It refers to general categories such as effectiveness and integrity within which are contained the more typical terms used to describe information such as relevance, timeliness and consistency. Other categories such as efficiency refer more to the process and technology costs used to provide information rather than to the information itself. The elements of information quality are less clearly apparent from these categories. These differences from traditional models possibly arise from the origin of COBIT as an IT governance model. The intent to place information quality criteria at the centre of an IT governance framework is admirable.

The continuous management of data quality is also built into COBIT. You will see in Chapter 11 that COBIT has a 'Delivery and support' objective to help control data quality. *DS11 manage data* refers to the need to achieve the business requirement that data remain complete, accurate and valid during input, update and storage.

Knowledge quality

Knowledge quality
Knowledge quality is dependent on the capability of people to attach significance to information to inform their decisions and the ability to convert it into information to convey to other people

As for information quality, relevance is the key to knowledge quality. The knowledge must be relevant to analyse information, take a particular decision or inform actions. 'Knowledge quality' is not a concept that is as frequently used as 'data quality' or 'information quality', but English (1999) has developed a similar equation to that for information presented above, suggesting the relationship between knowledge and the factors that determine its quality:

$$\text{Knowledge quality} = f(\text{people} + \text{Information} + \text{Significance})$$

Table 10.1 COBIT requirements of information quality

Information quality requirement	Definition	Example from Lo-cost Airline Company for route data introduced in Chapter 1
Effectiveness	Deals with information being relevant and pertinent to the business process as well as being delivered in a timely, correct, consistent and usable manner.	The provision of flight capacity information for an individual route which can be used to improve the process of making and scheduling flights on a route.
Efficiency	Concerns the provision of information through the optimal (most productive and economical) use of resources.	The cost of collection and dissemination of the information above should be economic.
Confidentiality	Concerns the protection of sensitive information from unauthorised disclosure.	The information above should be protected from release to outside sources.
Integrity	Relates to the accuracy and completeness of information as well as to its validity in accordance with business values and expectations.	Refers to data quality of above information, i.e. whether it is correct (although confusingly this term is also used under 'effectiveness').
Availability	Relates to information being available when required by the business process now and in the future. It also concerns the safeguarding of necessary resources and associated capabilities.	Is this information timely, i.e. how long does it take for the reports on capacity to be produced? Note again, this is also referred to under 'effectiveness'.
Compliance	Deals with complying with those laws, regulations and contractual arrangements to which the business process is subject, i.e. externally imposed business criteria.	Since the company is registered in the US, flight data will have to comply with Sarbanes–Oxley, i.e. it will have to be accurate.
Reliability	Relates to the provision of appropriate information for management to operate the entity and for management to exercise its financial and compliance reporting responsibilities.	Requires that the information above be consistently of good quality, i.e. relevant, accurate, timely, secure, etc. This also overlaps with other categories.

Source: COBIT (2000)

In other words, knowledge quality is dependent on the capability (or experience) of the people who use the information, the quality of the information they hold in their minds and available to support them, and their ability to apply the knowledge for a relevant or significant purpose. Significance also implies the value of unique knowledge or innovative knowledge which can help an organization gain a competitive advantage. Similar attributes to knowledge also apply to information – for example, is it relevant, complete and can it be represented (explained) clearly?

In Chapter 4 we saw how a knowledge audit is used to assess knowledge quality within an organization. The knowledge audit uses a similar process to an information audit, but its focus is different. The key difference is that an information audit is more focused on information 'objects', whereas the knowledge audit is 'people-centric', focused on employee know-how and knowledge flow. The elements of the ASHEN model introduced in Chapter 5 are effectively elements of knowledge quality. They are:

- *Artefacts*. Anything made by people, processes, documents, tools in which knowledge is embedded.
- *Skills*. Abilities that can be trained and measured without ambiguity.
- *Heuristics*. Rules of thumb, the outcome of experience, the main repository of knowledge, mostly unarticulated.
- *Experience*. Accumulated experience of failure and success which allows the right pattern to be triggered in the right context.
- *Natural talent*. Some people are just better at doing things than other people – and they are often not the people you expect.

The ASHEN factors can be used to assess knowledge quality at different knowledge disclosure points:

- Decisions
- Problems resolution
- Solution creation
- Judgement
- Learning points.

To apply the concept of knowledge quality to a real example, complete Activity 10.2.

Activity 10.2	Management of knowledge quality at AstraZeneca

Purpose

This activity is based on a case study upon which the concepts of data quality, information quality and knowledge quality can be applied.

Activity

For this particular case identify the characteristics or attributes of data quality, information quality and knowledge quality and explain the relationships between them.

Tip As you read the case study, map out the quality attributes of the different elements of the DIKAR model using Figure 10.2.

Case study

Like all major pharmaceutical companies, AstraZeneca invests heavily in its own research and development but also generates revenue from drugs that contain products that are under licence from other companies. Typically, around 20–30% of revenue in the industry comes from licensed-in products.

The route in for a licensed product can be varied and complicated. During a Cranfield survey, Roger Lloyd of AstraZeneca's business development group reported that there were up to 15 legitimate contact points between AstraZeneca and prospective licensors. Approaches to AstraZeneca can run to thousands a year. The process for handling all this lacked focus and was vulnerable to duplication and misunderstanding. It was also too slow.

Just under two years ago, Fred Brown, AstraZeneca's internal knowledge management consultant, initiated a KM approach to the issue. There were two bodies of knowledge that needed managing: the scientific and commercial knowledge, and the knowledge scattered all around the company about the status of any particular product under consideration.

The first step for Brown and Lloyd was to understand fully the process of transferring products and technology into the company's R&D and commercial activities. The next step was to secure agreement on the roles of knowledge owners and experts within that process. Clarifying ownership of each stage of the process and its key knowledge components was vital; only when they had fully understood the process, its owners and the knowledge required did Brown and Lloyd employ technology. They created, in effect, a virtual global department a community of the various experts needed to manage external investment activities. While they now act in concert with each other, the experts remain in their previous functional and geographical locations, where they are most valuable. The supporting technology (named Concert) allows structured and managed contact to occur among the relevant experts and the project manager at each stage of the external investment process.

The results have already been rewarding. The weeding-out process is much sharper; serious evaluation which might lead to contractual commitment can involve up to 60 or 70 people, so making sure unsuitable candidates do not get far means that scarce expertise can be focused on what really matters.

Source: Murray (2000)

Actions and results quality – performance management systems

Performance management system
A process used to evaluate and improve the efficiency and effectiveness of an organization and its processes

Effectiveness
Meeting process objectives, delivering the required outputs and outcomes – 'doing the right thing'

Efficiency
Minimizing resources or time needed to complete a process – 'doing the thing right'

The quality of actions taken by managers and results delivered in an organization depends on the processes and systems used to manage and control the direction of the organization. The processes and systems intended to monitor and improve the performance of an organization are known as 'performance management systems'. Performance is measured primarily through information on process effectiveness and efficiency. Put simply, effectiveness is 'doing the right thing'. 'Doing the right thing' means conducting the right activities and using the best strategies. From a process viewpoint it is producing the required outputs and outcomes, in other words meeting objectives. Efficiency is 'doing the thing right' – it defines whether processes are completed using the least resources and in the shortest time possible.

The importance of information to performance measurement is suggested by the definition used by Andy Neely of Cranfield School of Management's Centre for Business Performance. He defines performance measurement as

the process of quantifying the efficiency and effectiveness of past actions through acquisition, collation, sorting, analysis, interpretation and dissemination of appropriate data.

(Neely, 1998)

The imperative for performance management systems

The profile and significance of performance management systems in business have increased greatly over the past decade. One reason for this is the management trend to improving control and profitability in organizations through the creation of frameworks of metrics such as the balanced scorecard discussed later in the chapter. This has been coupled with the increased volume of performance data that is available through the introduction of enterprise-wide information systems associated with e-business initiatives such as supply chain management and customer relationship management systems. Such systems increase the potential availability of metrics and it is part of their value that they enable better control of processes. Managers require visibility of performance across different parts of the organization and this has led to the development of specialist corporate or business performance management software, described below, to address this need. A further reason for a focus on performance management systems is the introduction of laws such as Sarbanes–Oxley in the US and Basel II in Europe which require that organizations increase the transparency of their processes for managing financial and customer information. These laws are described in more detail in Chapter 12.

Figure 10.7 shows how information is used by managers to control the organization at the level of either an individual process or the organization as a whole. Information is one of the inputs to any process and also one of its key outputs. Deciding on the appropriate information to use and, as Neely suggests, how to cap-

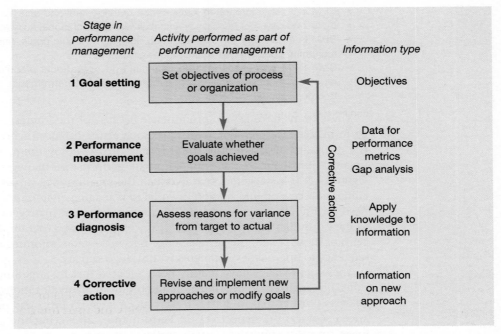

Figure 10.7 The role of information in controlling organizational performance

ture, store, analyse, interpret, disseminate and act on it is a vital activity for any organization. If assessment of performance measures is not approached in a disciplined way, problems in managing the business efficiently occur, as is illustrated by the mini case study 'Jigsaws always have more than one piece'.

Corporate performance management

The past decade has seen the development of many different frameworks of performance metrics, and the selection of metrics and the collection, analysis and dissemination of information to achieve this are an important part of any organization. The importance of the concept of performance measurement in the modern organization is evidenced by the range of management approaches used to evaluate and improve performance, including total quality management, activity-based costing, the balanced scorecard (see below) and Six Sigma (see below).

IT research analysts and vendors refer to software and processes which deliver information to support these management approaches as **corporate or business performance management**. Cognos, a vendor of applications to support corporate performance management, describes it thus:

> The aim of Corporate Performance Management (CPM) is to integrate a number of hitherto discrete applications into a single environment that includes all the necessary elements of performance management. These include: strategic and tactical planning; financial considerations such as budgeting and consolidation; the use of key performance indicators to support scorecard and analytic applications; the ability to monitor events on a real-time basis and to notify managers accordingly; and, of course, conventional query and reporting capabilities.

The related concept of business peformance management (BPM) is supported by the BPM standards group of analysts and vendors who are seeking to create standardized processes for process (see **www.bpmstandardsgroup.org**). They define BPM thus:

Corporate or business performance management
A process for improving the performance of organizations based on performance metrics

- BPM is a set of integrated, closed-loop management and analytic processes, supported by technology, that address financial as well as operational activities.
- BPM is an enabler for businesses in defining strategic goals, and then measuring and managing performance against those goals.
- Core BPM processes include financial and operational planning, consolidation and reporting, modeling, analysis, and monitoring of key performance indicators (KPIs) linked to organizational strategy.

These terms have gained prominence because of the interest of managers in using performance measurement approaches such as the balanced scorecard combined with the difficulty in assembling the information to deploy them. The difficulty many organizations have in achieving corporate performance management is indicated by Figure 10.8. It is staggering that over half the organizations surveyed admitted to difficulties in accessing information essential to managing organizational performance. The need for improved approaches to business information management is also suggested in the Consultants Advisory (2003) survey which showed that for three-quarters (76 per cent) of those polled, the key challenge is to make more informed decisions, with more reference to internal developments within the company.

These approaches have mainly been adopted first by large international organizations, but are likely to become more important in all organizations. It was estimated by analysts Gartner that in 2001, 70 per cent of large US firms had implemented the balanced scorecard (Perspectives on Performance, 2003), but this proportion is much lower for most countries. The importance of corporate performance management is also indicated by research by the Hackett Group which showed that 25,000 person-days are spent on planning and measuring performance per billion dollars of sales (Perspectives on Performance, 2003). Performance measurement is now also increasingly used in public-sector organizations such as local government, healthcare and schools in an attempt by governments to improve return on investment of public funds. For example, league tables and service delivery standards are now widely used for such organizations. Software companies such as Business Objects (**www.business objects.com**), Pilot Software (**www.pilotsoftware.com**) and Cognos (**www.cognos.com**) have developed to meet this need.

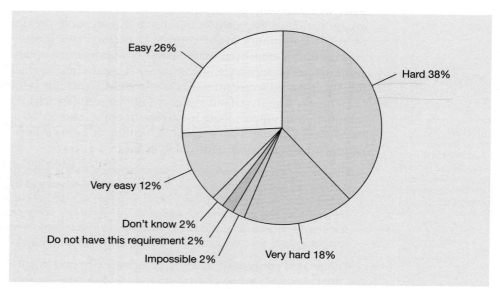

Figure 10.8 Response to question: 'How easy is it for decision makers in your organization to combine operational and financial information, and to do so when measured against corporate objectives?'

Figure 10.9 shows an example of how internal and external information can be summarized for busy managers and delivered as a **performance dashboard** or **corporate information portal or intranet** (see Chapters 2 and 8).

Now read Mini case study 10.2 'Jigsaws always have more than one piece' and complete Activity 10.3 to better understand the need for corporate performance management.

Performance dashboard
A summary of key performance indicators and drivers from which more detailed information can be obtained

Corporate information portal or intranet
A portal is a gateway offering web-based access to internal and external information sources for company employees

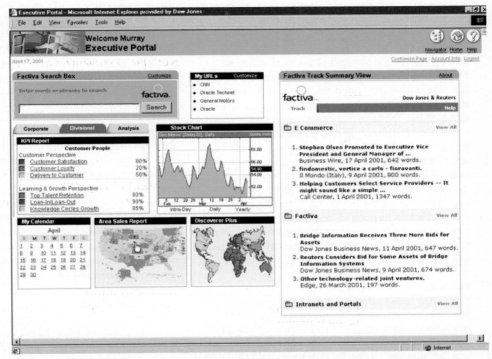

Figure 10.9 Factiva.com executive information portal showing summary of external and internal business information

Source: www.factiva.com

Activity 10.3	Capabilities of a corporate performance management system
Purpose	Explores the need for and requirements of a performance management system.
Activity	Read Mini case study 10.2 'Jigsaws always have more than one piece' and the description of performance management and then identify between five and ten requirements of a corporate performance management system. For example, the case shows that business decisions have many dimensions. In order to make the best business decisions you need to see the complete picture from different perspectives and different levels of detail.

Mini case study 10.2	Jigsaws always have more than one piece

This mini case study is written by David Stephens who has over ten years of experience in the IT industry specializing in management reporting and analysis. He wrote this fictitious tale of management information problems based on similar experience of misinterpretation of business metrics from real-world settings.

Piece 1

Paul Hutchins is the Managing Director of Hutchins Engineering Ltd, a medium-sized manufacturing company supplying valves and control equipment to the food and drinks industry. Paul was quite happy with what he saw that morning. The large bulky sales report had thumped on his desk and he had started to flick through it, he got to the entry for Bainbridge, he knew that Bainbridge was one of their biggest customers and was keen to see how sales were going. There it was, in black and white, it was 5% up on the same month last year, and this was an important figure as the Bainbridge account was almost 20% of the total turnover of the company. Seeing this he resolved to take an early lunch and a quick round of golf to try and improve his handicap, but what Paul had seen was just the first piece in the jigsaw.

Piece 2

If Paul had cross-referenced the Bainbridge entry in the sales report to the costings report, also on his desk, he would have seen that the costs involved in producing the inverse flow valve which was the main product supplied to Bainbridges were quite high and the profit margins were slim.

Piece 3

If Paul had double-checked with Jill Liddle who was the account manager with the responsibility for the Bainbridge account he would have found that information contained in Jill's spreadsheets showed that Bainbridge had recently negotiated further discounts on the inverse flow valve. The thin margins in the standard costing were being further eroded; in fact they would be lucky if they were breaking even on the Bainbridge account.

Piece 4

If Paul had checked with the production yield figures he would have found that there were major problems with producing the inverse flow valve. It was complex to produce and the yield was low, there was considerable re-working of defects in the product and the waste was high. In fact the true cost of producing it was much higher than the standard costings suggested. This information was held in the department's Microsoft Access database.

Piece 5

If Paul had checked with the Quality Assurance department he would have found that there were also problems with the quality of the inverse flow valve. Returns were running at almost 8% of shipped finished product and this was creating a backlog of paperwork for refunds. The QA information was very detailed but was all held on paper forms.

Piece 6

If Paul had checked the latest aged debtor report he would have seen a significant increase in debt for the Bainbridge account because they had been withholding payment until the refunds backlog was resolved. Paul was on the distribution list for the aged debt report but rarely looked at it because of its bulk and confusing format.

Piece 7

If Paul's sales report had been a bit more comprehensive it would have shown him that although the current month's sales figure were higher than the same month last year, in fact, the sales trend for the Bainbridge account had been falling every month for the last 6 months.

Piece 8

If Paul had seen the latest report from the logistics department he would have seen that many of the deliveries to Bainbridges were late, sometimes by weeks. Paul had asked for access to delivery information on a number of occasions but the IT staff hadn't got round to adding this option to his menu screen.

Piece 9

If Paul had checked the engineering trade press he would have found that his competitors Spears Engineering had opened a new modern production facility and were aggressively marketing to fill their new capacity.

Piece 10 (the final piece)

The phone rang, it was Jill Liddle, and she told Paul that they had just lost the Bainbridge account to Spears Engineering. Paul decided that he better postpone his round of golf.

Source: With permission of the author, David Stephens of Business Intelligence Solutions (www.bi-solutions.co.uk)

Performance metrics

Performance metrics
Measures that are used to evaluate and improve the efficiency and effectiveness of business processes

Key performance indicators (KPIs)
Metrics used to assess the performance of a process

Specific **performance metrics** are used to evaluate and improve the efficiency and effectiveness of a process. As we have noted, efficiency refers to how well the process makes use of its resources and effectiveness refers to whether the process is meeting its goals. **Key performance indicators (KPIs)** are a special type of performance metric which indicate the overall performance of a process or its sub-processes. An example of KPIs in a performance management system for an online electrical goods retailer is shown in Figure 10.10. The KPI is the total online sales figure. For a traditional retailer, this could be compared as a percentage to other retail channels such as mail order or retail stores. It can be seen that this KPI is dependent on performance drivers (e.g. Olve et al., 1999), such as number of site visits or average order value, which combine to govern this KPI. The concept of the KPI is similar to that of the critical success factor referred to in Chapter 6. Running the e-commerce site involves using the techniques on the left of the diagram to improve the performance drivers and so the KPI.

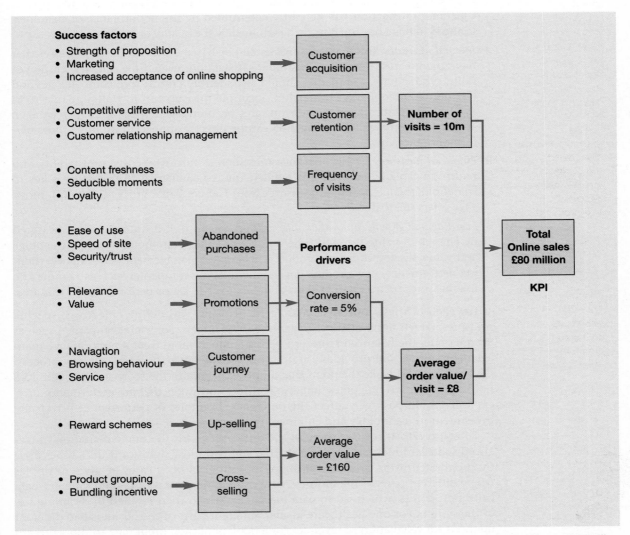

Figure 10.10 An example of a performance measurement system for an e-commerce electrical goods retailer

Source: Friedlein (2002)

The balanced scorecard

Balanced scorecard
A framework for setting
and monitoring business
performance. Metrics are
structured according to
customer issues, internal
efficiency measures,
financial measures and
innovation

The **balanced scorecard** is a corporate performance management system. It has become widely used as a means of translating organizational strategies into objectives and then providing metrics to monitor the execution of the strategy. The balanced scorecard, popularized in a *Harvard Business Review* article by Kaplan and Norton (1993), can be used to translate vision and strategy into objectives. In part, it was a response to over-reliance on financial metrics such as turnover and profitability and a tendency for these measures to be retrospective rather than looking at future potential as indicated by innovation, customer satisfaction and employee development. In addition to financial data, the balanced scorecard uses operational measures such as customer satisfaction, efficiency of internal processes and also the organization's innovation and improvement activities, including staff development.

Four main areas of organizational performance are managed through the balanced scorecard. These are:

1 *Customer concerns.* These include time (lead time, time to quote, etc.), quality, performance, service and cost. An example measure for Halifax Bank from Olve et al. (1999) is satisfaction of mystery shoppers visiting branches and from branch customer surveys. Customer satisfaction will be partly determined by the performance of customer-facing IS in branches and directly determined by the quality of online banking.

2 *Internal measures.* Internal measures should be based on the business processes that have the greatest impact on customer satisfaction: cycle time, quality, employee skills, productivity. Companies should also identify critical core competencies and try to guarantee market leadership. Example measures from Halifax Bank: ATM availability (percentage), conversion rates on mortgage applications (percentage), arrears on mortgage (percentage). IS can be directly applied to improve these performance measures.

3 *Financial measures.* Traditional measures such as turnover, costs, profitability and return on capital employed. For publicly quoted companies this measure is key to shareholder value. Example measures from Halifax bank: gross receipts (£), mortgage offers (£), loans (£).

4 *Learning and growth (innovation and staff development).* Innovation can be measured by change in value through time (employee value, shareholder value, percentage and value of sales from new products). Examples: management performance, training performance, new product development. Some companies such as Skandia Life use measures such as staff IT skills or access to IT to assess performance in this area.

For each of these four areas management teams will define objectives, specific measures, targets and initiatives to achieve these targets. For some companies, such as Skandia Life, the balanced scorecard becomes much more than a performance management system and provides a framework for the entire business strategy process. Olve et al. (1999) make the point that a further benefit of the scorecard is that it does not solely focus on outcomes, but also considers measures that are performance drivers that should positively affect the outcomes. Examples of performance drivers are investment in technology and employee training.

Tillmann (2004) reviews some of the difficulties with the implementation of balanced scorecard metrics. He suggests that the two most significant difficulties arise from data definition and the timing of reporting. In both cases he gives examples where different parts of the business were using different measures and different data collection points, which led to data inaccuracy which then resulted in declining use of the system. For one healthcare insurer, different parts of the business had different methods for calculation of revenue. For a book publisher, input data to the scorecard at different levels of detail were collected at different times of the month, which led to lack of trust in the scorecard. Additionally, he points out that many managers are sceptical about scorecards or do not want to be compared to managers in other departments through numbers alone, so they may try to sabotage the project by directly criticizing it or submitting metrics late. Tillmann suggests that many metrics projects may fail for this reason.

Six Sigma quality improvement

Six Sigma
A quality measure and improvement programme developed by Motorola that focuses on the control of a process to the point of ±six sigma (standard deviations) from a centreline, or 3.4 defects per million items

'Six Sigma' is a label for a quality measure and improvement programme originally developed at Motorola that focuses on the control of process to the point of ± six sigma (standard deviations) from a centreline, or 3.4 defects per million items. As the standard deviation increases towards six sigma, the number of faults decreases and the quality of a process or service increases, as shown in Table 10.2.

Table 10.2 Relationship between Six Sigma and faults for an electricity company

Six Sigma value	Faults or events per million opportunities	Percentage of faults or events	Time without electricity per month
1	691,462	30.85%	464h
2	308,538	69.15%	207h
3	66,807	93.32%	45h
4	6,210	99.38%	4h
5	233	99.78%	9min
6	3.4	99.99%	8s

It initially focused on statistical control of processes such as the manufacture of engineered items to a particular tolerance, but now has a much wider management application. Truscott (2003) describes its purpose as:

> to provide a universal performance metric, or measure, that can be applied to any product, process, service regardless of its relative complexity; a world class performance benchmark and the marketing name for the Six Sigma improvement initiative.

Six Sigma can be applied to assess the efficiency of a wide range of business processes at different scales. Examples include faults in manufactured products, delays to a transport service, complaints received by customers, purchase orders or invoices processed without manual intervention or even a method of measuring data or information quality! Mercury Interactive has developed solutions for IT governance using Six Sigma which consider IT projects and levels of service. It is apparent that the efficiency of each stage of a project can in theory be assessed using Six Sigma, although the interdependencies between project phases and iterative processes described in Chapter 7 mean that Six Sigma has not been widely adopted for IT governance.

Companies put in place Six Sigma projects with training and changes to business process and staff incentivization in order to strive for Six Sigma. Staff development is identified by a series of 'belts', from green belt to black belt, similar to judo! Considering transport delays, for instance, it can be seen that achieving Six Sigma 3.4 delays per million journeys or even 3.4 delays of less than 30 minutes is often not a realistic goal. Rather, Six Sigma gives a benchmark – between different forms of transport such as rail and air travel or between different train operators. An individual train operator can use Six Sigma to set targets for improvement and measure achievement against results. Techniques such as value analysis to reduce costs and Potential

Failure Mode and Effects Analysis (PFMEA) are used to analyse and refine processes. The overall approach of improvement using Six Sigma is usually summarized as DMAIC (Define–Measure–Analyse–Implement–Control), but Truscott (2003) has a useful elaboration to these eight stages of a Six Sigma project:

1　Identify the project.

2　Define the project.

3　Measure current process performance.

4　Analyse current process.

5　Develop the improvements, pilot and verify.

6　Implement the changes, achieve breakthroughs in performance.

7　Control at new level; institutionalize to hold the gains.

8　Communicate new knowledge gained; transfer solution to similar areas.

It is obvious that information quality and information systems quality are vital to Six Sigma quality improvement programmes!

Six Sigma is the most recent manifestation of many quality improvement initiatives such as total quality management (TQM), the European Foundation for Quality Management (EFQM), quality circles and zero defects. But it seems to be gaining in popularity, particularly in large US-based manufacturing organizations such as 3M, Intel and General Electric which then transfer the skills to other countries where they have offices. In its 2000 annual report, General Electric claimed $6.6 billion in savings by implementing Six Sigma. Motorola has measured nearly $20 billion in savings. Truscott (2003) summarizes the differences of this quality initiative as: business-oriented, company-wide initiative, scientific method, addresses performance gaps, focus on adding value and catalyst for cultural change.

Assessing the quality of business performance metrics

An alternative view of the attributes of information quality which applies specifically to business metrics is provided by the widely used SMART mnemonic. SMART is an assessment for information quality that applies specifically to the quality of the business metrics for managers (see Chapter 1). SMART is used to assess the suitability of objectives set to drive different strategies or the improvement of business processes. SMART stands for:

- *Specific* – Is the detail in the information sufficient to pinpoint problems or opportunities?
- *Measurable* – Can a quantitative or qualitative attribute be applied to create a metric?
- *Actionable* – Can the information be used to improve performance?
- *Relevant* – Can the information be applied to the specific problem faced by the manager?
- *Time-related* – Can the information be viewed through time to identify trends?

An alternative viewpoint of the quality of business performance metrics is presented in the Research insight 10.1 'Successful metrics guidelines'.

Case study 10.1

NHS Operating Room Management Information System (ORMIS)

Operating Room Management Information System (ORMIS) is used in operating theatres in the NHS to monitor and control both patients and resources (www.isoftplc.com/corporate/mediafiles/ORMIS.pdf).

The system oversees equipment and material stocks, tracks patient admission and discharge, records important patient statistics in real time and allows this data to be viewed graphically by staff and management.

The real-time capture of patient data, which is collated into a document known as a care-plan, is perhaps the most interesting aspect of ORMIS. It is recorded perioperatively (before surgery), intraoperatively (during surgery) and postoperatively (after surgery) by the theatre staff who enter details into ORMIS via touchscreens.

The data has several uses:

- It is used to highlight where delays occur and enables staff and management to continuously improve the efficiency of the department.
- It can be analysed to identify trends in treatment and recovery, such as the relative effectiveness of anaesthetic drugs or clinical practices.
- It may also be used to check that patients had been cared for in the most appropriate way according to their condition.

Data capture – times

In order to monitor the rate at which patients are processed several 'key times' are recorded:

- Time patient enters pre-op waiting area
- Time patient enters anaesthetic room
- Induction time
- Time patient enters theatre
- Knife to skin time
- Dressing on (time)
- Time out of theatre and into recovery

There is also a facility for recording the nature and duration of any delays that occur perioperatively. Interestingly, a 'delay' is considered to be any unplanned event that causes the time between Patient Entering Preop and Patient Entering Anaesthetic Room to exceed 15 minutes. Such delays are often caused by consent forms being incorrectly filled in, or the surgeon or anaesthetist being late.

There is some debate over the definition of Induction Time. It is defined by some hospital managements as:

'The time that the patient first sees the Anaesthetist in the Anaesthetic Room.'

Whereas the medical definition is:

'The time that the patient actually receives their anaesthetic.'

Adopting the first definition effectively means that the Induction Time is the same as the time that the patient enters the Anaesthetic Room. Using this definition allows the data to be analysed for any delays in the process of preparing a patient for their surgery in Preop, and for any delays in the time that it takes to administer an anaesthetic to the patient.

Adopting the second definition enables the data to be analysed for any delays between the patient entering the Anaesthetic Room and then receiving their anaesthetic, and the time taken between them receiving their anaesthetic and then entering the theatre.

The first definition allows the processes of patient preparation and administering anaesthetic to be assessed for delay whereas the second definition allows the combined processes of patient preparation and administering anaesthetic to be examined along with the rapidity of the anaesthetic drug. The former can be interpreted as a purely managerial performance metric whereas the second is a combination of managerial and clinical metrics.

These competing measures would appear to be driven by the need to improve patient care throughout as hospital waiting lists remain long and the desire of hospital managers, doctors, nurses and clinical practitioners to improve the well-being of patients often through programmes such as the Anaesthesia in Partnership initiative (www.npsa.nhs.uk/patientsafety/improvingpatientsafety/patientsafety initiatives/anaesthesiapartnership).

Data capture – staff

The names of all staff working in a particular operating theatre are also recorded every day via ORMIS. If the 'Anaesthetist' button is pressed on screen a list of all the Anaesthetists within the particular NHS trust (group of local hospitals) will appear from which the attending Anaesthetist may be selected – this is known as context relevant listing. The same happens when 'Surgeon', 'ODP, 'Scrub' or 'Support Staff' buttons are pressed. It can be appreciated that there may be hundreds or even thousands of staff in each category and scrolling through the list of available names can be very time consuming.

It is not uncommon for theatre staff to change during the course of a day: many staff work shifts and specialist staff are sometimes brought in to assist with specific cases.

ORMIS though does not have a provision for recording staff changes. This is not usually a problem but it does prevent the collation of complete and accurate records.

Data capture – patients

The type of monitoring equipment that is used is also recorded via ORMIS along with specific patient data. This may require the capture of significant amounts of data, including:

- Temperature monitoring equipment, whether invasive (internal) or non-invasive (external)
- Type of temperature and blood pressure warning equipment used.
- Type of prophylaxis (preventative) measures used, such as elasticated stockings to prevent Deep Vein Thrombosis (DVT).
- Patient temperature, blood pressure and oxygen levels before, during and after surgery.
- Patient position and the type of supports and restraints that are used.

Some of the problems with the data that is recorded are attributable to the type of equipment that is used: for example, some non-invasive thermometers are highly sensitive items of equipment and are more accurate than others. Recording less accurate temperature readings results in a deterioration of the quality of data that is stored by ORMIS and consequently the less accurate that any subsequent analysis will be (Refer to Chapter 10 for further discussion about data and information quality).

Recording this array of data requires the member of theatre staff to access each individual item on the patient care plan and enter the appropriate measurement or description. Understandably, during complex surgery or whenever patients require heightened levels of care and attention it is difficult to find time to record much of the less vital information. This enables staff to focus upon the patient's wellbeing but does result in incomplete care-plans and department metrics being recorded.

Even though ORMIS offers context relevant lists for much of the equipment that is used, the level of detail that is recorded is highly subjective. It is dependent upon the personal preferences of the member of staff inputting the data and the amount of time that they have available to complete the task.

This may be a significant issue if a patient suffers post-operative complications, for example complaining of a bruised arm following surgery on their hand. Normal practice may be to protect the arm with padded supports and this would be recorded on the patient care-plan in ORMIS. If no record had been made of the type of supports used under the arm during surgery then it would be difficult to ascertain if the bruising was due to staff failing to ensure adequate arm support or whether the bruise was caused by some medical ailment which would require further investigation and treatment.

Questions

1 Consider the differences between the data requirements of the people involved. What data are important for the hospital management, the surgeons and the anaesthetic staff.

2 How could the system be used more effectively?

3 How would you approach the development of a system to replace ORMIS?

Research insight 10.1 | Successful metrics guidelines

Andy Neely and colleagues from the Performance Measurement Group at Cranfield School of Management have developed a more sophisticated form of the SMART mnemonic, by research into problems in the way business metrics are used both individually and collectively (Neely et al., 2002). They present the Ten Measures Design Test which can also be viewed as an assessment of information quality.

The Ten Measures design tests

1 *The truth test*. Are we really measuring what we set out to measure?
2 *The focus test*. Are we only measuring what we set out to measure?
3 *The relevancy test*. Is it the right measure of the performance measure we want to track?
4 *The consistency test*. Will the data always be collected in the same way whoever measures it?
5 *The access test*. Is it easy to locate and capture the data needed to make the measurement?
6 *The clarity test*. Is any ambiguity possible in interpreting the results?
7 *The so-what test*. Can and will the data be acted upon?

8 *The timeliness test.* Can the data be accessed rapidly and frequently enough for action?

9 *The cost test.* Is the measure worth the cost of measurement?

10 *The gaming test.* Is the measure likely to encourage undesirable or inappropriate behaviours?

Why measure?

Traditional

11 To track recent/current actual performance against targets/predictions/history.

12 To track recent/current performance against external regulations or internal policies.

13 To track perceptions of performance deficiencies and monitor their improvement.

14 To motivate managers and employees to achieve specific performance objectives.

Emerging

1 To help predict future trends.

2 To validate or challenge existing assumptions.

3 To discover new insights (through data analysis).

4 To stimulate the creation of new initiatives, objectives and targets.

Ultimately

1 To aid decisions and substantiate improvement/investment recommendations.

2 To show the achievement/realisation of anticipated benefits resultant from actions.

Source: Neely et al. (2002)

Conduct information audit

Now that we have defined information quality and its relationship to data and knowledge quality, we turn our attention to a key tool for improving information quality – the **information audit**.

Information audit
An evaluation of the usage and flows of information within an organization in supporting organizational objectives

What is an information audit?

The information audit was introduced in Chapter 4 as a key part of developing a structured information strategy. We saw that the information audit is an essential analytical tool to help in creating a foundation for using information strategically. The similar process involved in the knowledge audit was covered in Chapter 4. In this section we look at what is involved in an information audit in more detail.

An information audit has been defined by the Aslib Information Resources Management Network, referenced in Orna (1999), as:

> a systematic examination of information use, resources and flows, with a verification by reference to both people and existing documents, in order to establish the extent to which they are contributing to an organization's objectives.

This definition does not refer directly to improving information quality, but it does so indirectly since information quality is dependent on how well the information resources and usage contribute to an organization's objectives. Information audits are sometimes explained to staff in other ways because of the negative connotations of the term 'audit'. Di Mattia and Blumenstein (2000) report on an information audit conducted by Trudy Katz, director of the Mastercard Information Center. She initially referred to the project as an information audit until financial staff told her that 'audit' connoted a restriction or change and would scare people away. She chose to label it 'the corporate information survey' for a more positive response.

Although the scope of information audits will often apply to all management information within an organization, within a larger organization it may be infeasible or unnecessary to audit all information. Information audits may target a number of specific information management needs or applications, which might include:

1 creation or refinement of an intranet or extranet;

2 improvement of library or information centre services;

3 reduction in time spent by staff searching for internal or external information;

4 corporate performance management;

5 an individual business process, department or data type, e.g. financial data, inventory data or customer data;

6 competitive intelligence about an organization's marketplace and competitors;

7 knowledge management (see Chapter 6 which defines the process for a knowledge audit, which is one form of information audit).

What is the purpose of an information audit?

According to Orna (1999), there are both short-term and long-term benefits of completing an information audit, as is shown in Table 10.3. Furthermore, she suggests that if an information audit is not conducted, then possible consequences are:

● information activities inappropriate since not driven by organizational objectives;

● new production development or other processes may fail due to poor communications;

● a poor correlation between corporate and IT or information strategy;

● decision making poor since it will be difficult to bring together relevant information from a range of sources to make quick, effective decisions;

● poor response to threats and opportunities since information-sensing capabilities are limited.

Nigel Oxbrow, managing director of TFPL, a London- and New York-based company specializing in information audits, sees the benefits of information audit as

a database of information resources, improved understanding of information costs and value, and improved quality of information services. An increase in awareness about

Table 10.3 **Benefits of conducting an Information Audit**

Short-term benefits	Long-term benefits
● Attention to immediate threats, and exploitation of opportunities	● Enriched understanding of what information and knowledge mean throughout the organization
● Quick financial and efficiency gains from making information more available and usable	● Development of a strategy for managing knowledge and information
● Increasing awareness of presence and location of all necessary information	● Better use of information in supporting key business processes
	● Integrated management of the full range of information

Source: Orna (1999)

information, accompanied by changes in user expectations and patterns of sharing are also expected by products.

(Di Mattia and Blumenstein, 2000)

He describes the risks in terms of information and knowledge quality of not conducting the audit as:

duplicate, incomplete or inaccurate resources and work; inefficient use of an intranet; innovative ideas that don't get shared; and intellectual assets that are not fully utilised.

From the description above, the information audit might be considered as a one-off event. However, Sue Henczel, author of *The Information Audit: A Practical Guide*, views it as a cyclical process where planning, data collection, data analysis, data evaluation, communicating recommendations and implementation are repeated at regular intervals (Henczel, 2001).

What is the procedure for an information audit?

Orna (1999) acknowledges that there is no standard procedure for an information audit. It is unlike a systems development methodology, for example. However, she suggests that there is a common core to the audit. This involves identifying the objectives of an organizational process, whether it be a high-level or a low-level process. Then the information required to support the process and assess whether the objectives are achieved is defined. This is then compared to the actual information provision. Assessing the actual information provision is the core of the information audit. Orna (1999) frames several key questions about information resources which are typically part of an information audit. We will illustrate them relative to investor relations (IR) information for the Lo-cost Airline Company. The questions about the information resources are:

1 *What are they*? Details on company performance.

2 *Where are they*? They are produced in paper form for distribution when requested. Also available online in PDF and HTML formats.

3 *Who is responsible for them*? Responsibility for the timely delivery of investor relations' information belongs to the Head of Investor Relations. The accuracy of information is the responsibility of the chief financial officer and, as mentioned earlier, is now subject to the Sarbanes–Oxley Act described at the start of Chapter 12. The production of investor relations' information is outsourced to a specialist IR company (**www.huginonline.com**).

4 *What kind of information do they contain*? Financial statements, quarterly company trading statements, annual reports and presentations by the management team.

5 *How do people who manage them define the users and the way they use information*? The information needs of different users of IR information need to be reviewed to ensure the information is fit for purpose. This has not been thought through (see point 7) since it is a legal requirement to produce them and if people such as investors require them they will be sought out.

6 *What do the users themselves say*? The users would include potential and actual investors, the media and researchers including other companies. Key users such as potential investors could be asked to assess the data.

7 Are there other people who could make good use of this resource who:
   – *Don't know about it*? Newly joined managers may find this information useful in induction, but they are not currently made aware of it.
   – *Know about it, but don't have access to it?* Not relevant since available online.

We should also think about information quality and information lifecycle issues such as:

● *What are the attributes of quality information in this category?* Timeliness – the information needs to be made public within 30 days of the end of each quarterly trading period. Presentation – the presentation is key. Currently competitors produce an improved presentation, which needs to be reviewed. Accessibility is covered in the information audit by reviewing information flows using information mapping.

● *How long are data sources such as database records or documents kept?* Are they archived and backed up? This is the responsibility of the company maintaining the records – it needs to be clarified.

Swash (1997) stresses these issues of information quality in her summary of questions needed in the information audit. She recommends:

Audit questions should seek to identify what information is central to business need, what sources are actively used and how often. These data should preferably be weighted in order of priority. The problems arising through the non-availability of timely and accurate information should be recorded and any discrepancies between perceived and actual needs quantified. Further questions should be included to explore the use of primary contacts, both internal and external which will frequently be more highly valued than published sources.

Gap analysis
Assesses the current information provision against that required to support an organization's objectives

A **gap analysis** between the required and actual information is also performed to assess whether the appropriate information is available to measure and support progress to these objectives. The types of question used to inform the gap analysis are summarized in Figure 10.11.

Research insight 10.2 'An information audit at the University of Glamorgan' illustrates a typical information audit process. It highlights five typical stages of an information audit. The auditing parts which are used to complete a gap analysis are

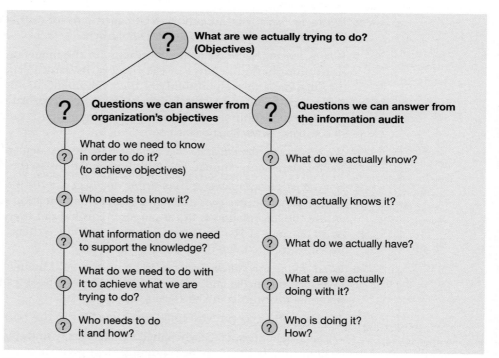

Figure 10.11 Information audit questions relating to an organization's objectives
Source: Orna (1999), Figure 4.5, p. 85

stages 1 to 3, which are followed by further actions. You will see that the process for an information audit is similar to that for a knowledge audit suggested in Chapter 4. At stage 2, similar audit tools are used, such as questionnaires, interviews, focus groups and narrative techniques. In addition, observation of use of information systems may be used. These can be conducted either by internal staff or by external specialists. There is debate in the literature (see for example Swash, 1997) on whether the internal or external approach is best. Swash says that internal auditors require less time to understand the business of the organization, but they may be seen as aligned to particular organizational interests. Furthermore, frank views may not be expressed. Clearly consultants will take longer to understand the business, but the external perspective can help clarify relevant information and provide an objective view on information management resources and processes.

Research insight 10.2   An information audit at the University of Glamorgan

In 2000, the University of Glamorgan took part in a research project arranged through the Information strategies initiative of JISC (Joint Information Systems Committee) which promotes best practice in information management in the UK.

The aim of the project was to develop an Information Strategy Process Framework (ISPF) methodology. The ISPF was intended to underpin a strategic programme of the University by providing a direct mechanism for identifying and monitoring the information needs directly related to the strategic goals and objectives of the University.

We take one example of an organizational process that was selected for an information audit – the recruitment of new students. In this case, the strategic goal was to 'Attract and Retain Sufficient students' or more specifically to 'Identify, annually, the number of students to be recruited in the following September to meet our income, Higher Education Funding Committee targets, standards and participation targets'.

Stage 1: Define information requirements
This stage involves identifying the organizational objectives, which can be at different levels such as strategic, departmental or process level. The information required for achieving and monitoring progress of these objectives is also required.

An analysis was undertaken on the types and kind of information that would be required to achieve and monitor performance against this strategic goal. The following were identified as principal topic areas:

- In what form does information on student numbers, applications figures, target numbers, mode of study etc. need to be produced and by whom?
- In what form should information on students be held within the University and by whom? In what form should this information be disseminated by school/department or by university as a whole, to whom should this information be disseminated to?
- What medium should be used to store different categories of information on students?
- How should information on student numbers etc. be disseminated effectively?
- The use of technology – what technologies should be used to support the dissemination of student information?
- What information is needed to assess the performance of the University in student recruitment?

In summary, the key metrics were:

- Information on full- and part-time student numbers
- Information on how the University is currently progressing against its student retention targets
- Up-to-date information on admissions and enrolments

Stage 2: Assess current information provision
This analysis assesses the information actually available against that ideally required to achieve or monitor progress.

Current provision was established through a thorough analysis of the student progression, retention information available to the University.

Stage 3: Gap analysis of difference between information requirements and provision

This summarizes the main problems with information resources by assessing the difference between required information at stage 1 and actual information at stage 2.

Identification of the perceived gaps involved an analysis of all the problems with the current information provision and related to matters such as inaccuracy, untimely information, duplication of information, lack of relevant information, inadequate dissemination channels [information quality issues]. In this example the data illustrated that there was a lack of information on part-time students within the University. The University had no adequate system in place for analysing part-time numbers in relation to national performance indicators and national comparators. The University had a good performance on recruiting part-time students but an ineffective system for analysing the make-up of these numbers.

Stage 4: Identification of potential solutions

Solutions to remove the information gap are devised; these may include the provision of certain types of information, new processes or new technology.

1 An effective system for monitoring part-time numbers
2 Increased marketing by schools to attract more part-time students
3 To analyse the number of part-time students studying within the Community Studies section of the University.
4 To develop a marketing plan to enhance the portfolio/opportunity for delivering by alternative modes – particularly part-time (on campus) and distance learning

Stage 5: Develop action plan

Specific action points including provision of information and changes to processes. In this example, the action points were:

1 To include in departmental plans, objectives to enhance part-time (on campus) and distance-learning numbers through increased school/departmental marketing of existing part-time courses and enhanced portfolios of part-time courses.
   Action by: Head of Marketing and Heads School/Department.
2 To develop a marketing plan to increase part-time student numbers
   Action by: Head of Marketing
3 To develop a web page specifically for part-time students
   Action by: Head of Marketing and Departmental Web Co-ordinators

The role of the information audit in influencing the strategy of the university was acknowledged by Mr John O'Shea, Academic Registrar, University of Glamorgan who said:

The information provided by the ISPF made the University realize that in order to achieve our mission we needed to become more market and demand led. One outcome of this was the action to encourage those students that would not have traditionally applied to go to University.

Source: JISC (2000)

To conclude this section, see Case study 10.2, which provides a further example of an information audit – the case summarizes the results from an information audit. You have to perform a simple gap analysis.

Case study 10.2

FT

An information audit at an SME

This case illustrates the types of information assessed during a real information audit. This is based on a real audit conducted by Mike Swain and Oliver Crook of Liverpool John Moores University for an SME (a chartered surveyors) as part of a Knowledge Transfer Programme (KTP).

Information requirements

Interviews have identified several key information requirements for the business which are illustrated in Table 10.4.

One partner suggested that the level of information required will be dependent on the output required and that different services and clients specify different levels of required detail. This does not reduce quality to the client, as customer expectations/requirements are still met. He acknowledged the importance of information: 'You can only be as good as the information you are given.'

Information availability

Financial information

The company produces a spreadsheet summarizing actual and projected incoming cash on a monthly basis. This shows revenues split by client/type of client/services delivered etc. An interview with a partner showed some areas for development, such as changing the headings which are dated. One issue that was raised was the 'Other' category accounting for nearly 30% of revenues. This is worth further investigation.

One partner said 'we often do not know how much it is costing us to deliver certain services to the client'. He suggested that it would be useful to have a breakdown of costs, allocated to clients. This would identify sectors where work is particularly profitable, clients who are not as profitable, etc. This would then form the basis of subsequent relationship marketing campaigns.

Sales and marketing information

Most respondents suggested that more detailed information regarding the direction being taken by competitors would be useful (however, all accepted that this will be hard to identify).

One key information gap experienced in most cases is feedback on previous work completed and on unsuccessful submissions. One partner responded, 'We need to implement a feedback system ... by email/post/telephone/face-to-face.' Having this kind of information would enable organizational learning to take place and therefore lead to improvements in future bids. The same partner stated that further 'internal meetings to discuss successful and unsuccessful bids and work completed would be very useful to allow us to learn from our mistakes and take advantage of many more opportunities'.

Information for submissions

All of the partners commented that the information required to complete submissions is not readily available in one place. One partner estimated that the company are completing between 2–5 submissions per week at a cost of £000's worth of partner time. This is a significant cost and should be reduced.

Interviews with certain senior staff identified the same issue, and one response was that a database of regular questions occurring on submission forms should be produced. This would save a great deal of time and also improve the effectiveness of the submissions. It would enable learning to occur, especially if combined with a feedback system.

Another suggestion from one partner that should be implemented in line with the above point is a submissions template to be used as a starting point for each submission, with all regular sections included. This database

Table 10.4 Information requirements

Partners	Staff
Financial information	Costing information from published sources
Information for submissions	Costing information from past work
Staffing levels and capacity	Details on the task in hand – what they are doing/ what the end result needs to be/deadlines/start dates/format it must be in
Details on previous/current/future clients and work carried out	Drawings and specifications Access to all information from any correspondence Site visits

would then make tailoring the submission to each individual commission quick and easy.

Partners are aware of the huge costs associated with wasted time in the development of submissions. Duplication of efforts on a regular basis is a huge and unnecessary drain on resources, in terms of actual and opportunity costs (partners' time would be better used on other activities).

Information on staffing/skills/capacity

When new work comes in, the partners or a selection of the partners discuss the available resources within the company and allocate the most suitable option. The partners have this information, as they are well aware of each person's skills, experience and levels of expertise.

It would be the recommendation of the auditing team that there should be a central database containing this information, ensuring that it continues to be simple and effective as more surveyors are employed, and as partners change, retire or leave the company. This would also provide the basis for staff to search for people who have completed similar tasks to current commissions. This will enable them to go to them for assistance in job-specific tasks.

One issue that arose from personal experience of the associate was the difficulty in finding where people are when out of the office, and when they are expected to return. There is a diary system, but this is in the reception and therefore is not easily accessible or accurate. A simple shared calendar system using the existing Outlook system would allow everyone to see at a glance where people are and when they are returning to the office. Receptionist staff agreed that this type of system would be useful.

Information on previous/current clients and client work

One partner responded that a more detailed database of client information would be useful. Items such as all previous work completed, all submissions sent, and any other general information should be included. This would enable all partners and staff to communicate intelligently with all clients when they call or meet. It was suggested that this should be very detailed, and include interesting conversational points, such as football teams supported etc. An example of where this would be useful occurred during one of the interviews, where a partner needed to return a call to a client and was trying to remember the name of the client's partner who had been ill.

This system would form the basis for an improvement in management information and would facilitate effective customer relationship management. It would also disseminate tacit knowledge on each individual client held within partners and staff, and create an impression of importance for every client.

Costing information from published sources

Most respondents were happy with the access to information from published sources. One minor issue was that there are only a few copies of the Price Books, and sometimes they are all out on people's desks. Respondents acknowledged that it is only very rarely that it becomes a problem, and that for everyone to have their own book(s) would be unnecessary.

The major issue to arise was Internet access. There are several different levels of Internet access within the company. These are free and easy access, no access, and access but requiring permission. Several people commented that although they have use of a communal Internet computer, sometimes they do not bother using it as they have to walk across the office, log-on etc. Another member of staff commented that not allowing access suggests a lack of trust, which becomes a de-motivating factor. They stated that the office is close-knit and felt that no one would abuse the privilege. If broadband access were installed (approximately £226 installation fee, £46 per month), then the dial-up costs associated with going onto the Internet would be eliminated. Open Internet access should be tested, or allow controlled access to only relevant sites. For a site to be added to the list a set procedure will be designed.

Costing information from previous work

This was an area shown by both staff and partners as a real area for potential improvement. The computer-based files are not held in a simple, logical structure due to people at present keeping their work within folders of their own name. There is also a carry-over from when all Word processing was carried out by receptionist staff, and their files were held separately. Therefore, one partner commented that if there is more than one surveyor working on a project, there could be 4+ locations for work on a single commission. Having everything in one central client folder would make the job easier for everyone.

One partner suggested several reasons for these issues. Everyone is very possessive of their work and wants it to be in their own folder and people have filing structures they are used to at home and this is carried forward to the office. However, the auditing team would suggest that both of these problems will be overcome because many people identified the same issues.

There is also a significant potential for improvement in the filing and storage of hard copy materials. There are two real issues in this area, the fact that people need access to certain printed information, and wasted space and poor image of boxes and files all around the office. There is actually a procedure that specifies the documents that need to be kept, for how long and where. This is not enforced or adhered to.

The costs associated with wasted time attempting to locate information are huge, as is the potential for making efficiency improvements. This will develop profitability of projects, and increase the capacity of the company to cope with increased sales resulting from other activities.

General task information

It was suggested that when work is allocated all of the required general task information is provided to the relevant member(s) of staff. An issue that came from the staff interviews was that certain information that would be relevant to the task is not disseminated throughout the organization. These include things such as the strategic importance of the client, how much other work has been completed for the client etc. This sort of information would enable staff to take control of their time and prioritize tasks more effectively, enabling empowerment and leading to higher motivation.

One member of staff commented that one regular occurrence is that people pass work on to each other, which may involve small tasks that only take a short amount of time. Often there is a temptation to act on a 'needs to know basis' and not pass on all of the general task information. He agreed that this is the wrong ethos/mentality to have.

> **Question**
>
> The information collected in the audit is summarized above. Imagine you are the information auditor. Develop a five-stage summary of the information audit using the example in Research insight 10.2 'An information audit at the University of Glamorgan'.

Define and implement information quality policy

Information policy
A statement of an organization's approach to information management

Information quality policy
Details organizational and individual approaches to reviewing, monitoring and improving the quality of information within an organization

In Chapter 4, we introduced the concept of the **information policy**. We saw that this supports an information strategy by setting out the high-level principles of how an organization should be organized. It refers to general aims such as using information to improve organizational performance, ambitions to share knowledge and the intention to secure information. It will also typically refer to identifying staff responsibilities for information management. What we believe is also needed in addition to this high-level policy is more detailed practical guidelines on managing information quality and data quality. This is an **information quality policy**. This includes procedures to evaluate and improve information quality. Information quality is controlled by staff actions and checks built into business applications and database. Such procedures need to be set out to minimize the problems of poor-quality data and information introduced at the start of the chapter. English (1999) stresses the need to manage information quality. He says that managing information quality involves:

1 raising awareness of the problems caused by poor-quality information (through education and training);
2 defining processes for measuring information quality (the information audit is the first stage in this);
3 defining processes for improving information quality;
4 providing education and guidance on facilitating the improvement in these processors;
5 measuring the cost savings and customer satisfaction that results from improved information quality.

Systems controls
Software is used to control data quality on entry and through data cleansing

Human controls
Staff control data quality at entry and through review

Xu et al. (2003) distinguish between **systems controls** and **human controls** on information quality – these are the means by which processes are put in place to improve information quality. In research on accountants these authors found that IT people tend to think that systems controls are most important, while accountants tend to think that human-related factors are more important. The accountants believed that system control rules cannot be built in for every aspect of data quality since judgement is required. They argue that education and training are critical.

In the following sections, we will look in more detail at key issues within an information quality policy. The coverage refers to approaches for:

- *Managing data quality* – issues include defining data quality, systems controls such as data validation, data quality auditing, profiling and data cleansing and human controls such as setting data quality targets, training and review.

- *Managing information quality* – defining information quality, human factors, responsibilities for information quality and controls on information quality.
- *Managing knowledge quality* – this is not referred to explicitly in this chapter since approaches to improving knowledge quality are covered in Chapter 5 on knowledge management strategy. Key issues are the models of knowledge sharing, staff motivation in knowledge management and the technology used to support knowledge management.

Approaches for managing data quality

To improve information quality a range of options are possible which can be recommended in the information policy to improve data quality. These measures can be divided into those that are used to control data quality when they are first entered into information systems and those that are used to control data quality once stored in the system when they can be reviewed and modified.

It also helps to understand the source of data quality problems to help devise strategies to improve information quality. A Data Warehousing Institute (2002) survey which looked at data quality in all types of database system found that the main causes of data quality problems were:

- Data entry by employees, for example when talking to a customer on the phone (76 per cent)
- Data entry by customers, for example when entering their details over the Internet (25 per cent)
- Changes to source systems, i.e. changes to database definitions made by database administrators without thinking through information quality implications (53 per cent)
- Data migration or conversion projects (48 per cent)
- Mixed expectations of data quality by users (46 per cent)
- Errors introduced by the import of external data (34 per cent)
- System errors causing corruption of data (26 per cent).

We will now review a range of approaches that can be used to manage and improve data quality.

The data dictionary

Data dictionary
A structured definition defining data objects and the relationship between them together with attributes and acceptable values

This survey confirms the importance of validation or checking data on entry and also shows the importance of clear definitions for data. A key method of controlling data is the use of common data definitions to establish a standard to refer to and check against. This is traditionally known as 'the **data dictionary**'. It consists of the verbal definitions of data and the relationship between the entities as introduced in Chapter 9. A data dictionary is a form of metadata, a concept introduced in Chapters 3 and 9. For data quality purposes it is essential that the data dictionary contain input checks or validation rules to enforce data quality, as explained in the section below. However, sometimes it is limited to a list of fields and descriptions of these fields.

Note that the survey results show a significant problem with changes to source systems. It is common for database fields to be added during the lifetime of a system. Adding fields is often a means to improve information quality. For example, in a marketing database of its business customers the company might decide it needs to know the size of the organization through either number of employees or turnover. While this will be useful for marketers, when the field is added it will be blank for all existing records on the database. In cases like this, procedures need to be put in place to populate this field, either through running through the database record by record, which is unlikely since the costs will exceed the returns, or by educating staff who contact these customers to add this information. Another possibility is to link to a third-party data source such as One Source (**www.onesource.com**) which will contain such data for millions of companies and can then be used to populate this and other fields which help users understand the customers better.

A common case of data definition in many organizations involves customer data. We saw in Mini case study 10.1 'Abbey Bank cuts costs through improving data quality' that in organizations where customer information is viewed as particularly important, such as a bank, specific information managers will be created. Often problems arise through multiple data sources, so a single source of data is produced which is clearly defined. This is sometime known as a 'single view of the customer'. It is created through a process known by analysts Gartner as '**customer data integration**' (CDI). They describe CDI as 'the consolidation of all data sources used to create a single view of the customer. The core technology layer of a CDI solution includes the cleaning, linking and grouping of customer data, as well as the technology for putting integrated customer data at the points where your business needs it – in the call center, in the mail room or even at the cash register.' A single view of the customer is typically produced for operational purposes, so that if a customer contacts a company their details or product delivery data can be readily accessed. A single view of the customer may also be produced for tactical purposes where the customer data are analysed to build up a model of different customer groupings which are then used in marketing campaigns to provide more relevant material.

Customer data integration
The process of creating a single view of each customer

Data validation

The problems of data quality or inherent information quality mentioned in the earlier section can be reduced and controlled by checks performed when data are entered into database systems. This is known as '**data validation**', a systems control process to improve the quality of data by checking that they have been entered correctly and prompting the user, informing them of incorrect data entry.

Validation is usually built into database systems such that when the information architecture is defined, and the database tables created, the following types of check can be created for different fields:

Data validation
A process to improve the quality of data by checking that they have been entered correctly and prompting the user to inform them of incorrect data entry

- *Data type checking.* Field types will be defined, such as text (alphanumeric), number, currency or date. Text characters will not be permitted in a number field and when a user enters a date, for example, the software will prompt the user if it is not a valid date.

- *Data range checking.* Since storage needs to be pre-allocated in databases, designers will specify the number of digits required for each field. For example, a field for holding the quantity of an item ordered would typically only need to vary from 1 to 999. So, three digits are required. If the user made an error and entered four digits, then they would be warned by the database that this was not possible.

- *Input limits.* This is another form of range checking when the input range cannot be specified through the number of digits alone. For example, if the maximum number of an item that could be ordered is 5, perhaps due to a special offer, this would be specified as a limit of 1–5. The user would not be permitted to enter 0.

- *Restricted value checking.* This usually occurs for text values that are used to describe particular attributes of an entity. For example, in a database for an airline, the type of booking would have to be stored. This could be a restricted choice of standard or business. Once the restricted choices have been specified, the software will ensure that only one of these choices is permitted, usually by prompting the user with a list of the available alternatives.

- *Unique value checking.* Unique values are required for the primary key fields used in tables to definitively identify each record. For example, each customer or product must have a distinct number. A database will reject a number for a key field that has already been used or can autogenerate a key field.

- *Multiple field validation.* If there are business rules which mean that allowable input is governed by more than one field, then these rules must be programmed in. For example, in the estate agent database, there could be a separate field for commission shown as a percentage of house price, such as 1.5 per cent, and a separate field showing the amount, such as £500. In this situation the programmer would have to write code that would automatically calculate the commission amount depending on the percentage entered.

- *Referential integrity checking.* This is a specialized case of multiple field validation – it is used to check that the primary and secondary key fields between records in different tables are correct. This is a built-in feature of many databases, but sometimes it is not switched on since it can degrade system performance.

Data quality auditing

Data quality auditing
A structured approach to assessing data quality using database queries and manual checking

We now turn to approaches that can be used to improve data quality once the data have been entered into the database. To improve data quality, a key approach is to understand what the level of data quality is. This process is known as '**data quality auditing**'. This is a combination of systems control and human control. Data quality auditing is performed on actual records in the database. This can be done on an ad-hoc basis through performing database queries designed to test data quality. This is easier for some aspects of data quality than others. Returning to the postal code example from earlier in the chapter it is relatively easy to test for field completeness and validity. To test the former a query can be performed to assess the number of records with a blank postal code. To check validity postal codes could be assessed against the known values of postal codes. It is more difficult to establish accuracy of data since the postal code may no longer be valid if the person has moved. This is difficult to test for, because of the time and cost of checking random entries in the database to identify errors. An audit will often use this combined approach, evaluating all records for aspects of data quality such as completeness, but using a sample to check for other aspects of data quality such as accuracy.

Data profiling
Data analysis performed to assess the data quality of attributes within a database

Another automated approach to data quality auditing is **data profiling** (Olson, 2002). This analyses the data quality within the context of the data dictionary. For example, a birth date field might be checked to assess the percentage of times it is complete and within the right format. Olson describes other data quality problems discovered through this technique, such as attributes documented for one use, but used for another, unused attributes and wrongly coded fields which should have a defined value. Software such as that from Evoke (**www.evokesoftware.com**) is now available to perform this type of analysis.

Data cleansing

Database cleansing
Typically an automated approach to improve the quality of a customer database

The quality of existing data can also be improved by database cleansing or **data cleansing**. This is also a systems control. Data cleansing is most commonly conducted on databases of customers or potential customers where it is important that customer details be up to date for inbound and outbound communications. An inbound communication to an organization such as a phone call requires that the customer details can be found easily and are accurate. For outbound communications by phone or post it is also important that accurate customer details are available. A common problem is where there is more than one record for each customer or household. This may result in contacting the wrong address or incurring cost or annoying customers as several communications are sent to the same address.

De-duplication
Reduces the occurrence of multiple records about the same customer through comparing fields

There are two main forms of database cleansing, which are known as 'de-duplication' and 'hygiene processing'. De-duplication is needed to reduce the occurrence of multiple records about the same customer. The process of de-duplication or 'de-duping' involves an initial matching on certain fields such as name and address to identify potential duplicates and then deleting these duplicates while minimizing overkill (to avoid deleting records which appear to be matched, but are different) and underkill (records that are not matched, but are, in fact, duplicates). Matchkey processing is most commonly used: this involves taking the first letter of the different components of name, position, company and address. Fuzzy logic algorithms are now used to identify similarities.

Hygiene processing
Automated improvement of data quality by modifying formats and checking for validity

Hygiene processing consists of three steps that are usually performed before 'de-duping':

1 *Formatting* – remove punctuation marks and extra blanks.
2 *Parsing* – identify main data elements, e.g. company names, street name, postcode, which may be in combined fields.
3 *Validation and enhancement* – e.g. a postcode used to check an address or the case correctly applied to first names and surnames.

Note that database cleansing does not solve the problem of poor-quality data, it simply attacks the symptoms. Information quality management also addresses the *causes* of poor-quality data such as data entry, as explained above. However, database cleansing is an activity that needs to occur in every company.

Data migration to data warehouses

An additional data quality issue for customer data is accessibility or rather the lack of accessibility where information is stored in separate silos. As we saw in Chapter 8, data stored in different operational databases can be migrated to a central data warehouse where it is used for analysis of customer characteristics. This is another approach to managing data quality where companies have large customer databases. Mini case study 10.1 'Abbey Bank cuts costs through improving data quality' outlines the approach used and illustrates some of the benefits that have been achieved.

Targets for data quality

Data quality targets
Targets for the level of data quality within a particular database

Once data quality auditing has been performed it will be useful to set **data quality targets**. These are specific numeric targets for individual fields: for example, to achieve 90 per cent completeness and 70 per cent accuracy in postcode fields. Through using targets, the importance of data quality can be communicated to staff and in some cases data entry staff or their managers can be assessed on whether they achieve these targets. The use of targets also implies an ongoing commitment to putting in place procedures to improve data quality and reviewing performance against targets. In some instances data quality can have a major impact on the costs of an organization. Take the example of a single field – an e-mail address. Imagine an airline with millions of customers. If it has not collected an e-mail address for a customer, it will have to send more direct mail communications to customers to inform them of offers and encourage future flights with the carrier. These will be more costly. Through setting a target such as increasing valid e-mail address coverage of the customer base from 50 to 70 per cent within one year, significant savings could be made. E-mail addresses are a particular challenge for data quality since many of us hold several e-mail addresses or change e-mail addresses, so if nothing is done to improve e-mail address

| Activity 10.4 | Procedures for managing information quality – the challenge of the e-mail address |

| Purpose | Explores the notion of data quality further together with approaches that can be defined by managers for improving data quality. |
| Activity | An organization has set the target of increasing from 50 to 80 per cent valid e-mail address data quality within its customer base. You have to devise approaches to ensure this level of data quality is reached. Your approach should include: |

1 Using definitions of data quality to specify what is meant by a 'valid e-mail address'.

2 Defining approaches to capture more e-mail addresses.

(*Tip* Consider how e-mail addresses can be collected at all contact points with customers – both online when they are using web services and also through direct or indirect contact offline.)

3 Defining approaches to ensure e-mail addresses which have been captured are up to date.

accuracy they will become out of date. Activity 10.4 explores this example of managing data quality further.

Human factors in data quality

The importance of data quality may not be immediately evident to staff involved in data entry or their managers. Furthermore, few staff would agree that data quality is interesting, rather work involved with data quality is 'a necessary evil'. However, as we have said, we do need human controls in addition to systems controls. So key management approaches here are building awareness of the importance of data quality, assigning responsibilities for data quality and training in approaches used to achieve data quality. To train staff to improve data quality, English (1999) suggests that those who create data must understand (1) the customers of the data, (2) the quality requirements of their customers, (3) how data are used and (4) the quality of non-quality data.

Definitions of clear responsibilities for data quality are essential for managing data quality. Through putting data quality responsibilities in job descriptions, the importance of data quality is highlighted and staff performance can be reviewed in this area during performance appraisal. Everyone in an organization has data quality management responsibilities. Molineux (2002) defines four typical responsibilities for customer data quality – providers, users, maintainers and owners. Figure 10.12 summarizes what needs to be identified about these different users in an information audit and how their responsibilities should be defined. Molineux notes that problems can occur when responsibilities are split across different departments or processes. These responsibilities can also be applied to other areas – at the end of the chapter we see that similar terms are used for information quality in accounting systems.

Mini case study 10.3 'Managing information quality at the Low-cost Airline Company gives an example of the importance of managing data quality and illustrates a range of methods used to improve data quality such as data cleansing and staff training, incentivization and 'name and shame'. We place more emphasis on human factors in the next section on information quality. We will see that many of the issues are shared with those for data quality.

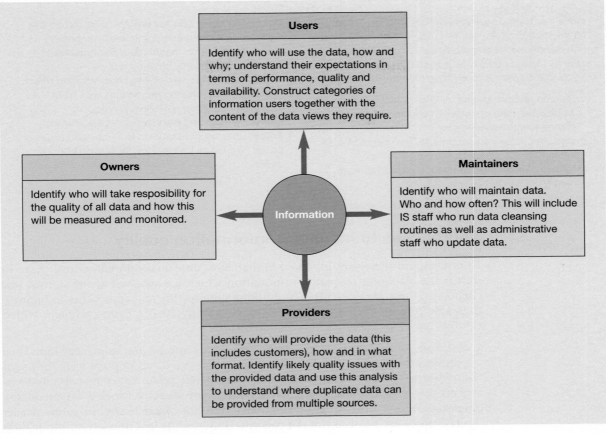

Figure 10.12 Data quality responsibilities
Source: Molineux (2002)

| Mini case study 10.3 | Managing data quality at the Lo-cost Airline Company |

The daily data processing needed for a major international company such as the Lo-cost Airline Company is significant. Each year over 20 million passengers book flights on over 200 routes serving 60 airports. These include both consumer and business bookings. Since its inception, the Lo-cost Airline has created a database of 80 million customer profiles each containing detailed information such as:

- Names and addresses
- Travel type – business or personal
- Inference of travel type – city breaks, stag-nights, packaged holidays, business travel, etc.
- Number of tickets in booking
- Frequency of routes flown
- Booking of related services such as travel packages, car hire and insurance

The company also holds customer communication preferences such as those who opt-in for the company e-newsletter or postal mailings and investor relations.

Customer data is captured through the website (90 per cent of bookings) or by phone bookings and then fed into an online database known as the 'Customer Information System' (CIS). The system screens for data quality. On average, 20 per cent of postal addresses are returned as un-mailable and a further 10 per cent are incomplete. Many of the e-mail addresses or postal addresses are incorrectly entered first time. In these cases a manual follow-up by phone is then completed to correct details where appropriate. If these details are not accurate then some of the millions of dollars used for direct marketing by post, e-mail and the website are wasted, due either to messages not getting through or the offers not being relevant.

The attention that the Lo-cost Airline Company attaches to data quality is indicated by these additional measures to improve data quality:

- Defined responsibilities for data quality assigned to a customer data manager who is part of a small customer intelligence team
- Training courses on data quality are part of all staff inductions
- Data quality targets are used for staff in the call-centre

- Data quality for customer profiles collected on the website is reported and continuously improved
- Quarterly CRM mini-boards for senior managers
- Quarterly data quality steering groups
- Reporting of responsiveness of customers to direct mail and e-mail offering promotions with RFM analysis of customers (Recency, Frequency, Monetary value and also category of bookings)
- Follow-up procedures for when e-mail addresses or postal addresses become invalid (e-mail bounce-backs).

Approaches to managing information quality

To understand the issues involved in managing information quality, one place to start is the attributes of quality information which we reviewed at the start of this chapter. To illustrate the attributes of information quality and approaches to improve them, we refer in each attribute to Mini case study 10.4 'A games retailer', which exhibits typical problems of information quality.

1 *Relevance*. Relevance means providing appropriate information to manage individual processes effectively and control the organization overall. As we have seen, the use of an information audit and the creation of corporate performance management systems are both important approaches which are directly focused on producing relevant information. An information audit was not conducted by the games retailer since they were not aware of the concept. However, the lack of relevant information was clear to managers in the organization and was a key driver for the project. The main lack of information was the lack of detailed information through drill-down. Putting in place controls to manage relevance is a key method of countering information overload. Automated systems controls can be helpful in achieving this. Take the example of an intranet. An information audit will identify information requirements in terms of types of information and frequency and then systems controls can be used to supply relevant information through different mechanisms. Consider a 'newswire' service such as PRNewswire eWatch (**www.prnewswire.com**). These types of service can provide relevant information about competitors and markets by e-mail alerts using a number of systems control techniques:

- *Keyword filtering* – only sends news articles that include keywords such as company names or product names.
- *Range filtering* – only sends information about a change in share price if it exceeds a certain percentage.
- *Grouping content* – e.g. by geography, industry, competitors.
- *Aggregated alerts* – options to receive individual alerts or digests for the entire day or week.

The Really Simple Syndication (RSS) approach described in Chapter 9, where any news or type of content is received by specialist reader software, offers a method of sending alerts and news to employees that uses a different broadcast method to e-mail and is not subject to the same conflicts with spam or spam filters (Chapter 12).

2 *Presentation*. Presentation is of less importance than relevance. It is not a quality issue that can be readily specified as a strategic requirement of information quality. Presentation is normally an issue that arises at the level of an individual application and the detailed issues in how information will be presented as graphs, tables

and documents is usually specified as part of the analysis in systems development. However, it is easier to achieve the required presentation if organizations have a strategic approach to information systems. The use of enterprise resource planning systems together with an enterprise-wide information architecture is essential to provide facilities such as roll-up summary information and drill-down to the level of detail required. Enterprise-wide databases and operational applications were already in place in the case of the games retailer; however, the correct level of information could not be presented. The data warehouse and business intelligence system were required to address this deficiency. These were provided from a separate vendor and essentially 'bolted on' to the existing infrastructure. Companies considered for these tools included Cognos (**www.cognos.com**) and Business Objects (**www.businessobjects.com**).

3 *Timeliness*. Like presentation, this attribute of information quality is to a great extent dependent on having the correct technology infrastructure and information architecture in place. If the right systems are in place, it will be possible to access real-time information. A further issue is how quickly internal performance information can be summarized for review at the end of accounting periods such as monthly, quarterly and annually. As well as having the right systems in place, targets and procedures for producing relevant reports more rapidly are required. For the games retailer, reducing the time to produce the 'report pack' at the end of reporting periods was a further requirement of the system.

4 *Accessibility*. Problems in accessing information are present in many organizations. In Chapter 2, we explained how information is often held in departmental silos. The use of enterprise resource planning systems which have a single or integrated information repository is one approach to avoiding this problem with information quality. We also in saw in Mini case study 10.1 'Abbey Bank cuts costs through improving data quality', at the start of this chapter, that migrating data into a single data warehouse will improve access to information.

For the games retailer described in the mini case study that follows, a further benefit of the new system was the capability to share information more widely within the organization. It was hoped that the new system would be used to share information with less senior managers and for them to be given greater responsibility. A further accessibility problem faced by the games company was the many different log-ins required.

From this brief review of the attributes of information quality it can be seen that common approaches to improve information quality are the selection of appropriate performance management or business intelligence applications (Chapters 2 and 6) and enterprise-wide information architecture (Chapter 8).

Mini case study 10.4   A games retailer

This UK-based company has a large product range, with over 10,000 current products available. It has direct sales operations in the UK, the US, Canada, France, Germany, Spain and Australia. Around three-quarters of sales are to international markets. Products are sold through its own own chain of 500 retail shops and over 5000 independent toy and hobby shops around the world. These outlets are complemented by the growing mail order and online sales businesses. Some games products are manufactured internally and some are sourced externally.

As a rapidly expanding international company, one of the challenges it faces is managing information about the manufacture, distribution and sales of products in its different markets. To help improve information quality a project to introduce new systems, including a data warehouse system, was implemented.

Existing applications portfolio
The organization uses different applications to support manufacturing, inventory management, sales at tills

and distribution. While this combination proved effective for managing the day-to-day operations of the company, it was believed that better understanding of product sales could improve the performance of the organization further. As part of the project, a data warehouse and business intelligence system were purchased to achieve this. The relationship between these applications is shown in Figure 10.13.

Aims – improving information quality

The main aim of the data warehouse project was to improve access to measures which could be evaluated in order to improve the performance of the business. The new system needed to be able to provide different levels of detail on the performance of different product lines, different channels to market such as retail, direct, trade and Internet, and different geographical markets. Drilling down as part of ad-hoc reporting was required from country level to find out the performance of an individual product in an individual store. Better-quality information on fast-moving lines was also required to be able to better respond to demand. Exception reports were also required to highlight underperforming regions or stores. To enable comparison between geographic markets, the retailer uses a measure of market penetration based on the average spend per head of population in a country.

In the previous reporting process, 'information packs' were produced monthly and quarterly in the finance and operations department. These contain standard information about financial performance necessary to run the business, such as sales figures and lists of debtors. A further requirement of the system was to improve the efficiency of this reporting. While it was not anticipated that costs would be reduced through a need for fewer staff, it was anticipated that the system would streamline the process of reporting and enable improved metrics and faster production of reports as the company expands. This would be achieved without the need to recruit further staff. A key reporting benefit envisaged from the new system was a reduction in lag between the end-of-month or end-of-quarter close and when reports can be distributed, analysed and acted on. As part of the change introduced with the system it was also intended to increase access to reporting information, enabling senior managers to delegate some aspects of process analysis and actioning.

The project also had to support elements of the retailer's long-term strategic IS vision. One aspect of this was a single access point to systems. Different log-ins were required for many of the systems shown in Figure 10.13 and some re-keying of data between systems was required. The new project also had to provide information through the company's intranet – a separate project to provide better access to company policies and procedures and share knowledge between staff.

Source: Fictitious case used in teaching

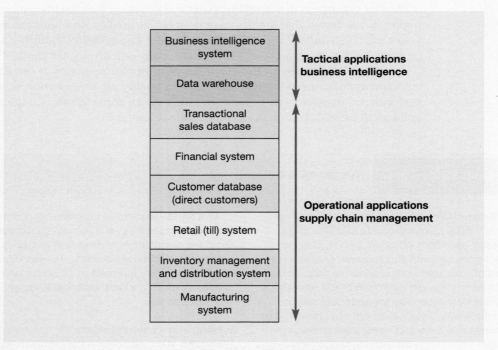

Figure 10.13 Relationship between the main applications at the games retailer

Human factors in information quality

Developing a successful human dimension to information quality is dependent on developing an appropriate **information behaviours and values capability**, according to Marchand et al. (2002). These authors have reviewed the human resources and management control literature to develop what they refer to as 'an integrated view of enhancing information use'. They identify six different dimensions of information behaviours and values capability and then for each dimension ask questions which assess organizational capability.

1 Proactiveness

Proactiveness is characterized by the willingness of staff to use information in an innovative way and to monitor and respond to changes in their environment.

Evaluated by asking whether staff:

- actively seek out information on changes and trends;
- use information to respond quickly to changes in the competitive environment;
- use information to create or enhance products and services;
- use market intelligence, using information to support.

2 Transparency

Transparency is characterized by openness about information, particularly that which may be sensitive. It is related to integrity and openness.

Evaluated by asking whether staff:

- trust one another to share information on failures;
- who are managers encourage openness.

3 Integrity

Integrity refers to the ethics and morality of using information at an individual and organizational level.

In this case the organization will want to discourage those behaviours which reduce the quality of information. The questions are evaluated negatively.

Evaluated by asking whether staff:

- knowingly pass on inaccurate information;
- distribute information to support decisions after the fact;
- keep information to themselves;
- exploit business information for personal gain.

4 Sharing

This dimension evaluates the sharing of both sensitive and non-sensitive information. Sometimes non-sensitive information is not shared since there is a sense of loss of control, but sharing information can be of value.

Evaluated by asking whether staff:

- share information within teams;
- share information across functional boundaries;
- share information across organizational boundariers, i.e. with customers, suppliers and partners.

5 Control

Control is characterized by the use of information to manage process and organizational performance.

Evaluated by asking:

- Is information on business performance presented to employees and does it influence working behaviour?
- Do staff use information to improve their performance?
- Is information so scattered that it is difficult to control people and processes (reverse scored)?
- Is information distributed on a 'need to know' basis, so employees know 'what to do', but 'do not know why they are doing it'?

6 Formality

The main concern with formality is whether informal, potentially unreliable sources are used in preference to formal, potentially more reliable sources.

Do staff:

- trust informal over formal sources of information;
- use informal information sources extensively even though formal sources are available and credible;
- use informal sources to verify and improve the quality of formal information sources?

Evaluating the information behaviours and values presented above is a powerful diagnostic tool through which organizations can assess the human element of their information management capability. It highlights aspects of information quality which are quite different from, but at least as important as, the pragmatic elements of information quality discussed earlier in the chapter, such as relevance, timeliness, presentation and accessibility. Of these four characteristics, relevance and accessibility are most closely related to information behaviours and values. Such factors are not traditionally a core element of an information audit, but they could readily be incorporated.

While it is relatively straightforward to put in place controls to improve data quality, it is relatively difficult to put in place controls to improve these human dimensions of information quality. We have seen that data quality controls work through defining data quality requirements and then putting in place procedures to improve data quality on entry and to maintain data through auditing and cleansing. With information quality it is much more difficult to define what is good-quality information. We can assess the data quality characteristics such as completeness or validity of records in a database relatively easily compared to assessing the relevance of information. Information may be irrelevant to certain people or tasks but highly relevant to others. Furthermore, the framework presented above tends to encourage openness in sharing information when it talks about dimensions such as proactiveness, transparency and sharing.

Responsibilities for information quality

An information quality policy should clearly identify responsibilities for information quality in order to improve quality.

Xu et al. (2003) suggest that five types of stakeholders in information quality have been identified in different information quality studies. They illustrate the types of person in the context of accounting information systems (AIS):

1 *Information producers (providers).* These create or collect information for the AIS. Ultimately, these are the people in the company who collect sales order details and the purchasing department who are involved in raising purchase orders and paying invoices.

2 *Information custodians (maintainers)*. Those who design, develop and operate the AIS.

3 *Information consumer (users)*. Those who use the accounting information in their work activities, i.e. the accountants.

4 *Information managers (owners)*. Those who are responsible for managing the information quality in the AIS.

5 *Internal auditors*. Those who monitor the information quality in the AIS.

It will be apparent that the first four are consistent with the different responsibilities for data quality defined in the section on data quality at the start of the chapter.

Summary

1 The DIKAR model (Data–Information–Knowledge–Action–Results) is useful for understanding different forms of information quality. Ultimately information quality is important in supporting decisions to produce organizational actions and results.

2 Data quality or inherent information quality describes the degree to which data accurately reflect the object they represent. Its main attributes are accuracy, completeness, validity and consistency.

3 Information quality refers to the degree of usefulness and value data have in context, to support organizational processes. Its main attributes are relevance, presentation, timeliness and availability.

4 Knowledge quality is dependent on the capability of people to attach significance to information to inform their decisions and the ability to convert it into information to convey to other people.

5 Corporate performance management is an important aspect of information quality which defines the capability of an organization to develop business metrics which can be used to improve its competitive performance.

6 The information audit assesses information and knowledge quality within an organization by analysis of information resources, usage and flows. It is a key tool in understanding information quality.

7 An information quality policy specifies systems controls (typically software controls) and human controls which are developed through training and education to improve information quality.

8 Data quality improvement is achieved through defining data quality, systems controls such as data validation, data quality auditing, profiling and data cleansing and human controls such as setting data quality targets, training and review.

9 Information quality control is achieved through defining information quality, understanding human factors and providing clear responsibilities for information quality.

Exercises

Self-assessment questions

1 Explain how the DIKAR model can be used to inform different aspects of information quality.

2 What is the difference between data quality, information quality and knowledge quality?

3 Explain the purpose and different applications of an information audit.

4 Describe the work involved in an information audit.

5 Summarize approaches to improve organizational data quality.

6 Summarize approaches to improve organizational information quality.

Essay and discussion questions

1 Assess the importance of information quality to organizations.

2 What approaches can organizations take to improve information quality?

3 Assess the extent of adoption of the information audit approach by businesses and explore reasons for your findings.

4 Write an essay on the importance of human controls on information quality.

5 Produce a report on approaches to improve information quality for accounting information systems.

6 You have recently been appointed to the newly created position of 'customer information quality manager' at the Lo-cost Airline Company. Create a plan to improve information quality. Your report will be read by senior managers at the airline so you will need to explain concepts and justify the approaches you suggest.

References

COBIT (2000) *COBIT Framework*, 3rd edn. Released by the COBIT Steering Committee and the IT Governance Institute. Available online at: www.isaca.org/cobit.

Computing (2008) £100 million Contract Aims to Avoid Friendly Fire. By Janie Davies. Available online at: www.computing.co.uk/computing/news/2213333/mod-boosts-ground-troop.

Consultants Advisory (2003) *Integrated Business Intelligence and Corporate Performance Management*. Report, September. Available online at: www.consultant-advisory.com.

Data Warehousing Institute (2002) *Data Quality and the Bottom Line. Achieving Business Success through a Commitment to High Quality Data*. Research report by Wayne Eckerson of Data Warehousing Institute. www.dw-institute.com/dqreport.

Di Mattia, S. and Blumenstein, L. (2000) In search of the information audit: essential tool or cumbersome process? *Library Journal*, 125(4), 48.

English, L. (1999) *Improving Data Warehouse and Business Information Quality. Methods for Reducing Costs and Increasing Profits*. Wiley, New York.

Friedlein, A. (2002) *Maintaining and Evolving Successful Commercial Websites: Managing Change, Content, Customer Relationships, and Site Measurement*. Morgan Kaufmann, London.

Henczel, S. (2001) *The Information Audit: A Practical Guide*. Springer Verlag, Heidelberg.

JISC (2000) Case Study on the development of an Information Strategy based on the JISC Guidelines into a practical tool for the support of the University of Glamorgan Strategic Planning Process. Project report. Published online at: www.jiscinfonet.ac.uk/Resources/external-resources/glamorgan-is-case-study/view.

Kaplan, R. S. and Norton, D. P. (1993) Putting the balanced scorecard to work. *Harvard Business Review,* September–October, 134–42.

Lillrank, P. (2003) The quality of information. *International Journal of Quality and Reliability Management*, 20(6), 691–703.

Marchand, D., Kettinger, W. and Rollins, J. (2002) *Information Orientation: The Link to Business Performance.* Oxford University Press, Oxford.

Miller, H. (1996) The multiple dimensions of information quality. *Information Systems Management*, 13,(2), 79.

Molineux, P. (2002) *Exploiting CRM. Connecting with Customers.* Hodder & Stoughton, London.

Murray, P. (2000) How smarter companies get results from KM. In D. Marchand, T. Davenport and T. Dickenson (eds) *Mastering Information Management.* Financial Times Prentice Hall, Harlow, pp. 187–92.

Neely, A. (1998) *Measuring Business Performance.* Profile Books, London.

Neely, A., Adams, C. and Kennerley, M. (2002) *The Performance Prism. The Scorecard for Measuring and Managing Business Success.* Financial Times Prentice Hall, Harlow.

Olson, J. (2002) Data profiling: the key to success in integration projects. Article in *Business Integration*, February. www.bijonline.com/PDF/Olsonr-rFebrissue.pdf.

Olve, N., Roy, J. and Wetter, M. (1999) *Performance Drivers. A Practical Guide to Using the Balanced Scorecard.* Wiley, Chichester.

Orna, E. (1999) *Practical Information Policies,* 2nd edn. Gower, Basingstoke.

Perspectives on Performance (2003) Gazing into the crystal ball: The future of performance measurement. *Newsletter of Performance Management Association*, 2(2), 12–14. www.som.cranfield.ac.uk/som/cbp/pma/newslettervol2issue.pdf.

Swash, G. (1997) The information audit. *The Journal of Managerial Psychology*, 12(5), 312–18.

Tillmann, G. (2004) A CIO's view of the balanced scorecard. *strategy+business*, Booz Allen Hamilton house magazine, Issue 34, IT section, pp. 1–5. www.strategy-business.com.

Truscott, W. (2003) *Six Sigma. Continual Improvement for Businesses.* Butterworth-Heinemann, Oxford.

Xu, H. and Koronios, A. (2004) Understanding information quality in e-business. *Journal of Computer Information Systems*, 45(2), 73–82.

Xu, H., Horn, J., Nord, G. and Lin, B. (2003) Key issues of accounting information quality management: Australian case studies. *Industrial Management and Data Systems*, 103(7), 461–70.

Further reading

English, L. (1999) *Improving Data Warehouse and Business Information Quality. Methods for Reducing Costs and Increasing Profits.* Wiley, New York. This book by Larry English provides a guide for managers on the characteristics of information quality and gives detailed guidelines on managing information quality.

Henczel, S. (2001) *The Information Audit: A Practical Guide.* Springer Verlag, Heidelberg. Describes an approach to completing an information audit; includes Australian case studies to illustrate the different stages of the information audit.

Lillrank, P. (2003) The quality of information. *International Journal of Quality and Reliability Management*, 20(6), 691–703. This paper provides a detailed review of information quality theory.

Orna, E. (1999) *Practical Information Policies,* 2nd edn. Gower, Basingstoke. Describes an alternative approach to completing an information audit; includes UK case studies.

visit the
www

Weblinks

Business Performance Innovation Network (www.bpinetwork.org).

The Data Warehouseing Institute site (www.dw-institute.com) Research company site with some free content on data quality.

InfoImpact (www.infoimpact.com) Website produced by Larry English containing articles on information quality.

Information Management (www.information-management.com) Publication focusing on data mining and business intelligence. Some articles on information quality.

Motorola University on Six Sigma (http://mu.motorola.com/sixsigma.shtml) A good summary from the originators.

For multiple-choice questions, and annotated weblinks relating to this chapter visit this book's website at: **www.pearsoned.co.uk/chaffey**

11

Managing information services quality

Objective

To evaluate management approaches for the delivery of cost-effective, high-quality information services to end-users.

Learning outcomes

After reading this chapter, you will be able to:

● Identify different types of information service delivery.

● Explain the concept of total cost of ownership.

● Define approaches for managing end-user computing and outsourcing.

Management issues

Typical questions facing managers related to this topic:

● How do we evaluate service levels delivered to end-users?

● How do we manage end-user development?

● How do we minimize total cost of ownership for information systems?

Links to other chapters

The main related chapters are:

➤ *Chapter 6* on IS strategy introduces the range of information services which are defined as part of an information systems strategy.

➤ *Chapter 8* on information architecture describes methods of securing systems against unauthorized access.

➤ *Chapter 12* on legal, ethical and security issues explains laws introduced to protect company information. It also integrates coverage of laws to protect unauthorized data access with a review of methods for protecting information.

Introduction

In the previous chapter we explored the approaches which organizations use to improve the quality of their information resources. Accessibility was one of the key attributes of information quality which was discussed. The current chapter is essentially about accessibility – how access to data, information and knowledge through information systems is managed and controlled. The degree of accessibility to information resources in an organization is dependent on a combination of the quality of the information and communications technology (ICT) infrastructure and the skills of the people with access to information, commonly known as their 'computer literacy'. In the era of the Internet, extranets and intranets, these people may be customers, partners or employees. Management of the ICT infrastructure is necessary to provide rapid, continuously available access to information. Effective management and development of the skills of information users through education and training is necessary to help them use the information and technology to its full capabilities to support their tasks. Requests from information users about problems with information access also need to be answered via support staff. The quality of the data also needs to be managed using the approaches described in the last chapter, such as data profiling, data validation, data cleansing and back-up. Controls also have to be put in place to minimize loss in productivity through staff using modern information resources such as e-mail and the World Wide Web. Protecting of information resources from deletion or corruption is also needed through access controls and back-up and restore procedures.

Information services delivery
Management of ICT infrastructure, information and support of information users in accessing a range of information resources

Together, the operational management of access to information and data management are known as 'information services delivery'. The type and name of the organizational unit which delivers information services vary widely according to the type of organization. Typical titles of this unit or department arranged from modern to traditional labels are:

- Information services
- Information and library services
- Information centre (typically a US term)
- Computing services
- IT department
- IT help-desk
- IS department
- Data processing (DP department).

Traditionally, information services have focused on management of the technology or data processing, hence descriptions such as IT or IS department and computing services. Increasingly the focus is on managing information delivery at an acceptable level of service quality. This focus is accentuated since many technology responsibilities are now 'outsourced' to a third-party supplier. Many public organizations such as the UK National Health Service now no longer have an 'IT department', rather there is an 'Information services unit'. In larger organizations, the responsibilities for management of the technology, information and user support may be split into different units. In keeping with modern parlance we refer to 'information services' in this chapter.

End-user computing
(1) The resourcing and delivery of information services to end-users, (2) the development of business applications by end-users

From an academic standpoint, the term 'end-user computing' has traditionally been used to refer to the study of the management issues involved with providing services for non-specialist users of information systems. That is essentially anyone who is not an IT specialist who may be involved in developing or supporting systems.

(Of course, IT staff can also be considered to be end-users of computing services.) End-user computing was a widely discussed issue within the information systems literature during the 1980s and early 1990s, but since then it has not achieved such prominence. Within industry, however, it remains significant, with the issues we will cover in this chapter, such as managing spam and viruses, help-desk management, reducing the total cost of ownership of hardware and software applications, outsourcing and employee monitoring, all prominent.

The 'end-user computing' concept also incorporates 'end-user development'. This refers to non-IS specialists creating their own applications to support their work. The best-known example of this is the creation of spreadsheet models and reporting systems and databases by end-users. With the capabilities of office tools such as the Microsoft Excel spreadsheet and the Access database, such tools are widely used by staff.

In this chapter we look at the many management issues involved with delivering information services to end-users. Some of these were introduced in Chapter 6 on IS strategy which outlines the range of information services which are defined as part of an information systems strategy. In this chapter we look at the operational and strategic issues in managing information services delivery in five areas. First, we look at the types of information service delivered, including information delivery and search services, information protection and counter-measures to protect end-users from the impact of disruption from viruses, spam and e-mail overload. Second, we consider the provision of help-desk services to answer user queries and give support on applications development. Third, we review controls needed on access to information services, including managing employee Internet access and monitoring employee use of websites and e-mail. This coverage is brief since this is covered in the final chapter together with the legal controls on monitoring. Fourth, we look at how the ICT infrastructure is used to deliver a good level of information delivery in terms of speed and availability. Finally, we look at approaches to resourcing information services. Here we examine the costs of managing information services and approaches to reduce the total cost of ownership. The scrapped PCs shown at the start of the chapter remind us that with the life of the average business PC at around three years, managing the direct costs of hardware and the indirect costs of supporting this hardware is an issue in all organizations. Outsourcing information services delivery to third parties is now a common approach to help reduce costs, but it is also contentious and we look at the benefits of this approach in some detail.

The different types of information service and the sequence in which they are covered in different parts of this chapter are summarized in Figure 11.1.

End-user development
The creation of applications by end-users (typically based on spreadsheets and databases)

What is information service quality?

Service quality gap model
A tool for assessing the level of service quality based on the difference between users expectations and the service experience delivered

To understand the nature of information service quality it is useful to look at a model used by researchers in marketing to assess customer service quality experienced by consumers, for example of a banking service. The service quality gap model was developed by Parasuraman et al. (1985) in order to understand the factors that affect customers' perception of the quality of a service. In a business information management context, the customers are the different types of end-user in an organization who use information to support them in their work, from senior management through employees across all departments to partners who access the company's information resources from outside the company. In this model, which is shown in Figure 11.2, the perception of the level of service quality is dependent on understanding the differences between expected performance and actual performance experience.

It can be seen from Figure 11.2 that expected service is influenced by three factors. The first factor is word-of-mouth communications from other employees in a differ-

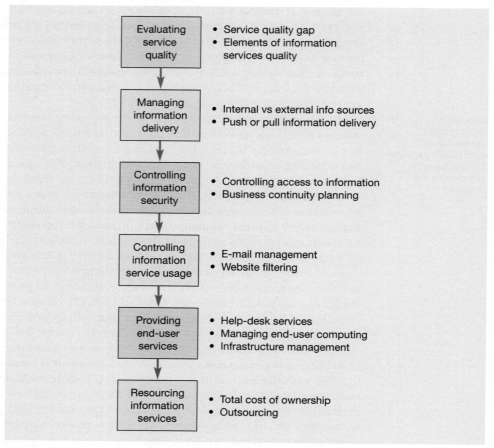

Figure 11.1 Different aspects of information service quality management

ent part of the organization who experience a different level of service, or more likely other employees in other organizations with whom they discuss the experience. The second and most important factor is personal needs – what the individual believes is necessary to do their work efficiently. The third factor is past experience from previous employment or use of information services at home such as an Internet service

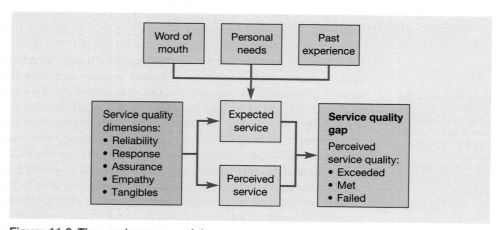

Figure 11.2 The service gap model
Source: Parasuraman et al. (1985)

provider. Based on these factors, the users of information services will form an opinion of the level of service compared to their expectations. Their opinion of different aspects of information service delivery will be that it meets their expectations, exceeds their expectations, or falls below them. Their overall opinion will be governed by subconsciously reviewing different aspects of service delivery, which in this model are referred to as: reliability, response, assurance, empathy, tangibles.

Attributes of service quality

What are the elements of service delivery shown in Figure 11.2 in an information management context? Well, they will vary according to the type of service, but are broadly similar for different services. Let's take the example of a company intranet. The elements of service quality depend on both human and technology contributions. We will take the original meaning from the work of Parasuraman et al. (1985) and then apply it to an intranet:

- *reliability* – the ability to perform the service dependably and accurately – for an intranet this would be influenced by the speed at which pages can be downloaded and the availability – the average amount of 'down-time' there is each day;
- *responsiveness* – a willingness to help customers and provide prompt service – for an intranet this could refer to response time to download information, but also how responsive the staff supporting the intranet were;
- *assurance* – the knowledge and courtesy of employees and their ability to convey trust and confidence – this is again something that is conveyed by the support or help-desk staff;
- *tangibles* – the physical appearance of facilities and communications – in the context of an intranet this is the information quality attributes such as relevance, accuracy, timeliness and presentation which are covered separately in the next section and in the previous chapter;
- *empathy* – providing caring, individualized attention – for an intranet this would refer to how helpful the staff supporting the intranet were. It could also refer to the overall 'look and feel' of the service, indicating the degree to which it could help solve users' tasks. Empathy could be increased by interactive services such as asking question online.

How can this model be applied by managers of information services? What are its implications? First, it suggests the importance of setting targets for service quality and measuring service quality. Current service quality perceptions can be evaluated by asking the customers, the end-users, about their opinions of different aspects of service such as information quality, the speed with which information is delivered over the network and how helpful the help-desk staff are. Information services users can be asked about the issues that most concern them and areas they would most like to see improved. Regular e-mail-based questionnaire surveys or focus groups and observation can also be used to assess service quality.

For some attributes of service quality such as information delivery and network or server reliability it is not necessary to ask users, since these can be measured directly. Information delivery can be measured in megabits per second and reliability can be measured as percentage reliability. For these types of numerical measure it will also be possible for IT managers to benchmark or compare service levels with those of other companies. This is similar to the service quality measures posted by airlines and railways about on-time arrival. For an intranet and extranet and other applications, the level of usage, which is one indication of satisfaction, can be measured automatically. The percentage of staff using these services can be measured through the number and frequency of log-ins and engagement with content such as the average number of pages viewed per day or queries completed, which can be assessed through a web log file. We will see later in the chapter that service-level agreements between an organization and its suppliers of information services are used to define acceptable parameters of and levels of service quality.

To summarize this discussion of information service quality, complete Activity 11.1 which places service quality in the context of different information users at a university.

Activity 11.1	End-user information service quality requirements

Purpose

To review the types of information services needed by end-users and their level of quality.

Activity

Assess the information service requirements of three different types of end-user at a university or college: (a) a student completing an assignment using a PC in a library, (b) a member of academic staff writing a research proposal and (c) an administrator involved in student recruitment. You should list their requirements or needs and the level of service quality they expect by answering these questions:

1 What will cause frustrations in the end-users' use of information systems?

2 What types of support may they expect from specialist information services staff?

3 What are the characteristics and types of information that are needed to support these end-users?

Assessing online service quality

Two of the most significant frameworks for assessing online service quality are:

- WEBQUAL (Loiacono et al., 2000), which considers 14 dimensions. It has been criticized for relating too much to functional design issues rather than service issues. The 14 dimensions are:

    1 *Information quality*. The concern that information provided is accurate, updated, and appropriate.
    2 *Functional fit to task*. The extent to which users believe that the website meets their needs.
    3 *Tailored communications*. Communications can be tailored to meet the user's needs.
    4 *Trust*. Secure communication and observance of information privacy.
    5 *Response time*. Time to get a response after a request or an interaction with a website.
    6 *Ease of understanding*. Easy to read and understand.
    7 *Intuitive operations*. Easy to operate and navigate.
    8 *Visual appeal*. The aesthetics of the site.
    9 *Innovativeness*. The creativity and uniqueness of the website.
    10 *Emotional appeal*. The emotional affect of using the website and intensity of involvement.
    11 *Consistent image*. The website does not create dissonance for the user by an image incompatible with that projected by the firm through other media.
    12 *On-line completeness*. Allowing all or most necessary transactions to be completed online (e.g. purchasing over the website).

13 *Relative advantage*. Equivalent or better than other means of interacting with the company.

14 *Customer service*. The response to customer inquiries, comments, and feedback when such response requires more than one interaction.

- E-SERVQUAL (Zeithaml et al., 2002), which contains seven dimensions. The first four dimensions are classified as the core service scale, and the latter three dimensions are regarded as a recovery scale, since they are only relevant when online customers have questions or problems:

1 *Efficiency* refers to the ability of the customers to get to the website, search for information or transact as required.

2 *Fulfilment* involves the accuracy of service promises, including products in stock availability and delivering the products in the promised time.

3 *Reliability* is associated with the technical functioning of the site, including availability and performance.

4 *Privacy* is related to assurance that shopping behaviour data are not shared and that credit card information is secure.

5 *Responsiveness* refers to the ability of e-tailers to provide appropriate support information to customers when requested.

6 *Compensation* involves returns facilities for refunds and return shipping and handling costs.

7 *Contact* is the ability of customers to talk to a live service agent online.

Both are useful frameworks which can be still applied to evaluate online service quality today, although arguably they omit the importance of accessibility, findability techniques, multi-channel integration and customer reviews and ratings (as discussed in the later section on merchandising as a determinant of satisfactory experience).

Case study 11.1

Multi-channel customer service

In 2008 Transversal conducted their third assessment of UK Companies' online customer service. The study of the 100 most popular websites establishes their ability to answer simple queries. After all, customers expect prompt answers without having to explore multiple screens and layers of Help and FAQ pages.

If answers cannot be provided via the website then the customer should be directed seamlessly to alternative modes of assistance. This investigation also assesses the organization's ability to deal with customers that subsequently make contact via e-mail or telephone.

A number of different sectors were covered:

- Banking
- Insurance
- Consumer electronics
- Utilities
- Travel
- Telecoms
- Grocery retail

- Fashion retail
- CD/DVD/games retail
- Consumer electronics retail

Like most studies of this type, the results were poor; often simple questions were best answered by telephoning an automated call-centre rather than by searching the website. Responses to customer e-mails had deteriorated since the previous studies were conducted, with many organizations focusing on the speed rather than the quality of the reply. Less than half of all replies were found to answer the customer query completely.

Summary of findings:

- Websites could answer only 50 per cent of customer queries.
- Average response time to e-mails was 46 hours.
- The Insurance sector provided the worst response to customer e-mails, with only 10 per cent giving complete answers.

- The Banking sector's response time to e-mails has deteriorated from 17 hours in 2005 to 22 hours in 2006 and 30 hours in 2007.
- E-mails to Consumer Electronics companies can wait an average of 36 hours for a response.
- E-mail response times in the Utilities sector have improved from 102 hours in 2006 to a still inadequate 53 hours in 2007.
- The quality of responses to e-mails in the Utilities sector has deteriorated from providing full and accurate replies to 70 per cent of queries in 2006 to just 15 per cent in 2007.
- Online Fashion Retailers were worst for replying to e-mails, taking 23 hours in 2006 and 116 hours in 2007.

- Grocery Retail also deteriorated in the quality and speed of e-mail response, taking on average 94 hours to reply and providing full and accurate responses to only 55 per cent of enquiries.
- CD/DVD Retailers proved that it is possible to provide high-quality service with the fastest response time of 1 hour and 80% accuracy of answer.

Question

If you were the Chief Information Officer (CIO) of a large retail organization, how would you undertake an analysis of the quality of your online services?

Costs of service delivery

The model of Figure 11.2 omits one key factor, and this is cost. Investment is needed to meet or exceed customer service quality standards. If companies could afford to continually update to the latest technology or could employ one member of support staff for every ten employees then this would be more likely to result in excellent service. However, investing in technology and support staff is expensive. The reality of the role of the information services manager is that they have to deliver the best service they can with a fixed budget which often declines year on year. If information service managers can reduce the cost of purchasing and maintaining hardware, software and networks then more money can be devoted to the human aspects of service delivery. We will return to this topic later in this chapter when we look in more detail at the factors that affect the total cost of ownership of hardware and software. Another approach that can help control costs is outsourcing information services to a third party. This is a common activity to which the final section is devoted.

Managing information delivery

Naturally a key role of an information services function is to manage delivery of quality information to end-users. In Chapters 2 and 6 we saw how enterprise resource planning and e-business systems are used to manage information for operational and tactical management of business processes. This information is based on business events where the business is directly involved in transactions such as customer purchases, organization purchases from suppliers and associated invoicing. Information is also held on objects involved in these events such as customers, suppliers and products. This is *internal information* and specific to an organization. In Chapter 6 we saw how an important part of IS strategy development is to define the applications portfolio which delivers this type of information. The information services function is responsible for managing the operation of these applications. This means monitoring reports of errors with the system, problems with data quality or suggestions for enhancements. In Chapter 7 we saw how applications enhancements are managed in the maintenance phase of the systems development lifecycle.

External information is also managed and delivered by an information services function which may be separate from the group that manages the ICT infrastructure such as software- and hardware-related support services. Large organizations often have a library or market research function to enable managers to sense and respond to changes in the marketplace. Such information services deliver market and competitive intelligence (see Chapter 5) such as reports on markets, sales achieved by competitors and mentions of the company in the media.

The advent of the World Wide Web has changed the nature of this information delivery. Before the advent of the web, a library or research function would purchase, store and deliver external market reports and intelligence based on their knowledge of the requirements of the information users. The knowledge of user requirements would be based on discussions with users and more formal approaches such as an information audit. Essentially this is the **push model of information delivery**. Information is pushed from the information function to the information users. With the advent of the web, information is more typically requested by information users, using search engines to find relevant information. This is a **pull model of information delivery**. Search engines are used to search external information and knowledge sources, but also internal sources. Mini case study 11.1 'The World Bank pulls information using the Google Search Appliance' illustrates the value of search in liberating internal information and knowledge. Note though that the pull approach is not entirely new since information users will often go to a library or research services department to request and discuss their information needs and the researcher will then complete the search. This discussion with an expert on information sources is not available in the online context. Although this benefit of traditional searching is lost, information is now available on a more timely basis and this suggests that gathering information to support decision making would be increased.

While online searches such as those used by the World Bank use a pull model, a combined pull and push model can prove effective for online information sources. Here the web is used to identify user requirements (pull model) and a push model is then used to deliver information via e-mail or RSS feeds which link through to a website with the detailed information. The push approach is valuable since information is delivered directly to the end-user's inbox. This information can be filtered according to whether the topic is of interest to an individual. For time-sensitive information, alerts can be sent to users to notify them of important news. These aspects of improving information quality through these types of tools were explained further in Chapter 10. This overcomes a major weakness of web-based information – information users will not have time to proactively visit intranet or Internet sources just in case information is available. E-mail provides them with a timely prompt when relevant information becomes available.

Push model of information delivery
Information is supplied from the information function to the information users

Pull model of information delivery
Visitors proactively seek online information sources using search engines or directories of links

---

Mini case study 11.1

The World Bank pulls information using the Google Search Appliance

Overview

The World Bank Group is one of the world's largest sources of financial assistance for developing countries. Its 8000 employees in Washington, DC and 2000 field staff work to raise living standards in poor countries around the world with technical assistance and a wide range of loan and grant programmes. In fiscal year 2009, this international agency provided more than US$24 billion in loans to client countries throughout Africa, the Middle East, Eastern Europe, Asia, Latin America and the Caribbean.

In doing its critical development work, the World Bank produces a vast array of research and data used extensively by organizations across the globe, including universities, government agencies, non-governmental organizations and the private sector.

The challenge

The Bank's global reach is reflected in its intranet, which hosts hundreds of independent websites with more than 200,000 files on 445 servers, all of which are maintained by some 400 internal content providers around the world. All 10,000 Bank employees have access through an intranet home page which provides a comprehensive picture of the Bank's online resources and consolidates internal and external organization-wide communications.

The World Bank intranet contains documents in all the standard business applications and in every format from HTML to PDF. Loan officers and economic development specialists, technical experts and field staff all use the World Bank intranet to locate myriad project documents, case studies, health and environmental reports and complex financial data.

Using a prior search tool, World Bank intranet users made about 1500 queries a day – but according to surveys, they were not satisfied with the results. The previous search application made it difficult to access all sites across the network, or return useful results on environmental assessment policy, education project details, or poverty statistics. 'Before, you pretty much had to go to each individual repository to find something', says Intranet Project Team Leader and Information Management Officer Maria Dolores Arribas-Banos.

'Not only did our users have to cope with a poor search tool', she says, 'but they could not conduct e-business efficiently. Add in the cost of overall site maintenance, and the fact that the volume of information on World Bank's sites doubles each year, and we had a major headache.'

The solution

Looking for a new solution, the team signed up to test the Google Search Appliance GB-1001 (see Figure 11.3). The initial setup took less than one hour, and even indexing a tiny sample of five intranet pages demonstrated how much content the Google Search Appliance uncovers, reported Arribas-Banos. 'A big portion of our site had not been updated in a long time. The need for cleaning up the content became very evident.'

During a month-long trial, the Bank's web team explored such Google Search Appliance features as interface customization, so users see search results in the same look and feel as the rest of the intranet. Beyond this integrated interface is a search engine that integrates seamlessly with the existing network. 'They don't have to pick among a bunch of incomplete or incomprehensible search repositories. Now they can search the whole intranet, or narrow their search to a particular section.'

Since the World Bank materials are often available in a number of languages, Google's ability to easily handle content searches and indicate which content is available in which languages is a big advantage. Users can also toggle back and forth through language versions, which makes the intranet overall and search results in particular more relevant and productive.

Since users already knew and liked Google, deploying GB-1001 throughout the organization was painless. Several organization-wide e-mail messages informed the staff of the switch, and the web team offered a few demonstrations. No formal training was necessary.

Results

The Google Search Appliance has proven to be a cost-effective search solution for the World Bank, reports Arribas-Banos: 'It takes no time to set up, and no developer resources.' Not only does the World Bank spend less time on search administration, but it also spends less money. Over the next two years, she estimates that the GB-1001 will cost the Bank less than one-fifth what the prior search tool would have cost for maintenance alone.

As the number of documents on the network continues to grow at a considerable pace, the Google Search Appliance easily handles double the number of user queries per month over the old system just one year ago. The web team can focus on other initiatives instead of fixing search-related problems, says

Figure 11.3 Different Google Search Appliance options
Source: Google, Mountain View California (www.google.com/appliances/products.html)

Arribas-Banos. 'Search was a huge win. People actually called us up to say how well it was working, which was a pleasant surprise.' Table 11.1 indicates the time savings available through using the Google Search Appliance.

Table 11.1 Time and financial savings through using the Google Search Appliance

	Heavy searchers	Medium searchers	Light searchers
Hours spent searching (annually)	150	50	38.7
Times saved by replacing poor search (%)	53.4%	53.4%	53.4%
Time saved (hours per week, per user)	1.54	0.51	0.40
Value of time saved (per user per year)	$2,311	$770	$596
Value of time saved (for 500 users)	$1,155 443	$385,148	$298,104
% of ROI for 500 users	6,540%	2,113%	1,613%
Payback period	11 days	33 days	42.6 days
% ROI for 250 users	3220%	1,007%	757%
Payback period	22 days	66 days	85.2 days

Source: The ROI case for intranet search white paper www.google.com/appliance

Managing the quality of information delivery

The quality of information delivered to employees within an organization is clearly an important part of the overall experience of information services quality. However, traditionally, it is not seen as an important part of services delivery by information technology services. Rather, in a larger organization, it will often be a separate function which delivers pure information services. Many texts cover management of IT helpdesks and end-user computing, but this does not typically refer to managing the quality of information delivered. For this reason, in this book, Chapter 10 was developed to highlight the importance of having an effective process to manage the quality of information delivered to employees. Chapter 10 describes a process which companies use to improve the quality of information delivered based on conducting an information audit and developing an information policy and information plan. In Chapter 10, we referred to the value of the COBIT IT governance model for Control Objectives for Information and related Technology since it is based on different attributes of information quality. The COBIT IT governance framework also has the benefit that it specifically refers to management of information services delivery and support in a way that refers not only to support of hardware and software and their users, but also the related data. COBIT identifies the following 'Delivery and Support' objectives:

- *DS1 define and manage service levels* – It suggests the use of service levels acceptable to information users be defined to assess quality.
- *DS2 manage third-party services* – It is suggested that third-party services be managed through service-level agreements.
- *DS3 manage performance and capacity* – This control is used to ensure that the combination of software and hardware delivers sufficient speed and storage capacity for user and business needs.
- *DS4 ensure continuous service* – This control is used in order to achieve 100 per cent availability of software and information to users.

- *DS5 ensure systems security* – Security of information is stressed throughout the COBIT framework.
- *DS6 identify and allocate costs* – This refers not only to costs of technology, but also people and information resources.
- *DS7 educate and train users* – We see in a later section on total cost of ownership that training is important in reducing costs. Training here refers not only to effective use of technology but also an awareness of the risks and responsibilities involved.
- *DS8 assist and advise customers* – This refers to help-desk and trouble-shooting services for end-users.
- *DS9 manage the configuration* – Maintenance of the technology and information architecture, including managing the portfolio of applications and licences.
- *DS10 manage problems and incidents* – This provides an approach to disaster recovery and dealing with incidents such as server failure.
- *DS11 manage data* – This is to achieve the business requirement that data remain complete, accurate and valid during their input, update and storage.
- *DS12 manage facilities* – To protect the organization's offices from security breaches.
- *DS13 manage operations* – Scheduling the workflow for IS staff such that service delivery to users is appropriate.

It is evident that there are many benefits of using a standard framework such as COBIT. It enables a focus on key issues such as performance, availability, security, risk management and user support. However, it is relatively weak on the area of information delivery, focusing more on ensuring that the conduits for information are of sufficient quality rather than on the information itself. It does refer to data management, but this is at a level of data quality (completeness, accuracy and validity) rather than information quality where relevance, timeliness and presentation are key to success. There seems to be little guidance on how information can be delivered for market knowledge, competitive intelligence or business performance management, for example. However, as we saw in Chapter 10, at a broader level, COBIT does aim to facilitate the delivery of relevant quality information.

Controlling information security

The varied risks faced by organizations as they manage their information assets are summarized in Figure 11.4. This shows the growing number of security breaches and how they often have the most severe impact on large organizations.

Approaches to securing information have been described previously as part of developing an information management strategy in Chapter 4 and as part of developing the information architecture in Chapter 9. In these chapters we saw that standards are available on which to base an information security policy, such as BS7799 to help structure the approach to defining security. It is clearly in organizations' interests to protect their information, as a valuable asset. Furthermore, in many countries, it is now required by law to put in place security controls. For example, in the UK the Information Commissioner suggests these questions that an organization needs to ask to ensure it has adequate security:

1 Does the data controller have a security policy setting out management commitment to information security within the organization?
2 Is responsibility for the organization's security policy clearly placed on a particular person or department?
3 Are sufficient resources and facilities made available to enable that responsibility to be fulfilled?

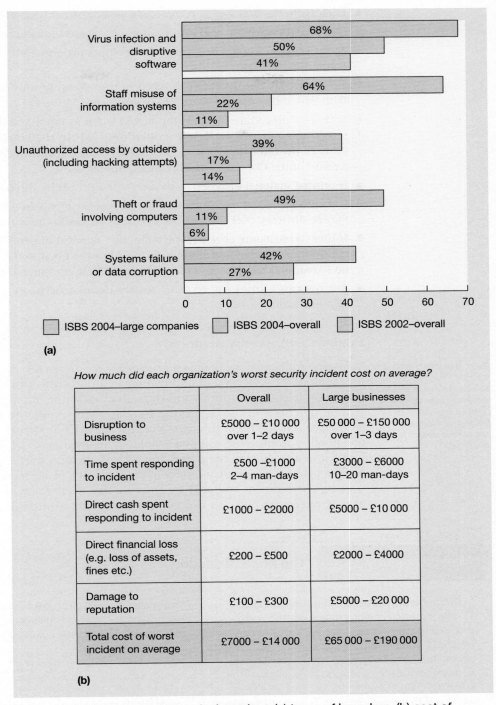

Figure 11.4 UK Information security breaches: (a) types of breaches, (b) cost of worst incident

Source: DTI (2004)

The concept of a data controller is described in Chapter 12 in the section on data protection and privacy legislation. As we saw in Chapter 9, the security policy typically sets out two areas: controlling access to information and achieving business continuity.

Controlling access to information is required to manage information theft or deliberate or accidental deletion of information. More detailed questions posed by the Information Commisioner to assess controlling access to information are:

- Is access to the building or room controlled or can anybody walk in?
- Can casual passers-by read information off screens or documents?
- Are passwords known only to authorized people and are the passwords changed regularly?
- Do passwords give access to all levels of the system or only to those personal data with which that employee should be concerned?
- Is there a procedure for cleaning media (such as tapes and disks) before they are reused or are new data merely written over old? In the latter case is there a possibility of the old data reaching somebody who is not authorized to receive it (e.g. as a result of the disposal of redundant equipment)?
- Is printed material disposed of securely, for example by shredding?
- Is there a procedure for authenticating the identity of a person to whom personal data may be disclosed over the telephone prior to the disclosure of the personal data?
- Is there a procedure covering the temporary removal of personal data from the data controller's premises, for example for staff to work on at home? What security measures are individual members of staff required to take in such circumstances?
- Are responsibilities for security clearly defined between a data processor and its customers?

Business continuity planning

Business continuity or disaster recovery
Measures taken to ensure that information can be restored and accessed if the original information and access method is destroyed

Managing for **business continuity or disaster recovery** seeks to control disruption if the methods for protection of information are insufficient. Disruption can result from malicious deletion of information through a hacker or employee or as a result of a virus as described in the 'Managing computer viruses' section later in this chapter. Disruption can also occur through so-called 'acts of God'. Here natural hazards such as fire, flood or storm cause computers holding information to be destroyed. Acts of terrorism can also destroy computers and the information they contain. Organizations need to plan for business continuity in the event of a major incident that destroys the working environment and/or IT by ensuring that if information or technology is lost or destroyed, the business can continue with the minimum disruption possible.

| Mini case study 11.2 | **The price of security** |

In December 2006 the company that operates TK Maxx warned customers that its credit card processing systems had been hacked. The intrusion affected the information systems of the multinational parent company TJX and affected several other companies under its umbrella. Speaking after the event, CEO Ben Cammarata said that they were working with the authorities to investigate the extent of the occurrence and with experts to improve their system security.

The way that global organizations share information makes it possible for customers to be affected by crimes that have been committed on the opposite side of the world and highlights the importance of implementing security measures such as encryption. TJX were subsequently criticized for their poor information security practices, including using less secure wireless systems than could be found in most homes (**www.theregister.co.uk/2007/05/04/txj_nonfeasance/**).

The loss of customer information, which included details such as social security numbers, had taken place over 17 months and resulted in the theft of 45.6 million credit card numbers (**www.theregister.co.uk/2007/10/24/tjx_breach_estimate_grows/**).

In fact, the true extent of the damage may be significantly greater and impossible to quantify accurately: later reports suggest that as many as 94 million credit card numbers had been stolen. TJX set aside $118 million against costs and potential liabilities (**www.theregister.co.uk/2007/08/16/tjx_charges/**).

This requires back-up of all data, often on a remote site which won't be affected by the same incident and the ability to deploy new servers and PCs in a new location if required. The approach used is known as 'business continuity' or 'disaster recovery planning'.

European data protection and privacy law requires that customer and employee information is adequately protected. The UK Information Commissioner gives guidelines based on asking these questions to check that protection measures are adequate to ensure business continuity:

- Are the precautions against burglary, fire or natural disaster adequate?
- Is the system capable of checking that the data are valid and initiating [automatically scheduling] the production of back-up copies?
- If so, is full use made of these facilities?
- Are back-up copies of all the data stored separately from the live files?
- Is there protection against corruption by viruses or other forms of intrusion?

Managing computer viruses

Computer virus
A program capable of self-replication allowing it to spread from one machine to another. It may be malicious and delete data or be benign

Computer viruses are a major threat to company and personal information since it is estimated that there are over 60,000 computer viruses. They are a specific instance of a security breach.

Types of virus

There are many different mechanisms by which computer viruses spread from one machine to another. All use some technique for the virus to reproduce itself or 'self-replicate' and then pass on to another machine. We will now review the main different types of computer virus which use different techniques to copy or replicate.

Boot-sector virus
Occupies boot record of hard and floppy disks and is activated during computer start-up

1 *Boot-sector virus*. Some of the most successful or most destructive viruses spread when floppy disks were widely used. These **boot-sector viruses** exist on the first sector on a floppy disk or hard disk known as the Master Boot Record (MBR). If a computer is switched on with an infected floppy disk in the drive this activates the virus which is then transferred to the hard disk and all floppy disks subsequently used in that machine.

'Brain' was one of the first boot-sector viruses which emerged in 1986. A more recent example from the start of the 1990s is 'Michelangelo' which was one of the most destructive boot-sector viruses. The name was given to it by a researcher who noticed that its trigger date was the same as Michelangelo's birthday, 6 March (1475). This is a **malicious virus** which overwrites part of the hard disk and floppy disk, thus destroying data.

Malicious virus
A virus that causes damage through destruction of data or software

Worm
A small program that self-replicates and transfers across a network from machine to machine. A form of virus

2 *Worms*. A **worm** is a small computer program that replicates itself and then transfers itself from one machine to the next. One of the first worms was developed in 1988 by Robert Morris and is described in the section on hacking in Chapter 12. Since then more malicious worms have been developed which now spread much more widely owing to the current scale of the World Wide Web. Since no human interaction is required, worms can spread very rapidly. For example, the 'Code Red' worm replicated itself over 250,000 times in just nine hours on 19 July 2001. In 2003, the 'Slammer' worm exploited a security loophole in the Microsoft SQL server database product and rapidly infected 75,000 machines. Each infected machine sent out so much traffic that many other servers failed also. This was one

of the fastest spreading viruses of all time, as Figure 11.5 shows. In future it seems that such worms will bring the Internet to a complete standstill.

3 *Macro-viruses*. Macro-viruses are a more recent phenomenon. They piggyback on documents created by office applications such as Microsoft Word and Excel. Office software such as this has a macro-facility to help users record common actions such as formatting or to develop more complex applications in Visual Basic for Applications (VBA). Macro-virus writers develop viruses that spread when a document is opened. Typically the virus will attach itself to all subsequent documents that are opened. Since documents and spreadsheets are commonly shared in and between offices, these viruses can spread very rapidly. UK government statistics show that 23 per cent of internet users had been affected by a computer virus that had resulted in lost information or time (**www.statistics.gov.uk/pdfdir/inta0807.pdf**).

One of the first Word macro-viruses was the Word 'Concept' virus from 1995. One of the best-known macro-viruses is 'Melissa'. This struck in March 1999 and it marked a new trend as it combined a macro-virus with one that accessed the address book of Microsoft Outlook to e-mail itself to new victims. This was one of the fastest-spreading viruses in history and it is estimated that it affected over a million PCs. In 2002, the author of the Melissa virus, David L. Smith, was sentenced to 20 months in prison in the US.

4 *E-mail attachment viruses*. These viruses are activated when a user of an e-mail program opens an attachment. 'Melissa' is an example of such a virus. They typically replicate by accessing the address book and sending copies of an e-mail with the same attachment to everyone in the address book. Effectively they are then acting as a worm. An even more destructive virus was launched in 2000. The 'Love Bug' virus contains the subject line 'I love you', while the message contains the text 'kindly check the attached LOVELETTER from me' which is an attached file called LOVE-LETTER-FOR-YOU.TXT.VBS. The virus deleted image and audio files and accessed Internet servers to send out different versions of itself. According to ClickZ (2003), it was estimated that nearly $9 billion of damage was done through this virus. Much of the cost is not the loss of data, but the cost of hiring specialists to rectify the problem and of staff time lost.

More recent e-mail worm viruses have been even more damaging. ClickZ (2003) reports that the e-mail worm viruses such as 'Klez', 'Blaster' and 'So-Big' cause billions of dollars of damage. 'So-Big' alone is estimated to have caused around $30

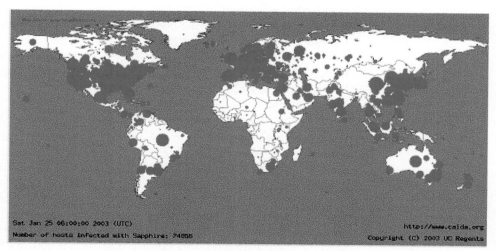

Figure 11.5 The geographic spread of the 'Slammer' worm 30 minutes after release
Source: University of Berkeley (www.cs.berkeley.edu/~nweaver/sapphire/)

billion of economic damage. 'So-Big' was activated by an attachment and spread widely since it used not only the address book to replicate to, but any e-mail addresses held in documents or HTML files on the hard disk of the computer. The virus even contained its own e-mail engine to enable replication.

5 *Trojan viruses.* A **trojan** is a virus that masquerades as a bona fide application. They are named after the Greek myth of the giant wooden horse used by attackers to gain access to Troy in order to attack it. Examples include utilities such as a file-sharing program, a screensaver, upgrades to some system components or even imitation anti-virus programs. The advantage for virus writers is that the programs can be much larger. One of the most famous trojans is 'Back Orifice', reputedly developed by a hacking group known as 'Cult of the Dead Cow'. This could be attached to other larger files and gave hackers complete access to a machine.

Trojan
A virus that masquerades as a bona fide application

6 *Hoax e-mail viruses.* These are warnings about viruses that are not real viruses but ask the recipient to send the warning on to their friends. They are not usually malicious, but can contain instructions on how to remove the virus by deleting files which could cause damage. They cause disruption through time lost.

This is a typical example of a carefully crafted hoax e-mail which was widespread in 2003:

> To all of my email contacts,
>
> Unfortunately a virus has been passed to me and many other people, you may already have it from some other source – through an address book virus which also infected my address book. Since you are in my address book, you will probably find it in your computer, too. The virus (called jdbg.exe) is not detected by Norton or McAfee Anti-virus systems.
>
> The virus sits quietly for 14 days before damaging the system. It is sent automatically by 'messenger' and by address book, whether or not you sent e-mail to your contacts. Basically, that means you will pass it along unknowingly, as I did. I was sent this email and am now passing it on to you as to how to check for the virus and how to get rid of it. Please do this! It's very simple to do and takes about 3 mins.
>
> 1 Go to Start, then click your 'Find' or 'Search' option
> 2 In the folder option, type the name... jdbgmgr.exe
> ←more instructions follow→
>
> If you find the virus, you must contact all the people in your Address Book so that they may eradicate the virus from their own address books.
>
> To do this:
>
> 1 Open a new e-mail message
> 2 Click the icon Address Book next to 'TO'
> 3 Highlight every name and add to 'BCC'
> 4 Copy this message and paste to e-mail
>
> This will affect everyone in your address book. So send it now!

Protecting computer systems against viruses

All organizations require a policy to combat the potential impact of viruses, given the frequency with which new, damaging viruses are released. Even individual computer users at home should think through the steps they can take to counter viruses. There are two approaches that can be combined to counter viruses. These are using the right tools and educating staff to change practices.

Anti-virus software
Software to detect and eliminate viruses

Anti-virus software is well known as a tool to protect systems from viruses. Many businesses and homes now use products such as McAfee Virus Scan and Symantec Norton Anti-Virus to protect themselves against the threat of viruses. Unfortunately, a lot more action is required than initial purchase for the anti-virus software to be effective. We have seen above that new viruses are continually released. It is therefore essential that regular updates be obtained and this often doesn't happen since a process has to be in place to trigger updates such as a daily update. Typically updates to the entire software aren't required, but to the signature files which are used to identify viruses. In smaller organizations without a dedicated computer support team it is difficult to maintain up-to-date versions of the signature files. One effective solution is to use tools which provide automatic updates over the Internet as soon as a new release becomes available. This requires continuous access to the Internet to be effective and several new updates may be needed each week.

Companies also need to decide on the frequency of scanning memory and computer files, since a full-scan on start-up can take a long time. Most anti-virus software now seeks to identify viruses when they first arrive (real-time scanning). A further issue is how good the anti-virus tool is at identifying e-mail and macro-viruses, since it is less straightforward for these types of virus to be identified.

Managed e-mail service
Receipt and transmission of e-mails is managed by a third party

Another approach to counter e-mail viruses is to use an external **managed e-mail service** which scans e-mails before they arrive in the organization and then scans e-mails for virus before delivery. For example, Messagelabs (**www.messagelabs.com**) scans 30 million e-mails a day for 7500 companies worldwide. Managed e-mail services are likely to be more effective than using internal anti-virus software since the service providers are experts in this field. They will also be able to identify and respond to e-mail worm attacks more rapidly.

To summarize: organizations need a policy to be developed for use of anti-virus software. This should specify:

1 the preferred anti-virus software to be used on all machines;
2 the frequency and mechanism for updating anti-virus software;
3 the frequency with which the whole end-user PC is system-scanned for viruses;
4 organizational blocking of attachments with uncommon extensions;
5 organizational disabling of macros in office applications;
6 scanning to be performed on mail servers when e-mails are first received and before viruses are sent;
7 recommendations on use of spam filtering software;
8 back-up and recovery mechanisms.

Education of staff in identifying and then acting upon the different types of virus can also limit the impact of viruses. Apart from Internet worms which execute automatically, some steps can be taken to reduce the risks from all the types of viruses identified above. Some general instructions can then be developed as part of a policy to reduce the risk of virus infection and transmission. Many of these apply also to home machines; these are:

1 Do not open attachments to e-mails from people you don't know (reduces transmission of e-mail attachment viruses). Since some viruses will be sent from trusted sources, only open attachments which look legitimate, for example Word documents with relevant names. Some viruses use file extensions that are not commonly used, such as .pif, .scr or .vbs. Viewing documents rather than opening them for editing can also reduce the risk of transmission.
2 Download software only from the official source, and always check for viruses before installing the software (reduces risk of trojan horse viruses).
3 Disable or turn off macros in Word or Excel unless you use them regularly (reduces risk of macro viruses).
4 Back-up important files daily if this function is not performed by a system administrator.

Controlling information service usage

Issues in controlling information service typically involve one of two problems from the employer's perspective. First, hardware and software resources provided for work purposes are used for personal purposes, thus reducing productivity. Secondly, monitoring the use of information introduces legal issues of surveillance. Monitoring of information service usage includes checking for:

- use of e-mail for personal purposes;
- inappropriate use of e-mail, possibly leading to legal action against the company;
- use of Internet or websites for personal use.

The problems in e-mail usage are covered in the next section on e-mail management. Owing to the privacy issues with monitoring service usage, the legal issues and policies and filtering and blocking tools that companies can create to control information service usage are described in more detail in Chapter 12.

E-mail management

E-mail is now an essential business communication tool and is also widely used for personal use. The popularity of e-mail as a communication tool has resulted in billions of messages being sent each day as Research insight 11.1 'E-mail volume' shows. For the individual, managing these communications in their e-mail inbox is rapidly becoming unmanageable! For the information services manager and indeed any business manager, there are three main controls that need to be considered to reduce the amount of time effectively wasted by staff reading e-mail. Controls can be introduced as part of an e-mail management policy to minimize the volume of:

1 spam (unsolicited e-mail);
2 internal business e-mail;
3 external business e-mail;
4 personal e-mail (friends and family).

Despite the potential time loss through e-mail misuse, an AMA (2003) survey suggested that only 34 per cent of employers had a written e-mail retention and deletion policy in place. Furthermore, there are issues of legal liability about what employees say in their e-mail which also need to be considered. We will look at the risk and controls of each e-mail risk in turn.

1 Minimizing spam (unsolicited e-mail)

Spam
Unsolicited e-mail (usually bulk mailed and untargeted)

Spam is now a potential problem for every company and individual using the Internet, as suggested by Figure 11.6. Over just three years the proportion of e-mails that were spam or virus-related increased dramatically, unprotected in-boxes would have received hundreds of spam e-mails each day. Originally spam was best known as a tinned meat (a contraction of 'spiced ham'), but a modern acronym that has been devised is 'Sending Persistent Annoying e-Mail'. The negative perception of e-mail derives from the many unsolicited e-mails we all receive from unscrupulous 'get-rich-quick merchants'. The spammers rely on sending out millions of e-mails in the hope that even if there is only a 0.01 per cent response they may make some money, if not necessarily get rich.

Research insight 11.1   E-mail volume

Lyman and Varian (2003) have compiled research summarizing the volume of e-mail messaging:

- In 2002 it was estimated that there are 31 billion e-mails sent each day.
- The volume of e-mails amounts to 1829 terabytes per day or 3.35 petabytes per year.
- By 2009, e-mail volumes had increased to 247 billion per day.
- The volume and proportion of spam has increased dramatically from 1 in every 1000 e-mails in 2001 to 1 in every 1.08 e-mails in August 2010 (92.2 per cent, as shown in Figure 11.6). Hungary topped the list of the most spammed countries, with a spam rate of 96.3 per cent.
- The time spent reading and writing e-mail can amount to well over two hours per working day. Incredibly, a 2003 survey by the American Management Association found that the average employee spends 25 per cent of the workday on e-mail, with 8 per cent of workers devoting over four hours a day to e-mail! This highlights the importance of making e-mail use efficient.
- Despite these problems, 86 per cent of respondents still agreed that e-mail has made them more efficient.

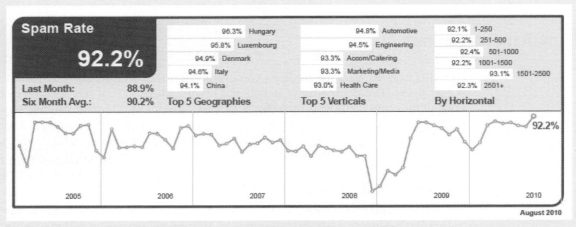

Figure 11.6 Proportion of global e-mail traffic that is spam

Source: MessageLabs, August 2010, *MessageLabs Intelligence* report, http://www.messagelabs.co.uk/resources/mlireports

Legal measures to combat spam have had limited success, so many information services managers are now using a range of methods to control spam. Figure 11.7 summarizes alternative techniques to combat spam: (a) is the original situation where all mail is allowed into an in-box; (b) uses different techniques to reduce the volume of e-mail through identification and blocking of spam; (c) is a closed in-box where only known, trusted e-mails are allowed into an organization.

The full range of techniques that can be used in combination to combat spam include:

1 *Avoid harvesting of addresses.* Spammers harvest e-mails from e-mail addresses published on web pages and even the program code used to convert online form content to an e-mail to a company. By reducing the number of e-mail addresses published, or changing their format, the number of e-mail addresses can be reduced.

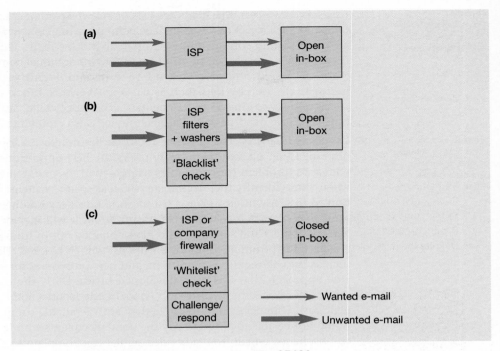

Figure 11.7 Progression of attempts to combat SPAM

2 *Educate staff not to reply to spam.* The worst thing an individual can do on receiving a spam is to reply to it to complain or to attempt to unsubscribe. This merely confirms to the spammer that the address is valid and they are likely to send more junk e-mail and sell your address on to other spammers. In Microsoft Outlook 2003 images are not enabled since downloading images in an HTML e-mail is a sign to spammers that yours is a valid address.

3 *Use filters.* Filtering software can identify spam from keywords and phrases such as 'For Free', 'Sex', or 'Viagra' contained in the subject line, 'from' address and body copy of the e-mail. **E-mail filters** are provided for users of web-based e-mail such as Hotmail and Yahoo! Mail with e-mails placed in a Junk Mail folder. Microsoft Outlook Express has its own filter. Filtering software such as Mailwasher (**www.mailwasher.net**) or McAfee Spamkiller (**www.mcafee.com**) can also be installed. Unfortunately, many spammers know how to avoid the keywords in the filters. The problem with filters and other services is that there can be 'false positives', or valid e-mails that are classified as junk. Additionally, spammers find ways to work around filters by putting 'gobbledygook' in the footer of their messages that is not recognized by the filters or using variants of words such as V1agra, or Via-gra. Review of these may still be necessary. This technique is represented by Figure 11.7(b).

4 *Use 'peer-to-peer' blocking services.* These take advantage of humans being good at identifying spam and then notifying a central server which keeps an index of all spam. SPAMNet from CloudMark (**www.cloudmark.com**) requires users to identify spam by pressing a 'Block' button in Outlook Express which then updates a central server, so when others download the same message at a later time it is automatically identified as spam. This technique is represented by Figure 11.7(b).

E-mail filter
Software used to identify spam according to its characteristics such as keywords

Blacklist
A compilation of known
sources of spam that are
used to block e-mail

5 *Use blacklist services.* Blacklists are lists of known spammers such as those reported to Spamhaus Project (**www.spamhaus.com**) or SpamCop (**www.spamcop.net**). They are often used in conjunction with filters to block e-mails. One of the most widely used systems, developed by Brightmail (**www.brightmail.com**), uses a global network of e-mail addresses set up to trap and identify spam. Brightmail is increasingly used by ISPs such as BT OpenWorld to block spam, but it is not a cheap service, costing $5 to $15 per year. This price could easily be justified by the time staff save over the year. This technique is also represented by Figure 11.7(b).

Whitelist
A compilation of trusted
sources of e-mail that are
permitted to enter an
in-box

6 *Use whitelist services.* The whitelist approach has not been adopted widely since it is difficult to set up, but it probably offers the best opportunity for the future. An increasing problem for companies using e-mail for marketing is 'false positives' – where filters identify their legitimate e-mail as spam. Whitelist services are one solution to this. A whitelist gives a list of bona fide e-mail addresses that are likely to want to contact people within an organization. It will include all employees, partners, customers and suppliers who have obtained opt-in from employees to receive e-mail. E-mail from anyone not on the list will be blocked. However, maintaining such as list will require new software and new procedures for keeping it up to date. One approach that has been developed in the US is the concept of a 'bonded sender' developed by Return Path (**www.bondedsender.com**). Senders of opt-in e-mail post a financial bond to prove they are a reputable company. Senders of spam would not be able to afford to pay the bond. Recipients who feel they have received an unsolicited e-mail from a bonded sender can complain to their ISP, IT manager, or IronPort and a financial charge is debited from the bond. Another approach rapidly gaining acceptance is Habeas (**www.habeas.com**) where special text (a 'warrant mark') is sent in outbound mail, which allows filtering systems to identify the e-mail as 'not spam'. This technique is represented by Figure 11.7(c).

In early 2004, there was an announcement of intent for international cooperation by governments to encourage ISPs to create an effective infrastructure to limit spam, by reducing the ease with which spammers can spoof or mask their real address in e-mail headers by replacing it with another domain name. This would prevent spammers using common domain names such as Yahoo.com or Hotmail.com, but some believe it will not prevent spoofing of less well-known names. Providers such as Sendmail (**www.sendmail.com**) are developing 'sender authentication technology' which allows organizations to verify the source of a message before accepting it by automatically checking if an e-mail came from where it claims it did. The raft of measures described in this section should eventually spell the end for spammers, but when is unclear. Also at this time, Bill Gates of Microsoft announced at the annual Davos meeting of business leaders that Microsoft would develop technology to rid the world of spam within two years. Clearly this technology has not been developed, and spam remains a significant problem. An additional component of future approaches could be charging a small amount for each e-mail sent using money or computation time, particularly where multiple messages are sent. This would eliminate the economic incentive for spammers, particularly if they could not hide the source address.

**Challenge/respond
system**
An e-mail from an
unknown source is
challenged by another e-
mail which is used to
prove the originator is a
valid sender

A further approach is challenge/respond. Here, if a message is received from a person who is not on the whitelist, a message is sent to that person requesting that they click on a link to verify that they are a genuine person and not a spammer (spammers would not have time to verify all addresses since it cannot be done automatically). Of course, this presents a problem for legitimate commercial e-mail marketers.

7 *Ensure anti-virus software and blocking is effective* (Chapter 12). E-mail viruses are increasingly perpetrated by spammers since they are a method of harvesting e-mail addresses. Virus protection needs to be updated daily with new signatures if addresses are not be captured through viruses.

2 Minimizing internal business e-mail

The ease and low cost of sending e-mails to a distribution list or copying people in on a message can lead to each person in an organization receiving many messages each day from colleagues within the organization. This problem tends to be worse in large organizations, simply because each individual has a larger address book of colleagues.

A press release from the British Computer Society summarizing research conducted by the Henley Management College released on 20 December 2002 suggested that a lot of time is wasted by managers when processing irrelevant e-mails. It suggested that: 'UK management is now suffering acute stress from "Information Overload" with executives "complaining of being deluged by e-mail"'. The report found that e-mail demands a daily average of two hours of executive time; and that nearly a third of e-mail received is deemed to be irrelevant and much is rated of poor quality. Further findings included:

- Of seven common management tasks, meetings took up 2.8 hours on average, dealing with e-mail came second with an average of 1.7 hours and accessing information from the Internet accounted for a further 0.75 hour.
- Respondents reported receiving on average 52 e-mails per day while 7 per cent received 100 e-mails per day or more.
- Managers reported that less than half of e-mails (42 per cent) warranted a response, 35 per cent were read for information only and nearly a quarter were deleted immediately. On average only 30 per cent of e-mails were classified as essential, 37 per cent as important and 33 per cent as irrelevant and unnecessary.
- Despite the reservations about the quality and volume of e-mails received the majority of respondents (81 per cent) regarded e-mail as the communications technology which has had the most positive impact on the way they carried out their job, alongside the Internet and the mobile phone.

To overcome this type of business e-mail overuse, companies are starting to develop e-mail policies which explain best practice. For example, considering the way that the authors of this book use their e-mail, we quickly devised these guidelines:

- Only send an e-mail to employees for whom it is essential to inform or act upon.
- Ban certain types of e-mail, such as the classic 'e-mail to the person who sits next to you' or individuals in the same office (although there are strong arguments for this since e-mail is an asynchronous medium and colleagues are not always available or don't wish to be disturbed).
- Avoid 'flaming' – these are aggressive e-mails which often put voice to feelings that wouldn't be said face-to-face. If you receive an annoying e-mail it is best to wait 10 minutes to cool down rather than 'flame' the sender.
- Avoid 'trolls' – these are a species of e-mail closely related to flame-mails. They are postings to a newsgroup deliberately posted to 'wind up' the recipient. They are best ignored.
- Combine items from separate e-mails during the day/week into a single e-mail for the day/week.
- Write clear subject lines.

- Structure e-mails so that they can be scanned quickly using sub-heads, numbered and bulleted lists.
- Make follow-up actions clear.
- When reading e-mail, use folders to categorize e-mails according to content and priority.
- Perform e-mail reading and checking in batches, e.g. once per morning/afternoon rather than being alerted to and opening every e-mail that arrives.
- Delete e-mails which are not required for future reference (large volumes are taken up on servers through staff not deleting e-mails and their attachments).
- Etc. – all common-sense guidelines, but often common sense isn't common!

3 Minimizing external business e-mail

As well as spam which is unsolicited and usually untargeted, people within an organization can also receive many e-mails from legitimate suppliers. For example, an IT manager might receive e-mails from hardware and software manufacturers, service providers, event/conference organizers and e-newsletters from magazines. This source of e-mail is not usually controlled through company e-mail policies, since it is usually left to the judgement of the individual employee to select appropriate e-newsletters. The technologies to block e-mails such as SPAM filters will not usually block such messages, but primitive filters may, if they block words such as 'Offer' or 'Free' which also appear in legitimate business e-mails. The challenge/respond system will still enable such e-mails to be received. Additionally, technology described in Chapter 12 is available to block access to certain websites such as news or entertainment sites, and this software renders e-newsletters less effective since images are not downloaded from blocked sites. An approach used by many individuals to help control information from these sources is to use a separate e-mail address from the main in-box when opting in. This could be a Hotmail or Yahoo! Mail address and this form of e-newsletter can be read in the office or at home and is also available when the individual changes jobs.

4 Minimizing personal e-mail (friends and family)

Although there are many surveys about the volume of spam and amount of time spent processing e-mail at work, there is relatively little data published on the amount of time spent writing personal e-mails. Most of it is not independent; it is commissioned by vendors of software for monitoring e-mail use. However, using e-mail for personal use is going to occur if there are no measures to stop it.

One example of misuse of e-mails was highlighted in 2003, when UK mobile phone retailer phones 4U became the first UK company to ban the use of internal e-mail across the entire business. This was partly as a result of use of e-mail for personal purposes and partly due to the management feeling that other methods were better for internal communication. Similar smaller-scale e-mail bans came from Nestlé Rowntree and Liverpool City Council. *Computer Weekly* (2003) claimed that the move will save each employee three hours a day, adding up to £1m per month. Surprisingly, the article reported that '13,000 internal e-mails passing through its system every week, individual e-mail accounts were taking up too much of the IT department's time, the company said'. Communication between phones 4U head office and its stores now occurs by telephone, and the company intranet, which is used for ordering equipment and services, is already showing positive results.

The move was instigated by John Caudwell, the company's multi-millionaire owner, who believed his 2500 staff had been spending too much time sending and receiving e-mails and not enough time dealing face-to-face with customers. He was quoted as saying:

> I saw that email was insidiously invading phones 4U so I banned it immediately. Management and staff at HQ and in the stores were beginning to show signs of being constrained by email proliferation – the ban brought an instant, dramatic and positive effect. Phones 4U staff have been told to get off the keyboards, get face-to-face or on the phone to colleagues.

It doesn't seem as if all companies will follow suit: Charles Dunstone, chief executive of rival Carphone Warehouse, said: 'We trust our people to know how to use e-mail properly.'

To minimize this problem and some of the problems of overusing e-mail for business use, the following steps can be taken:

1 Create written guidelines defining the policy on acceptable e-mail use and disciplinary procedures for when guidelines are breached.

2 Use increasing levels of control or sanctions for breaches, including: performance reviews, verbal warnings, removal of e-mail privileges, termination and legal action.

3 Provide training for staff on acceptable and efficient e-mail use.

4 Monitor e-mails for signatures of personal use and any breaches of the policy, e.g. swearing, and take action accordingly.

AMA (2003) suggests that all these approaches are becoming more commonplace, but although the majority of companies now have monitoring tools for external e-mail, only 20 per cent have such tools for monitoring internal e-mail.

Debate 11.1   *All firms should take the lead from phones 4U and ban all internal e-mail.*

5 Legal liability

A further risk when e-mail is not used prudently by employees is that legal action may be taken against the company. Defamation through e-mail is one example. E-mail defamation is where someone makes a statement that could potentially damage an individual or a company. A well-known example from 2000 involved a statement made on the Norwich Union Healthcare internal e-mail system in England which was defamatory towards a rival company, WPA. The statement falsely alleged that WPA were under investigation and that regulators had forced them to stop accepting new business. The posting was published on the internal e-mail system to various members of Norwich Union Healthcare staff. Although this was only on an internal system, it was not contained and became more widespread. WPA sued for libel and the case was settled in an out-of-court settlement when Norwich Union paid £415,000 to WPA. Despite this, such cases are relatively rare.

E-mail is also increasingly used as evidence in courts, for both criminal prosecutions and enquiries into government actions. Employees also need to be made aware of this. It may be unethical, but there are some business discussions that should only be made verbally and not through e-mail. Certain information should be retained inside companies, but it is difficult if employees are working remotely or consultants are employed to analyse data.

Staff should also be reminded that office banter, particularly of a prurient nature, can make them famous or rather infamous internationally, as is shown by the Claire Swire incident (**www.dazereader.com/claireswire.htm**) where millions of people gained intimate knowledge of an office worker's sexual preferences! Due to reputational damage to the companies involved, several of those who wrote or forwarded the e-mail were suspended.

End-user support

Most medium and large organizations have an IT help-desk or IT support staff to which users can turn for assistance when there are problems with their use of computer technology and information. In the UK, such services are often referred to as 'IT' or 'computer' help-desks, but elsewhere, following the trend in the US, they are often known as 'information centres'.

The types of service offered by a typical information centre or IT help-desk are:

1 *Help-desk support for user problems*. These are typically problems with hardware or using software. An indication of the types of problems faced by users is given in Research insight 11.2 'Press Delete for IT time wasters'. Most queries seem to be about applying hardware and software rather than information management.

2 *Advice on software purchase*. This ensures that the software is suitable for its purpose and is compatible with hardware, other software and company purchasing schemes and standards.

3 *Advice on hardware purchase*. This will usually be a centralized standard, again to take advantage of discounts and limiting support contracts.

4 *Advice on how end-user development should be approached*. The support person will suggest the best approaches for developing software, such as following the main parts of the lifecycle described in Chapter 7. These can be supported through more detailed training and advice on how to use applications building tools such as Visual Basic which are intended for end-user development.

5 *Application development*. For larger systems, the information centre staff may be involved in performing the systems analysis and design or more difficult aspects of the programming.

6 *Training*. In particular, on packages or development techniques.

7 *Data management*. Management and supply of data to end-users or explanations of formats used.

It can be seen that the information centre plays a role not only in providing advice, but also in maintaining control of purchases of software and hardware from preferred suppliers. All purchases have to be authorized by the information centre to achieve this type of control.

The survey shows that many of the problems are trivial operational issues such as printer jams and exceeding e-mail capacity. The survey suggests that more education and training of end-users could potentially save money since fewer support staff would be required. Alternatively, support staff could put more time into value-adding activities such as using information and tools.

End-user development

End-user development
Development of applications and management of information by non-IT specialists

End-user development (EUD) of applications represents a major trend in the use of information technology in organizations. An increasing number of users are writing their own software or spreadsheet models to help in decision making. This was not possible before there was a PC on every desktop and all development was performed in the data processing department. Since the IS department focused on strategic applications, the users' requests for small-scale applications would often be ignored.

End-user development tools such as macros in office applications and Visual Basic for Applications have empowered end-users. Office applications such as spreadsheets and databases have built-in functions that can be considered for development – using a formula or creating a pivot table in a spreadsheet can be considered end-user development.

Research insight 11.2	Press Delete for IT time wasters

IT staff waste an average of 20 hours a month solving simple problems that today's office workers should be computer-literate enough to do themselves, according to research from Computer People, the UK's leading IT recruitment consultancy.

The research was conducted among 500 IT professionals by Computer People in order to gauge the amount of time IT staff spend answering questions posed by office workers each month that could be spent on more important IT issues. The results reveal the following top five IT time-wasting problems:

1 Why isn't my monitor working?
2 My printer's jammed – can you make it print properly?
3 Why can't I send any more e-mails?
4 Please could you format this for me?

Problems such as these are usually easily solved and 86 per cent of the time they don't require IT support. However, 64 per cent of IT professionals are surprised at how often they are called out to look at 'broken' monitors only to find they aren't plugged in, 52 per cent claim that they are regularly asked to unblock paper jams in printers and 54 per cent are often asked to change toners!

Forty-six per cent of IT professionals say they are repeatedly questioned by employees who have simply run out of storage space on e-mail, even though this can be easily avoided simply by deleting e-mails regularly. Thirty-five per cent of support staff despaired at those who didn't take the disk lock off before trying to save documents.

Carole Hepburn, Commercial Director for Computer People says, 'In this age of technology there is no excuse for office workers not spending a couple of minutes trying to think through the problem, rather than being too quick to pick up the phone and call for unnecessary help. The amount of time IT professionals spend each month solving the simple problems that today's workers should be able to do themselves is equivalent to nearly three working days.

'This could be avoided if IT staff identify the top time-wasting problems complete with their solutions and make the rest of the workers aware of them. Of course, some problems can only be dealt with by the IT department, and when that is the case the following tips may help.'

Computer People's top tips to help IT professionals when those around are fretting about their computer problems:

- Send weekly Top Tips – an excellent way not only to let all the computer users in the office know how to solve any simple problems that may arise, but also to pass on timesharing shortcuts you may have.
- Always appear willing to help – don't forget this is what you are trained in! Those needing help aren't, so try to be as patient and helpful as possible even if the problem is very simple.
- Keep calm and be reassuring – if a major predicament occurs, the worker may panic and show distress. To help calm them down, give lots of reassurance and keep calm yourself.
- Talk in non-technical language – there will be a far better chance of workers understanding what the problem is and how it can be avoided in the future if they understand what you are saying.

Source: www.computerpeople.com

There is a wide range of possible applications for end-user development. These include:

- Reports from an enterprise database or data warehouse using ad-hoc or standard queries to databases defined by the user. For someone in an airline, for example, these might include access to a frequent flier database, customer reservation system or crew rostering system to monitor performance of each.

- What-if? analysis using tools such as spreadsheet models or more specialized tools such as risk or financial management packages or business intelligence software, used for monitoring sales and marketing performance of information stored in a data warehouse.

- Creating company information for a company intranet page.

- Development of applications such as a job costing tool or production scheduling system, using easy-to-use, high-level tools such as application generators, PC database management systems such as Microsoft Access, or visual programming environments such as Microsoft Visual Basic, Borland Delphi, Powerbuilder or Centura.

The stage model of Huff et al. (1988) indicates how the use of end-user (EU) computing might develop in a typical organization. This is loosely based on Nolan's stage model of computing use in organizations (Chapter 6). The stages of development are:

1 *Isolation*. A few scattered pioneers of EUD develop small-scale business tools within their area. Initially, little support from central IS.

2 *Stand-alone*. Larger-scale applications are developed that may be of importance to a department. Examples might include a staff rostering system or an application for anticipating demand for raw materials. At this stage, an information centre may be developed to support an increase in demand for user computing services.

3 *Manual integration*. Here, different EU applications need to exchange data. This happens through manual intervention, with files being transferred by memory stick or across the network or even with rekeying of information. IC development has continued to support the needs of these larger-scale applications by providing training and skills and specifying standards for hardware, software and the development process.

4 *Automated integration*. Users start to link into corporate applications to gain seamless access to information. For example, end-users may download information from a central data warehouse, which is then used to profile customers for a new product launch or marketing campaign.

5 *Distributed integration*. At this stage of development, there is a good level of integration between different end-user applications and corporate systems. Good standards of metadata (or data describing data in a data dictionary) are required to help achieve this.

Since this model was proposed, experience indicates that although a natural progression can be seen in many organizations, the development beyond Stage 3 may not be practical or desirable. Once end-user-developed applications become important or 'mission-critical' to a department or an organization, the question which must be asked is: 'Are end-users the right people to maintain an application of this importance?' The answer will usually be 'no', since end-users will not have the skills to develop such an application and if they are trained to levels necessary to do this, they will no longer be end-users fulfilling their original function, but specialist application developers!

Management of end-user development is required to ensure that the right tools are available to staff and that they have the skills to use them. Many information management tools such as spreadsheets are easy to use, but errors can be costly. There are cases where a single error in a spreadsheet formula has cost companies millions of dollars. We saw in Chapter 7 that it is difficult for IS professionals to deliver on time IS projects which meet the requirements of users. For staff who are untrained in systems development there is a great risk that there will be a high level of errors which could have costly implications. The types of problem that can occur through the systems development lifecycle are shown in Table 11.2.

There are also the general risks or misuse of information associated with end-user-developed information systems, which include:

- using information that is out of date;
- information requires export from other information systems before it can be analysed by the end-user application;

Table 11.2 Review of problems associated with end-user development and where they occur in the systems development lifecycle (SDLC)

Stage of SDLC	Typical problem
Initiation	*Absent or limited feasibility study*. If omitted, the user may be developing a system that is not required or solving a problem that has been solved before. *Insufficient review of cost–benefit and acquisition alternatives*. Other end-user software with the same function may be available elsewhere in the organization. Off-the-shelf software may also be available.
Analysis	*Limited analysis*. Since the end-user may know their own requirements, they may not consult others in the company who may have a different perspective. This may alienate potential users and mean that the software is unsuitable for its application.
Design	*Omitted completely!* This stage is often omitted and programming will occur straightaway. This may occur since users may not have the design skills or understand the importance of design. This will adversely affect the usability, speed and security of the software.
Build	Programming will occur as normal – the problem is that ancillary activities may be omitted. *Documenting* the work and *testing* are areas that should not be omitted.
Implementation	Implementation becomes more difficult for large systems. For a stand-alone piece of end-user-developed software, there should not be too many problems.
Maintenance	Problems at this stage are minor compared to those that may have happened before. Users may not keep an adequate list of problems that need to be fixed. There is also a tendency to release updates to the software without good version control.

- corruption of centrally held data by uploading erroneous data;
- development of insecure systems without password control that are vulnerable to accidental and deliberate damage.

An additional problem is the hazard of personal or private systems that are unreadable, undocumented and not transferable to any other users. This is a particular problem if the developer of the software leaves. This can be a common scenario with end-user-developed software. The only solution to this problem is often to rewrite the software, since the source code and documentation may be impossible to follow or be non-existent.

End-user development strategy
A structured approach is defined for the management and control of applications development by non-IS professionals

An **end-user development strategy** can help provide the support and the tools to minimize the problems shown in Table 11.2. This can potentially be part of the information policy described in Chapter 10, but it is often not considered because the policy tends to centre on use and consumption of information rather than creation of applications and information.

End-user development needs to be recognized as part of the IS strategy or information policy and guidelines should be developed that cover the techniques below. However, references to end-user development both in the literature and in the professional trade press are limited. Techniques that are commonly used in organizations where end-user development is acknowledged as an information service management issue include:

1 *Training*. Provision of relevant training courses both in how to program or use the tools and in how to approach systems development in a structured way (the second of these is often omitted).

2 *Suitability review*. Authorization of major new end-user developments by business and IS managers to check that they are necessary (this should not be necessary for smaller-scale developments since otherwise creativity may be stifled).

3 *Standards for development.* Such standards will recommend that documentation and structured testing of all user-developed software occurs. Detailed standards might include clear data definitions, validation rules, back-up and recovery routines and security measures.

4 *Guidance from end-user support personnel.* IC or help-desk staff can provide training in techniques used to develop software.

5 *Software and data audits.* There should be regular audits for data and application quality of software produced by end-users. There is an apocryphal story of a company that had an end-user-developed spreadsheet for making investment decisions which had an error in a formula that lost the company millions of pounds each year!

6 *Ensuring corporate data security.* Ensure that users are not permitted to enter data directly into enterprise databases except via applications especially written for the purpose by the IS department which have the necessary validation rules to ensure data quality. For analysis of corporate data, data should regularly be downloaded from the central database to the PC for analysis, where they can be analysed without causing performance problems for the corporate system.

It is apparent from this list of potential measures that a careful balance has to be struck between being over-restrictive, which may cause a stifling of innovation, and being too open, which will result in the types of problem referred to above.

ICT infrastructure

If there are problems with ICT infrastructure including hardware, software or network then information service quality falls. This is surprisingly common as indicated by Research insight 11.3 'Service quality disruptions'. The research refers to the introduction of an 'IT quality policy' in an attempt to reduce this problem. Such policies involve analysis to identify the source of problems. Current levels of service quality and the source of the disruption are identified. Measures are then put in place to tackle the source of the problem and targets are set to improve the overall availability. ICT infrastructure is often managed through the information centre or IT help-desk, although normally in a larger organization it is not the customer-facing staff who will manage problems with the infrastructure. Instead a separate team will constantly monitor service levels and adjust them accordingly.

Research insight 11.3	Service quality disruptions

Reduction in the quality of service delivery caused by problems with ICT infrastructure is relatively common according to a survey of 450 IT directors in the UK, France and Germany by research analyst IDC. The majority of those surveyed said they sometimes suffered 'major faults' with their IT systems, with 6 per cent saying that such problems were common.

Just under two-thirds of companies admitted to slowed-down applications, while 59 per cent admitted to particular functions becoming unusable and 38 per cent said problems rendered applications completely unavailable.

Companies are leaving themselves open to major system faults because they lack an IT quality policy, according to research by analyst IDC.

In the report, IDC found that three-quarters of companies with no IT quality policy in place are faced with major faults. Half of UK companies said they had a policy in place to improve the quality of IT by making systems more flexible, scalable and free of faults or downtime. Half said they planned to introduce a policy, with 80 per cent of those claiming it would be in the next year.

Source: Steve Ranger, Firms suffer from lack of IT quality, *IT Week*, 19 May 2003

Where internal or external networks and computers are managed by a third party through an outsourcing arrangement, **service-level agreements (SLAs)** are used to control the quality of service. As part of the contract with the suppliers, the SLA will define confirmed standards of percentage availability and performance measured in terms of the *latency* or network delay when information is passed from one point to another on the network. The SLA also defines notification to the customer detailing when the web service becomes unavailable, with reasons why and estimates of when the service will be restored, with possible penalty payments if the agreed service level is not met.

Service-level agreements (SLAs)
A contractual specification of service standards a contractor must meet

Resourcing information services

As we mentioned at the start of the chapter, management of information services is a balance between delivering service quality and the cost of service delivery. In the final section of this chapter, we look at two approaches which are used to control costs, while at the same time achieving appropriate service levels. These two approaches are managing service costs, better known as 'the total cost of ownership' of technology; and outsourcing, using a third party to deliver information services.

Managing service costs

The costs of delivering information services in a large organization can be significant. The section on outsourcing shows that it is not uncommon for outsourcing contracts to exceed $1 billion over several years. One of the reasons that this cost is high arises from the cost of maintenance and support – every application supported and every piece of hardware and software not only has a purchase cost, but also a maintenance cost. Since the modern organization requires many different types of hardware and software, there can be large savings if both purchase price and maintenance costs can be reduced. As a consequence, the person responsible for information services or IT is constantly looking for ways to reduce the **total cost of ownership (TCO)** of hardware and software, whether it is the finance director or owner-manager in a small-to-medium enterprise or the IT director or chief information officer in a larger company.

Total cost of ownership (TCO)
The lifetime cost of purchasing, maintaining and supporting any technology component

The concept of TCO originated with studies by analyst Gartner in the mid-1990s on the TCO of PCs, which showed that the average annual TCO for a PC was $8,000! Costs were attributed to 'desktop costs', related to the PC hardware and software, and 'network costs', related to managing communications and the network operating system. Desktop costs accounted for about two-thirds of the TCO. A relatively small proportion was spent on capital and all the other costs can be considered as aspects of supporting end-user computing. Further studies have shown that if companies carefully manage their PC resources, they can achieve cost savings of up to $3,100 per PC per annum. Figure 11.8 illustrates desktop PC annual TCO by refresh rate.

The concept of TCO can be usefully applied to other IT infrastructure components such as printers or servers or software such as operating systems software or even applications software such as enterprise resource planning or accounting systems. In the following sections we will look at approaches to reducing TCO for these different components.

The hardware vendor Compaq provides good resources on TCO management (subsequently acquired by HP). It suggests that organizations reduce TCO most effectively when they make three complementary investments: (1) training people, (2) streamlining processes and (3) acquiring technologies that are easy to manage, service and support. It summarizes the approach as follows:

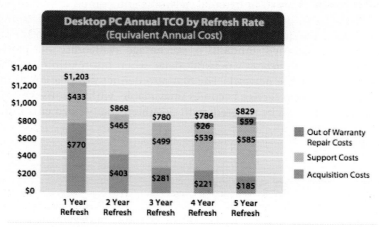

Figure 11.8 Breakdown of the total cost of ownership of a PC

Source: The Register®, http://whitepapers.theregister.co.uk/paper/view/1379/industrywhitepaperusingtcodetermine optimalpcrefreshlifecycles.pdf

- *people* – training end-users and IT staff to make optimal use of cost-controlling processes and technologies;
- *processes* – automating some tasks and streamlining others, ranging from asset tracking to software updating;
- *technologies* – deploying information technologies that minimize and in some cases eliminate the widest range of labor-intensive tasks.

Education and training are significant since this is one of the main elements of TCO. TCO cannot be improved by deploying software alone. Gartner estimates that untrained software users require twice as much official support services as trained users.

Reducing the TCO of client computers

A more detailed review of the different costs of managing client computers is presented in Table 11.3. Note that the table has been developed by Citrix, a manufacturer of lower-cost workstations, to justify the purchase of its computers, but it does provide a realistic breakdown of all the different costs incurred. You can see that the cost of maintaining client computers breaks down into human resource costs, application costs and hardware/network costs. Human resource costs include time wasted by end-users when their PCs are not working due to problems with hardware or software or while training and the time spent by help-desk staff in solving these problems. Software costs include the cost of purchase, installing and upgrading. Applications that are web-based or hosted on a central server have a lower maintenance and usually a lower purchase cost than applications where the software must be installed on each machine. Hardware costs include the costs of purchase and upgrades to clients, servers and networks.

Software audits
A formal assessment of software types used and level of usage

Understanding the range of software used in a company through **software audits** is now common as a means of complying with licence agreements – the risks to companies where software piracy occurs are discussed in Chapter 12. Tools such as that shown in Figure 11.9 are used to monitor the number of software applications installed and their level of usage. Such tools can also assist in reducing TCO. *IT Week* (2004b) gives the example of US mobile communications provider Cingular Wireless as one company that has set up such a centralized system. The company found that there was an overspend of $2 million on a single piece of software which was installed on many PCs, but not used on all. The company has over 200 strategic software contracts and potential savings can occur on all of them.

Table 11.3 Major cost elements of maintaining client computers

Category	Description	Business implication
Desktop environment [Client computer purchase and upgrade]	Number, type, and cost of desktops, notebooks, and thin-client devices used	Management costs increase with the number of desktops, notebooks, and thin-client devices. Multi-platform requirements also drive costs higher, especially in the area of support.
Human resources [End-user time wasted with client computer software problems and configuration]	Salary of various employees and number of working days in a year	The loss of productivity affects the bottom line in a way that is directly tied to worker compensation.
Help Desk and support	Time spent supporting users by help desk staff	The complexity of the environment and applications can lead to significant support costs.
Loss of productivity [End-user time wasted with client hardware problems]	Amount of downtime, both on the server side, client side, and network	Users that cannot access applications due to hardware downtime are less productive, leading to a higher cost structure.
Training	Administrator and user training time	Most technology requires user training, which is costly in terms of time away from work and tuition. However, effective training reduces overall support and help desk costs.
Application software [Software licences and upgrades]	Number, type, and platform of application software in use	The types of applications that need to be deployed and managed can drastically affect maintenance and upgrade costs. Client/server applications are more costly to deploy than Web-based applications.
Heterogeneous cross platform applications access [Supporting communications between hardware and software from different vendors]	Number of users who will need access to and from other platforms, like UNIX	Cross-platform access requirements generally require investment in new software to help bridge incompatible technologies.
Network and secure remote access	Requirements for secure access to applications by outside users (including partners and/or remote employees)	There are significant costs associated with remote access software. Bandwidth requirements are also an important consideration.
Operating system upgrade and maintenance	Time to test and upgrade to a new release of an operating system	Operating system upgrades are one of the most costly of maintenance upfront tasks. They usually require extensive testing and even longer deployment cycles.
Desktop application upgrade and maintenance	Time to test and upgrade applications on managed or unmanaged desktops	Although not as extensive as operating system upgrades, the number of updates generally increases, pushing costs higher.
Server cost	Server hardware pricing, as well as the cost of maintenance	Servers are more costly than desktops, but a single server, deployed properly, can support many users.
Back-up and utilities	Back-up software and hardware, back-up media, and related utilities	Especially important in server-centric computing environments where back-up of application data is critical for disaster recovery. Advanced back-up infrastructure can be costly.

Source: Doculabs paper produced for Citrix (www.acecostanalyzer.com/NewUserInfo.asp)

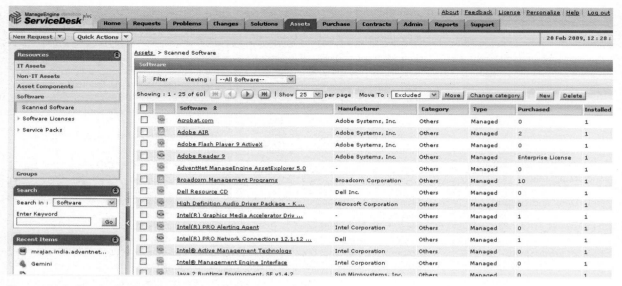

Figure 11.9 ServiceDesk Plus used for software tracking

Source: ManageEngine, ServiceDesk Plus, http://www.manageengine.com/products/service-desk/software-asset-management.html?
gclid=CLCB1sbviaQCFUc_4wodbFJR4Q

For medium-to-large organizations, Microsoft has recognized the TCO issue and has developed a product known as Systems Management Server (SMS) which is aimed at reducing the cost of distributing and maintaining software. SMS provides:

● automated software distribution and upgrades including security fixes and 'patches';
● metering of which applications are being used;
● hardware and software inventory for each machine;
● trouble-shooting diagnostics of each machine from a remote location (i.e. users' machines can be monitored from a help-desk).

Another approach to reducing the TCO of software is the use of open-source software for operating systems such as Linux or office software such as StarOffice or OpenOffice, for which there is no or a low licence fee (see Chapter 2 for details). A further approach for TCO reduction is reducing the need for physical copies of software to be installed on each client. In the application service provider (ASP) approach described in Chapter 2, applications running on remote servers are accessed via the web. This means that the costs of installing, configuring and upgrading software are effectively removed.

The cost of information provision

Studies of TCO have traditionally focused on the costs associated with software, hardware and the people who use and manage the equipment. There is less emphasis on the cost of provision of pure information services through library services or through groups preparing and distributing management reports, for example spreadsheets summarizing business performance management. It can be argued that this is also part of the total cost of ownership. There are significant costs in people to manage library services and business performance management. Both functions may also require the purchase of external research data about the market and competitors (competitive intelligence). These costs are also likely to be considerable. Such costs can be better measured with a holistic approach that considers both technology and information management.

Case study 11.2

How long before we scrap that PC?

This case explores the arguments for and against extending the lifetime of PC hardware.

Keith Cooke's hard drives were starting to crash and his monitors were beginning to flicker. As manager of IT services at Progress Energy's nuclear division, Mr Cooke had replaced his group's 3,000 personal computers in 1999 in advance of Y2K [a problem arising in date arithmetic in software and hardware in 2000, known popularly as 'the millennium bug']. Four years on, the failure rate of those machines had increased fourfold.

So Mr Cooke's company, which serves almost 3m customers in three south-eastern US states, in January 2003 replaced the ageing PCs with new machines from IBM. The new PCs ran Windows XP, Microsoft's latest operating system, and could thus cope with Progress's weighty but critical enterprise asset management software.

Upgrading PCs was a no-brainer for Mr Cooke. Applications performance improved by 70 per cent and employees no longer complained about sluggish desktops and notebooks.

And the new machines enabled Mr Cooke's department to cut support and maintenance costs sharply. The investment, he said, would pay off in just one year.

But in 2003 the PC industry was mired in a slump, so Mr Cooke was something of an anomaly – albeit the kind of IT manager that PC makers would like to see more often. Even though PC makers such as Dell Computer, Hewlett-Packard and IBM all said there were compelling reasons to buy new machines, cash-strapped companies worldwide were still delaying new PC purchases as long as possible.

Forecasts were not positive. PC unit sales in 2002 had inched back into positive territory after contracting more than 4 per cent in 2001. But, with average selling prices in an inexorable downward spiral, the industry's revenues contracted in 2002 after plunging in 2001.

The industry recovered but the global economic downturn at the end of the decade struck PC makers hard once again. By early 2010, there started to be signs of recovery.

'The technology downturn of 2008 and 2009 is unofficially over,' said Andrew Bartels, analyst at Forrester Research. 'All the pieces are in place for a 2010 tech spending rebound.'

The PC market can only start growing solidly again when corporations such as Progress Energy reach a point at which they can no longer afford to hang on to ageing machines. The corporate market is crucial to the likes of Dell, HP and IBM – it accounts for as much as 69 per cent of all PC sales, according to some estimates.

The upgrade, or refresh, cycle is particularly critical to the health of the PC industry. PC makers used to be able to count on the regular cycle by which corporations upgraded their computers every 3.5 years or so. A Merrill Lynch report suggested the cycle shortened to three years in the late 1990s, in part because buyers needed faster machines to run the latest 'killer applications'.

Concern over the Y2K bug also fuelled a corporate buying binge in 1999. But the dotcom bust, the lack of new applications and the anaemic economy all helped push the upgrade cycle to an estimated four years by 2002. Worse yet, the brokerage estimated the upgrade cycle could on average stretch to 4.5 years by 2004 if there was no discernible pickup in demand.

In 2010, Forrester Research predicted that businesses and governments around the world would start investing in IT in a six- to seven-year cycle of growth and innovation. This would be part of a significant rise in global IT spending – of which software and computer hardware would be the biggest growth sector. This would be offset, however, by the fact that average selling prices have fallen significantly, particularly as consumers lean towards cheaper netbooks.

With pressing financial pressures, it is hardly surprising that many companies move conservatively on the PC front. Industry insiders say it is not uncommon to hear from a CIO who wants to upgrade technology but is ultimately overruled by the company's chief financial officer.

'The CFOs are winning more than the CIOs. I think right now, the onus is on the CIO to really prove what the return on IT is going to be', said Jim McDonnell, vice-president for marketing at HP personal systems, in 2003. The same is true today.

Fortunately for PC makers, CIOs do have some valid arguments with which to make their cases. The most common argument, as Mr Cooke noted, is simply that upgrading PCs is cheaper – and not necessarily in the long run.

The rule of thumb for hardware is that acquisition costs account for roughly 20 per cent of overall cost. Maintenance and support accounts for the remainder. After three to four years, CIOs say they start to see a noticeable increase in the number of hard drives, fans or memory chips that fail, pushing up break-fix costs or preventative expenditure.

Doug Busch, Intel's chief information officer, recalls how accountants had earmarked roughly $1m to replace batteries for notebook PCs that were more than 3 years old and were going to be replaced at some point in the near future. The obvious solution – buy new notebooks right away and put the $1m to better use.

Another factor is that a PC software load tends to increase over time, meaning that older machines might require new components or additional memory to prevent them from getting bogged down under the increased demand of more complex software.

Equally important, but harder to demonstrate, is the argument that newer machines will boost worker productivity. IBM says studies show that new PCs can reduce hourglass time – the amount of time workers waste staring at a PC's onscreen hourglass while the machines process commands – by an average of 40 hours per year per employee. In other words, a new PC can bolster a worker's productivity by about one week per year.

A further factor regulating PC consumption is leasing agreements, which account for perhaps one-quarter of the overall market. Most leases run for three years with a one-year extension. After that point, it makes less economic sense to continue leasing older PCs.

Microsoft could also have some influence over the PC refresh cycle. An issue will be the company's decision to stop providing technical support for older versions of its Windows desk operating system.

This is particularly worrisome because the older operating platforms are riddled with security flaws that constantly require tweaking. Mr Busch at Intel, for example, said he was particularly motivated by security concerns and hoped to step up his PC purchases. Optimists hope that security concerns and the end to Microsoft's support would compel companies to purchase new machines that could run a more robust operating system.

A final growth driver is the advent of new technologies that facilitate ease of working.

While there appear to be any number of reasons for companies to upgrade their PCs, financial concerns are likely to take precedence for some time.

Source: Scott Morrison, Working life gets longer for corporate PCs, FT.com, 7 May 2003. Chris Nuttall, Spending rebound set to spur IT revival, FT.com, 14 January 2010.

Questions

You are a chief information officer (CIO) for an organization with a holding of several hundred PCs. The average age of a PC is approaching three years, and you think it is time to upgrade the PCs. However, the chief financial office (CFO) believes that PCs only need to be replaced every five years. Using the article:

1 Summarize the argument that the CFO is likely to use to argue for a five-year upgrade cycle.

2 Develop your own argument to counter the CFO's case.

Outsourcing of information services

Outsourcing
Business activities that are contracted to a third party

Outsourcing refers to an organization using a third party to complete business activities. Typically these activities have previously been completed in-house. Operations that are commonly outsourced include catering, cleaning, public relations, call-centres and information systems. Outsourcing of all types is a common business activity. Outsourcing of information services is no exception. An important role of CIOs and IT managers is deciding which information services to outsource and to whom. We will see that many pitfalls await the unwary, but, despite the potential problems, IT outsourcing remains popular.

In more recent years all these types of outsourcing have been referred to by consultants as BPO or 'business process outsourcing'. In this chapter we refer specifically to information systems outsourcing. **IT outsourcing** involves outsourcing a range of information services to third parties. These can include IT infrastructure and data management (the IBM contract) and applications development or help-desk support (the Xansa contract). Often, large-scale outsourcing also involves transfer of information services staff from the organization outsourcing its services to the company delivering the services.

Business process outsourcing
Specific business processes are contracted to a third party

IT outsourcing
Different information technology functions are performed by a third party over a contract period, for example, hardware and software purchase and maintenance, application development and IT help-desk services

The Boots–IBM contract is just one example of many large-scale IT outsourcing deals and their volume continues to increase. In 2003 analyst Datamonitor reported that its IT Services Contract Tracker – which monitors all new outsourcing, systems integration and consulting deals worth more than $1 million – found that the number of deals with a value greater than $100 million increased by 49 per cent to 244, and deals worth more than $1 billion more than doubled to 29. A snapshot of recent major IT outsourcing deals includes:

- Consumer goods maker Unilever extended its €1bn outsourcing contract with BT Global Services in a technology refresh deal worth an extra €173m (£144m).

- UK-based travel agent giant TUI Travel has awarded a five-year network infrastructure outsourcing contract reported to be worth €100m (£88.2m) to Deutsche Telekom's corporate customer arm T-Systems.

- India's fifth-largest IT services company HCL Technologies has recently been awarded a $500-million strategic IT outsourcing contract from the US-based pharmaceutical company Merck Sharp and Dohme (MSD).

- In a three-year deal, Infosys will manage the internal IT services for Microsoft worldwide, including IT help desk, desktop management, and infrastructure and application support, from multiple Infosys centres. The deal covers applications, devices, and databases in 450 Microsoft locations across 104 countries.

- Tata Consulting Services (TCS) will help Telenor Norway with application maintenance and development services and work with the company to update its application portfolio across fixed, mobile, data warehouse and accounting system domains to customers in 13 markets across Asia and Europe.

Source: *Computing*, www.computing.co.uk, Incisive Media (2010)

Note that although there is a trend to shorter IT outsourcing deals since this is a lower-risk option for the company outsourcing its services, long-term, 10-year contracts are still common, largely because these have the most favourable cost-savings associated with them. Yet, we will see that IT outsourcing is not only the preserve of the large company; many small–medium companies can also outsource different aspects of their information services.

Mini case study 11.3   Outsourcing

In 2008 Welwyn Hatfield Borough Council engaged in a £31 million contract to outsource their services over 12 years. IT services, council tax, benefits, contact centre, reception and switchboard will all be managed by Steria and is expected to deliver £500,000 in cost benefits over the life of the contract.

The deal will not result in job losses, redundant positions being moved from the local council to Steria.

Selection of the partner to take over the provision of these services was based primarily on quality, not cost, so that quality of service was maintained or even improved.

Historically India has been the recipient of much outsourcing, due to its relative low costs and high concentration of IT expertise. The downturn on global economies seen during 2008 is expected to shift that balance. Influential US finance, banking and insurance firms account for 40% of India's outsourcing revenue and their fall will result in a corresponding collapse of India's economy which has seen spectacular growth in recent years.

Source: silicon.com, www.silicon.com/publicsector/
0,3800010403,39336511,00.htm; zdnet.com;
http://news.zdnet.com/2424-9595_22-238208.html?tag=nl.e550

Types of information services outsourcing

Outsourcing of information systems, information technology and information management functions is a well-established practice which has proved popular over the past 20 years. Outsourcing of information services can vary greatly in scope. Sometimes all information services activities are outsourced to a single company – from IS strategy, hardware purchasing and applications delivery through to IT help-desk support. This is a 'total outsourcing' approach. 'Selective outsourcing' refers to a situation in which different IT services are outsourced to different companies. There is a trend away from 'total outsourcing' such as that signed between the Inland Revenue and EDS in the 1990s which had some project management delays. Today virtually all organizations will outsource some of their information services. For example, if an organization has a website which is hosted externally by an Internet service provider, as many do, then they are using information services outsourcing. It follows that the main management decisions related to outsourcing are ones of degree – to what extent should services be outsourced? The range of services that can be outsourced is indicated in Figure 11.10. It can be seen that hardware and software maintenance are the most commonly outsourced functions, while applications development is also common.

Total outsourcing
All IT services are outsourced to a single company

Selective outsourcing
Different IT services are outsourced to different companies

Offshore outsourcing or 'offshoring'

Offshore outsourcing is a major trend in outsourcing. It refers to a company's processes being undertaken by staff who are located in another country, typically with lower wages for employees. Lower wages and overheads lead to more cost-effective outsourcing. The best-known example is financial services. Today, if you phone your bank with an account enquiry they are probably not based in your (high-wage) country, but overseas in a country such as India which is one of the main locations for 'offshoring'. Phone staff are even trained in the idiosyncrasies of the customers in the country they are talking to. Offshoring is actually a longer-established approach for IT outsourcing.

Offshoring for IT mainly involves application development, with managing of infrastructure and help-desks less common. In 1992, Ed Yourdon, a commentator on

Offshore outsourcing
A company's processes are undertaken by staff who are located in another country, typically with lower wages for employees

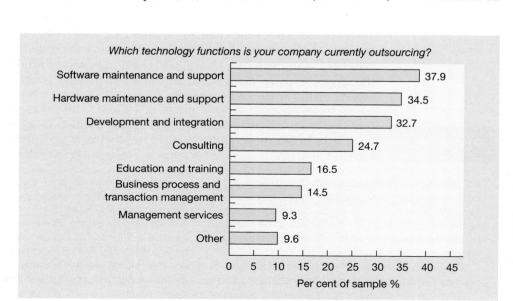

Figure 11.10 **Types of information services functions outsourced**
Source: IT Toolbox (2003)

software development, wrote a book called *The Decline and Fall of the American Programmer*. This foresaw the trend to increased IT offshoring, since at that time many applications were already being developed overseas and this trend has continued since. In 2003, the *Financial Times* reported that Tata Consultancy Services (TCS) had become the first Indian software and services company to earn $1 billion in annual revenue. *Financial Times* (2003) reported that this activity does not only occur in India since applications development may also need to occur on the company's site. Nearly a quarter of TCS's 24,000 software professionals are abroad for periods of between two weeks and two years. About half of Wipro's 13,000 IT engineers are overseas on short-term assignments, while some 4000 out of Infosys's 14,000 engineers are on overseas assignments at any one time. The number of staff involved in India's three largest IT companies shows the significance of this trend. IT staff in India are university educated, but the salaries are such that the overall costs of outsourcing are typically reduced by a third. In 2003, the average Indian programmer salary was $5,880 a year; this is $18–25 an hour which is around a quarter of the minimum salary in a developed country. With overheads and margins, the outsourcing company typically charges twice as much to the company for each member of staff they pay.

CIO (2003) catalogues what it refers to as 'the new TCO – the Total Cost of Offshoring'. Additional costs including selecting and visiting the supplier, which can cost up to 2 per cent of the contract. One of the most expensive additional costs is managing the change in the first six to nine months of the contract – it's not as simple as switching on a light. Staff from the outsourcing company need to travel to the business they are working for to understand the application and the business. If they are working in the company, the offshore company's margin improves since they don't have to provide office space. So they tend to encourage this type of in-company working. Additional travel and accommodation costs are involved. Costs are such that if around 25 per cent of the offshore workforce is in fact 'onshore' (a not uncommon figure), then the contract benefits become insignificant. The article reports that if this face-to-face meeting doesn't happen, then specifications are often insufficient to define application needs and a poor-quality system results. Once the contract is set up, the staff time involved in managing the contract can add another 6–10 per cent to the total cost of the contract.

Secure, dedicated network links can also cost tens of thousands of dollars each month. The cost of reducing headcount is high also, with severance and retention bonuses – it is not possible to sack staff immediately since skills transfer needs to happen. There are also morale problems and change management issues for those employees left who have lost their former colleagues and now have to spend much of their time not programming but explaining the basics of the business to their new counterparts. The article also mentions the cultural issue – the productivity or value added by an offshore programmer may be lower since they don't understand the business or customer needs as well and their English usage will be different. Yet another issue is turnover in the outsourcing company. Staff attrition can reach 35 per cent in India, which results in disruption and training new staff in the business. So it is apparent that there are many additional costs, some of which are intangible, which need to be accounted for in the decision to outsource. Despite these issues, *CIO* (2003) reports that nearly half of large US companies use offshore outsourcing, so the cost arguments are such that it is a question of managing the contract risks – the overall benefits are still clear.

These Indian outsourcing companies have built on their success and are now serving emerging markets in Asia such as China, in South and North America via a Spanish-language-based centre in Tijuana, Mexico and in Eastern Europe where they have created multilingual support centres. Lower-cost options are also being explored in the Philippines, Malaysia and Mauritius. Offshoring is truly a global business!

Outsourcing for small and medium organizations

Aside from the large-scale outsourcing deals where staff are transferred to the outsourcing companies, what are the opportunities for small and medium enterprises to reduce costs through outsourcing? It would at first appear that these are limited since a small company with 25 to 100 staff is unlikely to have its own in-house application development team and one manager and one technology support manager can effectively manage the purchase of all hardware, software and support delivery. If this work were outsourced, there would still be one person needed to liaise with the outsourcing company. It is also difficult to imagine small companies resorting to offshoring.

In fact, two broad types of IT outsourcing are practical for small-to-medium companies (SMEs). First, they can use an outsourcing service specifically developed for small companies. For example, IT outsourcing specialists such as IT Department UK (**www.itdepartmentuk.com**) or IT Lab (**www.itlab.co.uk**) have services specifically for SMEs. These types of company offer continuous phone support, remote monitoring of network performance, network management, plus one or two scheduled visits each month to solve non-urgent maintenance problems for a fixed fee of much less than £100 per PC depending on the number of PCs.

Another approach to outsourcing that can be used by small companies is the application service provider (ASP) services introduced in Chapter 2. This approach has made the cost savings provided through outsourcing more readily available to small and medium companies. Examples of information services outsourcing that can be performed through use of ASPs include:

- E-mail services which scan, filter and archive all inbound and outbound e-mail so that no e-mail server needs to be managed inside the company.

- Website management – all files are hosted on a third-party server which provides support.

- Remote data back-up services such as IBackup (**www.ibackup.com**). Data are automatically backed-up to external servers.

- Internal network outsourcing. The network and firewalls can be administered externally and maintenance staff supplied to fix problems.

Benefits of information services outsourcing

The single most important reason for IT outsourcing is cost reduction. The reason why the company performing the outsourcing can deliver the equivalent service more cheaply depends on the type of service that is outsourced. In hardware and software purchase and maintenance, the outsourcing company will make higher-volume purchases and this gives economy of scale. Furthermore, if the outsourcing company also manufactures hardware and software, then cost savings arise from direct purchase as part of the overall contract. Over the past ten years, technology suppliers such as IBM and Hewlett-Packard have changed their business models from a focus on technology to a blend of technology and consulting and outsourcing services since they are in a better position to deliver value compared to pure consulting or outsourcing companies such as EDS, Accenture or Cap-Gemini. Cost savings also accrue when staff who previously developed applications or provided IT support are transferred. The overhead of paying for insurance and holiday pay and providing office space for these staff is transferred (although many staff will remain 'on-site' in their original company). A clear summary of the main reasons for all types of outsourcing is provided by the Outsourcing Institute (more detail provided at **www.outsourcing.com**). This survey was conducted in 1998, but the reasons remain current. The main reasons for outsourcing in order of importance are:

1 Reduce and control operating costs.

2 Improve company focus.

3 Gain access to world-class capabilities.

4 Free internal resources for other purposes.

5 Resources are not available internally.

6 Accelerate re-engineering benefits.

7 Function difficult to manage or out of control.

8 Make capital funds available.

9 Share risks.

10 Cash infusion.

It can be seen that every one of these reasons is relevant to IT outsourcing. Although cost is sometimes thought of as the only real driver for outsourcing, quality is another significant reason. Through outsourcing IS functions such as applications development to a company which is expert in its field, it should be possible to deliver better-quality services to both internal and external customers. Better quality could be delivered in the form of systems that are more reliable and have appropriate features, a more reliable company network and better phone support. Better-quality services can also be delivered and projects are more likely to hit deadlines simply because the company and its partner are in a contractual arrangement. The contract will often state service quality standards and if these are not met there may be penalties, and there is always the threat of outsourcing to another company when the contract ends.

Another common reason given for all types of outsourcing is achieving focus. Through outsourcing a company can concentrate its energies on what it is familiar with, i.e. its market and customers, rather than being distracted by information systems development. This particular argument is weak in some industries such as the financial services sector where information systems are critical to operating in a particular market. In these cases selective outsourcing may be undertaken, where hardware and basic IT support will be outsourced but applications development and information management will be retained in-house.

The results of a survey specifically about IT outsourcing, dating from 2003, around the time when there was a high level of growth in outsourcing, are presented in Figure 11.11. It can be seen that many of the reasons are similar to the general reasons for outsourcing.

Problems with information services outsourcing

Collins and Millen (1995) reviewed management issues arising with information systems outsourcing. Of the 100 companies surveyed from the largest US companies, 90 per cent of respondents reported difficulties in implementation. The most frequently cited obstacle to implementation was developing working relations between in-house and outside personnel, which was cited by 61 per cent of the respondents. The need to train outside staff in the business issues of the company was mentioned by 48 per cent of the respondents. They note that outside personnel may be technically adept, but will often have to acquire business-specific knowledge. Other concerns mentioned include a sense of loss of control of information systems, security worries and the negative impact on morale of existing staff.

Debate 11.2

Companies that outsource information services lose their capability to use information to create competitive advantage.

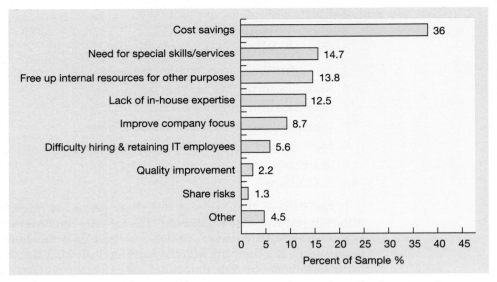

Figure 11.11 Responses to the question 'What is your main strategic reason for outsourcing IT services?'
Source: IT Toolbox (2003)

Further difficulties are indicated by the fact that some companies are shortening the length of their outsourcing contracts, changing suppliers or even bringing some outsourced services in-house. According to *IT Week* (2004a), companies are now renegotiating technology contracts more frequently. Eighty per cent of European firms now look to renegotiate contracts every six months, but in the past the average was every three years. Of the 100 procurement directors surveyed, three-quarters mentioned that overall quality of service was the main reason for negotiating. This implies a high level of dissatisfaction with service quality, although renegotiation is also necessary to improve the cost-effectiveness of services.

There are also problems with outsourcing which involve the loss of jobs or transfer of staff to the company performing the outsourcing. While there have been protracted disputes with unions, organizations now offer incentives to staff to reduce the likelihood of this. *IT Week* (2004a) reported that a bank offered an additional three months' pay for staff transfers for redundancies.

Further problems with outsourcing are indicated when there are contractual disputes over outsourcing such as those described in Chapter 7. Outsourcing undertaken by government departments is also open to scrutiny.

Summary

1 The service quality gap model is useful for understanding the requirements of information services. User satisfaction and service quality must be monitored and measured to support improvements to the process.

2 Management of information delivery is one information services function. This includes both internal information delivered to employees and partners via applications, intranets and extranets and external information on the marketplace delivered to employees' desktops.

3 Information security controls can be divided into restricting access to information and planning for business continuity if data are compromised.

4 Issues in controlling information service usage include the use of e-mail for personal purposes, inappropriate use of e-mail possibly leading to legal action against the company, and the use of Internet and websites for personal use.

5 End-user support services known as 'help-desks' are needed to answer questions that users have about their software or hardware. The ICT infrastructure is usually also managed by this group, which may use service-level agreements to control the level of service quality.

6 Control of the total cost of ownership (TCO) is important in reducing the cost of information services. TCO refers to purchase and all maintenance support costs associated with hardware or software.

7 Outsourcing information services to a third party in a long-term contractual arrangement is a common activity. The benefits include cost reduction and increasing capacity to focus on core competencies. The risks in outsourcing include hidden costs in application development and issues involved with the transfer of staff.

Exercises

Self-assessment questions

1 Explain the relevance of the service quality gap model to information service delivery.

2 What types of information delivery are information services responsible for?

3 Outline approaches for protecting the information resource.

4 Describe the typical problems with e-mail usage by staff which need to be managed.

5 Explain the concept of the total cost of ownership.

6 Summarize the different types of information service outsourcing.

7 Explain the benefits and risks associated with information service outsourcing.

8 What are the management issues involved with offshore outsourcing for information services?

Essay and discussion questions

1 Discuss the future of information services outsourcing.

2 Write an essay on e-mail management.

3 You are CIO at a European-based airline which currently uses a mix of internal application development (with a team of 100 developers) and additional specialist external contract staff. You have been following the trend in offshore outsourcing and want to assess the business case for offshore outsourcing. Produce a business case clearly presenting the arguments for and against offshore outsourcing.

4 Create a plan for the same organization for improving the quality of the delivery of external market information – competitive intelligence.

5 Assess the opportunities and risks of outsourcing knowledge management activities.

6 Explain how the concept of 'total cost of ownership' can be used to control information service delivery.

References

AMA (2003) American Management Association 2003 E-Mail Rules, Policies and Practices Survey. www.amanet.org/research/pdfs/EmailrPoliciesrPractices.pdf. Self-selecting survey of over 1000 respondents in a range of organizations.

CIO (2003) The hidden costs of offshore outsourcing, *CIO*, 1 September. www.cio.com/archive/ 090103/money.html.

ClickZ (2003) Virus damage worst on record for August 2003. News alert published online at ClickZ. Jupiterweb networks. www.clickz.com/stats/bigrpicture/applications/article.php/1301r3071131.

Collins, J. and Millen, R. (1995) Information systems outsourcing by large American firms: Choices and impacts. *Information Resources Management Journal*, 8(1) (Winter), 9–14.

Computer Weekly (2003) Phones 4U bans internal e-mail, Daniel Thomas, 19 September. www.computerweekly.com/articles/article.asp?liArticleID=125010&liArticleTypeID=1&liCategoryID=2&liChannelID=30&liFlavourID=1&sSearch=&nPage=1.

DTI (2004) Department of Trade and Industry Information Security Breaches Survey Executive Summary. www.pwc.com/images/gx/eng/about/svcs/grms/2004Execr Summ.pdf.

Financial Times (2003) Services wave ripples outwards, Khozem Merchant, 2 July.

Gartner Group (1996) Total Cost of Ownership: Reducing PC/LAN Costs in the Enterprise. 9 February. The Gartner Group, Boston, MA.

Huff, S., Munro, M. and Martin, B. (1988) Growth stages of end-user computing. *Communications of the ACM*, 31(5), 542–50.

IT Toolbox (2003) 2003 IT Toolbox Outsourcing Survey. http://crm.ittoolbox.com/research/survey.asp?survey=outsourcingrsurvey&p=1. Global survey of 600 IT professionals (self-selecting) on August 20 to August 22, 2003.

IT Week (2004a) IT deals stay under review. *IT Week*, 12 January.

IT Week (2004b) Audit tools bring savings. *IT Week*, 12 January.

Loiacono, E., Watson, R. and Goodhue, D. (2000) WEBQUAL: A measure of website quality. In K. Evans and L. Scheer (eds) *Marketing Theory and Applications*, Vol. 13. American Marketing Association, Chicago, 2002, pp. 432–9.

Lyman, P. and Varian, H. (2003) How Much Information? – online research summary. Available online at: www.sims.berkeley.edu/research/projects/how-much-info-2003/.

Parasuraman, A., Zeithaml, V. and Berry, L. (1985) A conceptual model of service quality and its implications for future research. *Journal of Marketing*, 49 (Fall), 48.

Zeithaml, V., Parasuraman, A. and Malhotra, A. (2002) Service quality delivery through web sites: A critical review of extant knowledge. *Academy of Marketing Science*, 30(4), 368.

Further reading

Regan, E. and O'Connor, B. (2002) *End-user Information Systems. Implementing Individual and Work Group Technologies*, 2nd edn. Prentice-Hall, Upper Saddle River, NJ. This textbook has an end-user computing orientation which gives an 'employee-centric' approach to managing information systems.

Ward, J. and Peppard, J. (2002) *Strategic Planning for Information Systems*, 3rd edn. Wiley, Chichester. Chapter 11 is entitled 'Managing the supply of IT services, applications and Infrastructure'. It also covers outsourcing. It does not refer in depth to end-user development or the issues with e-mail management.

visit the www

Weblinks

E-policy Institute (www.epolicyinstitute.com) Commercial site with examples of e-mail problems faced by companies and sample guidelines.

Outsourcing Institute (www.outsourcing.com) A comprehensive review of success factors and best practice in all types of outsourcing.

Outsourcing Project (www.outsourcingproject.com) Collection of white papers co-ordinated by Montgomery Research-Accenture. Includes knowledge management outsourcing and ROI studies.

Security Survey (www.security-survey.gov.uk). Results of twice-yearly security surveys in the UK.

For multiple-choice questions, and annotated weblinks relating to this chapter visit this book's website at: www.pearsoned.co.uk/chaffey

12

Managing ethical and legal issues

Objective

To recognize the legal and ethical issues involved in business information management.

Learning outcomes

After reading this chapter, you will be able to:

● Understand the implications of privacy and data protection legislation for managers.

● Assess approaches to providing and monitoring employee access to information.

● Define the risks of unauthorized data access and solutions to counter them.

Management issues

Typical questions facing managers related to this topic:

● What are the legal constraints on managing customer and employee data?

● What are the risks of unauthorized access to data and how can we minimize these?

● What is the balance between business imperative and moral stance for monitoring and controlling employee data access?

Links to other chapters

The main related chapters are:

➤ *Chapter 5* introduces the need to manage legal, ethical and security issues as part of information management strategy.

➤ *Chapter 8* on information architecture describes how security can be built into the design of information systems.

Introduction

The widespread adoption of information and communications technology by organizations has increased both the volume of data held digitally and the options for accessing them. Although organizations may have good intentions in protecting the privacy of their customers' data and securing all data resources, other business priorities may mean that data protection measures are inadequate. The image at the opening of the chapter suggests the challenge of managing ethical and legal issues – it is a 'knotty' problem attempting to unravel the ever-changing ethics and laws, and often organizations 'take their eye off the ball' since traditionally it has not been a business priority.

How organizations manage personal data related to individual customers or employees is a particular concern in modern society because if these data are mismanaged it may have serious implications for the individual. If their personal details are not secured correctly, then their details may be accessed by third parties such as criminals or journalists, for example, who will seek to gain from access to data whether it be a credit card number or details of a hospital visit. Legal deterrents and control measures also need to be in place to discourage or prevent third parties from gaining unauthorized access to organization data of all types. Furthermore, employees in an organization may deliberately or inadvertently access or use information from other companies to which they do not have any rights.

Given the extent of the threats to personal data and privacy, laws relating to business information management have been introduced in many countries. It is important that managers be aware of these laws, so they can ensure that their information processing activities are legal, and so that they can seek redress when their information resources are misused or abused.

In the final chapter of *Business Information Management* we review the laws that have been introduced to control information management and we assess their implications for organizations. But in the first section of the chapter we look at ethical issues of business information management. Many ethical decisions that managers previously needed to make about how they dealt with customer and employee information are now covered by law. These ethical decisions often involve balancing business benefits of using data against whether the practice is acceptable to customers or wider society.

We then start to look at legislation on privacy and data protection law, an important law which affects all companies. Many organizations now monitor employee use of computer systems and this also has legal implications. We then look at how laws seek to reduce unauthorized access to information through activities such as hacking and viruses. We also look at the increasing problem of identity theft, where criminals steal personal data and then seek to commit fraud by impersonation. Since legislation is a last resort in countering unauthorized data access, we also describe how companies can prevent access to information before it occurs, without the need for recourse to the law. To protect information, managers need to understand threats such as hackers and viruses and we will explore the different forms of threat and control measures to reduce them.

In the next section, we look at how organizations protect their valuable digital information resources such as articles, books, film, music and software from unauthorized copying.

Many of the laws to safeguard digital information are only newly established. As a consequence, some issues about how information is managed are not determined by law but by the ethical approach of the business. Managers have to make ethical decisions continually about how they use its information resources. For example, laws have been recently introduced to control the sending of unsolicited e-mail known as spam, but before these laws existed, individual businesses had to decide how to approach the sending of unsolicited e-mail. Did they agree to send it because they thought they would ultimately achieve more revenue or did they decide not to send unsolicited e-mail because they thought it unethical?

Ethics in information management

Ethical standards
Practice or behaviour which is morally acceptable to society

Ethical standards are personal or business practices or behaviour generally considered acceptable by society. Acceptable ethics can be described as moral or just and unethical practices as immoral or unjust. Sometimes it is possible that business practices are within the law, but cannot be considered ethical. We will touch on ethical issues as we discuss all the different laws that have been developed, but in this first section of the chapter we also review specific ethical issues that aren't well controlled in law, including those that affect wider society. We now live in an 'information society' which creates many opportunities for those with access to technology. But society and governments also need to consider problems such as social exclusion through technology where those in society who do not have access to technology may be disadvantaged. One example of a difficult information ethics question concerns Iceland, where the government sold access to the DNA data for the entire population to a company called Decode for $200 million! All individuals were included, unless they knew about the sale and objected.

In the following sections in this chapter we will see that many laws have now been enacted to protect the privacy of individuals and employees as their details are stored and their activities are monitored through online networks. Previously these required ethical decisions by managers and organizations.

Business ethics
Moral principles concerning acceptable and unacceptable behaviour by corporations and individual business people

With the increasing detail in law of how personal information and privacy should be protected on computer systems, there is arguably now less need for reflection on the **business ethics** of information management. We can say that what would previously have been considered unethical business practices in information management are now punishable through law. Unethical business practices that are now covered by law include:

1. sending unsolicited e-mail communications;
2. passing sensitive personal information on to a third party;
3. unauthorized access to competitor data;
4. copyright infringements.

Sarbanes–Oxley Act
A law defining acceptable accounting practices including audit and control of financial information

The Enron case, where senior managers and their accountants colluded to misstate company financial details, has had a significant impact on law. Such practice was clearly unethical and also illegal, but when the extent of the malpractice became apparent new laws were enacted to reduce the risk of such behaviour. This is typical of the pattern seen throughout this chapter where new laws are introduced to control unethical use of information. In 2002, the US government passed the **Sarbanes–Oxley Act** (Sarbox or SOX for short), which redefines legally acceptable accounting practices. Essentially, the law requires senior management to be responsible for the accuracy of their financial reporting, in other words information quality. The key clause is:

Section 302: Corporate Responsibility for Financial Reports.

The CEO and CFO of each issuer shall prepare a statement to accompany the audit report to certify the 'appropriateness of the financial statements and disclosures contained in the periodic report, and that those financial statements and disclosures fairly present, in all material respects, the operations and financial condition of the issuer'.

Furthermore, Section 404: Management Assessment of Internal Controls requires

an 'internal control report', which shall:

(1) state the responsibility of management for establishing and maintaining an adequate internal control structure and procedures for financial reporting; and
(2) contain an assessment, as of the end of the issuer's fiscal year, of the effectiveness of the internal control structure and procedures of the issuer for financial reporting.

This law affects not only US companies, but any company which has a listing or is registered in the US.

Such laws essentially mandate the use of systems to manage corporate performance management and electronic records management. It is a boon for many technology suppliers since it has stimulated demand for their products.

Owing to advances in technology and business practice, the law may not account for all unethical practices, so ethical decisions still have to be taken. In addition to the moral reasons for ethical practices, there are now financial reasons for them. Negative publicity about ethical practices can damage a company's or brand's reputation. Furthermore, some consumers and investors will avoid doing business with companies they consider unethical.

An unrelated law, with more limited relevance to organizations, but an opportunity for hardware and software organizations, is Basel II. This required that by the end of 2006 banks have at least three years of back-dated customer and operational information. The Basel II Accords are recommendations from the Basel, Switzerland, Bank for International Settlements' Basel Committee on Banking Supervision. They provide official guidelines for financial institutions that standardize measurements of credit risks, market risks and operational risk.

Basel II
Official guidelines for financial institutions that standardize measurements of credit risks, market risks and operational risk

The role of professional bodies

Guidance in ethical issues of information management is often provided by professional bodies which different types of manager may join. These are examples from the UK of some professional bodies whose members often have to make ethical decisions with respect to information management:

- *Chartered Institute of Marketing* (**www.cim.co.uk**). Marketers are typically responsible for customer information.
- *Chartered Institute of Personnel and Development* (**www.cipd.co.uk**). Human resources managers are typically responsible for employee information.
- *British Computer Society* (**www.bcs.org.uk**). The developers of information systems and the associated databases, also have ethical decisions to take about customer and employee information.
- *The Association for Information Management* (**www.aslib.co.uk**). Likewise, all information professionals and researchers will take ethical decisions about information.
- *Chartered Institute of Library and Information Professionals* (**www.cilip.org.uk**). Another group specifically for information professionals, with many librarians as members.
- *The Records Management Society* (**www.rms-gb.org.uk**). This society provides a lot of information on how its members must deal with the Freedom of Information Act.

Such organizations provide guidance notes and training courses which often cover laws related to information management, but where laws are less fully developed they will issue guidelines that are intended to support the professionalism of their industry. For example, specific legislation for e-mail marketing did not become available until late 2003 in many countries. However, guidelines and charters on acceptable practice were issued in many countries over five years before that point. This shows the important role such bodies have to play. They also have a role to play in commenting on new legal proposals to ensure that commercial interests are not disregarded.

Ethics within the information society

A further ethical issue with information management is the level of access to information resources and services available to different types of groups and individuals within society. This is inevitable where we have an information society, as explained in the first chapter. The social impact of the Internet has concerned many commentators since the Internet may have the effect of accentuating the differences in quality of life, both *within* a society in a single country and *between* different nations. The United Nations (1999), in a report on human development, noted that parallel worlds are developing where

> those with income, education and – literally – connections have cheap and instantaneous access to information. The rest are left with uncertain, slow and costly access ... the advantage of being connected will overpower the marginal and impoverished, cutting off their voices and concerns from the global conversation.

Where individuals are disadvantaged in this way, this is known as 'social exclusion'. The UK's Social Exclusion Unit (**www.socialexclusionunit.gov.uk**) describes social exclusion as:

> a shorthand term for what can happen when people or areas suffer from a combination of linked problems such as unemployment, poor skills, low incomes, poor housing, high crime environments, bad health and family breakdown.

While access to information is not paramount to people in this predicament, a moral argument can be made that they should not be further disadvantaged through lack of access to information that may help them. Indeed, there is much valuable information on the Internet from government agencies and charities that can help address specific problems or develop skills and careers.

Governments have an important role to play in ensuring that information is readily available to all who need it. In recognition of this, the European Community (EC) Information Society initiative (i2010) (**http://ec.europa.eu/informationsociety/eeuropa/i2010/index_en.htm**) was launched in 1998 with the aims of increasing public awareness of the impact of the information society and stimulating the participation of all in society. The strategy is ended in 2010 to be followed by a new initiative – the Digital Agenda (**http://ec.europa.eu/information_society/digital-agenda**). The information society was defined in 1997 by the UK INSINC working party on social inclusion in the information society as:

Information society
A society with widespread access and transfer of digital information within business and the community

> A society characterised by a high level of information intensity in the everyday life of most citizens, in most organisations and workplaces; by the use of common or compatible technology for a wide range of personal, social, educational and business activities; and by the ability to transmit and receive digital data rapidly between places irrespective of distance.

UNESCO (the United Nations Educational, Scientific and Cultural Organization) has also been active in advancing the information society in less developed countries (**http://portal.unesco.org/ci/**).

As part of the EC Information Society initiative, the EC eEurope Action Plan was launched in May 2000 with objectives of 'a cheaper, faster, more secure Internet; investing in people's skills and access; and stimulating the use of the Internet'. The Commission intends to increase Internet access relative to the US, in order to make Europe more competitive.

Also in May 2000, the EC announced that it wanted the supply of 'local loops', that is, the copper cables that link homes to telephone exchanges, to be unbundled so that newer companies can compete with traditional telecommunications suppliers. The objective here was the provision of widespread broadband services.

In member countries of the EU, different initatives have been launched. An example from the UK was the launch in 1999 of a 'UK Online' campaign (**www.ukonline.gov.uk**), initiatives and investment aimed at moving people, business and government itself online. An e-envoy and an e-minister were appointed. The then prime minister, Tony Blair, said:

> There is a revolution going on in our economy. A fundamental change, not a dot-com fad, but a real transformation towards a knowledge economy. So, today, I am announcing a new campaign. Its goal is to get the UK online. To meet the three stretching targets we have set: for Britain to be the best place in the world for e-commerce, with universal access to the Internet and all government services on the net. In short, the UK online campaign aims to get business, people and government online.

Quayle (2002) summarizes six strands of the UK government strategy for e-commerce:

1 To establish a brand in e-commerce both domestically and internationally.

2 To transform existing businesses.

3 To foster e-commerce creation and growth.

4 To expand the e-commerce talent pool (skills).

5 To provide leadership in international e-commerce policy development.

6 Government online should be a priority.

Some of these goals, such as 2, 3, 4 and 6, are typical for many countries, but the UK is unusual in seeking to take leadership (1 and 5). It can be expected that as widespread adoption of the Internet occurs, expenditures on these initiatives will decrease.

Specific targets have been set for the proportion of people and businesses that have access, including public access points for those who cannot currently afford the technology. Businesses that are aware of these initiatives can tap into sources of funding for development or free training to support their online initiatives.

Booz Allen Hamilton (2002) reviews approaches used by governments to encourage use of the Internet. They identify five broad themes in policy:

1 *Increasing the penetration of 'access devices'*. Approaches include either home access through Sweden's PC Tax Reform, or in public places, as in France's programme to develop 7000 access points by 2003. France also offers a tax incentive scheme, where firms can make tax-free gifts of PCs to staff for personal use.

2 *Increasing skills and confidence of target groups*. These may target potentially excluded groups, as with France's significant €150m campaign to train the unemployed. Japan's IT training programmes use existing mentors.

3 *Establishing 'driving licences' or 'passport' qualifications*. France, Italy and the UK have schemes which grant simple IT qualifications, aimed particularly at low-skilled groups such as the long-term unemployed.

4 *Building trust or allaying fears*. An example of this in the US is the 1998 Child Online Protection Act which used schemes to provide 'kitemark'-type verification, or certification of safe services.

5 *Direct marketing campaigns*. According to the report, only the UK, with its UK Online campaign, is marketing directly to citizens on a large scale.

A further approach is to provide access to government services; this is part of e-government.

Internet governance

The Internet raises many ethical and legal issues to be considered by society, such as:

- Can Internet content and activity be controlled?
- To what extent should this be enforced?
- What is the relationship between the Internet and freedom of speech?
- What role should government take?
- What role should industry and business take?

Internet governance
Control of the operation
and use of the Internet

Esther Dyson, author of *Release 2.0: A Design for Living in the Digital Age* (1998), who is influential in advising on the impact of Internet on society, describes 'Internet governance' as the control put in place to manage the growth of the Internet and its usage. Governance is traditionally undertaken by government, but the global nature of the Internet makes it less practical for a government to control cyberspace. She says:

> Now, with the advent of the Net, we are privatising government in a new way – not only in the traditional sense of selling things off to the private sector, but by allowing organisations independent of traditional governments to take on certain 'government' regulatory roles. These new international regulatory agencies will perform former government functions in counterpoint to increasingly global large companies and also to individuals and smaller private organisations who can operate globally over the Net.

Dyson (1998) describes different layers of jurisdiction. These are:

1 physical space comprising each individual country where its own laws such as those governing taxation, privacy and trading and advertising standards hold;
2 ISPs – the connection between the physical world and the virtual world.

The Internet is quite different from all previous communication media since it is much less easy for governments to control and shape its development. Think of print, TV, phone and radio and you can see that governments can exercise a fair degree of control on what they find acceptable. With the Internet, governments can pass laws, but their control is diminished since it is global and there are far more media owners to be monitored and controlled – everyone with Internet access becomes a potential publisher or media owner. It is relatively easy to control media owners such as newspapers and TV channels, but on the Internet there are millions of individual publishers. Online publication can be anonymous, again making control difficult. ISPs have an important role in Internet governance. ISPs transmit and archive Internet content such as e-mails and web pages and also hold vast amounts of data on user activity on the Internet – some of which is sold commercially through services such as Hitwise (**www.hitwise.com**). There have been limited attempts to control ISPs by government in Europe and the US, partly because it is against the ethics of free speech in these countries and the general ethics of Internet use. However, consider the ethics of allowing information to be freely available about making nuclear bombs or inciting racial hatred or child abuse. In these cases, society requires that governments act, and specific laws and associated monitoring services have been created as described later in this chapter. Typically, the burden has not been placed on ISPs to make them responsible for this content. A related issue is auction sites such as e-Bay which may contain distasteful information – a search on eBay for 'Nazi' reveals many memorabilia. However, this is not the most curious item allegedly put up for sale. The BBC e-commerce channel has reported on these items being placed for sale, often as a hoax:

- A Scottish castle (asking price £4m).
- An 8-year-old in Germany (asking price €1) – a 'joke' by her mother?

- Swansea University campus (asking price $2) – a protest against tuition fees.
- The seller (asking price $2) – a virtual date from a US woman sold for £25.
- A US Navy jet worth $28 million in 1997 – yours assembled for $9 million.
- A kidney (initial price, $25,000) – bidding stopped by eBay when bids reached $6 million.

Jurisdiction
The scope or extent of control of a law geographically – who it applies to

Jurisdiction in control of online content and activities is a further issue. While governments can readily create laws to control their own citizens and organizations, this is more difficult with international information transfer. Cross-national supra-government groups such as the European Union can improve coordination and control between countries. Since governments can control only their limited sphere of influence, activities illegal in one country may simply move to another. For example, spammers resident in the US moved to China and then moved again once new controls were introduced there. Efforts to introduce laws to prevent unsolicited commercial e-mail (spam) in the US and Europe have had limited success since much spam originates in other countries. Here cooperation between ISPs in different countries is required and governments have started to play a role in facilitating this.

Independent supra-government organizations

There are a number of established non-profit-making organizations that exert control and influence on different aspects of the Internet. These are sometimes called 'supra-governmental organizations' since their control is above government level.

Independent lobbying bodies that are concerned about privacy have a valuable role to play. For example, the Internet Watch Foundation (**www.iwf.org.uk**) works in partnership with ISPs, telcos, mobile operators, software providers, police and government, to minimize the availability of illegal Internet content such as child abuse or racist images. At the same time, other non-profit organizations such as Cyber Rights (**www.cyber-rights.org**) campaign for free speech (although they do not condone all material online). Cyber Rights describes its mission as 'to promote free speech and privacy on the Internet and raise public awareness of these important issues'. It seems difficult for society and governments to identify the line between what is generally acceptable and what is dangerous. In an article entitled 'Is it time to scrap the Internet?' (BBC, 2004), BBC reporter Bill Thompson describes a case of a sexually motivated murder where the perpetrator was influenced by images available over the Internet. The partner of the murderer was reported as speaking for many when he said: 'Jane would still be here if it wasn't for the Internet.'

Thompson argues for creation of a new network which, unlike the Internet, has controls to protect privacy and at the same time control criminal activity built in from the start. We are sure that this will happen, but when it will happen or whether it will be based on enhancement to current Internet standards we are unsure

There are also supra-government organizations that control different aspects of the technology described in Chapter 2, such as ICANN and the Internet Society. Their role tends to be limited to technology standards rather than ethical standards.

E-government

E-government
The application of e-commerce technologies to government and public services

Not to be confused with Internet governance, **e-government** refers to the application of e-commerce technologies to government and public services. It is one facet of the move to the information society as government aims to make its services or control processes available to all organizations and individuals via Internet technology. In the same way that e-business can be understood as transactions with customers (citizens), suppliers and internal communications, e-government covers a similar range of applications:

- Citizens – facilities for dissemination of information – for example, in 2002 Hansard, the record of the UK parliament, was received in paper form by only two individuals in the UK, while over 300,000 per month access it online. Such communications can occur at both national and local government levels. Transactions with citizens potentially include electronic voting, which has been trialled in the UK, the US and Sweden, and requests for local government services. Filing of tax electronically is another e-government application for citizens.
- Suppliers – government departments have a vast network of suppliers. They can achieve the same benefits of e-procurement as businesses.
- Internal communications – the use of intranets for information collection and dissemination and e-mail and workflow systems for improving efficiency can be deployed in government departments.

To achieve e-government, some governments have set targets for both buy and sell side. In the UK, the government's main target was that by 2005, 100 per cent of dealings with government should be capable of being delivered electronically, where there is a demand. According to E-envoy (2002), other aims in the 'electronic service delivery' programme were:

- Refine analysis of customer groupings and carry out customer needs analyses and the Office of the e-Envoy will work with departments to introduce e-business strategies for key customer segments.
- Ensure that there is a strategy, with a measurable baseline, to maximize take-up of e-services.
- Re-engineer departmental business processes to fully exploit new technologies.
- Ensure that key transactional services are e-enabled via the Government Gateway.
- Drive forward citizen participation in democracy.
- Further develop a cross-government knowledge management system.
- Continue to drive forward e-procurement and e-tendering.

In Australia, the National Office for the Information Economy (NOIE) (**www.noie. gov.au**) has created a strategic framework which has the following themes. This summarizes the types of actions that many governments are taking to encourage e-business within their countries.

- *Access, participation and skills* – Encouraging all sectors of the community to actively participate in the information economy.
- *Adoption of e-business* – The government is working to provide more efficient communication between businesses to help improve the productivity of the Australian economy. A priority focus for 2002/2003 was to promote the uptake of electronic procurement and broader electronic business processes, especially by small and medium enterprises.
- *Confidence, trust and security* – The government is working to build public trust and confidence in going online, and addressing barriers to consumer confidence in e-commerce and other areas of online content and activity.
- *e-Government strategies and implementation* – The use of new technologies for government information provision, service delivery and administration has the potential to transform government. This transformation will improve the lives of Australians. NOIE provides a framework and coordinates whole-of-government approaches to support Commonwealth agency efforts in this area.
- *Environment for information economy firms* – Provide research on the environmental variables that drive innovation and growth in the information economy and underpin its future development.

- *International dimensions* – NOIE, in cooperation with other government bodies, represents Australia in world forums where decisions that may affect national interests in the information economy are made.

Booz Allen Hamilton (2002) reported that the leading countries in e-government are Sweden, Australia and Germany. In Sweden, for example, local authorities allow public participation via the Internet in council meetings. However, the report notes that:

> Generally, delivery of services on the internet has been approached as an opportunity to automate services over an additional channel rather than opportunity for service innovation, and so comprehensive process redesign is only just beginning to emerge.

More recent assessments of different countries are available from the iEurope (2010) site: **http://ec.europe.eu/information_society/eeuropa/i2010/index_en.htm**.

Many innovative schemes (such as e-voting) remain at the pilot stage and, as a result, evidence for real impact is scarce. Furthermore, with currently low levels of uptake of e-government services compared to offline channels, even in the leading countries, tangible impact on costs and efficiency is yet to be felt.

A rare example of both process redesign and tangible efficiency gains is Italy's e-procurement platform, Consip. Another example is the German student loan authority, which has moved to paperless administration with savings of €4.5m annually.

Privacy

Privacy
The right of an individual to control the personal information held about them by third parties

Personal data
Any information about an individual stored by companies concerning their customers or employees

One of the most important issues in managing information which has both legal and ethical implications for managers is privacy. In the context of information, 'privacy' refers to an individual's rights as a customer, employee or citizen concerning what **personal data** are held about them by third parties such as companies, employers and government agencies and how they are used. 'Personal data' refers to contact details such as name, address, phone number and e-mail. For a customer it also includes details such as products purchased, credit history, when a website has been visited or which e-mails have been viewed. For an employee it can also include details such as salary, sickness and holiday records. Users of government services such as councils or healthcare also hold personal data which may include age, sex, religion, ethnic background and services used. Think about how many organizations hold your personal data, what they know about you and how often they contact you by mail, phone or e-mail. Does this worry you or is it an acceptable part of business practice?

Mason (1986) has usefully divided issues related to privacy into four areas:

- *Privacy* – what information is held about the individual? Are personal details held which are not arguably relevant to the business?
- *Accuracy* – is it correct? Incorrect information may disadvantage an individual.
- *Property* – who owns it and how can ownership be transferred?
- *Accessibility* – who is allowed to access this information, and under which conditions? This is the security concern.

Fletcher (2001) provides an alternative perspective, raising these issues of concern for both the individual and the marketer:

- *Transparency* – who is collecting what information?
- *Security* – how is information protected once it is collected by a company?
- *Liability* – who is responsible if data are abused?

Mini case study 12.1   **Google privacy**

Following concerns from a number of users and privacy campaigners, plus being ranked as having the worst privacy policy of the major Internet organizations (Google, 2007a), Google altered the way in which its cookies operated. Previously, like most cookies that store information about the user's website preferences, they would reside on the user's machine indefinitely. Increasing privacy concerns, though, have prompted Google to set a maximum lifespan of two years on all its cookies. After this time has elapsed they will automatically be deleted (Google, 2007b).

Google point out that users can delete any cookies stored on their computers at any time through their Internet controls.

As well as making the change to the cookies, Google posted comprehensive explanatory materials via its official blog to reassure and educate its community of users about its Privacy Policy – **http://googleblog.blogspot.com/2007/08/google-search-privacy-plain-and-simple.html**.

Google also committed to reducing the length of time that it stores details of web searches that have been made, including the user's IP address (Google, 2007c).

A further key issue not highlighted by these authors is how an individual's data are used. For instance, if personal data are used for intrusive marketing then this can also be considered an infringement of privacy. We will now explore some examples of potential data use or abuse.

Data held about individuals are commonly used for marketing products to potential or existing customers. Your name will be available for purchase or rental from a database traditionally known by marketers as a 'cold list', so called because the company that purchases the data from a third party does not know you. Your name will also be stored on a **house list** of companies you have purchased from. We will examine what rights the individual has and what the company is allowed to do. Such decisions are often not straightforward. Think of your bank; if you have a current account you would probably think it was acceptable for them to send you details about other product offerings such as a savings account. But what if they passed your details on to a related company which offered you insurance or a loan – are these product-related? Many would feel this was infringement of their personal data.

Large companies such as Claritas (**www.claritas.com**) and Experian (**www.experian.com**) which operate in Europe and beyond can provide cold lists with postal and e-mail addresses for millions of consumers. These lists not only include contact details, but also characterize individuals in different ways such as according to income or social group or the company they work for. This is often based on their postcode since similar types of people generally live in a small postal sector. Customers that share common characteristics are grouped together so that marketers can send more relevant offers to the groups. This process is known as '**customer segmentation**'. One example of a system used for customer segmentation is MOSAIC. According to Experian, 'it is available in 20 different countries throughout the world and classifies more than 800 million people into distinct groups which can be used by organizations to drive intelligent decisioning'. MOSAIC is sometimes referred to as 'lifestyle data' since it categorizes people. For example, as part of MOSAIC for financial services you will be placed in one of the following groups according to where you live: 'adventurous spenders', 'burdened borrowers', 'indebted strugglers', 'just about surviving', and targeted with offers to invest or borrow accordingly.

Applications of MOSAIC for marketers include:

- *Database segmentation and customer profiling.* Identifying different types of consumers in their database according to their neighbourhood since people with similar characteristics tend to live in any area.

Cold list
Data about individuals that are rented or sold by a third party

House list
Data about existing customers used to market products to encourage future purchase

Customer segmentation
Customers are grouped according to their characteristics such as income

Direct marketing
Communications with customers or potential customers using media such as mail, phone or e-mail, encouraging response leading to a sale or further dialogue

- *Customer acquisition and retention.* Once customers have been grouped into different categories, marketing communications or **direct marketing** can be used to encourage them to purchase services. For instance, a marketer offering health club membership could target consumers above a certain income who read a particular newspaper.
- *Branch location and planning.* If a company such as a supermarket plans a new store opening, then it can create models of its potential revenue according to the spending power of consumers who live in its vicinity.
- *Media planning.* Local adverts on TV or in print can also be scheduled according to consumer characteristics.
- *Category management.* This is a process that involves managing product categories such as soft drinks or cereals as business units and customizing them on a store-by-store basis to satisfy different customer needs.

Unsolicited postal direct marketing remains legal in many countries such as the UK and France, but there are exceptions – it is outlawed in Germany. In countries such as the UK and France the business practice could be considered to be unethical because it seems unpopular – many people complain about direct marketing. However, proponents of direct marketing would argue that such countries provide consumers with a choice in receiving information since they can ask to be removed from mailing lists if they wish and businesses would argue that many consumers do respond to direct marketing – suggesting that it meets a need from consumers and other businesses.

Debate 12.1

The sending of unsolicited direct marketing to consumers or businesses should not be permitted by law in any country.

Perhaps of more concern is information held about individuals' finances. Credit checking agencies such as Equifax (**www.equifax.com**), which operates both in Europe and the Americas, hold information about the financial holdings of individuals and their ability to pay. The information held by such agencies, which, for a fee, is shared with financial services organizations such as banks, can make it difficult for an individual to obtain loans. It is vital that this information be of good quality.

Data protection and privacy legislation

Data protection legislation
Law intended to protect the privacy of consumers' data through defining how organizations can gather, store, process and disclose personal information

Protecting the privacy of consumers has been accepted by many governments as an important issue and they have enacted laws to control the use of personal information by companies. In Europe, the legislation is known as '**data protection legislation**'. This legislation is well established; the European Union introduced legislation for its member countries in the 1980s and this is continually revised to reflect changes to the technology. In Nordic countries, which are not all in the European Union, similar laws exist which acknowledge the use of a personal identity code for each person in an ID card scheme.

This type of legislation does not go unchallenged. While this is clearly in consumers' interests, some companies see the practice as restrictive. In 2002, ten companies, including IBM, Oracle and VeriSign, which refer to themselves as the 'Global Privacy Alliance (GPA)' lobbied the EU, saying that it put too much emphasis on the protection of individuals' privacy, and not enough on ensuring the free flow of information between companies! More recently a directive has been introduced to add additional protection to privacy related to electronic communications such as the Internet and e-mail. This is summarized in a later section.

Similar laws exist in many countries and are documented by Privacy International (**www.privacyinternational.org**). In Australia the law is known as 'privacy law' (**www.privacy.gov.au**). In the US, there is a privacy initiative aimed at education of consumers and business (**www.ftc.gov/privacy**), but legislation is more limited.

Data protection legislation is there to protect the individual, to protect their privacy and to prevent misuse of their personal data. Indeed, the first article of the European Union Directive 95/46/EC, on which legislation in individual European countries is based, specifically refers to personal data. It says:

> Member states shall protect the fundamental rights and freedoms of natural persons [i.e. a named individual at home or at work], and in particular their right to privacy with respect to the processing of personal data.

In Europe, individual countries develop or enact their own laws, based on the Directive, which hold to the principles, but may differ in detail. For example, German law does not permit any unsolicited direct mail communications, which are permitted in the UK, although consumers can request not to receive these as explained later in this section. In the UK, the enactment of the European legislation is the Data Protection Act 1984, 1998 (DPA), which is managed by the 'Information Commissioner' and summarized at **www.informationcommissioner.gov.uk**. Any company that holds personal data on computers or on file about customers or employees must be registered with a data protection registrar (although there are some exceptions which may exclude small businesses). This process is known as **notification**.

There are eight enforceable principles of good practice arising from the Directive 95/46/EC and the Data Protection Act that any organization processing **personal data** (even the smallest business processing customer data may need to be registered) must comply with. Since it is useful for managers to be conversant with the terms associated with data protection such as 'data subject', 'data controller' and 'subject access request', we will now explore the implications of the eight data protection principles or requirements in more detail. The eight principles are only meaningful if a more detailed interpretation and examples are given. The guidelines on the eight data protection principles are produced by Information Commissioner (1998), on which this overview is based. These principles state that personal data should be:

Notification
The process whereby companies register with the Data Protection Register to inform it about their data holdings

Personal data
Any information about an individual stored by companies concerning their customers or employees

1 Fairly and lawfully processed

In full: *'Personal data shall be processed fairly and lawfully and, in particular, shall not be processed unless – at least one of the conditions in Schedule 2 is met; and in the case of sensitive personal data, at least one of the conditions in Schedule 3 is also met.'*

The Information Commissioner has produced a 'fair processing code' which suggests how an organization needs to achieve 'fair and lawful processing' under the details of Schedules 2 and 3 of the Act. This requires:

Data controller
Each company must have a defined person responsible for data protection

Data subject
The legal term to refer to the individual whose data are held

- Appointment of a **data controller** who is a person with defined responsibility for data protection within a company.

- Clear details in communications such as on a website or direct mail of how a '**data subject**' can contact the data controller or a representative.

- Before data processing 'the data subject has given his consent' or the processing must be *necessary* either for a 'contract to which the data subject is a party' (for example, as part of a sale of a product) or because it is required by other laws. Consent is defined in the published guidelines as *'any freely given specific and informed indication of his wishes by which the data subject signifies his agreement to personal data relating to him being processed'.*

- Sensitive personal data require particular care; this includes
  - the racial or ethnic origin of the data subject;
  - political opinions;
  - religious beliefs or other beliefs of a similar nature;
  - membership of a trade union;
  - physical or mental health or condition;
  - sexual life;
  - the commission or alleged commission or proceedings of any offence;
- No other laws must be broken in processing the data.

2 Processed for limited purposes

In full: *'Personal data shall be obtained only for one or more specified and lawful purposes, and shall not be further processed in any manner incompatible with that purpose or those purposes.'*

This implies that the organization must make it clear why and how the data will be processed at the point of collection. For example, an organization has to explain how your data will be used if you provide your details on a website when entering a prize draw. You would also have to agree (give consent) for further communications from the company.

Figure 12.1 suggests some of the issues that should be considered when a data subject is informed of how the data will be used. Important issues are:

- whether future communications will be sent to the individual (explicit consent is required for this in online channels; this is clarified by the related Privacy and Electronic Communications Regulation Act which is referred to below);
- whether the data will be passed on to third parties (again explicit consent is required);
- how long the data will be kept.

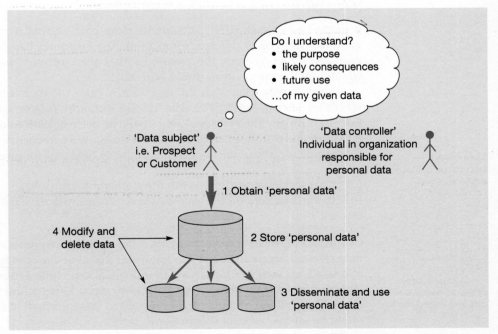

Figure 12.1 Information flows that need to be understood for compliance with data protection legislation

3 Adequate, relevant and not excessive

In full: *'Personal data shall be adequate, relevant and not excessive in relation to the purpose or purposes for which they are processed.'*

This specifies that the minimum necessary amount of data is requested for processing. For example, it would not be applicable in the Lo-cost Airline Company example for the company to ask about your credit history. There is difficulty in reconciling this provision between the needs of the individual and the needs of the company. The more details that an organization has about a customer, the better they can understand that customer and so develop products and marketing communications specific to that customer to which they are more likely to respond.

4 Accurate

In full: *'Personal data shall be accurate and, where necessary, kept up to date.'*

It is clearly also in the interest of an organization in an ongoing relationship with a partner that the data be kept accurate and up to date. The guidelines on the Act suggest that additional steps should be taken to check that data are accurate, in case they are in error, for example due to mis-keying by the data subject, organization or some other reason. Inaccurate data is defined in the guidelines as: 'incorrect or misleading as to any matter of fact'.

The guidelines go on to discuss the importance of keeping information up to date. This is only necessary where there is an ongoing relationship and the rights of the individual may be affected if they are not up to date. This implies, for example, that a credit-checking agency should keep credit scores up to date.

5 Not kept longer than necessary

In full: *'Personal data processed for any purpose or purposes shall not be kept for longer than is necessary for that purpose or those purposes.'*

The guidelines state: *'To comply with this Principle, data controllers will need to review their personal data regularly and to delete the information which is no longer required for their purposes.'*

It might be in a company's interests to 'clean data' so that records that are not relevant are archived or deleted, for example if a customer has not purchased for ten years. However, there is the possibility that the customer may still buy again, in which case the information would be useful.

If a relationship between the organization and the data subject ends, then data should be deleted. This will be clear in some instances, for example when an employee leaves a company their personal data should be deleted. With a consumer who has purchased products from a company this is less clear since frequency of purchase will vary, for example a car manufacturer could justifiably hold data for several years.

6 Processed in accordance with the data subject's rights

In full: *'Personal data shall be processed in accordance with the rights of data subjects under this Act.'*

Subject access request
A request by a data subject to view personal data from an organization

One aspect of the data subject's rights is the option to request a copy of their personal data from an organization; this is known as a 'subject access request'. For payment of a small fee such as £10 or £30, an individual can request information which must be supplied by the organization within 40 days. This includes all information on paper files and on computer. If you requested this information from your bank there might be several boxes of transactions!

Other aspects of a data subject's rights which the law upholds are designed to prevent or control processing which:

- causes damage or distress (for example, repeatedly sending mailshots to someone who has died);
- is used for direct marketing (for example, in the UK consumers can subscribe to the mail, e-mail or telephone preference services to avoid unsolicited mailings, e-mails or phone calls). This invaluable service is provided by the Direct Marketing Association (**www.dmaconsumers.org**). If you subscribe to these services organizations must check against these 'exclusion lists' before contacting you. If they don't, and some don't, they are breaking the law;
- is used for automatic decision taking – automated credit checks, for example, may result in unjust decisions on taking a loan – these can be investigated if you feel the decision is unfair.

7 Secure

In full: *'Appropriate technical and organizational measures shall be taken against unauthorised or unlawful processing of personal data and against accidental loss or destruction of, or damage to, personal data.'*

This guideline places a legal imperative on organizations to prevent unauthorized internal or external access to information and also its modification or destruction. Of course, most organizations would want to do this anyway since the information has value to their organization. Techniques for managing data security were discussed in Chapter 9.

Of course, the cost of security measures will vary according to the level of security required. The Act allows for this through this provision:

> (i) Taking into account the state of technological development at any time and the cost of implementing any measures, the measures must ensure a level of security appropriate to: (a) the harm that might result from a breach of security; and (b) the nature of the data to be protected. (ii) The data controller must take reasonable steps to ensure the reliability of staff having access to the personal data.

8 Not transferred to countries without adequate protection

In full: *'Personal data shall not be transferred to a country or territory outside the European Economic Area, unless that country or territory ensures an adequate level of protection of the rights and freedoms of data subjects in relation to the processing of personal data.'*

Transfer of data beyond Europe is likely for multinational companies. This principle prevents export of data to countries that do not have sound data processing laws. If the transfer is required in concluding a sale or contract or if the data subject agrees to it, then transfer is legal.

To help understand the application of the data protection guidelines to an organization, complete Activity 12.1.

Debate 12.2

Most large retail firms have the opportunity to capture large amounts of customer data, including their names and addresses, credit card details and purchasing habits and preferences.

The Internet provides a medium through which masses of consumer information can be collected relatively easily and cost-effectively. Often this information is provided freely, by web shoppers for instance when making a purchase. Sometimes, however, data are gathered without the surfer's knowledge. Even data that are gathered with the consent of the individual may later be sold to third parties without their knowing (Sipior, Ward and Rongione, 2004).

Ask yourself, does this enable the stores to provide a tailored marketing service that draws your attention to products and services that you are interested in, or does it enable them to use a targeted marketing service that highlights products and services that you are likely to procure?

Activity 12.1	Data protection guidelines

Purpose

Many managers are required to interpret the relevance of the data protection guidelines to their organizations. This activity applies the eight principles to a university or college as part of an organization.

Activity

You are responsible for data protection at a university and need to develop guidelines for staff. You are comparing or benchmarking your current guidelines against those of other universities in your country.

visit the www

Perform a Google search to find data protection guidelines for universities or colleges in your country. For example, in the UK, type: ["data protection guidelines" site:ac.uk] to restrict the search to academic institutions.

Produce a brief summary of how each of the eight principles of the Data Protection Act applies to management of personal data of students in the university context.

Tip You may also find it useful to refer to the guidelines on data protection developed by the Office of the Information Commissioner and summarized at **www.informationcommissioner. gov.uk.**

Regulations on privacy and electronic communications

While the Data Protection Directive 95/46 afforded a reasonable level of protection for consumers, it was quickly superseded by advances in technology. One of the most significant issues was the volume of unsolicited electronic e-mail, commonly known as spam, which was discussed in Chapter 11. As a result, in 2002 the European Union passed an act '2002/58/EC Directive on Privacy and Electronic Communications' to complement previous data protection law. This act is significant from an information technology perspective since it applies specifically to electronic communications such as e-mail and the monitoring of websites.

As with other European laws, this law was implemented differently in different countries. Some countries considered infringements more seriously. A company which is in breach of the directive in Italy is threatened by fines of up to €66,000 while in the UK the maximum fine is £5,000. It is clearly important for managers to have access to legal advice which applies not only to their country, but also other European countries.

In the US in January 2004, a new federal law known as the CAN-SPAM Act was introduced to assist in the control of unsolicited e-mail. CAN-SPAM stands for Controlling the Assault of Non-Solicited Pornography and Marketing Act. This harmonized separate laws in different US states, but was less strict than in some states such as California. The Act requires unsolicited commercial e-mail messages to be labelled (though not by a standard method) and to include opt-out instructions and the sender's physical address. It prohibits the use of deceptive subject lines and false headers in such messages. Anti-spam legislation in other countries can be accessed at **www.spamlaws.com.**

We will now review the implications for managers of the UK enactment of 2002/58/EC Directive on Privacy and Electronic Communications. This came into force in the UK on 11 December 2003 as the **Privacy and Electronic Communications Regulations Act.** The law (PECR) is published at: **www.hmso.gov.uk/si/si2003/ 20032426.htm.**

Privacy and Electronic Communications Regulations Act
A law intended to control the distribution of e-mail and other online communications including cookies

It is a surprisingly accessible and common-sense document – many marketers were practising similar principles already. Clauses 22 to 24 are the main clauses relevant to e-mail communications. We will summarize the main implications of the law by picking out key phrases. The new PECR law:

1 Applies to consumer marketing using e-mail or SMS text messages

22 (1) applies to '*individual subscribers*'. 'Individual subscribers' means consumers, although the Information Commissioner has stated that this may be reviewed in future and include business subscribers, as is the case in some other countries such as Italy and Germany.

Although this sounds like great news for business-to-business (B2B) marketers and some take the view that '*great, the new law doesn't apply to us*', this could be dangerous. There has been adjudication by the Advertising Standards Agency which found against a B2B organization that had unwittingly e-mailed consumers from what they believed was an in-house list of B2B customers. Distinguishing between those working for large organizations and small partnerships may be difficult, and what about the many business users who opt-in for business e-mail communications using their personal Hotmail or Yahoo! Mail account?

2 Is an 'opt-in' regime

Opt-in
A customer proactively agrees to receive further information

The law applies to '*unsolicited communications*' (22 (1)). It was introduced with a view to reducing spam or unsolicited commercial e-mail, although we all know that its impact will be limited on spammers beyond Europe. The relevant phrase is part of 22 (2) where the recipient must have '*previously notified the sender that he consents*' or has proactively agreed to receiving commercial e-mail. This is **opt-in**. Opt-in can be achieved online or offline through asking people whether they want to receive e-mail. Online this is often done through a tick box. The ASA CAP code (see below) refers to '*explicit consent*', which suggests that a proactive action at the point of opt-in is required. On a web profiling form this means actively selecting the option to receive e-mail by ticking a box. The main options are shown in Figure 12.2. Figure 12.2(a) is opt-out and it can be considered that this is against the spirit of the law since someone may sign up to receive e-mail communications without realizing it. Figure 12.2(b) is opt-in since the subscriber has to explicitly check the box. Figure 12.2(c) is also opt-in, but it is a more subtle approach. The consumer cannot enter the prize draw unless they complete the form.

Permission marketing
Customers agree (opt in) to be involved in an organization's marketing activities usually as a result of an incentive

The approach required by the law, in common with many aspects of data protection and privacy law, has been used by many organizations for some time. In other words, sending unsolicited e-mails was thought to be unethical and also not in the best interests of the company because of the risk of annoying customers. In fact, the law conforms to an established approach known as '**Permission marketing**', a term coined by US commentator Seth Godin. Godin (1999) notes that with the advent of the web and digital TV we now receive over 3000 messages a day! From the marketing organization's viewpoint, this leads to a dilution in the effectiveness of the messages – how can the communications of any one company stand out? From the customer's viewpoint, Godin says that 'time is seemingly in ever-shorter supply, customers are losing patience and expect reward for their attention, time and information'. Godin refers to the traditional approach as 'interruption marketing'. Permission marketing is about seeking the customer's permission before engaging them in a relationship and providing something in exchange. The classic exchange is based on information or entertainment – a B2B site can offer a free report in exchange for a customer sharing their e-mail address which will be used to maintain a dialogue; a B2C site can offer a screensaver in exchange. Godin says that marketing communications should be anticipated, relevant and personal (see **www.permission.com**).

3 Requires an opt-out option in all communications

Opt-out
A customer declines the offer to receive further information

An **opt-out** or method of 'unsubscribing' is required so that the recipient does not receive future communications. In a database this means that a 'do not e-mail' field must be created to avoid e-mailing these customers. The law states that a 'simple means of refusing' future communications is required both when the details are first collected and in each subsequent communication.

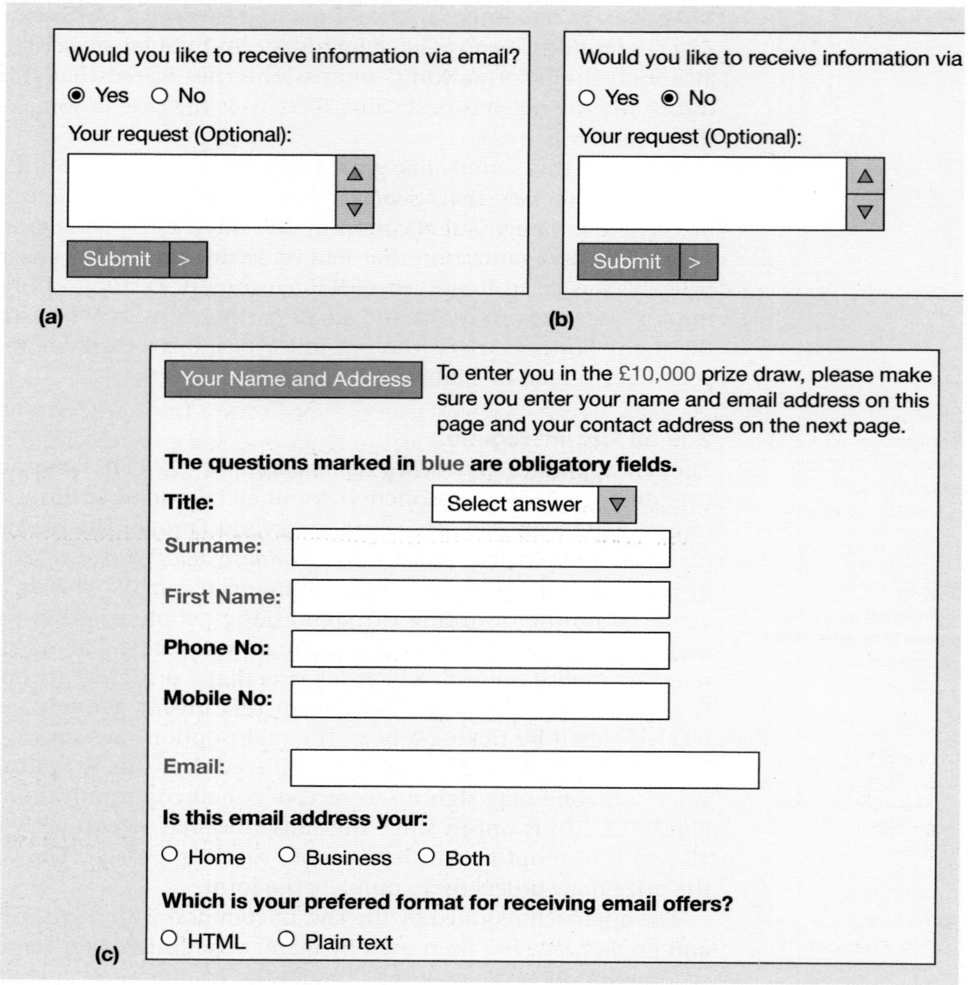

Would you like to receive information via email?	Would you like to receive information via
● Yes ○ No	○ Yes ● No
Your request (Optional):	Your request (Optional):
[text box] △ ▽	[text box] △ ▽
Submit >	Submit >
(a)	(b)

Your Name and Address   To enter you in the £10,000 prize draw, please make sure you enter your name and email address on this page and your contact address on the next page.

The questions marked in blue are obligatory fields.

Title: Select answer ▽

Surname: [text box]

First Name: [text box]

Phone No: [text box]

Mobile No: [text box]

Email: [text box]

Is this email address your:

○ Home   ○ Business   ○ Both

Which is your prefered format for receiving email offers?

○ HTML   ○ Plain text

(c)

Figure 12.2 Online forms: (a) opt-in, (b) opt-out, (c) implicit opt-in

4 Does not apply to existing customers when marketing similar products

This common-sense clause (22 (3) (a)) states that previous opt-in is not required if the contact details were obtained during the course of the sale or negotiations for the sale of a product or service. This is sometimes known as 'soft opt-in'. While this is great news for retailers, it is less clear where this leaves not-for-profit organizations such as charities or public sector organizations where the concept of a sale does not apply.

Clause 22 (3) (b) adds that when marketing to existing customers the marketer may market 'similar products and services only'. Case law will help in clarifying this. For example, for a bank, it is not clear whether a customer with an insurance policy could be targeted for a loan.

5 Contact details must be provided

It is not sufficient to send an e-mail with a simple sign-off from 'The Marketing team' or 'Web team' with no further contact details. The law requires a name, address or phone number to whom a recipient can complain.

6 The 'From' identification of the sender must be clear

Spammers aim to disguise the e-mail originator. The law says that the identity of the person who sends the communication must not be 'disguised or concealed' and that a valid address to 'send a request that such communications cease' should be provided.

7 Applies to direct marketing communications

The communications that the legislation refers to are for 'direct marketing'. This suggests that other communications involved with customer service, such as an e-mail about a monthly phone statement, are not covered, so the opt-out choice may not be required here.

8 Restricts the use of cookies

Some privacy campaigners consider that the user's privacy is invaded by planting cookies or electronic tags on the end-user's computer. The concept of the cookie and its associated law is not straightforward, so it warrants separate discussion.

Cookies and the law

Cookies
Cookies are small text files stored on an end-user's computer to enable websites to identify them

A 'cookie' is a data file placed on your computer that identifies an individual computer. 'Cookie' derives from the Unix operating system term 'magic cookie' which meant something passed between routines or programs that enables the receiver to perform some operation.

The cookie is placed on the computer via the web browser by the website you visit. This could be considered to be unethical since the organization is tracking the behaviour of individuals. However, it is a powerful technique from a marketing point of view since it is used to identify a particular customer and tailor the web session accordingly. One of the powerful features of cookies for a website owner is the ability to match an individual to their personal details such as name, address, job and preferences such as information delivery required. This is helpful for the site owner since they can use **personalization** (recommendations based on the preferences and characteristics of the individual). It can be argued that this is ethical since it provides the customer with a better service – many users of Amazon, for example, benefit from the recommendations made to them about other books to purchase.

Personalization
Recommendations based on the preferences and characteristics of the individual

Session cookie
A cookie used to manage a single visitor session

There are two forms of cookies: **session cookies** and **persistent cookies.** Session cookies are used to manage a single visitor session, for example they manage the process of adding items to a shopping basket and then checking out; as the website visitor moves from page to page they are still recognized. Persistent cookies remain on the computer after a visitor session has ended. Their main purpose is the identification of returning visitors. Without the use of persistent cookies it is not possible to uniquely identify an individual returning to a website without requesting that they identify themselves through a username.

Persistent cookie
Cookies remaining on the computer after a visitor session has ended. Used to recognize returning visitors

Cookies are stored as individual text files in a directory on a personal computer. There is usually one file per website. For example: daverchaffey@british-airways.txt. This file contains encoded information as follows:

> FLTrVIS |K:bapzRnGdxBYUU|D:Jul-25-2010| british-airways.com/ 0 425259904 29357426 1170747936 29284034 *

The information in the cookie file is essentially just an identification number and a date of the last visit, although other information can be stored.

Cookies are specific to a particular browser and computer, so if a user connects from a different computer such as at work or starts using a different browser, the website will not identify him or her as a similar user.

Some examples of cookie use

The following are common applications of cookies:

● Cookies are used to identify users and retrieve their preferences from a database. For example, I subscribe to the E-consultancy service (**www.econsultancy.com**) for the latest information about e-business; each time I return I do not have the annoyance of having to log in because it remembers my previous visit. Many sites feature a 'Remember Me' option.

- Retailers such as Amazon can also recognize returning visitors and can recommend related books purchased by other readers.

- Advertising networks use cookies to track the number of times a particular computer has been shown a particular banner advertisement; they can also track adverts served on sites across an ad network and there was an individual rights outcry in the late 1990s because Doubleclick was using this to profile customers. Doubleclick no longer operates an ad network.

- Software such as Webtrends (**www.webtrends.com**) which analyses statistics on visitors to websites relies on persistent cookies to find the proportion of repeat visitors to a website.

Privacy issues with cookie use

Many distrust cookies since they indicate that a 'big brother' is monitoring your actions. Others fear that their personal details or credit card details may be accessed by other websites. This is very unlikely since all the cookies contain is a short identifier or number that is used to link you to your record in a database. Anyone who found the cookie wouldn't be able to log-on to the database without your password. Cookies do not contain passwords, credit card information or any personal details as many people seem to think. These are held on the site servers protected by firewalls and usernames and passwords. In most cases, the worst that someone who gets access to your cookies can do is to find out which sites you have been visiting.

A technical issue with cookies is that they do not identify an individual unless only one person uses a machine, and sometimes it may be several. Although cookies such as those on Amazon provide convenience since it is not necessary to log-on to the site each time you visit, they may also be a security risk. If someone else uses a machine you have used they could potentially access your information or even buy a book, although the site will usually prompt again for a password after a short interval.

It is possible to block cookies if the user finds out how to block them, but this is not straightforward and many customers either do not know or do not mind that their privacy may be infringed. In 2003 an interesting survey on perception and behaviour with regard to cookies was conducted in the UK (RedEye, 2003). Of the 1,000 respondents:

- 50 per cent had used more than one computer in the last three months;
- 70 per cent said that their computer was used by more than one person;
- 94 per cent said they either accepted cookies or did know what they were, although 20 per cent said they only accepted session cookies;
- 71 per cent were aware of cookies and accepted them; of these, only 18 per cent did not know how to delete a cookie, and 55 per cent of them were deleting them on a monthly basis;
- 89 per cent knew what cookies were and how to delete them and said that they had deleted them once in the last three months.

Legal constraints on cookies

The PECR law limits the use of cookies. It states:

a person shall *not* use an electronic communications *network to store information*, or to gain access to information stored, in the terminal equipment of a subscriber or user unless the following requirements are met.

The requirements are:

(a) the user is provided with *clear and comprehensive information about the purposes of the storage of*, or access to, that information; and

(b) is *given the opportunity to refuse the storage* of or access to that information.

(a) suggests that it is important that there is a clear **privacy statement** and (b) suggests that opt-in to cookies is required. In other words, on the first visit to the site, a box would have to be ticked to agree to the use of cookies. This was thought by many commentators to be a curious provision since this facility is already available in the web browser. A further provision clarifies this. The law states: 'where such storage or access is *strictly necessary* for the provision of an information society service requested by the subscriber or user.' This indicates that for an e-commerce service session cookies are legitimate without the need for opt-in. It is arguable whether the identification of return visitors is 'strictly necessary' and this is why some sites have a 'Remember me' tick box next to the log-in. Through doing this they are compliant with the law. Using cookies for tracking return visits alone would seem to be outlawed, but we will have to see how case law develops over the coming years before this is resolved.

Viral e-mail marketing

One widespread business practice that is not covered explicitly in the PECR law at the time of writing is '**viral marketing**'. The network of people referred to in the definition is more powerful in an online context where e-mail is used to transmit the virus – rather like a cold or flu virus. The combination of the viral offer and the transmission medium is sometimes referred to as the 'viral agent'.

Examples of online viral marketing which build awareness through video clips from brands such as Virgin, T-Mobile and Microsoft are viewable at DMC (**www.dmc.co.uk**). For example, Mazda has commissioned several awareness-building campaigns based around humorous video clips for new car launches.

The following categories of online viral marketing can be identified:

1 *Pass-along e-mail viral*. This is where e-mail alone is used to spread the message. Towards the end of a commercial e-mail it does no harm to prompt the first recipient to forward the e-mail along to interested friends or colleagues. Even if only one in 100 responds to this prompt, it is still worth it. The dramatic growth of Hotmail, reaching 10 million subscribers in just over a year, was effectively down to pass-along as people received e-mails with a signature promoting the service. Word-of-mouth helped too.

   Pass-along or forwarding has worked well for video clips, either where they are attached to the e-mail or the e-mail contains a link to download the clip. If the e-mail induces a big reaction it will be forwarded. Example virals in this category can be viewed at the Viral Bank (**www.viralbank.com**) and one of the most popular UK websites, **http://viral.lycos.co.uk**.

   Since the e-mails are forwarded by friends, this form of viral marketing is permissible under the new law.

2 *Web-facilitated viral (e-mail prompt)*. Here, the e-mail contains a link/graphic to a web page with 'E-mail a friend' or 'E-mail a colleague'. A web form is used to collect data of the e-mail address to which the e-mail should be forwarded, sometimes with an optional message. The company then sends a separate message to the friend or colleague.

3 *Web-facilitated viral (web prompt)*. Here it is the web page such as a product catalogue or white paper which contains a link/graphic to 'E-mail a friend' or colleague. A web form is again used to collect data and an e-mail is subsequently sent.

Although, strictly speaking, categories 2 and 3 are unsolicited communications received from an organization, they are not instigated by the company and the Information Commissioner has indicated in comments that these forms of viral marketing will be permissible.

4 *Incentivized viral*. In this case, offering some reward for providing someone else's address is used and this can dramatically increase referrals. A common offer is to gain an additional entry for entry into a prize draw. Referring more friends gains more entries to the prize draw. With the right offer, this can more than double the response. The incentive is offered either by e-mail (option 2 above) or on a web page (option 3). For example, in 2001, Virgin Atlantic ran a 'free flights for life' campaign which received 200,000 entries, although only 100,000 people were contacted initially. Entrants received an extra entry if they supplied a friend's e-mail address and the friends were then e-mailed with the offer to enter. Many did. Over 100,000 e-mails were added to the in-house list for Virgin Atlantic since these customers agreed to receive further communications such as e-newsletters and promotions from Virgin Atlantic.

This form of viral marketing could be considered to be unethical since marketers are taking advantage of a person's personal contact to improve the reach (number of people contacted) of their marketing campaign. However, marketers would argue that they are providing the referred friends with an offer which may benefit them. Initial indications are that this form of viral marketing could be outlawed since the friend's e-mail addresses are not freely given. We will have to see whether any test cases are brought in this area.

5 *Web-link viral*. Online viral marketing isn't just limited to e-mail. If you click on any web link referring you to another site, then that can also be considered to be online viral marketing or you could call it 'online public relations'. Links in discussion group postings or blogs which are from an individual are also in this category.

Consumer marketers in the UK also need to heed the April 2003 Code of Advertising Practice from the Advertising Standards Agency (ASA CAP code, **www.asa.org.uk**). This has broadly similar aims and places similar restrictions on marketers to the PECR law.

Problems introduced by data protection and privacy legislation

It is also worth remembering that laws put in place to protect individuals or organizations can sometimes cause harm. For example, in December 2003 an elderly couple in the UK died through hypothermia after their utility company had cut off their gas supply. Initially the press supported the company, suggesting that the utility supplier had made every effort to assist the couple, but data protection laws prevented them passing sensitive personal data on to social welfare and charity organizations. However, such comments may have arisen through the tendency of some media to criticize government laws. The Information Commissioner reacted angrily to these claims. *Guardian* (2004) quoted the commissioner as saying that organizations used the Act as a '*smokescreen for their own shortcomings*'. He suggested that common sense should be applied. Commenting on the utilities case he said: '*Where a gas company is disconnecting people they know to be vulnerable, I don't have a problem with telling social services. I would find it wholly unacceptable if they told a bank or credit card company.*' In a further case, information about someone with sex allegations against them was not passed on from one police authority to another when he was checked for a job as a caretaker and he subsequently murdered students because of fears of passing on the caretaker's personal data. Commenting on this case, the Commissioner said he had been 'just astonished' by the police force's claim that the Act required them to delete information about allegations about individuals that did not lead to a prosecution. In fact the law enables holding of data for a long period for legitimate purposes.

Electronic commerce legislation

Transactional e-commerce, where goods are purchased via the Internet, has also had specific legislation enacted. There are eight legal issues which need to be considered by e-commerce managers, according to Sparrow (2000).

1 *Marketing your e-commerce business.* Arguably, the first stage of marketing an e-commerce business is purchasing a domain name for its website. A company may own several domains, perhaps for different product lines, countries or specific marketing campaigns. Domain name disputes can arise when an individual or company has registered a domain name which another company claims they have the right to. This is sometimes referred to as 'cybersquatting'. One of the best-known cases was brought in 1998 by Marks and Spencers and other high-street retailers, since another company, 'One In a Million Limited', had registered names such as marks&spencer.com, britishtelecom.net and sainsbury.com. It then tried to sell these names for a profit. The companies already had sites with more familiar addresses such as **www.marksandspencers. co.uk**, but had not taken the precaution of registering all related domains with different forms of spelling and different top-level domains such as .net. Unsurprisingly, an injunction was issued against One in a Million which was no longer able to use these names. Other cases may be less clear-cut, particularly when two companies have similar rights to the name; for instance; **www.prince.com** caused a problem since there was a British company with the name Prince, in addition to the well-known US sportsgear manufacturer. In this case Prince UK had registered first, and had a valid claim to the name, so were allowed to keep the name when taken to court by Prince US. Although many companies have successfully registered their domain names as .com or country domain, disputes can still exist, for instance for the relatively new .info and .biz domains. Additionally, companies often need to renew domain names. For example, the .co.uk domain must be renewed every two years. Companies that don't manage this process potentially risk losing their domain name. Nominent, the UK register, has surveyed UK businesses and has identified that around half of companies are unaware that they need to renew their domain names.

Metatags, which are part of the HTML code of a site, are used to market websites by enabling them to appear more prominently in some search engines (see Chapter 3). Some companies have tried putting the name of a competitor company name within the metatags. This is not legal since case law has found against companies that have used this approach.

A further issue of marketing-related law is e-mail marketing, which was considered in the previous section.

2 *Forming an electronic contract (contract law).* The contract formed between a buyer and a seller on a website will need to be subject to the laws of a particular country. In Europe, many such laws are specified at the regional (European Union) level, but are interpreted differently in different countries. This raises the issue of which law applies – is it that for the buyer, for example located in Germany, or the seller (merchant) whose site is based in France? Although this has been unclear, in 2002 attempts were made by the EU to adopt the '*country of origin principle*'. This means that the law for the contract will be that where the merchant is located. This also applies to e-mail marketing, where it is the location of the sender in the EU, not

the location of the recipient, which is relevant. Of course, the web server could be located outside the EU, but from a legal perspective (although not a tax perspective), it is the main location of the company that is important.

Sparrow (2000) advises that different forms of disclaimers be used to protect the retailer. For example, if a retailer made an error with the price or product details were in error, then the retailer is not bound to honour a contract, since it was only displaying the products as 'an invitation to treat', not a fixed offer. Disclaimers can also be used to limit liability if the website service causes a problem for the user, such as a financial loss resulting from an action based on erroneous content. Furthermore, he suggests that terms and conditions should be developed to refer to issues such as timing of delivery and damage or loss of goods.

The Distance Selling Directive also has a bearing on e-commerce contracts in the European Union. It was originally developed to protect people using mail-order (by post or phone). The main requirement is that e-commerce sites must supply:

- the company's identity, including address;
- main characteristics of the goods or services;
- prices and tax should be clearly specified;
- the right of the consumer to withdraw.

One of the most important aspects of the regulations is the way in which products are presented to website visitors, e.g. the customer. The website effectively operates as a shop window rather than an 'offer to sell' in the language of lawyers. A well-known case was when the online retailer Argos offered televisions for £2.99 owing to an error in pricing a £299 product. Numerous purchases were made, but Argos claimed that a contract had not been established simply by accepting the online order, although the customers did not see it that way! Unfortunately, no legal precedent was established in this case since it did not come to trial.

3 *Making and accepting payment.* For B2C sites, the relevant laws are those referring to liability between a credit card issuer, the merchant and the buyer. The merchant needs to be aware of their liability for different situations, such as the customer making a fraudulent transaction.

4 *Authenticating contracts concluded over the Internet.* Authentication refers to establishing the identity of the purchaser. For example, to help prove a credit card owner is the valid owner, many sites now ask for a 3-digit authentication code which is separate from the credit card number. This helps reduce the risk of someone who has, for instance, found a credit card number from a traditional shopping purchase buying fraudulently. The Electronic Communications Act 2000 specified that electronic signatures would be valid for commercial contracts. It also provided for contracts expressed in the form of e-mail to be valid. All price indications online must be clear and unambiguous and indicate whether they are inclusive of packaging or delivery costs. There are several cases of e-commerce posting offers such as TVs for several euros which have caused dispute.

5 *E-mail risks.* One of the main risks with e-mail is infringing an individual's privacy. Laws have been and are being developed to avoid unsolicited commercial e-mail as explained previously in this chapter.

A further issue with e-mail is defamation. This is where someone makes a statement that is potentially damaging to an individual or a company. A well-known example was the financial services company Norwich Union against WPA which was described in the section in Chapter 11 on controls for e-mail.

6 *Protecting intellectual property.* Intellectual property (IP) describes designs, ideas and inventions and includes content and services developed for e-commerce sites. For example, Amazon has patented its 'One-click' purchasing option. Further information on copyright of web pages is provided later in this chapter.

7 *Advertising on the Internet.* Advertising standards that are enforced by independent agencies such as UK's Advertising Standards Agencies also apply in the Internet environment.

8 *Data protection.* Data protection has been referred to in depth in the previous section.

The Freedom of Information Act (FOIA)

This law was introduced in the UK in 2000 to supplement data protection law and follows a similar law established in the US in 1966 and Australia in 1982. Similar laws exist in many countries. But they are quite variable within the EU. For example, France and Belgium have a form of FOIAs, but Germany does not. Most Scandinavian countries have established FOIAs, some dating back to the 20th century.

The UK FOIA does not address personal data and privacy, rather it is to encourage openness amongst public authorities. It is intended to give citizens access to information held by public authorities, enabling them to participate 'in the discussion of policy issues and so improve the quality of government decision making' and 'holding government and other bodies to account'.

This law applies specifically to information held by public services, such as local government and central government. Public authorities are broadly defined in the Act, and include not only government departments, local authorities and many other public bodies (such as the Post Office, the National Gallery and the Parole Board), but also schools, colleges and universities. Private entities – such as spin-off companies of universities – that are wholly or largely owned by a 'public authority' will also be subject to the Act.

The FOIA requires such public authorities to adopt and maintain publication schemes, in order to improve the amount and quality of information made available to the public.

Effective from January 2005, anyone has the right to ask public authorities for any information they hold. According to the Information Commissioner's website (**www.informationcommissioner.gov.uk**), this will include people living abroad, non-UK citizens, journalists, political parties, lobby groups and commercial organizations.

Publication scheme
A list of the classes of information made available by the organization

By law, public organizations must produce a **publication scheme** which consists of the classes of information that are made available. See, for example, the Publication Schemes for Leicester University (**http://foi.le.ac.uk**), the Open University (**www.open.ac.uk/foi**) or the government Department for Education and Skills (**www.dfes.gov.uk/foischeme**). It would appear as if it would be interesting to look at the publication schemes for organizations such as British Nuclear Fuels, security bodies such as MI5, or universities. However, there are numerous exemptions to publication for sound reasons of national security, defence, law enforcement, personal information, commercial interests and so on. This means that much interesting information remains closed and one wonders whether the Act will be used to limit disclosure of information that would be damaging, such as the performance of a public authority.

One implication of the FOIA may be that organizations selling services to governments may be able to access what would formerly be thought of as confidential details about competitive bids. This may contain commercially sensitive information which will affect the outcomes of future bids. However, the Act does exempt trade secrets. In fact, businesses need to consider all types of information given to public bodies since it may be disclosed at a later date, although there are exemptions. For developments on the Freedom of Information Act see **http://foia.blogspot.com**.

There are major implications for UK public authorities in terms of the emphasis that has to be placed on records management. To quote the foreword to the Code of

Practice on Records Management published by the Lord Chancellor under section 46 of the Act, 'Any freedom of information legislation is only as good as the quality of the records to which it provides access'.

Writing in Issue 136 of the *Freepint* newsletter (**www.freepint.com/issues/010503.txt**) which is read by tens of thousands of information professionals worldwide, Steve Wood said that 'Freedom of Information will place a new focus on Information retrieval in the public sector. Research completed by the Home Office as preparation to the Act estimated that there would be approximately 40,000 requests in the first year of operation.' The Records Management Society provides further information on how its members must deal with the Freedom of Information Act (**www.rms-gb.org.uk**).

Monitoring of electronic communications

Electronic communications are regularly monitored by both government organizations and the organizations we work for. This is a complex area of legal ethics since many different laws can be invoked. It includes the Data Protection and Privacy laws referred to in previous sections, but employment laws are also involved. Some employees have also invoked the Human Rights Act (1998) to protect their privacy. Furthermore, in 2000, the UK government introduced the Regulation of Investigatory Powers Act (RIP) to enable UK government agencies to monitor employee communications. While the case for government agencies to monitor networks to prevent criminal or terrorist activity would seem justified to many, provided it is not used for other purposes, the same cannot be said for employee monitoring.

Employee communications monitoring
Companies monitor staff e-mails and websites they access

Employee communications monitoring or surveillance is used by organizations to reduce productivity losses through time wasting. Time can be wasted when a member of staff spends work time checking personal e-mail messages or accessing the Internet for personal interests.

Simple calculations highlight the wastage when staff time is spent on non-productive work. If an employee earning £25,000 per year spends 30 minutes each day of a 5-day week answering personal e-mails or visiting non-work-related websites, this will cost the company over £1,500 per year. For a company with 100 employees, where the average employee works 46 weeks per year, this amounts to over £150,000 per year or the cost of several new employees! Activities such as using streaming media to view the news or downloading audio clips can also place strain on the company networks if they are common. Case study 12.1 summarizes the extent of this problem and solutions that can be used.

A typical example of alleged time wasting where the company dismissed the employee concerned involved Lois Franxhi, a 28-year-old IT manager who was sacked in July 1998 for making nearly 150 searches over four days in office hours for a holiday. She claimed unfair dismissal – she was pregnant at the time of the dismissal. As with many unfair dismissals, the case was not clear-cut, with Mrs Franxhi claiming that the company sacked her because of sex discrimination. The tribunal dismissed these claims, finding that the employee had lied about the use of the Internet, saying she had only used it for one lunchtime when, in fact, records showed she had used it over four days.

Acceptable use policy
Statement of employee activities involving use of networked computers that are not considered acceptable by management

Communications monitoring of employees may also be warranted if it is felt they are sending or receiving e-mails or accessing websites which contain content the organization deems unacceptable. Typical examples of such content are pornography and racist material. However, some organizations even block access to news, sports or web-based e-mail sites because of the amount of time staff spend in accessing them. To define permissible content, many organizations now have **acceptable use policies**. For example, many universities, at log-in, or in computer labs and libraries have notices about 'acceptable use policy'. This will describe the types of material it is not acceptable to access and is also a means of explaining monitoring procedures.

Scanning and filtering are the two most common forms of monitoring. **Scanning software** identifies the content of e-mails sent or received and web pages accessed. Tools such as WebSense or NetIQ MailMarshall or WebMarshal will look for the occurrence of particular words or images – pornography is indicated by skin colour tones, for example. Rules will also be set up, for example to ban e-mail attachments over a particular size or containing swearing, as indicated by Figure 12.3. Such tools can also give a picture of the most popular types of site or content. This might show, for example, how much time is being wasted accessing news and sports sites.

Such software usually also has blocking or **filtering capabilities**. Filtering software such as WebSense (**www.websense.com**) can detect and block other activities such as:

- Peer-to-peer (P2P) file sharing, for example of MP3 audio files.
- Instant messaging using Yahoo! Messenger or Microsoft Instant Messenger.
- The use of streaming media (e.g. audio and video) and other high-bandwidth applications.
- Access to specified sites, e.g. some companies block all news sites such as **www.bbc.co.uk** or **www.msn.co.uk** since analysis has shown that staff spend so much time using them. Access to personal e-mail programs such as Yahoo! Mail or Hotmail may also be blocked. This would not be popular at universities!
- Spyware which seeks to send out information collected from computers.

Scanning software
Identifies e-mail or web page access that breaches company guidelines or acceptable use policies

Filtering software
Software that blocks specified content or activities

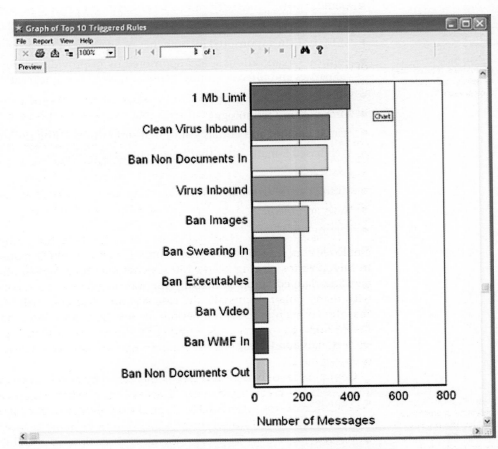

Figure 12.3 Example rules triggered by e-mail in NetIQ Mail Marshall

Source: NetIQ (www.netiq.com), www.netiq.com/news/pressrandranalysts/pressrkits/mediaekits.asp

- Adware programs which place adverts or pop-ups.
- Employee hacking.

WebSense and similar products can block sites in different categories, for different types of staff, according to the acceptable use policy of the organization using a database (**www.websense.com/products/about/database/categories.cfm**) that contains over 1.5 million websites in many categories, of which we list just some to illustrate the degree of control available to the employer. Examples of the categories include:

- Abortion or Pro-Choice or Pro-Life
- Adult Material
- Parent category that contains the categories: Adult Content, Lingerie and Swimsuit, Nudity, Sex, Sex Education
- Adult Content
- Advocacy Groups
- Business and Economy
- Financial Data and Services
- Drugs
- Education
- Entertainment
- Gambling
- Games
- Government
- Military – sites sponsored by branches or agencies of the armed services
- Political Organizations – sites sponsored by or providing information about political parties and interest groups focused on elections or legislation
- Health
- Information Technology
- Search Engines and Portals – sites that support searching the web
- Web-based E-mail – sites that host web-based e-mail
- Job Search
- Militancy and Extremist
- News and Media
- Racism and Hate
- Religion
- Shopping
- Professional and Worker Organizations
- Society and Lifestyles
- Hobbies
- Personals and Dating
- Sports
- Travel
- Vehicles
- Violence
- Weapons.

Consider how many of those listed above you may visit when studying, at business or at home. It will be apparent that if an employer wishes, they can block virtually every site. Some organizations in the UK block access to all news sites and even block access to search engines such as Google and web mail such as Hotmail and Yahoo! Mail. When search engines are blocked, management-grade employees are likely to be restricted in understanding the business environment and restricted from self-development! Employees are likely to view negatively an employer who does not trust them to use their time judiciously.

Employee monitoring legislation

Although employee monitoring falls within the remit of European data protection law, the Data Protection Act was not originally devised to cover employee monitoring. To help clarify the law on employee monitoring in the UK, in June 2003, the Office of the Information Commissioner published 'Monitoring at Work', the third part of the Employment Practices Data Protection Code. The code provides practical guidance for employers on how they should approach monitoring of employees in the workplace. These guidelines seek to achieve a balance between employees' wishes for privacy and the need for employers to run their businesses efficiently. The code does not prevent monitoring, but is based on the concept of proportionality. Proportionality means that any adverse impacts from monitoring must be justified by the benefits to the employer and others. This addresses an apparent anomaly in that data protection law refers to individual consent for processing of personal data being 'freely given' and it is not normal for employees to give this consent. The code makes it clear that individual consent is not required provided that an organization has undertaken an 'impact assessment' of monitoring activities.

Impact assessment
An assessment of the employee monitoring process in the workplace to identify improvements to minimize infringement of employee privacy

According to the code, an impact assessment involves:

- identifying clearly the *purpose(s)* behind the monitoring arrangement and the benefits it is likely to deliver;
- identifying any likely *adverse impact* of the monitoring arrangement;
- considering *alternatives* to monitoring or different ways in which it might be carried out;
- taking into account the *obligations* that arise from monitoring;
- judging whether monitoring is *justified*.

The code does not make specific recommendations about monitoring of e-mails or web traffic, but it does refer to them as typical monitoring activities which it suggests may be acceptable if staff are informed of them and an impact assessment has been conducted. The code does ask employers to consider whether alternatives may be better than systematic monitoring. Alternatives may include training or clear communication from managers and analysis of stored e-mails where it is thought an infringement has taken place rather than continuous monitoring. Automated monitoring is preferred to IT staff, for example, viewing personal e-mails of staff. The code also makes clear that the company should not undertake any covert monitoring, so it should be open about all the types of monitoring that occur. In universities, as mentioned above, at log-in, or in computer labs and libraries there is often a notice about 'acceptable use policy'. This will describe the types of material it is not acceptable to access and is also a means of explaining monitoring procedures. It does appear that if an employee were disciplined or dismissed for sending too many personal e-mails, for instance, they would have legitimate grounds to appeal if they had not been informed that monitoring was occurring and their managers had not made it clear that this was unacceptable practice.

Covert monitoring
Monitoring which the employer undertakes without notification of staff

Different European countries have different laws on monitoring. Some such as Germany are much more restrictive than the UK in terms of the level of monitoring that organizations are able to perform. Organizations opening offices abroad clearly need to be aware of local variations in legal constraints on employee monitoring and data protection.

Debate 12.3   *Organizations have no right to monitor employees' use of e-mail or the web.*

Case study 12.1

Prevention better than litigation? Monitoring of employee computer use

Summarizes the extent of non-work-related, computer-related activities in the workplace and explores approaches to limit these activities.

A quarter of UK companies have dismissed employees for internet misconduct, with the vast majority of sackings related to accessing or transmitting online pornography, according to WebSense, a provider of internet management solutions.

Misuse of the internet in the workplace is so widespread that 72 per cent of UK companies have had to deal with it, mostly by having a quiet word with the employee, followed by verbal warnings.

The company's research also shows that time wasting on the internet is an issue. In the US, workers spend more than one entire workday each week surfing non-work-related websites, with 18 per cent admitting that pornography sites were a big draw, only just behind shopping sites and online news.

In 2008, 5 months after being dismissed, a former employee was jailed after accessing his employer's website and opening the email server to spammers. He later stated his amazement at finding old passwords still working and there being no firewall in place (**www.techworld.com/security/news/index.cfm?newsid=106507**).

WebSense's products are now used by more than half of the Fortune 500, one-third of the Nikkei 225, and half of the FTSE 100 companies, indicating that online porn in the workplace is a fast-growing problem. But for employers, dealing with the issue is not always as straightforward as buying some software.

Ray Stanton, director of security at Unisys, has faced the problem head-on in previous jobs. He relates how an employee was caught sending e-mails around the organisation with 127MB (megabytes) of pornography attached, in the shape of games, pictures and text. The sheer size of the attachments caused the e-mail server to crash.

Of greater concern to Mr Stanton was that the volume of material was not coming into the organisation from the internet – even with broadband it would have taken too long to download. These megabytes of pornography were already on the corporate network.

When the business unit where that individual worked upgraded its desktops, an exercise which required the monitoring of file transfers, engineers discovered 20GB (gigabytes or billion bytes) of unacceptable material in corporate storage systems, the result of perhaps dozens of people's online activity. 'Apart from anything else, that represents a serious management cost, perhaps $250,000 worth', Mr Stanton says. The individual who sent the 127MB e-mail was disciplined under usual procedures.

Mr Stanton believes that the problem of online pornography is not going to go away and that it needs to be treated as a special case. In part, that is because it does not usually stop just with individuals looking at pornography.

'From experience in investigating many such cases, most start off as a joke and rapidly turn into a real problem', says Clifford May, principal forensic consultant at Integralis, the IT security solutions vendor. 'The immediacy of e-mail is the biggest danger, supported by the ease with which a large audience can be accessed – people attach images, hit send and think about it later – so-called clicker's remorse.'

Mr May adds that the circulation of explicit images as a joke is also a very real problem and in some cases has brought multi-million pound projects to a halt while development staff are investigated for circulating ever more outrageous material.

While measures such as filtering and blocking websites can help, it does not stop internet misuse.

'Companies need a policy in place to know how and when employees use the internet, with guidelines that they stick to', says Stephanie Slanickova, a solicitor at Tarlo Lyons, a law firm that specialised in IT issues.

'It is also important that companies get employee consent for monitoring, perhaps by [including] a clause in their contract. If a company just goes ahead with surveillance it could be in breach of the law. But they will be OK if they clearly set out what they are going to do', she adds.

After discovering that patient records had been lost in 2008 when a personal USB storage device had been mislaid NHS Lothian are encrypting their data. The solution, which needs to cover some 11,000 devices, will enable USBs to be connected but they will act in a read-only capacity (www.silicon.com/publicsector/0.3800010403,39337811,00.htm).

Disturbingly, the US Army has had to stop the use of USBs, CDs, flash drives after its systems came under attack from a network worm (http://blogs.zdnet.com/security/?p=2206&tag=nl.e589). In future, the use of personal removable media will be banned.

The legal situation varies in different parts of the world, and is still evolving. The general principle is that if a citizen's right to privacy is enshrined in a written constitution, companies need to be more careful about any surveillance they wish to carry out.

A good indicator of how the European Commission (EC) views the situation is provided by a working party document released in May 2002.

Personal e-mails are where the issue gets particularly thorny. 'The document announces that employees don't abandon their right to privacy and data protection at the door to the workplace', explains Michael Clinch, a partner at Picton Howell, the London law firm.

'They have a legitimate expectation of a certain degree of privacy. The EC recognises, however, that this has to be balanced with the employer's right to run a business', he says.

However, he believed that employers would not like the document, since the European Union has consistently taken the side of the individual on data protection issues.

The topic was reviewed during 2002 and 2003 with a view to harmonising national laws on e-mail monitoring at the end of that period. [See the sites listed at the end of the chapter for the latest developments in employee monitoring.]

Of course, if a company has to resort to the law, it already represents a breakdown in communication between employer and employee. This is why everyone advising on the matter stresses the need for clearly advertised and enforced policies and guidelines. Prevention is far better than litigation.

'Dismissing an employee for internet misuse is a substantial cost to the employer', says Jonathan Naylor, a barrister in the employment, pensions and benefits group of Morgan Cole, the UK law firm.

A study in 2001 by Incomes Data Services found that the costs of replacing key staff could be as much as 150 per cent of the employee's annual salary.

In addition, if the dismissal process is handled poorly by the employer, the organisation could also face employment tribunal proceedings, incurring further management time and costs.

Mr Stanton did not believe companies should panic, although they would need to be sensible and pragmatic since doing nothing was not an option.

'Any director of a large company can assume he has a problem', he says. 'It comes with the people.' But over time, through education, monitoring and some disciplinary action, companies can learn to deal with it.

Source: Mark Vernon, Prevention better than litigation? Monitoring of employee computer use, *Financial Times*; 2 October 2002

Questions

1 Summarize the benefits of using automated software tools to manage staff access to Internet content and e-mail.

2 What practices does the article suggest organizations should adopt to counter misuse of computer resources by employees? Can you suggest further measures?

3 Do you think it is ethical for organizations to monitor employees to detect access to pornography and then sack them if they have accessed it?

Identity theft

Identity theft is an increasing problem in the information society. According to *Guardian* (2003a), quoting the Credit Industry Fraud Avoidance System (CIFAS), the UK's fraud prevention service, it is the fastest-growing white-collar crime, generating a criminal cashflow of £10m a day. In 1999, there were 20,264 reported cases of identity theft in the UK; but by 2010, 102,327 cases of identity theft were reported by CIFAS members. Although the main source of identity theft is commonly considered to be online 'phishing' attacks where unwitting web users give their personal details, sometimes theft will occur through employee collusion or hacker attacks. Sometimes employees may pass on the details of many customers of the company they work for and these are then sold on to the highest bidder (CIFAS 2010).

CIFAS defines identity theft as follows:

> Identity Theft is the misappropriation of the identity of another person, without their knowledge or consent. Broadly speaking, identity theft is another name for impersonation fraud. The name and other personal details of another individual are used to obtain goods and services in that person's name. The kind of information used may include date of birth, current address or previous addresses – the kind of detail used to help establish identity in an application for all kinds of services, ranging from credit products to bank accounts, from insurance to utilities.

Of course, for the person who gains a new identity, it is identity creation, albeit criminal creation of a false identity. Identity theft is commonly associated with the Internet. Hackers can find out personal details and credit card numbers and then use them to purchase items online. However, it is still widespread in the offline world – one of the authors has twice had his identity stolen offline through copying of credit card numbers when the card has been removed or stolen. In this case 'identity theft' is just jargon for 'having your wallet stolen'. This is a serious form of identity theft since if the driving licence or passport is stolen and these do not have photos to identify the individual, large sums can be stolen through impersonating – according to *Guardian* (2003a) this could be as much as £5,000 to £8,000 on average. Another form of theft is through 'skimming' where a shop assistant or waiter can scan the credit card number and security code in a legally bought scanning device and collect £50 for each number they skim. Such fraud, according to CIFAS, cost industry £148m in 2003, a relatively small amount since the perpetrator can use this credit line only for as long as its real owner doesn't spot the extra spending.

More sophisticated forms of identity theft involve setting up false bank or credit card accounts or even passports using the stolen identity – these often use discarded bills and receipts which may be thrown out with the household rubbish. CIFAS reported, in an analysis of 400 domestic bins, that 72 per cent contained a full name and address, 40 per cent contained a credit card number and expiry date linked to an individual, and 20 per cent held a bank account number and sort code alongside a name. Experian reported in 2002 that 53 out of 71 local authorities reported that bin raiding was taking place in their areas, and getting noticeably worse.

Guardian (2003a) explained how a more complex identity theft might be orchestrated:

> Stealing an ID is a careful, meditated process undertaken by organized gangs. It involves getting hold of some sort of identifying documentation as a starting point, and then building a complex ID portfolio around it. So, for instance, a bank statement will provide a name, address and account details. A utility bill is a commonly accepted proof of ID. With a credit card receipt, it is possible to trace a name, address and bank. If I have found a name I like, I can get a replacement or fake birth certificate or driver's licence in that name, which will give me more solid indicators of ID. Scratch around a bit more and I can find your passwords: mother's maiden name? It's on your birth certificate. Name of first school? You left that on friendsreunited.

Reassuringly, surveys shows the money involved in identity theft cases in recent years as down by two-thirds as agencies develop ever more sophisticated methods to combat it, and individuals become more savvy about protecting their personal information.

Approaches to countering identity theft

A number of approaches have been suggested to reduce the risk of identity theft. For purchases, such measures must work both when a person is present when making the purchase and when purchasing over the phone, Internet or mail-order, known as 'card holder not present'.

Identity cards

In the first category of identity theft, the introduction of photographs on credit cards and driving licences is a useful measure that has occurred in many countries. Identity cards have been introduced in many countries, although in others, such as the UK, they have not proved acceptable to the population.

For access to buildings and aircraft, some suggest that further measures are necessary to definitively identify people. These are biometrics identifiers, which can be based on the iris or retina, voice, fingerprints, DNA or even handwriting. Another alternative is the use of under-skin chips that has been proposed by some futurologists. They have developed a rice-grain-sized subdermal radio frequency identification microchip (RFID), named VeriChip, which would beam out card details to special readers. While such applications may sound futuristic, we can imagine that owing to concerns about terrorism, such approaches will be adopted in the future – it is a question of when.

Guardian (2003b) reported that credit card company Mastercard was already developing similar technology. A Mastercard spokesman was quoted as saying '*It could be embedded in anything – maybe even under the skin*'. The article asks about the risk of surgical muggers attempting to gouge a chip out of your arm. Matthew Cossolotto of ADS, who has had himself chipped, says: 'We do hear concerns about this. If you don't want it any more ... you can go to a doctor and have it removed.' By 2004 a business application for RFID chips inserted into the arm had been identified – clubbers at a nightclub in Spain could automatically gain 'VIP access' to part of the club, as part of a membership package. Although many civil liberties campaigners and squeamish people seem likely to intervene, there have also been complaints on a religious basis – is this the biblical 'mark of the beast' mentioned in the Book of Revelation? Certainly such technology raises serious ethical issues of individual freedom against excessive government control.

When a card holder is not present, one simple approach for identification that has worked quite well is the three-digit identifier that is on the back of the credit card. This is not included when the card number appears on statements or receipts, so criminals will only have access to it if they have physically stolen the card. A further approach is for digital certificates which are unique to an individual to be used in online purchase. Although digital certificates are used in online purchases using secure sockets layer (SSL) technology, individual digital certificates have not been widely adopted.

Biometrics identifiers
Techniques to identify an individual based on their physical characteristics or behaviours

Radio frequency identification microchip (RFID)
Tags which can respond to a radio signal with a unique identification code to identify different types of object to which they are attached

Other applications of RFID

RFID tags are already widely used for logistics purposes. They can be attached to individual product items in a warehouse or in a retail location. With appropriate scanning technology they can then be used to assess stock levels – they can be read at a distance of 1 to 6 metres. Other usages are more sinister. A supermarket in the UK experimented by attaching RFID tags to high-value items, such as spirits, commonly targeted by shoplifters. Theft of these products could then be readily identified. While approaches using similar, but less obtrusive technology are widely used in music and clothing retail, there were complaints about this technology from some groups. A group known as 'No Tags' (**www.notags.co.uk**) protested against RFID trials at UK retailer Tesco since it felt that the company wasn't being frank about the types of surveillance that might occur in the future. While most people would not see a problem in a retailer protecting their products against theft, they might be concerned about the RFID tags, which are very small, being incorporated into the products to identify and market to customers. For example, a music retailer could use RFID to identify customers who frequently try to retain refunds after burning a CD when they return to the store. Similarly, a clothing vendor could potentially track visitors who wear its clothing. Figure 12.4 shows a spoof advert produced by a company concerned about such activities.

Credit cards from some banks already contain RFID tags. These could be used to profile a customer entering a branch and recommend appropriate products. Civil liberties groups protest about lack of disclosure in such cases.

It is important that managers of computer systems 'know their enemy' – the type of people who try to gain unauthorized access to their systems and the techniques they use. In this section we will review three of the most common methods by which access is gained to computer systems: hacking, 'phishing' and viruses. For each we will look at possible techniques that can be used to prevent access. In these cases, legal redress is insufficient – it is important to prevent the problem before it happens.

Figure 12.4 Spoof advert produced by Junkbusters about the threat of RFID-tagged clothing

Source: Junkbusters (www.junkbusters.com)

Techniques used to gain unauthorized access to computer systems

Hacking

'**Hacking**' refers to the process of gaining unauthorized access to computer systems, typically across a network. Hacking can take different forms. Hacking for monetary gain is usually aimed at identity theft where personal details and credit card details are accessed for the purpose of fraud as described in the previous section. Hacking could also occur with malicious intent. For example, a former employee might gain access to a network with a view to deleting files or passing information on to a competitor. Some of the notorious hackers who have been prosecuted, but often seem to have ultimately gained from their misdemeanours, are:

- *Robert Morris* – The son of the chief scientist at the US National Computer Security Center, this graduate student created a destructive Internet worm in 1988 which took advantage of a security flaw in the Unix operating system. When unleashed it caused thousands of computers to crash. The disruption was partly accidental and he released instructions to system administrators on how to resolve the problem. He was sentenced to three years of probation, 400 hours of community service and a fine of $10,050. He is now an assistant professor at MIT, where he originally released his worm to disguise its creation at Cornell University.

- *Kevin Poulsen* – In 1990 Poulsen took over all telephone lines into the Los Angeles radio station KIIS-FM, assuring that he would be the 102nd caller. Poulsen won a Porsche 944 S2. This was one of many hacks conducted while he worked for hi-tech company SRI International by day and hacked at night. He was eventually traced and, in June 1994, he pleaded guilty to seven counts of mail, wire and computer fraud, money laundering and obstruction of justice, and was sentenced to 51 months in prison and ordered to pay $56,000 in restitution. It was the longest sentence ever given for hacking. He is now a computer security journalist.

- *Kevin Mitnick* – The first hacker to be featured on an FBI 'Most wanted' poster, Mitnick was arrested in 1995. He later pleaded guilty to four counts of wire fraud, two counts of computer fraud and one count of illegally intercepting a wire communication. He admitted that he broke into computer systems and stole proprietary software belonging to Motorola, Novell, Fujitsu, Sun Microsystems and other companies. He was sentenced to 46 months. Following his sentence he became a security consultant. He is now a leading commentator on security and has made many TV appearances and written books and articles.

- *Vladimir Levin* – A graduate mathematician who was part of a Russian gang that reputedly masterminded a $10 million fraud of Citibank. Arrested by Interpol at Heathrow airport in 1995.

- *Alexey Ivanov* – A June 2001 indictment against Ivanov alleged that he gained unauthorized access into CTS Network Services, a San Diego-based Internet service provider. Ivanov allegedly used a stolen credit card number to open an account with CTS, and once inside the company's computers he hacked the systems to gain control of the computers. Ivanov then used CTS computers to launch a series of computer attacks against e-commerce companies, including two credit card processors – Sterling Microsystems of Anaheim and Transmark of Rancho Cucamonga – and NaraBank of Los Angeles. Ivanov allegedly stole customer financial information, such as credit card and bank account numbers, leading to fraud of $25 million. A prison sentence of three years was given.

Hacking may not be directly related to theft or damage, rather gaining access to a system may be perceived by the hacker as a technical challenge. The term 'hacking' traditionally refers to process of creating program code, another form of technical challenge. This can almost be considered as a pastime, albeit an unethical one. While not as popular as watching sports, hacking appears to be more than one or two people in each country. BBC (2003) reported that TruSecure, a US hacking monitoring organization, tracked more than 11,000 individuals in about 900 different hacking groups and gangs.

Three main forms of gaining unauthorized access to computer systems can be identified. First, the normal entry points to systems through usernames and passwords can be used. For example, many system log-ins have a username of 'administrator' by default. Sometimes the password will be the same. Other common passwords are days of the week or children's names. Tools are available to try different alternative log-ins, although most modern systems will refuse access after several attempts. Hacking can be combined with identity theft to gain an idea of the passwords used.

The second form of hacking exploits known vulnerabilities in systems. Although these vulnerabilities in operating systems such as Windows or Linux or web browsers such as Internet Explorer are publicly known and will be posted on the vendor's website and specialist security websites, there will be many system administrators who have not updated their systems with the latest security update or 'patch'. This is partly because there are many security vulnerabilities, with new ones being announced every week.

Social engineering
Exploiting human behaviour to gain access to computer security information from employees or individuals

Thirdly, Kevin Mitnick refers to '**social engineering**', which typically involves impersonating employees of an organization to access security details. One example, given in Mitnick and Simon (2002), is when the attacker contacts a new employee and advises them of the need to comply with security policies. They then ask the user for their password to check it is in line with the policy of choosing a difficult-to-guess password. Once the user reveals their password, the caller makes recommendations to construct future passwords in such a way that the attacker will be able to guess it.

Protecting computer systems against hackers

Protecting computer systems against hackers involves creating countermeasures to the three main types of hacking outlined above. For gaining access to systems via passwords, policies can be developed to reduce the risk of access. One simple approach is to mandate that new passwords are required every month and that they contain at least one number and a mix of upper and lower case. This prevents users using simple passwords which are easily guessed. Education is required to reduce the risk of passwords falsely obtained through 'social engineering', but this will never completely remove the threat.

Firewall
A specialized software application typically mounted on a server at the point where the company is connected to the Internet. Its purpose is to prevent unauthorized access into the company

Computer systems can also be protected by limiting access at the point where the external network enters the company. **Firewalls** are essential when extranets are used to ensure that outside access to confidential information does not occur. Firewalls are usually created as software mounted on a separate server at the point where the company is connected to the Internet. Firewall software can then be configured to accept links only from trusted domains representing other offices in the company.

The use of firewalls within the infrastructure of a company is illustrated in Figure 12.5. It is evident that multiple firewalls can be used to protect information on the company. The information made available to third parties over the Internet and extranet is partitioned by another firewall using what is referred to as 'the demilitarized zone' (DMZ). Corporate data on the intranet is then mounted on other servers inside the company.

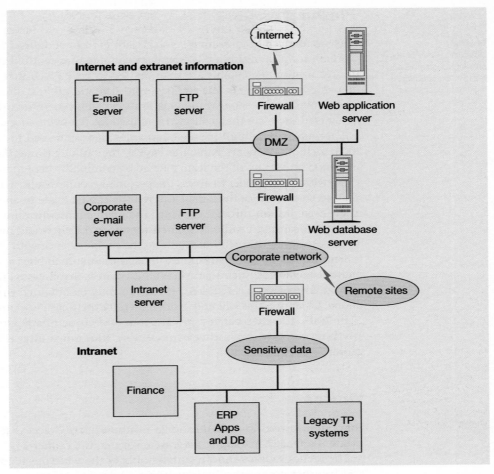

Figure 12.5 Firewall positions within an organization's network

Measures must also be put in place to stop access to systems through published security vulnerabilities. BBC (2003) reported that in 2003 there were 5500 security vulnerabilities that could be used. A policy on updating operating systems and other software with the latest versions is also required. It is not practical to make all updates, but new vulnerabilities must be monitored and patches applied to the highest-risk categories. This is a specialist task and is often outsourced. TruSecure (**www.trusecure.com**) is an example of a specialist company that monitors security vulnerabilities and advises organizations on prevention. TruSecure estimates that only 80 or 90 per cent of vulnerabilities are being used regularly, so patches should prioritize on these. TruSecure provides a service for hundreds of organizations to see whether they possess these vulnerabilities. They also employ a team of people who attempt to infiltrate hacker groups to determine the latest techniques. TruSecure gave the FBI over 200 documents about the Melissa virus author. Although they did not know his real name, they knew his three aliases and had built a detailed profile of the author. These undercover groups have to know the latest lingo such as using 'k3wl' instead of 'cool' and replacing 'a' by '4'.

Ethical hackers
Hackers employed legitimately to test the quality of system security. The term 'white hats' is sometimes used to describe ethical hackers and 'black hats' for criminal hackers.

A further approach that organizations use to check their defences against hacking is to employ '**ethical hackers**'. These are former hackers who now apply their skills to test the vulnerabilities of existing systems.

Although all of the examples of hacking above involve computer networks, sometimes 'low-tech' techniques can be used too. *Guardian* (2003a) reported cases where criminals had impersonated call-centre staff in order to gain access to customer accounts.

'Phishing'

Phishing (derived from 'fishing') is a specialized form of online identity theft. The most common form of 'phishing' is where a spam e-mail is sent out purporting to be from an organization. Recipients are then invited to visit a website to update their details after entering their username and password. The web address directs them to a false site appearing to be the same as the organization's site. When the username and password are entered these are then collected and used for removing money from the recipient's real account. Some high-profile companies were subjected to this form of attack in 2003, including Barclays Bank and PayPal, the online payment company. Such scams are a modern version of the scam devised by criminals where they install a false ATM in a wall with a card reader to access the person's account details. This form of scam is difficult to counter since the e-mail and website can be made to appear identical to those of the organization through copying. The main countermeasure is education of users, so banks for instance will tell their customers that they would never send this form of e-mail. However, this will not eradicate the problem since with millions of online customers some will always respond to such scams. A further approach is the use of multiple passwords, such that when an account is first accessed from a new system an additional password is required which can only be obtained through the mail or by phone. Of course, this will only work if identity theft hasn't occurred.

In 2003, the sites barclaysprivate.com and eurocitibank.com – neither of them anything to do with existing banks – were shut down after they had been used to garner ID details for fraud.

Viruses

Computer viruses are another form of unauthorized access to computer systems. Issues involved in managing these were covered in Chapter 11.

The sections above show examples of how the widespread adoption of computers and Internet companies has encouraged criminal activity. Some of this activity is simply traditional crimes such as theft and fraud conducted in an online setting. But some of the activity such as hacking and the propagation of viruses is new. To cover both traditional and new forms of crime achieved over computer networks, many companies have introduced laws as a deterrent and punishment.

In the UK, the Computer Misuse Act (1990) was introduced with the intention of reducing online criminal activity. The Act recognizes three types of criminal activity:

1 *Unauthorized access to computer material.* The Act is worded to protect systems both from hacking and from employee access to material that they do not normally have access to. Specific intent to access a particular type of information is not required for the law to be broken – merely gaining unauthorized access is an offence, with a payment of a fine or imprisonment up to a period of 6 months. The law states:

    (1) A person is guilty of an offence if—
        (a) he causes a computer to perform any function with intent to secure access to any program or data held in any computer;
        (b) the access he intends to secure is unauthorized; and
        (c) he knows at the time when he causes the computer to perform the function that that is the case.

    (2) The intent a person has to have to commit an offence under this section need not be directed at—
        (a) any particular program or data;
        (b) a program or data of any particular kind; or
        (c) a program or data held in any particular computer.

2 *Unauthorized access with intent to commit or facilitate commission of further offences.* In this case, it is found that there is a specific intention to destroy data, cause damage or commit fraud. A fine and/or five-year prison sentence can occur in this situation.

3 *Unauthorized modification of computer material.* The law adjudges this to have occurred when there is an act committed which: *'causes an unauthorized modification of the contents of any computer.'* These specific examples of the purpose of modification are given:

    (a) to impair the operation of any computer;
    (b) to prevent or hinder access to any program or data held in any computer; or
    (c) to impair the operation of any such program or the reliability of any such data.

The Computer Misuse Act has been in existence for 20 years now, yet we saw in the previous section how computer crimes such as online identity theft have increased in importance. Many now feel that the laws do not have 'sufficient teeth'. *Guardian* (2003b) reported that the average sentence for identity theft is nine months and that the criminals may still have access to the millions they acquired through fraud.

The law originated before the widespread adoption of the World Wide Web and this has led to some loopholes. For example, in 2001, a 19-year-old computer student from Wales was arrested after he retrieved the details of thousands of credit cards from commercial websites and posted them on the Internet. He pleaded guilty to the charge, but in fact the law does not specifically refer to this situation.

Denial-of-service attacks
Websites are disabled through bombardment with many requests for information originating from computers around the world that have been hijacked

The law also does not cover other forms of illegal access such as **denial-of-service attacks**. In denial-of-service attacks, websites are bombarded with many requests for information, or e-mails, originating from computers around the world that have been hijacked solely to request information. For example, in 2000 Yahoo! servers suffered a denial-of-service attack where servers were bombarded with a billion hits per minute. This caused direct losses in advertising and online shopping revenue. More recently, denial-of-service attacks have been used for extortion, with online retailers and bookmakers asked to pay a ransom or face an attack which could cause them to lose millions in revenue. It is expected that future updates to the law will include new aspects of misuse such as denial-of-service attacks and phishing.

Disability and accessibility legislation

Accessibility legislation
Legislation intended to protect website users with disabilities including visual disability

A further aspect of legislation, developed in some countries, is intended to protect medically disabled Internet users; this is usually referred to as **accessibility legislation**. The most common problems in using computers for the 10–20 per cent of the population who are disabled are related to visual impairment – for example, some users need to enlarge the text of websites, and, although browsers provide this facility, sites may be written in such a way that the text cannot enlarge. Some users are mainly interested in text content rather than graphical content, particularly those using text recognition technology (screen readers) to read out the pages of sites. To cater for these users, alternative text views of sites should be available.

Internet standards organizations such as the World Wide Web Consortium have been active in promoting guidelines for web accessibility (**www.w3.org/WAI**). This site describes common accessibility problems as:

images without alternative text; lack of alternative text for imagemap hot-spots; misleading use of structural elements on pages; uncaptioned audio or undescribed video; lack of alternative information for users who cannot access frames or scripts; tables that are difficult to decipher when linearized; or sites with poor color contrast.

A tool provided to assess the WWW standards is BOBBY (**http://bobby.cast.org**).

A case that highlights the need for website accessibility is that brought by Bruce Maguire, a blind Internet user who uses a refreshable Braille display, against the Sydney Organizing Committee for the Olympic Games in 2000. Maguire successfully demonstrated deficiencies in the site which prevented him using it adequately, which were not successfully remedied. He was protected under the 1992 Australian Disability Discrimination Act and the defendant was ordered to pay A$20,000. This was the first case brought in the world, and it showed organizations in all countries that they could be guilty of discrimination if they did not audit their sites against accessibility guidelines, since many countries such as the US and UK have similar discrimination acts. Such acts are now being amended in many countries to specifically refer to online discrimination. See **www.uiaccess.com** or **www.rnib.org.uk/professionals/webaccessibility** for further developments.

Copyright law and IPR

Copyright
The legal protection for different forms of works such as books, films, music and software against unauthorized copying

Intellectual property rights (IPR)
A generic term applying to different forms of rights to ownership of works including copyright, trademarks, patents and design

Copyright law is designed to protect authors, producers, broadcasters and performers through ensuring that they see some returns from their works every time they are experienced. The first Copyright Act, in 1709, became necessary with the widespread adoption of the printing press. This first Act gave an author or their publishers the right for exclusive production of a book for a period of 28 years. Since that time, copyright law has been updated in line with changes in technology and media, thus film (1911), television (1956) and software (1985) were protected in later modifications to the Act. The latest UK copyright amendment was in 1988. The rights that the originators or owners of such works hold are known as '**intellectual property rights (IPR)**'. A more recent European Directive of Copyright (2001/29/EC) came into force in many countries in 2003. This is a significant update to the law which covers new technologies and approaches such as streaming a broadcast via the Internet. It also covers the case where ISPs may hold copies of work during transmission. A significant change is that taking copies of a work for research and private study was permitted. This is now excluded if the research or study is for a commercial purpose such as teaching, training or research – it is for individual study only. This suggests that universities and colleges have to pay for all types of copied articles and other works in addition to those they have previously paid for, such as book extracts. A further change concerns digital rights management – for example, a digital photo provider such as Corbis (**www.corbis.com**) uses a digital code to protect copyright on its images. This is now permitted in law and using any method to circumvent this technology to break copyright is now illegal. Rights management features are now built into software such as Microsoft Word and Media Player (for music downloads).

Protection of software from copying by other developers

Source code
The lines that are compiled and executed as a computer program

Protection of software from imitation by other software vendors through copyright is far more difficult than for books or films. There are two main reasons for this. First, as in the case of a book, it is possible to copy part of a software program if its **source code** becomes available. Since source code is typically compiled into a binary executable file (.exe) to run it, the copied source code is no longer visible. It has been alleged in court that some components of Microsoft DOS, Windows and even the open-source software Linux have been based on a pre-existing source. The original source code may become available through a security breach, typically caused by a disgruntled employee or industrial espionage. Furthermore, it is also possible to 'reverse-engineer' executable software programs using special tools to determine the form of their original code. Secondly, it may be difficult to protect key elements of software such as the design of the interface. Early versions of Microsoft Windows used similar screen elements such as windows, icons, menus and pointers (the so-called 'WIMPS' graphical user interface (GUI)) to the Apple Macintosh. According to Wikipedia (2004), in 1988 Apple filed a court case claiming that the 'look and feel' of the Macintosh operating system had been copied. The difficulty of settling such cases is indicated by the fact that it took six years before the decision was dismissed on appeal. This followed an analysis of 189 GUI elements, with the judge deciding that 179 of these elements had been licensed to Microsoft in the Windows 1.0 agreement, and most of the remaining 10 elements were not copyrightable. Mid-way through the trial, Xerox, which originated the GUI concept some time before Apple, also filed a suit against Apple. This case was also dismissed. If Apple Computer had filed a **software patent** on some aspects of the interface it might have had more success with the original claim. Amazon famously obtained a patent on its 'One-click' ordering system which many disputed.

Software patent
Patents protect innovations from imitation in law

Protection of software from unauthorized copying

A further risk for software vendors is that their software may be copied and freely distributed without the software developer achieving a return on their investment in developing and marketing the software. The potential loss in revenue globally is large, as Figure 12.6 shows.

There are many ways in which software can be illegally copied which are facilitated by its digital form. These include:

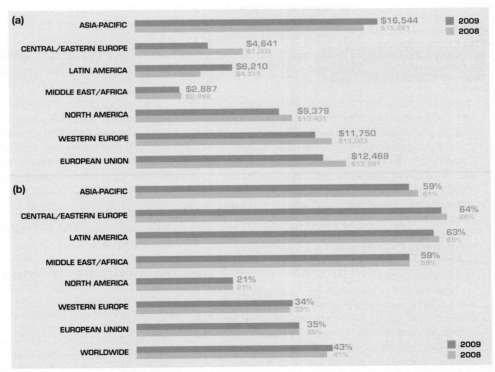

Figure 12.6 Software piracy: (a) commercial value of unlicensed software by region (in millions of US dollars) [Note: six of the seven shown are mutually exclusive; the seventh – the European Union – includes economies from Western Europe and Central and Eastern Europe.] **(b) rates by region**

Source: Figure 4 in the *Seventh Annual BSA/IDC Global Software Piracy Study*, Business Software Alliance (2010)

- Direct copying of media, for example 'burning' a distribution CD for software on to another CD and then selling it. This can be on a large scale, as Mini case study 12.2 'Software piracy' shows. Often international criminal gangs are involved in this activity.

- Sale of original copies of software through online auction houses such as eBay and Yahoo! auctions.

- Exchange of software through peer-to-peer file sharing services such as Limewire, Napster and Kazaa (see next section).

- Online hosting of pirated software or software activation codes on sites known variously as 'Warez' and 'Crackz'.

Software vendors naturally take a number of measures to avoid unauthorized copying of their software to protect their revenue. Managers need to be aware of these measures, since they may be breaking the law if unlicensed software is being used in the area of the business they are responsible for. Table 12.1 shows that piracy levels in Western Europe remain relatively high in some countries, suggesting that many managers could still be open to prosecution. Measures that manufacturers take to reduce software piracy include:

- Producing a numbered software licence for each copy of software purchased, together with a legal warning against copying.

- Producing activation codes or serial numbers for software which are usually contained on the CD jewel-case and have to be manually entered when the software is first used.

- Online or phone-based registration of products coupled with limiting the number of authorized installations for each serial number.

Peer-to-peer file sharing
Files containing music, software and video are shared between the hard disks of Internet users through intermediary services which provide an index of the users and the content they have on their machines

---

Mini case study 12.2   Software piracy

In early December 2002, Operation Wolf was concluded after nine months of investigation by the ELSPA [Entertainment and Leisure Software Publishers] Anti Piracy Unit, when the internet trader known as Brian Green Software Café was put out of business. The unnamed trader and his accomplices allegedly operated by 'spamming' internet adverts worldwide and offered a massive range of pirate product. He produced a disc containing a list of the items available each month, which ran to 890 A4 pages. He offered a huge selection of video games as well as music, film and business software.

Near the end of his operation, he also began to offer a service whereby customers sent their hard drives to him and he would then download on to them a large amount of illegal content. He moved premises in the UK three times and his ISP from the UK to southern Ireland and then to Canada. He is also suspected of changing his UK postal 'drop' address twice. ELSPA made numerous test purchases over the internet and obtained fingerprint evidence from the discs and DNA from the stamps.

Working closely with the South Wales Police, Financial Investigation Team revealed a lucrative lifestyle with over £100,000 believed to be passing through two bank accounts. On the morning of the raid by ELSPA, trading standards and police at a house in South Wales, the trader's packed bags were found on the landing as he was thought to be intending to move out that day. A search revealed a server and two PCs with ten DVD and CD copiers. Approximately 5,500 master discs were found and a large proportion contained zip files. A large amount of paperwork and packaging, necessary for a worldwide operation, was discovered. Two further bank account details were also found and are now being investigated by police financial investigators. That same morning, his 'drop' address in Cardiff was searched and orders from the UK, US, Canada and Europe were seized.

Microsoft lists numerous further examples where individuals and organisations have been prosecuted for selling illegal copies of software (**www.microsoft.com/hk/licenses/cases.htm**).

Source: Proving the Connection links between intellectual property theft and organised crime. Paper produced by Alliance Against Counterfeiting and Privacy. www.aacp.org.uk

- Producing hardware devices (known bizarrely as 'dongles') which must be plugged into a serial port on the back of the system unit in order for the software to run.

- Membership of organizations such as the Business Software Alliance (BSA) and the Foundation against Software Theft (FAST), which may enter a company and take action against it, was highlighted in the open-source software section in Chapter 2, which described how a company was fined $90,000 when, after an unannounced raid by armed US marshals instigated by the BSA, it was found to have eight unlicensed copies of Microsoft Office.

- Use of different software distribution and payment models. The adoption of the application service provider (ASP) model for hosting software where it is accessed over the Internet (introduced in Chapter 2) effectively reduces piracy.

- With ASP services such as those for CRM from Salesforce (**www.salesforce.com**) and Oracle CRM On Demand (**www.crmondemand.com**), each user has to log-in with a separate password so piracy is no longer a relevant concept.

The range of measures taken by manufacturers, as listed above, has been successful in reducing piracy rates in many countries. A significant amount of potential software revenue is still lost, which suggests that companies may become more active in protecting their intellectual property.

Given the possibility of a raid, it is important that managers have a policy on holding legal copies and software. The BSA offer employees a reward for anonymous reporting of the use of the unlicensed software in their business. Such measures and education about software theft seems to have had impact. The BSA noted that in 2009, installations of unlicensed software on PCs dropped in 54 of the 111 individual

Table 12.1 PC software piracy rates in Western Europe

Country	Piracy rates %	
	2009	2008
Austria	25	24
Belgium	25	25
Denmark	26	25
Finland	25	26
France	40	41
Germany	28	27
Greece	58	57
Ireland	35	34
Italy	49	48
Netherlands	28	28
Norway	29	28
Portugal	40	42
Spain	42	42
Sweden	25	25
Switzerland	25	25
UK	27	27
TOTAL W. EUROPE	34	33

Source: Table 3 in the *Seventh Annual BSA/IDC Global Software Piracy Study*, Business Software Alliance (2010)

economies studied, and rose in only 19. However, the value of unlicensed software still amounted to $51.4 billion worldwide. This figure suggests why software vendors are keen to move to a 'Software as a Service' model where software is accessed online through a login, so reducing the need for software installed on each PC.

Since employees may bring in their own software, the only way to be sure that legitimate copies of software are installed is to conduct regular software audit. These audits can be carried out in all companies with a network, using software tools for 'asset management' designed for this purpose, including tools available free from the BSA (**www.bsa.org**).

Software audit
A check taken to assess the software used on each machine

Management controls also need to be put in place to control the different forms of software piracy that can occur in an organization. The BSA website recognizes five common types:

1 *End-user piracy.* This occurs when a company employee reproduces copies of software without authorization. End-user piracy can take the following forms:
   - using one licensed copy to install a program on multiple computers;
   - copying disks for installation and distribution;
   - taking advantage of upgrade offers without having a legal copy of the version to be upgraded;
   - acquiring academic or other restricted or non-retail software without a licence for commercial use;
   - swapping disks in or outside the workplace.

2 *Client–server overuse.* This type of piracy occurs when too many employees on a network are using a central copy of a program at the same time. If you have a local-area network and install programs on the server for several people to use, you have to be sure that your licence entitles you to do so. If you have more users than allowed by the licence, that's 'overuse'.

3 *Internet piracy.* This occurs when software is downloaded from the Internet. The same purchasing rules should apply to online software purchase as for those bought in traditional ways. Internet piracy can take the following forms:
   - pirate websites that make software available for free download or in exchange for uploaded programs;
   - Internet auction sites that offer counterfeit, out-of-channel, infringing copyright software;
   - peer-to-peer networks that enable unauthorized transfer of copyrighted programs.

4 *Hard-disk loading.* This occurs when a business that sells new computers loads illegal copies of software on to the hard disks to make the purchase of the machines more attractive. The same concerns and issues apply to value-added resellers (VARs) that sell or install new software on to computers in the workplace.

5 *Software counterfeiting.* This type of piracy is the illegal duplication and sale of copyrighted material with the intent of directly imitating the copyrighted product. In the case of packaged software, it is common to find counterfeit copies of the CDs or diskettes incorporating the software programs, as well as related packaging, manuals, licence agreements, labels, registration cards and security features.

Copyright protection of online information resources

The Internet has had a similar impact on copyright to the advent of the printing press: it has made infringements of copyright easier. Website material can be copyrighted through the addition of the copyright notice '©' to the website. This will provide protection in law for text, graphics, data and code through the law. However, copying of web materials is straightforward, as the examples in the previous section on phishing show. Aside from the copying of parts of the website for fraudulent purposes, there are two main concerns for organizations. First, a company, particularly a media company, such as an online newspaper or magazine, will have invested considerable amounts in developing its copyrighted material. If it is copied by a third party, it is losing some of its return on the material. One of the landmark cases concerned the *Shetland Times* vs the *Shetland News* where the latter website linked to content on the *Shetland Times* site. The case was settled in 1996 before it went to court since it was agreed that the *Shetland News* site was designed in such a way that it appeared to be passing off copyrighted material as its own. An agreement was reached where the *Shetland Times* was clearly attributed and shown in a separate window.

Secondly, by using copyrighted material or material related to a company such as trademarks on their sites, the company may be misrepresented. To reduce the risk of this, some large organizations use 'reputation management' services to assess how their brand is represented on the World Wide Web. This also includes comments posted in chatrooms and on bulletin boards. Furthermore, companies such as Dell strictly limit how images and trademarks related to the company can be used online.

Plagiarism
Passing off another person's previously written material or concepts as your own

A final issue associated with the ease of access to information online, which is relevant to all educational institutions, is plagiarism. Read Case study 12.2 to review the approaches used by students and the techniques which can be used to combat plagiarism.

Case study 12.2   **FT**

MBA students swap integrity for plagiarism

A professor at a well-known business school was recently grading papers for a required ethics course. In two of the papers he saw obvious signs of plagiarism. Students were not required to put their names on their papers, just a number identifiable by the administration. Before escalating the problem, the professor e-mailed his entire class saying that the guilty parties could avoid sanction by coming forward now. He received eight e-mails, in addition to the two he had already spotted, admitting to cheating.

Such stories bolster the academic research that suggests business students, both at graduate and undergraduate level, are more inclined to cheat than students in other disciplines. Critics of business and business education leap on such findings to say that this explains Enron, dodgy hedge funds and crooked sub-prime mortgage lenders. They say the whole system is built on fraud. This impression was reinforced further in March when the dean of Durham University's business school in the UK, Tony Antoniou, was fired for having plagiarised academic work 20 years earlier.

However, in their enthusiasm to eviscerate, the critics may be overlooking some vital differences between a business education and one in, for example, philosophy or electrical engineering.

In spite of their long history – Harvard Business School celebrates its centenary this year – business schools still strain for academic respectability, especially in the minds of their students. For many, the purpose of attending business school is not to receive an academic education, but to get a job.

'The academic values of integrity and honesty in your work can seem to be less relevant than the instrumental goal of getting a good job,' says Craig Smith, a professor of business ethics and corporate responsibility at Insead, France.

Dispiriting research, he says, indicates that MBA students actually become less ethical over the course of their education. 'The focus on maximising shareholder value causes some students to minimise other important codes of behaviour,' he says. He adds that the number of graduates of prominent business schools being caught in corrupt practices has forced a 'period of useful introspection' at the schools.

The accessibility of information online has affected the definition of plagiarism. Don McCabe, a professor at Rutgers Business School in the US, has conducted extensive research into plagiarism among business school students. He says that by far the most commonplace form these days is cutting and pasting from the Internet. This generally involves using a few sentences from multiple sources, either verbatim or paraphrased.

▶

'Many students are very equivocal as to whether this is actually cheating or not,' says Prof McCabe. 'Especially if they paraphrase from a source.' 40 per cent of students in Prof McCabe's research admitted to cutting and pasting, although he assumes the figure is probably higher.

He adds that students today, both in business schools and beyond, feel much freer than their forebears to define what constitutes cheating for themselves, regardless of their teacher's instructions. One example is that when a teacher requires individual work, many students see no problem in collaborating with each other.

'They argue that they can produce much better work and that they learn more when working together. Business students seem to be more ready to justify such behaviour by noting the emphasis corporations are putting on hiring people who can work together in teams. They argue that their collaboration, even when not permitted, is simply gaining practice at a skill they need to acquire to get a good job and advance,' he says. 'And faculty who do not encourage or allow such collaborative work are simply out of touch.'

Prof McCabe says that from the faculty's perspective, aside from purely ethical issues, it is hard to give academic credit to students who copy other people's work. Whether the students cheat to inflate their grade or simply as a "time-management" solution to an academic requirement, they become difficult for professors to grade. Different schools adopt different strategies to deal with plagiarism. Some delegate policing to faculty, while others put it in the hands of students and a strict honour code. The latter is generally more effective.

At Dartmouth's Tuck School of Business in the US, students are taught the honour code from the first day they arrive on campus, when they must also participate in some form of community service. 'It's a way of telling them that they are not here just to learn about the bottom line, but how to become responsible citizens of society,' says Aine Donovan, executive director of Dartmouth's Ethics Institute. Tuck's pedagogical approach also minimises the opportunities to cheat, with lots of teamwork and few written papers. Ethics is not a required course at the school, but it is an oversubscribed elective.

'It allows students the chance to think about things which have been bothering them in the rest of their course,' says Ms Donovan.

Most ethics teaching at business schools tends to focus on cases where poor ethical judgments have been made, rather than issues of basic honesty. These cases, such as Enron and Exxon-Valdez, look at the situations in which individuals and companies made appalling decisions. They examine the twilight zone in which business decisions, subsequently seen as "ethical", were made and the stresses on the people who made them. This tends to provide students with a sliding scale of right and wrong rather than a set of absolutes.

Addressing the more hum-drum issue of plagiarism, Ms Donovan says, can make ethics more personal. Students tend to be much harsher on each other than faculty. They know stepping outside the lines might yield enormous personal rewards, but comes with equal risk and can be lethal for a community.

Business school students are more likely to self-report cheating, she believes, because they are 'more forthright, willing to say "sure I shave corners to get ahead", but then have a reason for it. A philosophy or comparative literature student will never admit to cheating.'

Ms Donovan used to teach at the US Naval Academy, where cheating on an engineering test might mean being unprepared when a problem arose on a battle ship. The consequences of plagiarism were dire.

While cheating on a business school paper might not be quite so grave, 'these graduates from top business schools are expected to come in to businesses and dazzle. If they've short-changed themselves, they will be found out very quickly', she adds.

Source: MBA students swap integrity for plagiarism, FT.com, 19/05/2008, by Philip Delves Broughton.

Questions

1 Define 'plagiarism' using your understanding of the term, the article and the definition at **www.plagiarism.org/**.

2 Discuss the prevalence of plagiarism at your place of study!

3 Assess the suitability of techniques described in the article to counter plagiarism.

Summary

1 Laws have been enacted in many countries to protect the privacy of personal information and also to protect organizational data from unauthorized access. Managers need to be aware of these laws to comply with them.

2 Some controls on information management are not covered fully by law. In these cases, managers need to make ethical judgements about what activities are acceptable.

3 Data protection and privacy legislation have been enacted in many countries to protect personal data and so maintain privacy of individuals.

4 In the EU, laws have been developed to end unsolicited e-mail and limit the use of website cookies for monitoring.

5 The monitoring of employee communications is now commonplace, using scanning and filtering software to prevent access to categories of websites and transmission of certain types of e-mail. Legal constraints require companies to adopt appropriate monitoring and be open with employees about this.

6 Identity theft is becoming increasingly common through access to individuals' information both online and offline.

7 Managers need to be aware of the range of external and internal threats of unauthorized access to computer systems such as hacking and viruses. Suitable countermeasures can then be put in place.

8 Intellectual property law protects the rights of the originators of online information resources such as articles, music, film and software through copyright, trademarks and patent laws.

Exercises

Self-assessment questions

1 Distinguish between legal and ethical constraints on the management of business information.

2 Explain the requirements that data protection and privacy legislation places on organizations in your country.

3 How is intellectual property of resources available through the Internet protected? What are the constraints on individuals and organizations using such resources?

4 How can the need for organizations to monitor employee use of networked computer systems be reconciled with the legal and ethical constraints on monitoring?

5 Describe the different forms of threats from hacking and solutions to counter them.

6 What are the different types of computer virus? What steps can be taken by an organization to limit the impact of viruses?

7 Outline the measures that can be taken by an organization to stop software piracy.

8 Define e-government and give examples of different approaches to e-government.

Essay and discussion questions

1 In your role as information manager you are giving a one-day workshop on data protection and privacy legislation to managers. Develop a set of ten slides which explain the principles and requirements of UK law.

2 You have recently been appointed as IT manager in an organization with 200 staff. You have been told that some unlicensed software is in use. You want to avoid the company being reported and fined for software piracy. Detail the measures you would take to end software piracy in the organization.

3 Assess the different risks of unauthorized external access to information systems and suggest countermeasures.

4 What are the threats from computer viruses and how should companies protect their systems from computer viruses?

5 Write an essay assessing the extent to which George Orwell's prophecies about 'Big Brother' monitoring citizens made in his novel *1984* have become today's reality.

6 Assess the role of e-government in managing equitable access to online information resources and services.

References

BBC (2003) Cracking the hacker underground. *BBC News Online*. http://news.bbc.co. uk/1/hi/technology/3246375.stm.

BBC (2004) Is it time to scrap the Internet? How to control what is online. BBC Interactive. 6 February. http://news.bbc.co.uk/1/hi/technology/3465383.stm.

Booz Allen Hamilton (2002) *International E-Economy: Benchmarking the World's Most Effective Policies for the E-Economy*. Report published 19 November, London. www.e-envoy.gov.uk/oee/oee.nsf/sections/esummit-benchmarking/$file/indexpage.htm.

BSA (2002) Global Survey of Software Piracy. Press release issed by Business Software Alliance (www.bas.org).

BSA (2010) Seventh Annual BSA/IDC Global Software Piracy Study. Business Software Alliance. http://portal.bsa.org/globalpiracy2009/studies/globalpiracystudy2009.pdf

CIFAS (2010) *Fraudscape: Depicting the UK's fraud landscape*. Research report published February at: http://www.cifas.org.uk/default.asp?edit_id=979-57

Dyson, E. (1998) *Release 2.1 Design for Living in the Digital Age*. Penguin, London.

E-envoy (2002) UK Online Action Plan. Office of the E-envoy. http://e-government.cabinetoffice.gov.uk/ EStrategy/ActionPlan/.

Fletcher, K. (2001) Privacy: The Achilles heel of the new marketing. *Interactive Marketing*, 3(2).

Godin, S. (1999) *Permission Marketing*. Simon and Schuster, New York.

Google (2007a) Google ranked worst on privacy. Available online at: http://news.bbc.co.uk/1/hi/technology/6740075.stm.

Google (2007b) Google cookies will 'auto delete'. Available online at: http://news.bbc.co.uk/1/hi/technology/6901946.stm.

Google (2007c) Google cuts data retention times. Available online at: http://news.bbc.co.uk/1/hi/technology/6745191.stm.

Guardian (2003a) Hijacked your bank balance, your identity, your life, *Guardian*, 25 October. www.guardian.co.uk/weekend/story/0,3605,1069646,00.html.

Guardian (2003b) City diary. Richard Adams, *Guardian*, 27 November.

Guardian (2004) Data act 'often unfairly blamed'. *Guardian*, 14 January.

Information Commissioner (1998) *Legal Guidelines on the 1998 UK Data Protection Act.* Available online at: www.informationcommissioner.gov.uk.

Mason, R. (1986) Four ethical issues of the information age. *MIS Quarterly*, March.

Mitnick, K. and Simon, W. (2002) *The Art of Deception: Controlling the Human Element of Security*. Wiley, New York.

Quayle, M. (2002) E-commerce: The challenge for UK SMEs in the twenty-first century. *International Journal of Operation and Production Management*, 22(10), 1148–61.

RedEye (2003) A study into the accuracy of IP and cookie-based online management information. The RedEye Report. Available online at: www.redeye.com.

Sipior, J. C., Ward, B. T. and Rongione, N. M. (2004) Ethics of collecting and using consumer internet data. *Information Systems Management*, 21(1), 58–66.

Sparrow, A. (2000) *E-Commerce and the Law. The Legal Implications of Doing Business Online.* Financial Times Management Briefings. Financial Times Prentice Hall, Harlow, UK.

United Nations (1999) *New Technologies and the Global Race for Knowledge*. Human Development Report. UN, New York.

Wikipedia (2004) Apple v. Microsoft. Entry from Wikipedia, the collaboratively produced 'free enyclopedia'. Available online at: http://en2.wikipedia.org/wiki/ Applerv.rMicrosoft.

Further reading

Sparrow, A. (2000) *E-Commerce and the Law. The Legal Implications of Doing Business Online.* Financial Times Management Briefings. Financial Times Prentice Hall, Harlow, UK. This book summarizes all the legal constraints covered in this chapter.

visit the www

Weblinks

European Data Protection (http://ec.europa.eu/justice/policies/privacy/index_en.htm) Site for European Union countries on data protection.

Freedom of Information Act UK blog (http://foia.blogspot.com) Summary of FOIA developments produced by Steve Wood.

Information Commissioner (www.ico.gov.uk) The latest developments and guidelines on data protection and personal information-related law in the UK.

Information Security Breaches Survey (www.security-survey.gov.uk) Regular survey conducted by PricewaterhouseCoopers on behalf of the UK government.

IWS – The Information Warfare Site (www.iwar.org.uk/) This is an online resource that aims to stimulate debate on a variety of issues involving information security, information operations, computer network operations, homeland security and more. It is the aim of the site to develop a special emphasis on offensive and defensive information operations.

Marketing Law (www.marketinglaw.co.uk) Up-to-date source on all forms of law related to marketing activities.

Privacy International (PI) (www.privacyinternational.org) A human rights group formed in 1990 as a watchdog on surveillance by governments and corporations. Has details on regulations in different countries in areas of privacy.

RNIB Accessibility resources (www.rnib.org.uk/professionals/webaccessibility). The UK Royal National Institution for the Blind is one of the leading advisory groups on accessibility.

> For multiple-choice questions, and annotated weblinks relating to this chapter visit this book's website at: **www.pearsoned.co.uk/chaffey**

Glossary

Note: Well-known abbreviations such as RAM or ROM are used in preference to the full form of the term.

3G Third generation of mobile phone technology with high speed data transfer enabling video calling

A

Acceptable use policy Specified rules for using information systems and networks from a user perspective

Access control system Restricts use of files and resources through a log-in and password system and corresponding permissions for files

Accessibility legislation Legislation intended to protect website users with disabilities, including visual disability

Actor Someone or something (person, organization or external system) that interacts with the system

ADSL (asymmetric digital subscriber line) A communications technique for making use of existing telephone lines to provide very high data transfer rates

Agents Software programs that can assist humans to perform tasks

Agile software or system development Development methodologies that aim to overcome the limitations of traditional approaches

Anthony model A simple framework for categorizing applications according to their support for planning and control at the strategic, tactical or operational levels

Anticipatory change An organization initiates change without an immediate need to respond

Anti-virus software Software to detect and eliminate viruses

Application hosting provider (AHP) Service for hosting an organization's application separately

Applications portfolio The mix of software applications used in an organization or department

Applications programming interfaces (APIs) A standard method of exchanging data and instructions between different development software

Applications service provider (ASP) A software supplier that offers hosted solutions to a range of customers

Applications software A computer program that delivers services to support business processes and their managers

Arithmetic and logic unit (ALU) Part of the *processor* that executes operations or performs calculations

Assistive technologies Technology that has been developed for use by persons with impaired abilities

Asymmetric architecture The design of information systems that comprise global standardization with locally tailored elements

Audit See *Information audit, Knowledge audit*

B

Backbones High-speed communications links used to enable Internet communications across a country and internationally

Back-up devices Storage using optical media such as a CD-ROM or magnetic tape to keep a copy of documents

Balanced scorecard A framework for setting and monitoring business performance. Metrics are structured according to customer issues, internal efficiency measures, financial measures and innovation

Barcode A graphical representation of data that can be read with a barcode-reader

Basel II Official guidelines for financial institutions that standardize measurements of credit risks, market risks and operational risk

Berkeley Open Infrastructure for Network Computing (BOINC) Software platform for enabling distributed computing

Bespoke development Information system development specifically for purpose

Best of breed Software is not purchased from a single vendor, but from multiple vendors that are considered to be the best for specialist applications

Biometrics identifiers Techniques to identify an individual based on their physical characteristics or behaviours

BIOS (binary input and output system) Activated when a computer is first switched on, before the operating system is loaded from the hard disk. Starts up hardware and operating system

Bit See *Byte*

Blacklist A compilation of known sources of spam that are used to block e-mail

Blade servers Compact 'high-density' servers comprising microprocessors and memory on a single circuit board. Developed to be low-cost servers which can easily be added to as capacity requirement changes

Blog An online, publicly accessible diary or news source prepared by an individual or a group of people. See also *Transaction log files, web log*

Bluetooth A wireless standard for transmission of data between devices over short ranges (less than 10 m)

Boot-sector virus Occupies boot record of hard and floppy disks and activated during computer start-up

Bottom-up method of IS strategy definition The selection of the IS applications portfolio partially or completely determines the emphasis of IS strategy and how it impacts corporate objectives

Bridges and routers Devices used to connect networks and control the flow of data between them

Broadband services Internet services that offer high-speed data transfer

Burning Recording through optical storage devices

Business alignment An approach to IS strategy where innovative approaches to deploying applications are used to gain competitive advantage by influencing an organization's strategy

Business continuity or disaster recovery Measures taken to ensure that information can be restored and accessed if the original information and access method is destroyed

Business data Detailed objective facts about events or items related to business processes and the external environment

Business ethics Moral principles concerning acceptable and unacceptable behaviour by corporations and individual business people

Business event A financial or non-financial transaction within or between organizations that happens at a point in time

Business impacting An approach to IS strategy where innovative approaches to deploying applications are used to gain competitive advantage by influencing an organization's strategy. Typically a bottom-up approach to IS strategy generation

Business information Data that have been transformed into a meaningful, organized form relevant to those who require them to manage business processes

Business information management The process of managing information as a strategic resource for improving organizational performance. This process involves developing strategies and introducing systems and controls to improve information quality to deliver value

Business intelligence Internal information about the performance of an organization reviewed at either a detailed or summary level

Business intelligence software Software used to analyse and improve business processes through the provision of analysis and reporting capabilities

Business performance management (BPM) A process for improving the performance of organizations based on performance metrics

Business process An activity undertaken by an organization to develop and deliver products or services to stakeholders

Business process automation (BPA) Automating existing ways of working manually through information technology

Business process improvement (BPI) Optimizing existing processes typically coupled with enhancements in information technology

Business process management (BPM) An approach supported by software tools intended to increase process efficiency by improving information flows between people as they perform business tasks

Business process outsourcing (BPO) Specific business processes are contracted to a third party

Business process re-engineering (BPR) Identifying radical, new ways of carrying out business operations, often enabled by new IT capabilities

Business-to-business (B2B) Commercial transactions between an organization and other organizations

Business-to-consumer (B2C) Commercial transactions between an organization and consumers

Business transformation Significant changes to organizational processes implemented to improve organizational performance

Business views Different reports available from a system from summary to detailed level to support different types of manager and decision

Buy-side e-commerce E-commerce transactions between a purchasing organization and its suppliers, possibly through intermediaries

Byte A unit of storage – made up of 8 bits used to represent a single character or digit

Cache (processor) A temporary storage area used by the *processor*

Case management An approach to managing all the tasks involved with a process concerning an individual customer such as a job or credit applicant or an insurance claimant

CASE management tools Computer-aided software engineering tools provide an automated process for graphical representation of systems development. The purpose of CASE tools is to simplify and manage the analysis and design stages of systems development if a level of complexity is reached

Central processing unit (CPU) The traditional terminology for the processor

Centralized computing A single mainframe or mini-computer performs processing and provides storage for many users

Centralized IS location approach All IS services and support are managed and located centrally

Challenge–respond system An e-mail from an unknown source is challenged by another e-mail which is used to prove the originator is a valid sender

Change The transition between two dynamic states. See *Anticipatory change, Reactive change*

Change management Managing process, structural, technical, staff and culture change within an organization

Changeover The method of migrating users and data from the old system to the new system

Chief information officer Manager with responsibility for information assets and/or information systems strategy

Chief knowledge officer The organizational knowledge management champion who will provide the KM vision and strategy

Chipset A grouping of processor and memory chips integrated together to perform a particular function such as sounds or video

Client An end-user computer

Client/server model A system architecture in which end-user machines such as PCs known as clients run applications while accessing data and possibly software programs from a server

Clock speed An indication of how fast instructions are processed by the processor, measured as 'cycles per second'

Cloud computing Computing resources and technologies that are off-site and not under the direct control of the organization that uses them

Clustering Servers are connected to increase stability and performance. If one server fails, another will take over; if there is a high load then this will be shared between servers

Cold list Data about individuals that is rented or sold by a third party

Communications networks Communications media and communications processors used for transfer of data between systems

Community of practice A group (often interdisciplinary) linked by their shared interest in a subject area; the group will organically evolve over time in terms of membership and scope. The purpose will be to learn and share

Competitive intelligence A process that transform disaggregated information into relevant, accurate and usable strategic knowledge about competitors, position, performance, capabilities and intentions

Computer network A communication system that links two or more computers and peripheral devices to enable transfer of data between these computers

Computer virus A program capable of self-replication allowing it to spread from one machine to another. It may be malicious and delete data or be benign

Content management system (CMS) A software tool for creating, editing and updating documents accessed by intranet, extranet or the Internet

Control Changes to the system through modification of system inputs or resources

Control unit Part of the processor that fetches instructions from memory and then decodes them to produce signals which control other parts of the computer

Controlled vocabulary A list of equivalent terms, often enumerated

Cookies Cookies are small text files stored on an end-user's computer to enable websites to identify them

Copyright The legal protection for different forms of works such as books, films, music and software against unauthorized copying

Corporate information portal A portal is a gateway offering web-based access to internal and external information sources for company employees

Corporate or business performance management A process for improving the performance of organizations based on performance metrics

Covert monitoring Monitoring which the employer undertakes without notification of staff

CRC card A collection of physical index cards used in sessions with users and key system stakeholders to model classes

Critical path A sequence of activities which, if delayed, will delay the whole project

Critical success factor (CSF) A performance measure which must be achieved in order for business objectives to be met

Customer data integration The process of creating a single view of each customer

Customer extension Techniques to encourage customers to increase their involvement with an organization

Customer relationship management (CRM) An approach to building and sustaining long-term business with customers

Customer retention Techniques to maintain relationships with existing customers

Customer segmentation Customers are grouped according to their characteristics such as income

Customer selection Picking the ideal customers for acquisition, retention and extension

Data Discrete, objective facts about events. Data are transformed into information by adding value through context, categorization, calculations, corrections and condensation

Data controller A defined person in an organization with the responsibility for data protection

Data dictionary (1) A structured definition defining data objects and the relationship between them together with attributes, and acceptable values

(2) Special type of metadata definition used in databases, acts as a catalogue of all data elements, containing their names and structures and information about their usage

Data flow diagram A graphical representation in the form of a diagram illustrating external sources, flows, processes and data stores

Data migration Transfer of data from old systems to new systems

Data mining A technique used to identify patterns within data that may prove valuable in understanding customer behaviour or enable targeting

Data profiling Data analysis performed to assess the data quality of attributes within a database

Data protection legislation Law intended to protect the privacy of consumers' data through defining how organizations can gather, store, process and disclose personal information

Data quality auditing A structured approach to assessing data quality using database queries and manual checking

Data quality targets Targets for the level of data quality within a particular database

Data redundancy The storage of duplicate data

Data subject The legal term to refer to the individual whose data are held

Data validation A process to improve the quality of data by checking that they have been entered correctly and prompting the user to inform them of incorrect data entry

Data warehouses Large database systems containing detailed company data on sales transactions which are analysed to assist in improving the marketing and financial performance of companies

Database cleansing Typically an automated approach to improve the quality of a customer database

Database system Software for management of structured data

Database table Each database comprises several tables, each related to a single *entity*

Decentralized IS location approach All aspects of IS management are distributed at other points in the organization

De-duplication Reduces the occurrence of multiple records about the same customer through comparing fields

Deliverable An outcome from a phase of the project such as a specification or a version of the software

Denial-of-service attacks Websites are disabled through bombardment with many requests for information originating from computers around the world that have been hijacked

Departmental applications Specialist software used to support workers in one area of the business which is not closely integrated with other areas of the business

Device convergence The functionality of different digital devices is united into a single device

Direct marketing Communications with customers or potential customers using media such as mail, phone or e-mail encouraging response leading to a sale or further dialogue

Directory services Provided as part of the network operating system and are used to manage objects associated with the network such as user accounts and servers

Discontinuous change Change involving a major transformation in an industry

Distributed computing Clients are networked with multiple servers. The organization's data are physically located on different servers

Domain model Representation of business concepts relevant to problem space

Dot pitch The absolute size of a dot on-screen in millimetres

Dots per inch (DPI) A measure of printer resolution

Drill-down An information system provides the capability to visualize more detailed information

Dublin Core A *metadata* initiative for defining a common way to refer to documents

Dynamic Systems Development Method (DSDM) A structured approach to iterative design and prototyping

Dynamic web page A page that is created in real time, often with reference to a database query, in response to a user request

E-business (Electronic business) All digital information exchanges supporting business processes that are mediated through Internet technology including transactions within and between organizations

E-business applications Information management applications supporting business processes which are enabled through Internet technology

E-commerce (Electronic commerce) All financial and informational electronically mediated exchanges between an organization and its external stakeholders

E-government The application of e-commerce technologies to government and public services

E-learning The use of electronic networks and software to deliver training or facilitate learning processes

E-mail filter Software used to identify spam according to its characteristics such as key words

EDI (electronic data interchange) The exchange, using digital media, of structured business information, particularly for sales transactions such as purchase orders and invoices between buyers and sellers

Effectiveness Meeting process objectives, delivering the required outputs and outcomes. 'Doing the right thing'

Efficiency Minimizing resources or time needed to complete a process. 'Doing the thing right'

Effort time Total amount of work to complete a task, usually expressed in days

Elapsed time Length of time, or duration required to complete a task

Electronic document management systems (EDMS) Used to create, distribute and maintain organizational documentation

Electronic funds transfer (EFT) Automated digital transmission of money between organizations and banks

Employee communications monitoring Companies monitor staff e-mails and websites they access

End-user computing (1) The resourcing and delivery of information services to end-users. (2) The development of business applications by end-users

End-user development The creation of applications by end-users (typically based on spreadsheets and databases)

End-user development strategy A structured approach is defined for the management and control of applications development by non-IS professionals

Enterprise applications Integrated applications used across large parts of an organization

Enterprise resource planning (ERP) software
Enterprise applications used to manage information about organizational resources such as raw materials, products, staff and customers as part of delivery of a product or service

Entity A self-contained piece of data that can be referenced as a unit

Entity relationship diagrams A graphical representation that displays entities, relationships and attributes

Environment The external influence on a system with which it interacts

Environmental scanning or sensing The process of continuously monitoring the environment and events and responding accordingly

Ethical hacker Hacker employed legitimately to test the quality of system security

Ethical standards Practice or behaviour which is morally acceptable to society. See *Business ethics*

Explicit knowledge Codified knowledge that can be readily expressed and understood such as business procedures

Extranet Formed by extending selected intranet services beyond an organization to its customers, suppliers and collaborators

Extreme Programming (XP) A feature of this approach is that programming is completed in pairs with a view to producing more effective, maintainable and less error-prone code

Feasibility study A report assessing the viability of the system

Feedback Output that is used to evaluate the performance of the system

Fields Attributes of products, such as date of birth

File server A computer system used to share files from different PCs

Filtering software Software that blocks specified content or activities

Firewall Hardware used to increase security of part of a network through preventing unauthorized access from beyond the network

Flash RAM Non-volatile RAM storage

Freedom of Information Act (FOIA) Intended to give citizens access to information held by public authorities, enabling them to participate 'in the discussion of policy issues and so improve the quality of government decision making' and 'holding government and other bodies to account'

Gantt chart A bar chart with project activities and milestones listed down the left-hand side with dates shown across the top, and activity duration shown as horizontal bars

Gap analysis Identification of the requirements from information systems by comparing the current systems and information availability to what is required by users

Gigabyte A unit of storage equivalent to 1024 *megabytes*

Governance See *IT governance, Internet governance*

Graphical user interface A visual method to enable the user to control the computer using mouse and keyboard

Graphics card A separate card for improved graphics performance, sometimes known as the 'video-adapter'

Green computing The concept of reducing the environmental impact of technology

Grid computing The need for powerful servers is reduced by this approach which shares the power of client machines to solve computational problems – the clients are effectively joined to become a powerful server

Groupware Software supporting group-working and collaboration by employees

Guided media Communications channels that use cables and wires

Hacking The process of gaining unauthorized access to computer systems, typically across a network

Hard copy Printed output from a system, distinct from soft or electronic copy

Hard disks The most common form of permanent storage on computer systems

Hardware The physical components of a computer system such as its input devices, processor, memory, storage and output devices

Hidden Web Data and information held by organizations that is not readily accessible by web-based browsers

High-level languages Relatively simple programming languages

Hosted solution Standard software which is managed externally on the supplier's server

House list Data about existing customers used to market products to encourage future purchase

HTML (Hypertext Markup Language) A standard format used to define the text and layout of web pages. HTML files usually have the extension .HTML or .HTM

HTML meta tags Standard HTML codes used to specify the content and characteristics of the document

HTTP, the Hypertext Transfer Protocol A standard method for web browsers and servers to transfer requests for delivery of web pages and their embedded graphics

Hubs Used to connect groups of computers to a network

Human controls Staff control data quality at entry and through review

Hygiene processing Automated improvement of data quality by modifying formats and checking for validity

Hyperlink A method of moving between one web-site page and another, indicated to the user by an image or text highlighted by underlining and/or a different colour

i-mode A mobile access platform widely used in Japan that enables display of colour graphics and content subscription services

Identity theft The misappropriation of the identity of another person, without their knowledge or consent

Impact assessment An assessment of the employee monitoring process in the workplace to identify improvements to minimize infringement of employee privacy

Inbound e-marketing activities The Internet is used to support enquiries to an organization referred by offline communications such as advertising or online communications such as search engines, online adverts or e-mail enquiries

Incremental change Relatively small adjustments required by an organization in response to their business environment

Informatics (organizational) The study of the development and use of information and information technology within organization with a focus on the effects on the organization's human resources

Information Organized data, meaningful and contextually relevant. Used for decision making

Information accessibilty An assessment of the ease with which an employee can access an online or offline information source

Information architecture Definition and structure of organizational information related to information systems

Information architecture strategy Overall information architecture framework for an organization related to higher-level strategies

Information audit An approach to review and improve information usage and information quality within an organization

Information behaviours and values capability A measure of how well an organization instils and promotes appropriate information behaviours and values amongst its staff

Information and communication technology (ICT or IT) The software applications, computer hardware and network used to create information systems

Information consistency Similar data items have different values in different databases

Information duplication Similar types of data are repeated in databases in separate parts of the organization

Information economy An economy that is highly dependent upon the collection, storage and exchange of information

Information flow diagram A simple high-level diagram illustrating information flows

Information lifecycle The sequence of activities involved in information management from creation through to permanent deletion of information

Information lifecycle management (ILM) Workflow systems to control the creation, storage, modification and deletion of documents

Information management See *Business information management*

Information management strategy Definition of management approaches to the organization: control and application of organizational information resources through coordination of people and technology resources in order to support organizational strategy and processes

Information mapping An approach for identifying the value of, and relationships between organizational information resources

Information model A conceptual model of information related to organizational functions or processes

Information orientation A concept or metric used to assess how effectively people use information and IT to inprove business performance

Information overload The capacity of individuals and systems within an organization to derive value from information is exceeded by the volume and complexity of information

Information policy A formal declaration of how information management will be managed and information quality will be improved within an organization

Information quality The suitability of *information* for the purpose required by its users. See *Pragmatic information quality, Inherent information quality*

Information quality policy Details organizational and individual approaches to reviewing, monitoring and improving the quality of information within an organization

Information security management system An organizational process to protect information assets

Information services delivery Management of ICT infrastructure, information and support of information users in accessing a range of information resources

Information silos Information is stored in separate databases which are not linked

Information society A society with widespread access and transfer of digital information within business and the community

Information strategy A plan with a defined timeframe setting information management objectives and tactics and controls to achieve them

Information system A computerized or manual system to capture data and transform them into information and/or knowledge

Information systems The means by which organizations and people, using information technologies, gather, process, store, use and disseminate information

Information systems location Refers both to where the IS services are physically located and where they are managed or controlled

Information systems stages of growth model A six-stage evolutionary model of how IS can be applied within a business

Information systems strategy The formulation of approaches and planning needed to deploy information systems resources to support organizational strategy

Information technology (IT) The information and communications technologies used to capture, process, store and transport information in digital form

Infrastructure See *Technology infrastructure*

Inherent information quality The degree to which data accurately define real-world objects

Initiation phase The first phase of a systems development project. It establishes project feasibility and produces a plan

Inputs The physical and virtual resources that feed into a system

Integrated development environment (IDE) Tools used to create new software using programming languages and databases

Integration risk Potential project overruns caused by additional work involved with integrating the output from separate activities

Internet The physical network that links computers across the globe. It consists of the infrastructure of network servers and communication links between them that are used to hold and transport information between the client PCs and web servers

Internet EDI Use of EDI data standards delivered across non-proprietary IP networks

Internet governance Control of the operation and use of the Internet

Internet marketing or e-marketing The application of the Internet and e-mail to support all forms of marketing exchanges with customers and other stakeholders

Internet service provider (ISP) A provider providing home or business users with a connection to access the Internet. They can also host web-based applications

Interoperability The application of computer systems to work together, conforming to common standards

Interview A series of questions (orally delivered) by one person (an interviewer) in which the responses of the interviewee are recorded

Intranet A private network within a single organization using Internet standards to enable employees to share information using e-mail and web publishing

Investment appraisal Evaluation of the return on investment on IS strategy at firm or application level

IP address The unique numerical address of a computer

ISDN (integrated services digital network) A data communications technique for transfer of digital data using phone lines

IT governance Management of the processes to direct and control the enterprise use of IT in order to achieve the enterprise's goals by adding value while balancing risk versus return over IT and its processes

IT outsourcing Different information technology functions are performed by a third party over a contract period, for example hardware and software purchase and maintenance, application development and IT help-desk services

Jurisdiction The scope or extent of control of a law geographically – who it applies to

Key performance indicator (KPI) A specific measure used to determine the progress in achieving critical success factors.

Kilobyte A unit of storage equivalent to 1024 *bytes*

Knowledge The combination of data and information to which is added expert opinion, skills and experience to result in a valuable asset which can be used to make decisions. See *Explicit knowledge, Tacit knowledge*

Knowledge audit Systematic, formal assessment of organizational knowledge assets, processes and flows

Knowledge management The combination of strategies, techniques and tools used to capture and share knowledge within an organization

Knowledge management strategy Defined and coordinated plan of actions to enable core business processes using knowledge management techniques

Knowledge manager Manager who will implement the knowledge management strategy

Knowledge map A visual representation of organizational knowledge assets, flows and relationships

Knowledge quality Knowledge quality is dependent on the capability of people to attach significance to

information to inform their decisions and the ability to convert it into information to convey to other people

Knowledge workers A term referring to employees who spend a large part of their time searching, analysing and disseminating information within an organization

Legacy systems Existing systems with which new systems must integrate

Linux Open-source operating systems software initially developed by Linus Torvalds

Local-area network (LAN) A computer network that spans a limited geographic area such as a single office or building

Logical In the information systems context, a logical representation is an abstraction of the real situation developed in order to give the user view of how the system must be organized and structured

Low-level languages Relatively complex programming languages which interact more directly with the hardware

Macro-environment Broader forces affecting all organizations in the marketplace such as social, technological, economic, political and legal

Magnetic storage Storage on iron-ferrite-based disks such as the hard disk

Mainframe Powerful computer used for large-scale data processing

Malicious virus A virus that causes damage through destruction of data or software

Managed e-mail service Receipt and transmission of e-mails is managed by a third party

Management sponsor for IS strategy A senior manager who chairs the steering committee for IS strategy development and execution

Market intelligence External information about a specific market which is used to understand a company's competitive position

Maturity models Enable auditing of IS capabilities for comparison on a standard scale

Megabyte A unit of storage equivalent to 1024 *kilobytes*

Meta tags See *HTML meta tags*

Metcalfe's law The value of a network grows by the square of the size of the network

Micro-computer Typically used to refer to a PC or similar sized client workstation

Micro-environment Specific forces on an organization generated by its stakeholders

Microprocessor A modern small-scale *processor*

Middleware Software used to facilitate communications between business applications including data transfer and control

Milestone A control point in the project marking the completion of a major project phase

Mini-computer A general term, often referred to as 'midrange', typically for computers smaller than micro-computers and PCs, but larger than mainframes

Modem Modulator–demodulator used to convert data between digital and analogue form when transmitting data over telephone lines

Module design Defines operation of individual subsystems within the system

Monitor An *output device* for visualizing software outputs on a screen

Motherboard Circuit board on which is located processor, chipsets, memory and other components

MTBF (mean time before failure) The life expectancy of a piece of equipment

Multi-tasking Management of memory and processor requirements enabling different applications to run simultaneously

Network diagram A graphic showing different project activities and the dependencies between them

Network interface card (NIC) Used to connect a computer with a corporate network

Network operating system (NOS) Systems software used to control the access to and flow of information on a network

Non-volatile storage Storage is permanent

Normalization A process to structure data, carried out to minimize duplication and inconsistencies. Usually involves breaking down a single table into two or more tables and creating relationships

Notification The process whereby companies register with the Data Protection Register to inform about their data holdings

Objects A person, a thing or concept. Building blocks of object-oriented systems. Objects know things and do things

Object-oriented A programming method that uses objects as building blocks in software applications

Office software Basic document management applications including word processor, spreadsheet, database, presentation packages and e-mail software

Offshore outsourcing A company's processes are undertaken by staff who are located in another country, typically with lower wages for employees

On-demand computing This term, equivalent to *utility computing*, was coined by IBM

Ontology An explicit formal specification of how to represent the objects, concepts and other entities that are assumed to exist in some area of interest and the relationships that hold between them. A term sometimes used by knowledge managers when dealing with organizational relationships

Open-source software Program code, usually developed collaboratively, freely available for inspection, compilation and use

Operating systems software Software that interacts with the hardware and applications software of a computer system to control its operation

Opt-in A customer proactively agrees to receive further information

Opt-out A customer declines the offer to receive further information

Optical storage Storage using optical media such as CD and DVD that are accessed using a laser

Organizational change Includes both incremental and discontinuous change to organizations

Organizational culture The values and beliefs shared by members of an organization

Organizational strategy Definition of the future direction and actions of an organization specified as approaches and allocation of resources to achieve specific objectives

Outbound e-marketing activities The Internet is used to communicate proactively with customers and potential customers using e-mail campaigns and e-newsletters

Outputs The physical and virtual products that are created by a system

Output devices Used for viewing outputs from a system

Outsourcing See *IS, IT outsourcing*

 P

Packaged implementation Standard software is installed with limited configuration required

Packet Each Internet message such as an e-mail or HTTP request is broken down into smaller parts for ease of transmission

Pages per minute (PPM) A measure of printer speed

Peer-to-peer computing Each computer is used in a client or a server capacity

Peer-to-peer file sharing Files containing music, software and video are shared between the hard disks of Internet users through intermediary services which provide an index of the users and the content they have on their machines

Performance dashboard A summary of key performance indicators and drivers from which more detailed information can be obtained

Performance management system A process used to evaluate and improve the efficiency and effectiveness of an organization and its processes

Performance metrics Measures that are used to evaluate and improve the efficiency and effectiveness of business processes

Permission marketing Customers agree (opt-in) to be involved in an organization's marketing activities usually as a result of an incentive

Personal computer (PC) The most widely used client machine, originally developed by IBM and now produced by many manufacturers

Personal computing Individual PCs are used for performing users' tasks and storing data

Personal data Any information about an individual stored by companies concerning their customers or employees

Personal digital assistants (PDAs) Handheld computers used for managing an individual's tasks

Personal productivity software Software application to support staff in administrative tasks

Personalization Relevant products and messages are offered to users of the Internet via websites or e-mails dependent upon their profiles and behaviour

Political Economical Sociological Technological Legal Environmental (PESTLE) The external factors that affect organizations

Phishing Obtaining personal details online through sites and e-mails masquerading as legitimate businesses

Pixel A dot on a screen, short for 'picture element'

Plagiarism Passing off another person's previously written material or concepts as your own

Portal See *Corporate information portal*, *Web portal*

Portfolio management A structured approach to the selection and management of IS projects (the *applications portfolio*)

Pragmatic information quality The degree to which information quality is of value to those who use it and the organization as a whole

Primary key The field that uniquely identifies each record in a table

Printer An *output device* used for visualizing software outputs on paper

Privacy The right of an individual to control the personal information held about them by third parties

Processor The computer component that controls the operation of the computer through processing instructions and issuing signals to control other parts of the system

Productivity paradox Research results indicating a poor correlation between organizational investment in information technology and organizational performance measured by return on equity

Programming languages Programme code used to help develop new systems

Project management methodologies Guidelines defining a standard process for the project management process

Project management office (PMO) A function in larger organizations for coordinating projects

Project tolerance A project control mechanism used to escalate an issue to management attention when the actual project deviates from planned by a pre-agreed amount

Project views Alternative methods of visualizing the project tasks, resources and plans

Prototype A preliminary version of part or all of an information system reviewed by its users and business sponsors

Prototyping An iterative process in which website users suggest modifications before further prototypes and the live version of the site are developed

Publication scheme A list of the classes of information made available by the organization

Pull model of information delivery Users seek information for themselves, using search engines and specialist online information portals

Push model of information delivery Information is supplied from the information function to the information users

Quick Response (QR) Code A two-dimensional development of barcoding

RAD (rapid application development) An approach to information systems development that includes incremental development using prototypes

Radio-frequency identification (RFID) microchip Tags which can respond to a radio signal with a unique identification code to identify different types of object to which they are attached

RAID (redundant array of individual disks) An arrangement of hard disks that can provide protection from data loss

RAM (random-access memory) Temporary storage for programs and data accessed by the *processor*

Reactive change A direct response by an organization to a change in the organization's environment

Real time Information is available for analysis almost immediately events or transactions occur

Record A document or an instance of an entity within a business. In a *database*, a collection of fields for one instance of an entity, for example Customer Smith

Records management The process of managing the creation and maintenance of and access to documents and records about individuals and events related to an organization through the information lifecycle

Redundancy See *Data redundancy*

Repeater Device used to increase efficiency of transmission over long distances

Repetitive strain injury (RSI) Damage to soft tissues and sometimes joints caused by repeated movements or a strained position

Requirements creep Incremental changes to the specification of an IS project during implementation

Resistance to change Staff actively or passively demonstrate opposition to new working practices

Resolution An indication of the clarity of the screen image

Resource definition framework An element of HTML intended to facilitate standardized metadata

Return on investment (ROI) A measure of the benefits delivered by the software in comparison to the costs incurred in its purchase and maintenance

Reverse design Taking a physical database design from a database application and presenting it as a logical model

Risk management Assessing potential reasons for failure for projects and developing strategies to reduce risks

ROM (read-only memory) Permanent memory used to store the BIOS

RSS (Really Simple Syndication) A version of XML and RDF that offers a standardized way of syndicating news headlines (or similar types of content) across the World Wide Web

Sample frame An assessment of the characteristics of a survey determining whether the sample is representative

Sample size The number of respondents to a survey

Sarbanes–Oxley Act A law defining acceptable accounting practices including audit and control of financial information

Scalable Infrastructure will operate under different capacities

Scanning software Identifies e-mail or web-page access that breaches company guidelines or acceptable use policies

Search engines Automated tools known as 'spiders' or 'robots' index registered sites. Users use a search engine by typing a key phrase and are presented with a list of pages from the index ranked by relevance to the key phrase

Secondary key A field that is used to link tables, by linking to a primary key in another table

Selective outsourcing Different IT services are outsourced to different companies

Sell-side e-commerce E-commerce transactions between a supplier organization and its customers, possibly through intermediaries

Semantic web A concept describing the use of metadata or self-description of WWW documents to enable context-understanding programs to selectively find what users want through more efficient location and exchange of data

Server A computer that provides services such as storage or application to other (client) computers

Service-level agreement A contractual specification of service standards a contractor must meet

Service quality gap model A tool for assessing the level of service quality based on the difference between users expectations and the service experience delivered

Session cookie A cookie used to manage a single visitor session

Short message service (SMS) The formal name for text messaging

Single view of the customer All information related to a customer can be readily accessed using an integrated system

Six Sigma A quality measure and improvement programme developed by Motorola that focuses on the control of a process to the point of ±six sigma (standard deviations) from a centreline, or 3.4 defects per million items

Social engineering Exploiting human behaviour to gain access to computer security information from employees or individuals

Social network analysis (SNA) The mapping and measuring of relationships and flows between people, groups, organizations, computers or other information or knowledge processing entities

Soft systems methodology (SSM) A systems analysis methodology that determines requirements needed from a system and identifies changes to the organization and processes needed

Software The instructions or programs used to control a computer system through interaction with hardware

Software audits A formal assessment of software types used, licences held and level of usage

Software patents Patents protect innovations from imitation in law

Software or web services Information management facilities are accessed from an external provider – the software is not installed within the company

Sound card A separate PC card used for audio reproduction

Source code The lines that are compiled and executed as a computer program

Spam Unsolicited e-mail (usually bulk mailed and untargeted)

Stakeholder An individual or group with an interest in the success of an information system or an individual or group that will be affected by the outcome of the information system. A stakeholder has a vested interest in the information system

Static web page A page on the web server that is invariant

Sociological Technological Economical Environmental Political Legal Ethical (STEEPLE) The external factors that affect an organization, an extension of PESTLE

Storage area network (SAN) Server clustering is used to connect and manage networked storage devices. This helps ensure that all data are backed up and if new storage capacity is needed, it can be added without disruption of service

Storage device A unit used for reading and writing data from and to the storage media

Storage media The form of material used for storing information

Strategic information systems planning (SISP) Term used to refer to IS strategy formulation and planning

Strategy development process A framework for approaching strategy development in a series of logical steps

Supply chain management The coordination of all supply activities of an organization from its suppliers and partners to its customers

System bus Used for transferring data between the components on the motherboard

System unit The main body of the PC which is used to house processor and storage

Systems A collection of interrelated components that work together towards a collective goal

Systems analysis Process of researching and identifying organizational and user requirements

Systems avoidance End-users of a system show resistance to change through non-use or reduced use of a system

Systems controls Software is used to control data quality on entry and through data cleansing

Systems design Defines the overall structure of the system and its inputs and outputs

Systems design phase Defines how the completed system will operate

Systems development phase Creation of the system through programming, database management and configuration

Systems implementation The new information system is introduced into the business

Systems requirements Define how an IS will be used within the business through detailed specification of the feature

Systems software Controls the resources of the computer system as it performs tasks for the end-user through acting as a 'bridge' between the hardware and applications software

Systems theory A model of the interdependence between different elements or resources in organizations and the natural world

Table See *Database table*

Tacit knowledge Mainly intangible knowledge that is typically intuitive and difficult to record

Tailored development The standard solution requires major configuration or integration of different modules

Tape storage Magnetic tape is used for data storage

Taxonomy A browsable hierarchy of organizational classification terms

TCP/IP The Transmission Control Protocol is a transport layer protocol that moves data between applications. The Internet Protocol is a network-layer protocol that moves data between host computers

Technology infrastructure resources The hardware and communications networks used to store, process and transmit the software and information in an organization

Telecommunications systems The systems used to transmit information between different locations

Terabyte A unit of storage equivalent to 1024 *gigabytes*

Terminal A simple computer typically consisting of display, keyboard and mouse. The number of processors and amount of memory are minimized to reduce cost

Text messaging See *Short message service*

Thin client An end-user access device (terminal) where computing requirements such as processing and storage (and so cost) are minimized

Three-tier client/server The first tier is the client that handles display, the second is application logic and business rules, the third is database storage

Timebox A fixed period within a DSDM project for the development of specific deliverables

Top-down method of IS strategy definition The IS applications portfolio is determined by alignment with corporate objectives

Total cost of ownership (TCO) The sum of all cost elements of managing information systems for end-users including purchase, support *and* maintenance

Total data quality management (TDQM) The philosophy of aspiring toward excellence in all areas of data capture, storage and use

Total outsourcing All IT services are outsourced to a single company

Transaction log files A web-server file that records all page requests

Transformation process The mechanism by which inputs are transformed into outputs.

Transistors Switches or amplifiers used in a circuit

Trojan A virus that masquerades as a bona fide application

Unguided media Communications channels which are wireless

Unified modelling language(UML) A visual modelling methodology covering the notation and ways of specifying, modelling and documenting object-oriented systems

Uniform (universal) resource locator (URL) A web address used to locate a web page on a web server

Usability The ability of systems to meet the defined needs of users

Use case analysis A view of describing the sequence of actions and functionality a system should deliver, facilitating the work of actors

Utility computing IT resources and in particular software and hardware are utilized on a pay-per-use basis

Validation See *Data validation*

Value-added network (VAN) A secure wide-area network that uses proprietary rather than Internet technology

Value chain A model for analysis of how supply chain activities can add value to products and services delivered to the customer

Value network The links between an organization and its strategic and non-strategic partners that form its external value chain

Valued outcome A benefit that occurs to employees during their employment such as pay or favourable working conditions

Vendor-managed inventory (VMI) Suppliers monitor information about the level of demand for products by their customers through shared systems and provide goods to match this demand

Viral marketing Refers to a powerful offer transmitted via a network of people to reach a large audience cost-effectively to generate prospects, build brand awareness and so increase sales

Virtual memory Memory that is allocated from the hard disk to supplement RAM

Virtual private networks (VPN) A secure, encrypted (tunnelled) connection between two points using the Internet, typically created by ISPs for organizations wanting to conduct secure Internet trading

Virus See *Computer virus*

Volatile storage Memory such as RAM which isn't permanent

Voluntary Computing An approach to networking that uses redundant processing power of individual's computers

Web blueprint An overview sitemap indicating pages, types and page components and their relationship to the home page

Web browsers Browsers such as Microsoft Internet Explorer provide an easy method of accessing and viewing information stored as web documents on different web servers

Web classification The process of arranging a way of organizing objects on the websites in a consistent manner

Web log See *Blog*

Web portal A gateway website to further information on broad or narrow topics

Web servers Store and present the web pages accessed by web browsers

Web services Information management facilities are accessed from an external provider – the software is not installed within the company

Whitelist A compilation of trusted sources of e-mail that are permitted to enter an inbox

Wide-area network Computer networks covering a large area which connects businesses in different parts of the country or different countries

Wi-Fi (wireless fidelity) A high-speed wireless local-area network enabling wireless access to the Internet for mobile, office and home users

Wireframe Also known as 'schematics', a way of illustrating the layout of an individual web page

Wireless Application Protocol (WAP) A technical standard for transferring information to wireless devices, such as mobile phones

Wireless networking Local-area networking using wireless media

Workflow management Applications to manage the flow of information required when several stages and/or different resources are used to process this information

World Wide Web (WWW) A method for accessing information published on the Internet. It is accessed through web browsers which display web pages and graphics downloaded from web browsers

Worm A small program that self-replicates and transfers across a network from machine to machine without human intervention. A form of virus

XML or eXtensible Markup Language A standard based on customized tags that enable the definition, validation and interpretation of data, and so facilitates the transfer of data within and between applications and organizations

XML schemas A set of rules in XML language for specifying the structures of XML document types. Documents that reference schemas must conform to the rules specified

Index

Note: Page numbers for glossary entries and margin definitions are in **bold** type.

26 01 666 826

web blueprints 439
web services **39**, **60**, **G13**
wireframes 440–2
web logs 83–4, 461, **G15**
websites
  blueprints for **439**, **G15**
  and browsers **49**, **134**
  classification of **428**, **G15**
  design of 438–45
  for display 140
  pages in 135
  and portals **G15**
  self-service type **69**
  and servers **99**, **134**, **G11**, **G15**
  and services **G15**
Websense (software) 597–8, 600–1
Wegner, E. 216, 239
Wei Choo, Chun 97
Welch, J. 381
Welwyn-Hatfield Borough Council 561
Whinston, A. 71
White, G. 343, 357
White, M. 246, 438
whitelists of e-mail sources **546**, **G15**
Whitman, M.E. 466

wide area networks (WANs) **127**, **G15**
wi-fi (wireless fidelity) **129**
Wikipedia 133
Willard, N. (and Willard model) 182
Willcocks, L. 367
Williams–Sonoma (company) 277
Wipro (company) 563
wireframes **440**
Wireless Application Protocol (WAP) **149**, **G11**, **G15**
wireless fidelity *see* wi-fi
wireless Internet 149–51
wireless networks 127
Wodke, C. 440
workflow management applications (software) **51**, **G15**
Working Party on Social Inclusion in the Information Society 4
World Bank 243, 533–4
World Wide Web (WWW) 22, 39, 69, **132**–3, 148, 295, 526, 539, 615, **G11**, **G15**
World Wide Web Consortium 137, 140, 609

worms 539, **G15**
WPA (company) 549–50, 594
Wurman, R. 413
Wurster, W. 5, 10
WWW *see* World Wide Web
Wylie, J. 453
Wynekoop, J.L. 343

XML (eXtensible markup language) **141**–9, 155, 460–3
  schemas for **460**, **G15**
XP *see* extreme programming
Xu, H. 483, 509, 520

Yahoo! 22, 453
  Messenger 50
yellow pages, corporate 246–7
Yourdon, E. (and Yourdon systems methodology) 344

Zak, M. 215, 231, 235–6
ZDNet 188
Zwass, V. 71